THEORY OF INSTRUCTION:

PRINCIPLES AND APPLICATIONS

By Siegfried Engelmann
and Douglas Carnine

Revised edition

NIFDI PRESS
1140 Willagillespie Rd, STE 18
Eugene, Oregon, 97440

Layout: Ashly Cupit
Subject Index: Patricia McFadden

Copyright © 1991 by Siegfried Engelmann
Revised edition, 2016 (NIFDI Press)

All rights reserved. No part of this publication may be reproduced, distributed, or transmitted in any form or by any means, including photocopying, recording, or other electronic or mechanical methods, without the prior written permission of the publisher, except in the case of brief quotations embodied in critical reviews and certain other noncommercial uses permitted by copyright law. For permission requests, write to the publisher at the address below.

National Institute for Direct Instruction
1140 Willagillespie Rd, STE 18
Eugene, Oregon, 97401.
www.nifdi.org

Printed in the United States of America

ISBN: 978-1-939851-30-7

Library of Congress Control Number: 2016910052

Foreword, 1991 Edition

by Robert Dixon

Many questions regarding *Theory of Instruction: Principles and Applications* have arisen in the years since the publication of the first edition in 1982. Is it a textbook? Why wasn't it named, *Theory of DIRECT Instruction?* Why is it so difficult to read? How relevant is it to the current *Zeitgeist* of educational philosophy? And last-and least-is the cover of the 1982 edition red or orange?

I propose at this publication of the revised edition, that *Theory of Instruction* is exactly what the title implies, and further that my proposition is of potentially inestimable significance to the field of education.

Theory

First and foremost, *Theory of Instruction* is the articulation of a theory-not in the atheoretical sense "theory" is used in educational jargon, but in the more precise sense well-established among scientists and philosophers of science.

Engelmann and Carnine's theory evolved the same way original natural science theories have evolved, through the scrupulous application of logical analysis to existing empirical observation. The Engelmann and Carnine theory possesses the most critical attributes of natural science theories: (1) it is *exhaustive* in that it covers everything from the most basic motor skill instruction to the highest of the "higher order" thinking skills, and (2) it does so *economically*. In short, it is parsimonious.

Engelmann and Carnine's theory builds logically from just two initial assumptions: that learners perceive qualities, and that they generalize upon the basis of *sameness* of qualities. (This is not unlike the way Euclidean geometry derives logically from a minimum of unproven and unprovable assumptions about points and lines.) If we accept Engelmann and Carnine's simple assumptions and if we were to employ rigorous logic to any instructional problem, then the instruction we would derive would fall within the constraints of the Engelmann and Carnine theory. We wouldn't come up with *the same instruction*, but rather, with the same or similar instructional principles.

That is highly significant. Engelmann and Carnine don't look at the book when they develop instruction; they developed most of their instruction before they wrote their book. They haven't memorized various sequences from their own book, either. They simply apply the logic of their own theory to new content, and essentially recreate manifestations of their theory. Put another way, one very good indication that Engelmann and Carnine are operating within the framework of a theory is that *they are constrained to adhere to their own theory.* One can only religiously conform to a theory that exists. It strikes me as absolutely fantastic that the published Direct Instruction programs–before or after the theory book–are consistent in terms of how examples of given types are ordered and sequenced. (Some variation exists due directly to refinements in the theory.) Absolutely no other published programs of any type demonstrate such consistency, at such a level of detail. Absolutely no other published programs have an underlying, consistent rationale for the examples they use and the order they use them in. It's quite likely that few authors of published educational materials have ever given the slightest thought to the *fact* that when we change the examples, we change the information that is communicated to the learner.

The Engelmann and Carnine theory provides a basis for making predictions that can be tested. In the absence of a theory, experimentation is driven by random hypotheses based upon "plausible ideas" or intellectual frolicking. If such hypotheses prove to be false, little is gained, save the rejection of one of an infinite set of plausible (but wrong) ideas. If such hypotheses prove to be true, very little is *still* gained: there's an idea that shows promise, but where does it fit? How does it relate to other ideas that show promise? The current state-of-the-art in educational experimentation is characterized by this kind of tinkering with plausibility.

If a hypothesis generated by a theory proves false, on the other hand, not only is the hypothesis itself questionable, but because of the logical interconnectedness of the theory's components, the entire theory becomes questionable. But if a hypothesis generated by a theory is verified, then the veracity of the entire theory is strengthened. Theory-based research is worth the time and effort; plausible idea-based theory isn't. When *Time* charged that the longest running joke on most university campuses is the Education Department, the black humor tended to obfuscate the reason that so many non-education academics might feel that way: conducting research in the absence of a theory might be funny, were it not for the unconscionable waste of money and human resources.

A true theory not only predicts, but explains. For example, if we are interested in *why* cognitive psychologists have, after several years of research, concluded that the extent to which learning transfers is dependent upon the relative salience of surface and structural features of examples, this theory will explain that for us. If we are interested in why a typical textbook presentation of a new concept *must* fail to communicate accurately to many learners, this theory will explain that, too.

Instruction

Theory of Instruction, again as the name implies, is a theory of *instruction*, not a theory of learning. Learning theories (if they are really theories at all) are no doubt of value to those interested in how humans learn in the absence of instruction (which generally is inefficiently).

Theory of (DIRECT) Instruction

There is a relatively simple fact about the Engelmann and Carnine theory that many educators appear to find disturbing: it is the *only* theory of instruction and therefore, does not require the "direct" qualifier. Although we hear of all kinds of "theories" of learning and even a few "theories" of instruction, this book represents the only theory of instruction that would withstand the rigorous tests of theories required by philosophers of science—disciplined logical interconnectedness, predictive value, parsimony, etc.

Theory of Instruction does not prescribe any "one best way," but rather, describes a range of best ways, and suggests an infinite range of ineffective ways. (If I were to set out to intentionally design the *worst* instruction possible, I would still look to *Theory of Instruction* for guidance on how to precisely lead students far astray.)

I have even heard serious educational researchers express the fear that if *Theory of Instruction* is the first and only theory of instruction, then there would be nothing left for anyone else to do. That is like arguing that Newton's *Principia* and Lavoisier's *Chemistry* killed physics and chemistry. The emergence of a first theory in a field opens that field to countless opportunities for inquiry, closing off only those practices akin to changing lead to gold. (Geocentrism died because it was untrue, not because it was unpopular.)

Reading the Theory

I've never heard of anyone who found *Theory of Instruction* to be an easy read. In general, any written theory, in the presence of either no competing theory or no similar theory, will be hard to read. The reader will not possess a frame of reference necessary for easy comprehension. That's one way of characterizing the purpose of a theory: to create a new frame of reference. I doubt that *Principia* was anyone's leisure reading when it first appeared.

Engelmann and Carnine's *Theory of Instruction* is as clear as it can be for whom I believe to be the principal intended audience: Engelmann and Carnine. Imagine carrying around in your head a theory so exhaustive, so economical, on a subject so broad and complicated. My conjecture is that a crucial stage in the development of any true theory is for that theory to be written down, first and foremost for the benefit of the theorist(s), and then only secondarily for any of the rest of us who might be interested. The theory seems complex because it is complex.

Summary

Theory of Instruction could easily be the most important educational book ever written, bar none. (Yes, I am aware of Aristotle and Dewey and Piaget and Skinner, etc.) Instruction is at the heart of education, and *Theory of Instruction* is the first true theory that cuts to the heart of instruction. Although I believe the theory of instruction to be fundamentally correct, even that judgment is secondary to the importance of a theory existing in the field of instruction. My contentions herein may seem like exorbitant fanaticism. Time and experience will tell.

Acknowledgments

The authors would like to acknowledge these original patient readers—particularly Galen Alessi, Robert Dixon, Joseph Jenkins, Martin Siegel, and Marcy Stein. Final scrutiny came from our editor, Wesley Becker. We are very grateful to these people. We are also heavily indebted to the graduate students and colleagues who provided us with the research data on specific instructional or theoretical issues: Abby Adams, Craig Darch, Phil Dommes, Ruth Falco, Bill Fink, Roger Freschi, Russell Gersten, Patty Hickman, Ed Kameenui, John Kryzanowski, Alex and Robyn Maggs, Dorothy Ross, Randy Sprick, Bob Taylor, and Paul Williams.

We are grateful to the teacher-trainers and site supervisors we have worked with, because they provided us with ongoing reminders of what people could do if they had a highly technical understanding of instruction. Each of the following people has provided incredible demonstrations of teaching the unteachable—Geoffrey Colvin, Karen Davis, Alex Granzin, Glenda Hewlett, Deborah Lamson, Carol Morimitsu, Linda Olen, and Linda Youngmayr.

Finally, we are grateful to the people who have developed instructional programs with us and have helped us learn about the amazing difference that good programs can make in the performance of children Carl Bereiter, Elaine Bruner, Linda Carnine, Gary Davis, Robert Dixon, Gary Johnson, Jean Osborn, Jerry Silbert, Leslie Zoref, and perhaps more than anyone else, Susan Hanner.

Introduction, 2016 Edition

What is Instruction?

The words instruction and teaching do not occur very often in the education literature. In fact, the word instruction appeared only 18 times in the 230 pages of the Common Core standards. The words teach or teaching appeared only 5 times. Ironically, instruction or teaching is what is supposed to occur in the classroom. Specifically, if the learners do not have a particular skill or bit of knowledge, the assumption is that the learners will acquire these through some form of "interaction" or process in the classroom. The interaction or process that is designed to transmit skill or knowledge is teaching. It may be disguised as a "learning activity" and may be configured so the teacher has no role in directly transmitting a specific skill or information, but instead does something that is designed to change the learner's cognition in specific ways. Practically and pragmatically, whatever the teacher does that is supposed to result in specific changes in the learner's repertoire and behavior is "teaching."

In a rational system, teaching is related to three other processes–standards, curriculum, and testing. The four processes occur in a fixed order that starts with standards and ends with testing.

Standards➜curriculum➜teaching➜testing

The order is justified on rational grounds. The sequence couldn't start with teaching without specifying what to teach and how what is taught is related to other skills and knowledge that are scheduled for students to learn. Logically the curriculum and standards must be in place before specific teaching occurs. Without these prerequisite processes there would be no safeguards against first-grade teachers presenting material that is neither appropriate for the subject being taught nor for the grade level.

1. Standards:

If the curriculum is math level K or 1, a possible appropriate standard would indicate that learners are to "Count backward from 20 to 0." The standard, "use information from the text to draw conclusions about where Columbus would go next" is more advanced (possibly grade 4 or 5) and is not a math standard but a geography, history, or science standard.

2. Curriculum:

The standards imply specific features of the curriculum. If a skill or informational item is specified in a standard, there necessarily must be a specific segment of the curriculum that provides the instruction needed to teach the skill or information. If this provision is not honored, there would be no rational basis for relating the standards to the curriculum.

A proper curriculum scrupulously details both the order of things that are to be taught and the requirements for adequate or appropriate teaching.

The curriculum is often packaged as an instructional program. A properly developed curriculum would have detailed "lesson plans" that provide adequate directions for the sequence and content of what is to be presented first, next, and next in each successive lesson.

Introduction

The degree to which the teacher's presentation behavior is specified by a lesson script varies greatly across programs, but the goal of all instructional programs is the same—to provide students with the skills and information specified by the standards.

Questions about the adequacy of the teacher presentation are answered empirically, by facts about student performance. If the teacher presents lesson material the way it is specified, and students learn the skills and content, whatever training and scripting the program provided are judged to be adequate. Conversely, if students tend to fail, the presentation the teacher provided is flawed. It may require observations to determine why it failed and what has to change for the teacher to be successful. Note, however, that it is not possible to observe the presentation in one part of the program and extrapolate to unobserved portions of the program. A program could have parts that are quite good with respect to teaching students, and have other parts that are quite bad.

3. Teaching:

Teaching is the process that follows the specifications provided by the curriculum. The relationship is simple: the teaching must transmit to the students all the new skills and knowledge specified in the curriculum. A test of a valid curriculum would show that students did not have specific knowledge and skills before the teacher taught them. The posttest that is presented after instruction shows that students uniformly have the skills. The conclusion is that a process occurred between the pretest and posttest and caused the specific changes in student performance.

The evaluation of a curriculum that occurs when a high percentage of students *fail* the posttest is more complicated. The failure could have been caused by a flawed curriculum, by flawed standards, by a flawed presentation, or by a combination of flawed curriculum, standards, and presentation. If the grade-one standards have items that assume skills that are not usually taught until grade 4 or 5, the teacher fails when she tries to teach her first graders these skills, and the students fail the test items that require these skills.

It is not possible to look at the outcome data alone and infer why the failure of these items occurred. We have to analyze what knowledge and skills students would need to pass these items, and identify the instructional sequence that would be needed to teach this information and skill set.

4. Testing:

The final process is testing. Its purpose is to document the extent to which the student performance meets the standard. Also the testing should be designed to disclose information about each standard. As noted above, if students fail items on the pretest and pass items of the same type on the posttest, we assume that teaching accounted for the change in performance.

Ideally the testing would occur shortly after students have completed the teaching. The testing should be fair and extensive enough to generate specific information about the standards, the curriculum, and the teaching.

Standards that are unreasonably difficult or inadequately taught are identified by examining test results of the highest-performing classrooms. Any items that are failed by more than half of the students are possibly poor items or items that test material that is poorly taught. The most direct way to obtain more specific information about the failed content is to work with students who failed specific items and observe what they tend to do wrong or what information they don't know.

Benefits of Theory of Instruction

Instruction is the essential operation that drives standards, curriculum, and assessment. Instruction provides the basic evidence of what can be achieved in altering student performance. These facts of achievement, in turn, provide the basic foundation for standards, curricula, and testing. The problem with current instructional practices is that there are no widely accepted rules for what instruction is capable of achieving or of the essential details of successful instruction.

This paucity of information occurs because there are no widely accepted guidelines for using facts about teaching to formulate standards or assessments. Stated differently, there is no widely recognized theory of instruction that lays out basic principals of teaching and that provides various empirical tests to facilitate refinement of instructional practices.

Theory of Instruction fills this gap. It articulates principles of effective instruction in sufficient detail to permit educational practitioners to develop effective instruction. The effectiveness of the instruction may be measured by comparing results generated by *Theory of Instruction* with results of other educational approaches.

A final implication is that if educational institutions have clear information about the extent to which students of all levels can be accelerated, the institutions are then able to develop and install reasonable standards, effective curricula, and fair assessments.

Contents

SECTION I – OVERVIEW OF STRATEGIES ... 1
- Chapter 1 – Theoretical Foundations ... 3
- Chapter 2 – Analysis of Basic Communications ... 11
- Chapter 3 – Knowledge Systems ... 23

SECTION II – BASIC FORMS ... 41
- Chapter 4 – Facts and Rules About Communicating Through Examples ... 45
- Chapter 5 – Non-Comparative Sequences ... 53
- Chapter 6 – Nouns ... 65
- Chapter 7 – Comparative Single-Dimension Concepts ... 79

SECTION III – JOINING FORMS ... 91
- Chapter 8 – Single-Transformation Sequences ... 93
- Chapter 9 – Correlated-Features Sequence ... 111

SECTION IV – PROGRAMS ... 127
- Chapter 10 – Introducing Coordinate Members to a Set ... 131
- Chapter 11 – Hierarchical Class Programs ... 147
- Chapter 12 – Programs Derived from Tasks ... 161
- Chapter 13 – Double Transformation Programs ... 173
- Chapter 14 – Programs for Teaching Fact Systems ... 187

SECTION V – COMPLETE TEACHING ... 203
- Chapter 15 – Expanded Teaching ... 205
- Chapter 16 – Worksheet Items ... 215

SECTION VI – CONSTRUCTING COGNITIVE ROUTINES ... 227
- Chapter 17 – Cognitive Routines ... 231
- Chapter 18 – Illustrations of Cognitive Routines ... 245
- Chapter 19 – Scheduling Routines and Their Examples ... 257

Chapter 20 – Prompting Examples 269

Chapter 21 – Covertization 285

SECTION VII – RESPONSE-LOCUS ANALYSIS 297

Chapter 22 – New Response Teaching Procedures 301

Chapter 23 – Strategies for Teaching New Complex Responses 315

Chapter 24 – Expanded Chains 329

Chapter 25 – Expanded Programs for Cognitive Skills 347

SECTION VIII – DIAGNOSIS AND CORRECTIONS 367

Chapter 26 – Diagnosis and Remedies 369

Chapter 27 – Mechanics of Correcting Mistakes 381

Chapter 28 – Program Revision and Implementation 397

SECTION IX – RESEARCH AND PHILOSOPHICAL ISSUES 413

Chapter 29 – Instructional Research: Communication Variables 415

Chapter 30 – Instructional Research: Programs 429

Chapter 31 – Theoretical Issues 449

References 463

Subject Index 469

SECTION I
OVERVIEW OF STRATEGIES

Section I provides the theoretical foundations for the analysis of cognitive skills and the implications that are derived therefrom for how to teach those skills.

The precise analysis of cognitive learning is difficult, if not elusive, because it stands at the juncture of three separate analyses–the analysis of behavior, the analysis of stimuli used as teaching communications, and the analysis of knowledge systems or the content to be taught. (See Figure I.1)

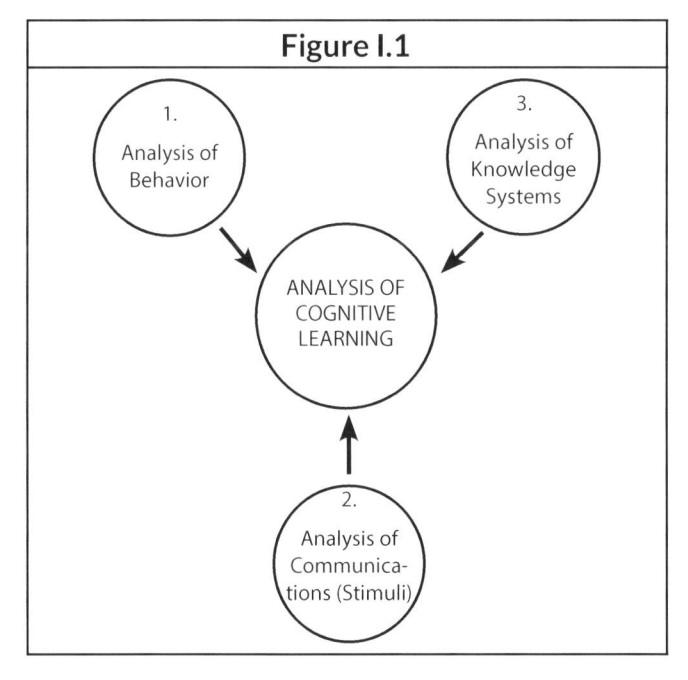

Figure I.1

1. Analysis of Behavior
2. Analysis of Communications (Stimuli)
3. Analysis of Knowledge Systems

→ ANALYSIS OF COGNITIVE LEARNING

1. *The analysis of behavior* seeks *empirically-based* principles that tell what is universally true about the ways in which the environment influences behavior for different classes of learners.
2. *The analysis of communications* seeks principles for the *logical* design of communications that effectively transmit knowledge. These principles allow one to describe the range of generalizations that should logically occur when the learner receives specific sets of examples. The analysis of communications focuses on the ways in which examples are the *same* and how they *differ*.
3. *The analysis of knowledge systems* is concerned with *logically* organizing knowledge so that relatively efficient communications are possible for related knowledge.

The analysis that has received the most attention from psychological theories is the analysis of behavior (Hilgard & Bower, 1975). Although the other two analyses have received some theoretical attention (e.g. Gagne, 1970; Bloom, 1956; Markle & Tiemann, 1974), there has been little systematic effort to develop *precise* principles of communications used in instruction or to analyze knowledge systems.[*] This book frames behavior theory within a three-way analysis of human cognitive learning.

The three areas of analysis derive directly from the nature of cognitive learning. The first aspect of cognitive learning is that the *learner learns from the environment*, which means that the environment is somehow capable of communicating concepts or skills to the learner. The analysis of communications provides rules for designing these communications so they are effective transmitters.

Another aspect of cognitive learning is that it *always involves some topic or content*. When we think, we think about something, even if that something is a process. This aspect of cognitive knowledge carries basic implications for designing the communications that we present to the learner. We cannot communicate with the learner without communicating *something*. Conversely, if we are to understand how to communicate a particular bit of knowledge (such as knowledge of the color **red**, or knowledge about the operation of **square root**), we must understand the essential features of the particular concept that we are attempting to convey. Only if we understand what it is and how it differs from related concepts can

---

[*] Although analyses such as Gagne's deal with learning and with the teaching of concepts, principals, etc., the theoretical development is at best a beginning.

we design a communication that effectively conveys the concept to the learner.

The final aspect of cognitive learning has to do with the relationship of a given concept to other concepts. The word **large** is related to the word **blue** because both function as adjectives. The color **blue** is related to the color **red** because both have the properties of color. The relatedness of cognitive knowledge suggests that it is possible to develop a classification system for various types of knowledge (circle 3 in Figure I.1). If this classification system is to be of value to the instructional designer, the system should be designed so that the classification of a particular skill carries information about how to communicate that skill to a learner. Concepts that are structurally the same in some respects can be processed through communications that are the same in some respects.

Both the analysis of communications and the analysis of knowledge systems are *logical analyses* that involve assumptions about the learner. The analysis of behavior, however, investigates the learner and how the learner responds to specific communications. Chapter 1 presents an overview of the strategy that we will use to unite the three parts of the analysis; Chapter 2 further develops the analysis of communications; Chapter 3 outlines the organization of knowledge types that will be used throughout the book.

Chapter 1
Theoretical Foundations

A theory of instruction begins with the assumption that the environment is the primary variable in accounting for what the learner learns. The different skills learned by people in different environments suggest that the assumption is reasonable. People who live in primitive societies learn skills quite different from those learned by people who live in urban societies. Although the environment is assumed to be the primary cause of what is learned, it is not assumed to be the total cause. Within any group of people there are individual differences. Also, there are differences that correlate with the age of the learner. Therefore, the learner is also a variable.

To show the relationship between the role of the environment and the learner, we are faced with the basic problem of experimental control. We must control one of these variables (the environment or the learner) before we can make precise observations about the other variable. Ideally, we would rule out or eliminate one of these variables (either the environment or the learner) and observe the remaining variable in a pure state. This solution is not possible. A possible solution is to control one of the variables so that it functioned as if it were ruled out. We cannot readily achieve such control over the learner because we do not know precisely how to do it. However, such control is possible with the environment. We can design communications that are, ideally, faultless. Faultless communications are designed to convey only one interpretation. From a logical standpoint, these communications would be capable of teaching any learner the intended concept or skill. When we present such a communication to the learner, we effectively rule out the environment as a *variable*. The communication is not merely standardized; it is analytically or logically capable of transmitting the concept or skill to *any learner who possesses certain minimal attributes discussed later.* The learner either responds to the faultless communication by learning the intended concept, or the learner fails to learn the intended concept. In either case, the learner's performance is framed as the dependent variable. The extent to which the learner's performance deviates from the performance that would occur if the learner responded perfectly to the communication provides us with precise information about the learner. The deviations indicate the extent to which the learner is not a perfect "mirror" of the environment. Furthermore, these deviations are caused by the learner (not the environment, which has been controlled so that it is faultless).

The strategy of making the communication faultless and then observing the performance of the learner is the basis for the theory of instructions that we will develop. We will use this strategy in designing instructional sequences and in deriving principles for communicating with the learner. The following is a summary of the steps in our strategy, showing where logical analysis is used and where behavior analysis comes into play:

1. Design communications that are faultless using a *logical analysis* of the stimuli, not a *behavioral analysis* of the learner.

2. Predict that the learner will learn the concept conveyed by the faultless presentation. If the communication is logically flawless and if the learner has the capacity to respond to the logic of the presentation, the learner will learn the concept conveyed by the communication.

3. Present the communication to the learner and observe whether the learner actually learns the intended concept or whether the learner has trouble. This information (derived from a behavioral analysis) shows the extent to which the learner does or does not possess the mechanisms necessary to respond to the faultless presentation of the concept.

4. Design instruction for the unsuccessful learner that will modify the learner's capacity to respond to the faultless presentation. This instruction is not based on a logical analysis of the communication, *but on a behavior analysis of the learner.*

Note that the behavioral analysis comes into play only after the communication has been designed so that it is faultless. The faultless presentation rules out the possibility that the learner's inability to respond appropriately to the presentation, or to generalize in the predicted way, is caused by a flawed communication rather than by learner characteristics.

Assumptions About the Learner

The primary problem that we face in pursuing this strategy is that we do not know what constitutes a faultless communication *unless we make some assumptions about the learner*. Stated differently, assumptions about the learner and the communication vary together. The greater the assumed capabilities of the learner, the less the assumed responsibility of the communication. If we assume that the learner will learn from any exposure to the environment, we will provide communications that do not control details of the presentation. If we assume that the learner is not capable of learning from communications that are ambiguous, we will approach the design of communications quite differently. To provide for control of the maximum number of communication variables, we must postulate a *simple* learning mechanism. Also, we must assume that the learner's behavior is lawful, which means the learner who possesses the assumed mechanism will learn what the communication demonstrates or teaches.

The learning mechanism that we postulate has two attributes:

1. The capacity to learn any quality that is exemplified through examples (from the quality of **redness** to the quality of **inconsistency**).
2. The capacity to generalize to new examples on the basis of sameness of quality (and only on the basis of sameness).

These attributes suggest the capacities that we would have to build into a computer that functions the way a human does. Note that we are not asserting that these are the only attributes that a human possesses, merely that by assuming the two attributes we can account for nearly all observed *cognitive behavior*.

1. The Capacity to Learn Any Quality from Examples

This assumption indicates *what* the mechanism is capable of learning, not how it learns. A quality is any irreducible feature of the example. The simplest way to identify qualities is to begin with a concrete example. Any example (such as a pencil) has thousands of qualities, which relate to shape, position, parts, color, texture, etc. All differences between a given concrete example and any other concrete example are differences in quality. Also, anything we do to change the example we start with is a change in quality. We can make the pencil shorter, break the point, paint it, change its position, and so forth. Each change is related to a quality of the original example.

The assumption that the learner mechanism learns qualities means simply that if an example possesses a quality, no matter how subtle, the mechanism has the capacity to learn that quality. The only factor that limits the learner mechanism is the acuity of the sensory mechanism that receives information about qualities. This mechanism, however, is capable of learning qualities as subtle as the unique tone of a particular violin or qualities that involve the correlation of events (such as the relationship of events on the sun to weather on the earth).

2. The Capacity to Generalize on the Basis of Sameness of Quality

Attribute 1 above indicates what the learner is capable of learning. Attribute 2 suggests *how* learning occurs. According to this attribute, the learning mechanism somehow "makes up a rule" that indicates which qualities are common to the set of examples presented to teach a concept. By using this rule, the mechanism classifies new examples as either positive examples of the concept or negative examples. A new example is positive if it has the same quality(ies) possessed by all the positive examples presented earlier. It is a negative example if it does not have the same quality(ies).

According to the assumption about the generalization attribute, there is no sharp line between initial learning and generalization. The rule-construction of the learning mechanism is assumed to begin as soon as examples are presented. In formulating a rule, the mechanism does nothing more than "note" *sameness of quality*. Once the mechanism "has determined" what is the same about the examples of a particular concept, generalization occurs. The only possible basis for generalization is sameness of quality. If the example to which the learner is to generalize is not the same as the earlier examples with respect to specific qualities it is impossible for generalization to occur unless the learning mechanism is empowered with magical properties.

A further implication of attribute 2 is that the generalizations the learning mechanism achieves are completely explained in terms of the examples presented to the learner and the qualities that are common to these examples.

Table 1.1 illustrates how the learning of **conservation of substance** is the same as the learning of **red.**

Table 1.1	
Learning of a Cognitive Operation (e.g., Conservation of Substance)	Learning of Red
Before exposure to examples, the learner has no knowledge of concept.	Before exposure to examples, the learner has no knowledge of concept.
Only some possible examples are examples of this concept.	Only some possible examples are examples of this concept.
The learner demonstrates mastery of concept by treating selected concrete examples of the concept in specified ways.	The learner demonstrates mastery of concept by treating selected concrete examples of the concept in specified ways.
The learner generalizes to new examples of the concept.	The learner generalizes to new examples of the concept.
The appropriate generalizations are to examples that possess the quality of the concept.	The appropriate generalizations are to examples that possess the quality of the concept.

Both concepts are learned in the same way—through a communication from the environment that shows the nature of the concept. The only difference is *what* is learned. And the "whatness" is the quality that comes from the examples, not the learner. For the learner to learn these diversely different qualities, the learner must have the ability to detect both the quality of **redness** and the quality common to the **conservation** examples (e.g., the relationship between changes in appearance and changes in amount).

The Structural Basis for Generalization

The assumptions about the two-attribute learning mechanism imply the type of structure that we must provide to cause specific generalizations. The two-attribute learning mechanism suggests that the learner operates on qualities and sameness, and that both the qualities and samenesses come from the concrete examples that have the same quality and provide information that these concrete examples are the same in a relevant way.

The most general implication of the two-attribute mechanism is the nature of the analysis that we must use for cognitive learning. If the only primary difference between such disparate cognitive skills as learning the color **red** and learning **conservation of substance** is the quality that is to be learned, and if the quality comes from concrete examples (and not from the learner), the primary analysis of cognitive learning must be an analysis of *qualities of examples and of the communications that present these qualities to the learner*. This analysis focuses on the stimuli that the learner receives. We refer to this analysis as the *stimulus-locus* analysis (which is developed further in this and subsequent chapters).

More specific implications of the two-attribute learning mechanisms suggest the general parameters of a communication that is capable of inducing a particular generalization. This communication must meet these structural conditions:

1. The set of positive examples presented through the communication must possess one and only one distinguishing quality. If we assume that the learner learns qualities that are presented through examples, we must make sure that the set of examples presented demonstrates *only one identifiable sameness in quality*—not more than one. If every positive example in the set that is presented to the learner possesses two distinct qualities, at least two distinct generalizations are implied by the communication. Since one of these generalizations is inappropriate, the set of examples does not meet the structural conditions necessary for inducing the intended generalization. For instance, if every example of **red** presented to the learner was a circle and every example that was **not-red** was box-shaped, at least two generalizations are implied by the same communication. Possibly the learner will generalize according to sameness in shape (calling any circle "red" regardless of shape). Both generalizations are possible because both are based on the qualities and samenesses shown by the demonstration examples. Since a given learner is assumed to have no preknowledge of the concept and must base the generalization solely on the quality and sameness of demonstrated examples, a given learner may learn an inappropriate generalization from the demonstration of red circles.

To avoid this problem, we must eliminate the inappropriate quality from the demonstration examples. Different techniques are possible for achieving this goal;

however, the simplest is to modify the set of examples so that some of the examples identified by the teacher as "not red" are circles. With this modification, the set does not present *circularity* as a distinguishing quality of the positive examples.

2. The communication must also provide a signal that accompanies each example that has the quality to be generalized. This signal is the only means we have for *treating examples in the same way*. When we present examples that are physically different (such as two examples of **red** that are not the same shade) we must use some form of signal to tell the learner, in effect, that these examples are the same and that the learner must discover how they are the same. The signal, typically a behavior such as saying "red" for all examples that are red, also provides the learner with a basis for communicating with us. The learner can use the same signal, "red," to let us know which generalization examples have the quality of **redness.**

The assumption about the signal accompanying the various examples is necessary because our goal is to induce a particular generalization. However, if we simply present a group of examples that share a particular quality, we cannot guarantee that: (a) the learner will attend to the common quality; or (b) we will be able to communicate about this quality, even if the learner does attend to it. For instance, if we present a group of objects that are red, how do we know that the learner is attending to the sameness in the quality these examples share? We face other problems if we wish to test the learner to see if the generalization was induced. How does the learner indicate which generalization examples have the quality? Unless we use some signal to suggest sameness (such as putting all red objects in one place or calling them "red" or associating some other unique signal with each example), we cannot demonstrate sameness; we cannot test sameness; and we cannot correct the learner who responds inappropriately.

For the most basic type of communication, two signals are implied. One is used for examples that have the quality. Another is used for examples that do not have the quality.

3. The communication must present a range of examples that show the physical variation of the examples that exhibit a common quality. If every example that the communication presents to the learner is exactly the same shade of red, the communication does not provide adequate information about the range of variation in the quality that is to be labeled as "red." Since this demonstration does not imply that other shades of red share the quality of **redness**, the communication is incapable of inducing the appropriate generalization to examples of other shades of **red.**

To show the quality that is to be generalized, the communication must demonstrate (through examples) the range of variation that typifies the concept. In other words, the communication must present positive examples that are physically different, but that share the quality that is to be generalized.

The requirement of showing a range of positive variation derives directly from our assumptions about the learning mechanism. We assume that the learner is capable of learning any quality exemplified through examples. For most concepts, the quality is something that is common to variations that are physically different. We assume that the learner has the capacity to make up a "rule" about this range of variation. We further assume that if we do not show an appropriate range of variation, the learner is not provided with the information that is necessary to formulate the appropriate "rule." Therefore, if the communication fails to demonstrate the range, the learner cannot be expected to generalize appropriately.

4. A basic communication must present negative examples to show the limits of the variation in quality that is permissible for a given concept. If we show the learner a range of red examples that differ in shades of redness, the communication may appropriately induce a generalization to new examples that are red. (The learner with the two-attribute learning mechanism should appropriately classify any example that falls within the demonstrated range of variation as "red.") However, this communication does not show the boundaries for the generalization, which means that on a test of generalization, the learner may call pink examples "red."

To show the learner basic concepts, the communication must demonstrate the boundaries for the range of permissible generalization. All negatives presented to demonstrate the limits of permissible variation are the same in that they possess the quality of being "not red." To signal that these negative examples are the same, a common behavior is presented with each example. To assure that the learner does not classify these examples in the same way that the positive examples are classified, the communication presents a different signal for the negatives (for example, "not red"). The basic communication, therefore, presents *two* sets of examples (one for the positives and one for the negatives) and two distinct signals (one to signal each positive and the other to signal each negative).

5. The communication must provide a test to assure that the learner has received the information provided by the communication. The test should present positive examples and negative examples that had not been demonstrated earlier, but that are implied by the range of variation of quality demonstrated for the positives and the negatives. If the learner has formulated an appropriate "rule" for the quality that had been demonstrated through the demonstration examples, the learner should be able to respond appropriately to new examples that fall within the range of variation previously demonstrated. A variation of the same signals that are used to demonstrate positive and negative examples is used when the generalization examples are tested.

In summary, the two-attribute learning mechanism implies that a communication for basic concepts must meet these structural requirements.

1. The communication must present a set of examples that are the same with respect to one and only one distinguishing quality (the quality that is to serve as the basis for generalization).

2. The communication must provide two signals—one for every example that possesses the quality that is to be generalized, the second to signal every example that does not have this quality.

3. The communication must demonstrate a range of variation for the positive examples (to induce a rule that is appropriate for classifying new examples on the basis of sameness).

4. The communication must show the limits of permissible variation by presenting negative examples.

5. The communication must provide a test of generalization that involves new examples that fall within the range of quality variation demonstrated earlier.

Analyzing Whether Communications are Faultless

In addition to serving as guidelines for creating faultless communications, the five points above provide the basis for analyzing communications to determine whether they are faultless. The primary analysis for the communication involves no reference to a particular learner. The analysis does not deal with empirical information, but with the structural basis for generalization that is provided by the communication. A communication is judged faultless if it meets the five structural requirements outlined above. The set of examples presented to the learner must be unambiguous about the quality that is to be generalized. The examples must be designed so that only one quality is unique to all positive examples. The range of positive variation exemplified by the set of demonstration examples must be sufficient to imply the appropriate generalization. The negatives should be precise in demonstrating the boundaries of a permissible generalization. The signals presented with the examples must unambiguously provide the basis for classifying examples as either positives or negatives. The test of generalization that is presented as part of the communication must assure that the learner appropriately responds to new positive and negative examples that are clearly implied by the set of demonstration examples. In summary, the communication is judged faultless if it adequately provides the learner with information about *quality* and *sameness*.

The structural requirements that must be met if a communication is to be judged faultless do not refer to specific techniques that are used to correct an inappropriate communication or to design one efficiently. However, these techniques (which are discussed in later chapters) follow from the structural requirements. If we understand that a communication must show that a particular quality is unique to the positive examples, we will investigate possible techniques that achieve this goal. From the possibilities we will select those that are most efficient and those that show the uniqueness most emphatically. Similarly, the design of the test examples can be reduced to some how-to-do-it formula once we understand what the test examples must do.

The five structural requirements derive directly from our assumptions about the learner. We can appreciate the implications of the two-attribute learning mechanism by considering how the structural basis for a generalization would change if we changed our assumptions about the learning mechanism. For instance, if we assumed that the learner generalized on the basis of *similarity,* not sameness, we would not be provided with a strict standard about whether the communication that we design presents examples that are *"similar."* The notion of similarity is not precise and it begs the question of how the *"similar"* examples are the same. If examples are similar, they must be the same with respect to some quality, but the notion of similarity does not require us to identify this qualitative sameness. Therefore, similarity leads to an imprecise standard for evaluating our communication. By assuming that the learner generalizes only on the basis of sameness, we are required to create examples that are the *same* in some identifiable way, and the standard we use is objectively stronger.

If we assumed that the learner's generalizations are not clearly determined by the common quality of the concrete examples of a concept, we would not be provided with a standard for judging whether a communication adequately shows both the quality and the range of variation in the quality across various examples. We might assume that the generalization would occur simply if the learner received some "exposure" to the concept. But we would not have any analytical yardsticks for determining whether the "exposure" presented through a particular communication was adequate.

With the assumed two-attribute learning mechanism, however, we are provided both with general guidelines for creating structures that will induce specific generalizations, and with more specific implications about what the communication must do and what it must avoid doing.

Predictions of Generalizations

The procedure for determining flaws in a communication is a logical one, based on observable details of the communication. The procedure therefore permits us to make predictions about what the learner will learn. These predictions are independent of the learner. The basic form that these predictions take is that if the communication is flawless (adequately meets the five structural requirements), the learner will learn the generalization that is conveyed through the communication. The learner will respond appropriately to the examples that test the generalization and will respond to additional examples that are implied by the demonstration examples. Conversely, if the communication has flaws, some learners who receive this communication will learn the inappropriate quality demonstrated by the flawed aspect of the communication.

Equally important, the development of procedures for determining whether a communication is faultless permits us to engage in a very precise study of the learner. A faultless communication serves as a *standard* against which we compare the learner's performance. If this communication is analytically faultless (with respect to clarity in communicating one and only one possible generalization), any learner who possesses the two-attribute learning mechanism will learn the concept that is presented by the communication. If a learner does not perform in the predicted manner, we immediately know three things about that learner:

1. We know that the learner does not have (or is not using) the two-attribute mechanism.

2. We know the precise ways that the learner's performance deviated from the predicted performance.

3. Because we know that the problem resides with the learner and not with the communication (which is judged faultless), and because we know precisely how the learner has deviated from the predicted standard, we know how we must modify the learner so that the learner is capable of performing acceptably in response to the communication.

We are able to make these strong inferences about the learner because we have ruled out the possibility that the learner's poor performance can be accounted for by the presentation. Furthermore (as we observed earlier), we would not be able to draw precise conclusions about the learner unless we ruled out the possibility that the communication has flaws and that the learner is responding in a logically reasonable way to the flawed communication. If the learner generalized to circles following the communication that presented circularity as a quality common to all positive examples of **red**, we would be presumptuous if we interpreted this generalization as an indication of a "faulty" learning mechanism. Only if the communication is faultless can we make strong inferences about the learner.

Stimulus-Locus and Response-Locus Analyses

Although the major goal of this book is to describe procedures for designing effective instructional communications, not to study the learner's behavior, the procedure that we use parallels the one that we would use to study the learner. We use two analyses. The primary analysis is a *stimulus-locus analysis,* which deals with an analysis of the stimuli or communications the learner receives. The second analysis is the *response-locus analysis,* which focuses on the learner. This analysis comes into play if the learner is unable (for whatever reason) to produce the responses that are called for by the communication. The response-locus analysis consists of techniques for modifying the learner's capacity to produce responses. If the learner does not respond in the predicted manner to a faultless communication, the assumed "fault" lies not with the communication, but with the learner. Therefore, we must switch our focus. This switch involves a complete change in orientation, from a concern with the analyses of communicating quality and sameness in a precise manner, to the laws of behavior. These laws provide us with specific guides about the amount of practice, the massing and distribution of trials, the schedules of reinforcement, and other variables that cause the growth or strengthening of the learner's response to take place. For example, if the learner apparently forgets the word **red** and cannot respond to various examples in a faultless presentation that asks the learner, "What color is this?", we modify the learner's capacity to "remember" how to produce the name. When the learner reliably remembers the words, we return to the original communication. The learner is now assumed to be an adequate receiver, capable of responding according to the predictions of the stimulus-locus analysis.

The basic difference between the response-locus analysis and the stimulus-locus analysis is that the stimulus-locus analysis does not involve the learner. It involves the logic of *ruling out all the possibilities but the one* to be conveyed through a teaching communication. The response-locus analysis is based on empirical findings on learning.

When instruction in skills involves teaching new responses (those the learner has never produced before in response to any signal), we use the stimulus-locus analysis to design the sequence of skills to minimize possible conceptual confusion. We also use response-locus techniques to assure that the new responses are induced efficiently. However, even for the teaching of "motor skills" (such as shoe-tying, ball-throwing, etc.), the stimulus-locus analysis is the primary one. The reason is that the communications must be clear and must be organized so that the appropriate generalizations are induced and the appropriate response generalizations are implied. These communications, however, rely heavily on the application of behavioral principles.

Extending the Stimulus-Locus Analysis to Types of Knowledge

If we follow the stimulus-locus assumptions to their conclusion, we discover that knowledge may be classified according to the *samenesses of communications* used to teach various concepts. The samenesses in features of the communication parallel samenesses in the concepts that are to be taught. Viewed differently, the extent to which concepts are the same provides a precise measure of the extent to which faultless communications for these concepts may have the same features or attributes. Let's say that we design a faultless presentation for a particular concept. The communication isolates the quality presented to the learner, unambiguously signals the quality through examples, and provides additional examples for testing the learner's generalizations. To design a faultless communication for a concept that is highly similar to the original one, we would create a communication that is highly similar to the original one. The close logical parallel between the structure of the concepts we wish to teach and the structure of the communications that convey these concepts faultlessly results because the two concepts are the same with respect to many qualities. The samenesses in quality of the concepts is reflected in the samenesses in the communications that convey these qualities. Conversely, if two concepts differ in many ways, the faultless communications that communicate them will have many differences.

By extending the notion of the parallel between the structure of concepts and the structure of communications that convey them faultlessly, we are provided with general guidelines for creating *classes of cognitive skills.* For this classification, each category consists of concepts or skills that are the same with respect to important *structural* features. *Since the concepts in each category share samenesses, all concepts within a given category can be processed through simple variations or transformations of the same basic communication or form.* To classify a concept within this system is to be provided with an algorithm for communicating the concept to a learner who is assumed to possess the two-attribute learning mechanism.

Summary

The design and analysis of communications are based on assumptions about the kind of information the learner is capable of extracting from the communication. For analytical purposes, we postulated a learning mechanism that has these attributes: the capacity to learn any stimulus quality shown through examples, and the capacity to generalize a sameness of quality to new examples. This assumed mechanism implies that the primary analysis of cognitive learning must focus on quality and sameness of the examples presented to the learner. Further implications suggest the structural criteria that must be met by a communication if the communication is to induce a generalization for a basic concept.

1. The positive examples of the concept must be distinguished by one and only one quality.
2. An unambiguous signal must accompany each positive example, and a different signal must accompany each negative example.
3. The examples must demonstrate the range of variation to which the learner will be expected to generalize.
4. Negative examples must clearly show the boundaries of permissible positive variation.
5. Test examples, different from those presented to demonstrate the concept, assure that the generalization has occurred.

These criteria serve as guidelines for designing faultless communications and for determining whether a particular communication is faultless. The analysis of communications according to the structural features of the communication is the stimulus-locus analysis. The stimulus-locus analysis assumes that the learner is a "receiver" capable of attending to the information presented through a "faultless" communication. However, a particular learner may not learn in the predicted manner. The difference between the learner's actual performance and that predicted by the stimulus-locus analysis suggests the extent to which the learner does not respond to the basic logic of the communication (the logic of quality and sameness). If the learner is incapable of producing responses that are implied by the stimulus-locus analysis, our focus shifts from the stimulus-locus analysis to the response-locus analysis. Behavioral principles are used to induce new responses and to maintain responses.

Chapter 2
Analysis of Basic Communications

This chapter describes basic communications, elaborates the procedures by which sameness and difference are conveyed to the learner, and outlines a new type of diagnosis of learning failure that is implied by stimulus-locus analysis.

Basic Communications

Basic communications play a very important role in a theory of instruction. They are the simplest forms that are used to communicate concepts. More elaborate forms are extensions of basic communications.

A communication occurs when the learner is presented with examples and verbal descriptions that demonstrate *how to respond to particular stimuli*. For the stimulus-locus analysis, *the most basic communications are those that deal with generalizations*. A non-generalization item, such as the task, "What's your name?" is perhaps more adequately viewed through a response-locus analysis. Even this task becomes involved in a generalization when the learner must discriminate who is to respond when "What is your name?" is presented to different people.

The most basic communication for the stimulus-locus analysis has the following features:

1. *A set of examples* or instances.
2. *Some behavioral signal* provided by the teacher with each example.

The set of examples consists of the things or events shown to the learner. All positive examples of the concept within a set have the quality that is being taught.

The behavior signal demonstrates whether a particular example has the quality. The signal may be complicated or simple. In the simplest form, the teacher uses two behaviors, the first for signaling, "Yes, this example has the features you are to attend to." The other behavior signals, "No, this example does not have the features." Any two behaviors can be used to communicate information about the "yes-no" classification of the examples in the set.

Any sameness shared by all examples that are treated in the same way describes a generalization. If the examples treated in the same way share quality **A** and if the learner has the capacity to abstract this sameness, the learner will generalize to examples that have quality **A.**

If we hand a toddler a crayon and say, "Red," then present another crayon and say, "Red," we are asserting that there is something the same about both examples. If there were no structural sameness in the object, *we would have no basis for treating them in the same way.* By treating things the same way, we do not guarantee that we communicate *how* they are the same. We merely signal that *something* about the situations is the same. Perhaps the act of receiving a crayon is "red;" perhaps the act of coloring is "red;" perhaps anything you can scribble with is "red." All possibilities are suggested by the communication above, because both examples that were treated the same way share these structural features.

This list of facts in Table 2.1 shows some "samenesses" possessed by both examples. The samenesses are the possible bases for generalizations.

Table 2.1		
If Object 1:	And Object 2:	Then the sameness being demonstrated is:
Was handed to the child	Was handed to the child	Handing something
Was colored red	Was colored red	Colored red
Was wrapped in paper	Was wrapped in paper	Wrapped in paper
Was used for coloring	Was used for coloring	Used for coloring

The last column shows that many samenesses are logically implied by the communication. Which will the learner select? The answer is beyond the stimulus-locus analysis. We do not assume that the child has any preknowledge of the appropriate sameness. We therefore assume that the possibilities are "equal." We might modify this conclusion on the basis of empirical information of how learners respond.

Learning Sets

We might further modify our conclusion on the basis of what the learner has learned in the past. For example, if the presentation above has immediately followed the successful teaching of **green, yellow,** and **blue,** there would be very little doubt that the presentation would teach **red.**

The reason, however, is that the teacher is treating various objects in the same way.

- If coordinate objects in group 1 have a particular color (green),
- and coordinate objects in group 2 have a particular color (yellow),
- then coordinate objects in group 3 have a particular color (red).

This is a rather sophisticated extension of the sameness application. The idea is basically simple. The learner is prompted to attend to a particular set of features because the previous communications have shown that these features are the basis for the preceding discriminations. The present communication involves examples that have many of the same visual properties the preceding communications had. The present communication also involves teacher behavior that has many of the same features as the behavior presented with the earlier communications.

Research on "learning sets" (Harlow, 1959) has shown that learners tend to learn faster or better on subsequent examples of the same type (e.g., oddity problems). The process can be explained by referring to what is the *same* about the various examples and the behavior used to signal them. Puzzles of a given type have solution features that are *the same.* By learning to respond successfully to different puzzles, the learner learns how to treat the puzzles in that same way. Therefore, subsequent puzzles involve less new learning than initial puzzles. The learner has learned to process the later puzzles through the same strategy steps that led to solutions with the earlier puzzles.

Tests of Generalization

The stimulus-locus approach treats generalizations as the product of the communication. Samenesses, which form the structural basis for generalization, are shown through the communication. The learner will select one of the generalizations communicated. For us to determine whether this selection has occurred, we must test the learner. The simplest test is to present the learner with examples and see if the learner treats each in the appropriate manner. If we deal with a very simple communication (one that uses a "yes" signal for some examples and a "no" signal for others), we would present the learner with *new examples that share a particular sameness with the examples identified earlier as "yes" and new examples that share the sameness with examples identified as "no."* From the learner's pattern of responses we can determine whether or not the learner has learned a particular sameness. Note that the new examples we present may be physically different from the examples presented during the communication with the learner so long as they clearly possess a sameness shared by all the "yes" examples or by all the "no" examples.

The tests of generalization are limited to certain objective facets of the communication. We do not assume, however, that the communication conveys only these samenesses. If the receiver of the communication is capable of learning samenesses that are intentionally shown by the communication, the learner is also capable of learning many other "associations." The teacher's green dress may be the same as someone's dress in a past situation of some import; the sound that occurs in the background may be the same as sounds in other learning situations. These "associations" will certainly occur. For instructional design purposes, however, we do not deal with these generalizations because we are unable to control them. No matter how carefully we control the ambient aspects of the learning situation, many uncontrolled generalizations will be possible.

Basic Concepts and Examples

A basic concept is one that cannot be fully described with other words (other than synonyms). A communication for a basic concept, therefore, is one that requires concrete examples. We cannot explain **red** to a blind person in a way that would permit the person to discriminate between red and not-red objects. Similarly, concepts such as **smooth, heavy, over, toward, happy,** etc., require concrete examples unless the learner already knows the concept by a different label (**unrough, unlight, above, closer, glad**). Examples are needed to teach these concepts because the words that we use are not containers of the concept. They are merely symbols that stand for particular qualities. Unless the communication presents the learner with the actual experience of the quality being symbolized, the communication provides no basis for understanding which quality or property the symbol represents.

A problem with concepts and their analysis is their potential confusion with words. A basic concept is not a word and does not logically imply words. The qualities (the samenesses that exist in sets of examples) are "real" and objective. The words used to refer to them are creations. These creations are useful if they serve their primary functions of signaling the quality. They may have a secondary function of fitting into grammar and possibly possessing features that are shared by other words that refer to similar events. (The word **sixty** is related to the word **six** because both have a common part and that part refers to a common feature of reality.) *But the word is not the concept and does not imply the concept to a naive person.*

Inducing Patterns of Responses

If we used only one word for each quality we would have no problem with words. The fact that one word has many possible meanings, however, suggests that if we begin with the analysis of words, we may become so embroiled in word games that we fail to observe that this approach is irrelevant. We should begin with the *idea* (basic sensory concept) that we wish to teach, not the word. Here's how we could test an idea. We simply test the learner's response pattern by requiring the learner to point to different examples that show a concept. For instance, after instruction, we could tell the learner: "Point to all the objects that are **over** the table." The *pattern* of responses for pointing does not require the learner to use words. However, the pattern shows the generalization. The same pattern would be observed if we substituted a verbal response for the pointing response.

If the question presented with each example is, "Is this object over the table?" the learner would say, "Yes" for every object that had been touched and "No" for every example not touched. If we tell the learner, "Tell me 'over' or 'not-over'," the learner would say, "Over," for every object previously touched. If the same examples are responded to in one way when we require pointing to objects, when we require the learner to say "Yes," and when we require the learner to say "Over," something

must be the same about those objects. If the only observable sameness is the quality of being **over,** we conclude that: (1) we have induced this quality or idea; and (2) the idea does not depend on any particular response. (The pattern of responses remains stable over different responses.)

The words that we use are merely signals for the qualities of examples. We make no assumption that teaching the particular meanings signaled by **over** will induce the understanding of **over** when it is used in this way: "The party is over." Furthermore, we make no judgment about the relative *value* of the word **over** to describe the position, or about whether the learner should be taught the other meanings that are conventionally labeled with the word **over.** ("She's done that paper over four times.") The objective of a teaching communication is to convey *one meaning,* calling the learner's attention to a *particular* sameness. We *select* a word that is conventionally acceptable for this purpose. Then we teach the learner about the relevant sameness, using the word that we have selected.

Concrete Examples

We have already alluded to the notion that a *set* of examples must be shown to induce basic concepts. It is logically impossible to present a single example of a basic concept that shows *only* one concept. The reason is that an example capable of showing only one concept would have to possess only one quality or property. It would have to exist without any features that are irrelevant to the concept. If we are teaching **redness,** the example would have to show only redness—not space, position, duration, shape, or other identifiable non-color features. Such examples do not exist.

To determine the other concepts or qualities that a particular example of **red** exhibits, we ask, "Could this object be used as an example of ____?" Let's say that a concrete example of **red** is a rectangular piece of red felt placed on a felt board. The test of the other concepts this example exhibits discloses that the example could be used to demonstrate an indefinitely large number of *other* concepts. The concrete example is an example of **cloth,** of **felt cloth,** of **felt cloth of a particular shape,** of **felt cloth in a particular place,** of **an object,** of **a solid object,** of **an object smaller than a breadbox,** of **an object smaller than a dog,** of **an object smaller than. . .,** of the number **1,** of the number **4** (four corners), of **on,** of **above the floor,** of . . . The list continues indefinitely. Furthermore, a similar indefinitely long list can be constructed for any example that is presented to show a basic concept.

Although a concrete presentation is an example of thousands and thousands of concepts, the *set of concepts* generated by one concrete example is never the same as the set generated by another example. The reason is that if the sets were identical, the examples would be the same in every conceivable detail, which means that they would occupy the same place at the same time. They would therefore be the same example. Given that they are different examples, there is a difference between them, which means that we can make observations about one of the examples that we cannot make about the other. By manipulating the differences of examples, we can rule out irrelevant qualities that are inevitably present in the isolated example.

Analysis of Communicating Sameness

The learning of basic discriminations or concepts is *inductive*. The teacher treats concept examples one way (uses a common signal). The learner must identify the qualities that are referred to and learn that the word serves to signal the qualities.

Figure 2.1 shows five examples, each of which is labeled "glert." The word **glert**, therefore, stands for some particular feature or combination of features. The features of each example are represented by the letters **A**, **B**, **C** and **D**. Example 1 is presented first, and example 5 last.

Figure 2.1					
Examples	1	2	3	4	5
Features Within Examples	A B C D	A B C D	A B C Not-D	A B Not-C D	A B Not-C Not-D
Teacher Behavior	"glert"	"glert"	"glert"	"glert"	"glert"

Example 3 shows that **D** is not necessarily a feature of **glert**. This communication is achieved through the following inferences: the examples of **glert** can be treated the same way only if they are structurally the same. Example 3 is treated the same way as examples 1 and 2. Example 3 does not possess feature **D**. Therefore, feature **D** is not a necessary feature of **glert**.

The communication provided by the *entire set* of five examples suggests that **A** and **B** are necessary for **glert**. Both **A** and **B** appear in all examples and they are the only features common to all examples. However, the communication provides the following possibilities:

Glert refers to **A**.
Glert refers to **B**.
Glert refers to **A** and **B**.

A communication that is effective in showing that **A** is the only feature relevant to **glert** follows a *juxtaposition rule* for showing sameness. The rule: *To show sameness, juxtapose examples that are greatly different; treat each example in the same way*. (To juxtapose examples, present one immediately after the other or position the examples next to each other.)

Figure 2.2 draws a set of five examples that is consistent with the rule. All examples are positive instances of **glert**. All are treated in the same way (by being referred to as "glert"). And the sequence juxtaposes maximally different examples. The first example has four features (**A**, **B**, **C**, **D**). The second example has one feature **A**. Since both examples are called "glert," the concept of **glert** cannot be associated with what is different about the two examples, but only with what is the same—feature **A**. Different arrangements of examples would be as effective as the one given; however, any effective arrangement should juxtapose examples that are greatly different.

Figure 2.2					
Examples	1	2	3	4	5
Features	A B C D	A Not-B Not-C Not-D	A B Not-C Not-D	A Not-B C Not-D	A B Not-C Not-D
Teacher Behavior	"glert"	"glert"	"glert"	"glert"	"glert"

Analysis of Communicating Differences

Just as structural sameness is implied if all examples are treated in the same way, a structural difference is implied if two examples are treated in a different way. The difference assumption is: If two things are treated differently, the examples must be different with respect to some feature. A poor communication is one that presents negative examples that are greatly different from the positive examples of the concept. Figure 2.3 shows why large differences are ineffective.

Figure 2.3		
Examples	1	2
Features	A B C D	Not-A Not-B Not-C Not-D
Teacher Behavior	"glert"	"not-glert"

These juxtaposed examples differ in **A**, **B**, **C** and **D**. The behavior of the teacher signals that there is a structural difference between the examples (calling one example "glert" and the other "not-glert"). The problem is that there are many differences between example 1 and example 2. The only difference that "causes" example 2 to be treated differently from example 1 is the absence of **A**. All the other features are structurally irrelevant. The communication provided by the juxtaposition of these examples, however, provides many possible options about which features *cause* the change in the teacher's behavior. Stated differently, if a capable learner received the information provided by the communication above, the learner might not identify the example in Figure 2.4 as "not-glert."

Figure 2.4
Not-A
B
C
Not-D

The learner may identify it as "glert" or as "not-glert." Both possibilities exist because the presentation of the two demonstration examples is not specific about the minimum difference between "glert" and "not-glert."

Figure 2.5		
Examples	1	2
Features	A B C D	Not-A B C D
Teacher Behavior	"glert"	"not-glert"

The rule for articulately communicating differences through examples is: *To show difference, juxtapose examples that are only minimally different and treat them differently.*

Any structural difference observed in the juxtaposed examples can function as a possible basis for the different treatment of the examples. There is only one structural difference between examples 1 and 2 above in Figure 2.5. Therefore, there can be only one structural basis for the different treatment—the absence of feature A. This prescription for showing differences is contraintuitive, but logically compelling. If the only difference between the two juxtaposed examples is a small difference and if the examples are treated differently, the small difference must be solely responsible for the different behavior. Communication of the very small difference logically implies that differences that are larger than the one shown would also lead to the examples being identified as "not-glert."

Operations to Induce Generalizations

Although the procedures for demonstrating sameness and difference will achieve the desired communication goal, a deeper analysis of operations used to induce generalization provides a clearer understanding of why these operations work. This analysis identifies three specific operations: *interpolation, extrapolation,* and *stipulation*.

Interpolation. In its most basic form, the operation of interpolation assumes changes along a single stimulus dimension, such as color, size or position. Figure 2.6 shows color gradations, from light blue to dark blue. The display does not suggest that all features of color (hue, saturation, intensity) are taken into account, merely that the examples are arranged progressively from light to dark.

Figure 2.6				
X	P	X	O	X
Light blue				Dark blue

The three **X**'s indicate examples that are communicated to the learner as being the same. If they are the same, then what is being labeled as "blue" must be what they have in common (the range of the color value being labeled "blue"). According to the operation of interpolation, *if the learner receives the communication about the three examples, the learner will identify any example that is intermediate in blueness as "blue."* For example, the learner should identify examples **O** and **P** as "blue." (No example shown above would *be presented* on a continuum. The continuum is used only to indicate darkness and lightness of our examples.)

There are other forms of interpolation. One form involves the addition or subtraction of parts. Although this form deals with a generically different type of interpolation, the basic operation is the same. If the generalization example falls *within the range of interpolation* described by the demonstration examples, sufficient information for generalization is implied.

If we deal with very complex examples, we might not be able to precisely express the nature of the various features that change from one positive example to another. However, if we show examples that are greatly different from each other, and if we treat these examples in the same way, we imply interpolation of most new examples. The reason is that the examples we show initially would not be placed close to each other on a continuum. Any new example would probably fall somewhere between the examples demonstrated. Therefore, interpolation is implied.

The examples that are used to demonstrate **blue** would not predict that the learner would generalize to a shade of blue that is quite white and unsaturated. The reason is that this shade does not clearly fall on the continuum implied by the examples that we had presented. To solve this problem, we must present a larger number of examples. Let's say that we present three variations for each shade of **blue**–each variation presents a different saturation and hue (see Figure 2.7).

Figure 2.7					
Shade 1	X	P	X	O	X
Shade 2	X'	P'	X'	O'	X
Shade 3	X"	P"	X"	O"	X"
Light blue					Dark blue

The presentation consists of nine examples (the **X**'s). The test of generalization involves six. The six examples are clearly interpolated within the range of variation described by the nine demonstration examples; therefore, the communication implies that all variations of **O** and **P** would be identified as **blue.**

Extrapolation. According to the principle of extrapolation, if a small change makes a positive example negative, larger changes will also make the example negative. The differences of the various examples in Figure 2.8 is indicated by their position on the continuum of change. The learner is shown three examples. Two are labeled "blue" (the **X**'s) and one "not-blue" (the **Y**). The last two examples are quite close to each other on the continuum (to communicate difference). If the examples are only minimally different and are treated differently (one called "blue," the other "not-blue") the structural basis for the different label is unambiguous, because there is only one apparent difference in the examples.

Figure 2.8				
X	X	Y	O	P
blue	blue	not-blue		

Extrapolation is based on this idea: The difference between the second **X** and the **Y** is sufficient to make **Y** a negative example. *Any difference that is greater than this difference implies that the examples will also be negative.* The difference between **X** and **O** is greater than the difference between **Y** and **O**; **Y** is negative. Therefore, **O** must be negative also. Similarly, the difference between **X** and **P** is greater than the difference between **X** and **Y**. Therefore, **P** must be negative.

Another way to conceive of this sort of extrapolation is to visualize a concrete example, such as a patch of dark blue. Now consider how much change in the example is needed to convert the example into something that is not-blue. Changes greater *than the amount* create examples that are obviously not blue.

Stipulation. Stipulation involves repeatedly demonstrating examples that are highly similar and presenting only these examples. Each example is treated in the same way. The stipulated set of examples implies that any examples falling outside the range that had been demonstrated *are not* to be treated in the same way.

Figure 2.9 shows that the non-naive learner is presented with eight examples that are quite similar to each other in every respect (**X**'s). The communication does not present any additional demonstration examples. When tested on example **P** or example **O,** the learner would probably treat it as a negative example. The outcome is problematic because the learner is not given precise information about the range of variation that is permissible for the **X**'s. The communication shows only that when the examples of a particular type are presented, they are treated in the same way. Examples **O** and **P** are not the same type (because their obvious structural differences sets them apart from any examples that had been demonstrated). Therefore, a reasonable inference is that they are probably not the same as the **X**'s, and are therefore negatives.

Figure 2.9		
	XX	
	XX	
	XX	
P	XX	O

Stipulation depends on the number of examples that are presented. If we presented the learner with this single example | and labeled it "glup," we would not be surprised if the learner identified this test example as "glup": ∕ . However, if we presented the learner with 20 vertical examples and labeled each as "glup," the probability is greatly increased that the learner would identify the slanted test example as "not-glup."

One way to understand what is happening when stipulation occurs is to think of a particular concrete example and the various features it has (see Figure 2.10).

Figure 2.10
A
B
C
D

If we repeat this example again and again, we imply that the essential sameness possessed by the positive examples includes all features, **A**, **B**, **C**, **D**. If we later present an example that is different—one that has only **A** and **B**— the learner will probably reject it because features that have been implied to be essential are missing.

Examples of Complex Concepts

When we deal with complex learning, the communications involve a combination of stipulation, interpolation, and extrapolation. Consider the situation in which we present an operation for figuring out how to add numbers. The operation involves the same counting steps when it is applied to different examples. The operation therefore *stipulates* some behavior for all examples encountered. The examples presented show some range of variation. Some examples involve one-digit numbers, some involve two. Some problems present the largest number first. These examples communicate sameness by demonstrating that the same addition operation holds for a range of counting numbers and arrangements. Also, if the examples suggest that a change from one digit to two digits does not affect the operation and that a change from smaller numbers to larger numbers does not affect it, the learner could reasonably be expected to "extrapolate" and conclude that the operation holds for any number.

In summary, we communicate with the learner through examples. The game is something like trying to view a vista through a very small peephole, a glimpse at a time. The learner has the capacity to make a consistent "whole" or gestalt from what we show. The glimpses we provide are examples. The idea is to provide the learner with enough information to make a consistent whole from the examples. We do not want to induce distortion or misrules by showing poorly-selected glimpses.

One and Only One Generalization

Our objective, as noted earlier, is to design communications that lead to only a single generalization or interpretation. In other words, a communication should be faultless. Only if it is faultless do we receive unambiguous information about the learner. If there is more than one sameness for the various examples that are treated in the same way, the communication has faults. The learner may respond to an inappropriate sameness. Each sameness describes a generalization. Therefore, the inappropriate samenesses imply inappropriate generalizations. Conversely, if there is only one sameness that is possessed by all positive examples, there is only one possible generalization.

A communication that is analytically faultless is faultless for any learner. Viewed differently, any naive learner needs the same information about the nature of the concept—about which changes create negative examples, and about which changes do not. Although, by chance, a learner may pick up the appropriate information from a presentation that has faults, the learner is as likely to pick up inappropriate generalizations. This situation is possible whether the learner is "very bright," or "slow." The variable is not the learner, but the communication.

Faultless communication *does not imply that there is only one possible communication that will work for "all" learners.* Since there are countless examples of a given concept, there are potentially countless variations of faultless communications. Each variation would use different examples. However, all variations would be the same in many respects. All are based on the quality or concept being taught.

Let's say we wish to teach the naive learner the grade of a hill, angle of the hill, or slant of the hill. Our goal is to teach one of these labels, and to show the learner what it means. Let's say that we choose to refer to the **steepness** of the hill.

The most efficient way to communicate with the learner is through the *continuous conversion* of examples. *Continuous conversion occurs when we change one example into the next example without interruption of any sort.* Hold up your hand in an angle about like this: ∕. Give a behavioral indication for this example: "See this." Now move your hand to about this angle: ∕. Say: "It got steeper." You have created an example through continuous conversion. You change the first display into the example ("It got steeper"). Continuous conversion of examples logically provides the most precise communication with the learner. The reasons are:

1. Many aspects of the display appear in all examples and are therefore shown to be irrelevant. If you presented a series of continuous conversion examples with your hand, your hand would be in every example. The hand, therefore, could not account for the fact that some examples are "positive" (**steeper**) and some are "negative" (**not-steeper**). The differences in the slant of the various examples would be the only basis for difference in the labels of the examples.

2. It is possible to show *only those changes in the example that lead to a change in label*. Let's say that you start with your hand in a particular position. You then create the simplest change that permits the next example to be labeled "it became more slanted." You *must* change the aspects of the display that have to do with slantedness (you must rotate your hand). No other change will achieve the objective of creating an example more slanted. *It is possible to make that change and no other change when examples are presented through continuous conversion.*

3. It is possible to show the type of changes in the relevant dimensions that do *not* lead to a change in label. The relevant dimension is the one that is used to create a position from a negative example or vice-versa (rotation of the hand for the concept **slanted**). If we show the learner that certain changes in this dimension lead to changes in the label, we should also show a very small movement of the hand that is labeled, "It got steeper," and a very large movement that is labeled, "It got steeper." Both involve rotation, but both are obviously different from each other. The amount of change from positive example to positive example, therefore, is not relevant to "It got steeper."

For many concepts, continuous conversion is not possible. However, the communication through continuous conversion provides us with the guide or model for creating non-continuous-conversion sequences. The controls that are automatic in a continuous conversion sequence must be carefully constructed if we are required to present static examples to communicate the same information so well provided through continuous conversion.

Individualized instruction as it occurs in the home (when the mother instructs the child) often involves continuous conversion. The mother tells the child to do something: "Put a fork here." The child makes mistakes, putting a spoon in the designated place. The mother converts one example to the next: "No, honey, a fork, not a spoon. Here's a fork." The spoon is replaced with the fork and the learner receives specific information on the correlation between the differences in label and difference in example.

A Faultless Sequence

A faultless communication consists of two parts. The first shows what controls how the example is treated. The second shows more about the context in which the concept or quality may occur. Figure 2.11 shows a faultless presentation for the concept **getting steeper.**

The first 11 examples show what controls **getting steeper.** The first five are "modeled" by the teacher, which means that the teacher tells the answers. The next six examples are tested. Following example 11 are examples that show the learner something about the range of contextual variation in which **steeper** occurs. The examples present objects not shown in the initial part of the communication (lines, pencils, hills) and different types of tasks (touching, naming a hill, etc.).

Different examples in the first part of the sequence have different functions. Some show differences (examples 1-3 and 5-6). Minimally different examples are juxtaposed and are treated differently. Sameness is shown by

Figure 2.11		
Example		Teacher Wording
		Watch my hand, I'll tell you if it gets steeper.
1		It didn't get steeper.
2		It didn't get steeper.
3		It got steeper.
4		It got steeper.
5		It got steeper.
6		Did it get steeper?
7		Did it get steeper?
8		Did it get steeper?
9		Did it get steeper?
10		Did it get steeper?
11		Did it get steeper?
12		Touch the line that is steeper.
13		Hold up a pencil so that it is steeper than this pencil.
14		Which hill is steeper? Hill A or Hill B?

examples 3-4-5. Greatly different juxtaposed examples are treated in the same way. Examples 6 through 11 have the functions of testing the learner and of presenting examples whose values are implied by interpolation or extrapolation created with the first five examples.

The communication should be nearly faultless because it does an adequate job of demonstrating what controls the label and of not stipulating that the label is used only in connection with the presentation of hands. Examples 12 through 14 are different enough from hands to prompt the extrapolation of the concept to a wide range of examples not shown in the teaching. The presentation for **getting steeper** is faultless enough to permit rigorous study of the learner. If the learner does not generalize to new examples that are presented with the hands or does not extrapolate to new examples that do not involve the hands, the outcome cannot be explained with reference to the communication or the "stimulus." An explanation must be sought by reference to the learner.

Related Sequences for Related Concepts

The presentation above is adequate to communicate the structure of the concept **getting steeper.** With modifications, it is adequate for communicating any closely-related concept. Any changes in the structure of the concept, however, imply changes in the communication. If we present the concept **greater grade** instead of **getting steeper,** we could use the same examples and change only the label that we use. The reason is that the only difference is the label. If we change the concept so that both the label and the structure change, additional changes are needed. For instance, if we present **getting faster,** the label must change and the nature of the examples must change. We cannot demonstrate "faster" by showing "steeper." However, since both concepts (**getting steeper** and **getting faster**) are comparatives, they have structural details that are the same. These structural details imply samenesses that should be retained in the communication.

To teach **getting faster,** we can start with something that is moving. We can then model the changes that occur in the example after the type of changes that occur in the sequence for **getting steeper.** If there is a big change in the positive direction to create an example in the **getting-steeper** sequence, we will introduce a big change in the positive direction for the corresponding example of **getting faster.** If there is a small positive change in the **getting-steeper** sequence, we will make the corresponding example for the **getting-faster** sequence by introducing a small change in the positive direction. Figure 2.12 shows the first five examples of a positive sequence for **getting faster.** For all examples, the object moves in a circle. The size of the circle and the direction of the object remain the same for all examples.

Figure 2.12

Examples	Wording
Object moves 40 revolutions per minute.	Watch the dot. I'll tell you if it goes faster.
1. Object moving 30 revolutions per minute.	It's not going faster.
2. Object continues moving 30 revolutions per minute.	It's not going faster.
3. Object begins moving 40 revolutions per minute.	It's going faster.
4. Object begins moving 70 revolutions per minute.	It's going faster.
5. Object begins moving 90 revolutions per minute.	It's going faster.

These examples precisely parallel the first five examples of the sequence for **getting steeper.** The structural aspects of the two that are the same appear in both sequences—particularly the size of the change from example to example and the direction of the change. The prediction would be that if the sequence for **getting steeper** is faultless and if the concept of **getting faster** has the structural samenesses that are reflected in the samenesses of the two sequences, the sequence for getting faster should also be faultless.

Stimulus-Locus Diagnosis of Learning Failure

An implication of the stimulus-locus analysis is that the primary diagnosis of learning failure should be a diagnosis of the instruction the learner receives. If the learner fails to generalize, the problem may lie with the learner or with the communication the learner receives. We can rule out one of these possibilities by *assuming* that the communication is responsible for the observed problem. The remedy is to identify faults in the communication the learner is receiving and correct them so that the communication is faultless. If the faultless instruction fails, we know that the problem is with the learner and not with the communication. If the faultless instruction succeeds, we know that the initial problem was indeed with the communication.

This diagnostic procedure is the opposite of the traditional diagnostic procedure, which assumes that the learner is at fault for any learning inadequacies. The fact that the traditional diagnostic procedures hold the learner responsible can be ascertained by referring to the percentage of case histories in which the learner's deficiency in reading, for instance, is judged to be caused by poor teaching. The percentage consistently hovers around zero, implying that the traditional diagnostic paradigm assumes that the learner has the deficiency. Not only is this position improbable, it is also illogical. Any diagnosis begins with an observation of *behavior.* This behavior may be influenced both by deficiencies in instruction and deficiencies in the learner. To assert that the behavior is "caused" either by learner inadequacy or by teaching inadequacies is to go far beyond the data.

The value of the initial hypothesis of the problem (that the teaching is the sole cause of the learner's problem) is that *it requires us to rule out the possibility that instructional variables could account for learner failure.* The hypothesis requires us to identify flaws in the instruction the learner has received and to provide faultless instruction. The prediction is that when we provide faultless instruction, the learner's problems will be solved.

Regardless of the outcome of this test, we will receive very precise information about the actual status of the learner's problem—the extent to which the problem is caused by learner inadequacy and the extent to which it is caused by instructional deficiencies. If the learner responds to the faultless instruction by learning the samenesses or generalization conveyed by the faultless instruction, we conclude that the learner's initial problem was caused primarily (or solely) by instruction. If the learner remains virtually unchanged after the introduction of the faultless communication, we conclude that the learner's original problem was inadequacies in the learner, not inadequacies in the instruction. An intermediate outcome provides us with an intermediate conclusion: part of the learner's problems are caused by the learner, and part by the faulty communication.

If we accept the traditional approach to learning failure, we receive no diagnostic information that translates readily into instruction. If the learner's deficiencies are caused by learner inadequacies, how do we perform an instructional remedy that will reduce the learner inadequacies? The instruction is not suspect, so there is no reason to change it.

Illustration

Let's say that we observe a naive learner who has been taught speech behavior by one teacher in the same setting and the learner does not practice the newly-learned behaviors with other people in other settings. The instruction has a serious fault. Specifically, it is guilty of stipulation. All examples of learning language or speech skills have a large set of common features–the teacher, the details of the setting, and nature of the tasks. A prediction based on this fault is that the learner will not perform with other people. The skills will not "transfer."

If we attempt to diagnose the learner instead of the instruction, we will probably conclude that the learner is poor at generalizing, implying that the problem is caused by learner inadequacy. This diagnosis does not suggest how we can make the learner adequate or how we can rule out the possibility that the learner has responded in a perfectly reasonable way to the communication.

The stimulus-locus diagnosis assumes that although the learner clearly failed to "transfer," this failure is not caused by learner inadequacies, but is consistent with the instruction received. The solution is to modify the instruction.

Summary

Basic communications are the most important units for a technology of instruction. They present concepts or qualities that cannot be fully described to the learner in words because the learner lacks knowledge of which quality is being labeled. The communication consists of examples and behavioral signals presented with the examples.

Any samenesses shared by all examples treated the same way describes a generalization.

The test of this sameness may be performed with any stable response from the learner. For the simplest form of the test, the learner is presented with a series of test examples (some of which may be different from those presented during the earlier demonstration) and the learner indicates whether each is an example of the concept. If we test the learner first by requiring a pointing response, then by requiring some other response to the same examples, we discover that the *pattern maintains,* although the response changes. Since all that remains is the pattern, the teacher must have introduced this pattern.

The examples that are used in a basic-communication sequence have an indefinitely large number of qualities, each of which could theoretically serve as the basis for possible generalizations. One example, therefore, cannot possibly teach. Subsequent examples must be used to rule out some possible generalizations and to confirm others. In the end, the teaching of the concept requires a set of examples. The learning process is inductive. The learner is simply shown which examples are the same. The learner must identify the sameness that binds them.

In manipulating the examples to rule out particular interpretations, we follow juxtaposition principles.

To show sameness, we juxtapose examples that are greatly different and we treat each example in the same way.

To show difference, we juxtapose examples that are only minimally different and we treat the examples differently.

The three operations that describe our primary manipulations with the set of examples are: *interpolation, extrapolation,* and *stipulation*. Interpolation is based on a display that treats obviously different examples in the same way. If the range of variation shown by these examples does not cause the label to change, an intermediate value or change should also be treated in the same way.

Extrapolation is efficient for ruling out a range of negative examples. If the change from a given positive example to a minimally different negative causes the negative to be labeled differently, a greater change in the same direction from the positive will also result in a negative example.

Stipulation is the repeated presentation of examples that have a great many samenesses. The presentation implies that all features of these examples are necessary to the label. The result is that if the learner is presented with variations in any features, the learner will not treat the example in the same way as the original examples.

The most efficient way to show relevant changes in the examples and to label these unambiguously is through the process of continuous conversion. The process involves presenting an example and then converting it into the next example, providing the learner with a demonstration of only the difference between the examples. The difference is then labeled. The two examples are either treated in the same way (implying that the change was relevant to sameness) or in a different way (implying that the change caused a change in the label).

By combining the principles of showing sameness, showing difference, and testing on generalizations, we can create a basic communication—a set of examples accompanied with wording that *tells* and wording that *tests*. If a given presentation proves to be faultless, we are provided with a possible model for creating faultless sequences for discriminations that share many structural features with the concept taught in the original sequence. We simply change the parts of the sequence that process structural details that are different.

Finally, we may use the analysis of communication as the basis for diagnosis of learning failure. Instead of diagnosing the learner, we begin by diagnosing the instruction. We identify flaws in the instruction and correct them, with the assumption that the learner's problems were caused by flaws in the instruction. This hypothesis requires us to control the instruction or communications and then test the learner. Regardless of the outcome, we will receive very precise information about the learner.

Chapter 3
Knowledge Systems

Chapter 2 demonstrated that concepts with the same basic structure (**getting steeper** and **getting faster**) could be processed through faultless sequences that had the same basic structure. By extending the relationship of sameness in concept structure and sameness in communication, we are provided with a basis for categorizing types of knowledge. In this categorization, concepts that have the same structure are placed in the same class. Concepts within a class share structural similarities. Because these structural similarities parallel similarities in the structure of the communication used to convey the concepts to naive learners, concepts within the same class may be processed through variations of the same communication.

The two objectives of organizing different types of knowledge are:

1. To provide an exhaustive system that permits classification of any cognitive operation, from simple discriminations to complex operations.

2. To link the classification system with instructional procedures, so that all concepts within a particular class or category may be processed through variations of the same communication form.

This chapter describes the classification system. Subsequent chapters articulate the instructional procedures implied by the various categories of the classification system. We will first examine the stimulus-locus classification for cognitive skills (based on analysis of the cognitive operations). We will then outline the response-locus classification (based on analysis of learner's characteristics when learning new responses).

Classifications for Cognitive Knowledge

Basic Forms (sensory-feature concepts)
- Non-comparatives
- Comparatives
- Nouns

Joining Forms (relationships between sensory-feature concepts)
- Transformations
- Correlated-features relationships

Complex Forms (chains of joining forms)
- Cognitive problem-solving routines
- Communications about events (fact systems)

The three major categories within this system are presented in order of ascending complexity. Concepts within the first category (basic forms) are the simplest concepts. The communications that are appropriate for communicating them present single-step tasks or questions with the same, single question used for all examples in the sequence. **Getting steeper** is a basic form concept. Each test item for this concept asks a single question: "Did it get steeper?" All positive examples are responded to with the same response, "Yes." The goal of each of these communications is to teach a single concept.

The communications for the second category, joining forms, are more complicated. For some of these sequences, more than one question or task is presented with each example. For others, a single question is presented with each task; however, the appropriate response changes from positive example to positive example. The goal of each communication within this category is not to teach a single concept, but to teach a single relationship.

The communications for the third category, complex forms, are more complicated than the joining-form communications. For each example presented in a complex form communication, the learner must perform a series of steps. These communications are not designed to teach a single concept or a single relationship. Rather, each is designed to teach a *set of relationships* that are appropriate either for solving problems of particular types or for learning about the set of features that distinguishes one event from another. In either case, the communication presents a series of familiar concepts or relationships that are combined in a unique manner.

The classification indicates the most precise communication that is logically possible for each type of concept. The most precise communication possible for basic forms is basic forms. The most precise communication possible for joining forms is joining forms; however, it is possible to treat any joining form concept as a basic-form concept. Similarly, it is possible to treat any complex form as a joining form or as a basic form. The matrix below shows the relationship between the type of concept and the classification options available for that type. The cells in which the X is circled show how each type of cognitive operation is classified in the system. According to the matrix, any concept may be treated as a basic concept. If we were to treat the concept of carrying out a long-division operation as a basic form, we would present it through a communication that follows the same pattern used for all basic forms. We would present examples of working long division problems. For the examples that test the learner, we would ask the learner, "Is that the right way?" For some examples, the answer would be "yes" and for others, "no." This is not the most precise communication that is possible for the concept of the long division operation (or of a particular algorithm for working long division problems). A more precise way would be to show the learner the steps involved in working the problem. The concept of a long-division operation is a complex form—one that involves many steps, many concepts, and discriminations linked together.

Type of Concept	Classified As		
	Basic	Joining	Complex
Basic	Ⓧ		
Joining	X	Ⓧ	
Complex	X	X	Ⓧ

Basic Forms

Basic-form concepts are the simplest form because *they cannot be reduced to simpler forms,* and they cannot be clarified through verbal explanations. Basic-form concepts refer to specific meanings of words like **red, under, back, truck, door, sit, horizontal,** and **girl.** To communicate any basic form, we must present examples, some of which show what the concept is (positive examples), and some of which show what the concept is not (negative examples). There are several ways to test a concept to determine whether it is a basic form concept. The simplest way is to start with any sentence that conveys a relatively specific meaning, such as:

"Look at the red block under the table."

Earlier we noted that we are not dealing with words when we analyze concepts, merely meanings. The use of a sentence as a starting point does not contradict the earlier statement. In fact, the use of the sentence illustrates the difference between analyzing words and analyzing concepts. In the sentence, each word has a single, clear meaning. However, each word in the sentence has many possible meanings when the word is considered apart from the meaning conveyed in the sentence. **Look** could be a noun or a verb. It could refer to the appearance of something ("The new look"). Similarly, the word **red** apart from the sentence could refer to color or anger ("I saw red"). The sentence conveys the various meanings that we are to deal with. It also presents conventional labels for each meaning. The meanings that we will consider are those conveyed by the sentence. The words that we will use to signal each meaning are those contained in the sentence.

The smallest conceptual units signaled in the sentence are basic-form concepts. The concept **look** is a basic-form concept. So are the concepts **red, block, under,** and **table.** We cannot reduce these concepts or break them into components. If the learner does not know the concept **under,** we gain nothing by telling the learner, "It's **under** because it is **below,**" or "When it's **beneath,** we say it's **under.**" We would still need to teach the meaning of the new word that we introduce in the explanation—**beneath** or **below.** Since these words have the same communication function in the sentence as **under,** we would create an unnecessary step by introducing the synonym. The most direct and precise communication would be one that teaches the meaning of **under** that is used in the sentence. To convey this meaning, we would present different examples that show an object in different positions with respect to another object. We would label some examples "under" and some "not-under." Then, we would require the learner to respond to additional examples, answering this question for each example: "Is it under?"

Variations of the same procedure are used for all basic-form concepts. The basic form concept **under** is a *non-comparative*, which means that a given static example that shows something under is always an example of **under**. The concepts of **getting steeper** and **getting faster** are different. They are *comparatives*. An example of a particular grade is not always an example of **steeper.** It is steeper only when compared to an example that is less steep.

The final type of basic-form concept is a *noun concept.* Nouns are the meanings referred to by words like **shoe, building, magazine, chalk,** and other noun words. Nouns are basic forms that are structurally different from both comparatives and non-comparatives with respect to the number of dimensions that can be operated on to change a positive example of the concept into a negative. For non-comparatives (like **under**), only a single change in a positive example will make it a negative example. (For **under,** this change involves the spatial relationship between the two objects in the example.) Similarly, for comparatives (like **getting steeper**), changes in only one dimension will convert positive examples into negatives (for the concept of **getting steeper,** the change is the slope of the object). Both comparatives and non-comparatives are single-dimension concepts. Nouns are multiple-dimension concepts, which means that it is possible to change a positive example of a noun into a negative example by manipulating many dimensions of the object. (We can change a jacket into a non-jacket by changing the material, length, shape, by removing parts, and by adding parts.) The structural uniqueness of nouns suggests some unique features of communications that convey nouns faultlessly. However, nouns, like comparatives and non-comparatives, are simple, irreducible concepts that are based on the sensory features of objects or examples.

Joining Forms

Non-comparatives, comparatives, and nouns are signaled by a single label or by a group of words that functions as a single label. *Joining forms,* in contrast, involve relationships between basic-form concepts. Therefore, joining forms involve two independent labels that are related in some way. The joining forms are the simplest ways that logically unrelated concepts such as **under** and **table** may be combined. We can illustrate the relationship between basic forms and joining forms by referring to the concept **under**. After the learner has mastered the discrimination of **under–not-under** (basic form discrimination), we may combine **under** with other concepts that are logically unrelated to **under.**

One way to create a link between **under** and another concept is through a *transformation.* A transformation is systematic ordering of examples and a parallel ordering of symbols used to describe the examples. If the learner knows the positional meaning of **under** and understands the meaning of basic noun labels, such as **table, shoe,** etc., and we could combine these concepts with **under** using a transformation sequence. We would present different examples of an object in different positions. The learner, however, would not simply indicate whether the object is "under," or "not-under." Instead, the learner would produce a unique verbal response for each test example by telling where the object is. The learner's responses to different examples would be: "Under the table . . . under the shoe . . . under the bed . . . under the shelf . . . under the book . . ." If the sequence used to communicate the joining that occurs when **under** is linked with these objects is faultless, the learner *should be able to generalize to a new example,* one that had not been presented during instruction. For instance, if the learner is able to identify "pencil," the learner should be able to produce the new, appropriate response, "Under the pencil," when presented with an example that shows the target object under the pencil. Note that this response is one the learner had never produced before. The fact that the learner produces it implies that the learner has learned the transformation procedure for how to express the basic way that **under** is joined with other basic-form concepts.

Another way that basic-form concepts are joined together is the *correlated-feature joining.* This joining is not based on a system of ordered responses that change according to a transformation rule, but rather on *empirical associations.* If two things happen together, they are correlated. However, the two things involved in this correlation are logically unrelated, which means that the learner could exhibit complete basic-form understanding of both things involved in the correlation and yet not know the correlation. The following sentence expresses a correlated-feature joining involving **under:** "If it is under, it is below." The learner could be proficient at identifying all possible examples that require the learner to label the example as "under" or "not-under" without understanding that each example has another label–**below.** The relationship between the words is based on an empirical fact—by convention, examples of **under** have another label, **below**.

To teach the relationship between **under** and **below**, we would use the same sequence of *examples* used to communicate **under**. The reason is that **under** and **below** vary together. If something is labeled **under**, it is always labeled **below**. If the object is **non-under**, it is **not-below**. Therefore, the same set of examples and sequence of examples used to communicate under would effectively show what controls the label of **below**. To assure that the relationship between **under** and **below** is made explicit, however, we would not ask the same question that we use in the sequence for **under** ("Is it under?"). Instead, we would present a pair of different questions to show the relationship. The first requires the use of the new label (**below**). The second requires the learner to express the correlation between **under** and **below**.

Figure 3.1 shows the first three examples from a possible faultless sequence.

Figure 3.1	
Example	Teacher Wording
1	My turn: Is the ball below? No. How do I know? Because it isn't under.
2	My turn: Is the ball below? No. How do I know? Because it isn't under.
3	Your turn: Is the ball below?... How do you know?
4	Is the ball below?...How do you know?

Since all correlated-feature relationships are the same (based on an empirical relationship between the basic-form concept that is known to the learner and the concept that is correlated with it), we can use the same communication procedures to faultlessly convey any correlated-feature concept. Figure 3.2 shows the first part of a correlated feature concept that involves **steeper grade.** Note that the sequence of examples is the same as that used to communicate **steeper grade.** However, the questions are changed to assure that the learner learns the relationship between the grade and the speed of the object.

Whether the joining form involves a transformation or correlated features, the concept is not a basic form concept. It is a relationship between basic-form concepts, and the *relationship* cannot be reduced to

Figure 3.2	
Example	Teaching Wording
	Watch my hand. It shows how steep the grade of the stream is. I'll tell you if the water moves faster down the grade.
1	Did it move faster? No. How do I know? Because the grade did not get steeper.
2	Did it move faster? No. How do I know? Because the grade did not get steeper.
3	Did it move faster? Yes. How do I know? Because the grade got steeper.

simpler concepts. The relationship is irreducible because knowledge of any basic form concept does not imply its relationship to other concepts. Knowledge of **under** does not imply the system of ordered responses used to refer to "under the table . . . under the chair . . ." etc. Knowledge of **under** does not imply knowledge of the word **below**. Knowledge of **steeper grade** does not imply knowledge of **moving faster.** To connect these logically unrelated concepts, we use communication forms that show how the basic concept that is familiar to the learner is related either to the system of ordered responses or to some empirically associated concept.

Complex Forms

There are two types of complex forms—*cognitive problem-solving routines* and *communications about events* (fact systems). Both cognitive problem-solving routines and communications about events require the learner to attend to *various* details present in the example. The various details require multiple responses from the learner—each dealing with different aspects of the problem or event. Therefore, complex forms are distinguished from simpler forms by the multiple responses involved in processing each example.

If complex forms are to be unambiguously introduced to the learner, they should process concepts through a series of verbal instructions or directions. The directions tell the learner what to do, what to attend to, or how to label some features of the examples. Since any series of verbal instructions is composed entirely of basic-form concepts or joining-form concepts, the complex forms are of a higher order than either joining forms or basic forms.

Cognitive Problem-Solving Routines

The juxtaposition pattern for the complex forms is different from that of basic or joining forms. A sequence for a basic form presents juxtaposed examples that involve the *same response dimension.* The sequence strongly prompts the learner to attend to this dimension, because attention is never drawn from the single response dimension. With slight exceptions, the joining forms work in the same way. The juxtaposed examples deal with the same relationship and there is very little interruption between presentations of examples involving the response dimension being taught. (An exception is the correlated-feature sequence, which presents two questions with each example. However, both questions deal with different facts of the *same relationship:* "Would it move faster? . . "How do you know?" . . .)

With complex forms, the same response dimension is not referred to in juxtaposed tasks or questions. Figure 3.3 shows a cognitive problem-solving routine for working problems of the form: 5−3=☐.

Figure 3.3	
Teacher 5 − 3 = ☐	Learner
1. Read it	Five minus three equals how many?
2. (Touches under 5.) What does this tell us?	Start with five.
3. Do it.	(Learner makes 5 lines: 5−3=☐) /////
4. (Points to −3.) What does this tell us?	Minus three.
5. Do it.	(Learner crosses out 3 lines: 5−3=☐) ####//
6. (Points to equal sign.) What does this tell us?	We must have the same number on both sides.
7. What number is that?	Two.
8. Make the sides equal.	(Learner makes lines and writes answer:) 5−3=2 ####// //
9. Read the problem and the answer.	Five minus three equals two.

Notice that the entire routine deals with one subtraction problem (one example). Obviously, variations of the routine could be used for any problem within the same class as 5−3=☐; however, each example would be processed through the same nine steps. And no two steps deal with the same relationship. In step 2, the learner responds that the 5 tells us to "start with five." If the number were different, the response would be different. Therefore, the first step would have been pretaught as a transformation, with the teacher presenting different beginning numbers and asking about each, "What does this tell us?" (The responses are ordered according to ordered changes in the examples; therefore, a transformation is involved.)

This transformation is dealt with in only one step of the routine, however. Step 3 tells the learner to start with 5 and the learner makes five lines. A different transformation is involved in this step (one that would also be pretaught). Step 4 involves another transformation, in which the learner's responses vary as the symbols in the problem vary. Note that each step deals with a new feature or step in the solution to the problem. Note also that each step is composed entirely of basic concepts or joining-form concepts.

Cognitive problem-solving routines are appropriate for any task that may be treated as a series of steps that lead to a solution. The judgment of whether a routine is possible depends on whether the learner is logically required to process a series of concepts, details, or discriminations to arrive at the appropriate solution. An assumption is that if the logical analysis of the operation under consideration discloses that the learner must attend to a variety of discriminations, a cognitive routine is more appropriate than any other form for communicating the structure.

For example, simple word decoding for the learner who is assumed to be naive, logically implies attention to the different letters in the word and to their order. If the learner does not attend to the **m** in **mat,** the learner logically may confuse **mat** with **hat, cat** or **at.** If the learner does not attend to the **a,** the learner may confuse the word with **met.** If the learner does not attend to the **t,** the learner may confuse **mat** with **mad** or **map.** This analysis suggests that we should design a routine that deals with all the various discriminations or concepts. This routine should permit the learner to produce strong behavioral signals that leave little doubt about whether the learner is appropriately processing the various discriminations.

Figure 3.4 shows a possible routine for teaching initial word-reading.

Figure 3.4

Teacher	Learner
mat	
(Touches ball of arrow.) When I touch under each sound, say that sound. Keep saying it until I touch the next sound.	
Touches under **m**, **a**, **t**.	Says "mmmmaaat" without pausing between sounds.
Say it fast.	"Mat."

The routine assures that the sounds are produced, processed in order, and then transformed (through "say it fast") into the word spoken at a normal speaking rate.

We observed earlier that any complex cognitive operation may be treated either as a joining form or a basic-form concept, we would simply present examples of words and give the learner instructions to say the words that we show ("look and say"). The cognitive routine is logically superior to procedures that leave the steps of the operation covert because the routine reduces the possibilities for misgeneralization. When many steps are involved in a solution, and the steps are not explicit, the learner may learn spurious strategies that work in the initial-teaching situation but that will not work later. If the initial set of words to be read contains only one three-letter word that begins with **m** (**mat**), the learner who is taught to decode **mat** as if it were a basic-form concept may process the example by attending to the length of the word and the beginning letter. Although this strategy will permit the learner to discriminate between **mat** and the other words introduced early in the sequence, the learner will encounter serious problems when **mad** and **man** are introduced, because the learner's strategy will lead to these words being identified as "mat."

The highly overt procedure provided by the cognitive routine is superior to the procedure that leaves the steps covert because of the nature of all cognitive operations. These operations are quite different from physical operations. Yet many tacitly stated analogies about cognitive operations proposed by some cognitive psychologists are based on assumed parallels between physical operations and cognitive ones. The two primary differences between physical and cognitive operations are:

1. The physical environment provides continuous and usually unambiguous feedback to the learner who is trying to learn physical operations, but does not respond to the learning attempts for cognitive operations.

2. There is no *necessary* overt behavior associated with any cognitive operation.

The physical environment provides feedback to the learner for all applications of physical operations. Physical operations include fitting jigsaw puzzles together, throwing a ball, "nesting" cups together, swimming, buttoning a coat. When the learner performs any physical operation, the physical environment provides feedback. This feedback takes the form of contingencies that occur if the operation is not being performed correctly. The physical environment, when viewed as an active agent, either prevents the learner from continuing or provides some unpleasant consequences for the inappropriate action. If the learner is not performing the operation of buttoning a coat properly, the physical environment "prevents" the coat from being buttoned. If the learner is not nesting a series of bowls correctly, the physical environment "prevents" the nesting from occurring. If the learner does not carry out the operation of hopping correctly, the physical environment "interferes" when the operation is not being performed correctly. The "responses" from the physical environment (the negative consequences or the prevention of the operation from continuing) have a precise communication value. They indicate that some behavior must change if the task is to be completed.

For any physical operation, we can state the behaviors that account for the completion of the operation. Also, we can completely account for any outcome by referring to the overt behaviors produced by the learner. The learner cannot open the door without producing certain overt behaviors. Furthermore, if the door has been opened by the learner, we can account for every aspect of the outcome by referring to the different overt, observable things the learner did.

For any cognitive operation, *there are no necessary overt behaviors to account for the outcome that is achieved.* The practiced learner does not have to "write out" formulas to solve complex problems. The learner may solve them covertly. Cognitive operations do not exist in the sense that physical operations exist. We cannot account for the "silent reading" of a practiced learner by referring only to the overt behaviors that the learner produces. Clearly, if we are to observe the behaviors that lead to the outcome of a cognitive operation, we must design the steps so they are overt and so the outcome is accounted for by these overt steps.

The physical environment does not provide feedback when the learner is engaged in cognitive operations. If the learner misreads a word, the physical environment does nothing. It does not prevent the learner from saying the wrong word. It does not produce an unpleasant consequence. The learner could look at the word **form** and call it "Yesterday" without receiving any response from the physical environment.

The basic properties of cognitive operations–from long division to inferential reading–suggest both that the naive learner *cannot* consistently benefit from unguided practice or from unguided discovery of cognitive operations. Unless the learner is provided with some logical basis for figuring out possible inconsistencies (which is usually not available to the naive learner), practicing the skill without human feedback is likely to promote mistakes.

To build adequate communications, we design operations or routines that do what the physical operations do. The test of a routine's adequacy is this: Can any observed outcome be totally explained in terms of the overt behaviors the learner produces? If the answer is "Yes," the cognitive routine is designed so that adequate feedback is possible. To design the routine in this way, however, we must convert *thinking* into *doing*.

Although cognitive routines are composed entirely of basic-form and joining-form concepts, the routine is not a good vehicle for teaching these concepts. The reason has to do with the pattern of juxtapositions that occurs in a routine. Often only one step of the routine presents a particular discrimination. If the routine has five steps, a great deal of interference occurs before the learner receives a second example of the concept in a particular step. The learner does not receive massed practice on the critical concept (because the routine does not present juxtaposed examples that deal with this concept). Therefore, the learner's memory requirements are increased enormously and the total amount of time needed to teach the concept is increased. Components,

concepts, and skills should be pretaught before bringing them together in the routine.

A final point about cognitive problem-solving routines: they should be designed so they apply to the widest possible range of examples. Cognitive routines are *inventions*. Two opposing considerations are involved in the inventing process. The first is the need to make the learner's processing steps overt. The opposing consideration is the generalizability of the routine. If each routine applies to only a very small class of problems, many different routines would be required to teach the learner how to process the entire range of problems encountered. This situation is ineffective because: (1) each routine involves preteaching (and with many routines, a great deal of preteaching is involved); and (2) if the learner must select from a variety of routines, additional discrimination training is required.

Figure 3.5 shows an example of a generalizable routine. The teacher wording is the same wording presented in the routine for processing 5–3=☐. The example, however, is a negative-number problem.

Figure 3.5	
Teacher	Learner
3 – 5 = ☐	
1. Read it.	Three minus five equals how many?
2. (Touches under 3.) What does this tell us?	Start with three.
3. Do it.	(Learner makes 3 lines:) 3–5=☐ ///
4. (Points to –5.) What does this tell us?	Minus five.
5. Do it.	(Learner crosses out 5 lines:) 3–5=☐ ///--
6. (Points to equal sign.) What does this tell us?	We must have the same number on both sides.
7. What number is that?	Minus two.
8. Make the sides equal.	(Learner makes lines and writes answer:) 3–5=-2 ///-- --
9. Read the problem and the answer.	"Three minus five equals minus two."

The routine exhibits the basic properties of a well-designed routine.

1. Details that appear in one problem are treated in the same way when they appear in another problem (such as making lines for each positive counter and slashes for each negative counter).

2. The approach is maximally overtized, which means that the routine requires the learner to "show" exactly which steps the learner takes in solving the problem. Also, the learner must respond to the various details that are logically necessary to the solution.

3. Because the learner responds overtly to every detail that is logically necessary to solve the problem, the operation has the same feedback potential as a physical operation. The outcome is totally explained in terms of the overt behaviors. We know what the learner is "thinking" and we can respond to the overt steps that are functionally necessary for performing a physical operation. *This feedback must be provided by humans or machines.*

Fading. Successful teaching of cognitive problem-solving routines involves "fading out" the overt steps and "covertizing" the operation so that the learner performs independently. This feature further distinguishes cognitive routines from physical operations. Fading of steps is never necessary for physical operations because such steps are always overt.

The judgments about how quickly the routine should be covertized is made by considering two competing facts: (1) the learner's proficiency, and (2) the problem of stipulation. We should not covertize the routine until the learner is reasonably proficient with overtized routines. If our communication is to be consistent with a single interpretation, we must make sure that the learner is performing the appropriate steps. We will have this assurance only if we know that the learner performs appropriately when the steps of a routine are overt. However, the longer we work on the problem overtly, a step at a time, the more reliant we make the learner on the teacher direction. The covertizing process must proceed as quickly as it reasonably can (to reduce the stipulation problem). However, the process must not begin until the learner is proficient with the overt routine.

Communications About Events

These complex communications are like cognitive problem-solving routines in several ways. The communications are composed of steps that guide the learner. Also, juxtaposed steps deal with different response dimensions or features of the example. The primary difference between cognitive problem-solving routines and communications about events is that communications about events deal with learning about a new "whole" by learning about unique relationships of the different parts that make up this whole. The whole may be an object, such as a particular refrigerator. However, the goal is not to use that refrigerator as an example of some concept that is common to many other refrigerators. Instead, the goal is to attend to the features that make the particular refrigerator unique. To appreciate the uniqueness, the learner must attend to the sum of details that distinguish it from other refrigerators. Each distinguishing feature is expressed as a *fact*. "It has a scratch on this side . . . it is yellow . . . it has two handles . . ." etc.

There are many applications of communications about events. The primary one is the "expansion" of basic and joining form concepts that have been taught. Once a concept such as **yellow** has been taught through a basic-form sequence, the initial teaching has been accomplished. However, the use of the concept has not been established. To demonstrate the use, the concept now becomes a step in various communications about events. Let's say that the learner has recently been taught numerals, their relationship to counting, colors and the comparative concept of **bigger**. For an expansion activity, the teacher writes 2, 7, and 5 on the chalkboard. The numerals 2 and 7 are white; 5 is yellow. 5 is also written bigger than the other two numerals.

Teacher points to 5. "What numeral is this? . . . What number does it tell you to count to? . . . Let's hear you count to five . . . .What color is this numeral? . . . Yes, it's yellow. Tell me if it's bigger than the other numbers or not bigger . . . .Yes, it's bigger."

Unlike the steps in a cognitive routine, the steps that the teacher presents for communication about an event do not occur in a particular order, because the objective is not to convey a procedure for solving a problem (which requires a particular ordering of steps), but to deal with the features that make the 5 unique. These features may be presented in any order. In the case of the expansion activity above, the communication also plays an important role in demonstrating that the various concepts that have been taught are useful components in formulating a precise understanding of what makes the five unique. Knowledge of each component concept adds to the learner's ability to express details of the 5's uniqueness.

One of the more sophisticated types of communications about events involves a *symbolic event* that is created to teach a *system of facts*. Figure 3.6 shows a display that shows how factories work. The display functions as the event. The features that distinguish this display or event from others have to do with the unique spatial arrangement of details and the specific words that appear on the display. The display functions like a super outline that shows higher-order and lower-order relationships (the relationship between *raw material is changed into product*

and the more specific instances that derive from this rule: "Cotton is changed into cloth," etc.).

If the learner memorizes the words that appear in different parts of the display, the learner will be provided with an outline of how factories operate. Therefore, the goal of the communication is to teach the learner to memorize the wording in the various cells.

To achieve this goal, the communication first rehearses the learner on the wording in the various cells, then tests the learner with a display that is the same as the original, except that the cells are empty. The learner has to indicate the words that go in each cell.

Table 3.1 shows the communication for the teaching of the display followed by testing with the empty-cell display (Figure 3.7).

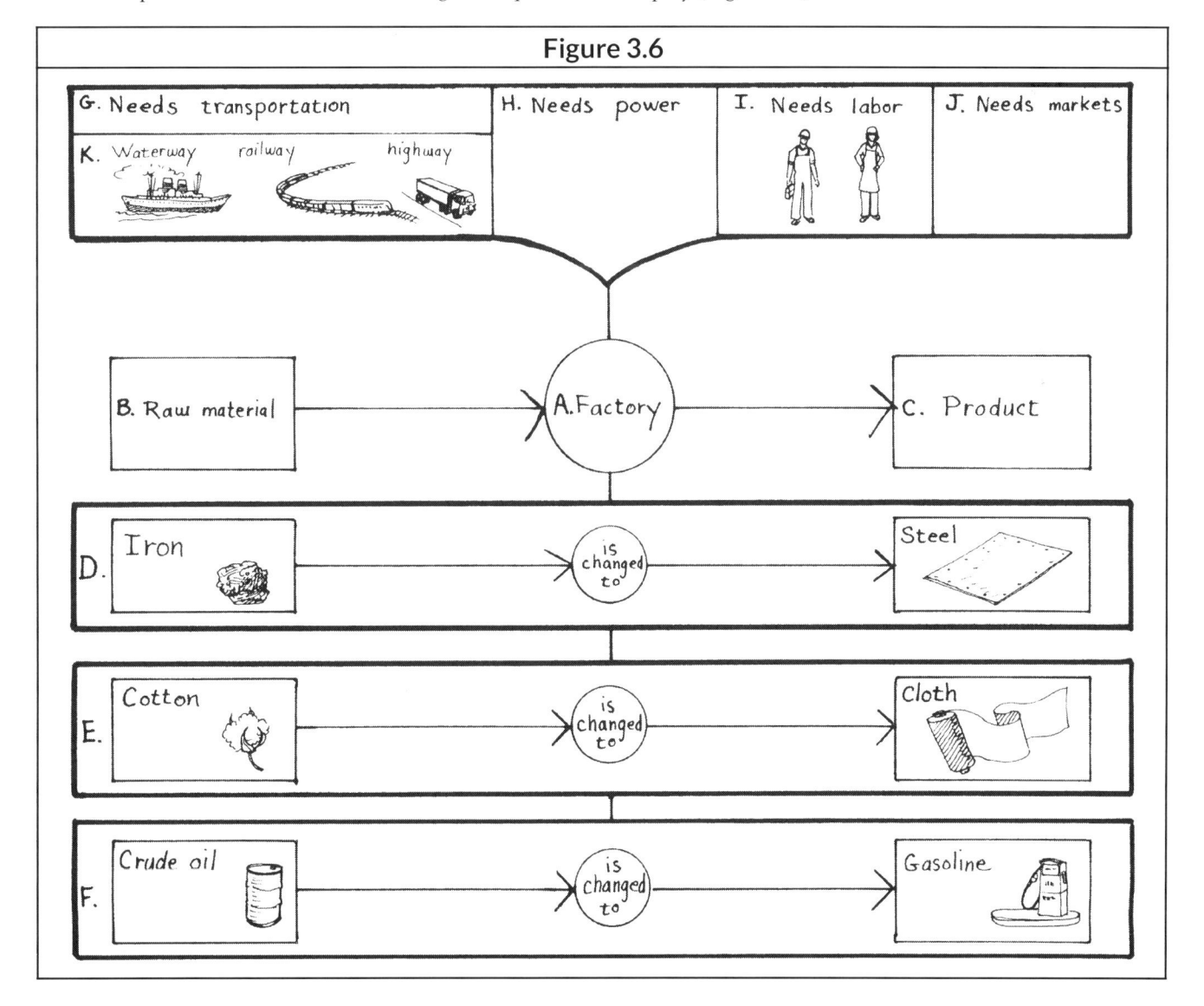

Figure 3.6

Section I | Overview of Strategies

Table 3.1

Teacher Does	Teacher Says and Does	Students Say	Teacher Does	Teacher Says and Does	Students Say
1. Present Figure 3.6 Touch A.	This chart shows what a factory does. **Factory.** Say it. *(Signal.)* A factory takes *(touch B)* raw material and changes it into *(touch C)* a product. Remember: *(follow arrow from B to A.)* **Raw material** goes **into** a factory. *(Follow arrow from A to C.)* A **product** comes **out** of the factory.	Factory.		Say it. *(Signal.)* *(Touch each space as children respond.)* Some factories take crude oil and boil it and put things in it. When they are done, they have changed the crude oil to gasoline. Crude oil also makes plastic and oil. But the big product is gasoline. Remember: **crude oil is changed to gasoline.**	Crude oil is changed to gasoline.
2. Touch B. Touch iron, cotton, crude oil.	First I'll tell you about some raw materials. **Raw material.** Say it. *(Signal.)* Remember: Raw material goes **into** a factory.	Raw material.	10. Touch A. Touch G.	A factory needs things if it is to change raw material into products. Here are the things it needs. A factory **needs transportation**.	
3. Touch iron.	**Iron.** Say it. *(Signal.)* Iron is a raw material. Iron comes from iron mines.	Iron.	Touch H.	It **needs power**.	
4. Touch cotton.	**Cotton.** Say it. *(Signal.)* Cotton is a raw material. It grows on plants.	Cotton.	Touch I.	It **needs labor**, and	
5. Touch crude oil.	**Crude oil.** Say it. *(Signal.)* Crude oil is a raw material. It comes **from under the ground**.	Crude oil.	Touch J.	It **needs markets**.	
6.	A factory takes a raw material and changes it into a product. **Product.** Say it. *(Signal.)*	Product.	11. Touch G.	A factory needs transportation. **Needs transportation.** Say it. *(Signal.)* Transportation is what we do when we move something from one place to another. We need transportation to bring the raw material to the factory. We need transportation to move the product from the factory to some place where we can see it.	Needs transportation.
Touch steel, cloth, gasoline.	These are products. Remember: A product comes **out** of a factory.				
7. Touch D.	*(Follow arrow and touch each space as you say:)* **Iron is changed to steel.** Say it. *(Signal.)* *(Follow arrow and touch each space as children respond.)* Steel is used to make many things – cars, lawn mowers, cans, and hundreds of other products. Remember: **iron is changed to steel.**	Iron is changed to steel.	Touch K.	Here are the big types of transportation used by factories: waterway, railway, highway. **Waterway, railway, highway.** Say it. *(Signal.)* *(Touch boat.)* A waterway is what boats use. A waterway is a river or a lake or an ocean. *(Touch train.)* A railway is what trains use. *(Touch truck.)* A highway is what trucks use. Remember: waterway for boats, railway for trains, highway for trucks.	Waterway, railway, highway.
8. Touch E.	*(Follow arrow and touch each space as you say:)* **Cotton is changed to cloth.** Say it. *(Signal.)* *(Touch each space as children respond.)* Some factories take the raw material cotton and change it into cotton cloth. Some shirts and blue jeans and sheets are made of cotton cloth. Remember: **cotton is changed to cloth.**	Cotton is changed to cloth.	12. Touch H.	A factory needs power. **Needs power.** Say it. *(Signal.)* Some factories use steam power. They heat water with coal until the water turns into steam. Then the steam runs the machinery in the factory. Some factories use electric power. The electricity runs the machinery. Remember: *(touch A)* a factory *(touch G)* needs transportation and *(touch H)* needs power.	Needs power.
9. Touch F.	*(Follow arrow and touch each space as you say:)* **Crude oil is changed to gasoline.**				

Table 3.1 Continued					
Teacher Does	Teacher Says and Does	Students Say	Teacher Does	Teacher Says and Does	Students Say
13. Touch I.	A factory needs labor. **Needs labor.** Say it. (*Signal.*)	Needs labor.	Touch I.	Say it. (*Signal.*)	Needs labor.
	Labor is another name for the workers who operate the machines in a factory. A lot of work is done by the machines, but some products need a lot of labor. Remember: *(touch A)* a factory *(touch G)* needs transportation and *(touch H)* needs power and *(touch I)* needs labor.		Touch J.	Say it. (*Signal.*)	Needs markets.
			16.	Get ready to tell me all the facts about a factory.	
14. Touch J.	The last thing a factory needs is a market. **Needs markets.** Say it. (*Signal.*) A market is a place where the product is sold. The big markets are the big cities. The big cities are big markets because there are a lot of people in the big cities. Remember: **needs markets**.	Needs markets.	17. Touch the spaces in this order: (A, B, C, D, E, F, G-K, H, I, J)	(*For each space, say:*) Say it. (*Signal.*) (Repeat until firm.)	(Children respond.)
			18. Remove Figure 3.6.		
			19. Present Figure 3.7.	The spaces are empty on this chart. Get ready to tell me the exact words that go in each space.	
15.	Let's go over the needs of a factory one more time.	Needs transportation.			
Touch G.	Say it. (*Signal.*)		20. Touch the spaces in this order: (A, B, C, D, E, F, G-K, H, I, J)	(*For each space, say:*) Say it. (*Signal.*)	(Children respond.)
Touch K.	What kinds of transportation are there? (*Signal.*)	Waterway, railway, highway.			
Touch H.	Say it. (*Signal.*)	Needs powers.			

Although the classification system of cognitive skills is exhaustive and is capable of generating specific information about how to communicate any concept within a given category, the specificity of the teaching information is less for the complex forms than it is for either the basic forms or the joining forms. There are two reasons for this reduced specificity.

1. The procedure or event may be approached in different ways (each way leading to a different arrangement of steps or facts).

2. Different wording is possible for each step or fact and for each response the learner is to produce.

Even with the less specific guidelines for complex forms, the classification system is capable of providing important information about the structure of any concept, and therefore carries important implications about how to teach the concept.

Response-Locus Classification

The primary analysis for all cognitive operations is the stimulus-locus analysis. The development of sequences and routines does not place heavy emphasis on teaching the learner to produce new responses. The primary domain for new responses is the physical world. However, once a routine is designed, it functions a great deal like a physical operation. The learner is presented with specific stimuli that call for specific, overt responses. The learner may not be able to produce the responses acceptably. For instance, the learner may be completely incapable of saying the word "four" so that it is impossible to distinguish the response from the learner's response for "five." At this point, we enter the domain of response-locus analysis. We must modify the learner so that the learner is capable of producing the new response. Similar problems occur if the learner is not able to make lines for numerals, or even if the learner tends to forget the label for the numeral 5.

The response-locus analysis is also appropriate for teaching any simple physical response or chain of

Section I | Overview of Strategies

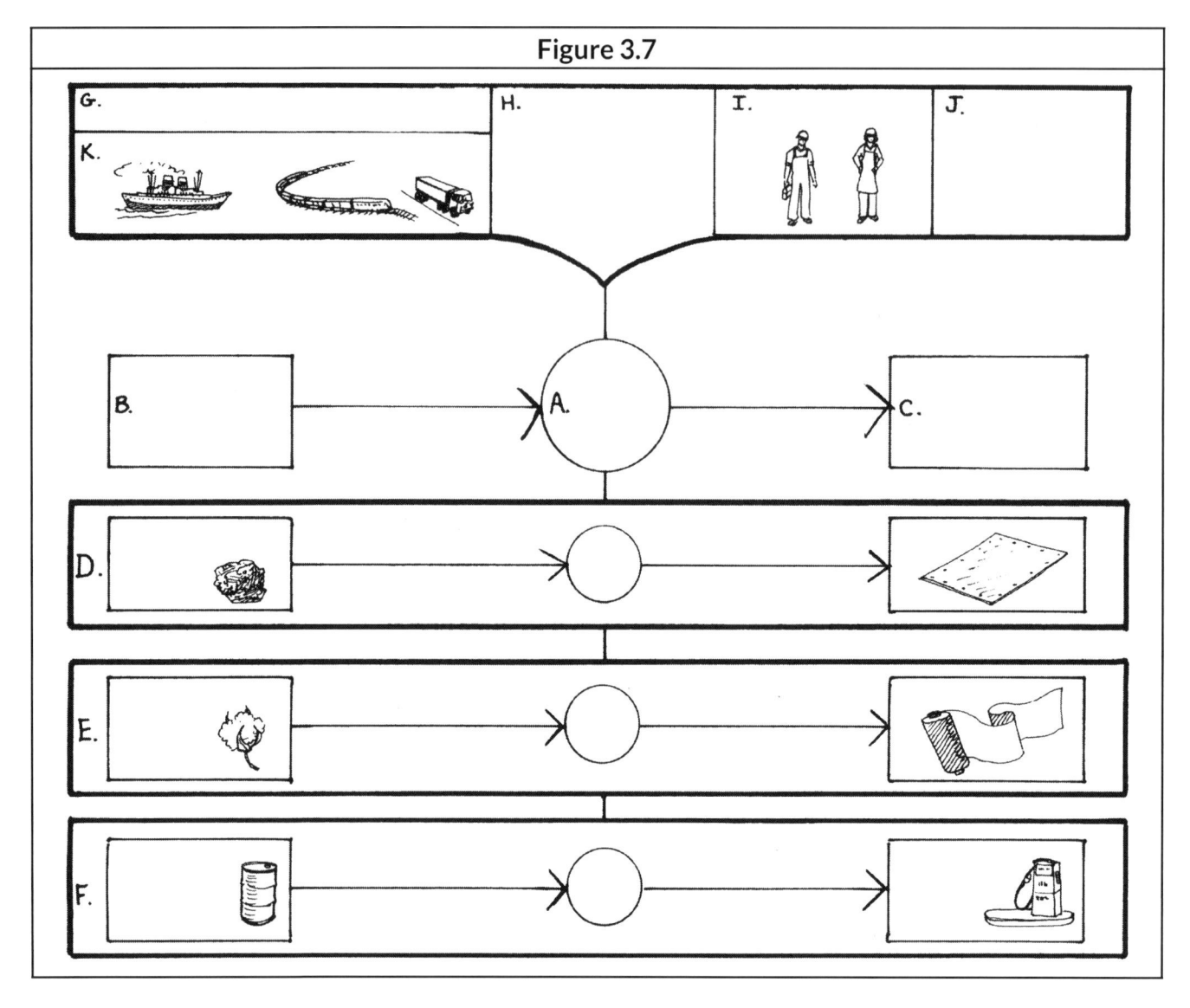

Figure 3.7

responses used for a complex physical operation. The learner may not be able to turn a door knob. Although the physical environment will assist in the teaching of this operation (by providing the learner with feedback on every trial), we can simplify the operation, streamline it, and provide the learner with prompts about how to approach the task.

Classifications for Response-Locus Communications

Simple Responses
- Response-context shaping
- Response-form shaping

Complex physical problem-solving operations

Simple Responses

Context and form. There are two primary types of response-locus instruction.

The first is *context instruction*. This type of communication is appropriate if the learner can produce the desired response in some contexts, but not in the context of the operation being taught. For instance, the learner can assume a "tuck" position while lying on the gym mat, but not in the response context of doing a back somersault from the diving board. The context of the response must therefore be shaped or changed so the learner learns to perform in the desired context. A different type of context-shaping problem is one in which the learner can say a word, such as **stegosaurus**, within the context of the task, "Say stegosaurus," but not within the context

34 Theory of Instruction: Principles and Applications

of the situation in which the learner is asked, "What's the name of this dinosaur?" For whatever reason, the learner is unable to remember the name.

The second type of response-locus instruction has to do with *form*. The learner cannot produce the response *in any context*. The learner is told to "Say stegosaurus," and the learner responds with something like, "Dedgustus." When we try other contexts, we can find no behavioral context in which the learner produces the desired response.

Shaping. The analysis of the learner discloses that practice is the primary variable for learning new contexts for responses or learning responses of a new form. The technique used to provide effective practice is *shaping.* There are two generically different ways a task may be made easier for the learner. The *context of the task* can be made relatively easier and then progressively modified to shape behavior in the new context. (The context for the task is easier if the task immediately follows a successful trial on the same task.) Also, the *criterion for an acceptable response* can also be made progressively more demanding. Instead of requiring the learner to produce a response of a certain configuration, we initially permit the learner to produce an approximation—any response that falls within a broader range of variation.

In summary, if the learner can produce the response called for by the task but not within the specified task context, the shaping focuses on *context changes*. If the learner can produce only an approximation, the shaping focuses on the *response form.*

Response-locus communications are unlike stimulus-locus communications in that they do not involve a particular number of trials. The reason for this difference becomes apparent if we consider what these two analyses deal with. The stimulus-locus analysis deals with concepts and determines the type of information that is needed to communicate how the concept works—which changes affect it and which do not. The response-locus analysis is an analysis of the learner and how the learner learns. Without possessing a great deal of information about the particular learner for whom the analysis is being used, we don't know how many trials are required to bring the learner to an acceptable criterion. Instead of introducing a specific sequence, therefore, the response-locus communication involves general rules about how to change the example or tasks when the learner performs unacceptably on initial tasks.

Context shaping. The context-shaping procedure sequences contexts of varying difficulty. The easiest context is one in which an example of the task is juxtaposed to another example of that task. The most difficult context is one in which the task is temporarily removed from another example of that task. For the sake of simplicity, context-shaping may be conceived of as involving three levels of context difficulty:

Level 1. A (A)
Level 2. A B (A)
Level 3. A B C D... (A)

The circled **A** in each context is the target task. Level 1 shows the task immediately preceded by a successful presentation of the same task. Level 2 shows the task preceded by the task and by some interference. **B** is a familiar task that is not similar to **A**. Level 3 shows more interference in the form of familiar tasks **B, C, D,** and possibly other familiar tasks not highly similar to **A**. The memory requirements for **A** on level 3 are far more difficult than those required for levels 1 and 2.

The teacher stays on a particular level until the learner is able to perform correctly on perhaps four consecutive trials. The teacher then moves to the next level. The goal is consistent performance on level 3. Throughout the training the learner will most probably receive reinforcement on at least 70 percent of the trials. Corrections, whether they occur within the current task training program or later after the skill is supposed to have been learned, involve returning to step 1 and quickly going through the various levels before repeating the task in the context in which the mistake occurred.

Form shaping. The procedures for shifting the response criterion in form shaping involve transitions similar to those indicated for context shaping. By observing the learner on a number of trials, we can determine the learner's baseline of performance. We establish a criterion that permits the learner to receive reinforcement on at least 70 percent of the trials if the learner performs no better than on baseline. When the learner's performance improves to perhaps 85 percent, the criterion is changed. The cycle is then repeated. An effective variation is to have standards for single reinforcement and for double reinforcement. The requirement for "doubles" is higher than for "singles." The higher requirement for double reinforcement gives the learner more immediate information about the direction in which the shaping will proceed. (The difference between responses that receive singles and those that receive doubles suggests the desired direction in which the responses are to be modified.)

Complex Physical Operations

Complex physical operations, such as swimming, hitting a baseball, throwing a baseball, soldering, and dialing a number on the telephone, have some of the same features as complex routines designed to teach cognitive problem-solving behavior. Both the physical operation and the routine involve discrete steps. Both involve creating a desired outcome by performing in a certain way. Both are composed of *components* that can be removed from the context of the complex behavior.

The samenesses suggest that we can use some of the same techniques designed for communicating cognitive operations when we teach physical operations; however, the approach must be modified to accommodate *shaping,* our primary technique for inducing the desired behavior,

Features of complex operations. All complex physical operations have *component behaviors.* A component behavior is one that retains the same form it has in the complex operation when it occurs in other contexts. (In other words, the same component can be identified in other tasks.)

There are two types of components—*essential behaviors* and *enablers* (or non-essential components). Essential behaviors are those *that account for the outcome of the task.* Enablers are behaviors that must be performed if the essential behaviors are to be performed. The essential behavior for the operation of brushing teeth is moving the brush while it is in contact with the teeth. One enabling behavior is holding the toothbrush. (If the learner does not hold the toothbrush, the direct behavior of bringing it into contact with the teeth cannot be achieved.) Note that the essential behavior occurs at the same time as the enabler. This situation is common to physical operations. The learning of physical operations, therefore, implies teaching not only the component behaviors, but also the coordination of these. Conversely, the operation would be analytically easier if it required less coordination because it would require less learning.

There are three basic strategies for beginning the instruction in a way that requires less coordination. They are:

1. The essential-response-feature approach.
2. The non-essential-response-feature approach.
3. The removed-component approach.

The essential-response-feature approach begins with an operation that has been simplified by eliminating some of the enabler-response components. The learner produces the essential-response components and thereby produces the behaviors responsible for achieving the outcome of the operation. (In the toothbrushing example, the learner would do the brushing; however, the toothbrush is rigidly attached to a glove, which means that the learner does not have to grasp it. The enabling component–grasping–is eliminated so that the learner performs on a simplified version of the operations. Note that the learner does the actual brushing.)

For the first step in the non-essential-response-feature approach, the learner produces the enabling or non-essential features of the operation, but is not responsible for the essential response feature. (The learner would put the toothpaste on the toothbrush, and possibly hold the toothbrush; however. the act of brushing would be performed by somebody else.) The learner would perform only the components that accompany the essential behavior.

The third approach, the removed-component approach, begins with a particular component *removed from the context of the operation in which it is to occur.* The instruction may begin by requiring the learner to hold an object like a pencil horizontally and then move it up and down while maintaining the horizontal orientation.

In practicing this behavior with the wrist turned in different positions, the learner practices a component of the brushing operation. The context is simplified because it does not require maintaining contact with teeth or turning the brush so the bristles are oriented properly, etc.

The three different strategies dictate different first steps of instruction. Shaping is used to achieve the desired performance. After the first step, the learner is given increasing responsibility for the total response until the learner is performing the operation with no prompts.

Each approach has the basic problem of *distortion.* Distortion is the counterpart of stipulation. It comes about because the learner is permitted to perform in a way that will not transfer to new examples or applications of the operation. The first step of the essential-response-feature program provides the learner with a very easy example. If the learner works too long on this presentation, the learner may learn to perform the response successfully, but not exactly the way it should be performed when the non-essential components are included in the operation. Although it *is possible* for the learner to perform on this example in a manner that is perfectly continuous with all examples of the operation (including the very difficult ones), the learner will probably perform in a way that is not perfectly continuous. *The more response latitude the easy example permits, the greater the probability that serious distortion will be evident when new more difficult applications are presented.*

Consider the problem of teaching the learner to button. If we begin with a very large button, we are providing the learner with a great deal of response latitude. The probability is therefore great that the learner will learn behaviors that achieve the goal of the operation, but that will have to be modified when more difficult examples are introduced. (The learner may grab the flat sides of the button between the thumb and index finger, a behavior that cannot readily be performed with smaller buttons.) The same sort of distortion is implied when the learner performs the non-essential response features of the operation. Distortion is observed when the components are integrated or when more difficult examples are introduced. Some distortion is inevitable because the simplified operation is just that—simplified. Therefore, component responses that are produced in this context are not under the constraints they will be under when they are integrated with other component responses.

To reduce the amount of distortion resulting from the initial practice, we may alternate from "easy" to "hard" examples. For instance, part of the time the learner works on a removed component; part of the time on the entire operation *with no prompting.* When the learner works on the entire operation, heavy use of reinforcement is used for shaping specific features of the operation. However, the primary value of this work would be to provide the learner with some sort of "advance-organizer" information about the direction the learning is to take and about the relationship between the removed component and the entire operation. A variation of this strategy can be used with either the essential-response-feature approach or the non-essential-response-feature approach. For instance, the learner might use something like a walker when learning to walk (non-essential-feature approach); however, instead of permitting the walker to support 100 percent of the learner's weight, we would use a spring-loaded walker so that the amount of support it provided varied. During one practice session, the learner might do some walking when 90 percent of the body weight is supported by the walker, some when 60 percent of the weight is supported, and some when 45 percent is supported. The percentages would change as the learner becomes more proficient at each of the initial percentages.

Effective strategies for teaching physical operations provide a great deal of practice. Children do not become proficient at cursive writing, at typing, or at dribbling a basketball without a great deal of practice. Within the framework of providing practice, however, the approach must be an effective communication. The complex operation should not be presented as something that is atomized into a number of pieces that can be put together through a backward chain. The *best programs are the simplest,* with the learner performing actual instances of the operation as quickly as possible.

Communicating physical operations to the learner is different from communicating simple discriminations only in the sense that if the learner does not respond quickly or well to the initial instruction, the learner needs practice. However, the basic stimulus-locus principles of communication still hold. If the learner works too long on a particular set of examples, serious stipulation or distortion will probably occur. If the examples that are practiced show a range of difference and show that the same basic response can be used for all applications, the communication implies a *generalization.* (It shows sameness of response across a range of examples.) To show differences in responses, we would use basically the same technique that we would use to show differences in examples of a concept. When dealing with physical operations, however, we must overlay the stimulus-locus procedures with the facts about practice. Even though we know that we are working on a particular example or application too long, we may be faced with a double-bind problem. We cannot go on to more difficult examples until the learner performs. However, the learner will not perform without distortion unless we proceed to other examples. The solution is a compromise. We must make the tasks easy enough to assure that the learner will succeed. At the same time, we must try to minimize the potential misgeneralization that occurs if the learner works too long on the easy examples. We reduce misgeneralization by interspersing some difficult examples early in the program. In the end, the communication that we provide will violate some principles, either in creating the initial examples or in providing the amount of practice the learner needs. The principles are violated only when necessary.

Summary

The classifications for cognitive knowledge forms and for response forms are as follows:

Cognitive Knowledge Forms (stimulus-locus analysis)

    Basic Forms

        Non-comparatives (single-dimension concepts)

        Comparatives (single-dimension concepts)

        Nouns (multiple-dimension concepts)

    Joining Forms

        Transformations

        Correlated feature relationships

    Complex Forms

        Cognitive problem-solving routines

        Communications about events (fact systems)

Physical Operation Forms (response-locus analysis)

    Simple Responses

        Context shaping

        Form shaping

    Complex Physical Problem-Solving Operations

The basic forms are the simplest concepts. By considering the various labels that occur in a sentence, we are provided with a single meaning of each label. The Basic-form communications consist of a series of examples that focus on the specific meaning that has been determined for a label. The sequence shows which features of the examples lead to changes in the label and which features do not affect the label. The sequence begins with a series of examples that are paired with statements about the label, followed by a series of examples that test the learner. Juxtaposed examples in the sequence deal with the same concept.

Joining forms do not deal with single labels. They involve the relationship between two logically unrelated basic-form concepts. The two types of simple relationships are a *transformation* and a *correlated-feature* relationship. The transformation sequence shows the learner how changes in the examples lead to ordered changes in the responses, thereby inducing a generalization that permits the learner to produce new responses to examples that have not been presented earlier. The goal of the transformation communication is to teach the relationship between the features of the examples and systematic changes in the responses. The correlated feature sequence shows empirical relationships between two things that occur together. This relationship is based on empirical fact. If it is an empirical fact that a steeper grade is correlated with faster movement of an object down the grade, a correlated-feature sequence is implied. The communication for this relationship presents the same set of examples that would be used to teach **steeper grade**; however, the questions are different. The first asks about "faster." (Did the object go faster?) The second links this conclusion with the evidence presented in the example. (How do you know?)

Complex forms are characterized by the logical requirements that the learner must attend to various dimensions or features of the example to understand the concept. The communication makes the learner's attention to these dimensions or features explicit or covert. Because the communication deals with sets of relationships rather than a single relationship (which is what the joining forms communicate), the juxtaposed questions or tasks in the complex communication do not deal with the same details or features and do not call for responses that deal with only one dimension. Therefore, these communications are not well designed to teach basic-form concepts or joining-form concepts.

The two types of complex communications are *cognitive problem-solving routines* and *communications about events*. The problem-solving routine is a cognitive counterpart of a physical operation—a creation that provides the learner with the various steps that are logically required to solve any problems of a specific type. (In other words, the same series of steps would be presented for all problems of a given type.) The routine is designed so that the learner produces overt responses for the various discriminations or details that logically must be processed if the learner is to solve the problem. The overt character of the processing assures that the teacher is able to observe the relevant details of the learner's processing and therefore is able to provide feedback (in the same way that the physical environment provides feedback on the learner's attempts to perform physical operations). The cognitive problem-solving routine is an initial-teaching communication. After the learner has mastered the overt routine, the steps are "faded" or made covert so that the learner processes these steps independently.

Communications about events consist of a series of tasks and instructions that are designed to articulate the unique character of events by pointing out the unique character of the individual features and the relationships that exist among the features. Unlike cognitive routines, the communications about events do not involve a particular order for processing the information. Communications about events, therefore, require the learner to learn the parts and relationships when these are referred to in any order. The visual-spatial display represents a sophisticated event that functions as a super outline showing the key relationships between various facets of a system of facts.

The *response-locus-analysis* is an analysis of the learner and therefore involves a classification system quite different from that for cognitive operations. Since the learner learns new responses and overcomes response deficiencies slowly, it is not possible for these communications to specify a set number and type of example to teach a particular skill. Instead, the classification is based on procedures for inducing simple responses and more complex ones.

The two response-induction procedures for simple responses involve shaping. *Context shaping* is used if the learner is capable of producing the desired response in some contexts but not in others. The context is systematically modified, from the one that the learner can perform into the targeted context. If the learner can answer a question such as, "What's your name?" only immediately following the answer to the question, this juxtaposition context is the starting point—the simplest context. Interruptions between presentations of "What's your name?" are systematically presented until the learner is able to perform when a great deal of interference and time is presented between presentations of the task, "What's your name?"

Form shaping is different. This technique is used if the learner is unable to produce the desired response in any context. The learner is able to produce only an approximation of the response. The shaping procedure involves establishing a criterion for reinforcing the learner so that the learner will be able to receive reinforcement for producing approximations that are as good as or better than those the learner typically produces. The criterion for reinforcing the learner shifts as the learner improves until the learner is reinforced for producing responses that are deemed *appropriate*.

The final response-locus category involves *communications for complex physical operations* (opening a door, tying a shoe, working a jigsaw puzzle, etc.). These operations involve *parts* that are to be chained together (in much the same way that a cognitive problem-solving routine chains parts or steps together to form a solution to the problem). The communication for inducing these operations is a program.

The key difference between these programs has to do with how they start. For the essential-response-features program, the first step may require the learner to perform the operation when the operation has been simplified. The first step for the enabler-response program requires the learner to produce the behaviors that are not essential to the outcome of the operation. The removed-component program initially presents practice in a context that is different from that of the operation.

SECTION II
BASIC FORMS

Section I presented the rationale for the stimulus-locus analysis, its relationship to the response-locus analysis, and an overview of the classification system that is based on common structural features of knowledge and skills. Section I provided a perspective of the major topics that will be dealt with in the following sections of this book.

Section II and the sections that immediately follow it shift from an emphasis on broad descriptions to a focus on specific how-to-do-it issues. The goal of these sections is to provide the degree of specificity needed for a person interested in creating faultless sequences to classify the concept being taught and to generate an acceptable sequence.

Chapter 4 provides a restatement of some of the facts and principles presented in Chapters 1 and 2. These principles are important because they apply to virtually all the communications that we will discuss. They indicate how to show samenesses, how to show differences, and how to test to assure that the generalization has been transmitted to the learner.

Each of the remaining chapters in Section 2 deals with a specific type of basic-form communication. Chapter 5 presents procedures for creating non-comparative sequences; Chapter 6 deals with nouns; and Chapter 7 deals with comparatives.

The communications that are developed for the basic-form concepts in Chapters 5, 6, and 7 are *initial teaching sequences*, designed to show the learner what controls the concept being taught and how the examples of the concept are to be labeled. The communications do not indicate how to *expand* the concept and incorporate it in contexts other than the initial-teaching sequence.

These initial-teaching communications are quite close to being faultless. They are probably more faultless than many instructional situations require. However, if you understand how to construct these communications, you will have little trouble creating approximations that are not as intricate or carefully controlled. The value in studying the more faultless forms is that when the communication must be very precise, you will be able to respond to the situation. Also, fewer problems are created if the communication errs in the direction of providing too much information rather than too little.

The forms that we will work with serve as models of faultless presentations. They also serve as a basis for evaluating communications that are less than faultless.

However, there are alternative ways to present various concepts that may actually be preferable to the forms that we will develop. For example, if we wished to teach **getting wider**, our first choice would be a communication based on the sequence presented in Chapter 7. However, the teacher would have to follow it precisely. The potential of the communication would be achieved only if the teacher did what the sequence specifies to do. If the teacher did not appropriately time the presentation of each example and use the wording presented for the example, the communication might fail. If the teacher talked and moved the hand at the same time, the learner might not understand the relationship between the talking and the changes. The teacher must show the change; stop; and then produce the specified wording. Since these and other behaviors are highly relevant to the transmission of the communication, we must control them. We can do this by giving the teacher an elaborate list of do's and don't's, by having a master teacher present the examples or by using the printed page. When we use the printed page, however, our examples must become *static* because we cannot readily use continuous conversion. Those details that are controlled so gracefully through continuous conversion must now be approximated through contrivances that exaggerate samenesses or differences and that provide for "relatively easy" comparison of examples. In the process, we make many compromises. Necessity usually dictates that we reduce the number of examples and deviate from the ideal in other ways. Often these deviations work reasonably well; however, they must be seen as "good solutions," rather than the ideal.

Although *single dimension non-comparatives, nouns,* and *single dimension comparatives* are different in structure, they comprise the sensory-based concepts, generalizations or discriminations. We will use the terms *concept, discrimination,* and *generalization* interchangeably. A concept is a generalization to the appropriate range of examples. A generalization is not possible unless a discrimination is involved. (You cannot generalize something unless what you generalize is specific and different from other possible things that might be generalized.) The basic nature of a concept is a qualitative irreducible feature that makes the particular concept different from all others. If such qualitative structure cannot be identified, we can reduce the concept to another, simpler concept (or concepts). We can avoid possibly confusing discussions about the nature of concepts by referring to *sets of examples*. If a set of examples has an observable sameness, that sameness is a concept, the basis for a discrimination or a generalization.

As noted in Chapter 3, communications for sensory-based discriminations share these features:

1. The communication involves presenting concrete examples and labeling each.
2. All positive examples receive the same response.
3. Negative examples receive responses that are different. (The set of negatives may receive a single response, "No," or a variety of responses, each different from the response used for positive examples.)

Examples of non-comparative single-dimension concepts include: **horizontal, between, over, three, more than one, gradual, convex, curved.**

Examples of nouns include: **dog, factory, car, shoe, quotation mark, sentence, adverb, animal.**

Examples of comparative single dimension concepts include: **steeper, louder, hotter, faster, getting cloudier, becoming more intense.**

The structure of the different concepts is summarized in Table II.1.

Both non-comparatives and comparatives are the same with respect to how positives and negatives are created. For both types, changes in a single dimension create the examples. For instance, positive examples of the non-comparative concept **over** are created by manipulating the position of the target object. By manipulating the

Table II.1		
Single Dimension on-Comparatives	Nouns	Single Dimension Comparatives
Changes in **single dimension** create positives and negatives.	Changes in **many dimensions** create negatives.	Changes in **single dimension** create positives and negatives.
Positive and negatives have an **absolute value** and a **fairly precise boundary**.	Positives and negatives have an **absolute value** and an **imprecise boundary**.	Positives and negatives have **a relative value** and **a precise boundary**.

position of the object, negative examples are created. For the comparative concept **faster**, changes in the speed of the object create positive examples, changes in the speed also create negatives. Nouns are "conjunctive" concepts, which means that an example is positive *only if a number of features are present*. For an object to be a **shoe**, it must have different parts, dimensions, relationships. We can change the object into a **non-shoe** by manipulating any of these dimensions or features.

The precision of the boundaries between positives and negatives varies considerably for the three types of sensory-based concepts. For single dimension non-comparatives, the boundaries are fairly precise; however, there may be some ambiguous examples. For instance, when is a stationary object **over** another object? Clearly, if the target object is in a "shadow" projected upward from the other object, the target is **over**. But what if the target is on the edge of this projection? Precisely when is it called **over**? The area of uncertainty for the non-comparatives is typically quite limited.

The boundary for comparatives is usually quite precise. Either something is **louder**, or **not louder** than another example of an audible signal. If we present the concept through sensory examples, we must make sure that the differences are perceptible through sensory observation. However, even if the differences are very small, the example is not ambiguous because the dividing line between positives and negatives is usually very precise for comparatives.

For nouns, the dividing line is very vague. When a **shoe** becomes a **not-shoe** is not known by knowledgeable adults because a precise dividing line does not exist and must become a matter of personal interpretation.

The three types of sensory-based concepts also differ with respect to the absolute value of the examples. The question that determines whether the concept is absolute is: Is a positive example of the concept always a positive example of that concept? For non-comparatives, the answer is, "Yes." An example of **over the table**, is always an example of **over the table**. Also, an example of a noun, such as **dog** is always an example of **dog**. Comparatives, however, are different. "Is this line longer?"

———————————————

The answer depends on the line to which the line is compared. The same line can be used as an example of **longer** and of **not longer**.

The structural samenesses and differences of these sensory-based concepts suggest structural samenesses and differences of the communications designed to teach them faultlessly. The sequences for teaching nouns must address the structural problem that nouns do not have a precise boundary between positive and negative examples. The sequences for teaching comparatives must somehow show that a given outcome (such as the line above) may be positive or negative.

Chapter 4
Facts and Rules About Communicating Through Examples

When we teach a concept, we must communicate a message to the learner. Our communication must be unambiguous—consistent with only one interpretation—and complete enough to permit the learner to apply what has been taught to different situations. To achieve the teaching we present a series of examples that:

1. Show the difference between positives and negatives.
2. Show the range of positive examples.
3. Provide a fairly thorough test of the learner's understanding of the concept.

Facts About Presenting Examples

Basic cognitive teaching involves presenting the learner with some examples that will induce a generalization to other examples. There are logical facts about these communications with the learner and there are rules or principles for achieving different communication goals, such as showing how things are the same or how they are different.

The facts and principles will be illustrated by referring to sensory-based concepts that are shown by presenting concrete examples and labeling each example.

Fact 1. It is impossible to teach a concept through the presentation of one example.

The teacher presents a positive example of a concept by showing the object below and labeling it: "This is glerm."

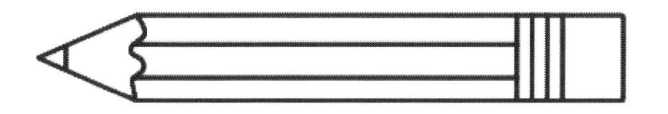

Glerm could refer to any feature of this example or any combination of features. Since the example has an enormous number of features, **glerm** could mean any one of an enormous number of things. The learner might select the right interpretation; however, the learner's chances are not very good. **Glerm** could mean "horizontal," "straight," "pointed," "made of wood," "writing instrument," "object with eraser," "something that floats," etc.

Fact 2. It is impossible to present a group of positive examples that communicates only one interpretation.

We can limit the number of possible interpretations by presenting positive examples only. This presentation may strongly *imply* the desired interpretation; however, a set of positive examples is always capable of generating more than one possible interpretation. Therefore the sequence of examples must contain negatives as well as positives.

Fact 3. Any sameness shared by both positive and negative examples rules out a possible interpretation.

The behavior that the teacher uses to signal positive examples is different from that used for negatives. Any sameness that is observed in both the positive and the negative examples, therefore, *cannot account for treating the negative examples differently.*

If we present example **A** as a positive example of **flot** and example **B** as a negative example of **flot**, any samenesses in the examples rules out possible interpretations.

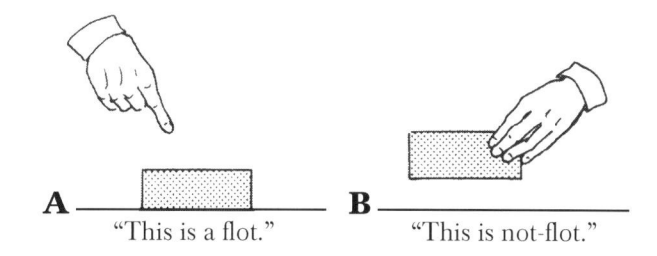

A ———— "This is a flot."   B ———— "This is not-flot."

The block is the same in both positive and negative example, therefore, **flot** cannot mean **block**. The horizontal orientation is the same in both examples, therefore, **flot** cannot refer to the **horizontal orientation**. Since any feature that is the same in both examples cannot be the basis for referring to one example as **flot** and the other as **not-flot**, the difference in behavior must be explained by reference to the features that are *different* from one example to another.

Theory of Instruction: Principles and Applications

This fact about how negative examples rule out possible interpretations has great implications for teaching. To rule out a particular interpretation, we simply show the same feature in the positive example and a corresponding negative example.

Fact 4. A negative example rules out the maximum number of interpretations when the negative example is least different from some positive example.

If negative examples rule out possible interpretations, it follows that, the more samenesses shared by positives and negatives, the more interpretations the negatives rule out. The reason is that these negatives show that a greater number of features do *not* play a role in determining whether the object is positive or negative. Figure 4.1 shows negatives that are increasingly more like the positive:

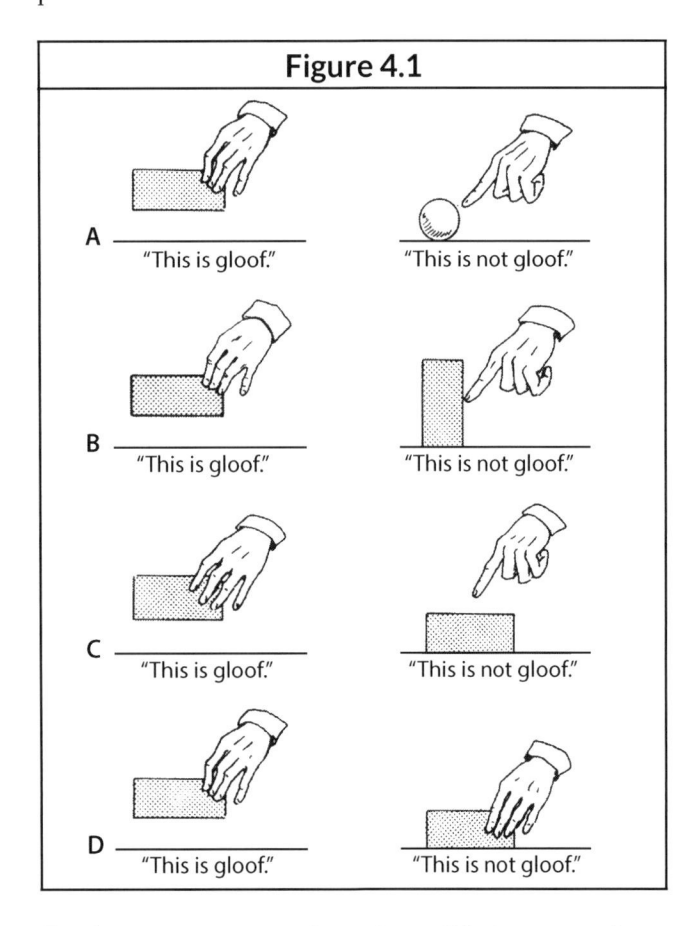

Figure 4.1

A. "This is gloof." / "This is not gloof."
B. "This is gloof." / "This is not gloof."
C. "This is gloof." / "This is not gloof."
D. "This is gloof." / "This is not gloof."

Set **A** generates a number of possible interpretations, including: **gloof** means "being held in the hand"; **gloof** means "something with corners"; **gloof** means "higher than"; **gloof** means "dark."

By changing the negative example (as in set **B**) so that it has more of the same features observed in the positive example, we can reduce the number of possible interpretations.

Some of the interpretations that were generated by set **A** are ruled out by the negative in set **B**. "Gloof" cannot mean **block**, because the block is present in both the positive and the negative. "Gloof" cannot mean **dark**, because darkness is a feature of both the positive and the negative examples. "Gloof" could mean **higher than**, or **in the hand**, or **horizontally-oriented**.

Set **C** rules out the interpretation that "gloof" means **horizontally-oriented** because the horizontal orientation is now in both the positive example and the negative example, and therefore cannot be the basis for determining what **gloof** is: "Gloof" could still mean **being in the hand**.

Set **D** rules out this interpretation by making **being in the hand** a feature of both positive examples and negative examples.

Set **D** generates only a few possible interpretations of "gloof." Perhaps it means **suspended**. To clarify the precise meaning of **gloof**, we would need more examples—both positive and negative.

The fact about samenesses shared by positive and negative examples is important in designing communications. If we design a negative example so that it is highly similar to a positive example, we rule out the greatest number of possible interpretations. Only the difference between the positive and the negative can account for one example being positive and the other negative. Since there is only a minimum difference, that difference must be the basis for treating the examples differently.

In summary, the four facts indicate the basic ways that we can control the possible interpretations communicated through the examples by controlling the details of the examples. If we use a single positive example, we communicate an enormous range of possible interpretations. Additional positive examples rule out possible interpretations. For a feature to be the basis for a possible interpretation, that feature must be present in *all* positives. If it is present in only some, the feature cannot be a basis for classifying the examples as a positive. By presenting a wide variety of positives, we show which features are relevant to the concept.

Negative examples rule out possible interpretations when samenesses occur in both positives and negatives. For a feature to be the basis for classifying the example as positive, that feature must be present in all positives *and in no negatives*. Therefore, any feature that is present in a positive and in a negative cannot be the basis for a possible interpretation. The negatives that rule out the greatest number of possible interpretations are those that are least different from some positive. In this situation, the differences are few, so the range of possible interpretation is limited.

Juxtaposition Principles

The fact that a set of examples must be presented to convey a concept to the learner introduces a new variable—juxtaposition of the items. *The examples that precede an example make that example relatively difficult or easy.* There are five principles of juxtaposition. These are expressed as how-to-do-it rules.

1. The wording principle: To make the sequence of examples as clear as possible, use the same wording on juxtaposed examples (or wording that is as similar as possible).

By using the same wording with all examples, we assure that the learner focuses on the details of the example and is not misled by variations in the wording. If the wording presented with each example is the same, the learner is shown that each example is processed in the same way.

We can make an example more difficult by changing the wording on juxtaposed items. The sequence below makes this task relatively *easy*: "Say the last letter in the word **hog**."

1. Say the last letter in the word **man**.
2. Say the last letter in the word **dog**.
3. Say the last letter in the word **hog**.

To make the task relatively difficult, we precede it with a series of tasks that require the learner to perform a *different* operation. Here is such a sequence:

1. Say the first letter in the word **man**.
2. Say the first letter in the word **dog**.
3. Say the first letter in the word **frog**.
4. Say the last letter in the word **hog**.

This procedure is similar to that used in the game "Simon Says." The leader presents a series of tasks in which he does the same thing he says. He then presents a task in which he does one thing and says another.

Easy juxtapositions are those in which the learner does the same thing with different examples, because these juxtapositions do not require the learner to process as much information. The learner does the same thing with all examples.

2. The setup principle: To minimize the number of examples needed to demonstrate a concept, juxtapose examples that share the greatest possible number of features.

This juxtaposition principle deals with the *examples* in the same way the first principle deals with *wording*. The greater the number of variables shown in the juxtaposed examples, the greater the number of total examples needed to demonstrate a concept. If we teach under by using a dog or a cat that is under a table or chair, we need quite a few examples. We must show:

1. The cat under the chair, the cat not-under the chair (on it, next to it, etc.),
2. The cat under the table, the cat not-under the table,
3. The dog under the table, the dog not-under the table,
4. The dog under the chair, the dog not-under the chair.

To show each of these positions, more than one example would be needed.

If we increase the number of features shared by juxtaposed examples, we decrease the number of examples needed to demonstrate the concept. If we eliminate the cat and use only the dog, we are required to show only:

1. The dog under the table, the dog not-under the table.
2. The dog under the chair, the dog not-under the chair.

If we eliminate the chair, we are required to show only:

1. The dog under the table, the dog not-under the table.

All juxtaposed examples contain the same dog and the same table. The only variable from example to example will be the relative position of the dog, which is the variable relevant to **under**.

The setup principle provides an easy formula for constructing the shortest, most efficient sequence: *construct all examples so they share the greatest possible number of features.* Not only will this formula permit us to demonstrate how the concept works with fewer examples, it will facilitate showing the learner which features are critical to the concept. If examples share the maximum number of features, they differ in the minimum number of ways. These are the ways that are relevant to the concept. The probability is therefore great that the learner will attend to the features and changes that are relevant to the concept.

3. The difference principle: To show differences between examples, juxtapose examples that are minimally different and treat the examples differently.

Positive and negative examples provide the maximum information when they differ only slightly from each other; however, positive and negative examples must be juxtaposed to guarantee that this information will be transmitted to the learner. Consider example set **A** in Figure 4.2. There are two minimally different examples created through continuous conversion.

Figure 4.2	
Set A	
Example	Teacher Wording
1	This line is not horizontal.
2	This line is horizontal.
Set B	
1	This line is horizontal.
2	This line is not horizontal.
3	This line is not horizontal.
4	This line is not horizontal.

When these examples are juxtaposed (one immediately following the other in time), the difference is conveyed relatively easily because the only change occurring from one example to the next is a slight change in orientation. When other examples are interpolated, however, the learner is not provided with a demonstration that shows this difference. Consider examples 1 and 4 in set **B**. They are the same examples that appear in set **A**. Although examples 1 and 4 are slightly different from each other and are labeled differently, the difference is not obvious because they are not juxtaposed.

When we juxtapose differently labeled examples that show the minimum difference, we call the learner's attention to the fact that the small difference is the only basis for the change in labels.

4. The sameness principle: To show samenesses across examples, juxtapose examples that are greatly different and indicate that the examples have the same label.

If we show **under** using only a table top and eraser, we can create many different positive examples of **under**. Some would be close to the table; others farther away; some would be near the middle of the table; others would be near the ends. The juxtaposed examples in Figure 4.3 show sameness. Note that the examples follow the wording principle (same wording for all examples), the setup principle (same objects appearing in juxtaposed examples), and the sameness principle (great difference from example to example with the same label from example to example).

Figure 4.3	
Example	Teacher Wording
1	The eraser is under.
2	The eraser is under.
3	The eraser is under.
4	The eraser is under.

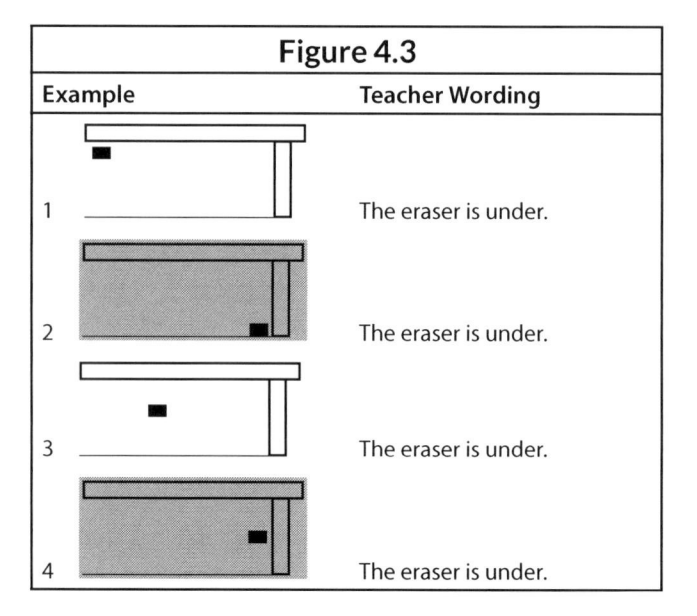

Since juxtaposed examples are treated in the same way ("The eraser is under"), the changes from example to example are shown not to affect the label. The learner

Chapter 4 | Facts and Rules About Communicating Through Examples

is told in effect, "These examples are the same, so whatever difference you observe in them is a difference that is irrelevant to **under**."

5. The testing principle: To test the learner, juxtapose examples that bear no predictable relationship to each other.

After the learner has been shown sameness and difference, the learner is tested on the generalizations implied by the communication. If the demonstration is adequate, the learner should be able to handle some new examples of the concept that are presented within the constraints of the setup principle. Note that the testing principle refers to the test that is provided immediately after the demonstration of sameness and difference. This test involves the same setup features as the sameness and difference demonstration. Following successful performance on this immediate test, the learner will be given *expansion tests* that involve new setups and new wording. The most immediate communication question, however, is: Did the learner receive the information needed to generalize to new examples presented within the original setup? The test that immediately follows the demonstration examples answers this question.

According to the testing principle, no pattern of responses should be evident from one test example to the next. (For example, no alternating sequence from positive to negative examples.) Examples presented in the test may be similar or dissimilar. The response called for by these examples may be the same or may be different. The test segment should repeat some examples that had been used to demonstrate difference and sameness. The segment should also contain new examples.

Applying the Five Principles

To provide a clear initial-teaching communication to the learner, we must design a sequence that takes into account all the facts and all five juxtaposition principles. The sequence must show relevant samenesses and relevant differences in the examples. The wording associated with the various examples must be precise. The setup must be designed to permit the smallest number of examples. And the learner must be provided with an immediate test, one that requires the learner to respond to examples created within the setup.

The sequence in Figure 4.4 is consistent with the five principles. As shown in Figure 4.4, different examples are designed to meet the requirements of different juxtaposition principles. The sequence is a comparative sequence designed for the initial teaching of the concept, **getting wider**. Each example involves a space (diagrammed as a line with a marker at either end). To present the sequence above, hold your hands about a foot apart and say: "Watch the space." Then hold your hands stationary and say the wording for example 1: "It didn't get wider." Move one hand in slightly, stop, and say the wording for example 2: "It didn't get wider." Move the same hand out slightly. Then say the wording for example 3: "It got wider." Continue in this manner for the remaining examples.

Figure 4.4

Symbol	Principle	Examples
A1, A2	The wording principle	1-13
B	The set-up principle	1-13
C	The difference principle	2-3, 5-6
D	The sameness principle	3-5
E	The testing principle	6-13

Example	Model	Teacher Wording
1		Watch the space.
1		It didn't get wider.
2		It didn't get wider.
3		It got wider.
4		It got wider.
5		It got wider.
6		Did it get wider?
7		Did it get wider?
8		Did it get wider?
9		Did it get wider?
10		Did it get wider?
11		Did it get wider?
12		Did it get wider?
13		Did it get wider?

Bracket **A** shows that the "same wording" is used for all examples. The wording could have been made even more uniform if the teacher demonstrated on examples 1 to 5 by asking the same question presented to the learner and then answering it: "Did it get wider? No....Did it get wider? No...." etc. The wording used in the illustration above is fairly uniform, however. All demonstration examples and all test examples refer to the same response dimension: **getting wider.**

Bracket **B** shows that all examples involve the maximum number of common setup features. Note that only one hand is involved in changing an example to the next example. (The same hand moves in all examples that involve movement.) The hands appear in all examples. The orientation of the hands, the background, and other features of the situation remain the same. Therefore, the setup principle is satisfied. The set of examples contains the maximum number of common features.

Bracket **C** shows that the difference is shown in two parts of the sequence. Both involve small differences in the juxtaposed examples that *lead to different wording.*

Bracket **D** shows sameness, created by juxtaposing examples that differ as greatly as possible within the constraints of the setup. Note that the size of the change from example to example is controlled for this concept because the communication must convey the idea that the *size of the change* has nothing to do with **getting wider.** The change from 2 to 3 is a very small change. The change from 3 to 4 is quite large. The change from 5 to 6 is intermediate. All are labeled in the same way: "It got wider."

Bracket **E** shows the test juxtaposition, an unpredictable sequence that contains some minimum-difference examples and some greater difference examples. The test sequence attempts to avoid any pattern such as an alternating pattern of positive, negative, positive, etc.

Continuous Conversion

As noted earlier, the procedure by which you present the examples when you change one example into the next (e.g., holding your hands up and then moving one of the hands to create the different examples) is called *continuous conversion.* The use of continuous conversion forces you to create *relevant changes in the examples.* When you create examples through continuous conversion, you do not create total examples, only changes. The learner is therefore not required to attend to all details of the examples, merely those involved in the change. The fact that you must change examples in a way that changes positives to negatives means that you will create changes that are relevant to the concept.

To appreciate the difference in communication potential between continuous conversion and non-continuous conversion, present the sequence of examples for *getting wider* non-continuously. To do this, use exactly the same set of examples you used before. However, between each example, put your hands at your sides. Then put your hands up again to create the next example. Start with your hands about a foot apart. Say, "Watch my hands." Put them at your sides. Raise them to where they had been and say, "They didn't get wider" (example 1). Again put your hands down. Return them, this time slightly closer together and say, "They didn't get wider." Continue through all examples in this manner.

The advantages of the continuous conversion sequence become immediately apparent when examples are presented non-continuously. It would be difficult for the learner to see that the space for example 2 is slightly less than that for example 1. The reason is that non-continuous conversion *requires creation of all details for each example.* First, all details of example 1 are created. Then all details of example 2 are created. To compare two examples, the learner is required to compare the two sets of details and observe possible differences. This task is logically more difficult than one in which the first example is changed into the next.

Continuous conversion makes small changes perceptible because one example is changed just enough to create the next example. If the two examples are highly similar, only a small change occurs; however, it is easy to detect because it is the only thing that happens.

Analyzing Concepts By Using Continuous Conversion

Continuous conversion of examples can be used to show us which dimensions are relevant to the concept. If we are in doubt about what causes an example to be positive or negative, we use continuous conversion to provide the answer. First we start with a negative example and, through continuous conversion, change it into a positive example. The dimension that we changed is a relevant dimension. (If we changed position, position is relevant; if we changed intensity, intensity is relevant, etc.) Next, we see how much change along the relevant dimension we can apply to a positive example without making it negative. We must operate within the constraints of the setup. For example, after observing that moving the hands in a certain direction causes an example to change from negative to positive, we conclude that movement of the hands is a dimension that is relevant to the concept. Next we see the extent to which we can move our hands *without* changing a positive example into a negative. This variation of the relevant dimension shows the range of positive variation that is possible within the constraints of the setup.

By applying the two-step conversion described above, we discover that many concepts are single-dimension concepts, which means that if we start with a negative example we can change it into a positive example only if we manipulate one dimension. We discover that other concepts are multiple-dimension concepts, which means that it is possible to change a positive into a negative by manipulating various dimensions.

Not all concepts can be presented through continuous conversion. If the example is the verbally presented statement, "The crow flew over the tree," we cannot continuously convert that example into another verbal example. However, if we pretend that examples can be created continuously, we more readily see which changes are relevant to the concept, how the various examples are the same, and how they differ.

Perspective. The rules and principles presented in this section apply in some form to any instructional design problem, because all these problems start with some "need." You want to show how things are the same or how they are different. You want to reduce the variables and make the relevant changes as obvious as possible. You want to test the learner on non-trivial generalizations of what you have taught. The principles apply because they are logical principles about examples.

Learn the principles of juxtaposition, and try to think of them as logical rules that apply to any situation that involves communicating through examples.

Summary

The most basic communications for teaching discriminations or concepts are ones that present *examples* and that permit the learner to perform on examples not shown in the initial presentation. Basic communication facts and principles are described in the context of communicating through examples. The facts deal with basic logical properties of communications that involve examples. The principles tell how to achieve particular communication goals, such as showing sameness, or showing difference.

The first *fact* is that the presentation of only one example cannot logically show one concept. The reason is that any concrete example is an example of thousands of concepts because it has thousands of features. The labeling of the concept does not indicate which features are being referred to.

The addition of different positive examples rules out possible concepts if the examples differ in various ways, but are labeled in the same way. The common label must relate to how the examples are the same, not how they are different. All observed differences among the examples are ruled out.

By presenting only positives examples, it is possible to strongly imply a concept, but logically impossible to show it precisely. The addition of negative examples rules out possible interpretations by calling attention to differences in the examples that are correlated with differences in the labels. The smallest differences provide the greatest information. If a very small change occurs and that change is associated with a change in the label, that change must be the cause of the different label. Furthermore, since it was a very small change, the identified cause is very precise. The change marks the boundary between the positives examples and the negatives.

A final fact is that samenesses and differences of examples are more obvious when the examples are juxtaposed. This fact implies that the continuous conversion of examples provides the clearest presentation of samenesses and, differences because it creates the *changes* that occur from one example to the next.

The *principles* of juxtaposition are based on the notion that the examples must be presented in sequence to the learner. The order of the examples is important. The general procedure in presenting sequences is to demonstrate with some examples and test on others.

Five principles provide specific direction for designing the wording, the setup, demonstrations of sameness, demonstrations of difference, and the test. These principles of juxtaposition are:

1. **The wording principle.** To make the sequence of examples as clear as possible, use the same wording on juxtaposed examples.

2. **The setup principle.** To minimize the number of examples needed to demonstrate a concept,

juxtapose examples that share the greatest possible number of features.

3. **The difference principle.** To show differences between examples, juxtapose examples that are minimally different and indicate that the examples have different labels.
4. **The sameness principle.** To show sameness across examples, juxtapose examples that are greatly different and treat the examples in the same way.
5. **The testing principle.** To test the learner, juxtapose examples that bear no predictable relationship to each other.

For a sequence to communicate unambiguously, *all* principles must come into play. The wording must be uniform, and the setup efficiently designed. The demonstrations of sameness and difference must precede the test examples. The test involves the same setup as the demonstration, and provides the most fundamental information about the sequence: Does the learner generalize within the setup? If so, the sequence is immediately followed by one that uses variant setups and variant wordings. However, our first concern is the performance within the setup.

The principles of juxtaposition apply to any set of examples. Become familiar with these principles before proceeding to the communications for sensory-based concepts.

Chapter 5
Non-Comparative Sequences

The non-comparative sequences that we will develop in this chapter are appropriate for teaching positional relationships (**under, near, in**); some actions (**running, hopping**); and simple adjective features (**pointed, bent, horizontal, red**). Variations of the basic non-comparative sequence are possibly appropriate for more advanced applications (adjectives such as **gradual** and **despondent**, actions such as **evade** and **inflect**).

There are two basic types of sequences for these concepts—positive-first sequences and negative-first sequences. As the labels imply, the positive-first sequences begin with demonstrations of positive examples. The negative-first sequences begin with demonstrations of negatives. Both sequences provide demonstrations of positives and negatives, followed by a test.

Figure 5.1 shows the basic formula or format for a negative-first sequence. By following this formula for any single dimension non-comparative concept, we can create an initial-teaching communication that is faultless. The concept taught through the sequence below is **slanted**, meaning not vertical and not horizontal. Note that the wording is not provided (merely the letters **N** and **P** to indicate whether each example is positive or negative) so that the focus on the positive and negative examples is more obvious. Present this sequence through continuous conversion, using a pencil. After creating the first example, rotate the pencil counter-clockwise. Then stop when the pencil is horizontal to produce example 2. Continue through the remaining examples by quickly rotating the pencil, then holding it stationary for the next example.

Juxtapositions

The sequence begins with two negatives. Both are minimally different from *some* positive examples, *but the negatives are not highly similar to each other.*

Following the negatives are three positives, juxtaposed to show sameness (examples 3, 4, 5).

Following the third positive is a negative (example 6).

Figure 5.1

Example		Example Type
1		N
2		N
3	C	P
4	D	P
5		P
6	C	N
7	B	P
8		N
9	E	N
10		P
11		N
12		P
13		P

The remainder of the sequence consists of examples in an unpredictable order with respect to whether they are positive or negative and with respect to the difference between juxtaposed examples.

The brackets next to the series of examples indicate that the sequence is consistent with juxtaposition principles:

  B. The setup involves your hand and the same pencil in all examples.

Section II | Basic Forms

C. Difference is created by juxtaposing two minimally different examples, each consisting of a positive and a negative (examples 2-3 and 5-6).

D. Sameness is created by juxtaposing maximally different examples 3, 4 and 5. The juxtaposed examples vary according to the direction of the point, the amount of rotation from the preceding example, and the absolute difference from the preceding examples.

E. Testing is provided by a series of examples that bear no predictable relationship to each other.

Constructing Non-Comparative Sequences

Negative-First Sequences

Since all non-comparatives have the same structure, all can be effectively conveyed through a sequence that is of the same form as the sequence above. To construct such a sequence for *any* single dimension non-comparative:

1. Begin with two negative examples that differ minimally from *some* positive example. For the sequence in Figure 5.1, we could have begun with any of the following pairs of examples: ←↑ ↓↑ ↓← or with the two used in the model sequence.

2. Make sure that the *second negative* (example 2) is minimally different from example 3. In the model sequence the second example is horizontal with the point facing right. Example 3 is slightly slanted with the point still facing right.

3. Make juxtaposed positive examples 3, 4 and 5 differ as much as possible from each other within the constraints of the setup. In the model sequence, example 3 points slightly downward, 4 points up and to the left, and 5 is pointed down and almost vertical. This order shows that the label of *slanted* does not have to do with the direction of the point or with the amount of slant. Each example differs in direction of point and in slant.

4. Make juxtaposed examples 5 and 6 minimally different, but *do not use the same minimum difference used in examples 2 and 3*. In the sequence above, examples 2 and 3 showed a minimum difference involving a *horizontal* example (2). Examples 5 and 6 show a minimum difference involving a *vertical* example.

5. Following example 6, present a series of 6 to 8 test examples that show no predictable order. The test segment should repeat some earlier examples; it should also contain new positives and new negatives. It should contain a sufficient number of positives to provide a good test of the learner's understanding, but it should not show a predictable order or pattern of positives (**P**) and negatives (**N**). The pattern for examples 6 through 13 in the sequence above is: **NPNNPNPP**. This pattern is acceptable. The following patterns are not acceptable: **NNPPNNPP** or **NPNPNPNP**.

Figure 5.2

Example		Example Type	Teacher wording
1		N	The block is not suspended
2		N	The block is not suspended
3		P	The block is suspended
4		P	The block is suspended
5		P	The block is suspended
6		N	Is the block suspended?
7		P	Is the block suspended?
8		P	Is the block suspended?
9		N	Is the block suspended?
10		P	Is the block suspended?
11		N	Is the block suspended?
12		P	Is the block suspended?

Illustration. The negative-first form (used to communicate **slanted**) is used in Figure 5.2 to communicate a different non-comparative–**suspended**. The sequence follows the same five rules:

1. The sequence begins with two negative examples, each of which is different from *some* positive example.

2. Example 3 is minimally different from example 2. (The only difference is that example 3 is held against the bottom surface of the table.)

3. Examples 3, 4 and 5 present sameness juxtapositions. Note the height and position of the block changes in all three of these examples.

4. A new minimum difference occurs between examples 5 and 6.

5. Beginning with example 6 is a series of 7 non-patterned test examples. (The sequence for **suspended** contains a total of 12 examples, compared to 13 for **slanted**. This difference is somewhat arbitrary. For some concepts more test items are needed to test the concept adequately.)

Present this sequence. Use any object and a table surface that has space beneath the surface. Follow the sequence of examples. First position an example. Then say the specified wording. Quickly position the next example and say the wording. As you present the examples, observe how the different possible interpretations are ruled out by the minimum-difference negative examples and the positive demonstration examples (3, 4, 5). Make sure that you hold the object in the same way for all examples.

Teacher wording. The teacher identifies the first five examples, saying either: "The block is suspended," or, "The block is not suspended." The teacher tests on the examples 6 through 12 by asking, "Is the block suspended?" The teacher wording could say, "Tell me suspended or not-suspended." This wording would be used for all test examples. The *positive* response for the question, "Is it suspended?" is "Yes." The positive response for "Tell me suspended or not-suspended" is "Suspended."

Variation Within the Setup

According to the setup principle, all examples should share as many features as possible. In the sequence above, all are held. All involve a horizontally-oriented object (not a vertical or slanted object). To show the range of positive variation (examples 3, 4 and 5), you might be tempted to present a **slanted** example. Such an example would certainly not make the sequence unacceptable, merely more difficult to construct. Here's why: When you violate the setup principle, you show a "variation" in some dimension that is incapable of changing an example from positive to negative. However, the learner does not know that this is the case. To show the learner that the variation is a change along some dimension other than the critical one you must therefore *add more examples to the sequence*. If you show a slanted positive example, you must show a slanted negative example to indicate that the slant of the object is unimportant and can appear in both positives and negatives. An easier way to show that it is unimportant is to remove it from the sequence. If no positive examples are slanted, the slant of the object cannot be relevant to whether the object is suspended. Similarly, if no objects have stripes, having stripes cannot be relevant to whether the object is suspended.

Determining Which Features Should Appear in All Examples

As noted earlier, the easiest test to determine which features should not be varied from example to example is to begin with a positive example and observe *all possible changes that will convert it into a negative example*. Will rotating the eraser convert a positive to a negative? No. *If a change does not convert a positive example to a negative, that change deals with an irrelevant feature.*

There are two basic ways to show that a feature of a positive example is irrelevant:

1. Present *another* example that does not have the feature, but is identical to the original in every *other* respect.

2. Present a negative example that *has the feature*, but is minimally different from the positive.

We could show that the vertical orientation of an object is irrelevant by:

1. Presenting another *positive* example that is not vertically oriented, but that is suspended over the same place of the table.

2. Presenting a *negative* example that is vertically oriented and that is in nearly the same place.

Figure 5.3 shows a 12-example sequence that parallels the model sequence of **suspended**. The only difference is that the orientation of the object shifts between being vertical and being horizontal. The addition of this variable creates a communication that does not rule out all possible misinterpretations. The sequence is consistent with the interpretation that a positive example in the middle of the table must be vertically oriented. Also a positive on the right end of the surface must be horizontal.

Figure 5.3			
Example		Example Type	Teacher wording
1		N	The block is not suspended
2		N	The block is not suspended
3		P	The block is suspended
4		P	The block is suspended
5		P	The block is suspended
6		N	Is the block suspended?
7		P	Is the block suspended?
8		P	Is the block suspended?
9		N	Is the block suspended?
10		P	Is the block suspended?
11		N	Is the block suspended?
12		P	Is the block suspended?

We could eliminate these misrules by adding 3 or 4 examples to the sequence. In the end, however, we would convey the same basic message that we convey through the 12 examples of the original sequence.

Stipulation

Stipulation occurs when the learner is repeatedly shown a limited range of positive variation. If the presentation shows **suspended** only with respect to an eraser and a table, the learner may conclude that the concept **suspended** is limited to the eraser and the table.

Stipulation is an "undergeneralization." The learner does not know the range to which this concept applies. *Misrules* are different from stipulation. Misrules occur when more than one cause for positive-negative changes is implied. It is a misgeneralization. The sequence provides a false idea of what makes an example positive or negative.

The initial teaching sequences for non-comparatives are guilty of stipulation. They clearly show the minimum necessary difference between positive and negative examples. They also show the range of variation that can be achieved within the constraints of the setup; however, each sequence is limited to one setup. All examples of **slanted** are shown with a pencil. All examples of **suspended** are shown with a block and a table.

The stipulation implied by these initial-teaching sequences is that the concept may be limited to a particular context. The learner, for example, may pick up the stipulation that the concept **suspended** applies only to blocks and tables. The sequence does not provide any examples to discredit this possible implication. To counteract stipulation, additional examples must follow the initial-teaching sequence. Following the learner's successful performance with the sequence that teaches **slanted**, for instance, the learner would be shown that **slanted** applies to hills, streets, floors, walls, and other objects. Following the presentation of **suspended**, the learner would be systematically exposed to a variety of suspended objects.

Stipulation of the type that occurs in initial-teaching sequences is not serious if additional examples are presented *immediately after the initial teaching sequence has been presented.* The longer the learner deals only with the examples shown in the original setup, the greater the probability that the learner will learn the stipulation. If the learner is presented with the new examples immediately following the initial teaching sequence, no significant new learning should be necessary. The learner is simply shown that the same dimension involved in the judgment that a block is suspended is involved in judgments involving other things and other tasks. (Remember, the initial teaching sequence requires only about one minute to present.)

To avoid stipulation during the initial teaching demonstration, we must violate two principles—the wording principle and the setup principle. The consequences of these violations are communications that are unfortunately elaborate and possibly unclear. To compensate for violations of the setup principle we must add examples. To compensate for violations of the wording principle, we must add examples. If both changes in setup and wording occur at the same time, a large number of examples must be added to make the sequence consistent with the desired interpretation. Even with these additional examples, however, the sequence will be "crude." The idea is not merely to make the sequence consistent with a single generalization, but to suggest that generalization as early in the sequence as possible. If the single generalization is apparent only after ten examples have been presented, the sequence is far inferior to one that reveals it after four. The simplest solution to the problem of stipulation is to follow the setup and wording principles. Then immediately follow the initial-teaching sequence with examples and tasks designed to counteract any possible stipulation. Follow-up sequences are discussed in Chapter 15.

Positive-First Sequences

Theoretically, negative-first sequences reveal the desired interpretation faster than positive-first sequences. However, for this interpretation to occur, the learner must be reasonably sophisticated and *must realize that the negatives shown first are related to the positives that will follow*. The first two examples show the sophisticated learner, "This is not it yet." The change involved in creating example 3 reveals to the learner, "Now you see what it is." At this point (example 3) the learner should have a very good idea of the concept. Some additional questions about how it works may still have to be answered through subsequent examples; however, the basic structure has been shown, through only three examples. Theoretically, positive-first sequences are not as capable as negative-first sequences in showing the concept as early. The reason is that the positive-first sequence starts with a positive example. Like all positive examples that are labeled, this positive is consistent with many possible interpretations. Some interpretations are ruled out by the positives that follow; however, possible misrules last until the negatives are introduced.

A possible communication problem with negative-first sequences occurs if the learner misunderstands the intent of identifying the first examples as "This is not slanted." The learner may conclude that the example *has nothing to do with* **slanted** and may ignore it. The result is that the learner does not benefit from the negatives.

In any case, the learner should be presented with some concepts through positive-first sequences and some through negative-first sequences. If only negative-first sequences were presented, the learner might develop the strategy of "memorizing" the pattern, rather than that of attending to the features of the example.

Constructing Positive-First Sequences

Here are the procedures for constructing positive-first sequences for any single dimension non-comparative.

1. Begin with three positives that are juxtaposed to show sameness (examples 1, 2, 3).

2. Follow with two negatives (examples 4, 5). The first is minimally different from example 3. The next is minimally different from example 6.

3. Follow with a positive (example 6) that is minimally different from example 5.

4. Follow with a series of 6 to 8 examples that follow the test-juxtaposition order.

5. Model the first five examples; test on the remaining examples.

Figure 5.4 illustrates a positive-first variation for **suspended.**

The sequence is created by rearranging the same set of examples presented in the negative-first sequence. The order of appearance for the examples in Figure 5.4 occur in the negative-first sequence (Figure 5.2) as: 7, 4, 5, 6, 2, 3, 1, 8, 10, 9, 11, 12.

One advantage of the positive-first sequence is that it permits us to show a wider range of positive variation. The negative-first sequence constrains the range of positives somewhat because there must be a minimum difference negative on either side of the positives. Since the positive-first sequence begins with positive examples, greater latitude is possible. The implication is that if you find it difficult to arrange the first three positives when working with a negative-first sequence, try a positive-first sequence.

Section II | Basic Forms

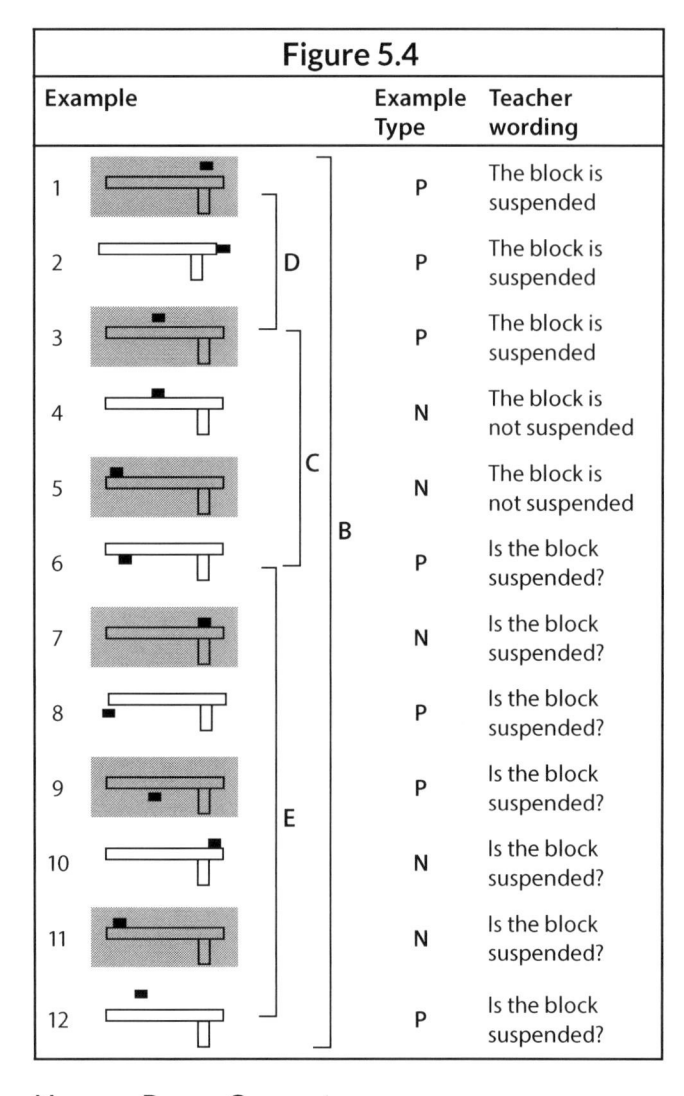

Figure 5.4			
Example		Example Type	Teacher wording
1		P	The block is suspended
2		P	The block is suspended
3		P	The block is suspended
4		N	The block is not suspended
5		N	The block is not suspended
6		P	Is the block suspended?
7		N	Is the block suspended?
8		P	Is the block suspended?
9		P	Is the block suspended?
10		N	Is the block suspended?
11		N	Is the block suspended?
12		P	Is the block suspended?

Narrow-Range Concepts

Some concepts have a very limited range of positive variation. (They can only be demonstrated through a setup that provides for a very narrow range of variation.) For instance, we could teach the concept **gradual turn** (meaning **not abrupt**) in a way that requires a great many variables; however, if we follow the setup principle and try to keep as many features as possible common to all examples, we will control the size of the turn, the object that is turning, and the direction of the turn. The boundary between **gradual** and **not-gradual** is not clear. (We can make it clear by teaching the concept **more gradual** and **not-more gradual**; however, this concept is a comparative.) If we keep the original concept—**gradual**—we must make some arbitrary decisions about what is **gradual** and what is not. The safest convention is this: Show all examples of **gradual turn** at one rate and all examples of **not-gradual turn** at a fast rate that is quite discriminable from that labeled **gradual**.

Figure 5.5 illustrates the resulting sequence. It begins with one positive and one negative.

Figure 5.5			
Example		Example Type	Teacher Wording
			Watch the turns that I trace with my finger:
1		(gradual) P	It turned gradually.
2		(abrupt) N	It didn't turn gradually.
3		(gradual) P	Did it turn gradually?
4		(gradual) P	Did it turn gradually?
5		(abrupt) N	Did it turn gradually?

To present this sequence, start with your finger pointing up. Turn it gradually clockwise 90 degrees. Stop and say the wording for example 1. Turn another 90 degrees abruptly in the same direction. Stop and say the wording for example 2. Note that you turn your hand 90 degrees for each example. You move it either abruptly or gradually. Try to present all abrupt examples at the same speed and all gradual ones at the same speed—a speed quite different from that shown for the abrupt examples.

The sequence might be improved if it contained more modeled examples at the beginning (possibly two positives and one negative). However, because the difference between positives and negatives is obvious and because there is no range of variation for the positives, one demonstration should be enough.

For all limited-range variations of non-comparatives, begin with either a positive or a negative, demonstrate on 1 to 3 examples and test on 3 to 5.

Conversely, for concepts that have an unusually wide range of variation, present more than three examples to show sameness. For concepts that have many types of negatives that are minimally different from positives, include more than two minimally different negatives in the demonstration part of the sequence.

Non-Continuous Conversion Sequence

Continuous conversions are not always possible or practical, particularly when we teach symbolic concepts. Assume that we wanted to teach the learner whether spoken words end in voiced sounds or not-voiced sounds. We cannot actually say words as a continuous vocalization. We say a word, then another word. This vocalization is *not* continuous. One word is presented. It disappears. Then another is presented. (The procedure is quite different from the presentation of **slanted**, which consists of examples that are retained until a change creates the next example.)

Figure 5.6

Examples	Example Type	Teacher Wording
		I'll say words. Then I'll tell you if each word ends in a voiced sound.
1 Mack	N	It doesn't end in a voiced sound.
2 Mass	N	It doesn't end in a voiced sound.
3 Maz	P	It ends in a voiced sound.
4 Mag	P	It ends in a voiced sound.
5 Mad	P	It ends in a voiced sound.
6 Mat	N	Does it end in a voiced sound?
7 Mass	N	Does it end in a voiced sound?
8 Mab	P	Does it end in a voiced sound?
9 Maff	N	Does it end in a voiced sound?
10 Mal	P	Does it end in a voiced sound?
11 Mat	N	Does it end in a voiced sound?
12 Mav	P	Does it end in a voiced sound?

The rule to follow in dealing with such cases is to design the sequence in basically the same way you would design it if continuous conversions were possible. Figure 5.6 shows a negative-first sequence for teaching whether spoken words end in a voiced sound or in a non-voiced sound. The brackets show that the same rules of juxtaposition used for the other sequences apply to this one.

To present the sequence, say the example, then say the specified wording for that example. Note that the teacher begins with an explanation of what the teaching will show. The **A** bracket shows that the wording principle is followed. The **B** bracket indicates that one part of each word (**ma**) is common to all examples. Each **C** bracket shows a pair of minimum-difference examples. The **D** bracket shows the three examples juxtaposed to convey sameness. The **E** bracket indicates the test examples.

Because these examples are presented verbally, they cannot be converted continuously. However, if we presented *written words* to the learner, we could present the same examples through continuous conversion.

The teacher would begin by writing the first word (**mack**) on the board and saying, "It doesn't end in a voiced sound." The teacher then erases only part of the word to create the next example. (The teacher erases **ck** and replaces it with **ss**. This change converts the first example into the second example.) Each following example would be created in the same way. The teacher would erase the ending of a word and replace it with another ending.

Remember, written examples can be continuously converted. Oral examples of words cannot. If we used written examples, however, we might choose to modify the teacher wording. The reason is that our communication depends on the learner correctly identifying the ending of each word. If the teacher simply says, "This word doesn't end with a voiced sound," there is a question about whether the learner was actually registering the correct pronunciation or whether the learner silently misread it. To reduce the ambiguity, the teacher would *say the word*, then tell about the ending or direct the learner to read each word aloud. (See Figure 5.7)

Figure 5.7

Example	Teacher Wording
1. mat	What word? Mat doesn't end in a voiced sound.
2. map	What word? Map doesn't end in a voiced sound.
3. mab	What word? Mab ends in a voiced sound.
Etc.	

Illustrations

Ordinarily pictorial illustrations do not permit continuous conversion because they are static and there is no easy way to change one picture into another. However, there are three ways that continuous conversion can be created with illustrations:

1. By covering or uncovering parts of the picture.
2. By adding or removing cutout parts to make a "background."
3. By pointing to parts of the picture.

The simplest procedure is to point to different parts. For some illustrations, however, this procedure is not practical.

We can illustrate the use of pictures with a sequence designed to teach the concept **they**. The teacher presents a group of illustrated characters, two girls, two boys, two men, two women, two dogs, and two cars. The teacher then creates continuous conversion by pointing to different characters or combinations of characters.

Figure 5.8 shows the first part of the sequence. The *examples* indicate what the teacher points to.

Figure 5.8

Example	Teacher Wording
	I'll tell you if I show **they**. Watch what I point to.
1. A boy	It doesn't show **they**.
2. A girl	It doesn't show **they**.
3. A girl and boy	It shows **they**.
4. Two dogs, a car, and a man	It shows **they**.
5. A dog and a woman	It shows **they**.
6. A dog	Does it show **they**?
Etc.	

By placing appropriate cutouts in a scene and by removing them, the teacher could create the same series of examples through continuous conversion. The teacher would first place the cutout of the boy in the scene. For item 2, a boy would be exchanged for a girl. For item 3, the girl would remain and a boy would be added to create a minimum-difference positive example. Example 4 would be created by removing the boy and girl and replacing them with two dogs, a car, and a man. This example is greatly different from example 3. The teacher treats it the same way example 3 was treated, thereby demonstrating sameness.

Note that the series of examples parallels the other negative-first series we have created, with respect to sameness and difference.

Two-Choice Tasks

These tasks present two choices, both of which are usually named in the task. "Tell me if it's pink or red." "Is this line vertical or horizontal?" "Is this fraction more than one or less than one?"

Two-choice tasks should be avoided in initial teaching sequences that are presented to relatively naive learners. The reason is that the tasks require the learner to use a more complicated formula for responding. The learner must remember which features of the examples go with each choice. Since there are two choices, *the task may induce reversals*. The tasks that are capable of inducing the most serious reversals are those that involve a transformation, with part of the response the same for both choices. The task, "Is this fraction more than one or less than one?" is such a task. The responses that the learner must produce (more *than one*, less *than one*) are the same except for a single word. Another example of choices with common parts is presented in this task: "Tell me if it is on *the table* or over *the table*."

Two-choice tasks that have common parts should be used with only the most facile learners or those who are already somewhat familiar with the responses that are being taught. Two-choice tasks that do not have common parts are more appropriate, even for facile learners. Examples of these tasks are: "Tell me if it is tilted or flat." Since the responses "Tilted" and "Flat" have no common parts and are highly dissimilar from each other, the probability of reversals is reduced.

For the more naive learner, single-choice tasks should be presented. "Tell me if it is tilted," "Is this fraction more than one?" "Is this on the table?" Sometimes the task may call for a response that involves the word **not**. If the learner is facile with this word, these tasks are not difficult; however, they may be quite difficult for the very naive learner who is not familiar with the meaning of **not**. For this learner, the task may function as a two-choice task that involves common response parts and therefore calls for a transformation, e.g., "Tell me if it is under or not-under." The learner may have mechanical problems in combining the word **not** with the appropriate features of the example.

Determining Positives in Two-Choice Tasks

For many teaching situations, we are required to teach facile learners related concepts, such as **tilted** and **flat**. Since no transformation is involved in the responses and the learners are facile, we could teach the concept through a two-choice task. The obvious advantage of this approach is that it is fast. With one demonstration, we could teach both words.

If we decide to pursue this approach, we are faced with the problem of deciding which we should make *the positive examples*–**tilted** or **flat**. This problem is unique to two-choice tasks. Here is a rule to follow: *Make the examples with the greatest range of positive variation the positive examples and the examples with the narrower range the negatives.*

For **tilted**-**flat**, the concept **tilted** has the greatest range of variation, so **tilted** becomes the positive and **flat** the negative. Figure 5.9 shows a possible beginning of a sequence. It is a positive-first sequence beginning with three examples of **tilted**. Note that there is only one modeled example of **flat** because, within the context of the setup, there is no range of variation for **flat**.

Figure 5.9		
Example	Example Type	Teacher Wording
		I'll tell you if it's tilted or flat.
1	P	It's tilted.
2	P	It's tilted.
3	P	It's tilted.
4	N	Now it's flat.
5	P	Tell me: tilted or flat.
6	N	Tell me: tilted or flat.
		Etc.

The only difference between this sequence and the earlier positive-first sequence comes after example 4. The reason is that there is only one negative in the sequence above. The teacher presents the same task or question for each test example; however, note that *the learner produces different responses.*

Non-Comparative Concepts as Components of Complex Tasks

In later sections we will deal with more complex forms of communication. These forms are composed of more basic forms. The following are two illustrations of how the basic non-comparative sequence is incorporated into more complex communications.

In our first example, we wish to teach the learner various spelling relationships that involve the discrimination of short vowel and not-short vowel. One relationship is:

- If the /**ch**/ sound immediately follows a short **a, e, i,** or **o**, it is spelled **t-c-h**.
- If the /**ch**/ sound does not immediately follow one of these vowels, it is spelled **c-h**.

We could teach at least part of the relationship through a sequence that begins like the one in Figure 5.10. This sequence is a non-comparative that follows the same pattern as the simpler non-comparatives.

Figure 5.10	
Example	Teacher Wording
Listen: Batch	Does a short vowel sound come just before the **ch** sound? Yes.
Listen: Hitch	Does a short vowel sound come just before the **ch** sound? Yes.
Listen: Itch	Does a short vowel come just before the **ch** sound? Yes.
Listen: Inch	Does a short vowel come just before the **ch** sound? No.
Listen: Pinch	Does a short vowel come just before the **ch** sound? No.
Listen: Pitch	Does a short vowel come just before the **ch** sound? Yes.

The sequence is a positive-first communication that presents a range of variation for the three positives at the beginning of the sequence, followed by two pairs of minimum-difference examples.

Note that the sequence above would not provide the entire teaching for the rule that the ending is spelled **tch** only if the ending is immediately preceded by a short **a, e, i** or **o** vowel. After the discrimination is taught, it would become a component in a cognitive routine that makes the entire operation of figuring out the appropriate spelling overt. Here is a possible routine:

1. Listen: Hatch. Say it. "Hatch."
2. Does a short vowel come just before the **ch** sound? "Yes."
3. So how is the **ch** ending spelled? "t-c-h."
4. Spell the word **hatch**. "H-a-t-c-h."

Note that step 2 in the routine is the same task that would have been pretaught through the non-comparative sequence above. The point is that non-comparatives are not merely simple discriminations; they may be quite complex and may require a long verbal explanation.

Before we leave the short-vowel illustration, we should note that instruction would not *begin* with the non-comparative sequence presented above. This sequence assumes that the learner is able to discriminate short-vowels from other vowels. Short vowels are interesting because they are not a single discrimination, but a group of different sounds that are arbitrarily called "short." They do not share a compelling set of sameness that would permit any sort of generalization from some of the short vowel sounds to others. (If we brought the learner to criterion on short **a**, short **o**, short **i**, there is no logical way for the learner to generalize to short **u** or short **e**. Therefore, we must teach each short sound as a separate discrimination and then combine them under the family name, "Short ____.")

Figure 5.11		
Example	Example Type	Wording
par	N	Is the a short? No.
pay	N	Is the a short? No.
pan	P	Is the a short? Yes.
pass	P	Is the a short? Yes.
patter	P	Is the a short? Yes.
pater	N	Is the a short?
pap	P	Is the a short?
pall	N	Is the a short?
pail	N	Is the a short?
pass	P	Is the a short?
pain	N	Is the a short?
pant	P	Is the a short?

To teach each of the short sounds, we could use a non-comparative sequence (or sequences). The biggest problem in designing these is to follow the setup principle. Although there are different solutions to the problem, perhaps the easiest is to keep the first part of each word constant. Figure 5.11 shows a negative-first sequence for teaching the short-**a** discrimination.

The decision about the range of positive variation is arbitrary. Perhaps the sequence should deal with only one-syllable words. Clearly, the sequence is not capable of teaching short **a** in all its contexts. It must be followed by parallel sequences. In the end, however, the sequence is a single dimension non-comparative.

In our second example, we wish to teach the learner to discriminate between story problems that involve multiplication and those that involve addition. The rule: *If a problem deals with the same number again and again, it is a multiplication problem; if it does not deal with the same number again and again, it is not a multiplication problem.* We could convey this idea to the learner through rules or through elaborate teacher-directed routines. The underpinnings of the rules or the routines, however, would be the non-comparative discrimination. In its simplest communication form, the concept of dealing with the same number again and again is presented through a series of stories that are similar in as many details as possible. Some problems make reference to using the same number again and again. Others do not.

Here are the first four examples from a possible negative-first sequence:

"I'm going to say parts of the problems. Some parts are from multiplication problems. Other parts are not from multiplication problems."

1. Listen: The man went to the store and bought five apples and two oranges. Is that a multiplication problem? No.
2. Listen: The man went to the store and bought five apples. Is that a multiplication problem? No.
3. Listen: Every time the man went to the store, he bought five apples. Is that a multiplication problem? Yes.
4. Listen: The man went to the store seven times. Is that a multiplication problem? Yes. Etc.

This sequence, like the one that taught the discrimination of the short-vowel sound immediately before **ch** involves a complex verbal example; however, it is clearly a non-comparative. The non-comparative sequence may not always be the best choice for processing these examples; however, if the decision is made to treat the discrimination or concept as a "yes-no" concept, and if the concept is absolute (rather than relative), the same form used for simple non-comparatives can be used to communicate the concept to the learner. The rules that apply to communicating the simpler non-comparatives apply to the more complex communications. Three juxtaposed examples show sameness; two pairs of minimum-difference examples show difference between positives and negatives; and a series of test examples follow the demonstrations of sameness and difference.

Summary

To construct non-comparative sequences, follow one of the basic forms shown in this section. After constructing it, modify it if a problem of communication exists. First decide whether the concept is a non-comparative single-dimension concept. The easiest way is to begin with a concrete example of the concept. If the example you select would always be a positive example of the concept, the concept is absolute, and you may be dealing with a non-comparative concept. Now change the positive example into a negative. If you can achieve this change only by manipulating a single dimension of the positive example, you are dealing with a non-comparative single-dimension concept.

To get more information about how to construct a sequence for teaching the concept, refer again to the concrete example. Figure out how to convert that example into other positive examples that are different from it. This exercise will reveal the sameness the examples share.

Now figure out the minimum-difference negatives. To do that, take a positive example and change it the very least possible amount to create a negative. Make sure that the conversion involves a perceptible manipulation. Our goal is not to obscure, but to amplify. The change may be small, but it must be quite perceptible.

Now follow the form, perhaps the negative-first form. Begin with two negatives, follow with a minimum difference and three positives, follow with a minimum difference, and end with a series of test examples.

Add a variation of the same wording for all examples. Model the first three to five examples and test on the others.

Test the sequence to make sure that it is consistent with only one interpretation. If it is not, change it. Perhaps more examples are needed (for concepts with a wide range of variation). Perhaps you can show the range better if you use a positive-first sequence rather than a negative-first.

Make sure that the single interpretation emerges as early as possible. It must occur by example 7; however, it should be strongly implied by example 5.

Check the minimum-difference negatives to make sure that they are different from each other.

Check the positives to make sure that they follow the juxtaposition principle for showing sameness.

Check the test examples to make sure that there are enough to provide a reasonable test, and that they are presented in an unpredictable order.

Make sure that the sequence is not needlessly laborious. If there is a very narrow range of positives or negatives, you can probably shorten it without jeopardizing the communication.

Use two-choice tasks as an economy measure if the learner is facile or already has some understanding of the concept. Try to avoid two-choice tasks that involve pairs of responses that have common words or part.

Chapter 6
Nouns

Nouns are labels for object classes: **bottles, things, solid objects, clouds, eyes, shoes, dogs, animals**. Also, symbols such as the letter **R** are nouns. The braille symbol **.:** is a noun, and so is the numeral **142**.

Some nouns have subtypes with names (**dogs** include **terriers, spaniels**, and other named subtypes; **vehicles** include **boats, cars**, and other named subtypes). These nouns are called higher-order nouns and will be covered later in this chapter.

Procedures for communicating the others—nouns such as **bottle, car, shoe**—are considered first.

Higher-order and "regular" nouns share a set of features. They are multiple-dimension concepts; differences between positives and negatives are not precise, but are absolute.

Concepts processed through a non-comparative sequence are *single dimension* concepts. We can make objects hot only by manipulating a single variable—the temperature of the object. In contrast, *nouns are multiple-dimension concepts*. In traditional terms, the noun is a "conjunctive" concept requiring the presence of more than one feature or attribute. When something is labeled **car** or **tree** or **bush**, the label stands for a number of features, each of which is necessary in some form. We could change a shoe into a non-shoe by adding parts (such as an upward extension, which would change a shoe to a boot); by subtracting parts (such as the entire upper, which would make the shoe a sandal); changing the material (such as the material of the sole, which would make the shoe a slipper); or by amplifying some of the features (filling the entire inside of the shoe with a solid-leather core, so that the shoe cannot function as a shoe). Some of these negatives are nameless, such as a shoe that is sewn to a pair of dress slacks.

Because non-comparatives are single-dimension concepts, it is usually practical to show relatively small difference between positives and negatives. Because nouns are multiple-dimension concepts, however, it is not only impractical to show minimum differences; it is virtually impossible, because even knowledgeable adults do not agree on the boundary line between positives and negatives of common nouns. To demonstrate this fact, present a group of adults with 20 examples of footwear and ask them to identify whether each object is **shoe** or **not-shoe**. Include tennis shoes, moccasins, flats, sandals, "ankle-high" shoes, and other "marginal" shoes. Although there will be perfect agreement on some items, there will be disagreement on tennis shoes, flats, and all other "marginal" shoes. In contrast, if we presented examples of **getting wider** to the same group, we would find virtually no disagreement.

The point of this demonstration is that with multiple-feature concepts *there is no precise minimum difference between positives and negatives*. Even if we tried to specify a definition or classification criterion for **shoe** that seemed totally precise, we would discover that we could create examples that are ambiguous because there are examples at the boundary line that cannot be classified. The interplay of the various features involved in the positive examples of nouns suggests that a precise formula for the positive examples is all but impossible. So it is with *all* nouns. The implication for instruction is that we should not try to create a precise boundary line (minimum differences) when very knowledgeable adults do not agree on one. Fortunately, teaching minimum-differences is not necessary.

Continuous conversions are not necessary and not practical for the initial teaching of most nouns. The purpose of continuous conversion of examples is to call the learner's attention to the precise details or differences between one example and the next. When we deal with nouns, there are not precise boundary lines between positives and negatives; therefore, the basic rationale for using continuous conversion is not present.

Since there are many differences between positives and negatives of most nouns, the probability is increased that the learner will attend to *some* feature that permits reliable discrimination of positives and negatives.

When dealing with the small difference between something that is on a surface and something that is not, the learner must attend to a specific difference. The situation with nouns is quite different. There may be 20 observable differences between a positive and the most highly similar negative of a noun. Because any one of these differences will serve the learner to discriminate between positives and negatives, we should not have to call attention to any particular difference, because any one of the differences will serve the learner in discriminating between positives and negatives.

Finally, there are *serious mechanical problems in trying to use continuous conversions with nouns.* Converting examples of **car** into some existing negative—**truck, bus, train**, etc.—could be achieved through animated motion pictures; however, for the resources that are generally available, continuous conversion sequences for nouns are impractical.

Constructing Initial-Teaching Sequences for Nouns

The structure of nouns suggests differences between the sequences for teaching non-comparatives and sequences for teaching nouns. The major features of the noun sequences are these:

1. Since it is impossible to determine precise boundaries between positives and negatives, the sequence does not show the smallest minimum differences that are possible. *Instead, the sequence limits the negatives to nouns already known by the learner.* They are the *least-different examples in the learner's repertoire from the noun being taught.* In other words, the learner should be able to already identify all negatives used in a noun sequence. When we refer to *minimum negatives* in a noun sequence, we do *not* mean the smallest differences that are possible, merely the smallest differences that are included in the sequence.

The noun sequence changes as the knowledge of the learner changes; therefore, the minimum differences are relative to what the learner knows. For one learner, the negatives in a sequence that teaches **train** may be trucks. For another learner, the negatives may be handcars and streetcars.

2. Since the names of negatives have already been taught, *the learner labels both negatives and positives in the noun sequence.* Instead of saying, "Not-pen" to indicate a negative of **pen**, the learner names the negative: "Crayon."

3. Because the learner names both positives and negatives, a new type of minimum difference may be present in the noun sequences—the similarity of **names**.

The symbols **b** and **v** are not similar in shape; however, *their names are minimally different.* If the learner already knows **b** when **v** is being taught, **b** would be a minimum difference negative based on similarity of name. Note, therefore, that the learner might confuse positives and negatives of nouns either because of similarity in name or because of similarity in features of the examples.

4. Because very small differences in examples are usually not shown in a noun sequence, the sequence is usually fairly short, consisting of enough positive examples to show the range of variation and those negatives that might be confused with the positives. The number of negatives and positives depends on the range of positive variation and on the negatives known to the learner.

Table 6.1 summarizes the major differences between non-comparative sequences and noun sequences.

Table 6.1	
Non-Comparatives	**Nouns**
Present minimum-difference negatives.	Do not present minimum-difference negatives, but the most highly similar negatives already known to the learner.
Usually require the learner to respond to negatives with "No" or "Not ___."	Require the learner to label or name the negatives.
Present examples through continuous conversion.	Present static examples (not created through continuous conversion).
Call for responses that do not involve minimum-differences in names.	Call for responses that may involve minimum-differences in names between positive and negative examples.
Call for the same response for all negatives.	Call for different responses for different negatives (because each negative is labeled).

The Sequence

Figure 6.1 shows a sequence designed to teach **truck** to a four-year old. The learner is able to identify **train, bus,** and **car**, which are the negatives in the sequence.

Chapter 6 | Nouns

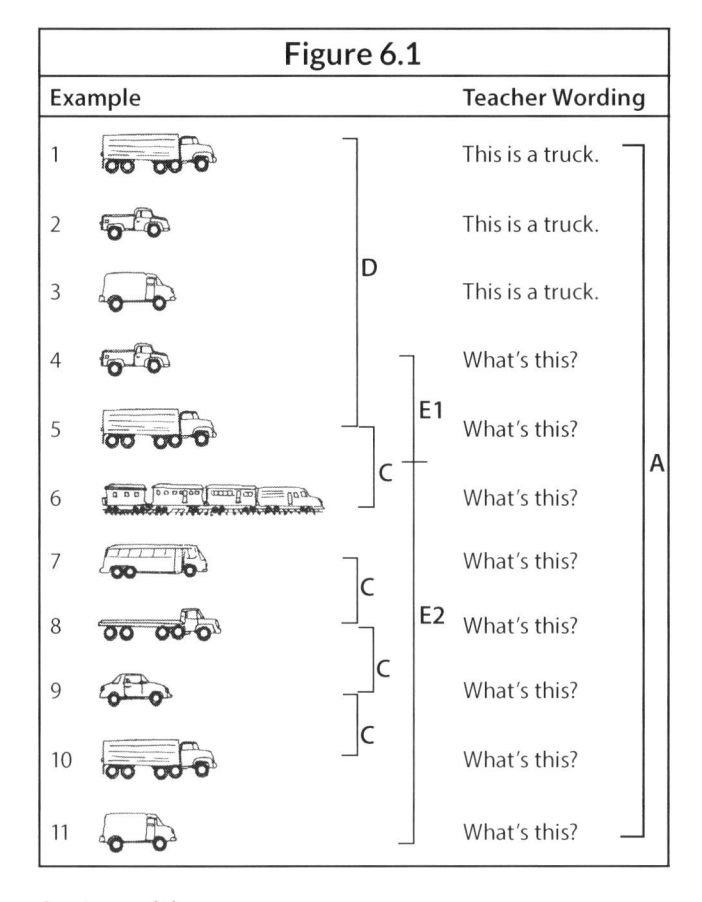

Figure 6.1

Example		Teacher Wording
1	[truck]	This is a truck.
2	[truck]	This is a truck.
3	[truck]	This is a truck.
4	[truck]	What's this?
5	[truck]	What's this?
6	[train]	What's this?
7	[bus]	What's this?
8	[truck]	What's this?
9	[car]	What's this?
10	[truck]	What's this?
11	[truck]	What's this?

Brackets: D covers 1–3; E1 covers 4–5; E2 covers 6–11; C brackets appear between 5–6, 7–8, 8–9, 9–10, 10–11; A covers all.

Juxtapositions

The **A** bracket shows that the wording principle is followed. Variation of the same wording is used for all examples.

The **B** bracket is missing, because the setup principle is not followed. All objects are presented at the same time and in the same place; however, there is no further attempt to increase the sameness shared by positives and negatives.

The **D** bracket shows that the sequence begins by showing sameness shared by positives. A noun sequence *always begins with positives*. The reason is that information about negatives does not *imply* anything about the positives. Many features change when we go from negatives to positives; therefore, the sequence does not begin by showing what the noun is not. It begins with positives. Greatly different examples are juxtaposed and labeled in the same way. This juxtaposition provides an idea about how examples are the same by showing some of the features they share.

The **C** brackets (showing difference) occur only in the test segment, after positives have been demonstrated. *All negatives are minimum-difference negatives* (with respect to the learner's knowledge). Therefore, each time a negative is juxtaposed with a positive, a minimum-difference juxtaposition occurs.

The **E** bracket is divided into **E1** and **E2**. The **E1** bracket is a test of *wording*. It is a test of two of the examples that had just been modeled in segment **D**. It assures that the learner can produce the labeling response for the positive examples. Following **E1** is the **E2** test, which requires the learner to discriminate between objects labeled **truck** and similar objects with other labels (**bus, car**).

Minimum-Difference Examples

The reason for including *only* minimally different *familiar* examples in the sequence is this: If the learner can discriminate between examples that differ in the smallest practical way, the learner should automatically discriminate between examples that differ in larger ways. If we make sure that the learner can discriminate between **truck** and those things or names known to the learner that are most highly similar to **truck**, we assure that the learner will not confuse **truck** with any other familiar discrimination or label. Knowledge of the difference between a truck and a train guarantees that the learner will never confuse a truck with a butterfly. Similarly, if the learner can discriminate between a chair and a couch, the learner will never confuse a chair with a dog.

Test Examples

No new examples of **truck** are included in the test segment. The sequence would not suffer from a greater variety of test examples; however, no generalization items are necessary in the test segment (if the range is adequately shown in the **D** segment). If you are in doubt, add items to the sequence. The test sequence should be long enough to assure that the learner can respond to the examples of the new noun when they occur within the context of familiar nouns.

Within the test segment, there should be more positive examples than negatives.

The Naive Learner

If the learner who is to be taught the noun **truck** is quite naive, we would use a different sequence from the one above. If the learner did not know **train, bus**, and **car**, these would not appear as negatives. If the learner could identify no objects that have reasonable similarity to **truck** (in name or in features of the example), we would simply select some objects that are familiar to the learner and include them in the **E2** segment of the series. These objects serve two functions. They provide a more difficult juxtaposition for responding to **truck** in the test sequence. They also assure that the learner is attending to details that discriminate **truck** from the other objects. Figure 6.2 shows a possible sequence.

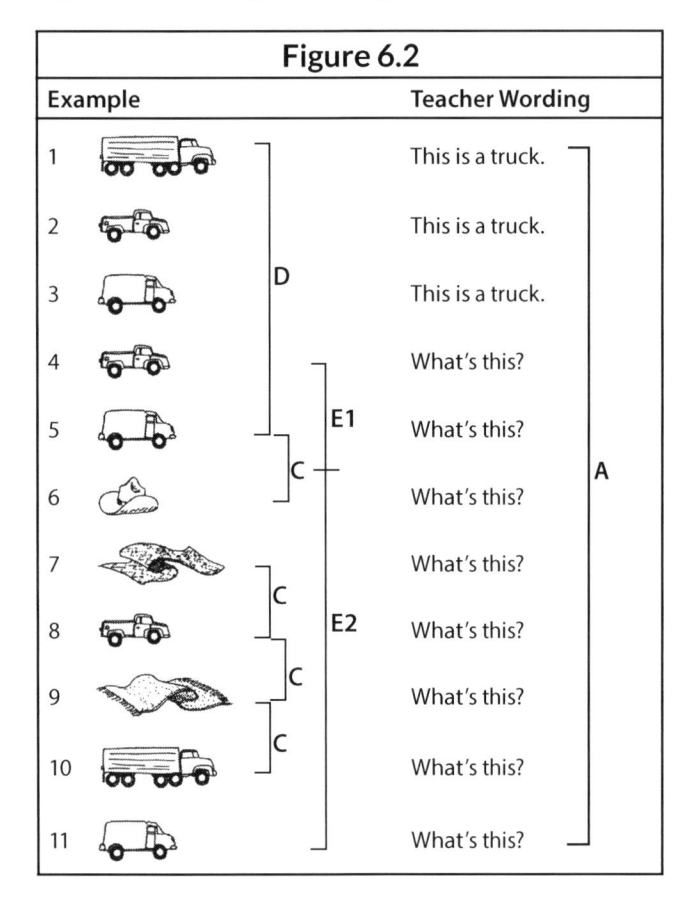

Figure 6.2

Example		Teacher Wording
1	[truck]	This is a truck.
2	[truck]	This is a truck.
3	[truck]	This is a truck.
4	[truck]	What's this?
5	[truck]	What's this?
6	[hat]	What's this?
7	[hat]	What's this?
8	[truck]	What's this?
9	[blanket]	What's this?
10	[truck]	What's this?
11	[truck]	What's this?

Remember, minimum differences are relative to the learner's knowledge. Do not create them where none exist for the learner. Although many objects are more highly similar to **truck** than **hats** and **blankets**, for this learner, **hats** and **blankets** are highly similar for the learner being taught the discrimination.

If no close minimum-difference negatives are apparent, or if you are in doubt about the learner's knowledge:

1. Present positives.
2. Follow with response test (**E1**).
3. Follow with a test segment that contains possibly two objects that are familiar to the learner. Create a pattern of juxtaposition appropriate for a test segment (**E2**).
4. Keep the sequence as brief as you practically can.

Narrow Range Sequence

The number of examples in a noun sequence depends on the range of positive variation and the differences between positives and negatives.

1. *The range of positive variation the learner is expected to deal with.* The range of positive variation for the letter **b** is very narrow. We can write the symbol **b** larger or smaller, in bolder print, and with other minor variations; however, the range of **b** is far less than the range of **truck**, **cup**, or **shoe**.

2. *The degree of difference between examples of familiar concepts and the new concept.* As a rule, add one or two examples of familiar concepts to the **E2** segment for every highly similar discrimination presented in the sequence.

Figure 6.3 illustrates the procedure with the teaching of **b**. If the learner has been taught no letters that are highly similar in name or in shape to **b**, but has been taught the letters **r** and **s**, we could use this sequence to teach the symbol **b**:

Figure 6.3

Example		Teacher Wording
1. b		This is b.
2. b		This is b.
3. b		What's this?
4. b		What's this?
5. s		What's this?
6. r		What's this?
7. b		What's this?
8. b		What's this?

Two examples of **b** appear in **E1** and two appear in **E2**. The sequence is short because the concept has a very narrow range and the learner had not been taught any names or shapes that are minimally different from **b**. (The sequence is a slightly shortened version of the noun sequence specified for **truck**).

If a learner had been taught the letters **h** and **q**, the sequence would be longer because symbols for **h** and **q** would appear in the minimum difference test segment (**E2**). See Figure 6.4.

Figure 6.4	
Example	Teacher Wording
1. b ⎤	This is b.
2. **b** ⎦ D	This is b.
3. b ⎤ E1	What's this?
4. b ⎦	What's this?
5. h ⎦ C	What's this?
6. q ⎦ C E2	What's this?
7. b ⎦	What's this?
8. q ⎦ C	What's this?
9. h ⎦ C	What's this?
10. b ⎦	What's this?
11. **b** ⎦	What's this?

The **D** segment remains unchanged because the range of positives has not changed. The **E2** segment of the sequence is longer, however, because highly similar negatives were included. Note that **h** and **q** replaced **r** and **s** because, for the learner being taught, **h** and **q** are the known symbols most highly similar in shape to **b**. The test of **h** and **q** is more elaborate than that of **r** and **s** because there is more reason to believe that the learner might reasonably confuse **h** or **q** with **b**.

Differences in Features and Responses

The rules for sequencing different types of negatives in the **E2** segment are:

1. Juxtapose minimum differences in *features* first.

2. Juxtapose minimum differences in *name* next.

3. Juxtapose minimum differences in *name and features* last.

The sequence involving **b**, **h** and **q** contains negatives that are different from **b** in shape only. If minimum differences in *name* were included, they would be tested after the shape differences in the **E2** segment.

By first dealing with shape difference in **E2**, we assure that the learner is attending to the *features* of the new concept. Next, we introduce examples that may create name confusion. At this point, *we know that any mistake the learner makes is a name mistake, not a mistake of understanding the features.*

Illustration. If the concept being taught is **f** and the negatives include **j**, **t**, and **s**, we would first present minimum difference juxtaposition of **f-j-t**. These examples are minimally different in shape, but their names are not similar. Next, we would present juxtapositions of **f** and **s**. These examples are not similar in shape, but in name. Since the set of **t-j-s** does not include a member that is highly similar to **f** in both name and shape, rule 3 does not apply to the sequence.

Illustration. The concept being taught is **d**.

The learner has been taught:

a (Minimally different in shape only.)

t (Minimally different in name only.)

p (Minimally different in shape and name.)

Figure 6.5 shows the sequence. Note the juxtaposition of **E2**.

Figure 6.5	
Example	Teacher Wording
1. d ⎤	This is d.
2. **d** ⎦ D	This is d.
3. d ⎤	What's this?
4. a ⎦ E1	What's this?
5. d ⎦ C	What's this?
6. d ⎦	What's this?
7. a ⎦ C E2	What's this?
8. t ⎦	What's this?
9. d ⎦ C	What's this?
10. p ⎦ C	What's this?
11. d ⎦	What's this?
12. p ⎦ C	What's this?

The **E2** segment first juxtaposes **d** and **a**, then **d** and **t**, and near the end of the sequence, the sequence begins to alternate between examples of the new concept and negatives. Although this alternation is not desirable, it is far less dangerous in a noun sequence than it is in the non-comparative. The reason is that the learner must produce a different response for each example. Instead of saying "Yes" and "No" or saying "Slanted" and "Not-slanted," the learner must identify everything that is shown. Because the response requirement is stronger for the noun sequence (less probably a function

Section II | Basic Forms

of guessing), the presence of the pattern is not a serious problem.

Dealing With Discriminations That Involve Small Minimum Differences

Because of the multiple-feature structure of nouns, they are usually easy to teach. The reason is that examples of the concept possess many features that are not shared by any discriminations in the learner's repertoire. If the learner does not attend to a particular difference between the new discrimination and a familiar one, no problem is created because there are usually many other differences available. All will serve to discriminate the positive (the new noun) from the negatives (familiar nouns).

If differences between concepts familiar to the learner and the new concept are very small, the learner may have serious problems learning the discrimination. As a rule of thumb, serious problems occur when highly similar names are involved. Problems are also possible, however, when sets of examples highly similar in features are presented. However, the most serious problems are those that involve examples similar in both name and features.

There are two ways to adjust the noun sequence for the learner who will probably have problems. The first involves presenting the noun sequence *a part at a time* rather than all at once. The second involves adding some "easy" items to the sequence, as well as presenting the sequence a part at a time.

Presenting the sequence a part at a time. Response problems are often predictable if the new discrimination calls for a response highly similar to that for a familiar discrimination. If response problems seem probable, present the part of the sequence that precedes the similar-name juxtapositions in **E2**. At a later time, when the learner is firm on the first part of the sequence, present the entire sequence. For instance, instead of presenting the entire sequence that involves the negatives **d**, **a**, and **t**, present examples 1 through 7 first. The learner is presented with **d**, tested on producing the response for **d**, and tested on discriminating between **d** and **a**. The learner is not yet required to deal with **t** (which is highly similar to **d** in name) or **p** (which is highly similar in shape and name).

During the next session with the learner, repeat the first part of the sequence. If the learner performs reasonably well on it, continue with examples 8 through 12 of the sequence. The point to remember is that the entire sequence does not have to be presented during the first session that introduces the new discrimination.

Adding easy examples to the sequence. If the type of learning required by the material is dissimilar from any kind the learner has achieved, anticipate more severe problems. If the learner has never learned from an adult in a teacher-learner situation, has never learned to discriminate between highly similar objects (such as letters), and has never been required to remember the various names for the objects, anticipate severe problems. The learner will probably exhibit *discrimination* problems as well as *response* problems. The learner may make mistakes on examples that require discrimination of **a** and **d**, which are similar in features, but not in label.

1. Include only those discriminations that are not similar to the new discrimination (**d**) in either shape or label.

2. Insert these easy discriminations immediately after the **E1** test.

3. End the sequence with the test of the new member (**d**) and the non-similar members.

Figure 6.6 illustrates these adjustments.

Figure 6.6		
Example		Teacher Wording
1	d	This is d.
2	d	This is d.
3	d	What's this?
4	d	What's this?
5	🚢	What's this?
6	d	What's this?
7	✂	What's this?
8	🚢	What's this?
9	d	What's this?
10	✂	What's this?
11	d	What's this?

Ultimately, we want the learner to respond to **d** in the context of **t** and **p**. The sequence in Figure 6.6 presents **d** in the context of highly discriminable negatives–**boat** and **scissors**. Confusion is minimized by this context. Although the context does not do much to facilitate the discrimination of **d** and **p**, it provides practice in producing the response for **d**.

This easy discrimination would be repeated until the learner performs well on the letter **d**. At other times during the day (or the lesson), the teacher continues to review **p** and **t**, but **p** and **t** do not occur in the same sequences as **d**. (More information about the nature of these reviews is provided in later chapters. The point here is that the familiar discriminations are kept firm while the new one is introduced within an easy context.)

The context in which **d** occurs becomes increasingly more difficult following success with the easiest context. The learner is introduced to the shape differences (**d** and **a**). Next, the name differences are added (**d**, **a** and **t**). Finally, the most difficult context is introduced: **d**, **a**, **t** and **p**.

We do not know the extent to which such a carefully staged introduction and modification of the context is needed: that remains an empirical question. However, it is possible to adjust the context level of difficulty from a very easy context to the terminal context. The context changes in the following ways:

- First, the new discrimination and non-similar negatives.
- Next, the new discrimination and negatives similar in shape only.
- Next, the new discriminations and negatives similar in shape, followed by negatives similar in name.
- Finally, the new discrimination, followed by negatives similar in shape, negatives similar in name, and negatives similar in shape and name.

Throughout the introduction all negatives should be reviewed in a context that does not involve the new discrimination.

Wide Range Nouns

The range of examples that we must show for a noun depends on what the learner knows and on the range of variation for the noun. The concept **dog** involves examples that vary far more than examples of **b**. The easiest way to show this wide range of variation is to include more positive examples in the sequence. The sequence illustrated in Figure 6.7 begins with 3 positives, followed by a response-production test (**E1**) on 2 of them. *New positives are introduced later in the sequence as test examples.*

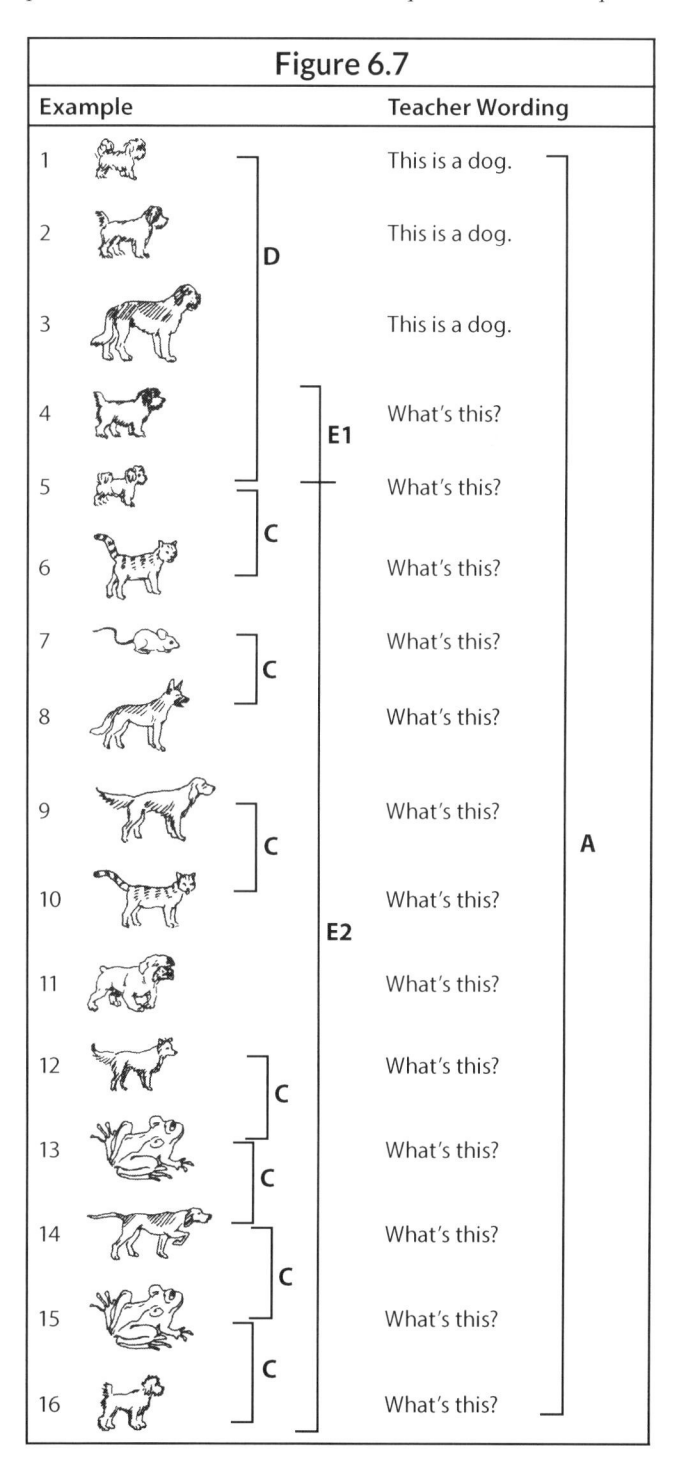

Figure 6.7

Example	Teacher Wording
1	This is a dog.
2	This is a dog.
3	This is a dog.
4	What's this?
5	What's this?
6	What's this?
7	What's this?
8	What's this?
9	What's this?
10	What's this?
11	What's this?
12	What's this?
13	What's this?
14	What's this?
15	What's this?
16	What's this?

The sequence in Figure 6.7 assumes that the learner has been taught **cat, dog,** and **mouse**.

The particular negatives in the **C** segments should not be inordinately similar to dogs. The learner should be expected to discriminate between most small dogs and cats that are roughly the same size; however, we should not search for cats that look unusually doglike.

The **E** juxtapositions first test examples that are minimally different in shape (**cat** and **mouse** versus **dog**) and later in the sequence, examples that are minimally different in name: **dog** and **frog**. Note that the **E** segment is quite long (13 examples) because the range of variation of **dog** is large. Note also that there are more examples of **dog** than of **not-dog** in the test summary.

The addition of new dogs to the **E2** segment is somewhat arbitrary. The sequence would not be a communication failure if none were added. Possibly the sequence could be modified so that it began with four models, instead of three, and no additional new examples were added in **E2**. However, as a general guide, when a noun has a large range of positive variation, add examples later in the sequence, if possible or practical.

Advanced Applications

The more the learner knows, the greater the amount of teacher wording that can be added to the sequence and the fewer the examples needed to assure learning.

Figure 6.8	
Example	Teacher Wording
	The mattock has a blade like a hoedad on one side and like a pick on the other.
1 (mattock)	This is a mattock. What is it?
2 (pick)	What's this?
3 (mattock)	What's this?
4 (hoedad)	What's this?

Suppose we wish to teach the discrimination between a mattock and other tools familiar to the learner, such as a hoedad and a pick. Figure 6.8 shows a possible presentation.

Suppose we wanted to teach the learner the difference between black oak leaves and white oak leaves. We could begin with a rule that expresses the difference and follow with a series of examples that shows the difference.

"If the lobes have points, it's a black oak leaf. If the lobes are rounded, it's a white oak leaf." (See Figure 6.9.)

Figure 6.9		
Example	Teacher Wording	Student Response
1	This is a black oak.	
2	This is a white oak.	
3	What's this?	White oak.
4	What's this?	Black oak.
5	What's this?	Black oak.
6	What's this?	White oak.

Suppose the learner is required to discriminate between black oaks (the new discrimination) and sycamores, maples, and white oaks (the familiar discriminations). The rule for identifying black oaks in this context is: *"Black oak leaves have the same vein pattern as the white oaks, but not the same lobe features. Black oaks have the same pointed lobe features as the sycamores and maples, but not the same vein pattern."* The rule points out the discrimination problems confronting the learner. The learner must discriminate between some examples on the basis of lobes (white versus black oaks) and discriminate between other examples on the basis of configuration or vein pattern (sycamores and maples, versus black oaks). The sequence must provide a sufficient number of examples to show these differences and to show the range of variation of black oaks. The sequence, therefore, must contain more examples than the sequence for showing black oaks and white oaks.

As shown in Figure 6.10, for each minimum difference negative, at least one example is added to **E2**.

This sequence adequately shows the difference between black oak leaves and the others. Possibly, we could reduce the number of examples if we preceded the sequences with a verbal rule, such as: "It is a black oak leaf if the *veins do not meet in one place and the lobes are pointed.*" (We will discuss verbal rules later.) Note that the example with minimum difference *name* (white oak) is presented near the end of the sequence.

The black oak sequence illustrates a critical design problem that comes about when several similar members are taught. Nouns are multiple-dimension concepts. Each dimension of the new member is a possible basis for similarity. The new member may be the same as familiar member **A** with respect to one dimension. It may be the same as familiar member **B** with respect to another dimension and the same as familiar member **C** with respect to another dimension.

For each minimum difference, add one or more test examples. If the sequence becomes too laborious, divide it into parts. Possibly, use verbal rules to call attention to the relevant details of the examples; however, do not use the verbal rule as a substitute for the examples. The sequence must provide a sufficient number of examples in **E2** to test the learner's application of the rule.

Higher-Order Nouns

A higher-order noun is one that has various subtypes, all of which have names. **Vehicles** is a higher-order noun that includes various named subtypes—cars, trucks, etc. **Games** is a higher-order type that includes a diverse group of named activities (from solitaire and chess to handball and baseball).

To teach a higher-order noun, use wording that preserves the critical nature of the concept. For the nouns that we have dealt with, *the negatives are coordinate with the positives.* The situation is different with higher-order nouns. If we present positive examples of **vehicle** and negatives that are labeled **chair, swing** and **motor**, we tend to imply that these negatives are coordinate with **vehicle**. To make them truly coordinate, however, we must classify them according to their "vehicleness." To achieve this goal, we refer to positive examples of higher-order nouns as "vehicles" and the negatives as "not vehicles." The higher-order noun sequence, therefore, becomes a

Figure 6.10			
Example		Teacher Wording	Student Response
1		This is a black oak.	
2		This is a black oak.	
3		This is a black oak.	
4		What's this?	Black oak.
5		What's this?	Black oak.
6		What's this?	Sycamore.
7		What's this?	Maple.
8		What's this?	Black oak.
9		What's this?	Black oak.
10		What's this?	Sycamore.
11		What's this?	Black oak.
12		What's this?	Maple.
13		What's this?	Black oak.
14		What's this?	Black oak.
15		What's this?	White oak.
16		What's this?	Black oak.
17		What's this?	White oak.
18		What's this?	Black oak.

Section II | Basic Forms

variation of the non-comparative sequence. All positives are responded to in the same way. A different response ("No," or "Not vehicle") is used for all negatives.

The learner may be familiar with lower-order class names for the positives that we present (**boats, trucks, cars**) and for the negative examples (**chair, swing, motor**). The practice that the learner has received with these names may have induced stipulation. The learner has learned one name, and the learner may resist calling the examples by another name. The sequence for higher-order noun concept counteracts this problem by requiring the learner to classify a series of juxtaposed examples as "vehicles" or "not vehicles." If the learner responds that a positive example is "a car," the teacher simply repeats the question, "But is it a vehicle?"

Figure 6.11 presents a sequence that teaches the higher-order concept **vehicle** to a learner who may be familiar with lower-order names for all the positives and negatives presented in the sequence.

Figure 6.11

Example		Teacher Wording
1	*boat*	This is a vehicle.
2	*train*	This is a vehicle.
3	*car*	This is a vehicle.
4	*truck*	This is a vehicle.
5	*swing*	This is not a vehicle.
6	*lawn mower*	This is not a vehicle.
7	*tractor*	Is this a vehicle?
8	*boat*	Is this a vehicle?
9	*drill*	Is this a vehicle?
10	*basket*	Is this a vehicle?
11	*car*	Is this a vehicle?

The sequence is a positive-first variation with six examples modeled. Negatives are selected to rule out possible misinterpretations. The swing rules out the notion that sitting and moving is sufficient for something to be a **vehicle**. The lawn mower rules out the possibility that moving and being motor-powered is adequate.

The same wording that is used for non-comparatives is used in the sequence. The teacher asks, "Is this a vehicle?" for each test example. Also, the same juxtaposition pattern used for non-comparatives is followed. Following four positive examples are the minimum-difference negatives, swing and lawn mower. Note that some new positives are introduced in the test segment. The examples in the sequence are created non-continuously (through illustration).

Selecting Negatives for Higher-Order Noun Sequences

The higher-order noun sequence has the same basic form as a non-comparative sequence. Although the sequence is the same for these two types of concepts, the concepts are different. Non-comparatives are usually single-dimension concepts. Higher-order noun sequences process *nouns*, and nouns are multiple-dimension concepts. Because they are multiple-dimension concepts, a positive example may be changed into a negative by manipulating various dimensions of the example. This fact carries implications for the negatives that we select for the higher-order sequence. We must select negatives that show the multiple-dimension nature of the concept. To achieve this goal, we use different negatives to rule out the possibility that a single feature is sufficient for the object to be a positive example. The last **black oak** sequence presented some negative examples to rule out the possibility that pointed lobes was sufficient for an example to be positive. Other negatives ruled out the possibility that a particular vein pattern was sufficient to make an example a positive. The **vehicle** sequence followed the same formula for using negatives. Some examples ruled out the possibility that movement is sufficient for an example to be a vehicle. Other negatives rules out the possibility that having a motor is sufficient, or that accommodating one in a sitting position is sufficient.

As a group, the negatives must show that *a set of features must be present before an example is a positive.* The strategy for showing the role of the various features derives from the difference principle: To show differences, juxtapose

Chapter 6 | Nouns

examples that are minimally different and treat them differently.

Suppose the *essential* features of a noun are **A, B** and **C**. If we juxtapose an example of the noun with a negative example having these features: **A, B, S**, *we show that* **C** *is an essential feature.* (The absence of **C** makes the example negative.) If we juxtapose **A, B,** and **C** with negative **B, C, S**, *we show that* **A** *is necessary also.* If we juxtapose a third positive with the negative (**A, C, S**), we show that **B** is necessary. Through this series of juxtapositions, we show that the positive condition is brought about only through the presence of **A** and **B** and **C**. The series of juxtapositions shows that all features are necessary.

The sequence for **vehicles** includes the examples boat, train, truck and car. If we present this set of positives to the naive learner with no negatives, misgeneralizations are implied. All the examples *move*, therefore a possible misrule is that anything that moves is a vehicle. All examples are associated with somebody sitting; therefore, another possible misgeneralization is implied.

The negatives must counteract these possible misinterpretations by showing the learner that: (1) the examples do move, but *moving is not a sufficient feature*; and (2) they may be associated with somebody sitting, *but somebody sitting is not a sufficient feature.*

If we present negatives of someone sitting in a seat swinging on a swing, *we rule out movement and sitting.* Note that the idea is not necessarily to find a single negative example that rules out all possible misrules. Identify different negatives, each designed to rule out a misgeneralization based on one of the features (or possibly two). Also make sure that your negatives are not questionable. For instance, are examples of someone on roller skates or someone on a pogo stick *negative* examples of vehicles?

The vehicles that we present as positives have a power unit. To rule out the possibility that anything with a power unit is a vehicle, we present a lawn mower (which also rules out movement).

Illustration. The concept **games** is difficult because games are diverse. All involve following a set of rules, a criterion for completion, and some sort of contingencies or unpredicted events that affect the completion. For some games, the contingency takes the form of chance, as in card games. For some, direct action of a competitor affects performance of the opponent (as in basketball, where shots can be blocked). For others, the contingency is independent performance of a competitor (as in bowling). In this case, you may lose even though you perform very well.

If we were to teach the higher-order noun **games** to a learner, we would create a group of positives and negatives. The positives would include a card game, a running game such as basketball, a game such as chess, and a contact game like football. The negatives must show that the presence of rules is not sufficient for something being labeled **game**, that a contingency or unpredicted outcome is not a game, or that the component motion (activity) is not sufficient for something to be a game.

The sequence in Figure 6.12 is of interest only as a model. We selected *games* for this example because it has been the subject of some philosophical discussions. In real life, any learner who knew a dozen games would probably already know how to classify any example as a game. The teaching of the discrimination **game** would therefore be completely unnecessary. The illustration below simply shows that very diverse subclasses of objects can be processed through a sequence that shows the common features of the positives.

Figure 6.12
Teacher Wording
1. Is **following traffic rules** a game? No.
2. Is **running** a game? No.
3. Is **running a relay race** a game? Yes.
4. Is **football** a game? Yes.
5. Is **playing cards** a game? Yes.
6. Is **shuffling** cards a game?
7. Is **following instructions** a game?
8. Is **basketball** a game?
9. Is **checkers** a game?
10. Is **counting stars** a game?
11. Is **fighting** a game?
12. Is **bowling** a game?
Etc.

The sequence begins with two negatives, followed by three positives. All these examples are modeled. Following is a series of seven test examples. The negatives rule out the notion that following rules is sufficient (examples 1 and 7), that component actions are sufficient (examples 2 and 6), and that score keeping or counting behaviors are sufficient (example 10).

Regular noun sequences always begin with *positives*. Higher-order sequences are modeled after non-comparatives and therefore may be either positive-first sequences or negative-first sequences.

Certainly examples could be added to the sequence and possibly better negatives could be created. However, the sequence above meets the objectives of communicating the higher-order concept. It implies what all games have in common, and it suggests that a set of common features is needed for an example to be a game.

Below is a summary of the steps to follow when designing a higher-order noun sequence.

1. First determine that it is a higher-order noun sequence. If it is, it is composed of subtypes that have names.

2. Select a set of positives that show the various subtypes. Juxtapose 3 to 6 examples to imply the sameness they share.

3. Determine the individual features that are shared by all the positives to be presented. Each feature suggests possible interpretation or generalization. (If all positives move, then movement is a possible basis for generalizing to new examples. If all positives involve action, the presence of action may become the basis for a generalization.)

4. Construct a negative that rules out each individual feature. *That negative will possess the feature to be ruled out, but will be a negative.* (An example that moves, but that is labeled as a negative, rules out a generalization based only on movement. An example that involves action, but that is negative, rules out a generalization based *only* on action.)

5. Design a sequence that begins with either positives or negatives. Juxtapose positives to show sameness. Juxtapose positives and negatives to show difference. (Minimum-difference juxtaposition consists of a positive and a negative that rules out a particular generalization.)

Model and test both positives and negatives.

Use non-comparative wording, requiring the learner to classify each example as a positive or negative example of the higher-order category (e.g., "Is this a vehicle?").

Noun labels for conglomerates. The higher-order sequence is based on the assumption that all members of the higher-order set possess the same quality or set of features. It is possible to design "nouns" that are simply conglomerates, nouns that cover a diverse group of entities that do not share a single quality or set of features. An example is **short vowels**. Another example is **sentence**. The type of utterances designated as sentences bears no compelling sameness. We could designate the letters **a**, **f**, **g**, **m**, **u**, and **w** as **frombers**. All other letters are **not-frombers**. The higher-order sequences would not be particularly appropriate for teaching **frombers** because no generalization is involved. A more appropriate procedure would be to present the group through a communication that treats each letter as an essential feature of a particular system. This communication would present a visual-spatial display. (See Chapter 14.)

Summary

The structure of nouns has intrigued philosophers, particularly the fact that diverse things can be classified according to the same noun label. Clearly, the learning of nouns cannot be the simple process of "associating" name with objects. Learning nouns involves learning the critical common features, with different features serving to distinguish the examples of a noun from various negatives.

From the standpoint of communicating nouns, the important facts are:

1. Nouns are multiple-feature concepts.

2. The boundary line between positive and negative examples of nouns is imprecise.

To teach nouns, first decide whether you are teaching it as a higher-order noun. If it is not higher-order, follow these steps:

- Present non-continuous examples.
- Use negatives that are known to the learner.
- Design the sequence with the test question, "What is this?"
- Always begin with positives.
- Juxtapose the positives to show sameness (great difference between juxtaposed examples). For wide-range nouns, show at least three examples. For narrow-range nouns, show one or two examples.

- Follow positives with two types of tests—response test followed by discrimination test. The response test (**E1**) presents examples that have been shown and requires the learner to label the examples in response to "What is this?" The discrimination test (**E2**) introduces negatives.
- Include only minimum-difference negatives for the sophisticated learner in **E2**.

  First test on negatives that are similar in shape.

  Then test on negatives that are similar in name.

  Then test on negatives that are similar in name and shape.
- For non-sophisticated learners, modify the sequence. Possibly divide it into parts and present the first part through the **E1** test, until the learner is facile; then add the remaining parts. Or, change the sequence by adding negatives that are not similar to the positive. When the learner is firm on this difference, add the minimum-difference negatives.
- Add new negatives to **E2** if the noun is a wide-range noun.
- Add one or two positives to **E2** for every minimum-difference negative.
- If you do not know whether the learner knows a particular negative, or if the sequence is to be presented to a group, either teach the negatives first or play it safe by eliminating all negatives that would be questionable. (The sequence will fail if the teacher must correct on negatives that are supposed to be known.)
- If the noun is higher-order, follow the same general procedures used for non-comparatives that are presented non-continuously. Use a question form that requires classification. ("Is this a ___?" or, "Tell me ___ or ___.")
- Begin the sequence with either positives or negatives.
- Design the negatives to rule out possible misrules.
- Select positives that sample from among the various subtypes that have names.
- Present an adequate number of test examples.

To show that a positive example must have multiple features, juxtapose negatives and positives that have a particular feature. This juxtaposition rules out the possibility that the single feature is adequate for an example to be positive.

Above all, remember that nouns have uncertain boundaries. Do not become embroiled over those examples that are questionable. If an example is not clearly negative or not clearly positive, do not use it. The communication with the learner is designed to convey what convention has already established, not to create classification conventions or precise boundaries where none exist.

Chapter 7
Comparative Single-Dimension Concepts

Comparatives include **getting wider, getting hotter, getting colder, getting heavier**, and similar concepts. The concept **full** is a non-comparative: **Getting fuller** is a comparative. **Green** becomes a comparative when we change the concept to **getting greener**. Similar conversions can be made for any non-comparative: **happy, worried, shiny, rough, troublesome, abrupt**, and **slanted**. In Chapter 5 the concept **abrupt** was presented as a non-comparative. By changing the concept to **more abrupt**, it becomes a comparative.

Comparatives are single-dimension concepts; therefore, they can frequently be processed through continuous conversion.

Comparatives have precise boundary lines between positives and negatives. Therefore, the communication should show minimum differences.

Comparatives are relative. The communication should demonstrate this relative nature.

The structure of comparatives indicates that they are quite similar to single-dimension non-comparatives. This similarity is deceptive. For non-comparatives, we label a particular event as the example in a continuous conversion sequence. For comparatives, *we label a change from one event to the next.* An event presented in a non-comparative sequence as a positive example is **always** a positive example. An event presented in a comparative sequence as a positive example, such as an object that is slanted 45°, is not always a positive example. Positive examples of a comparative always assume a reference point. A "small" star is not "large" or "larger" unless it is compared with other stars. An image that is "more brilliant" assumes some other images as the reference point.

The unique structure of comparatives suggests differences between the sequences designed to communicate comparatives and those for teaching non-comparatives and nouns. The following statements describe comparative sequences that use continuous conversions:

1. The comparative sequence always begins *with a starting point*—an example that is neither positive nor negative.

2. Every positive or negative example in the sequence is compared to the *preceding example* (with example 1 being compared to the starting point).

3. *The change* that occurs from example to example is the basis for determining whether the example is positive or negative.

4. When no change occurs, the example created is negative.

As point 4 above indicates, the *no-change negative* is unique to the comparative sequence. When comparatives are presented through a series of continuous-conversion examples, a change must occur to create a positive example. If we say, "It got wider," a change in width from the preceding example had to occur. If we say, "It got heavier," there was a change in weight from the preceding example. However, if we say, "It didn't get heavier," *it is possible that the weight did not change at all.* This possibility is the basis for the no-change negative. Two types of minimum-difference negatives are therefore used in the comparative sequence: *the minimum-difference negative change and the no-change negative.*

Negative-First Comparative Sequence

Figure 7.1 shows a model for the negative-first comparative sequence. The concept being taught is **getting heavier**. The learner's hand is placed, palm up, on a table surface. The teacher's finger presses downward against the learner's palm to create the sensation of the finger getting heavier and non-heavier. (The reason for placing the learner's hand on the table surface is to prevent it from moving down. We do not want the presentation to be consistent with the misrule that "getting heavier" means that it moves down further.)

The amount of weight or pressure is indicated in the middle column in Figure 7.1. The weight is indicated on a scale of 1-10. These units do not refer to actual weight.

Theory of Instruction: Principles and Applications

Section II | Basic Forms

Figure 7.1

Example			Teacher Wording	Example Type
Starting point:	Pressure	3	"Feel this."	
1.	Pressure	2	"It didn't get heavier."	−
2.	Pressure	2	"It didn't get heavier."	−
3.	Pressure	3	"It got heavier."	+
4.	Pressure	7	"It got heavier."	+
5.	Pressure	9	"Did it get heavier?"	+
6.	Pressure	9	"Did it get heavier?"	−
7.	Pressure	5	"Did it get heavier?"	−
8.	Pressure	6	"Did it get heavier?"	+
9.	Pressure	3	"Did it get heavier?"	−
10.	Pressure	4	"Did it get heavier?"	+
11.	Pressure	2	"Did it get heavier?"	−
12.	Pressure	5	"Did it get heavier?"	+
13.	Pressure	10	"Did it get heavier?"	+

Brackets: C (examples 2–3), D (examples 3–4), C (examples 5–6), B (examples 1–13), E (examples 7–10), A (examples 1–13).

They are arbitrary assignments designed to show how hard the teacher is pushing down with each example and the change in downward pressure from example to example. The least pressure that will be presented is 1. The greatest pressure is 10. A change from 4 to 5 is a slight change. A change from 4 to 8 is a fairly large change. Note that the teacher does not mention these numbers. The teacher says what appears in the third column.

The teacher begins by applying a pressure of 3 and saying "Feel this." This *starting point* is not a positive example or a negative example. It is a "starting point," a basis for showing the change that is to follow. The teacher then changes the pressure slightly (to 2), creating example 1. "It didn't get heavier."

Present the sequence to yourself, pressing in your own palm. You are not expected to maintain precise values for each of the pressures specified in the sequence; however, try to approximate each value. (Try to keep the value of 5 almost in the middle of the range of positive variation in your examples.)

The brackets **A**, **B**, **C**, **D**, and **E** are quite similar to the brackets for a negative-first non-comparative.

Wording. The **A** bracket shows that the wording for all examples refers to "heavier." Note, however, that the first pressure presented is not referred to as "heavier." The wording merely calls attention to the "feeling." The change from this example to the next is the basis for labeling example 1.

Setup. The **B** bracket indicates that all examples are created through the same setup—the finger creating pressure on the learner's palm.

Difference. All negatives modeled to show difference in a comparative sequence (through example 6) *involve either a small change or no change from the preceding example.* Example 2 is negative. It is created through a small change from example 1; example 1 is created through a small change from the "starting point" stimulus. This convention is unique to comparatives. Note that when we construct a negative-first non-comparative sequence, we begin with two negatives, each of which is minimally different from *some* positive, but not necessarily minimally different from each other. When we construct negative-first comparatives, however, *both negatives at the beginning of the sequence are related to each other*—created through a small change or through no change. A small change is used from negative example 2 to positive 3 and no-change from example 5 to example 6 (**C** brackets).

Sameness. The **D** brackets indicate that comparatives follow the same basic pattern used in the non-comparative sequence. Three positive examples are sandwiched between minimum-difference negatives. Examples 3, 4 and 5 show the range of positive variation within the constraints of the setup. *The amount of change* from example to example is not the same and is not progressive. If the same increase is shown from positive example to the next positive, a misrule is implied. Examples 3, 4, 5 below are unacceptable:

Example	Pressure	Change
2	3	–
3	5	+2
4	7	+2
5	9	+2

Each positive example is two units heavier than the preceding example. The misrule implied is that the increase must be of a certain amount for the example to be positive. Also, the sameness shared by positives is not clearly shown if the changes are ordered this way:

a change of 1

a change of 2

a change of 3

This ordering is progressive, implying that a given change must be progressively greater than the preceding change if the example is to be positive.

In the model sequence, the changes between examples 2 through 5 are 1, 4, 2–a small change, a quite-large change, and an intermediate change. *Follow this pattern for all comparatives.* It implies that any change in the positive direction creates a positive example.

Test items. Examples 5 through the end of the sequence are test items. For each, the teacher asks, "Did it get heavier?" The test segment could easily be reduced to seven examples. Note that it contains various positives, large negative changes, and minimum-difference negatives.

Summary. The steps to follow to construct a negative-first sequence for comparatives are:

1. Establish the "starting point" of your sequence slightly below the middle of the range you wish to demonstrate. If your range of variation is to be from 1 through 10, start with 3 or 4. If you are going to extend your arms all the way for the extreme example of **getting wider**, start with your arms slightly less than half-extended. If the extreme example of **getting fuller** is a glass that is entirely full, begin with an example that is slightly less than half-full. If your starting point is too high, you cannot show a great range of variation in the first positive examples that are designed to show sameness–examples

3, 4, and 5. If your starting point is 1, you cannot show a minimum-negative change.

2. For the negative-first sequence, open with two negative examples–a no-change negative and a minimum-negative change. It does not matter which comes first.

3. Follow the second negative with three positives. Each should differ from the preceding examples in: (a) absolute value, and (b) the amount of change required to create the example. If you were demonstrating **getting wider**, you would show an example that got wider through a very small increase in width, an example that got wider through a very large increase in width, and one that got wider through an intermediate-sized increase in width.

4. Make example 6 a negative that is minimally different from the preceding positive. This negative may be a no-change or a minimum-negative change. A minimum-negative change from a value of 7 is a value of 6; a minimum-negative change from something that is 50 centimeters long is something that is 48 centimeters long. To create a no-change negative, retain the same value as that of the preceding example. Example 6 in the **getting heavier** sequence is a no-change negative (example 5 has a value of 9, example 6 has the same value).

5. Follow with a series of unpredictably sequenced test examples.

   a. These should show some large differences, some small differences, and some no-changes.

   b. These should sample the range. (In the sequence for **heavier**, the test segment spanned a range from a pressure of 2 to a pressure of 10.)

   c. At least one value should be repeated as a positive and as a negative example. (In the test segment for **heavier**, the pressure of 5 is a positive example and, later, a negative example. Also, the pressure 9 is presented both as a positive example and as a negative.)

6. Limit the range of values shown to 1-10. Do not present examples of **no-pressure**, for instance, or **no-width**, or **no-fullness**, or **no-speed**. The basic question, "Did it get wider?" or "Did it get fuller?" does not make much sense with these examples. It did not get wider, but it has no width: therefore the question is not entirely fair for the introductory sequence. Save it for later amplifications of the concept.

Sensory Qualities and Perceptible Differences

The two most common mistakes that designers make when dealing with comparatives are: (1) to present *indirect* sequences that do not teach the basic sensory quality, and (2) to become preoccupied with "measuring" the absolute size of the "minimum differences."

Indirect sequences. *When teaching the naive learner, do not use numbers that refer to measurement units.* To teach **wider**, do not give the learner information about numbers such as, "The stream was *five feet wide*. Then it was *six feet wide*." These examples do not convey information about width to the naive learner. They convey information about numbers. If the learner knows how something looks or feels when it gets wider, then of course the learner can work from the numbers. But remember this about numbers: The same numbers may refer to *any* measurable relationship. "The stream was 4 glums. Then it was 5 glums." This information does not clarify the meaning of **glum**. (Does **glum** refer to a particular type of eddie on the surface, the speed, the width, the amount of pollution, the presence of sludge worms, or the temperature of the stream?) Numbers tell nothing unless you understand the *meaning of the units*. To teach these units, you must show changes in relevant dimensions. The basic sensory quality of **heavier** is not the appearance of a scale moving down. It is the *feeling* of downward pressure. The basic sensation of **hotter** is not something that is observed visually. The teaching of **hotter**, therefore, would involve examples that *are felt*. **Steeper** is something that can be felt or seen. Therefore, it can be presented either visually or tactually. **Greener** is something that is perceived visually and must be taught that way. Remember, a blind person can deal with measurements of **green** and deductions associated with **green**. (If it starts out with a greenness value of 4 and goes up to a greenness value of 6, it got **greener**.) However, after receiving information about **green**, a blind person knows no more about the basic quality we label **green** than before.

Perceptible differences. To construct minimum differences in the comparative sequence make sure that the differences are small, but quite perceptible. In the sequence for teaching **heavier**, the difference between a downward pressure of 3 and one of 4 is small but is assumed to be perceptible. Also, the difference between a downward pressure of 8 and one of 9 is small, but perceptible.

If we were teaching the concept **getting hotter**, for example, and were using a faucet that mixes hot and cold water, we would try out the sequence and determine small differences that are clearly perceptible. These small differences are not a simple product of so many physical units. The fact that we turn the faucet a certain amount (such as $1/_{12}$ of a turn) does not count for anything if the results of this physical manipulation is an imperceptible difference. Furthermore, we do not make assumptions about the "equality" of units. To make a perceptible change in the temperature range of cold water does not necessarily require the same physical manipulation as that required to make a perceptible change with hotter water. The question is empirical. The goal is to identify differences that are perceptible and *relatively* small. Do not try to identify the absolutely smallest difference that you can perceive. This difference leaves no margin of error. Try a difference that is slightly larger.

Wording

The teacher models the first four or five examples and then tests on the remaining examples. (In the sequence for **heavier**, the teacher modeled only four.) For modeling positive examples, the teacher says, "It got __," or answers a question, "Did it get __? Yes."

An addition to the teacher wording is required by the starting point. The teacher presents the starting point example and says, "Watch," or "Look at this," or "Feel this." The purpose of this instruction is simply to call the learner's attention to the example and to the subsequent change.

The test wording may be designed to call for "yes-no" responses. "Did it get __?" A stronger task is one that requires the learner to use the new word being taught. "Tell me hotter or not-hotter."

After presenting example 5, the teacher may give general *instructions* that apply to all test examples: "Your turn. Tell me if it gets heavier or not-heavier." For each test item, the teacher would then ask: "What happened?" or would say, "Tell me." The learner would respond, "It got heavier," or, "It didn't get heavier."

Illustration. A sequence for the concept getting hotter is shown in Figure 7.2. The setup is a stream of water from a faucet. The learner's hand is in the stream. The faucet is obscured from the learner's view so that the learner cannot see the teacher's manipulation of the hot and cold water handles. The units (1-10) referred to in the

Figure 7.2

Example				Teacher Wording	Type
Starting point:	Heat Level	4		"Feel this water."	
1.	Heat Level	4		"It didn't get hotter."	−
2.	Heat Level	3	⎤ C	"It didn't get hotter."	−
3.	Heat Level	4	⎦	"It got hotter."	+
4.	Heat Level	7	⎤ D	"It got hotter."	+
5.	Heat Level	9	⎦	"It got hotter."	+
			C	General instructions for test: "Your turn. Tell me whether the water gets hotter or not hotter."	
6.	Heat Level	8	⎤ B	"What happened?"	−
7.	Heat Level	10		"What happened?"	+
8.	Heat Level	4		"What happened?"	−
9.	Heat Level	1	⎤ E	"What happened?"	−
10.	Heat Level	4		"What happened?"	+
11.	Heat Level	2		"What happened?"	−
12.	Heat Level	4		"What happened?"	+
13.	Heat Level	5		"What happened?"	+
14.	Heat Level	8	⎦	"What happened?"	+

(Bracket A spans the entire sequence.)

sequence cover a range of temperatures from water that is very cold (1) to water that is on the verge of being uncomfortably hot (10).

Variations in the Negative-First Sequence

Although the sequence in Figure 7.2 is a negative-first comparative (like the sequence for **getting heavier**), and although it follows the same principles of juxtaposition, it differs from the earlier one in five ways:

1. The starting point of this sequence is a higher value (4) than the starting point of the sequence for **getting heavier**; furthermore, the values throughout the sequence are not identical.

2. The pattern of no-change and minimum-change negatives is different. In the getting-heavier sequence, the first negative (example 1) is a minimum-negative. In the **getting-hotter** sequence, the first negative is a no-change. Also, example 6 in the **getting-heavier** sequence is a no-change, while example 6 in the **getting-hotter** sequence is a minimum negative.

3. The number of examples modeled differs, with four items modeled for **getting-heavier** and 5 for **getting-hotter**.

4. The teacher wording is different, with the **getting-heavier** sequence calling for "yes-no" responses ("Did it get heavier?") and the **getting-hotter** sequence requiring the learner to use the name for the concept ("What happened?"). Associated with the use of this strong-response question for the **getting-hotter** sequence, general instructions are needed to show the learner which responses are expected. Without these, the learner might attempt to talk about "cooler" or "the same hotterness." The desired responses are "It got hotter," or "It didn't get hotter."

5. The number of examples in the sequences differ—13 in the **getting-heavier** sequence and 14 in the **getting-hotter** sequence.

Despite these differences, both sequences follow the same pattern of juxtapositions. The differences between them demonstrates the latitude that is available to the instructional designer, even within the constraints of a fairly "tight" formula.

Positive-First Comparatives Sequences

If the learner is to be taught six comparative concepts, approximately half should be presented through negative-first sequences and half through positive-first variations. Like the non-comparative positive-first sequences, the comparative positive-first *initially shows how positives are the same*, and then presents *minimum differences*, and finally *tests*. Figure 7.3 shows a positive-first presentation of the concept **closer together**. The setup is the teacher's hands, which are shown closer or farther apart. Note the general instructions after example 5 in the sequence.

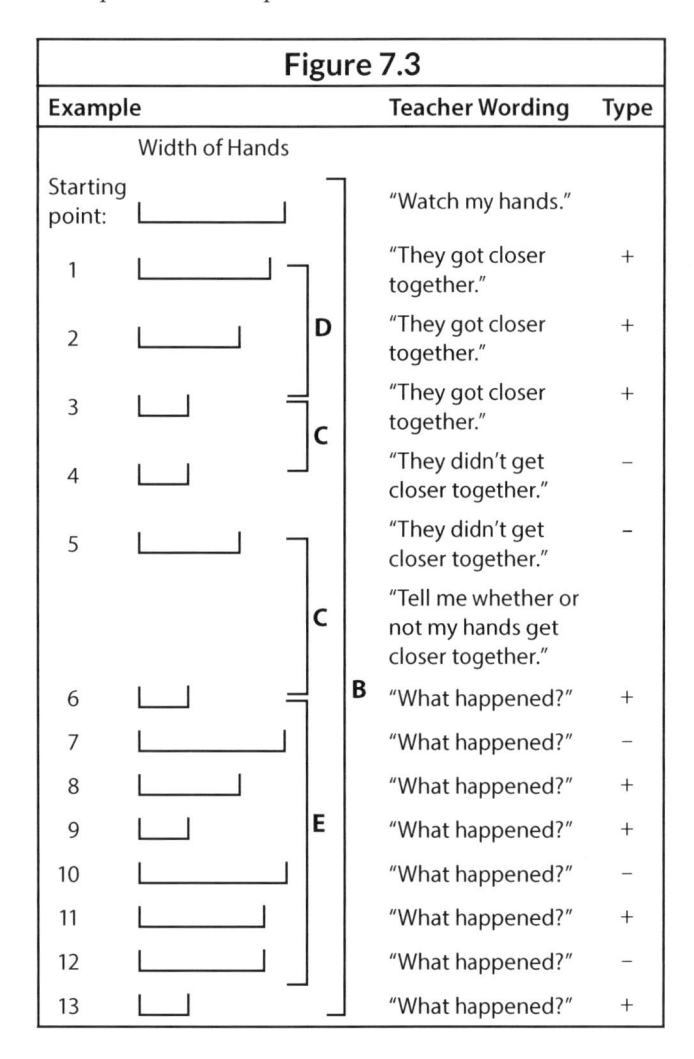

Figure 7.3

Example	Teacher Wording	Type
Starting point	"Watch my hands."	
1	"They got closer together."	+
2	"They got closer together."	+
3	"They got closer together."	+
4	"They didn't get closer together."	−
5	"They didn't get closer together."	−
	"Tell me whether or not my hands get closer together."	
6	"What happened?"	+
7	"What happened?"	−
8	"What happened?"	+
9	"What happened?"	+
10	"What happened?"	−
11	"What happened?"	+
12	"What happened?"	−
13	"What happened?"	+

Setup Features. For this sequence, the teacher moves only one hand. The changes could have been created so that each change involves two hands. However, to be consistent with the setup principle, the same sort of change used for one example should be used for all. If one hand moves to create one example, one hand must move to create all examples. If a two-hand change creates one example, that change must create all examples that involve a change.

Sameness. To show sameness, the same pattern used for the other sequences is presented in examples 1 to 3: a small change (example 1), a large change (example 2), and an intermediate change (example 3).

Difference. Two minimum differences are modeled, one that involves a minimum-negative change and one that involves no change. Note that all changes occurring in examples 3-6 of the positive-first comparative sequence are small.

Test items. The test items present a variety of types.

Advanced Applications

Advanced applications possibly involve two-choice wording, fewer examples, and a verbal explanation.

Two-choice wording. Many comparatives involve the words **more** and **less**. Something becomes **more intricate** or **less intricate**. It becomes **more strongly accented** or **less strongly accented**. If the learner has demonstrated ability to perform on some concepts that involve changes labeled **more** or **less**, two-choice variations in the test question can be presented for comparatives expressed with more ____ or less ____. If the learner is not facile with other concepts that refer to **more** or **less**, the two-choice variation should not be used.

Verbal explanation. Any explanation provided by the teacher should not be a highly-detailed description or a substitute for the examples. If the particular concept can be explained in a sentence (or two), the verbal explanation may precede the sequence. "I'll show things that get more involved. When something becomes more involved, it gets more parts." The explanation is not an attempt to exhaust the possible meanings of **getting more involved**, nor to specify every aspect of a particular meaning. The *examples* are expected to provide the details.

Number of examples. With sophisticated learners, 6 to 8 examples are usually enough. Two or 3 are modeled, followed by some test examples.

Illustration. Figure 7.4 shows a possible sequence designed to teach an advanced learner the meaning of **more permeable**. It incorporates verbal explanation, reduced number of examples, and a two-choice task.

Figure 7.4

Teacher: "When something is more permeable, liquid moves through it faster."

Teacher then presents an adjustable filter on the end of a hose. Initially, the water flows at a rate of 4.

Example	Water Flow	Teacher Wording	Student Response
Starting point:	4	Watch the water flow through this filter. I'll tell you what happens.	
1	5	The filter became more permeable.	
2	4	The filter became less permeable.	
		Your turn: Tell me if the filter becomes more permeable or less permeable.	
3	5	What happened?	It became more permeable.
4	4	What happened?	It became less permeable.
5	8	What happened?	It became more permeable.
6	10	What happened?	It became more permeable.

Note these points:

1. Only six examples are used in the sequence.
2. The teacher models one positive and one negative.
3. Test items include minimum negatives and a fair range of positives.

Two-Response Comparative Sequences for More Naive Learners

When dealing with **more permeable, less permeable**, the sophisticated learner actually deals with only one new word that is in a familiar context. When providing responses for **bigger-smaller**, however, the learner is required to use two words, both of which are new. The learner must also remember which new word goes with which observed change in the examples.

For teaching pairs such as, **faster-slower, bigger-smaller, older-younger**, or **happier-sadder** to naive learners, first introduce one of the labels (**slower, not-slower**). After the learner has applied this label in a range of activities, *introduce the two-response sequence*. The label taught earlier (**slower**) *would be the negative for the new sequence*; the new term (**faster**) would be the positive. The sequence would contain a fairly large number of examples to assure that the learner receives practice in applying both words. The general instructions would appear after positives and negatives are modeled: "Tell me if it moves faster or slower . . . What happened?"

Indirect Sequences

A direct sequence is one in which we present the learner with actual examples of the concept being taught. For **steeper grade**, we present examples that show the changes in the grade; for **more abrupt**, we present examples that show the abruptness the learner is to label. An indirect sequence does not present the actual sensory qualities for each example. Instead, a description of the quality is presented. The description often involves numbers. Indirect sequences should not be presented to the naive learner. If the learner knows the sensation that is associated with **getting hotter**, and understands that the temperature refers to how hot something is, we can use measurement numbers instead of sensory examples to teach concepts.

The following sequence teaches the concept **temperature increasing** to a sophisticated learner:

Teacher Wording

Listen. The temperature starts out at 45 degrees. Then it goes up to 46 degrees. My turn: What happened to the temperature? It increased.

Then it goes from 46 degrees to 73 degrees. My turn: What happened to the temperature? it increased.

Then it goes from 73 degrees to 73 degrees. My turn: What happened to the temperature? It didn't increase.

Your turn to tell me if the temperature increases or doesn't increase. It goes from 73 degrees to 72 degrees. What happened to the temperature?

It goes from 72 to 91 degrees. What happened to the temperature?

It goes from 91 to 91 degrees. What happened to the temperature?

It goes from 91 to 134 degrees. What happened to the temperature?

The sequence is a positive-first sequence that is modeled after the presentations for communicating basic sensory qualities. The differences are that:

1. Fewer examples are modeled and tested.
2. The examples are described verbally by the teacher.
3. Numbers are involved in the description of what happened.

Note, however, that the same pattern for showing sameness and difference used in earlier sequences applies to this sequence.

We could use a variation of this presentation for teaching **greater height**, **more permeable**, **longer distance**, **faster**, and other concepts for which conventional measurement units are available. The sequence can be designed as a negative-first or a positive-first sequence. Numbers, however, should not be used unless the learner is familiar with the sensory quality that is labeled by **height**, **permeable**, **distance**, **faster**, etc.

Other indirect sequences may be designed to illustrate the nature of the concept. For instance, if we were to teach the concept of **momentum**, we might begin with a sequence that teaches how momentum works. To achieve this goal, we might alter the concept so that it deals with **more momentum** and **less momentum**. The setup involves something moving and a means for measuring how resistant it is to stopping.

Teacher Wording

I'll tell you about a car that drives into a brick wall. Listen. The first time the car hits the wall, it goes through four feet of brick before it stops.

The next time it doesn't go through four feet of brick. It goes through three feet of brick before it stops. It had less momentum this time.

The next time, it doesn't go through three feet of brick. It goes through four feet of brick. It had more momentum.

The next time, it doesn't go through four feet of brick. It goes through seven feet of brick. Tell me about the momentum.

The next time, it doesn't go through seven feet of brick. It goes through five feet of brick. Tell me about the momentum.

The next time, it doesn't go through five feet of brick. It goes through nine feet of brick. Tell me about the momentum.

This sequence is basically the same as the others that we have developed. The wording is different, to assure that the learner will remember the two numbers that are involved in the comparison called for by each example.

A simpler variation of this sequence could be designed so the teacher draws a line into a representation of a brick wall to indicate how far into the wall the car moves on each trial.

- Here's how far the car goes into the wall the first time:
- Here's how far the car goes into the wall the next time:
  The car had more momentum.
  Etc.

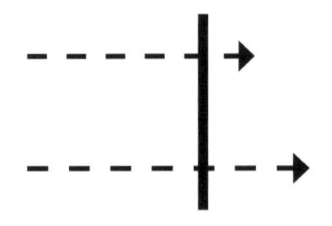

Note that for the second example, the teacher simply adds to the line or subtracts parts of it. The teacher does not draw a new line. The choice of which sequence to use is somewhat arbitrary. The verbal presentation has the advantage of forcing the learner to operate from number descriptions. If these descriptions are to be used later, the verbal description is probably preferable. The sensory presentation (using the line into the wall) provides a more compelling presentation. If there is some doubt about the learner's facility with the number descriptions, this sequence is preferable.

Identifying and Analyzing Comparatives

Some comparative concepts are not immediately apparent. The concept of **increasing** is a good example. Increasing means getting more of something (increasing speed, increasing duration, increasing other measurable qualities). The simplest way to analyze a concept to determine whether it is comparative is to see if it has the attributes of a comparative. To apply this strategy to **increasing**, start with an example of something increasing in some dimension. After you present the example, look at the display that you have created. (After showing **increasing in width**, look at the distance between your hands after you have shown the increase.) Ask: "Could that same *outcome* also be used as a negative example of **increasing**? It could. Therefore, the concept is a comparative. When we apply the same strategy to the concept of a fraction that is more than one, we see that although the label uses the word *more*, the concept is non-comparative. A particular concrete example of a fraction that is more than one is always an example of more than one—never of less than one.

Remember, start with a positive example of the concept; ask if the event that is presented in the example could possibly be used as a negative example of the concept. If the event could be positive in some cases and negative in others, the concept is comparative regardless of the wording used to describe the concept.

When to Make a Concept a Comparative

It is possible to change many non-comparatives into related comparative concepts. **Running** is a non-comparative discrimination, but **running faster** is a comparative. **Near** is a non-comparative; **nearer** is a comparative. Properties that are expressed through adjectives are particularly amenable to being converted into comparatives.

> **Happy** is a non-comparative. **Happier** is a comparative. **Angry** is a non-comparative. **Angrier** is a comparative. **High-pitched** is a non-comparative. **Higher-pitched** is a comparative.

When we convert a non-comparative into a comparative, we change the concept. A non-comparative requires the learner to classify the *example* as a positive example of the concept or as a negative. The difference that the learner must attend to is the difference between those qualities of the example that make the example positive and those that make it negative.

When we change the concept to a comparative, we deal with an entirely different difference. The difference now has to do with the kind of change that occurred. The simplest way to see how the concept changes when we convert a non-comparative concept into a comparative is to look at the negatives. The negatives for a non-comparative sequence are *non-examples* of the concept. A negative of the concept **moving** is **not-moving**. It has no movement. The negative of **moving faster** has movement, however. It moves, but not as fast as an example of **moving faster**. So it is with all comparatives. Below is a comparison of three other concepts:

Non-comparative

Positives	Negatives
turning	not-turning
running	not-running
typing	not-typing

Comparative

Positives	Negatives
turning sharper	turning, but not sharper
running farther	running, but not as far
typing faster	typing, but not as fast

The best test of whether the most appropriate sequence is a comparative or a non-comparative has to do with the *difference* that we want the learner to understand. If we want the learner to learn the difference between running and other actions that are not running, a non-comparative sequence is implied because it shows this difference. If our goal is to show the different speeds of running or different types of running, the difference implies a comparative (running faster, or running with larger steps, or running with more arm movement, etc.).

Comparative sequences are appropriate for showing changes within a type of action, quality, or event. Non-comparatives are appropriate for classifying a type of action, quality or event. Discriminations such as **big-little** (or **big, not-big**) may be taught with non-comparatives (with the **big** examples all the same size and all the **little** examples a different size). If the discrimination is taught as a comparative, the concept changes to **bigger**. The examples would show the basis for something becoming bigger or not-bigger. This sequence would actually show the basis for the concept better than the non-comparative sequence. As a rule, all polars (**wet-dry**, **fast-slow**, **fat-skinny**, **loud-soft**, etc.) are best presented as comparatives, introducing only one label in the initial-teaching sequence.

Identifying Concepts as Comparatives, Nouns, or Non-Comparatives

As noted in the earlier chapters, if we start with a sentence we can usually determine the type of concepts that are named in the sentence. Once we classify a concept, we know the basic procedures involved in communicating that concept faultlessly to the learner.

Below is a sentence that might be used to describe a procedure for reaching the top of a hill in a motor-driven vehicle.

> If you don't make it to the top of the hill, back the vehicle all the way down and go faster before you reach the steeper grade.

We can quickly identify some words or phrases.

> The **top** of something is a non-comparative.
> **Hill** is a noun.

Section II | Basic Forms

> **Back** or **back down** is a non-comparative.
> **Vehicle** is a noun.
> **Go faster** is a comparative.
> **Before something happens** is a non-comparative.
> **Reach something** is a non-comparative.
> The **steeper grade** is a comparative.

Each of these concepts that we identify would be taught so that the meaning conveyed in the sentence is transmitted through the initial-teaching sequence. For **hill**, we would present a noun sequence. The negatives might include **valley** and **mountain** (depending on the assumed knowledge of the learner).

For **back down**, we would present a non-comparative sequence. The negatives should include the vehicle backing up an incline and the vehicle going forward down an incline. The sequence, however, is a regular non-comparative sequence with the test question: "Did it back down?" presented with each test item.

Go faster is a comparative. The sequence used to teach this concept would show some object moving. The speed of the object would change from example to example. For the test examples, the learner would be required to label each example as either **moving faster** or **not-moving faster** (or answering the question: "Did it move faster?").

Reach something is a non-comparative. To communicate the concept, we could present a setup that shows an object moving toward something, like a truck moving toward a lake. The truck either reaches the lake or does not. The learner responds to "Did it reach the lake?" for each test example. (Some positive examples would show the truck just reaching the water line. Others would show the truck continuing farther into the water. Note that these examples would be presented through a diagram or by tracing the route of the truck on a picture that shows a road leading to a lake.)

Not all the concepts named in the sentence are best presented as non-comparatives, comparatives, or nouns. The concept **before something happens** may be presented as a non-comparative; however, it is best presented as a transformation (discussed in the following chapters).

In addition to identifying the single concepts named in the sentence, we can also identify the groups of concepts, described by the phrases in the sentence. For instance, instead of teaching **top** and **hill** as separate concepts, we could simply teach **top of the hill**. The concept is a non-comparative. It could be presented with a picture of the hill. For each example, the teacher touches part of the hill. For each test example, the teacher asks, "Did I touch the top of the hill?" Note that this concept is communicated through the basic sequence used for other non-comparatives. The fact that the label involves more than one word is irrelevant. The concept is a non-comparative with *minimum* negatives and a possible range of positive variations. The range of positive variation depends on the shape of the hill. If there is some clear boundary for the top (a flat place that is not so extensive that the hill becomes a plateau), a range of positive variation is possible.

Also, we could teach the concept of **make it to the top of the hill**. This concept is a non-comparative. The sequence is similar to that for **reach something**. The difference is that a hill is involved.

Back all the way down is another non-comparative. The negative examples would show **backing** but not **all the way down**, **going down all the way** but not **backing**, and **backing all the way up the hill**.

Finally, we could teach **Go faster before reaching the steeper grade** as a comparative concept. The negatives would show going the same speed (as the previous trial) before reaching the steeper grade, going slower before reaching the steeper grade, and possibly starting out fast but going slower before reaching the steeper grade.

If we understand the meanings conveyed by words and phrases of a sentence—any sentence—we can classify the concepts that are conveyed. We can immediately classify many of the individual words as comparatives, non-comparatives, and nouns. Furthermore, we can frequently group the words that occur in phrases (or possibly clauses) and classify each group of words as a comparative or as a non-comparative. Note that groups of words would rarely be classified as nouns. The phrase, "the little boy with the red cap" names several nouns, but is a non-comparative concept. The negatives are a little boy with a cap that is not red, a not-little boy with a red cap, a little girl with a red cap. By applying the test for determining whether the concept is a comparative or non-comparative (Is a positive example always a positive example?) we can readily determine how to classify the concept. To classify the word, phrase, or clause is to understand how to convey the meaning of that expression in a faultless manner. The power of the basic-form sequences becomes apparent when we recognize that any sentence is composed of basic-form concepts. In later chapters we will consider possibly more appropriate ways of presenting some concepts; however, the fact remains that any concept may be treated as a basic-form concept.

Practice with sentences. A useful exercise is to practice identifying how words or groups of words are classified. Do not become concerned over whether you exhaust all possible ways of grouping the words. A large number of groupings is possible when a sentence presents elaborate wording. You do not have to deal with all possible groupings. But you should become facile at classifying words, or groups of words, according to their most basic classification—as comparatives, non-comparatives, or nouns.

Summary

Comparatives are different from non-comparatives in the following ways:

- Comparatives assume a comparison of two things.
- Whether an example in a comparative sequence is positive or negative does not depend on the absolute value of the stimulus, but on the difference between that stimulus and the one with which it is compared.

Comparatives differ from nouns in the following ways:

- Comparatives involve precise minimum differences.
- Negatives for any particular comparative have the same label.

The procedures for creating continuous-conversion comparative sequences are:

1. Follow the same general wording rules and setup rules specified for non-comparative sequences. If possible, use continuous conversion of examples.
2. Begin the sentence with a *starting point*—a stimulus that is neither positive nor negative.
3. Make sure that the starting point is somewhere near the middle of the range that you will show. (This convention assures that you can "maneuver" toward either extreme.)
4. Follow the starting point with either positives or negatives.
    - For sequencing positives, show a small change, a large change, and a change of intermediate sizes, in that order.
    - For all modeled negatives, create a minimum difference from the preceding example.
    - Use two types of minimum differences—a very small negative change and a no-change negative. Model both positives and negatives. Four models are usually sufficient.
    - Construct the series of test examples according to the same rules used for non-comparatives.
5. Use shorter sequences for sophisticated learners.
6. Use two-choice tasks for comparatives if the same word appears in both the positive and negative changes (such as higher **pitch** and lower **pitch**, or more **pressure** and less **pressure**, or more **parallel** and less **parallel**). As a rule, do not use two-choice tasks for naive learners if different words are used to describe the positive change and the negative change (**bigger-smaller, faster-slower, happier-sadder**).

Convert polars such as **big-little** into comparatives (initially teaching **getting bigger**). This modification makes the basis of the concept precise.

The test of whether discriminations should be presented as comparatives has to do with the difference we wish to show. For most non-comparative concepts, such as **leaning, listening, lurching,** or **losing,** we wish to show how they differ from other conditions (**not-leaning, not-listening, not-lurching, not-losing**). To show this difference, we would use a non-comparative sequence. To show increases in an action—**leaning more, listening more carefully, lurching farther,** or **losing more**—we use comparatives.

SECTION III
JOINING FORMS

Anything that is immediately obvious in examples—anything that we can point to, sense, or show through the presentation of a concrete example—can be effectively communicated through one of the basic forms presented in Section II. Section III deals with the simplest forms that relate one concept to another. These are joining forms. As the name implies, they join basic form concepts. There are two types of joining forms—*transformations* and *correlated-feature relationships*.

A transformation is possible only when there is a systematic parallel between changes in examples and changes in responses for the examples. When a small change from one example to the next occurs, there is a corresponding small change in the response. The changes in the responses follow rules. They are not random changes.

The diagram below shows the nature of the relationship between examples and responses used for the examples.

Features of Examples	Responses
X	Y
XX	YY
XXX	YYY
XXXX	YYYY
XXXXX	YYYYY
Etc.	

The **X** column simply represents the way the examples change. The **Y** column shows that there is a parallel between the features of the example and the features of the response.

If the learner were provided with some examples and shown the response for these examples, the learner should be able to generalize to any example of the transformation.

There are two types of transformation relationships between example and response. For the first type, a part of the response changes as part of the example changes. (The example with the **X**'s and **Y**'s above demonstrate this type.) The other type of transformation is based on logical systems, such as the number system. A small change in the example may change the response totally; however, the response is logically a small change. The nature of this logic is evident only if the learner knows the system of responses. We can illustrate both types of transformations with the following comparison.

Type 1:

Example	Teacher Wording
000 00	Tell the numbers being added. (Three plus two)
0000 00	Tell the numbers being added. (Four plus two)

Type 2:

Example	Teacher Wording
000 00	Tell me how many. (Five)
0000 00	Tell me how many. (Six)

Type 1 shows that when one group of circles in an example changes, a corresponding *part* of the response changes. The group that remains the same is signaled by the *part* of the response that remains the same across both examples (plus two). This type of transformation is very important for many verbal skills.

Type 2 is different because no physical part of the response remains from example to example. One response is *five*, the other is *six*. No physical details of the response "five" are present when the response changes to "six." If we used this response for five: "one-one-one-one-one," and this response for six: "one-one-one-one-one-one," the transformation would be a type 1, with part of the response remaining constant. However, adding the one unit is not made explicit by the responses "five" and "six." The relationship between the change in the response and the change in the example is logical if one knows the nature of the counting numbers. A small change occurred in the second example (the addition of one counter), and the response reflects this change, a change in the total of the counting numbers. Obviously, the learner must know the *names* of the various counting numbers to use this transformation.

Whether the transformation is a type 1 or a type 2, it is a *system* for relating changes in the example to changes in their responses. It permits generalizations to new examples because all examples follow the same transformation rule.

The second type of joining form, the *correlated feature*, is completely different. It joins a given sensory discrimination to another discrimination that happens to occur with the first. The red line on a thermometer rises *and* the air gets hotter. These sensory events happen together. Observation of one therefore predicts the other. The sensory discrimination of the red line moving higher (a comparative concept) leads to the prediction that the sensory discrimination of "hotter air" *would be* experienced. Because these events are reliably correlated, the observer could predict the hotter air even if it is not experienced.

We can see the difference between the correlated event and the transformation by referring to a situation such as, "He fell down." A transformation would be a different situation expressed as, "She fell down," or a third situation expressed as, "He stood up." Parts of the original response are substituted to show changes in the situations. We treat the fact, "He fell down," quite differently when we deal with correlated features. If we have *factual information* that "He fell down," we know about events that occur together. **He** is correlated with **falling down**. If we are shown the person who is identified as **he**, we draw the conclusion that the person so identified **fell down**. Even if we do not observe the act of falling down, we can draw this conclusion. Every sentence that expresses a fact conveys the correlation of features expressed by the subject of the sentence (in this case, **he**) with the features expressed by the predicate (in this case, **fell down**).

All correlated feature joinings take the same form: a factual relationship exists between two sensory discriminations. When this *relationship* is conveyed to the learner, it serves as a "premise" for drawing a conclusion that is based on the observations of what is mentioned *first* in the fact. For the fact, **hotter things expand**, the observation involves hotter things and the conclusion drawn is about whether the object expands.

1. Fact: Hotter things expand.
    2. Observation: Thing getting hotter.
        3. Conclusion: Thing expands.

Note that the observer does not experience the expansion of the object, merely that it becomes hotter. As the diagram shows, the observation joins the discrimination observed directly (**getting hotter**) with the *fact* about an event that is correlated with **getting hotter**.

There are only two types of joining forms because there are only two ways that we can relate a given response for a specific sensory discrimination to other responses for other sensory discriminations. We can make the response to a sensory discrimination a part of an orderly, logical system of responses, or we can relate the sensory discrimination *empirically* to some other sensory discrimination. If we relate stimulus events and responses in a logically orderly way, we create a transformation. If we relate stimulus events empirically, we create a correlated-feature joining.

Chapter 8
Single-Transformation Sequences

The sequences that we have dealt with so far teach single labels (names for concepts). All positive examples in a basic-form sequence have the same label. A transformation sequence is different because the concepts that we teach through transformation sequences are different. The objective is not to teach a single label, but to teach a *system of responses* that applies not only to the examples that we present, but to a wide range of other examples. The only practical way to communicate the system of responses is to present various pairings of example and response.

A series of examples is used to demonstrate how each example is correlated with a particular response. After performing on a series of examples that sample a fair range of variation, the learner is provided with a basis for understanding what is the same across the various pairings of examples and responses. This sameness is a rule, an unstated relationship that indicates how responses are related to examples. With an understanding of this rule, the learner can produce *unique responses* to examples that had not been presented in the initial-teaching sequence. (Unique responses are possible because the new examples *are the same* as all other examples of the transformation with respect to the rule that governs the response.)

To assure that the learner receives clear information about the relationship between example and response, we will use a sequence that is different from basic form sequences in two primary ways:

1. The transformation sequence has no negatives.
2. The learner produces different responses for different positive examples.

Both of these features derive from the structure of transformation concepts.

There are no negatives in the transformation sequence because the sequence is designed to show pairings of different examples with different responses. Therefore, the task of wording that is used with each example requires the learner to produce a unique response. The two segments from sequences which follow show the basic differences between the concept of **rhyming with at** when it is treated as a transformation (the first sequence) and when it is treated as a non-comparative (the second sequence).

\multicolumn{2}{c}{Segment of Transformation Sequence}	
Example (visual)	Wording
m	Start with this letter and rhyme with **at**. (mat)
s	Start with this letter and rhyme with **at**. (sat)
f	Start with this letter and rhyme with **at**. (fat)
b	Start with this letter and rhyme with **at**. (bat)
Etc.	
\multicolumn{2}{c}{Segment of Non-Comparative Sequence}	
Example (visual)	Wording
mat	Does this word rhyme with **at**?
sat	Does this word rhyme with **at**?
sam	Does this word rhyme with **at**?
Etc.	

The teacher presents the same wording with each example in the transformation sequence. However, the wording for the transformation sequence requires the learner to produce different responses for different positive examples. When the learner starts with the letter **m** and rhymes with **at**, the learner produces the response "mat." When the learner starts with the letter **s** and rhymes with **at**, the learner produces the response "sat." No negatives are presented in the sequence because the learner rhymes with **at** for each example presented.

The non-comparative is different. All positive examples are responded to with the same response: "Yes." As we noted earlier, any concept can be treated as a basic-form concept. **Rhyming with at**, therefore, can be treated as a non-comparative. However, it is handled more effectively as a transformation, if our concern is with the learner actually *producing* the rhyming words rather than classifying or identifying them.

Identifying Transformation Concepts

The simplest way to identify transformations is to look at the task that is to be presented to the learner and the type of response the learner produces.

The answers to three questions determine whether a transformation is implied. If all are answered "Yes," a transformation is implied. The questions are:

1. Can the same task be used with a variety of examples of the same type?
2. Would the learner produce different symbolic responses for different examples?
3. Is there a sameness shared by all responses?

If we apply the three-criteria test to the task "Is this a cup?," we see that the same task can be used for a variety of examples. We could present various positive examples of cups, present them to the learner, and use the same task, "Is this a cup?"

When we test the task with the second criterion, however, we discover that the task does not imply a transformation. The reason is that for every positive example, the learner produces the same response: "Yes." The learner does not produce different symbolic responses for different examples.

If we test the task "Where is the dog?," we discover that it too can be used with a variety of examples of the same type (the dog under the bed, under the chair, under the table, etc.). For each different example, however, the learner produces a different response. Furthermore, there is an obvious sameness shared by all responses–the word **under**. Therefore, "Where is the dog?" implies a transformation. The task "Rhyme with this word" could be presented with a variety of examples of the same type (the words **mat, eat, fish, brother**, etc.). For each example that is different, the learner produces a different response. And there is an obvious sameness across all examples. The last part of each response contains the vowel sound and the ending of the word presented in the example. This pairing is the same for all words: **mat–sat, eat–meat, fish–dish, brother–mother**, etc.).

When we apply the three-criteria test to the task "When I stop counting, tell me the next number," we see that the same task can be applied to a variety of examples of the same type (counting to 5, to 7, to 34, to 3, etc.) We note that for examples that are different the learner produces responses that are different. They always present the number that occurs next in the counting order. (For 1, 2, 3, the response is 4. For 1, 2, 3, 4, 5, 6, the response is 7. This relationship of example to response is the same across all examples.)

The line between the transformation and basic forms depends on our criterion for judging a variety of examples to be "of the same type" (criterion 1). If we presented the task "What is this?" with examples of cups, the learner would not produce different responses for different examples. Instead, the learner would say "a cup" for every example. Therefore, within this context of "examples of the same type" the task does not imply a transformation. (It implies a noun classification.) If we judge any common object to be "of the same type," a transformation is implied, however, because the learner will produce different responses for different examples presented with "What is this?" (The learner would respond, "a cup," "a ball," "a pillow," "a dog," etc.) Furthermore, there is a sameness across all responses. All object names are preceded by **a**. (However, the learner would not be able to respond to an example unless the learner knew the object name.)

If the example presented to the learner is symbolic (a word, a sentence, a number, a numerical expression), and if the learner does anything but label the object as a word, a sentence, or a number, a transformation is clearly implied. If the learner reads the word, adds a past-tense ending to the word, spells the word, etc., the task that directs the learner implies a transformation.

If the example presented with a task is not symbolic, but the task requires the learner to respond symbolically, a transformation is probably implied. If the learner is directed to ask a question about the example, tell where the example is, count the parts of the example, say words that have the same initial sound as the example, etc., transformations are implied.

Transformation Sequences

Basic Structure

The three-criteria test suggests the basic structure of the transformation sequence:

1. The sequence presents the same wording with all examples.

2. The sequence requires different responses for different examples.
3. The communication clearly shows what is the same about all examples and how changes in the examples are correlated with changes in the responses.

The communication is designed to demonstrate the unstated rule that governs the transformation; therefore, the communication is designed to induce a generalization to new examples. Note, however, that the transformation sequence assumes that the learner understands the names or symbols that are related by the transformation. Transformations involving the counting numbers assume that the learner already knows the counting numbers. A communication that teaches the learner to identify the predicate of sentences assumes that the learner has some knowledge of sentences (at least the understanding of what they say).

The Single-Transformation Sequence

We will use a standard format for designing all single-transformation sequences. We will begin the sequence by juxtaposing examples to show *differences*. We will then juxtapose for *sameness*. By beginning with differences, we show how a small change in the example controls a corresponding small change in the response. After we show this relationship with a series of examples, we present sameness juxtapositions. These require the learner to apply the transformation to examples that do not carefully "prompt" the relationship between the example and response. The sameness juxtapositions provide the basis for generalizing to new examples.

Figure 8.1 shows a single-transformation sequence designed to communicate *making sides of an equation equal*. The sequence requires the learner to specify the missing number in different equations.

The sequence is created through continuous conversion. The teacher begins with the first problem written on a chalkboard, erases the **5**, and replaces it with **6**. The teacher models the first two examples by saying: "My turn," presenting the task to herself ("What makes the other side equal?"), and saying the answer. Beginning with example 3, the teacher asks, saying: "Your turn. What makes the other side equal?"

The sequence is continuous because part of the set up remains for all examples. That part is the equal sign.

Figure 8.1

Example		Teacher Wording
1.	15 =	My turn: What makes the other side equal? Fifteen.
2.	16 =	My turn: What makes the other side equal? Sixteen.
3.	61 =	Your turn: What makes the other side equal?
4.	6 =	What makes the other side equal?
5.	5 =	What makes the other side equal?
6.	5J =	What makes the other side equal?
7.	27M =	What makes the other side equal?
8.	9 =	What makes the other side equal?
9.	K =	What makes the other side equal?
10.	23 =	What makes the other side equal?
11.	0 =	What makes the other side equal?
12.	R =	What makes the other side equal?
13.	C + 1 =	What makes the other side equal?
14.	12 =	What makes the other side equal?

For all minimum-difference examples, only part of the preceding example is changed. The teacher can create the change from **16** to **61** by erasing only one digit. The **1** in **16** is erased and replaced by **1** after the **6**.

Juxtapositions. The **B** bracket indicates that the examples (created through continuous conversion) share the same "set up" features, the same equal sign. The sequence moves from showing differences (**C**) to showing sameness (**D**). The test (**E**) involves new examples. According to the sameness principle, we show sameness if we treat juxtaposed examples that are quite different in the same way. Note that the **D** segment achieves such juxtaposition. The same question applies to **27M** and **0**. The learner carries out the same operation with both examples. Therefore, the juxtaposition implies that **27M** and **0** are the same with respect to "equality." When the learner completes the sequence, the learner should be able to respond to a variety of new examples, such as: **3xr + 1**, or **340**.

Progressive minimum differences. The pattern for creating minimum differences in transformation sequences is *progressive*. Only *one change* occurs from one example to the next. The progression includes *the various types* of minimum difference changes that show the range of variation. For the sequence in Figure 8.1, example 1 is **15** and example 2 is **16**–a minimum difference involving *counting*. Example 3 involves a different type of change from the preceding example. The same digits are used (**1** and **6**); however, they are *reversed* from **16** to **61**. For the next example, one of the digits in **61** is removed, creating **6**. Example 5 is a minimum change in counting numbers **6** to **5**, and in example 6, a letter is added to the **5**, forming **5J**.

Obviously, other minimum differences could be introduced, such as those that involve fractions, decimals, and various operational signals, such as the times sign. Later, we will provide guidelines for identifying the variety of "types" that are to be included in the sequence. However, the basic rules apply for showing differences: *only one change occurs from example to example. That change is a small change.* The change from **5J** to **15J** is a relatively minimal change. The change from **5** to **15J** is not. It involves both the addition of a digit and a letter. A change from **5J** to **500J** is not relatively small, because it involves the addition of two **0**'s. The difference between **5J** and **50J** is a relatively small difference. Remember, to show difference, create one difference from example to example.

The analysis of minimum differences cannot determine which *type* of minimum difference is the "smallest," nor are we particularly interested in questions such as: "Does dropping a digit create a 'smaller' change or difference than reversing the digits?" The question is an empirical one. For us, it is irrelevant because *we should show both types.*

Constructing Single-Transformation Sequences

1. Begin the sequence with a mid-range example. If you are constructing a sequence that is designed to teach *the subject of sentences*, do not begin with an example that has a very long subject. ("The former president of the organization") or one that has a very short subject ("He"). Do not begin with one that is extreme in any way. Begin with a subject ("Five little ducks" or "That broken table") that can be converted into a shorter subject ("Five ducks," "That table") and that can be expanded ("Five fat little ducks," "That broken table in the hall"). Think of the starting example in the same terms as you would for the starting point of a comparative. If you start somewhere in the middle, you have latitude for showing a full range of changes.

2. Follow the first examples with 3 to 6 minimum-difference examples arranged progressively. Create each by making only one small change from the preceding example. Do not repeatedly change the preceding example in the same way.

A sequence for the beginning of a sequence for **subject of statements** could open with these examples:

   a. **Five little ducks** went walking.
   b. **Five ducks** went walking.
   c. **Five rabbits** went walking.
   d. **Five rabbits and a boy** went walking.

Each example is created by changing the preceding example in a relatively small way; however, each type of change is different. Example b is created by subtracting the word **little**. Example c is created by substituting **rabbits** for **ducks**. Example d adds the words **and a boy** to the subject.

3. Through the minimum-difference examples, try to show the learner the range of variation that will be covered in the test examples. If the test examples for the equality relationship are to include examples of this type: 4/3 = , include this type in the minimum-difference part of the sequence (perhaps preceding the example by: 4 =). If you cannot show all types of minimum differences in six progressively arranged examples, you should probably use more than one sequence.

4. Follow the minimum differences with a series of juxtaposed examples that are as different as possible within the constraints of the setup (and the types shown in segment C.) If the transformation has a fair range of variation, use as many as twelve examples in the C segment. For concepts that have a narrow range, use only 4 to 8 examples. **The entire sequence should not exceed 18 items**.

5. Model the first 2 to 5 examples. Test on the remaining examples. The simplest modeling procedure is to say, "My turn," and then present the same test wording that will be used with examples that are not modeled.

The test should always include at least two minimum-difference examples. If four examples are modeled at the beginning of the sequence, the sequence should have six minimum-difference examples. If only two examples are modeled, as few as four minimum-difference examples could appear at the beginning of the sequence.

The first test examples *may* be repetitions of examples that had been modeled. This procedure is appropriate if there is doubt about the learner's ability to produce the response. If there is no doubt, the first test example should be a new minimum difference.

Illustration. Figure 8.2 shows a single-transformation sequence for changing questions into positive statements. Each example is a question phrased in the past tense and beginning with the word **did**. The response that is called for is a past-tense statement.

The **C** bracket indicates that there are six examples progressively ordered. The changes show the range of variation that will occur in segment **D**. Not all possible minimum differences are included in the first six examples. Example three could have been: Did she laugh *loudly*? This example would certainly be acceptable. It includes all remaining words presented in the question, e.g., "Did the other girls come with you?" is changed by starting with the word after **did**: "The other girls came with you." However, the verb is changed to a past-tense verb. The minimum-difference examples show that the creation of the past-tense verb is not a mere mechanical operation. For the question, "Did those ducks fly high?" the learner does not respond by saying, "Those ducks flied high." Since these irregular verbs (Those ducks *flew* high.) are included in the test, they are demonstrated in the minimum-difference examples. Examples 4, 5, and 6 involve irregular verbs.

Note that this sequence nicely shows that what the learner must learn is a rule and that the rule may be quite complicated if we express it verbally. (Drop the word **did**. Start with the word that appears after **did**. Say all words as presented, but change the verb from present to past.)

Irregulars and Transformations

If responses are irregular, they are a subtype of examples that require knowledge beyond the knowledge implied for regular responses. If the learner does not know how to form the past-tense of words such as **eat**, these words should not be included in the sequence because they are irregular. If the learner is naive, but capable of handling regular past-tense transformations, we would expect the learner to produce responses such as: "She sitted with the clown," "They runned with the clowns," "Herman eated breakfast," "Those ducks flied high," "His sister buyed a car." Conversely, if we expect the "appropriate responses," we must make sure that the learner has the knowledge of how to produce them.

Subtypes

A subtype is a group of examples that have a set of common features not observed in any other examples. When we deal with transformations, we consider subtypes. The

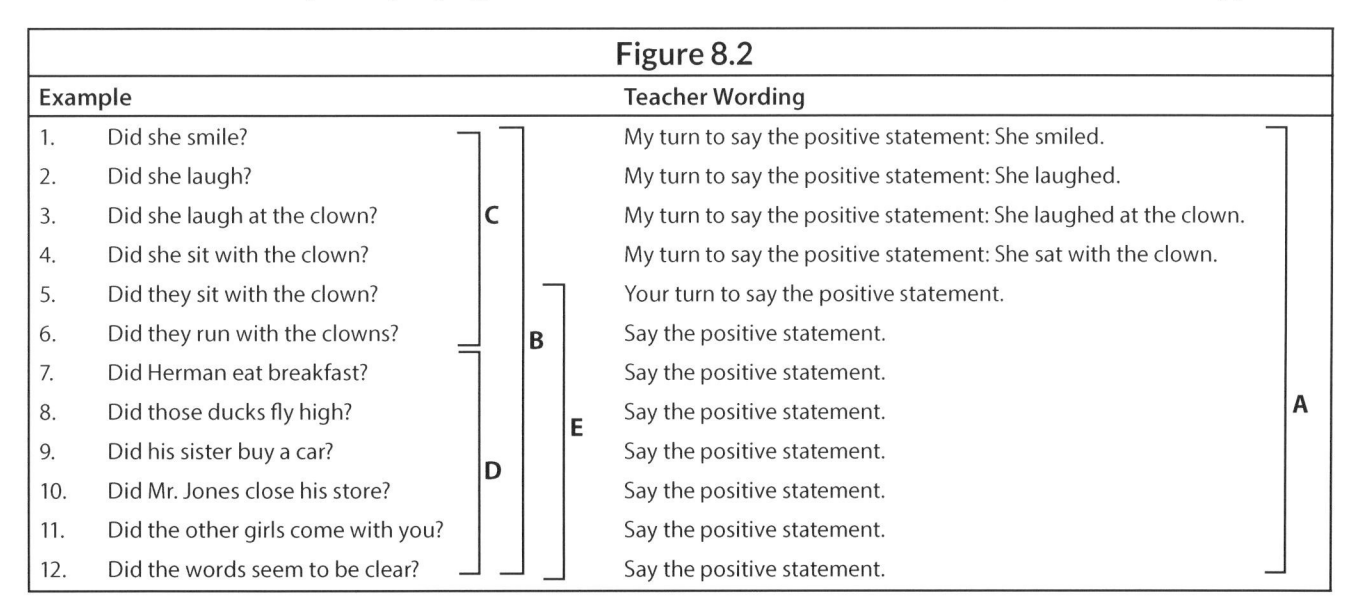

Figure 8.2		
Example		Teacher Wording
1. Did she smile?		My turn to say the positive statement: She smiled.
2. Did she laugh?		My turn to say the positive statement: She laughed.
3. Did she laugh at the clown?	C	My turn to say the positive statement: She laughed at the clown.
4. Did she sit with the clown?		My turn to say the positive statement: She sat with the clown.
5. Did they sit with the clown?		Your turn to say the positive statement.
6. Did they run with the clowns?	B	Say the positive statement.
7. Did Herman eat breakfast?		Say the positive statement.
8. Did those ducks fly high?	E	Say the positive statement.
9. Did his sister buy a car?	D	Say the positive statement.
10. Did Mr. Jones close his store?		Say the positive statement.
11. Did the other girls come with you?		Say the positive statement.
12. Did the words seem to be clear?		Say the positive statement.

(Bracket A encompasses all 12 examples.)

analysis of subtypes provides a better "guess" about difficulty of the sequence.

As the amount of sameness possessed by all members of a subtype increases, the number of examples in that subtype decreases. Consider extreme examples. An **elephant** and the word **if** are the same in some ways and can therefore be included in the class or type of entity. (They are the same because they are events observed on the planet Earth.) The number of examples in this class is very large because the samenesses are very few compared to samenesses possessed by a group that consists of the word **if** and other two-sound words that begin with vowel sounds (**if, in, on, up, at**, etc.). The membership of the two-sound-word class is smaller because things may be included in this class *only if they have many samenesses*. In addition to being events on Earth, they must also be verbal events; they must be words; they must be words of only two sounds; they must be words that begin with a vowel.

If we take the subtype classification to its extreme, we would create a subset for each word. The word **if** would be in a class composed only of two-sound words that begin with the sound /i/ and that end with /f/. The examples in this class have *more* samenesses than the examples in the class of two-sound words that begin with a vowel. The membership of the new class, however, would be smaller, because an example must have more sameness to be included in the class.

We may group examples according to many shared samenesses, or to relatively few shared samenesses. But the basis that we use for identifying subtypes is always the features of the examples. Conversely, if examples are of a given subtype, they will have common features not possessed by examples that are not of that subtype.

Subtypes that are irregular or difficult. Some subtypes should be difficult for the learner. These subtypes require: (1) additional behavior that is not required by the simpler examples, and (2) behavior that is contrary to that required by the larger set of examples.

All irregular subtypes require the learner to replace the behavior for producing a regular response with another behavior. Some irregular subtypes, however, require behavior that is contrary to that required by the regular subtypes.

Producing the response for, "Did she fly over the barn?" ("She flew over the barn") represents *additional* behavior.

In addition to expressing the verb as a past-tense verb, the learner must produce the word that is used conventionally to denote the past tense of **fly**.

An example of *contrary* behavior would be identifying the number of tens for teen numerals. For most two-digit numerals, the number of tens is mentioned first in the name—*forty*-six, *eighty*-six, etc. For teens, however, it is mentioned last: six*teen*, eigh*teen*. The formation is contrary to that of the larger group; therefore, we would predict problems with this subtype.

An easy way to find difficult subtypes is to make statements about the features of the examples or the responses, then see which examples have the features. The feature must be possessed by all members of a subset. Figure 8.3 presents a simple analysis of two-digit numerals. All **X**'s in the same *row* describe the membership for a given feature. All **X**'s in a column describe the features for a given subtype. The feature of **names of tens distorted** is possessed by the 20's, 30's, 50's, and by the teens. (We do not say "three-tee-two," we say, "thirty-two." We do not say "one-tee-four," we say "fourteen.")

If an **X** appears in a cell, all members listed at the top of the column have the feature indicated. For instance, all the listed numerals in column 5 have feature 6 (name of the ten distorted). We do not say "two-tee-three," for 23, but we do say six-tee-three for 63.

As Figure 8.3 shows, the samenesses shared by all the numerals 10 through 99 are fewer than the samenesses shared by members of any subset. Figure 8.3 also shows that membership in one subset does not exclude membership in another subset. The numerals 13 and 15 are in the subset of numerals with distorted *tens* names (we do not say thir*ten*), and distorted one's names (we do not say *three*teen). Thirteen is also in the group with the tens digit named last. To make this name regular, we would have to reverse the order of the parts of the name and straighten out the distortion of both the name of the tens and the name of the ones (calling the numeral one-tee-three).

Note that not all possible irregular subtypes are specified in Figure 8.3.

The various irregular features suggest where inappropriate generalizations will occur. Conversely, the irregulars must be taught separately to assure that the learner recognizes them as irregulars and does not generalize inappropriately.

		Full Set	Irregular Subtypes				
		10-99	ends in 0: (10, 20, 30...)	13-19	20's (21, 22, ...) 30's (31, 32, ...) 50's (51, 52, ...)	13, 15, all 20's, 30's, and 50's	11, 13, 15
1.	Numeral consists of 2 digits	X	X	X	X	X	X
2.	Name for each numeral	X	X	X	X	X	X
3.	Name refers to 10's digit only		X				
4.	Name refers to 10's digit first, ones next				X		
5.	Name refers to 10's digit last			X			
6.	Name to ten distorted			X	X	X	X
7.	Name of ones digit distorted						X

Figure 8.3

Figure 8.3 shows the product of grouping subtypes according to samenesses. This categorization is possible only after you have identified what is the same about all the subtypes. The simplest procedure for determining subtypes is that used in sequencing examples to show sameness. You are trying to discover unique samenesses; therefore, the sameness principles provide you with the most efficient guideline for demonstrating sameness.

1. Make a list of juxtaposed examples that differ greatly from each other. For the numerals, you might start with **52** and then follow with an example that is quite different from **52**, such as **17**. Then follow with an example that is greatly different from **17**, such as **90**. Continue until you have exhausted the range of variation of two-digit numerals.

2. Specify all the differences between the first three or four juxtaposed examples. How is **17** different from **52** with respect to the relationship of numerals and names? How is **90** different from **17**? etc.

3. For each difference that you describe, list all the numerals that share this difference. If you note that the name for **17** starts with "seven," list all the other numerals that have the feature of starting with the name for the ones number and not the tens number.

4. Cross out all examples farther down your list that differ from the preceding example in the manner that you have already described.

This procedure requires some trial and error. Expect some initial difficulty in expressing the differences from one example to the next. However, by following the procedure, you will probably identify all subtypes that are important and you will have a precise understanding of the features shared by all the examples within each subtype.

Setup for subtype variations. If a subtype involves additional behavior to form a response, or if a subtype calls for contrary behavior, **the subtype should not be presented in the initial sequence**.

For the setup features of the initial sequence, limit the examples to a *large* subtype that does not involve additional responses or contrary responses. If we deal with two-digit numbers, the initial sequence might contain only examples of the subtype that consists of regularly-formed numerals in the **40's, 60's, 70's, 80's** and **90's**. The group is large and generalizable. If we were teaching rhyming with single-sound beginnings, we might limit the examples in the initial sequence to those that involve **continuous sounds that are voiced**. This subtype is relatively large in membership and calls for responses that are relatively easy to produce. (Additional behavior is required by stop-sound beginnings **b, t, p, g** because the speaker must create a transition sound that is based on the sound that follows the stop-sound.)

Remember, for the introductory sequence, identify a relatively large subtype that involves producing the simplest class of responses.

The sequence presented in Figure 8.4 illustrates how the subtype analysis is translated into an initial sequence. This sequence teaches numerical expansion. The learner is presented with numerals, such as **46**, and says the addition fact for that numeral that is based on the two digits ("Forty-six equals forty plus six"). The initial sequence avoids all the irregular types (the **teen numbers, 20's, 30's, and 50's**).

	Figure 8.4	
Example		Teacher Wording
1.	79	My turn to say the addition fact for this numeral: Seventy-nine equals seventy plus nine.
2.	78	My turn again: Seventy-eight equals seventy plus eight.
3.	87	My turn again: Eighty-seven equals eighty plus seven.
4.	87	Your turn: Say the addition fact.
5.	97	Say the addition fact.
6.	96	Say the addition fact.
7.	69	Say the addition fact.
8.	42	Say the addition fact.
9.	88	Say the addition fact.
10.	71	Say the addition fact.
11.	45	Say the addition fact.
12.	93	Say the addition fact.
13.	64	Say the addition fact.

The sequence follows the same pattern as that for other transformations. The minimum differences continue through example 7. Note, however, that the same example is repeated as example 3 and example 4. The teacher models only three examples, then tests on the last modeled example. Following example 7 greatly different examples are juxtaposed to communicate sameness.

Following the learner's successful performance on this sequence, the learner would be able to generalize to all regularly-formed numerals. Obviously, however, the learner would not be able to generalize to the irregulars, particularly the teen numerals (because the teen names are formed in the reverse way the regulars are formed). The dilemma that faces us is that if we work too long on the regularly-formed numerals, we will stipulate this type and the learner will have great difficulty when the teens are introduced. On the other hand, if we introduce the teens before the learner is reasonably firm on the regulars, introduction of teens could lead to serious reversal problems, with the learner confusing the formulas for the regular numerals and the teens (calling **51** "ten plus five," for example).

Introducing the other subtypes would be relatively easy. The learner might generalize to the **20's, 30's, and 50's** following the initial format. Also, the numerals that end in zero (**40, 60**, etc.) should present little problem, because the numeral shows that the addition fact will refer to zero. ("Forty equals 40 plus zero"). Following the introduction of the initial sequence above, we could design a second sequence that introduces both the **20's, 30's, 50's** and the two-digit numerals that end in zero.

Application of the Subtype Analysis

The illustration with numerals shows the basic function of the subtype analysis, which is to identify the range of examples for which generalization will be possible, and to identify subtypes that will interfere with the generalization. The analysis suggests a strategy, which is to start with a relatively large, but easy subtype, then introduce the other subtypes systematically and integrate them with all subtypes that have been taught. The mechanics of this integration process is presented in Section IV, Programs. The issue that we are primarily concerned with here is that of identifying a good *initial* sequence, one that is efficient with respect to its generalization potential and yet one that is easy enough for the learner to master.

To show how the subtype analysis permits us both to identify problems and to solve them efficiently, we will take a relatively simple skill, oral blending, and apply the analysis to designing an initial sequence, creating a second sequence for one of the more difficult subtypes, and using the subtype analysis to diagnose problems the learner may have with a sequence. Although we will be dealing with a relatively simple skill, the same procedures would apply to any transformation concept because these concepts deal with symbolic manipulation (identifying the predicate of a sentence, expressing numerals as log functions, rhyming, converting commands into statements, etc.). One of the most prominent features of concepts that deal with symbolic manipulations is that they generate an incredibly large range of variation, which means that there are many possible minimum differences. These minimum differences may be categorized into subtypes, some of which should be more difficult than others.

Even if some of these subtypes are perfectly regular, they may involve additional behavior and should therefore be more difficult than subtypes that require less behavior. The skill of oral blending illustrates this situation. Although none of the subtypes that we identify when analyzing oral blending is irregular in the sense that the name for **15** is irregular, some subtypes are more difficult than others.

The same analysis that applies to the identification of irregulars applies to the identification of difficult subtypes. This subtype analysis will suggest where we should begin when teaching the skill to a naive learner.

For all examples of oral blending, the teacher says a word slowly. The learner then says the same word at a normal speaking rate. The subtype analysis of **words said slowly** reveals three large subtypes.

1. Words in which the parts are words familiar to the learner and there is a pause between the parts, e.g., **lawn** (pause) **mower**.

2. Words in which the individual continuous sounds of the word are held for a longer period of time than they are when the word is spoken at the normal speaking rate (**mmmmaaaannnn**). (Note that if a stop-sound occurs in the word, that sound would not be held: **mmmaaat**.)

3. Words in which the individual sounds are produced slowly and there are pauses between each sound, e.g., **mm** (pause) **aaa** (pause) **nnn**.

We can identify subtypes for these three main types. For instance, we could introduce words that have one part that is a word spoken at a normal speaking rate followed by sounds that are held for a longer than normal duration (**motorzzzzz**). Many other combinations are possible, such as sounds spoken at a normal rate with pauses between the sounds.

The subtype analysis shows us that the main groups are based on pauses (subtype 1) or exaggerating sounds (subtype 2). Subtype 3 is created by combining pauses and exaggerated sounds.

If we are to teach the skill of oral blending, we should teach all types. The most direct route would be to begin with subtype 3. This subtype would teach both the transformation created by pausing and that created by exaggerating sounds. Because this subtype presents both variations of the transformation, however, it is the most difficult subtype. We would arrive at the same conclusion if we simply asked which subtypes share the greatest amount of sameness with words spoken at a normal speaking rate. Subtype 3 obviously presents examples that share the least amount of sameness with the familiar word (the counterparts that are spoken at a normal speaking rate). Therefore, we would not introduce this subtype in the initial sequence if our goal is to begin with a sequence that is relatively easy.

Instead, we would consider either subtype 1 or subtype 2 for the initial transformation. Subtype 1 is the easiest subtype because the transformation involves only one alteration–eliminating a single pause. Subtype 2 involves transforming *each* sound to a sound of less duration. Since each sound must be modified, a more extensive transformation is implied.

Figure 8.5 presents a possible introductory sequence.

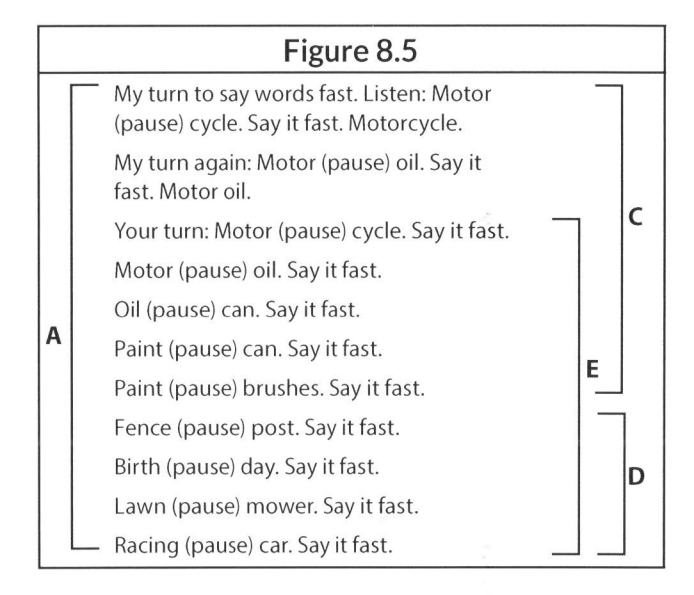

Figure 8.5

My turn to say words fast. Listen: Motor (pause) cycle. Say it fast. Motorcycle.

My turn again: Motor (pause) oil. Say it fast. Motor oil.

Your turn: Motor (pause) cycle. Say it fast.

Motor (pause) oil. Say it fast.

Oil (pause) can. Say it fast.

Paint (pause) can. Say it fast.

Paint (pause) brushes. Say it fast.

Fence (pause) post. Say it fast.

Birth (pause) day. Say it fast.

Lawn (pause) mower. Say it fast.

Racing (pause) car. Say it fast.

All examples in the series are of the same subtype. The first five words in the series are minimally different, arranged so that the change from one word to the next involves a minimum change. The changes are created by: (1) substituting a new last part while retaining the first part; (2) substituting the first part while retaining the last part; and (3) presenting a first part that had been the last part of the preceding word. The **D** segment of the sequence juxtaposes examples that are greatly different.

This subtype stipulates that the only way that unblended words are transformed into blended words (spoken at a normal speaking rate) is by eliminating pauses; therefore, we would introduce the subtype 2 as soon as the learner demonstrated a generalizable skill with the subtype 1 examples. This generalization should occur with the presentation of the first sequence or certainly with the presentation of a second sequence that introduces different subtype 1 examples.

Minimum Differences Within a Subtype

When we design a sequence for subtype 2, we discover that we are confronted with a new problem—a wide possible range of minimum-difference examples. According to our procedure for creating transformation sequences, we begin with a series of examples that are progressively minimally different (one change occurring from example to example). When we consider the range of variation that is possible within subtype 2, however, we discover that we may create examples that are so different that they may be difficult for the learner to discriminate. These minimum differences would be self-defeating because they would not show the learner how the transformation works.

The simplest way to determine whether the sequence attempts to include too wide a range of variation is to arrange the minimum-difference examples progressively (one change from example to example). *If it is not possible to cover the range of variation for a particular subtype through six minimum-difference examples, the subtype is too broad and will probably prove to be too difficult for the naive learner.* The remedy is to reduce the range of variation presented by the sequence or make the minimum-difference larger and therefore easier.

The sequence in Figure 8.6 illustrates the problem. The sequence attempts to show minimum differences for the full range of variations that would occur in a sequence that teaches the subtype 2 say-it-fast skill.

Figure 8.6	
Examples	Teacher Wording
Listen: aaammm	Say it fast.
Listen: aaannn	Say it fast.
Listen: iiinnn	Say it fast.
Listen: lllliit	Say it fast.
Listen: fffiiit	Say it fast.
Listen: fffllliiit	Say it fast.
Listen: fffllliiick	Say it fast.
Listen: fffllliiip	Say it fast.
Listen: sssllliiip	Say it fast.
Listen: sssiiip	Say it fast.
Listen: sssiiilll	Say it fast.
Listen: diiilll	Say it fast.
Listen: drrriiilll	Say it fast.
Listen: drrriiip	Say it fast.
Listen: trrriiip	Say it fast.

The seventeen examples in the sequence have not covered the range of variation for sounds in short words; therefore, presenting the smallest minimum differences for the subtype is probably unreasonable. The sequence would probably be too difficult for the naive learner. To correct the sequence, we would: (1) try to identify a range of variation that could be covered through no more than six progressively arranged minimum-difference examples; and (2) try not to create the smallest minimum differences available to us. (The examples that are particularly difficult in the sequence above are words like **flip, drill, drip,** and **trip**.)

The first six examples of a more appropriate sequence for introducing the subtype 2 say-it-fast words are presented in Figure 8.7.

Figure 8.7	
Examples	Teacher Wording
Listen: mmmeee	Say it fast.
Listen: mmmaaannn	Say it fast.
Listen: aaammm	Say it fast.
Listen: aaaat	Say it fast.
Listen: fffaaat	Say it fast.
Listen: fffeeet	Say it fast.

The sequence introduces two-sound words and three-sound words. It introduces words that begin with vowels, words that begin with a voiced consonant (**mmm**) and words that begin with an unvoiced consonant (**fff**). Only two vowel sounds are used in the words (**eee** and **aaa**). The minimum differences are not as fine as they could be (particularly with the first three examples). However, the sequence shows that changes in the vowel or changes in the consonants lead to changes in the word.

Feedback About Difficult Subtypes

The rule about limiting minimum-difference examples to six is a handy way to avoid possible difficulties. In the end, however, the subtype analysis will not provide us with precise information about how difficult the discriminations are for the learner. To determine difficulty, we must refer to the learner's performance. If we create a sequence that contains a subtype that is too "difficult," the learner's performance will provide clear evidence about the subtype. The learner will tend to miss items of that subtype and will not tend to miss items of other subtypes. Conversely, to analyze whether the learner has subtype problems, *we simply classify the errors the learner makes*. If all (or nearly all) items of a particular subtype are missed by the learner, the subtype is difficult. Note that the learner may make mistakes on items other than those of a particular subtype; however, if the learner misses nearly all items of a particular subtype, the sequence presents a subtype that is too difficult. To classify the items the learner misses, we determine if they are the same in some way. If we can identify features possessed only by these items (and not by other items), we identify the subtype.

Illustration. Let's say that the learner has trouble with the items marked with an **X** in the following say-it-fast sequence:

> My turn to say it fast: Listen: mmm-et. Say it fast: met.
> My turn again: vvv-et. Say it fast: vet.
> Your turn: fff-et. Say it fast. X
> j-et. Say it fast.
> b-et. Say it fast.
> p-et. Say it fast. X
> nnn-et. Say it fast. X
> sss-et. Say it fast. X
> mmm-et. Say it fast.

The learner misses four items: **fet, net, pet,** and **set**. We first try to determine if this set of items possesses a sameness not possessed by other items in the sequence. There does not seem to be any such sameness. Next, we see if we can identify a "trend." To do this, we try to find a sameness possessed by *most* of the mistaken items. Three of the missed items begin with an unvoiced sound (**fet, pet,** and **set**).

If the learner has trouble with this subtype, the learner should tend to miss items of the subtype whenever they appear. To determine the extent to which this happens, we examine the sequence to find unvoiced beginnings that were not missed. The conclusion is that although the learner missed the voiced-beginning word **net**, this miss was probably just a lapse of some sort. The major mistake tendency involves unvoiced beginnings.

To summarize the procedure for identifying subtype errors:

1. First determine if all items missed are of the same subtype.

2. If they are, examine the items not missed and determine the extent to which the learner consistently missed items of this subtype. A strong trend is indicated if the learner misses all items of a subtype.

3. If the items missed do not fall into an obvious subtype, try to divide them into groups based on common features. Identify the largest possible groups.

4. For each group identified, test the trend by examining the extent to which the learner consistently missed items of each subtype when they occurred in the sequence.

Remedies for Difficult Subtypes

If the learner's error pattern suggests a problem with a regular subtype (or subtypes), follow this procedure:

1. Create a sequence that is like the original sequence, but that does not contain the difficult subtype(s).

2. Create a second sequence that consists only of the difficult items. Present this sequence after the learner has mastered the first remedial sequence.

3. Present an integration sequence that consists of the subtypes that were presented in the original sequence and of the difficult-subtype items.

Note. This procedure would not necessarily be performed if the subtype was an irregular or contradictory subtype. The teaching and integration of such subtypes would be delayed until the learner is well-practiced in the regular subtypes.

Illustration. The mistakes on the earlier say-it-fast sequences suggest remedial sequences. First, a sequence is presented that is a variation of the original sequence with the difficult subtype removed (words that begin with unvoiced sounds).

> My turn to say it fast: Listen: mmm-et. Say it fast: met.
> My turn again: vvv-et. Say it fast: vet.
> Your turn: lll-et. Say it fast.
> j-et. Say it fast.
> w-et. Say it fast.
> b-et. Say it fast.
> nnn-et. Say it fast.
> g-et. Say it fast.
> y-et. Say it fast.

A second sequence would be presented next to teach the difficult subtype (unvoiced sounds).

> My turn to say it fast: Listen: sss-et. Say it fast: set.
> p-et. Say it fast: pet.
> Your turn: p-et. Say it fast.
> fff-et. Say it fast.
> t-et. Say it fast.
> sss-et. Say it fast. X
> ch-et. Say it fast. X

After the learner had successfully mastered both the remedial sequences, an integration sequence would be introduced. No examples would be modeled. The sequence would begin with minimum differences and would present both the difficult subtype and other subtypes. The integration sequence *begins with the most recently taught subtype or the most difficult subtype.* The reason is that performance on this subtype will tell whether the learner is "ready" for the remainder of the sequence. If not, we can add items to review the type before introducing the part of the sequence that presents the other types.

Advanced Applications

For sophisticated learners we may modify the transformation sequences in the same way we modify other sequences:

1. We do not model as many examples.
2. We do not model all subtypes.
3. We introduce new subtypes in the D segment of the sequence.
4. We shorten the entire sequence.

The use of transformation sequences is appropriate for teaching virtually any skill in which the learner is required to manipulate symbols. For the learner who is learning a foreign language, the sequence can be used to show how changes in the sentences signal changes in meaning. For the learner who is learning arithmetic, variations of the sequence may be designed to teach how to add ten to any number, how to multiply by a fraction to change any number into one, or how to express number values using exponents. The sequences are appropriate for teaching the learner what nouns, adjectives, and prepositions are. For each of these applications, the subtype analysis becomes important because of the wide range of minimally different types.

The sequence presented in Figure 8.8 shows the learner how to construct fractions that equal one.

Figure 8.8

1. My turn: If the top is twelve D, what's the fraction that equals one? Twelve D over twelve D.
2. My turn: If the top is twelve, what's the fraction that equals one? Twelve over twelve.
3. Your turn: If the top is two, what's the fraction that equals one?
4. If the top is seventeen, what's the fraction that equals one?
5. If the top is three plus R, what's the fraction that equals one?
6. If the top is 100 JD, what's the fraction that equals one?
7. If the top is nine over three halves, what's the fraction that equals one?
8. If the top is Z minus 5, what's the fraction that equals one?
9. If the top is two thirds, what's the fraction that equals one?
10. If the top is one, what's the fraction that equals one?

Items 1–2: C. Items 3–10: E. Items 4–10: D.

The **C** segment consists of three examples. Only two are modeled.

Examples 4 through 10 are juxtaposed to show sameness. Included in **D** are types that involve addition (**3 plus R**), subtraction (**Z minus 5**), fractions ($^2/_3$), and regular counting numbers (**17**).

Item 7 involves a fraction over a fraction (nine over three halves over nine over three halves). This subtype could be expected to present response-production problems for some learners (who may become confused about how many times to say the word **over**). The remedy would be: (1) remove the type from the sequence; (2) create a new sequence that involves only fractions over fractions; and (3) integrate the two types after the learner performs adequately on the fraction-over-fraction sequence.

The first part of a sequence to teach fractions over fractions follows:

1. My turn: If the top is two thirds, what's the fraction that equals one? Two thirds over two thirds.
2. My turn: If the top is twelve thirds, what's the fraction that equals one? Twelve thirds over twelve thirds.

3. Your turn: If the top is twelve thirds, what's the fraction that equals one?
4. If the top is three twelfths, what's the fraction that equals one?
5. If the top of the fraction is 12 over R, what's the fraction that equals one?
6. If the top of the fraction is A over 5, what's the fraction that equals one?

Etc.

Note that one of the modeled examples is presented as a test.

Each task in the sequences above begins with the same setup feature: "If the *top* is . . ." For the advanced learner there would be no particular problem with introducing a variation in the setup such as, "If the *bottom number* is . . ." To do this, we would add one more modeled example at the beginning of the sequence:

1. My turn: If the top number is twelve, what's the fraction that equals one? Twelve over twelve.
2. My turn: If the bottom number is twelve, what's the fraction that equals one? Twelve over twelve.
3. My turn: If the bottom number is twelve D, what's the fraction that equals one? Twelve D over twelve D.
4. Your turn: If the top number is 21 D, what's the fraction that equals one?
5. If the top number is two, what's the fraction that equals one?
6. If the bottom number is seventeen, what's the fraction that equals one?
7. If the bottom number is three plus R, what's the fraction that equals one?
8. If the top number is 100 JD, what's the bottom number?

Etc.

The items in the sequence after item 8 would refer to either the top number or the bottom number. Possibly, one or two more test items could be added to the sequence; however, the advanced learner probably would not need them.

Same-Response Minimum Difference

A unique minimum-difference is possible for many single-transformation concepts. This is the same-response minimum difference. This minimum difference involves a change in the example that results in no change in the response. Example 2 in the sequence just presented is a same-response minimum difference. Below is another example.

$$23 = \quad\quad \text{What's the answer? Twenty-three.}$$
$$= 23 \quad\quad \text{What's the answer? Twenty-three.}$$

The answer is the same even though a change has occurred in the example.

To decide whether same-response minimum differences should be introduced in the sequence, answer this question: Do *other* minimum differences involve the dimension or detail manipulated to create same-response minimum difference? If the answer is "Yes," same-response differences should be presented.

The example: =23 is created by moving the numeral across the equal sign. If we did not use this dimension of change (moving something across the equal sign) to create other minimum differences, the no-change minimum difference should not be introduced in the sequence.

Let's say that the equality sequence contained the following minimum-difference examples:

$$12 = (12)$$
$$12 + 1 = (13)$$

We showed that 12 is changed into 13 by adding a plus sign and a numeral. Since we introduced this dimension to show a change in value, we should introduce the same-response minimum differences involving the plus sign:

$$12 = (12)$$
$$12 + 10 = (12)$$
$$12 + 1 = (13)$$

The response to the first two examples is the same.

Consider another example, the beginning of a possible sequence for teaching the concept of **subject of a statement**:

Example	Teacher Wording
A fast runner went to the park.	My turn: What's the subject? A fast runner.
A runner went to the park.	My turn: What's the subject? A runner.
A little girl went to the park.	What's the subject?

The dimension manipulated is words in the sentence.

We can manipulate this dimension and *not change* the response from that of a particular example. We should therefore include same-response changes in the sequence as illustrated in Figure 8.9. The same-response minimum differences are in italics.

Figure 8.9	
Example	Teacher Wording
1. A fast runner went in the park.	My turn: What's the subject? A fast runner.
2. A runner went in the park.	My turn: What's the subject? A runner.
3. *A runner went up the hill.*	My turn: What's the subject? A runner.
4. Five girls went up the hill.	Your turn: What's the subject?
5. That girl went up the hill.	What's the subject?
6. *That girl sat on the hill.*	What's the subject?
7. Five men sat on the hill.	What's the subject?
8. A dog and five men sat on the hill.	What's the subject?
9. My cat ate beans.	What's the subject?
10. An old alligator was tired.	What's the subject?
11. He sang songs.	What's the subject?
12. My mother likes to cook.	What's the subject?
13. The yellow pencil and the white pencil are on the desk.	What's the subject?
14. She slept through breakfast.	What's the subject?
15. Phone books are very useful.	What's the subject?
16. A slow turtle sat on a log.	What's the subject?
17. They went in the park.	What's the subject?
18. Hank and Mary had an argument.	What's the subject?
19. That dream is interesting.	What's the subject?

This sequence may contain too many subtypes (suggested by the number of minimum-difference examples). The learner may have trouble with the single word subjects (**he, they, she**) and with the verbs other than action words (**is, has, are**). Note also that the sequence does not include subjects that contain **ing** words (*running is fun*), subjects that begin with the word to (*to work is fun*), or subjects that have verb words (*the best vacation we took was in Colorado*).

Figure 8.10 gives a sequence that presents a smaller range of sentences. The setup for this sequence is designed so that part of every predicate is the same. The same-response minimum differences are in italics.

The two sequences for presenting **subject of a sentence** represent extreme positions. The first sequence processes a wide range of subtypes and the second sequence involves a single relatively tightly circumscribed subtype. A very reasonable question is: Which sequence is appropriate for learner **X**? Stimulus-locus analysis is mute on this issue. The question is answered through a field tryout.

Figure 8.10	
Example	Teacher Wording
1. Fast runners went to the park.	My turn: What's the subject? Fast runners.
2. A runner went to the park.	My turn: What's the subject? A runner.
3. Five runners went to the park.	Your turn: What's the subject?
4. *Five runners played in the park.*	What's the subject?
5. That runner sat in the park.	What's the subject?
6. *That runner liked the park.*	What's the subject?
7. Henry's dog ran in the park.	What's the subject?
8. I went to the park.	What's the subject?
9. Those pigeons flew over the park.	What's the subject?
10. My brother hates the park.	What's the subject?
11. He wanted to go to the park.	What's the subject?
12. Her dog loves the park.	What's the subject?
13. Old people walk in the park.	What's the subject?

Recognize the limitations of the analysis. The analysis can tell us only how to achieve certain goals. If we want to show how two things are different from each other, the analysis provides us with specific procedures for doing so. The analysis suggests that if the sequence is guilty of stipulation, it must be followed by other sequences specifically designed to counteract this stipulation. If we decide that the learner should be able to handle a wide range of subtypes, the analysis suggests the most efficient procedures for communicating the sameness—juxtaposing examples that are greatly different (examples from various subtypes). If we discover that one of the subtypes included in the original sequence is difficult for the learner, the analysis suggests how we can make that subtype easier (by juxtaposing examples of the subtype with other examples of the same subtype so the learner does the same thing with juxtaposed examples). The fastest way to secure information about these "ifs" is to design a sequence that we judge to be slightly too difficult for the learner. This sequence could contain too many subtypes, too much variation, or subtypes that are too difficult. If our judgment is correct, we will observe a trend of mistakes.

Examples that Differ Only in Subtype Details

A final application of the subtype analysis is limited to some symbolic concepts. These concepts permit us to create a set of examples that is the same except for one part. For instance, if we were teaching the concept of **verb of a sentence**, we could create a series of examples that differ only in the verb. The other words in the sentence would remain constant. This type of sequence is, in one sense, analogous to the non-comparative and comparative sequences. The setup features are the same for every example and only a single dimension varies.

Figure 8.11

Example	Teacher Wording
1. She runs in the park.	My turn: The verb is run.
2. She ran in the park.	My turn: The verb is ran.
3. She will run in the park.	My turn: The verb is will run.
4. She would run in the park.	Your turn: What's the verb?
5. She was running in the park.	What's the verb?
6. She has run in the park.	What's the verb?
7. She ran in the park.	What's the verb?
8. She has been running in the park.	What's the verb?
9. She may have been running in the park.	What's the verb?
10. She should run in the park.	What's the verb?
11. She had been running in the park.	What's the verb?
12. She could have been running in the park.	What's the verb?
13. She is running in the park.	What's the verb?
14. She runs in the park.	What's the verb?
15. She might have run in the park.	What's the verb?

Figure 8.11 presents a sequence that employs this strategy. This sequence teaches the generalization of the different types of verbs. It shows that there are one-word verbs, two-word verbs, three-word verbs, and four-word verbs.

Note, however, that it does not teach different types of verbs. It stipulates that the verb may be limited to action words (or to the verb **run**). Subsequent sequences would be needed to introduce the different subtypes of verbs. The value of the sequence in Figure 8.11, however, is that it shows the general structure of all verbs.

Note that the sequence is based on subtype variations. The only difference from example to example is that the verb is of a different subtype.

To create subtype-variation sequences, follow these steps:

1. First determine whether it is possible to make examples that are identical except for the variation in the subtype.

2. Identify the various subtypes.

3. Follow the pattern (as closely as possible) for introducing minimum differences at the beginning of the sequence, followed by juxtaposed examples that differ as greatly as possible within the constraints of the setup.

Consider this type of sequence when the subtype analysis discloses that there is a staggering range of possible subtypes (as in the case of verbs). Instead of trying to design an initial teaching sequence that presents a single subtype (such as one-word verbs), consider an initial sequence that teaches a large group of subtypes. Usually, less stipulation will result from this strategy than results from the introduction of a single subtype. The reason is that the subtype sequence (with the only difference between examples being a subtype difference) shows the learner more about the concept than a series dealing with a single subtype can. If we initially introduce one-word verbs, we may induce serious stipulation about the structure of *all* verbs. We may have to introduce three or four subsequent sequences based on a single subtype before we effectively counteract this stipulation. *The subtype sequence shows the basic structure of all verbs through a single sequence.* The sequences that follow the first sequence simply show more about the range of variation (e.g., that the *subjects* can change without affecting the verb; that *different verbs* function the same way as **running** when they are substituted for **running**; that verbs function as verbs only when they follow the subject in a regular-order sentence; and that some words, such as **usually**, may split the verb). In the end, we are required to teach all these relationships. The subtype sequence provides us with the most efficient initial sequence.

Perspective

The subtype analysis raises an issue that we will encounter again—the easy-to-hard sequence. The traditional orientation to designing a program that proceeds smoothly is based on the idea that it is possible to identify examples of progressive difficulty. This orientation then draws the false conclusion that the most efficient program orders the introduction of the various subtypes identified in the easy-to-hard order, so the learner first masters the easiest subtype, then the second-easiest subtype, etc. There are two serious problems with this orientation. The most obvious is that it does not take into account the teaching of *sameness*. The easy-to-hard order is well designed not to show sameness across the subtypes, but instead to induce great stipulation. If we used this orientation to teach fractions, we would first introduce those that involve one piece of a pie ($1/2$ $1/3$ $1/4$). Working on this subtype first would induce serious stipulation. If we followed the example with another relatively easy type (whole numbers expressed as fractions over 1 ($5/1$ $7/1$ $4/1$), we would induce both reversals and further stipulation (that a fraction must have the number 1).

Certainly, the initial sequence should be easy. But ideally, it must also show the learner what is the same about all possible examples that the learner will deal with. Unless it conveys information about this sameness, it is a poor initial sequence.

A second problem created by the traditional easy-to-hard orientation is that the program typically begs the question of efficiency by using mastery criteria for each subtype. Although the sequence of subtypes from easy to difficult is poorly designed, the learner will most probably achieve mastery if enough trials are provided. However, the fact that the learner masters each subtype does not imply that the program is efficient. In fact, the mastery requirement may actually promote greater stipulation by requiring the learner to work on a relatively ungeneralizable subtype for a longer period of time than would be required if the mastery criterion were ignored.

We will return to the issue of easy-to-hard when we deal with more complex communications. The problem that we will deal with is the same one that emerged from the subtype analysis. We must show all types as quickly as possible. Only when we show the learner what is the same about all examples do we teach the concept. The longer we delay dealing with the full range, the more problematic the sequence of subtypes is.

Summary

We can present any concept as a choice-response discrimination. Some concepts, however, are transformations. Although there are many variations of transformation sequences, their structure is basically the same.

- Design the sequence so that the same wording is used for each test example and so this wording leads to different responses for examples that are different.

- Begin the sequence with a series of 4 to 6 minimum-difference examples. These should be arranged progressively, with a change in one detail occurring from example to example.

- Use no more than 6 minimum-difference examples to show the range of subtypes. If more than 6 are needed, the sequence probably covers too many subtypes. Adjust by removing some of the subtypes.

- If the total sequence involves more than eighteen examples, it is probably too long.

- After the minimum differences in the sequence, juxtapose examples that differ greatly (a change in more than one detail occurring from example to example).

- At least two examples should be modeled. Test on the rest. Limit the examples that are tested to those that are presented in the minimum-juxtapositions of the sequence. (For sophisticated learners, this requirement may be waived.)

- If the original sequence does not present the entire range of variation for the concept, it will be guilty of stipulation. Counteract the stipulation by following the original sequence with a sequence that counteracts the stipulation (negates it).

Two approaches are efficient for introducing a transformation that involves many subtypes:

1. Introduce a relatively large regular subtype and follow it with other regular or irregular subtypes.

2. Introduce a sequence in which the examples differ only in subtype differences; follow the sequence with others that expand the range of application for the various subtypes.

The second approach avoids possible stipulation more readily than the first; however, the first is analytically more predictable. We do not know how difficult an example of the second type will be. We can design the total teaching more easily if we use the first option, however. The reason is that this solution permits us to introduce one new subtype at a time.

Because transformations deal with concepts that have many possible minimum differences and a wide range of possible variation, the most efficient analysis of the concept involves identifying subtypes based on regularity (or generalizability) and difficulty (based on the number of behaviors called for to process the examples in a particular subtype). To perform the subtype analysis:

- Select a range of examples.
- Sequence them to show sameness.
- List the features that are the same for all members of a subtype.
- Apply the subtype analysis to determine possible initial sequences (a generalizable type that does not involve complicated behaviors).
- Apply the analysis to determine a strategy for introducing the other subtypes.
- Apply the analysis to determine whether the learner has difficulty with a particular subtype.
- Also use the analysis to deal with transformation skills that involve great variation across many dimensions.
- If the concept permits, design a transformation sequence in which the only difference from example to example is a subtype difference.

Transformations are very important concepts. The latitude that we have in introducing these concepts is much greater than that for basic-form concepts simply because transformations are joining-form concepts. Because they combine basic-form concepts, they generate a very large range of possibilities. If we combined the subjects (**he, she** and **it**) with the verbs (**runs, sits**, and **eats**) we have nine examples. If we include double and triple combinations (**he** and **she, sit** and **eat**), there are forty possibilities.

This great range of variation for transformation concepts suggests that there are many different strategies for approaching the teaching of a given transformation concept. A further implication is that we will not be able to teach the transformation through a single sequence. Although there are many possible efficient ways to approach a transformation, we must remember that the initial sequence is the most important. It should be very carefully designed to show as much as possible about the structure of the concept and the sameness across different examples. If the initial sequence is poorly designed (dealing with a small subset of examples), the teaching will become relatively inefficient. If in doubt about whether to start with a very easy (but possibly limited) subset, or to show sameness by including a wider range of variation in the initial sequence, show the sameness. The performance of the learner will indicate whether the subtype you select is too broad or difficult.

Chapter 9
Correlated-Features Sequence

The second-joining form, the correlated-features form, creates a joining quite different from the transformation joining. The transformation is a rule for replacing parts of a response with coordinate substitutions. The correlated-features joining involves linking things that happen to occur together. The goal of the correlated-features sequence is to teach the learner that the presence of specific stimulus features indicate *that other unobserved features or events also occur*. The features that are joined by correlated-features communications have names or labels. The joining involves two discriminations. One is shown; the other is not. The learner is asked to predict the status of the *unobserved discrimination* from the observed discrimination.

The communication of correlated-features is the transition between the immediately observable features of examples and the complete symbolized representation of events presented in facts (verbal statements). The correlated-features communication is most appropriate for teaching science rules, spelling rules, unfamiliar words that have familiar meanings, and similar applications.

Correlated-Features and Statements of Fact

The correlated-feature joining is the same type that occurs in statements of fact. By dealing with statements of fact, we observe the basic properties of the correlated-feature joining.

All facts may be regarded as having two parts and each part specifies a discrimination. The first part names an entity and the second part indicates the link or relationship between the entity named and some other features.

Here's a fact: **Ducks fly north in the spring**. The entity named is **ducks**. The discrimination correlated with **ducks** is **flying north in the spring**. If we accept this fact and saw a duck, we would know that the entity flies north in the spring. We would not have to observe this flying if we relied on the fact.

Another fact: **China cups are breakable**. The first-named entity is **China cups**. This entity is linked to **being breakable**.

Another fact: **Only small glerms with big ears hunt at night**. Even though we would not be able to identify concrete examples of "small glerms with big ears," this entity is named in the fact. The feature that it possesses is **hunting at night**. Therefore, if we are provided with information that a concrete entity is a small glerm with big ears, we would know that the entity hunts at night.

First-Mentioned Discriminations

All facts name two discriminations. Correlated-features joining is based on the discriminations that are joined in a particular fact.

The first-mentioned discrimination tells which examples are presented in a correlated-feature sequence. If we wish to teach the link that is expressed by this statement of fact: **hotter objects expand**, we would present hotter objects.

If the fact is: **ducks fly south in the spring**, we would present examples of ducks. If the fact is: **When the sound /oy/ occurs at the end of a word, the sound is probably spelled o-y**, we would present words with the sound /**oy**/ at the end.

How the Examples are Sequenced

The second part of the fact tells how the examples are arranged in the sequence. The second part implies either: (1) a transformation ordering of the examples; or (2) a simple single-dimension discrimination ordering.

Note that transformations are possible only if the first-mentioned entity is *symbolic*. The following fact implies a transformation: **Words rhyme with their ending**. (Rhyming with the ending can be demonstrated with a variety of words, each leading to a different rhyming response.)

The following fact does *not* imply a transformation: **Words are the basic unit of language communication**. (If something is a word, we draw one conclusion about it. It is the basic unit of language communication. The only response that is possible for any example of a word is that it is the basic unit of language communication or that it is not the basic unit of language communication.)

This fact does not imply a transformation: **Two digit numbers are bigger than nine**. (For any positive two-digit number, only one conclusion is possible: It is bigger than nine.)

This fact does imply a transformation: **The first digit of two-digit numbers tells the number of tens**. Every two-digit number has the property of telling the number of tens. (How many tens for this numeral?) Different answers are possible for different first digits.

If the second-named discrimination in a fact describes a transformation, arrange the examples as you would in a transformation sequence.

If the second-named discrimination in a fact does not describe a transformation, arrange the examples as you would for a basic sensory discrimination (either negative-first or positive-first).

Wording

The wording used for each example in a correlated-feature sequence consists of two questions.

The first question requires a conclusion. It asks about *what is not shown*.

The second question requires the learner to link the conclusion with the correlated-features of the examples. This question is: How do you know?

If the fact being taught is: **Hotter air rises**, we would show examples of hotter air and not-hotter air. We would first ask about *whether the air rises* (which outcome is now shown) and then, "How do you know?" The questions could be: "Will this air rise? . . . How do you know?" The instructions could be: "Tell me *rises* or *not-rises* . . . How do you know?" In responding to the two tasks, the learner responds to the *relationship* that is being taught.

Example	Wording	Response
Air gets hotter.	What will happen to this air?	It will rise.
	How do you know?	Because it got hotter.
Air does not get hotter.	What will happen to this air?	It will not rise.
	How do you know?	Because it didn't get hotter.

For positive examples of this relationship, the learner is saying "The air will rise . . . because it gets hotter," and for negatives "The air will not rise . . . because it didn't get hotter." The learner is predicting the outcome, by applying the rule to actual changes in the concrete examples. And the learner's pair of responses provide clear evidence that the learner is responding to the appropriate features of the examples and is linking these to the appropriate relationship.

Constructing Single-Dimension Sequences

1. To construct a single-dimension correlated feature sequence, we begin by constructing the fact that we wish to teach. That fact will provide us with the wording that we will use in the sequence. It will also imply the type of juxtapositions that we will use and the form of the primary task that we will present with each example.

If we wish to teach the notion that when free air becomes heated it rises, here is a possible expression of that idea: **Hotter air rises**.

2. We analyze the fact to determine whether the second part of the fact (rises) implies a transformation. Since the concept *rises*, *not-rises* is most appropriately treated as a single-dimension comparative, the second part of the fact does not imply a transformation.

3. We select the juxtaposition pattern that is appropriate for the second part of the fact. Since the second part of the fact **hotter air rises** does not name a transformation, we will use the juxtaposition pattern that is appropriate for single-dimension concepts.

4. We now create a sequence that would show the concept named in the first part of the fact (**hotter air**). We use the same juxtaposition pattern and the same examples that would be used to communicate **hotter air**.

5. We construct a pair of questions that is to be presented with each example, the first asking about *rising* or *not-rising*, the second asking "How do you know?"

Figure 9.1 presents a correlated-feature sequence for teaching the relationship between **hotter air** and **rising**. Note that the examples presented in this sequence are *sensory* examples. (The learner feels the differences from example to example. The numbers simply represent discriminable differences, with 4 and 5 being minimally different, but discriminably different.)

Figure 9.1

Heat Level of Example	Teacher Wording
4	I'm going to tell you whether this air would rise. Feel it now.
4	It won't rise. How do I know? Because it didn't get hotter.
3	It won't rise. How do I know? Because it didn't get hotter.
4	It will rise. How do I know? Because it got hotter.
7	Your turn: Will the air rise? How do you know?
9	Will the air rise? How do you know?
8	Will the air rise? How do you know?
1	Will the air rise? How do you know?
3	Will the air rise? How do you know?
2	Will the air rise? How do you know?
5	Will the air rise? How do you know?
5	Will the air rise? How do you know?
7	Will the air rise? How do you know?

Juxtapositions

The examples are the same as those used to teach **hotter** versus **not-hotter**. The juxtapositions are also the same as those used to teach **hotter** versus **not-hotter**. The sequence begins with a starting point, then two negatives, followed by three positives and a series of unpredictably ordered examples.

The A' bracket suggests a variation in wording conventions. Although the learner does the same thing with juxtaposed examples, the learner does more than one thing with each example. Therefore, an interruption occurs between answering different presentations of the question, "Will the air rise?" (Before another instance of this question is presented, the learner is presented with the question, "How do you know?")

Sequence Length

The sequence above is as long as it would be if we were designing a safe presentation for teaching **hotter** to a naive learner. The learner who is being taught the relationship **hotter air rises**, however, is not naive. The learner has already learned the component concepts, **hotter** and **rises**. Therefore, the sequence above is needlessly long. Remember, the goal is not to teach the component discriminations, but to establish the fact that rising depends solely on the relative temperature of the air (so far as the present relationship is concerned). Therefore, we can shorten the sequence. Figure 9.2 presents a shortened version that begins with one negative and two positives. Only the first two examples are modeled:

Figure 9.2

Heat Level of Example	Wording
4	Feel the air. I'm going to tell you if it would rise.
4	It won't rise. How do I know? Because it didn't get hotter.
5	It will rise. How do I know? Because it got hotter.
7	Your turn: Will it rise? How do you know?
7	Will it rise? How do you know?
2	Will it rise? How do you know?
5	Will it rise? How do you know?

The sequence consists of six examples, which is probably enough to establish the correlation.

Representations Rather than Real-Life Objects

Figure 9.3

Heat Level of Example	Wording
40	I'll tell you if the air rises. It starts out at 40 degrees.
40	Then it stays at 40 degrees. Did it rise? No. How do I know? Because it didn't get hotter.
50	Then the air goes up to 50 degrees. Did it rise? Yes. How do I know? Because it got hotter.
70	Then the air goes up to 70 degrees. Did it rise? How do you know?
70	The air stays at 70 degrees. Did it rise? How do you know?
20	The air goes to 20 degrees. Did it rise? How do you know?
50	The air goes to 50 degrees. Did it rise? How do you know?

We do not have to present sensory examples if there is no communication problem associated with representations of the sensory qualities. Let's assume that the learner understands the relationship between **heat increases**

Section III | Joining Forms

and **increases in number of degrees**. We could now teach the relationship **hotter air rises** by presenting *references to heat units* rather than direct sensory presentations. (See Figure 9.3.)

Note that the various temperature examples were created simply by adding a zero to each level shown in the preceding sequence.

Unambiguous Responses

The primary goal is to create communications that are consistent with a single interpretation. The sequence above prompts a possible misrule, which is that the **rising** refers simply to an increase in temperature (the temperature rises) not physical movement in the air. To correct this possible misrule, we could modify the primary response required by the learner. Instead of giving the learner the choice of labeling **rising** and **not-rising**, we could give the learner the choice of *showing* whether the air will rise or not rise. (See Figure 9.4.)

Figure 9.4
Wording
I'll point to show you which way the air moved as it got hotter and colder. It starts out at 40 degrees. Then it goes up to 50 degrees. Which way did it move?...How do I know it went up? Because it got hotter.
Then the air goes up to 40 degrees. Which way did it move?...How do I know it didn't go up? Because it didn't get hotter.
Then it goes to 20 degrees. Show me which way it moved.... How do you know it didn't go up?
Then it goes to 70 degrees. Show me which way it moved.... How do you know it did go up?
Then it goes to 90 degrees. Show me which way it moved.... How do you know it did go up?
Then it goes to 80 degrees. Show me which way it moved.... How do you know it didn't go up?

The wording is changed so that it refers to going up rather than rising. The reason is simply that the past tense of rising is *rose* and the question, "How do you know it rose?" does not parallel the question, "How do you know it didn't rise?"

The selection of examples is modified for practical reasons. There are no no-change negatives. The reason is that the fewer pointing conventions we introduce, the better. The sequence therefore presents a simple relationship. If the temperature goes up, you point up. If the temperature goes down, you point down.

Summary of Variations for Single-Dimension Sequences

We start with a fact that expresses a sensory-based link. If the second part of the fact does not suggest a transformation, we use the single-dimension sequence format. We *show* the first-mentioned discrimination in the fact. We present two questions. The first requires a conclusion about the feature *that is not observed*. The second question, "How do you know?" requires the learner to make an observation about the sensory evidence that led to the conclusion.

Because the learner already knows the component discriminations, we can shorten the sequence. We would retain at least one minimum difference juxtaposition, but we can probably shorten the sequence to 6 examples.

Because the learner is familiar with the component discriminations, we may be able to *describe* each example rather than presenting it as a sensory example.

Because the response the learner produces may be ambiguous, we can sometimes reduce the ambiguity by requiring the learner to point or to produce some other physical response.

Figure 9.5	
Example	Wording
40	This number tells how hot the object is. Watch the number. I'll tell you if the object gets hotter.
50	Did the object get hotter? Yes. How do I know? Because the number got bigger.
40	Did the object get hotter? No. How do I know? Because the number did not get bigger.
70	Your turn: Did the object get hotter? How do you know?
90	Did the object get hotter? How do you know?
80	Did the object get hotter? How do you know?
10	Did the object get hotter? How do you know?
50	Did the object get hotter? How do you know?

Illustration. If the learner does not know the conventions for expressing heat in degrees, we can design a correlated-feature sequence that demonstrates the relationship. We start with the fact: **When the number of degrees gets bigger, the object gets hotter.** This fact may seem backward. Why isn't it expressed this way: **When the object gets hotter, the number of degrees gets bigger?** The latter fact would require us to present examples of **hotter** and **not hotter**. The learner would have to respond by telling us if the number **gets bigger** or **not bigger**. If we present the numbers and require the learner to tell whether the object **gets hotter** or **not hotter** (or **hotter** or **colder**), however, we are provided with an unambiguous response. Figure 9.5 presents a possible sequence.

A variation of this procedure can be used to teach any measurement relationship. Note that the sequence assumes that the learner is attending to the numbers and does not misidentify them. The only way we would know whether this is the case, however, would be to require the learner to produce some sort of overt response. In other words, we would add an identification task to each example. Two test examples are shown in Figure 9.6.

Figure 9.6

Example	Wording
70	
90	How many degrees now? did the object get hotter? How do you know?
80	How many degrees now? Did the object get hotter? How do you know?

This procedure has both an advantage and a disadvantage. According to the wording-juxtaposition principle, the same wording on juxtaposed tasks is the easiest juxtaposition. The example that involves three tasks violates this principle, which means that the difficulty level of the sequence increases. The advantages are that: (1) the three-task examples permit us to introduce the label **degree**, and (2) they make all the steps overt, thereby reducing ambiguity about what the learner is doing to process the example.

Correcting Repeated Mistakes

If the learner has repeated problems with any correlated-feature presentation, the best procedure is to improve the wording juxtapositions. Simply remove the question, "How do you know?" from each example (and possibly increase the number of examples). If three-task examples are involved, eliminate two of them, retaining only the primary question. Figure 9.7 shows a correction sequence for mistakes on either of the temperature sequences above.

This sequence presents juxtaposed tasks that involve the same response dimension. The learner simply concludes

Figure 9.7

Example	Wording
40°	Watch the number. It tell how hot the air is. I'll tell you if the air gets hotter.
40°	The air didn't get hotter.
30°	The air didn't get hotter.
40°	The air got hotter.
70°	The air got hotter.
90°	Tell me about the air.
90°	Tell me about the air.
10°	Tell me about the air.
30°	Tell me about the air.
80°	Tell me about the air.

whether the air got hotter. The sequence presents a full range of examples. The same basic procedures would be used if the learner had trouble with the sequence for other relationships. Only *one task* would be presented with each example, the task requiring the learner to draw conclusions. Figure 9.8 below shows the first five examples of a possible simplified sequence for **hotter air rises**.

Figure 9.8

Example	Wording
40°	The number tells about the temperature of the air. I'll tell you whether that air goes up or doesn't go up.
30°	The air didn't go up.
30°	The air didn't go up.
40°	The air went up.
70°	Your turn: Tell me about the air.
90°	Tell me about the air.

The examples in these correction sequences are virtually identical to those used to teach sensory-based discriminations, but instead of asking about what is shown, *the question asks about a correlated feature.* It would be possible to present all correlated-feature sequences with only a single question. The problem is that this sequence suggests, for instance, that **going up** is simply another name for **getting hotter**. The question pairing that requires a conclusion and then an answer to, "How do you know?" prevents this possible misinterpretation. Following the presentation of the single-task sequence, we would again repeat the original sequence that requires answers to two questions for each example.

Section III | Joining Forms

Non-Comparative Correlated-Feature Sequence

The preceding examples have involved comparatives—the more one thing changes, the more another changes. Figure 9.9 shows a non-comparative correlated feature sequence.

Figure 9.9	
Example	Wording
	If a leaf that I show you has a pinnate pattern, it is an oak leaf.
	My turn: Is this an oak? No. How do I know? It doesn't have a pinnate pattern.
	My turn: Is this an oak? Yes. How do I know? It has a pinnate pattern.
	Your turn: Is this an oak? How do you know?
	Is this an oak? How do you know?
	Is this an oak? How do you know?

This sequence shows minimum-difference changes. Two examples are modeled (a positive and a negative) followed by three test examples. The sequence begins with a statement about the examples that are to be presented. The opening statement qualifies or limits the relationship to the set of examples that is to be shown. The teacher does not tell a "lie," which is what would happen if the teacher suggested that the presence of a pinnate pattern *always* predicts an oak leaf. The statement at the beginning of the sequence could be designed to make this point even clearer than it is in the sequence above: "I'm going to show some leaves that are oak leaves and some leaves that are not. The ones that are oak leaves have a pinnate pattern." A variation of this wording could be used in any case involving a relationship that is not limited to the concept shown. ("A rabbit has legs;" "Windows are pieces of glass," etc.)

Negative Wording

We might be tempted to avoid the problem of the qualified examples by using a negative rule, such as: "If a leaf has a *palmate* vein pattern, the leaf is not an oak leaf." Certainly this solves the problem from a logical standpoint. The problem comes when we create examples. Responses to *all* examples will contain negative wording, implying a tricky relationship between the vein pattern and the name. This wording creates a spurious transformation. (It's *not* an oak because it's palmate; It's an oak because it's not palmate.")

Figure 9.10 shows the first examples from a possible sequence based on negative wording:

Figure 9.10	
Example	Wording
	I'll tell you if these leaves are oak leaves. Is this an oak? No. How do I know? Because the vein pattern is palmate.
	Is this an oak? Yes. How do I know? Because the vein pattern is not palmate.

If possible avoid patterns in which the presence of something leads to a negative response. Try to make the rule of the form: *the presence of something signals the presence of something else.*

Correlations Involving and-or

Some relationships that we wish to teach involve the presence of more than one feature or the presence of either one feature or another feature. The structure of these relationships carries implications for the design of the sequence.

and. When dealing with a correlation that involves the conjunction of two properties (an **and** relationship), *begin with positive examples*. For example, this rule: "If it has stripes and it looks like a horse, it's a zebra," expresses an **and** relationship. For an example to be positive it must: (1) have stripes, **and** (2) look like a horse. If we begin with a positive example, *the first example* will *specify the criteria for classifying members as* **zebra** *or* **not-zebra**.

"My turn. Is this a zebra? Yes. How do I know? Because it has stripes **and** it looks like a horse."

If we begin with a sequence with a negative example (see Figure 9.11), however, both criteria are not mentioned with each example.

The presentation of two examples has not yet provided the information that *both* features must be present. The learner might believe that the criteria mentioned in examples 1 and 2 are two of many possibilities.

Figure 9.11

Example	Wording
(horse)	My turn: Is this a zebra? No. How do I know? Because it doesn't have stripes.
(tiger)	My turn again: Is this a zebra? No. How do I know? Because it doesn't look like a horse.

The problem is compounded if more than two criteria are used. "If the object grows, reproduces, and dies, the object is alive." This relationship would require a minimum of three negatives to present the three criteria. One positive would do the same job more clearly (e.g., "My turn: Is this object alive? Yes. How do I know? Because it grows, reproduces, and dies.").

or. Just as it is efficient to begin an **and** relationship with positives, it is efficient to begin an **or** sequence (disjunctive relationship) with negatives. By beginning with a negative for **or** relationships, we express both the criteria involved in the classification. Let's say the relationship is: "If it's a reptile, an amphibian, **or** a fish, it is cold-blooded." Figure 9.12 shows the information the learner receives through a negative example.

Figure 9.12

Example	Wording
Horse	My turn: Is this animal cold-blooded? No. How do I know? It's not a reptile or an amphibian or a fish.

If we begin the sequence with positives, we do not efficiently provide the learner with information about the criteria. Figure 9.13 shows a sequence that begins by presenting an alligator, a perch, and a frog.

At this point, the learner might assume that *all* vertebrates (including mammals and birds) are cold-blooded. After all, every type of vertebrate that is mentioned is cold-blooded.

Figure 9.13

Example	Wording
Alligator	My turn: Is this animal cold-blooded? Yes. How do I know? Because it's a reptile?
Perch	My turn: Is this animal cold-blooded? Yes. How do I know? Because it's a fish.
Frog	My turn: Is this animal cold-blooded? Yes. How do I know? Because it's an amphibian.

In summary, if a correlated-feature relationship involves **and**-criteria (the conjunction of two or more criteria), begin the sequence with positives.

If the correlated-feature relationship involves **or**-criteria (the disjunction of two or more criteria), begin the sentence with negatives.

Equivalent Meanings

An equivalent meaning is the substitution of one word or phrase for another that serves as an equivalent for the original. There are many different ways to teach equivalent meanings. Some are relatively faster and more efficient than others. We can teach a "definition" that indicates the relationship such as: "When something expands, it gets bigger." Then we can approach the definition problem as a transformation problem:

> I'll say things one way, you say them another way, using the word **expanded**.
>
> Listen: The cloud got bigger. Say it another way.
>
> Listen: The balloon got bigger. Say it another way.
>
> Listen: The steel ball got bigger. Say it another way.

A second way is to require the learner to correlate the meaning with actual examples. This procedure would be most appropriate for learners who had not demonstrated great proficiency in verbal transformations or who tended to play "word games" without actually attending to concrete examples. We would express the relationship as a fact: "When things get bigger, they expand." We would then present examples of things getting bigger or not-getting bigger. We would require the learner to indicate whether each example expands. Then we would require the learner to relate this conclusion to the features of the example. (Note that this treatment supposes that the learner already knows how to label examples as "bigger" and "not bigger.") This approach provides the most precise information about whether the learner is forming the appropriate relationship between sensory features, the familiar word (**bigger**), and the new word (**expand**). Figure 9.14 shows a possible sequence.

The primary question is designed so that the learner *produces* the word that is being taught. Instead of answering "yes" or "no" to a question such as, "Did the space expand?" the learner responds to, "What happened?" by using the word **expand**.

Remember, for equivalent meaning, ask first about the new word, then about the old. (The primary instruction could change to: "Tell me expand or not-expand." The second question would be: "How do you know it expanded?"

Figure 9.14

Example	Teacher Wording
Shows space between hands	
⌊⎯⎯⌋	Watch this space. I'll tell you if it expands or doesn't expand.
1. ⌊⎯⎯⌋	My turn: It didn't expand. How do I know? Because it didn't get bigger.
2. ⌊⎯⎯⎯⌋	My turn: It expanded. How do I know? Because it got bigger.
3. ⌊⎯⌋	Your turn: What happened? How do you know?
4. ⌊⎯⎯⎯⌋	What happened? How do you know?
5. ⌊⎯⎯⌋	What happened? How do you know?
6. ⌊⎯⎯⎯⎯⌋	What happened? How do you know?
7. ⌊⎯⎯⌋	What happened? How do you know?
8. ⌊⎯⎯⎯⌋	What happened? How do you know?

Verifying Conclusions

Developmentalists and those concerned with learning by doing, often exhibit an impractical approach to empirical relationships. The learner conducts an experiment and observes the outcome. From this conclusion, the learner is supposed to learn the correlation between the presence of some features and the presence of others. However, the communication is ambiguous. Let's say that an experiment is designed to show how low pressure affects the movement of air. One experiment involves turning on a shower and observing the direction in which the shower curtain moves. The learner concludes that the shower curtain moved toward the stream of water.

The learner might indeed learn about the correlation between the pressure of the air and the movement of the shower curtain from this presentation; however, the presentation is not designed to teach this relationship *because it shows the outcome before the learner predicts the outcome.* (The presentation is also poorly designed in a number of other ways. It does not provide for quick juxtaposition of examples that change along particular dimensions. It does not provide for wording that would assure precise communication of juxtaposed examples. It does not provide any sort of reasonable test of the generalization.) To communicate the desired relationship we would redo the communication to teach the fact: **Air moves toward a place of lower pressure**. (See Figure 9.15.)

Figure 9.15

Example	Wording
	My finger will point to the way the air moves. I'll tell you which is the place of lower pressure.
1. R (☝ J/P/T)	J is the place of lower pressure. How do I know? Because the air moved toward J.
2. R (☞ J/P/T)	Your turn: Which is the place of lower pressure? How do you know?
3. R (☝ J/P/T)	Which is the place of lower pressure? How do you know?
4. R (☟ J/P/T)	Which is the place of lower pressure? How do you know?

After the learner has demonstrated an understanding of the basic correlation, the learner could then apply the correlation to the actual-life situation (or an illustrated situation). This activity is perfectly reasonable as an application. However, it is not a reasonable presentation for teaching very much about the relationship. The learner who is first taught the basic relationship through a sequence such as the one in Figure 9.15 would be able to frame the application as a simple extension of the correlation. The learner is shown a diagram of a shower as in Figure 9.16.

Teacher: "The shower curtain doesn't move when the shower is not turned on. So circles R, J, P and T are not places of lower pressure." After the shower is turned on, the curtain moves toward R. (We can point to show the direction it moved.) "So which is the place of lower pressure?" (Point to R.) "How do we know? Because the air moved toward point R."

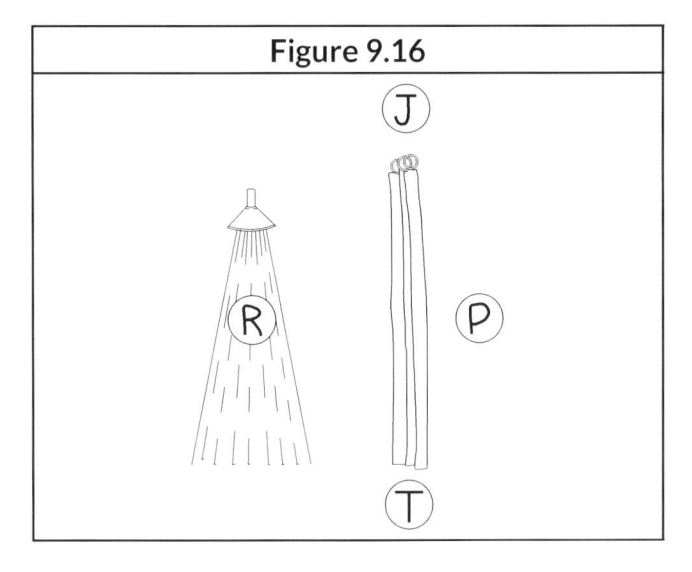

Figure 9.16

The application is now continuous with the general rule for air pressure. Similarly, every example of air movement can be diagrammed in exactly the same way as the shower problem.

When dealing with scientific facts, *provide the learner with verifications or demonstration that the "rule" does actually predict what will happen in real-life situations*. Provide this demonstration or verification, however, *after* the learner has demonstrated an understanding of the correlation of features implied by the fact. The initial instruction should require the learner to *predict* or draw a conclusion.

Correlated Features Involving Transformations

The sequences that we have dealt with are single-dimension sequences. The learner does not produce different responses for different examples. The learner, instead, classifies different examples—indicating whether each is a positive or a negative.

Correlated-features sequences that involve transformations are different. They do not require the learner to choose the class for various items, but to produce different responses.

The tasks require the learner to DO IT, not simply to CLASSIFY IT. This production requirement is a major difference between a transformation and a sensory discrimination. If the learner creates *different verbal responses* for different related examples, the correlated features is presented as a transformation.

If a transformation is involved, the fact we start with must meet two criteria:

1. It must begin by naming a class of things that are symbolic—any word, fractions that are more than 1, prime numbers, adjectives, contractions, vowels, inverted word orders, etc.

2. The second part of the fact must suggest a transformation relationship. If the second part describes a property that is possessed by a large number of examples, a transformation is implied. Any word that rhymes with its ending. Fractions that are more than one have numerators larger than denominators.

If a transformation is involved, it is possible to make up a number of examples, and each example will involve a different response.

We can demonstrate how a correlated-feature concept involving a transformation works by starting with this fact: **If you make the top and bottom of the fraction the same, you make a fraction that equals one whole**. The first part of the fact names a symbolic class—tops and bottoms of fractions. The second part of the fact suggests that a transformation is *possible*. If we try naming the fraction that equals one whole, we discover that there are many possible fractions that could be named. Therefore, we can design a task that requires the learner to name some of those fractions. The example could be fractions with either the numerator or denominator missing. The test tasks could be: "Make this fraction equal to one whole . . . How do you know it's equal to one whole now? . . ."

The transformation is not a necessity because *all discriminations* may be presented as choice discriminations (those that require the learner to classify examples). Only some, however, may be presented as transformations. Those are discriminations that deal with symbolic matter (words, numbers, etc.) organized in a manner that presents a parallel between changes in specific features of the examples and corresponding changes in specific parts of the responses.

Figure 9.17 and 9.18 show two sequences that derive from the fact: **If you make the top and bottom of a fraction the same, you make a fraction that equals**

Figure 9.17
A Choice-Response Sequence

Example	Wording
1. $\frac{5}{4}$	My turn: Does this fraction equal one? No. How do I know? Because the top and bottom are not the same.
2. $\frac{4}{4}$	My turn again: Does this fraction equal one? Yes. How do I know? Because the top and bottom number are the same.
3. $\frac{98}{98}$	Your turn: Does this fraction equal one? How do you know?
4. $\frac{7R}{7R}$	Does this fraction equal one? How do you know?
5. $\frac{7}{7R}$	Does this fraction equal one? How do you know?
6. $\frac{14}{8}$	Does this fraction equal one? How do you know?
7. $\frac{12}{12}$	Does this fraction equal one? How do you know?
8. $\frac{81}{5}$	Does this fraction equal one? How do you know?
9. $\frac{241P}{241P}$	Does this fraction equal one? How do you know?

Figure 9.18
A Transformation Sequence

Example	Wording
	I'm going to show fractions that equal one, but part of each fraction is missing.
1. $\frac{12D}{\square}$ =1	My turn to say the fraction that equals one: 12D over 12D. How do I know 12D over 12D equals one? Because the top and bottom are the same.
2. $\frac{12}{\square}$ =1	My turn again: What fraction equals one? 12 over 12. How do I know it equals one? Because the top and bottom are the same.
3. $\frac{2}{\square}$ =1	Your turn: Say the fraction that equals one. How do you know?
4. $\frac{\square}{2}$ =1	Say the fraction that equals one. How do you know?
5. $\frac{\square}{17}$ =1	Say the fraction that equals one. How do you know?
6. $\frac{\square}{3+R}$ =1	Say the fraction that equals one. How do you know?
7. $\frac{100R}{\square}$ =1	Say the fraction that equals one. How do you know?
8. $\frac{\square}{2/3}$ =1	Say the fraction that equals one. How do you know?
9. $\frac{5R/7}{\square}$ =1	Say the fraction that equals one. How do you know?

one whole. The first sequence treats the relationship as a single-dimension discrimination and uses a choice-response test. The second sequence treats the relationship as a transformation and requires the learner to produce the various transformation responses.

The sequence begins with a negative and three positives, followed by a range of test examples. The learner is required to classify each example.

The correlated feature transformation sequence in Figure 9.18 presents the same basic examples that appeared in Chapter 8 as a single-transformation sequence dealing with fractions equal to one.

The transformation sequence begins with progressive minimum differences, examples in which either the top part or the bottom part is missing. The fact that both bottom numbers and top numbers are replaced in the sequence may seem to be in violation of the setup principle. Actually, however, example four shows that the variation in setup is needed because it serves as a "same-response difference" (i.e., the response for example 4 is the same as that for 3).

The learner is required to say the fractions that equal one. The learner is then required to indicate why the fraction equals one.

To create a correlated-features transformation sequence, follow these procedures:

1. Create the same order of examples that would be used for a single-transformation, starting with a series of progressive minimum differences and then proceeding to greater differences.

2. Use the same primary question that would be used for a single transformation. (This question is the same one presented with each example.)

3. Follow with the same second question used for choice-response correlated features sequence– How do you know?

Creating a correlated-features transformation sequence is not difficult if you think of it as a single transformation sequence (perhaps somewhat abbreviated) with two questions for each example instead of one. The question that is added is: "How do you know?"

Which Sequence?

We have introduced four different sequences that could be used to teach concepts such as fractions that equal one—the single transformation, the correlated-feature choice response, the correlated-features transformation, and a choice-response single dimension discrimination sequence. Which sequence is most appropriate? In most cases, either the single transformation or one of the correlated-features sequences would be preferable. The reason is that these give us more information about what the learner is attending to. *These sequences make the responses that are relevant to processing the various examples more overt.* The more overt the procedure, the less ambiguity there is about what the learner actually does when making a mistake, and what sort of correction is implied.

When dealing with symbolic concepts, remember that it is possible to present either single-dimension discrimination sequences or transformation sequences. If it is possible to express a fact about correlated features (such as, **when the top and bottom of fractions are the same the fraction equals one**), a correlated-features sequence may be used. For the strongest responses from the learner, use a transformation sequence or a correlated-features sequence that is based on the transformation sequence. Figure 9.19 (pg 122) diagrams the choices.

Two important points about this decision flow chart are:

1. The question: "Can a fact be designed to express the relationship of correlated features?" can always be answered, "*yes*." If we know what the features are and how they work, we can always make up a fact that expresses the relationship. The test of whether we should use a particular fact depends on the amount of teaching required to prepare the learner. A fact names various discriminations. If it names many discriminations the learner probably does not know, a great deal of teaching must be provided before we can teach the new concept. Is it worth teaching these component skills so that we can teach the fact? If not, the option is to treat the discrimination as a single-transformation concept and not require the learner to express the relationship between correlated features.

2. The ease of producing the responses should be seriously considered in deciding whether to use a choice-response or a transformation. If the fact that we make up is very long, even though it involves no new concept, the juxtapositions are weakened. Think of the fact as interference that occurs between examples in which the learner does the same thing. The longer the fact, the greater the interference. The longer fact also increases the probability that the learner will have response problems. A similar problem occurs when the fact is shorter, but involves expressions that are difficult to produce. If we have reason to believe that the fact is "difficult," we should not introduce a correlated-features transformation sequence.

Applications

Many rules for arithmetic, spelling, decoding, and language comprehension can be processed through correlated-features transformation sequences.

Figure 9.20 shows a sequence in which a side of an equation is either "revalued" or "rewritten." It is revalued if the amount on the side is changed. The implication is that the other side must be changed by the same amount. The types of revaluing and rewriting are limited to operations and notations the learner already understands. Note: The teacher points to the left side when presenting all tasks.

This sequence may have too many minimum-difference examples for a transformation; however, the value on the left side for all examples is near 5; therefore, the minimum-difference does not apply in a strict fashion. There is a large difference between example 5 and example 6 although the amount on the right side is the same.

The presentation may be ambiguous because we do not know whether the learner is actually figuring out the amount on each side. To correct this problem, we could add a question for each example (e.g., *How many are on this side now?* What do we have to do with the other side? Why?).

The advantage of this solution is that it makes the operation overt. The problem with this solution is that it weakens the wording juxtaposition.

Another possible solution would be to use simpler examples, or to first go through the sequence asking the single question, "How many are on this side?" After the learner has responded correctly to the items in the sequence, we can present the two-question sequence with reasonable

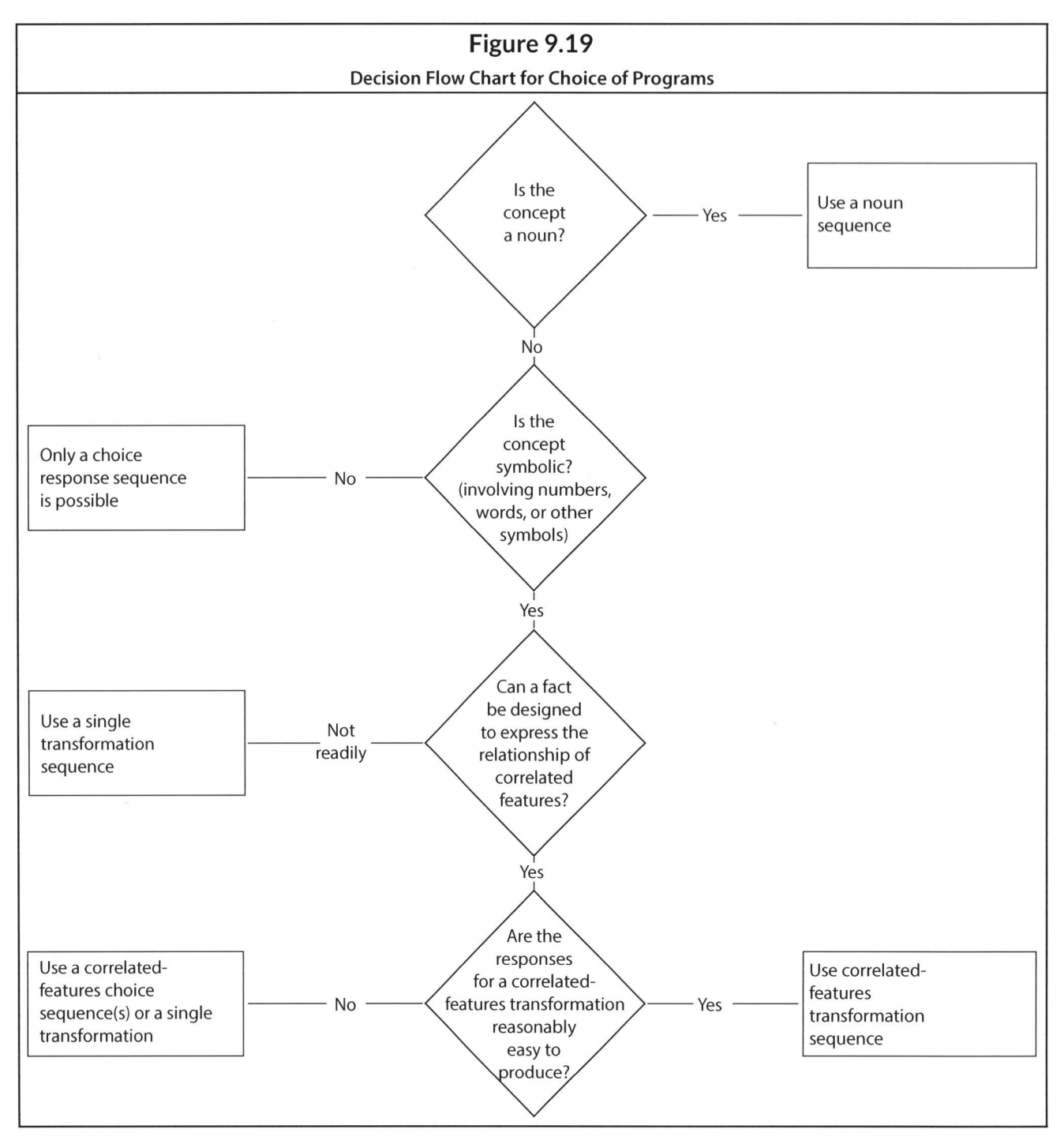

Figure 9.19
Decision Flow Chart for Choice of Programs

- Is the concept a noun? — Yes → Use a noun sequence
- No ↓
- Is the concept symbolic? (involving numbers, words, or other symbols) — No → Only a choice response sequence is possible
- Yes ↓
- Can a fact be designed to express the relationship of correlated features? — Not readily → Use a single transformation sequence
- Yes ↓
- Are the responses for a correlated-features transformation reasonably easy to produce? — No → Use a correlated-features choice sequence(s) or a single transformation
- Yes → Use correlated-features transformation sequence

certainty that the learner is correctly figuring out how many are on the left side.

The wording of the second question for the sequence above is, "Why?" This wording is sometimes possible and may be more appropriate than, "How do you know?" However, the wording, "How do you know?" can be used in nearly every situation, including the sequence in Figure 9.18. If in doubt, use the wording, "How do you know?"

The correlated-features transformation sequence may also be used for reading and spelling rules. Since these rules are not universal, the sequence must begin with some sort of limiting statement (see Figure 9.21).

Figure 9.20

Example	Wording
1. 5 = 5	Here's the equation we start with. I'll make changes. I'll tell you if each change means that we have to change the other side of the equation.
2. 4 + 1 = 5	My turn: What do we have to do with the other side? Nothing. Why? Because we didn't revalue the side.
3. 4 + 1 + <u>1</u> = 5	My turn again: What do we have to do with the other side? Add one. Why? Because we added one to this side.
4. 4 + 1 + <u>1 - 1</u> = 5	My turn again: What do we have to do with the other side? Nothing. Why? Because we didn't revalue this side.
5. 4 + 1 + <u>1 - 1 - 1</u> = 5	Your turn: What do we have to do with the other side? Why?
6. 6 - 1 = 5	What do we have to do with the other side? Why?
7. 6 - 2 = 5	What do we have to do with the other side? Why?
8. 5 x 3 = 5	What do we have to do with the other side? Why?
9. 5 x 2 = 5	What do we have to do with the other side? Why?
10. 5 x 1 = 5	What do we have to do with the other side? Why?

All words are presented in written form. Not all are real words. The instruction at the beginning of the sequence indicates that the vowel is either /ā/ or /ă/. A variation of the sequence would have to be repeated for other vowels (**o**, and **u** particularly).

Divergent Responses

A very difficult communication problem is associated with divergent responses, situations in which responses are acceptable and the learner produces a set of them. The teacher must have a solid understanding of responses that are not acceptable. Figure 9.22 shows the first part of a divergent-response sequence.

Often a modification is possible by restricting the learner's behaviors. For example, we might present a list of word beginnings: **s, st, l, b, bl, br** . . . We could then instruct the learner to use any one of these beginnings to make up a word that rhymes with **and**.

Figure 9.21

Example	Wording
	For some words below the vowel is /ā/. For others it is /ă/.
1. ate	My turn: What is the vowel in this word? /ā/. How do I know? Because the word ends with **v c** and **e**.
2. at	My turn: What is the vowel in this word? /ă/. How do I know? Because the word does not end with **v c** and **e**.
3. rat	Your turn: What's the vowel in this word? How do you know?
4. rate	What's the vowel in this word? How do you know?
5. rafte	What's the vowel in this word? How do you know?
6. rafe	What's the vowel in this word? How do you know?
7. safe	What's the vowel in this word? How do you know?
8. stand	What's the vowel in this word? How do you know?
9. ale	What's the vowel in this word? How do you know?
10. Stane	What's the vowel in this word? How do you know?
11. malte	What's the vowel in this word? How do you know?

Figure 9.22

Example	Wording
and	My turn: Band rhymes with **and**. How do I know? Because band ends in **and**.
and	Your turn: Make up another word that ends in **and**. How do you know that _____ rhymes with **and**? Etc.

For subsequent tasks, we could tell the learner: "Use another beginning to make up a word that rhymes with **and**." This procedure provides the learner with more options about the word that is created and about the order or sequence of examples. At the same time, it assures that the range of acceptable variation will be covered. There is nothing wrong with divergent-responses. Ultimately, we want the learner to produce examples of what we have taught. The problem is simply one of manageability. The communication must be effective. If we work one-to-one with the learner, such communications are easily created. Working with more than one learner implies much more careful treatment of divergent-responses, at least for the initial instruction.

Summary

The correlated-features relationship can be expressed as a fact. The first part of the fact tells about the particular entity or concept that is correlated with some other features. The second part of the fact describes these features. There are two basic types of correlated-features sequences—those that require choice-responses for each item and those that require production-responses. The choice-response sequences are science-type rules, non-symbolic relationships, or an expression that means the same thing as a familiar expression. The production-responses involve transformations and deal with symbolic matter.

To create a correlated-features sequence:

1. Start with a fact.
2. If the fact deals with things or events in the physical world, begin the fact by naming those things that lead to the outcome or the things that **cause** the event. Answer the question: "How do you make that outcome?" or "What must happen?"
3. If the fact deals with an equivalent meaning for a familiar expression, express the fact so that *the familiar expression comes first:* e.g., **If it is cut out of something, it is excised from that thing**. If the fact involves a transformation, express the fact so that the learner would be required to produce different responses for different examples. Remember, transformations are sometimes possible; however, they are *never* the only choice that is available. The second part of a statement of fact tells if a transformation is possible.

If the sequence does not involve a transformation, model the ordering of examples after the sensory-discrimination sequences.

1. Shorten the sequence.
2. Reduce the number of examples modeled.
3. Present two questions with each example. The first question directs the learner to respond to a discrimination that is not shown (the discrimination mentioned in the second part of the fact). The second question ("How do you know?") requires the learner to relate this conclusion to observable features of the example (the discrimination named in the first part of the fact). Stated simply, the examples show one thing and the learner uses this information to draw a conclusion about something else.
4. If the fact deals with conjunctive criteria (**and**), the sequence should begin with the modeling of a positive.
5. If the fact deals with disjunctive criteria (**or**), the sequence should begin with the modeling of a negative.
6. If the learner is familiar with the discrimination named in the first part of the fact, examples may be *described* rather than presented as sensory examples. We may describe the position, the temperature, the color, or whatever discrimination is named first.
7. If the learner's correct responses are possibly ambiguous, we could change the primary question into an instruction that requires the learner to produce a stronger response (pointing or producing some other unambiguous choice response).

Try to avoid wording that requires the learner to relate negative features of one thing to positive features of another. Avoid fact statements such as: "If it isn't ___, then it is ___." or "If it doesn't ___, then it is ___." Try to phrase the fact so the presence of one feature cues the presence of another. "If it is ___, then it is ___."

A correlated-features transformation sequence is desirable if:

1. The relationship deals with features of symbols.
2. The relationship can readily be expressed in words the learner understands.
3. The fact is not inordinately long and does not require responses that would probably be difficult.

To create a correlated-features transformation sequence:

1. Simply add a second question for each example in a regular transformation sequence. The question that is used for a single-transformation sequence is the primary question. The second question is "How do you know?" or "Why?"
2. If the fact used to generate the sequence is true only for a particular subtype, use general instructions

to limit the application of the fact to the examples that are presented. Instead of suggesting that the fact holds for all examples, start out by telling the learner that the fact applies only to the examples that are presented. This procedure is usually more effective than qualifying with the word *usually* or with longer explanations.

Remember, all discriminations can be treated as variations of basic sensory discriminations and can be processed through sequences that present choice-responses. Some discriminations may also be presented as transformations. Some transformations may be capable of being expressed as a fact that deals with all words or mathematical operations of a particular type, etc. For these, the correlated-features transformation sequence may be appropriate. However, many options are possible.

SECTION IV
PROGRAMS

A program is more than one sequence designed to achieve a given teaching objective. Although a wide variety of possible program formats exist, there are six basic functions for programs and therefore six types of basic cognitive-skill programs. These are:

1. Programs designed to introduce *coordinate members* or skills.
2. Programs designed to introduce *higher-order and lower-order members.*
3. Programs designed to teach the *component of a task that will be presented to the learner.*
4. Programs designed to teach *the relationship between sets of single-transformation concepts.*
5. Programs designed to teach the features of *an event or organization of related facts.*
6. Programs designed to *reduce prompting and stipulation* that occur as a function of the initial-teaching sequences.

1. Programs for Coordinate Members

A member is a stimulus that calls for a particular response or set of responses. When we teach the learner to identify the letter **m**, we teach a member: **m**. When we teach the learner **higher than**, the concept **higher than** is a member. When we teach the learner **under**, **under** is a member. The term *member* assumes that there are coordinate members that are the same in some ways as a given member. If **under** is a member, coordinate members would include **on, over, next to, between**, and other labels that function in the same way as **under** with respect to position. The simplest demonstration that the members are coordinate is that something cannot be both **under** and **on** the same target at the same time. (It is possible for the object to be **on** one target while being **under** another target; however, the concepts are the same with respect to their *function* in describing position.) Another way to identify members is to start with a sentence, such as "The ball is **under** the table." By replacing the word **under** with other words that refer to different positions, we identify various potential members.

If we teach the learner to identify the letter **e**, we teach a member. Coordinate members would include other letters: **t, m, b**, and so forth. These have the same symbolic role as **e**. All are in the class of things called "letters."

The programs that are designed to introduce coordinate members are based on objectives such as: "The child should be able to identify the individual letters;" or, "The learner is to discriminate various prepositions;" or, "The learner is to identify various parts of speech;" or, "The learner will read single-digit numerals."

The rules and suggestions for designing a coordinate-member program focus on procedures for separating highly similar members and for introducing new members at a reasonable rate. *These rules apply to concepts that are introduced in all program types.* The general rule is that highly similar teachings or members should be *separated* in time. Note that this rule applies to *programs, not to individual sequences.* The procedures that have been presented for sequences are not affected by what happens in a program. If we introduce the letter **b** as the first member to be identified in a program, we will not introduce **d** or **p** next. If we introduce the discrimination **on** as the first member, we will not introduce **under** next. If we introduce a rule for spelling words in which letters are dropped, we will not immediately follow it with a rule that presents an exception. Remember, we will not require the learner to learn one set of behaviors and then immediately learn new, highly similar behaviors. We will separate the instruction for the highly similar members.

2. Programs for Higher-Order and Lower-Order Members

This program is more complicated than that for the coordinate members because it introduces more than coordinate members. It also introduces a *higher-order relationship.* For instance, if we teach (from the beginning) a concept, such as **vehicles**, we must do more than introduce the coordinate members—**truck, car, bus**, etc. We must also introduce the relationships between these coordinate members and the higher-order label, **vehicle**. If the learner already knows many higher-order relationships and their conventions, the teaching of **vehicles** could be handled with little more effort than would be implied by the teaching of the coordinate members. If the learner is relatively unpracticed with the higher-order relationship, the program is fairly complicated.

Some complications result from the verbal conventions that we typically use to describe higher-order relationships. The convention problem can be seen by referring to a physical object, such as a truck. It is possible to say, "That truck is a vehicle." It is also possible to analyze the features of the truck that make it a vehicle (the features that **truck** shares with other objects that are vehicles). However, the statement "That truck is a vehicle" is quite different from the statement "That truck is red," or "That truck is on the table." **Red** and **on the table** refer to possible variables. Not all trucks are red, and not all trucks are on the table. The statement, "That truck is a vehicle" implies that **is a vehicle** is a variable; however, it is not. All trucks are vehicles. We must convey this fact to the learner.

3. Programs That Derive From Complex Tasks

Many instructional situations begin with the identification of an objective. This objective may be established as a task, such as, The learner will apply this rule: *The closer one is to the equator, the less the sun's rays will deviate from the perpendicular during any time of the year.* Note that we are neither suggesting that this rule is expressed well or that it should be introduced without reference to other things that are to be taught. If, for whatever reason, the rule is identified as something the learner is to be taught, we are provided with a basis for a possible program. The learner may not know **deviates from X, perpendicular during any time**, and **equator**. If the rule is introduced without preteaching these concepts, we will seriously violate our basic tenet of teaching only one thing at a time. A *program* is therefore implied by the task. Before we present the task (the rule), we will teach the meaning of the component discriminations contained in the task. Each skill identified in the task could be treated roughly as a "coordinate" member. The program therefore consists of teaching the coordinate members and then teaching the rule that integrates them.

4. Programs for Showing the Relationship Between Two Single-Transformations

The single-transformation concept involves an unstated rule that permits the generation of various responses. Single transformations, however, are often closely related to each other. For example, a single-transformation involves constructing fractions from pictures of pies. For a picture that shows two-thirds of the pie, the learner writes: $\frac{2}{3}$. Let's say that we wished the learner to express the same relationship as $3\overline{)2}$. If the learner knows how to construct fractions from the picture, the division notation can be taught as a relationship, not as a discrimination that is entirely new. The reason is that there is an unstated rule for converting any fraction into a division notation. That rule involves tipping the fraction over in a clockwise direction and modifying the line that separates the two numerals. For instance, if we start with $\frac{6}{2}$, we rotate it in a clockwise direction: $2|6$, and modify the line: $2\overline{)6}$. If the learner already knows one way to express a fraction, the most efficient program involves showing the learner the relationships between the familiar notation $\frac{2}{3}$; and the new notation $(2\overline{)3})$.

This relationship is referred to as a double-transformation. Any member of the first set (any fraction) can be converted into a member of the second set (the division notation) by performing the same transformation. Many relationships of this sort occur in instruction. To show the relationship, we first establish the original transformation (fractions). We then introduce the second transformation (the division notation) through juxtapositions that show *how the members of the new set are the same as members of the original set (their value) and how they are different (their notation).*

5. Programs for Teaching Systems of Related Facts

To explain the basic organization of the respiratory system, a communication would explain the role of the various features—providing information about the lungs, the tubes that transport air to the lungs, the movement of the diaphragm, the blood vessels, etc. This communication teaches a system of facts—not individual discriminations, but a set of discriminations. Another system might be the organization of a school—the administrator, the relationship of the school to the central board, the functions of the various departments and teachers within the school, and so forth. The program for teaching a system of related facts is different from any of the preceding programs because it requires strong emphasis on communicating information about how the various features of the system are related. The program involves presenting the preskills that may be needed before the total organization or system is presented. The program also involves techniques for teaching the system itself—showing how features are relevant to the system's structure or function.

6. Programs that Reduce Prompting and Stipulation of Initial Teaching Sequences

Initial-teaching sequences prompt the learner by juxtaposing examples that involve the same response dimension. These sequences also produce some stipulation. Instruction is therefore not completed when the learner performs successfully on an initial-teaching sequence. A program is needed to reduce the juxtaposition prompting that occurs in the initial teaching sequence and to counteract stipulation. The procedure for reducing juxtaposition prompting is to "shape the context" in which a given response is produced. A response to a test item in an initial teaching sequence is highly prompted because it immediately follows demonstration examples that prompt the response. To shape the context of the response, we change the juxtaposition pattern, so the learner is required to respond when the task is not immediately preceded by demonstration examples. To reduce stipulation, we present a much broader range of examples and tasks than the initial-teaching sequence provides. Following the initial teaching of **steeper**, the learner would be presented with a variety of tasks involving **steeper**. These would show objects different from those presented in the initial-teaching sequence. Also, the wording of these tasks would vary more.

Section IV presents the first five programs listed above. It does not present programs that reduce prompting and stipulation. The design of these programs is detailed in Section V (Complete Teaching), Section VI (Constructing Cognitive Routines), and Section VII (Response-Locus Analysis).

Chapter 10
Introducing Coordinate Members to a Set

New juxtaposition problems arise when we introduce a number of coordinate members to a set (such as the numerals 1 through 10, the letters **A** through **Z**, or the name of seven appliances). Each member has a new label and it involves new features. Both label and features must be discriminated from all other members that have been taught. The questions associated with the introduction of coordinate members are:

1. How should we expand or review the members that have been introduced before we introduce a new member?

2. What criterion should we require the learner to meet on discriminating between those members that have already been introduced before we introduce a new member?

3. Should the order of introduction juxtapose members that differ *minimally* from each other in either label or features, or should the order juxtapose members that exhibit large differences?

The Problem of Cumulative Review

When we introduce different members, we must provide *a cumulative review*. A cumulative review is a test of all coordinate members that have been taught (or a test limited to those members that have been taught and that might be confused with the new members on the basis of sameness of label or sameness of features). Let's say that we have introduced the reading words **hit, pot, pin,** and **it**. If we add the word **pit** to the set, we must make sure that the learner can discriminate between **pit** and all the other words. If the learner is not required to discriminate between all these words, the learner may not learn that the middle sound distinguishes **pit** and **pot, that the beginning sound distinguishes hit** and **pit** and **it,** and that the ending sound distinguishes **pin** and **pit**.

The cumulative review must be designed so the learner is required to deal with all the words, not with the words two at a time. An inappropriate procedure would involve first requiring the learner to discriminate between examples of **pit** and **hit,** then to discriminate between **pit** and **pin**, then to discriminate between **pit** and **it**, and then to discriminate between **pit** and **pot**. It is quite possible for the learner to learn from such a presentation. The procedure does not require the learner to discriminate between the features of **pit** *and the cumulative features of the set*. Therefore, it does not assure learning. A test that presents all the words—**pit, pot, pin, it, hit**—in a random order is much more difficult than the test involving pairs of them. The test involving pairs requires the learner to attend to *any difference* between a pair of words. Any difference will permit the learner to discriminate reliably and successfully. The cumulative test, which *requires the learner to discriminate all words, requires the learner to attend to the differences between the features of the word* **pit** *and the features of all the other words.*

The Discrimination Model

Table 10.1 shows a simplified representation of nine members of a set. The table refers to features **A** through **E**. Each member has some of these features. The letters that are not in parentheses stand for features that are possessed by a member. Letters in parentheses stand for features absent in the member. Any absent feature is present in some other members. The features **A** through **E** *do not exhaust the features of the members*. Each member may have hundreds of additional features. These features are not listed because they are shared by all nine members. The features that are listed are the only *differences* that are relevant to the task of discriminating between all members.

	Table 10.1 A Hypothetical Set of Members								
	Set Members								
	1	2	3	4	5	6	7	8	9
Features	A	A	A	A	A	A	A	(A)	(A)
	B	B	(B)	B	B	B	(B)	B	(B)
	C	(C)	C	C	C	(C)	C	C	(C)
	(D)	(D)	(D)	(D)	D	D	(D)	D	D
	(E)	(E)	(E)	E	(E)	(E)	E	E	E

Theory of Instruction: Principles and Applications

Assume that the members are introduced one at a time, starting with 1 and proceeding through 9. Unless the learner attends to all features of member 1 (features **A** through **E**), the learner will confuse member 1 with at least one of the other members when all nine have been introduced. Here is how an awareness of each feature helps the learner discriminate between member 1 and the other members.

Awareness of feature	Rules out
A	9, 8
A + B	9, 8, ⑦③
A + B + C	9, 8, 7, 3, ②
A + B + C + (D)	9, 8, 7, ⑥⑤, 3, 2
A + B + C + (D) + (E)	9, 8, 7, 6, 5, ④, 3, 2

The circled numbers indicate any additional members ruled out by awareness of the additional features. It is a logical axiom that if the learner attended to only feature **A**, the learner would discriminate consistently between member 1 when it was presented in the context of member 8 and member 9. However, the learner would not discriminate between 1 and any of the other members (2, 3, 4, 5, 6, 7).

The "concept" of a given member varies according to the composition of the set of members. Within the context of members 1, 8, and 9, the concept for member 1 can be any combination of features that reliably permits the learner to discriminate between member 1 and the other members in the set. The learner's concept could be **A** or absence of **D** or absence of **E** or any of these features in combination with other features.

As the membership of the set increases, the demands on the learner's "concept" increase. When all nine members have been introduced, we can infer that the learner's concept for member 1 is: **A, B, C, (D), (E)**. This unexpressed "rule" for identifying 1 is the only rule that will permit the learner to discriminate consistently between member 1 and the other members. Therefore, if the learner consistently discriminates between member 1 and the other members, we may assume that the learner's concept of member 1 must be: **A, B, C, (D), (E)**.

Perhaps the most difficult notion to grasp is that there is no absolute "concept" of member 1. The concept is relative to the composition of the group of members that must be discriminated. As the composition of the set changes, the concept for a given member changes. When the set is small, the learner's concept may be any of a *range of possible concepts* (possible references to different features). The concepts in this range include any combination of features that permit the learner to reliably discriminate between the members. As the composition of the set changes, the range of options available to the learner ultimately diminishes until the learner must attend to the only differences that actually discriminate the members from all the other members.

The Uncontrolled-Feature Misrule

The analysis of introducing members to a set suggests a new type of misrule. When members are added to a set, we begin with members that are different. They may be different in many ways. Only some of these differences are "valid" differences, which means that only some will serve the learner when other members are introduced to the set. We do not have a handy way to point out which features or differences are valid or functional. We can only show which are critical to the present discriminations.

There are two possible solutions to the problem:

1. Design the order of introducing members so that it juxtaposes *minimally-different* members.

2. Use procedures to assure that early in the program the learner attends to features other than those that distinguish members introduced early.

The problem with solution 1 is that it places severe memory demands on the learner. If members are highly similar in name, the learner must learn two names for highly similar members and must learn which name goes with which features of the examples. The naive learner may remember the names but may become confused about "associating" the right name with particular features. If the members are highly similar in form, the chances are increased that the learner will not attend to the small differences and may have "reversal" problems (confusing **n** and **h**, for example). Because of the problems associated with introducing members that are minimally different, we will not use this procedure, although it may be the most efficient procedure in some situations. The order of introduction that we will use juxtaposes *greatly different members.*

Solution 2, requiring the learner to attend to a wide range of features, can be achieved by *following the introduction of a member with application activities.* If the learner "constructs" examples of the early members or engages in activities that require the learner to use the discriminations in other contexts, the learner will attend to additional details of the members. If the learner is required to print or copy the letters when they are introduced, the learner will have far less trouble discriminating between **n** and **h** than the learner would if no such activities were introduced. The copying of the first letter introduced (**n**) *forces the learner to attend to details of the letter that are not needed to discriminate from greatly dissimilar members introduced early.* The assumption is that if the learner can copy or create an example, the learner has demonstrated an understanding of *all* features that are relevant to the member, and the learner should not have serious trouble discriminating the member from others as the set of members increases.

In summary, the order of introduction that we will use does *not* juxtapose minimally-different members. (If we introduce **b** as the first letter to be identified, we would not introduce **d** next.) We will use a *maximum-difference order*, which shapes the context of each member by increasing the sameness shared by that member and other members. First, the member is associated with members that differ from it in many ways. Identification of the member is relatively easy because: (1) any difference or combination of differences between the members serves as a reliable basis for the discrimination; and (2) the learner will probably attend to *some* differences. The members **s** and **b** differ in many ways. If the set contains only **s** and **b**, any difference between the members may be selected to discriminate between the members. The learner is not forced to select a *particular* feature.

As new members are introduced to the set, the context shaping occurs because the number of feature options available to the learner is reduced.

Following the introduction of each new member is a careful *expansion* of that member. The expansion calls attention to features of each member that are not essential and facilitates attention to essential features.

Rules for Ordering Members of a Set

We can arrive at a workable order of introduction by following two ordering rules. These rules take into account the fact that some members are quite similar to others and that highly similar members must be included in the set at some time.

Ordering rule 1. Arrange members so that minimally different (highly similar) members are separated by two or more non-similar members. Here is an order for introducing the letters **b** and **d**:

b n s e k **m** j v **d**

The letters **b** and **d** are separated by seven members. Note also that **m** is separated from the highly similar **n** by three members. This order, therefore, is consistent with the rule: separate highly similar members from each other by two or more members. The sequence below is not consistent with the rule.

b s e **m** k **n** v **d**

The members **m** and **n** are separated by only one dissimilar member.

Ordering rule 2. Separate introductions that involve minimum-differences by at least one introduction that does not involve minimum differences.

An introduction that involves minimum differences occurs *when the second members of a minimum-difference pair is introduced into the set*. In this set:

b m s e k

no serious minimum differences in features are involved. (There is a letter name minimum difference involved when **e** is introduced. The name for **e** is highly similar to that for **b**.) In the set below, however, **n** is added and a minimum difference in feature results. This minimum difference occurs when the second member of a minimum-difference pair is introduced.

b **m** s e k **n**

Rule 2 indicates that you should avoid successive introductions that involve minimum differences. Accordingly, the order below would be inappropriate because it introduces **d** (which is minimally different from **b**), immediately after **n** is introduced.

b **m** s e k **n** **d**

When **n** is introduced, minimum difference is involved (**m-n**). The next introduction introduced **d** and requires minimum difference labeling of **b-d**. Note that **d** is not similar to the preceding member, **n**. The introduction of **d**, however, calls for minimum-difference teaching. On two successive introductions, the learner is engaged in minimum differences. The learning requirements placed on the learner are reduced if we separate these minimum-difference introductions and interpolate introductions that do not involve minimum-differences. Here is an acceptable variation:

b m o e s n k d

This sequence violates rule 2:

p n s o k r b e j

A minimum difference introduction is required at **r** (for **n-r**). On the next introduction (**b**), minimum differences are involved for **p-b**. Here is one of many possible solutions:

n p s r o k b

The following sequence would not be acceptable, however, because it violates rule 1:

p n s r o k b

Although the introductions that involve minimum differences are separated by two members, **n** and **r** are separated by only a single member (**s**).

Minimum Differences in Examples and Labels

As we have seen from other minimum-difference sequencing problems, there may be minimum differences in the features of the examples, in the label, or in both. Members should be separated if they are minimally different in either features of the examples or in label. The best procedure for ordering members is to:

1. Identify the various minimum-difference pairs, whether they involve labels or features of the examples.
2. Position *one member* of each minimum-difference pair at the beginning of the sequence (unless the members of different pairs are similar to each other).

Let's say that we were sequencing some lower-case letters that are to be responded to with the letter *sound*. And let's say that these are the minimum-difference pairs: **n-ŭ, ĕ-ĭ, ŭ-ŏ**. Note that the last two pairs involve minimum differences in label or response (the letter sound), not in the features of the examples. The short-**e** sound is highly similar to the short-**i** sound. Also, the short-**u** sound is highly similar to the short-**o** sound. Here is a possible sequence:

u i s n t e k o

The introduction begins with **u** because **u** is involved in two minimum-difference pairings (**n-u** and **o-u**). The next member, **i**, is involved in one pairing (**e-i**). Neither **n** nor **o** appear near the beginning of the sequence because they are minimally different from **u**. The strategy of identifying the pairs of minimum differences and the placing of one member of each pair near the beginning of the sequence makes the job of ordering the members much easier.

Identifying minimum differences. Minimum differences are not absolute. They vary considerably from set to set. To determine which members are *relatively* minimally different from the others, use the principle of conversion. Begin with a member. Convert it into another member (convert **n** into **u**) and observe the number and type of steps that are involved in the conversion. Now compare that conversion with a conversion of the original member into a third member (convert **n** into **l**). Does one conversion *clearly* involve fewer steps or smaller steps? It is not always possible to specify which of the minimum-difference pairs is "most" minimally different. For instance, is the pair **n-u** more minimally different than the pair **n-r** or **n-h**? This question cannot be answered because a completely different type of conversion is involved. If there were three letters: **n, r, r**, we could specify that the pair **n-r** is more minimally different than **n-r** because fewer conversion steps are involved. Similarly, if there was the letter **ɲ**, we could specify that the pair **n-ɲ** is more minimally different than the pair **n-h**, again because fewer conversion steps are involved.

The comparison of **n-r, n-u,** and **n-h** is difficult because the conversions are generically different. One involves the position or orientation of the member, while the other two involve line deletion or line extension. Just as we cannot analytically determine whether **n-u** is more difficult than **n-r** or **n-h**, we cannot analytically determine whether **n-u** is more difficult than the short sounds **o-u**. One conversion involves *changes in the example*: however, **o-u** involves *changes in the letter sound*. (The short-**o** sound is more similar to the short-**u** sound than it is the short-**i** sound.)

Some members differ minimally from other members in *both* features and sound (**m** and **n**). If possible, design the order of introduction so that you separate each member from a counterpart that is highly similar. Try not to become embroiled over the issue of which members are *most* minimally different. You can compare minimum differences only if you can place the members on the same continuum of change (such as change in position or change in length of lines).

Other factors that determine the order of introduction. The similarity of members is not the only criterion for determining an order for introducing members of a set. *Immediate utility is an important consideration.* If our goal is to introduce letters that are most useful in making up regularly-spelled words, utility would be considered first. The letters **x, z,** and **q** would not occur early in the set of letters regardless of how dissimilar they are to other members. These letters are not as useful as **r** or **s**, **d** or **e**, in forming words that are familiar to the learners.

Finally, we may find through empirical investigation that some members are chronically confused, even though they are not highly similar in either appearance or name. For example, we may discover that many learners confuse the numerals 9 and 10. We can explain the confusion as a function of their proximity in the counting order. But this problem may not be obvious from an analysis of the members and their features. In any case, the confusion implies that the members should be separated.

In practice, it is impossible to specify an order of introduction that successfully meets three or more criteria. (As the applications above illustrate, it is difficult enough to sequence on the basis of a single criterion.) The instructional designer must strike a reasonable compromise. The most flagrant similarities in shape must be separated. The minimum-difference introductions should be distributed and not piled up at the end of the introduction sequence. An attempt must be made to introduce members that are useful. And the *most important* empirical information about members that are most chronically confused must be honored. The order, however, may not fully satisfy rules for separating members, the criterion of utility, and the mandate suggested by empirical information about specific members.

Scope of Rules

Although we have illustrated the application of the rules only with letters, the rules hold for anything that is taught. If we introduce three spelling rules that involve changing **y** to **i**, we do not sequence these rules so that one follows the other. We separate the **y**-to-**i** rules with spelling rules that have nothing to do with the letters **y** or **i**. We also separate the *introductions* of spelling rules that involve pairs of highly similar rules. The teaching of appliances, tree names, or operations for dealing with fractions are treated in the same manner. Each new thing taught is treated as a member. Also, introductions that involve minimum-difference pairs are separated by introductions that do not involve minimum differences.

The idea is to place each new thing taught in a context that is relatively easy for the learner. After the learner masters the member in this context, we change the context, making it more difficult and requiring attention to additional details.

Teaching Procedures for Introducing a New Member to the Set

Let's say that we have arrived at an order of introduction for the members of a set. We now consider the procedures for introducing each member. The first member must be introduced. Later, the fourth and fifth members are to be introduced. With the introduction of each member, three activities occur:

1. Initial teaching of the new member.
2. Expansion activities.
3. Cumulative review of the members already introduced.

Initial teaching. A new member should not be introduced until the learner is quite firm on all activities involving *members already introduced* to the set. The new member is taught through an appropriate sequence; comparative, non-comparative, noun, transformation, or correlated-feature. If we are teaching prepositions, the introduction of a new member would be achieved through a non-comparative sequence. If we are teaching names of numerals, each new member would be introduced through a noun sequence. If we are teaching a set of rules about pressure, we would introduce the new member (new rule) through a correlated-feature sequence.

Each new member would be taught through variations of the appropriate sequence *on two or three consecutive lessons.*

Expansion. Expansion activities begin immediately following the completion of an initial-teaching sequence (assuming that the learner successfully completes the initial-teaching sequence). These activities introduce new setups and new response forms. Worksheet activities may be part of this expansion. (These activities are outlined in Section V, Complete Teaching.)

Cumulative review activities. In its simplest form, the cumulative review is a series of test items containing examples of the most recently-taught member and some of the other members. The cumulative review also may be presented through worksheets or as a verbal activity.

If only a few members are to be introduced into the set, the cumulative review is easily achieved. Before the next member is introduced, the learner is presented with a "test" of *all* previous members that have been taught. The test is modeled after an E2 test of the noun sequence, with no predictable pattern to the juxtaposition of items. When the number of members in the set becomes large, however, the mechanical problems associated with the cumulative review become exaggerated because including all members becomes impractical.

Designing Reviews

The most difficult part of the procedures for introducing new members to a set is the review, particularly when a large number of members has already been introduced. To assure that each new member is presented within the context of the members that have already been taught, the review activities are designed according to these five criteria:

1. The review set should contain no more than six members (If you have taught 3 members before introducing the new members, the review set will consist of 3 members. If you have already taught 5, the review set will contain 5. If you have taught 34, the review set will contain 6.)

2. The member most similar to the new member is included in the review set.

3. The two members most recently introduced are included in the set. If the letters **l, s, p, m, o, t, e,** and **r** have been introduced in the order indicated, the two members preceding **r** are **t** and **e**. These members would be included in the review set that follows the initial teaching of **r**.

4. The member *most frequently missed* during previous review exercises is included. Let's say that learners most frequently misidentified **t**. This letter would be included in the review set.

5. The two members that have been *least* frequently presented during the last three or four review exercises should also be included.

Illustrations of Review Sets

1. The learner has been introduced to these letters: **m, o, t, e, r**. The next symbol to be taught is **v**. Here is the review set: **m, o, t, e, r**. Why are all members included? The number of members is less than six; therefore, all are included.

2. The learner has been introduced to these numerals: **1, 6, 4, 7, 5, 9, 8, 10**. The new member to be introduced is **3**.

    a. The member most highly similar to **3** is either **5** or **8**.

    b. **10** and **8** will be included in the set because each is a recently introduced member. (**5** therefore becomes the "highly similar" member.)

    c. **9** is the most frequently misidentified number, so it is added to the review set.

    d. The members **1** and **4** have been introduced least frequently during the last four review exercise. They are added, bringing the number of members in the review set to six: **10, 8, 5, 9, 1, 4**.

(Note that both **8** and **5** are introduced as highly similar members.)

Illustration of Initial Teaching, Expansion, and Review

To summarize, the three major activities involved in the introduction are introducing the new member, expanding the new member, and presenting a cumulative review that includes the new member.

If the new member is a noun, it is introduced according to the noun-sequence rules. Following the introduction of the new member comes the expansion activities. Following the expansion activities comes the cumulative review. All three activities may occur on the same day or lesson.

Initial teaching. Let's say that the learner has been introduced to these letters:

e s d m t o r

Chapter 10 | Introducing Coordinate Members to a Set

The learner identifies the letters by their sound, not the letter name. The next letter to be taught is **c**. The sequence used for initial teaching is a noun sequence. The "negatives" for a noun sequence are those members most highly similar to the members being taught. The letter **e** is similar in appearance to **c**. So is the letter **o**. The letter **t** is similar to **c** in sound. For the new teaching (to a fairly sophisticated learner), these three letters become the negatives. Here is a possible sequence:

Example	Teacher Wording
c	This is c.
c	What sound?
c	What sound?
o	What sound?
e	What sound?
t	What sound?
c	What sound?

Expansion Activities. Immediately following the initial teaching are *expansion activities*. The teacher presents a group of letters:

c o c t c c e c o t c

"See if I can fool you. When you hear me make a mistake, say 'stop'."

Teacher touches **c**. "This is c."
Teacher touches **o**. "This is c. What sound is it?"
Teacher touches **c**. "This is c."
Teacher touches **t**. "This is t."
Teacher touches **c**. "This is c. What sound is it?"

The teacher presents a worksheet activity:

"You're going to copy the new sound. What sound is it?
"Every time you make a **c**, you have to say the sound out loud. Put your pencil on the ball and follow the dotted lines for each c in the first row."

The instructions about saying the sound are important. If the learner does not say it, the connection between the features of the example and its name may not be established.

Cumulative review. On the next lesson, the initial teaching is repeated (with a sequence containing **c, o, e** and **t**). It is followed by another copying task. The copying task is followed by a cumulative review activity. The members included in the cumulative review with **c** are:

e and r	(the most recently taught)
o	(the most similar)
m and d	(the least frequently reviewed)
t	(the most frequently missed)

Example	Teacher Wording
m	What sound?
c	What sound?
d	What sound?
t	What sound?
c	What sound?
e	What sound?
r	What sound?
o	What sound?
c	What sound?

No examples are modeled. The examples are sequenced according to the sameness principle. Note these other points about the review sequences:

1. The most recently taught member (**c**) is included more than one time (three times in the sequence above).

2. Each of the other members appears only once; however, if the learner is particularly weak on one of the other members (such as **t**), this member could be repeated.

3. The order of examples in the sequence does *not* correspond to the order in which the members were originally introduced.

If the learner performs well on the sequence, a new member is introduced. If the learner performs poorly, the introduction of a new member could be delayed. This assures that the learner is firm on the discrimination of all members that have been introduced.

Theory of Instruction: Principles and Applications

The basic procedure outlined above for introducing, expanding, and reviewing would be used for teaching any new members to a set.

The initial teaching sequence teaches the relevant details of the new member. The expansion activities follow the initial teaching sequence and introduce an expanded context. The cumulative review assures that the learner learns the differences between the newly-taught member and the features of all other members in the set.

Minimum-Difference Introductions

When the second member of a pair of minimally-different members is introduced, the learner must discriminate between minimally-different examples. The circled members in the order of introduction below indicate the places at which minimum-difference discriminations occur.

b m s e k n j l d

When the letter **n** is introduced, the learner must discriminate between **n** and **m**. When **d** is introduced, the learner must discriminate between **d** and **b**. If the learner is quite naive and would be expected to have response problems, we follow the variations for teaching **n** that are described in Chapter 6. First **n** is introduced in an easy context (with highly dissimilar examples such as **s** and **b** as "negatives"). When the learner has demonstrated proficiency with **n** in this context, the regular noun sequence is introduced. This sequence consists of examples of **m** and **n**.

If no response problems are anticipated, the basic noun sequence can be presented for the initial-teaching sequence. A possible sequence follows. Note that the sequence is a "straight" noun sequence with only the most minimally-different member included in the sequence.

Example	Teacher Wording
n	This sound is *n*.
n	What sound?
n	What sound?
m	What sound?
n	What sound?
m	What sound?

Following the introduction of **n** is the introduction of **j**. This introduction occurs possibly two days after the first initial teaching of **n**. Since the learner has not been taught members that are highly similar to **j**, we are free to select negatives from any members that have been taught. The members **k** and **b** are more similar to **j** than the other members are because **k** and **b**, like **j**, are "taller" letters. Here is the first initial teaching sequence for **j**.

Example	Teacher Wording
j	This sound is j.
j	What sound?
b	What sound?
j	What sound?
b	What sound?
k	What sound?
j	What sound?

Possibly two lessons later, after **j** has been taught, expanded and reviewed, the next sound, **l** is introduced. Like **j**, it is not highly similar to any of the previously taught members; therefore, the initial teaching sequence would include **l** and possibly other tall examples–**j** and **k**, or **k** and **b**.

Following the expansion and review of **l**, the final member, **d**, would be introduced. The minimally different member known to the learner at this time is **b**. Therefore, **b** would be included in the initial teaching sequence (unless response problems were anticipated).

Example	Teacher Wording
d	This is d.
d	What sound?
b	What sound?
b	What sound?
d	What sound?

Charting a Schedule

When we deal with a large set, the integration of various activities–expansion, worksheets, reviews–is simplified by charting the introduction of members. When charting, follow these basic rules:

1. Provide initial teaching for at least two consecutive lessons.

2. Immediately follow the teaching with expansion activities.

3. Expansion activities continue after a member has been introduced.

4. Review occurs immediately **before** we introduce the next member.

By following these rules, we limit the rate at which items are introduced. We assure, however, that the introduction is careful and that the learner indeed learns each discrimination.

Figure 10.1 shows a schedule for introducing the meaning of new vocabulary words in a language program.

The first word is introduced on lesson 50, at which time the learner has already been taught fourteen vocabulary words.

The cumulative reviews occur immediately before the introduction of the next word (lessons 52, 55, 56, and 59). Note, however, that lesson 56 does not introduce a new word. It is a consolidation lesson (like 55) that involves expansion activities and review.

With facile learners it is possible to introduce the words faster, perhaps at the rate of one word a day. After ten lessons, however, we would have to provide a review before introducing the next block of words. The rate that is most appropriate for a group of learners can be determined by observing performance on the activities that are presented. A rule of thumb, however, would limit the rate of introduction to an average of one new item every two lessons.

The activities above do not comprise an entire lesson, merely a part. The time required by each activity should average no more than two minutes, which means that the vocabulary should require no more than six minutes a lesson.

Applications

As noted earlier, the principles for introducing members to a set apply to any set of coordinate or associated concepts, discriminations, or responses. For example, if we teach different hierarchical classes, each class is coordinate. Let's say that we plan to introduce: **tools, household appliances, furniture, articles of clothing, food, names of rooms in a house, animals, plants, things to read, vehicles** and **containers**. For each class, the learner would be required to use the class name and also to identify the various subclass members. ("This piece of furniture is a couch . . . this tool is a hammer.") Since each *class* is coordinate, each is treated as a *member*. The members are introduced according to the same procedures used for simple members. If **tools** is introduced first, **household appliances** would not follow, because household appliances are minimally different from tools. **Tools** would have to be separated from **household appliances** by some members that are not similar to tools–possibly animals or plants. Also, we would separate the teaching of **plants** and **food**. The teaching involved in the introduction, review, and expansion for the hierarchical classes is more involved than the teaching for letter names. Also, the discrimination teaching for similar members is more involved. However, the introduction sequence follows the same rules used in introducing members in a set.

Other types of coordinate members would be *facts* or *rules*. Let's say that we wish to teach the learner facts about different people and different dates. For each of these facts we ask a question, and the learner produces a verbal response. Like other members, facts may be similar to each other. These facts should be separated. The ordering of the different facts should follow the procedures outlined above.

Another type of coordinate members might be responses to different commands. You tell the learner, "Touch your nose," and the learner responds. The teaching involved for these responses is different from concept teaching. However, if we are going to teach more than one response, we should consider each task to be taught

Figure 10.1										
	sensitive	sensitive		articulate	articulate			obsession	obsession	
Initial Teaching	X	X		X	X			X	X	
Expansion	X	X	X	X	X	X	X	X	X	X
Cumulative Review			X			X	X			X
Lesson	50	51	52	53	54	55	56	57	58	59

a member, and we should order these members so that similar commands are separated. For example, we would not teach: "Touch your *nose*," "Touch your *mouth*," and "Touch your *knees*," in that order. We would separate the commands because they are similar to each other either with respect to the features of the command or the features of the response. Touching the nose and touching the mouth are similar responses. "Touch your nose" and "Touch your knees" are similar *sounding* commands. To separate these, we would interpolate commands that are quite dissimilar from them. Perhaps we would start with "Touch your nose." Follow it with the commands "Clap," "Smile," and "Touch the floor." Next, we could introduce "Touch your mouth."

Even complicated operations should be treated as members. Let's say that we wished to teach clearing the denominator and finding a common denominator. We treat each of these operations as members, and we separate them by interpolating members that are not similar (such as dealing with exponents and solving ratio problems).

Remember, if teachings are coordinate or associated, treat the teachings as members and separate them so that similar members are not juxtaposed in the order of introduction, and so that no juxtaposed members involve minimum-difference teachings.

Introducing Related Subtypes

The transformation chapter (Chapter 8) presented a procedure for analyzing subtypes. These subtypes are like unrelated members (such as **s** and **e**) in that the examples of a subtype are different from the examples of another subtype. However, subtypes are related. A variation of the same transformation applies to all regularly-formed subtypes.

To deal with transformations involving related subtypes, we use an order of introduction that is slightly different from that described for introducing unrelated members. We use two basic approaches: the **A-Z** *integration approach* and the *subtype-difference approach.*

We use the **A-Z** integration approach if we introduce one subtype at a time. We use the subtype-difference approach if we introduce the transformation through a sequence that shows *all* subtypes when these are presented within the context of examples that have many shared features.

The A-Z Approach

The letters **A** and **Z** refer to two different subtypes. Each subtype is processed through a sequence. All examples in the **A** sequence are from a single subtype. They share many common features. The sequence is therefore relatively easy (far easier than it would be if it showed the response variation of two or three subtypes). The **A** sequence, however, is guilty of stipulation. It implies that the transformation is limited to the subtype presented in the **A** sequence. To counter this stipulation, follow the **A** sequence with the **Z** sequence. The **Z** sequence is specifically designed to counteract the major stipulation implied by the **A** sequence. Examples in the **Z** sequence do not share the features that are stipulated by the **A** sequence; therefore, the **Z** sequence presents the transformation in a context that is greatly different from that of the **A** sequence. By following the **A** sequence with the **Z** sequence, we order the *sequences* to show sameness of the transformation across two greatly different contexts.

To assure that the learner masters this sameness, we follow the **Z** sequence with an integration sequence. This sequence presents a mix of examples from the **A** subtype and the **Z** subtypes.

The procedure is repeated by introducing a sequence that counteracts any possible stipulation created by the combination of **A** and **Z**. A third sequence (**B**) is introduced that counters this stipulation. This sequence is followed by a review. The cycle repeats until all subtypes have been introduced.

Table 10.2 presents a schedule for introducing four subtypes: **A, Z, B, Y**. Subtypes **Z, B,** and **Y** are designed to counteract whatever stipulation has been created by the subtypes that have been previously introduced.

Table 10.2							
Sequences	Lessons						
	1	2	3	4	5	6	7
Subtype **A**	X	X					
Subtype **Z**		X	X				
Subtype **B**				X	X		
Subtype **Y**						X	
Integration			A-Z	A-Z	A-Z-B	A-Z-B-Y	A-Z-B-Y

Each subtype is scheduled in the same basic manner used for any other group of coordinate members. Subtypes **A, Z** and **B** are each introduced on two successive lessons.

(Subtype **Y** is not because the preceding integrations have most probably overcome any possible stipulation.) The schedule presented in Table 10.2 may provide a too-careful introduction for many transformations; however, for those that involve complicated behaviors or fine discriminations (such as a transformation involving subject of a sentence) the schedule is reasonable. If we added expansion activities to the schedule, it would almost be identical to one for a group of coordinate members. The difference has to do with the procedure for determining which member should be introduced next.

Illustration of A-Z integration. Let's say that the learner is first presented with a sequence for say-it-fast in which word parts are presented with a pause between them: motor (pause) boat. This is the subtype **A** sequence and it is appropriate as the first sequence because it presents a large, but relatively easy, subtype. Another subtype of say-it-fast tasks presents *single continuous sounds*. (To present the sound **mmm**, simply say the sound for about two seconds.) This subtype counteracts the stipulation created by the **A** sequence (that all examples of *saying words fast* involve pauses between the word parts). This subtype becomes the **Z** subtype.

My turn to say it fast. Listen. **aaa**. Say it fast. **a**.
My turn again: **ooo**. Say it fast. **o**.
Your turn. **ooo**. Say it fast.
eee. Say it fast.
mmm. Say it fast.
sss. Say it fast.
rrr. Say it fast.
shshsh. Say it fast.
lllll. Say it fast.

Figure 10.2

Example	Wording	
mmmm	Say it fast.	C1
rrr	Say it fast.	
row (pause) boat	Say it fast.	C2
boat (pause) house	Say it fast.	
ssss	Say it fast.	E
drug (pause) store	Say it fast.	D
eeee	Say it fast.	
dog (pause) collar	Say it fast.	
fffff	Say it fast.	

(All bracketed on left as **A**.)

The initial sequence (**A**) implies that say-it-fast is achieved by eliminating a pause. The **Z** sequence shows that say-it-fast may involve increasing the rate of saying the sound. Following the presentation of the **Z** sequence, the integration sequence is presented. The integration sequence shown in Figure 10.2 follows the basic juxtaposition pattern used for single-transformation sequences; however, there are no modeled examples, simply test examples. An alternative integration sequence would simply present examples of the two subtypes, juxtaposed to show sameness.

Both subtypes appear in the minimum-difference segment of the sequence (**C1** and **C2**). The transition from one type to the other is fairly arbitrary. The word **rowboat** begins with the same sound that appeared in the preceding example. When constructing these transitions, you may not find a handy way to do it. In this case, just create an abrupt switch from progressively arranged examples of one subtype (**C1**) to progressively arranged examples of the next (**C2**).

The **D** segment of the integration series requires the learner to treat juxtaposed examples that are quite different (subtypes **A** and **Z** items) in the same way (operating on them by saying them fast).

Some slight stipulation occurs following the integration of **A** and **Z**, which is that only single sounds (not words) are speeded up. To counteract this stipulation, we would follow the integration of **A** and **Z** with a sequence that counteracts this stipulation (the **B** sequence). It would consist of words that are presented continuously (no pauses), but slowly. (Listen: **Mmmmeeee**. Say it fast.) After this subtype is taught, subtypes **A**, **Z** and **B** are integrated.

Listen: Motor (pause) boat.	Say it fast.
Listen: ēēē.	Say it fast.
Listen: mmmmeee.	Say it fast.
Listen: eeeet.	Say it fast.
Listen: Out (pause) fit.	Say it fast.
Listen: Sad (pause) ness.	Say it fast.
Listen: ōōō.	Say it fast.
Listen: Ō (pause) pen.	Say it fast.
Listen: O (pause)ther.	Say it fast.
Listen: mmmmaaaannnn.	Say it fast.

If the final subtype consists of words presented one sound at a time with pauses between the sounds, it would be presented as the final subtype (**Y**). (Listen: **mmm** (pause) **aaa** (pause) **t**. Say it fast.) This subtype would be delayed because it is a more difficult subtype. The goal of the earlier subtypes is to counteract the stipulation with the relatively easiest subtype that is available. Difficult subtypes should always be delayed until the easier subtypes have been practiced. Note that a subtype may be difficult because it involves a combination of behaviors (as in the case of words presented a sound at a time with pauses between the sounds) or because it is irregular.

Following the presentation of the **Y** subtype would be a sequence that integrates all types. Included in this sequence would be words separated by pauses, single sounds, words presented continuously with each sound held, and words presented a sound at a time with pauses between the sounds.

The order of introduction for the say-it-fast subtypes may be far more elaborate than we would need in many settings; however, if a careful introduction is required (for very naive learners), the **A-Z** integration procedure would assure that all subtypes are introduced and cumulatively integrated with the other subtypes.

Identifying a Subtype that Counteracts Stipulation

The simplest way to identify a sequence (or to design one) that counteracts the stipulation created by an initial sequence that presents a fairly easy subtype is:

1. Make up a list of the features that are shared by all examples in the original sequence.
2. Determine which of these features are unique to the subtype presented through the sequence.
3. Design a sequence with a subtype that has none of these subtype features (the ones that are shared by all examples within the sequence, but that are not shared by all examples of the transformation).
4. Make sure that the sequence that counteracts the stipulation presents a relatively easy subtype (one that involves neither complicated behaviors nor irregularly-formed examples).

Illustration. We can illustrate the procedures with a series of transformation sequences that teach adjectives. The first sequence (the **A** subtype) assumes that adjectives will be taught within the context of sentences or phrases. This sequence is relatively easy, presenting examples that consist of three-word phrases, the last word of which is always a noun. (See Figure 10.3.)

Figure 10.3
Subtype A

Example	Teacher Wording
1. The sad boy	My turn to name the adjectives: **the** and **sad**.
2. Those sad boys	My turn to name the adjectives: **those** and **sad**.
3. Five sad boys	Your turn: Name the adjectives.
4. Five sad dogs	Name the adjectives.
5. Five big dogs	Name the adjectives.
6. Our big dog	Name the adjectives.
7. A strong farmer	Name the adjectives.
8. My little brother	Name the adjectives.
9. A singing cat	Name the adjectives.
10. Those happy hours	Name the adjectives.
11. An unfortunate event	Name the adjectives.

The potential stipulation problems of the sequences are obvious. The learner may suppose that adjectives always occur in pairs or that they include all but the last word of the utterance. *Subtype* **Z** *should be designed to counteract this possible stipulation.*

Figure 10.4
Subtype Z

Example	Teacher Wording
1. The dog was sitting.	My turn: Name any adjectives: **the**.
2. The sitting dog was singing.	My turn: Name any adjectives: **the** and **sitting**.
3. That singing dog was sitting.	Your turn: Name any adjectives.
4. The sitting dog was panting.	Name any adjectives.
5. The dog was panting.	Name any adjectives.
6. A panting dog was sitting.	Name any adjectives.
7. Our dogs were panting and sitting.	Name any adjectives.
8. Her cat was sitting and panting.	Name any adjectives.
9. Her singing cat was panting.	Name any adjectives.

Many possible sequences may be designed to counteract the stipulation. The sequence in Figure 10.4 (the sequence for the **Z**-subtype) does not share the most highly stipulated features with the original sequence. The examples in the sequence do not end with a noun, and do not present a pair of adjectives.

The sequence shows that a word is an adjective only if it occupies a particular position in the sentence. The word **sitting** is not an adjective in example 1. **Sitting** is an adjective in example 2.

Figure 10.5	
Example	Teacher Wording
1. Five walking cats were crying.	Name any adjectives.
2. Five cats were walking.	Name any adjectives.
3. The silly cat.	Name any adjectives.
4. My silly brother.	Name any adjectives.
5. My brother was walking.	Name any adjectives.
6. That unusual song.	Name any adjectives.
7. A dog was snoring.	Name any adjectives.
Etc.	

Following successful completion of the preceding sequences is the integration sequence that requires the learner to respond to both types **A** and **Z**. Figure 10.5 shows the examples for the first part of the integration sequence.

Figure 10.6	
Subtype B	
Example	Teacher Wording
1. She met a happy man.	My turn to say any adjectives: **a** and **happy**.
2. She met five happy men.	My turn to say any adjectives: **five** and **happy**.
3. She met five old men.	Your turn: Say any adjectives.
4. She met that old man.	Say any adjectives.
5. She met my old dog.	Say any adjectives.
6. She met a tired mailman.	Say any adjectives.
7. She met a yellow moop.	Say any adjectives.
8. She met an unusual problem.	Say any adjectives.
9. She met four strange people.	Say any adjectives.
10. She met an unhappy ending.	Say any adjectives.
11. She met that silly hunter.	Say any adjectives.

The integration sequence counteracts some stipulation. The learner responds to adjectives in sentences and adjectives in phrases. The integration sequence is still guilty of stipulation, however. Adjectives are shown to occur only at the beginning of the utterance. To counteract this stipulation, we introduce subtype **B** (see Figure 10.6). This subtype presents adjectives in the predicate only. Note that this sequence presents a narrow subtype in which the first words are the same (**she met**) and the last word is a noun that is preceded by adjectives. The purpose of the subtype is to show the learner that adjectives are not limited to the beginning of an utterance.

Follow this sequence with another integration sequence with all subtypes—**A, Z,** and **B**. Figure 10.7 shows the first part of a possible sequence.

Figure 10.7	
Integration Sequence	
Example	Teacher Wording
1. I read about an old goat.	Say any adjectives.
2. I read about those old goats.	Say any adjectives.
3. Those silly goats.	Say any adjectives.
4. That silly cat was sleeping.	Say any adjectives.
5. That sleeping cat was running.	Say any adjectives.
6. I read about that sleeping cat.	Say any adjectives.
Etc.	

The integration of **A, Z,** and **B** fairly well conveys the different subtypes or contexts in which adjectives occur. The various examples presented so far stipulate that adjectives always precede the name of something. There is, however, the type of adjective that occurs in the predicate: "Johnny is happy." No noun follows **happy**. This type is irregular.

The problem that we may create if the irregular subtype is introduced too early is confusion of adjectives and verbs. Consider the sentence: **The running bear was happy**. The word **running** is an adjective, and **happy** is an adjective. We now reverse the two adjectives: **The happy bear was running**. The word **happy** is an adjective, but the word **running** is now a verb. A solution to the problem would to be: (1) teach the regular forms of adjectives; (2) teach the discrimination *verb*; and (3) introduce the irregular adjectives in the predicate. They would be easily identified as not-verbs and not-nouns. Therefore, they must be adjectives (with respect to what the learner has been taught).

Another possible solution would be to ignore the verb problem and use a different type of transformation to teach the irregulars after the learner has been firmed on the integration of **A, Z,** and **B**. Figure 10.8 shows the beginning of a possible sequence. Note that the sequence is preceded by a brief verbal explanation and that it does not deal with identifying adjectives, merely with restating the sentence.

Figure 10.8	
Example	Teacher Wording
	Some adjectives are funny. Before you can figure them out, you have to say the sentence another way.
1. The boy was happy.	My turn to say it another way: The boy was a happy boy.
2. The dog was happy.	My turn to say it another way: The dog was a happy dog.
3. The dog was big and frisky.	My turn to say it another way: The dog was a big and frisky dog.
4. The dog was big and frisky.	Your turn: Say it another way.
5. The dog was old and fat.	Say it another way.
6. The man was old and fat.	Say it another way.
Etc.	

After the learner has successfully completed the sequence, the sequence is repeated, this time with an additional task to be added to each example. Instead of simply directing the learner to say it another way, the teacher also directs the learner to say any adjectives at the end of the sentence. For example:

Example	Teacher Wording
The dog was big and frisky.	Say it another way.
	Now say the adjectives that are near the end of the sentence.

In summary, the **A-Z** integration strategy for dealing with subtypes is to introduce new subtypes one at a time and integrate each new type with all subtypes that have been taught.

1. Begin with a subtype (**A**) that has a relatively large membership.
2. Analyze the sequence to determine *the stipulation* that is implied.
3. Introduce a sequence involving a subtype (**Z**) *that does not have the features stipulated by the original sequence*. This sequence should be quite different from the original.
4. Create an integration sequence that begins with progressive minimum differences (which are tested) and that terminates in sameness juxtapositions of the two subtypes (**A** and **Z**).
5. Analyze the integration sequence for possible stipulation, and introduce a subtype (**B**) that does not have the features stipulated by the integration sequence.
6. Create an integration sequence that begins with progressive minimum differences and that terminates in sameness juxtapositions of the three subtypes (**A, Z, B**).
7. Repeat this procedure until all "regular" subtypes have been introduced.
8. Delay the introduction of irregular or contradictory subtypes until the learner is firm on the regulars. The irregularities may then be taught in a sequence followed by an integration sequence that processes all regular types that have been taught.

The Subtype-Difference Procedure

If we are required to introduce many subtypes for a given discrimination, we may elect to show all (or nearly all) of the regular subtypes in a single introductory sequence. We design this sequence so that the only differences between examples is a subtype difference. This type of sequence is possible for transformation concepts that have many subtypes.

Table 10.3						
Sequences	Lessons					
	1	2	3	4	5	6
Initial Sequence (I)	X	X				
Subtype **Z**		X	X			
Subtype **B**				X	X	
Integration			I-Z	I-Z	Z-B	Z-B

The subtype-difference procedure is basically the same as the **A-Z** integration procedure except that the first sequence shows all subtypes. Subsequent sequences expand the range of application for the various types presented in the initial sequence. The schedule in Table

10.3 presents a typical pattern of subtype-difference introductions.

Note that initial sequence (**I**) is not contained in the integration after **Z** and **B** become integrated. The reason is that the examples presented through **Z** and **B** present enough variation in examples to assure that the learner is attending to the sameness across the various possible subtypes.

Figure 10.9	
Example	Teacher Wording
1. She runs in the park.	The verb is **runs**.
2. She ran in the park.	What's the verb?
3. She will run in the park.	What's the verb?
4. She would run in the park.	What's the verb?
5. She was running in the park.	What's the verb?
Etc.	

Illustration. Let's say that the first sequence used to teach verbs is the one presented in Chapter 8. Figure 10.9 below is the first part of that sequence.

Although this sequence introduces a broad range of subtypes, it does not show any range of variation for each of the subtypes (such as the one-word verbs). The words "She ___ in the park" is common to all examples, and a form of the word **run** appears in all examples.

To counteract this sequence, we would introduce the initial sequence with one that expands a particular subtype. A possible **Z** sequence that presents one-word verbs and that tends to counteract the stipulation created by the original sequence (which is that verbs must have to deal with running) is as follows:

They ran in the park.
She sat in the park.
She is in the park.
She was in the park.
They were in the park.
They sat in a tree.
They sat.
They ate.
They climbed a tree.
They have a tree.
Etc.

The sequence may be attempting to introduce too many subtypes (suggested by the number of progressively minimum-difference examples that are required to cover the variation in one-word verbs). However, a single sequence or more than one sequence of this type would function well as a **Z** sequence to counteract the stipulation of the initial sequence. Following this sequence would be an integration of the type of examples presented in the initial sequence and the subtype that is elaborated in the **Z** sequence. Following this integration would be another sequence that introduced two-word verbs. Note that the type of examples presented in the initial sequence would be dropped following the introduction of the next subtype. This sequence would introduce three-word verbs. Another sequence might follow to introduce verbs when sentences are not in their regular subject-predicate order.

Perspective

We illustrated the integration of subtypes with transformation sequences. The same pattern of integration and the same options exist when we deal with different subtypes of examples that are processed through a cognitive routine or different subtypes of a physical operation (such as using a screwdriver with different types of blades—slotted, phillips, etc.). Our two major options are the **A-Z** integration or the subtype-difference approach. In both cases, the initial sequence introduces stipulation. It may show the range of subtypes but does so in a very restricted setup, or it may show the range of a single subtype without showing other subtypes. In both cases, subsequent sequences are needed to counteract the stipulation.

Summary

Members of a set are coordinate discriminations that are potentially confusing. To schedule the introduction for a group of members, we follow two basic ordering rules:

1. Arrange members so that minimally-different members are separated by two or more non-similar members.

2. Separate introductions that involve minimum-differences by at least one introduction that does not involve minimum differences.

Those members that are designed as "minimally different" are the most similar in features of the examples or in the labels.

The order of introduction is not wholly determined by the similarity of members. The criterion of immediate utility strongly influences selection. We introduce things because they are immediately useful to the learner. The greater the potential application, the stronger the argument for introducing it early.

Empirical investigation may disclose that some members are quite difficult for the learner and should perhaps be scheduled for late in the sequence. For instance, unvoiced sounds **f, s**, and **p** are more difficult for learners than their voiced counterparts **v, z**, and **b**. Also, stop sounds are more difficult than continuous sounds.

To introduce a member to a set, design three basic activities: *initial teaching, expansion*, and *cumulative review.*

When the set becomes large, do not review all members. Review the most similar, the most recently introduced, the most frequently misidentified, and the least frequently reviewed.

Limit the number of examples in the review set to six.

The initial teaching follows the procedures outlined in Chapters 4 to 9. If the set consists of nouns (which is characteristic of most large sets), a noun-sequence is used for the initial teaching of each member.

The expansion activities include foolers, manipulation activities, and tags. Also, worksheet activities are used to expand the newly-taught member. (See Section V.)

When designing activities to introduce each member, chart the schedule, allotting about two lessons for the introduction of each new member and providing periodic consolidations during which no new members are introduced.

The procedures for ordering members assures that the learner practices the earlier-taught members before the later, minimally-different, members are introduced. Hopefully, the amount of learning demanded when the second member is introduced is reduced because the learner is quite firm on the earlier-taught member. Confusions do not become chronic (the biggest single problem associated with members that are highly similar).

Modify the procedures for quite facile learners. The number and types of expansion activities can be reduced. The regularity of cumulative reviews can be disregarded somewhat. Intuition may suggest that *far less* teaching and expansion are needed to maintain new concepts; however, empirical investigation may disclose that the optimum amount of reduction is not as great as intuition suggests.

Procedures for introducing subtypes of transformations follow the same basic pattern as the introduction of coordinate members. Because subtypes are related, however, the procedure for identifying an order for the introduction of subtypes is different from that for ordering coordinate members.

Begin with a relatively easy sequence that either shows the full range of subtype variation in a restricted setup or presents a relatively large and easy subtype.

Follow with a subtype that counteracts the stipulation created by the initial sequence.

Integrate the subtypes.

Continue in this manner until all subtypes are introduced and integrated.

Chapter 11
Hierarchical Class Programs

A higher-order class is a group of objects or events that: (1) have a higher-order label, and (2) have different subtype labels.

The program for a higher-order or hierarchical class is more complicated than the program for introducing coordinate or associated members, because more teaching is involved. To teach various objects in the class **tool**, we must introduce a variety of tools. We must teach the name for the various *members* that are taught: **hammer, saw, pliers**, etc. This part of the program has the same requirements as the basic programs for ordering members of a set. Members are introduced one at a time. Some are minimally different from others and must be separated in time. For each member that is introduced, there should be initial teaching, expansion-activities, and some sort of review to assure that the member is being discriminated from all other members in the set. Introductions of members that require minimum-difference pairings of examples should be separated from other introductions that involve minimum differences.

All these features for higher-order teaching are shared by the basic program for teaching coordinate or associated members of a set. In addition to the basic teaching, however, we must provide for teaching of each member's *second name, the higher-order designation*. In addition to teaching the learner that the car is called "car," we must provide for the teaching of **vehicle**. This higher-order teaching suggests that we must show the learner how one label of the object (**car**) is based on some features, while the other label (**vehicle**) is based on other features. Also, we must show the learner that *although all cars are vehicles, not all vehicles are cars*. Finally, we must show the learner that not all things are vehicles. One of the biggest practical problems associated with the higher-order program is that of stipulation. If we teach the learner that an object is a car and we continue to reinforce the learner for responding to it only as a "car," we induce strong stipulation. The learner will later resist classifying the object as **vehicle**.

Each problem associated with the structure of higher order class can be solved by recognizing it and by providing the appropriate instructional remedy.

Structure of Higher-Order Relationships

The structure of higher-order relationships is intriguing. An understanding of this structure helps clarify the discriminations that must be taught. We will look at the structure two ways. First we will view the various hierarchical arrangements that are *implied by a single concrete example*. Then we will look at a series of progressively more inclusive higher-order classes.

Every concrete example has an indefinitely large number of features. The features (either individually or in groups) occur in other examples. Therefore, the features (either individually or in groups) serve as the basis for creating different *groups* in which the particular object would be placed on the basis of sameness of feature. Consider a particular pencil. It could be classified as **something that has erasers, something that is yellow, something longer than two inches, something with a point, something made of more than one material, something with wooden parts**, and so forth. Some of these classes are *more inclusive* than others. For instance, the pencil may be in the class of **things made of cedar wood**. It would also be in the class of **things made of wood**. All other members of the class, **things made of cedar wood**, would also be in the class **things made of wood**. Therefore, the class **things made of wood** includes the class **things made of cedar wood**. When all members of one class are included in another class, we say that a hierarchical or higher-order class relationship exists.

If we start with the concrete example described above (the particular pencil) and create higher-order classes based on color, we may identify the following classes: **middle-yellow objects, yellow objects, brightly-colored objects**, and **objects**. We can repeat the procedure for other classifications based on the hardness, weight, length, or any other discriminable characteristic

Section IV | Programs

of the object. The same pattern will emerge, however, for all the higher-order classes we specify. *The ultimate class that is named is* **objects**. The "objectness" is common to all possible higher-order arrangements that we can specify for something that is an object.

The diagram below shows the relationship between the features of a concrete object and various higher-order groups.

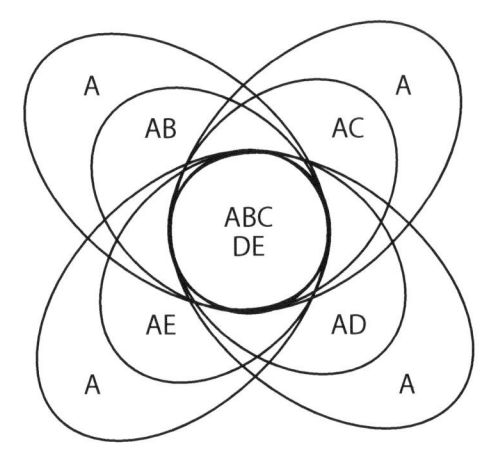

Each feature relevant to the various classifications is indicated by a letter: **A, B, C, D, E**. The center of the "flower" is the concrete object that is being classified in different ways. Each "petal" of the flower shows a simple higher-order program that consists of only two inclusive classes (such as **writing object** and **object**, or **yellow object** and **object**). (Letter **A** refers to **object**.)

As the diagram indicates, the basis for all possible higher-order classifications is the *set of features possessed by the concrete object* (the center of the flower). Different features are selected to create different higher-order arrangements. If feature **B** is "yellowness," the yellowness may be used as the basis for creating a higher-order class. The class would be **yellow objects**. The entities that would be included in this class would be the concrete object in the illustration and all other objects that have the feature of yellowness. Another feature of the concrete object is "pencilness." Therefore, **pencil objects** is a possible higher-order classification.

Although there is a progression of higher-order classes for any feature of the object (**yellow objects** and **objects**, for instance), each progression (petal) is independent of the other progressions (petals). The single concrete object that we start with, in other words, may be included as an example in any of the higher-order progressions that are identified. (The pencil is an example of **pencils**, of **yellow objects**, of **objects with points**, etc.) The membership of each of these categories, however, is different. (Many objects in the class **pencils** would not be in the class **yellow objects** or in the class **objects with points**.) This point is very important. For every feature of the concrete object, there is a possible progression of higher-order classes. Each progression, however, is independent of the others and describes a different criterion for grouping objects on the basis of common features.

The final point about the petal diagram is that as we proceed from the center to the end of any petal, we are using classification criteria that are increasingly inclusive. (All yellow objects are objects.) Therefore, the membership of each class is based on fewer and fewer common features as we progress toward the end of the petal. The objects in the class that has features **A, B, C, D**, and **E** have at least five common features. The objects in **AB** have only two common features. The objects in **A** have only one—"objectness."

Higher-Order Progressions

A single higher-order progression is represented as a petal in the flower diagram. Each petal in the diagram has only two divisions, or shows only two classes in the higher-order progression. Some progressions may consist of many classes, however. The diagram in Figure 11.1 presents a different perspective for higher-order progression. This diagram is a ladder, showing a progression of some of the possible classes for a particular object—an unripe Bing cherry. The value of the diagram is that it shows the three major relationships that characterize a higher-order progression. These relationships are:

- Relations of a shaded part to the row below it.
- The relationship of a shaded part to the other part of the same row.
- The relationship of a row to the shaded part in the row above.

Each row is divided into two parts. The first part names the positive (+) examples. The second part names the coordinate negative examples (−). For row 4 the positive examples are "Bing Cherries" and negative examples are "All Other Cherries." The negatives on each row suggest the positive classification for the row above. The positives on a row imply the row below. "Bing Cherries" implies different subtypes of **Bing Cherries**. The

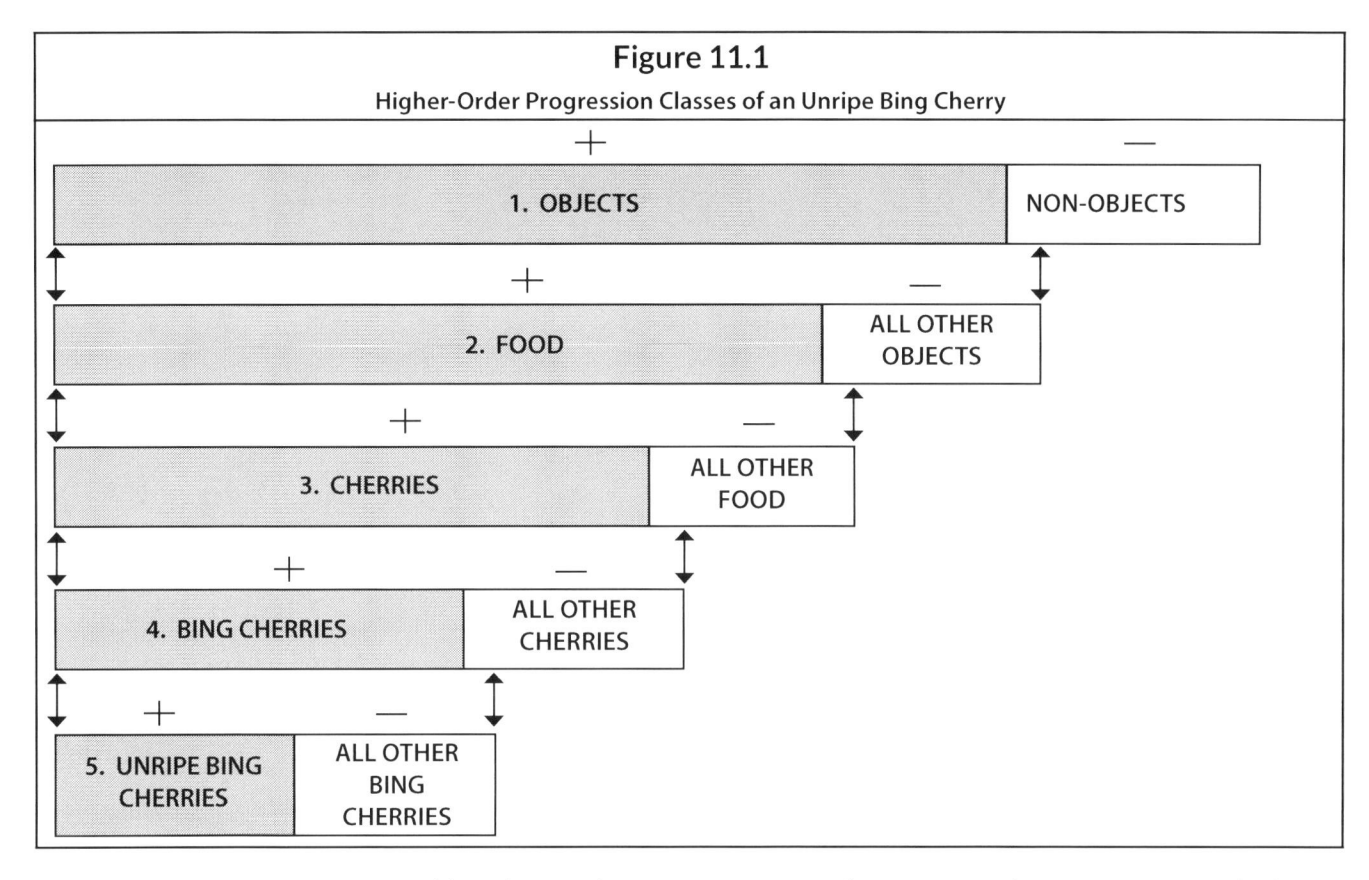

Figure 11.1
Higher-Order Progression Classes of an Unripe Bing Cherry

+	−
1. OBJECTS	NON-OBJECTS
2. FOOD	ALL OTHER OBJECTS
3. CHERRIES	ALL OTHER FOOD
4. BING CHERRIES	ALL OTHER CHERRIES
5. UNRIPE BING CHERRIES	ALL OTHER BING CHERRIES

positives on row 5 present a possible subtype of **Bing Cherries** ("Unripe Bing Cherries").

Row 5 shows that **Bing Cherries** are divided into two types—"Unripe Bing Cherries" and "All Other Bing Cherries." (There may be two *other types* or ten. We do not know the number. We only know that they are coordinate with **Unripe Bing Cherries**, which means that an object cannot be both an **Unripe Bing Cherry** and another subtype of **Bing Cherries**.)

Row 4 shows that there is a coordinate relationship between "Bing Cherries" and "All Other Cherries." This relationship suggests that we can divide **cherries** (arbitrarily) into two groups: the **Bing cherries** and the **non-Bing cherries**. This division shows that we can create a discrimination between cherries that are Bings and cherries that are not-Bings.

The relationship between "Bing Cherries" and the part above ("Cherries") provides a restatement of the fact that Bing cherries and all other cherries make up the class **cherries**, and that cherries are one type of **food**.

The structure of these discriminations suggests the teaching that is needed to introduce simple higher-order groups, such as various cherries, types of vehicles, or chemical elements.

Programs for Higher-Order Relationships

If we were to teach the higher-order name **cherry** and the lower-order membership **Bing, Queen Ann**, and **Lambert**, we would be responsible for teaching a total of four names, requiring three types of sequences.

1. A sequence for introducing the higher-order class discrimination (usually a variation of a non-comparative sequence).

2. A sequence for introducing *each* lower-class member (usually noun sequences).

3. Cumulative review sequences that begin after the second lower-class member has been introduced and that continue periodically throughout the program.

We teach the higher-order class discriminations first, then the various lower-order class names. There are many reasons for introducing the higher-order name first. Perhaps the most important is that if the higher-order name (**vehicle** or **cherries**) is taught, we can use the higher-order name in questions about the lower-order members. We can ask, "Is this cherry a **Bing cherry**?" "Is the vehicle a **truck**?" or, "What kind of **vehicle** is this?" These questions tell the learner that the object involved is a cherry or a vehicle, *but is also a particular type.* If we do not teach the higher-order discrimination first, we cannot express the relationship between higher-order and lower-order names. We must ask, "Is this a truck?" or "What is this?" As noted earlier, if the learner works with the lower-order labels for a long time before their higher-order name is taught, the presentation stipulates that the object identified as **boat** or **car** has only one noun-type label. The learner may resist the idea that these objects can also be called **vehicles**. In effect, the learner will insist that it is *not* a vehicle because it is a boat or because it is a car.

The problem is not easily remedied by pointing out that it is also a vehicle. The sentence, "This boat is a vehicle," does *not* convey the idea that "All boats are vehicles." The somewhat tricky relationship between **vehicle** and **car** can be taught quite simply and without serious stipulation by teaching the learner to identify all objects as **vehicles** and then by showing the types of vehicles. The statement, "This vehicle is a boat," clearly makes the point that the object has two labels.

Following the teaching of the higher-order discriminations, the various members are taught one at a time. The conventions used to introduce each member are basically the same as those specified in Chapter 10. Each introduction involves *initial teaching, expansion,* and *review.* A cumulative review appears periodically, starting before the introduction of the third member and continuing through the program.

The Sequences

1. The first initial-teaching sequence in the program is a non-comparative sequence that teaches the *higher-order class name.* If the higher-order name is **cherry**, the non-comparative sequence teaches **cherry, not-cherry**. If the higher-order name is **food**, the sequence teaches **food, not-food**. This first step would be used for any higher-order name: **dream, not-dream; gymnosperm, not-gymnosperm; condominium, not-condominium; vehicle, not-vehicle.**

2. The next group of sequences introduce the various *lower-class members,* usually through noun sequences. If the higher-order name is **vehicle**, different *noun sequences* would be used to introduce the subclasses **boat, car, truck,** etc. For each vehicle, a variation of the initial-teaching sequence would be provided on two consecutive lessons. Only one new member would be introduced at a time.

Note that the lower-order members introduced are ordered according to the rules for ordering coordinate members (specified in Chapter 10). Members that are highly similar in name or features are separated by dissimilar members. Also, introductions that involve minimum-difference introductions are separated.

3. Before the third lower-class member is introduced (usually on the second day of the initial teaching sequence for the second member), the cumulative review sequences begin. At least one cumulative sequence is introduced following the initial teaching of a new member.

The Program

Figure 11.2 shows a schedule for teaching the higher-order name and the name of five members. The first sequence teaches the higher-order name **vehicle**. Subsequent sequences introduce the various members, each being presented on two consecutive days before the next member is introduced.

The numbers at the top indicate the *lessons* or days of instruction. If the initial teaching of a member occurs on a particular lesson, an **X** appears on that lesson. As the pattern of **X**s shows, initial teaching is repeated on two consecutive lessons. On only two lessons (2 and 3) is there more than one initial-teaching sequence, and there is no initial teaching provided on lessons 7 and 12. More than one member is being taught on the early lessons (2 and 3), because the learner is not required to remember many new names on these lessons.

Below the heavy bar on the time-table are the schedules for expansion activities and cumulative review. The letters in the cells indicate which members are involved in activities. The expansion starts on lesson 2 (dealing with **A**, the **vehicle–not-vehicle** discrimination) and continues on a periodic schedule. The cumulative review begins on lesson 6 (after three lower-order members have been taught) and is presented before each new member is taught.

Figure 11.2

Concepts	Lessons											
	1	2	3	4	5	6	7	8	9	10	11	12
A. Vehicle (non-comparative)	X	X										
B. Truck (noun)		X	X									
C. Boat (noun)			X	X								
D. Wagon (noun)					X	X						
E. Train (noun)								X	X			
F. Car (noun)										X	X	
Expansion		A	AB	C	A	D	BCD	E		F	A	BCDEF
Cumulative Review						BCD			BCDE			BCDEF

Gaps in the Schedule

It is much more difficult to predict the difficulty of various responses when we deal with a program rather than a simple sequence. If one discrimination presents problems, a domino effect is sometimes created, with the learner confusing the difficult member with the one that is introduced next (or immediately before). This effect continues as subsequent members are introduced.

To avoid possible domino effects, we put "gaps" in the program. The program in Figure 11.2 above has one gap, which occurs on lesson 7. No new discrimination is taught on this day. The learner engages in expansions of the previously taught discriminations (**BCD**).

If we suspect problems, we space out the introduction so that there are more gaps or larger gaps. During the gap, we present either expansion activities or cumulative review sequences. We also provide a consolidation at the end of the sequence, which involves all the members taught in the sequence (lesson 12).

The cumulative review presents only the lower-order members (not the higher-order discrimination members) because the task form used for all items is, "What kind of vehicle is this?" This task does not accommodate **non-vehicles** and does not permit discrimination of **vehicles** and **not-vehicles**.

Before a new member is introduced, the learner performs on a cumulative sequence consisting of all the lower-class members that have been taught. If the learner does not perform well on the cumulative review, the next member should be delayed.

The Higher-Order Sequence

The higher-order sequence is the first taught in the program. It is a non-comparative sequence. The negative examples should be "minimally different;" however, we cannot easily present examples of most higher-order labels (such as **vehicle**, **not-vehicle**) through continuous conversion. We therefore use non-continuous examples and use the test instruction, "Tell me **vehicle** or **not-vehicle**." Figure 11.3 shows a possible sequence.

Figure 11.3

Example	Teacher Wording
Swing	This is not a vehicle.
Rocking horse	This is not a vehicle.
Bicycle	This is a vehicle.
Boat	This is a vehicle.
Trailer truck	Tell me vehicle or not-vehicle.
Large shed	Tell me.
Motorcycle	Tell me.
Car	Tell me.
Chair	Tell me.
Train	Tell me.
Swing	Tell me.
Wagon	Tell me.
Dog	Tell me.
Sled	Tell me.

The sequence above presents two negatives followed by three positives and then a series of test examples. Note that both opening negatives are objects that move; however, they are not vehicles. We could have presented an "exercycle" type of machine as one of the negatives.

The sequence is a higher-order non-continuous sequence. Examples are sequenced like non-comparatives, and a choice-response task is presented with each test item.

When the sequence for **vehicle** is presented on the second day, a variation could be introduced. Instead of opening with negatives, it could open with positives. The higher-order sequence should skip the modeled examples on the second day. Instead of containing 13 examples, it could contain 8 to 10 examples.

The strategy for identifying minimum-difference examples was discussed in Chapter 6. In review:

1. First consider the various misrules that would be implied by a presentation of positive examples. (All positives share the property of moving and the property of accommodating a passenger in a sitting position, etc.)

2. Identify negatives that have the particular feature involved in the misrule. (All vehicles move. The negative, therefore, should be something that moves but is not a vehicle.)

3. Eliminate questionable examples. What is a toy or a model? Are they vehicles? If the examples are not clear negatives, do not use them.

The Lower-Order Sequence for the First Member

The lower-order members are generally introduced through noun sequences. The question that accompanies each example tested is: "What kind of *vehicle* is this?" Note that the question contains the higher-order name.

There is one exception to the rule that lower-order members are introduced through noun sequences. *The first lower-order member to be taught should be introduced through a non-comparative sequence.* This sequence counters any possible stipulation created by the higher-order discrimination. The learner now responds to the various positive examples of vehicles as "truck" or "not-truck." Note that all examples are vehicles. Figure 11.4 gives a possible sequence for the initial teaching of the first lower-class member, **truck**.

The sequence is similar to the higher-order sequence. It is a non-comparative non-continuous sequence with "minimum-difference" negatives. *The negatives are vehicles that have not been taught yet.* They are the vehicles that are most highly similar to **truck**: **train** and **car**.

Figure 11.4

Example	Teacher Wording
1	These are vehicles. This vehicle is a truck.
2	The vehicle is a truck.
3	This vehicle is not a truck.
4	This vehicle is not a truck.
5	Your turn: Tell me if each vehicle is a truck or not a truck.
6	Tell me about this vehicle.
7	Tell me about this vehicle.
8	Tell me about this vehicle.
9	Tell me about this vehicle.

Note that the sequence uses the test wording, "Tell me about this vehicle." The label for the higher-order discrimination, **vehicle**, must appear in the task. Also, the test wording should call for a labeling response, not merely for a "yes" or "no" answer. *We want to make sure that the learner uses the lower-class name in response to objects that have previously been labeled with the higher-order name.* (The learner responds: "This vehicle is a truck," or "This vehicle is not a truck.")

Lower-Order Sequences for Other Members

After the first member is taught through a non-comparative sequence, all other members are taught through noun sequences. Here are the procedures for constructing these sequences:

- Limit the examples to the new member and to *minimally different members that have been previously taught.*

- Use non-continuous conversions.

- Use test wording that requires the learner to label all examples with the lower-class names ("What kind of vehicle is this?" or "Tell me about this vehicle.")

Figure 11.5 gives a sequence for introducing **boat**, the second lower-class member. Note that all **not-boats** are trucks. **Truck** is the only minimally-different member that has been taught. The sequence is fairly short because boats are greatly different from trucks, and because there should be no problems with responses.

Figure 11.5		
Example		Teacher Wording
1	*(boat)*	My turn: What kind of vehicle is this? A boat.
2	*(boat)*	My turn: What kind of vehicle is this? A boat.
3	*(canoe)*	Your turn: What kind of vehicle is this?
4	*(truck)*	What kind of vehicle is this?
5	*(kayak)*	What kind of vehicle is this?
6	*(sailboat)*	What kind of vehicle is this?
7	*(truck)*	What kind of vehicle is this?
8	*(boat)*	What kind of vehicle is this?

The initial-teaching sequence on the second day of teaching **boat** could be shorter and could have no modeled examples. Like the original sequence, it would begin with examples of the new member.

The next member to be introduced is **wagon**. The sequence for **wagon** is the same as that for **boat**. It presents examples of the new member, **wagon**, and examples of previously taught minimally-different members. The only two members that are known to the learner are **truck** and **boat**; therefore, these must serve as the minimally-different familiar members. Figure 11.6 gives a possible sequence.

For each subsequent noun sequence, not all known vehicles would be included in the sequence, only those that are minimally different from the new member that is being taught. As a rule, only two familiar members should be presented in the noun sequence. For the first three members that are taught, the decisions are easy.

Figure 11.6		
Example		Teacher Wording
		Here are some vehicles.
1	*(wagon)*	This vehicle is a wagon.
2	*(wagon)*	This vehicle is a wagon.
3	*(wagon)*	Tell me about this vehicle.
4	*(truck)*	Tell me about this vehicle.
5	*(wagon)*	Tell me about this vehicle.
6	*(boat)*	Tell me about this vehicle.
7	*(wagon)*	Tell me about this vehicle.
8	*(wagon)*	Tell me about this vehicle.
9	*(truck)*	Tell me about this vehicle.
10	*(wagon)*	Tell me about this vehicle.

The first member is taught through a non-comparative sequence, so we do not have to worry about which minimally-different members to include. (We select those that are minimally different in features.) The next member is taught through a noun sequence; however, there is only one known member, which automatically becomes the negative in the sequence. The same situation exists for the third member. Two members are known; therefore, they become the two negatives introduced in the sequence. After the third member has been taught, only two negatives will be included as *familiar members*. These two are the most similar (in name, shape, or name and shape) to the member that is being taught.

Cumulative Review Sequences

The schedule for teaching **vehicles** (Figure 11.2) shows that on lesson 6, three different activities are presented. The new member **wagon** is being taught for the second day. At some other time during the lesson, the learner receives expansion activities that involve **wagon**. At still another time, the cumulative review involving **truck, boat**, and **wagon** is presented. Note that these activities do not necessarily follow each other. The idea is to separate them in time. This separation achieves the following:

1. It helps distribute the learning by providing a "change up" or break between activities that involve the discriminations being taught. This break militates somewhat against possible fatigue or boredom.

2. The break also makes the juxtapositions more difficult by reducing juxtaposition prompting. The learner might be able to remember the name **wagon** when working within a sequence, because the learner has just heard the name and possibly just said it. This performance does not imply that the learner will remember the name one minute or ten minutes later. The performance within a sequence is easy because the sequence is designed to juxtapose examples in which the learner does the same thing (such as respond to, "Tell me about this vehicle.") When we present a break in the activity and later come back to the discrimination, the first examples in the cumulative review sequences are relatively difficult because the learner is not prompted by the same thing on preceding tasks.

3. The distribution of practice demonstrates that the learner will be expected to remember the names being taught. If the sequence always models the correct responses or immediately follows a sequence that models the correct responses, the learner may not understand that these names are to be remembered.

Figure 11.7 shows a cumulative review sequence that might be presented after **truck, boat,** and **wagon** have been introduced (lesson 6).

All the lower-order discriminations that have been taught are presented in the sequence. This procedure is used for all cumulative reviews.

Summary of Program Events for Hierarchical-Class Programs

In its simplest form, the hierarchical-class program is presented so that:

1. The higher-order class is taught as a higher-order noun (a non-cognitive sequence).

2. Each lower-order member is introduced, the first through a non-comparative sequence, all others through noun sequences.

3. The expansion activities for each member begin as soon as a member is taught (on either the first day or the second day of the discriminations' initial teaching sequence).

4. Cumulative review begins before the fourth member is introduced. An additional review sequence is presented before each subsequent member is introduced.

Advanced Applications

Three changes that occur in the basic procedures when we deal with advanced applications are:

1. Statements of facts or rules are sometimes used to indicate the basis for classifying members (implying the use of correlated-feature sequences).

2. The rate of introduction is accelerated.

3. The number and type of expansion and review activities is reduced.

If we were to teach **vehicles** as a more advanced application, we could possibly present a rule such as, "If it is made to take things from one place to another, it is a vehicle."

Figure 11.8 shows a possible sequence for the higher-order label. The sequence is a correlated-feature sequence. The first test question in each pair is designed so the learner responds to whether the objects are **vehicles** (the new name). Then the learner justifies the conclusion by

Figure 11.7

Example	Teacher Wording
	Here are some vehicles.
1	What kind of vehicle is this?
2	What kind of vehicle is this?
3	What kind of vehicle is this?
4	What kind of vehicle is this?
5	What kind of vehicle is this?
6	What kind of vehicle is this?

reference to whether the objects are designed "to take things from one place to another."

	Figure 11.8	
Example		Teacher Wording
1		My turn: Is this a vehicle? No. How do I know? Because it's not made to take things from one place to another.
2		My turn: Is this a vehicle? No. How do I know? Because it's not made to take things from one place to another.
3		My turn: Is this a vehicle? Yes. How do I know? Because it is made to take things from one place to another.
4		Your turn: Is this a vehicle? How do you know?
5		Is this a vehicle? How do you know?
6		Is this a vehicle? How do you know?
7		Is this a vehicle? How do you know?
8		Is this a vehicle? How do you know?

Correlated-feature sequences may be used for teaching lower-order members. For instance, in teaching varieties of **gymnosperm trees**, a correlated-features sequence might be used to show the difference between highly similar members such as **Sitka spruce** and **blue spruce**. Figure 11.9 shows a possible sequence that could be used when **blue spruce** is introduced. The sequence is a correlated-feature sequence. The first question in each pair requires the learner to identify the tree. The second question requires the learner to relate the conclusion to facts about whether the needle rolls.

Note that the test wording violates the rule about naming the higher-order class. The wording could be: "Is this gymnosperm needle from a Sitka spruce or a blue spruce?" However, the additional wording simply weakens the task, which clearly focuses on the type of spruce. With advanced applications, we do not have to be as rigid about naming the higher-order class in the test question as we are when dealing with the relatively naive learner.

	Figure 11.9	
Example		Teacher Wording
1		My turn: This is a blue spruce. How do I know? A needle rolls between my fingers.
2		My turn: This is from a Sitka spruce. How do I know? A needle does not roll between my fingers.
3		Your turn: Is this a blue spruce or a Sitka spruce? How do you know?
4		Is this from a blue spruce or a Sitka spruce? How do you know?

Adjusting the Sequence for the Learner's Prior Knowledge

Often, the learner is familiar with either the higher-order name or the names of some members. If the learner knows the higher-order name, but not the name of members, simply drop the teaching of the higher-order name and begin with the introduction of members. The introduction of members would follow the schedule for the scope-and-sequence for **vehicles**, except the sequence for teaching the higher-order name **vehicle** would be dropped.

If the learner knows some lower-order names, but does not know the higher-order name, a potentially awkward situation arises. A lower-order statement should mention the higher-order name first: "This tree is a larch." If the learner already knows lower-order names, we might be tempted to use a statement that reverses the order: "This Larch is a tree." This statement treats the "treeness" as a variable, which it is not. "Treeness," unlike "tallness," is common to *all* larches.

The simplest solution is to teach the higher-order name and *then* relate the higher-order name to the familiar lower-order names. If the learner knows the lower-order name **collie**, but not the higher-order name **dog**, we could start with the higher-order noun sequence given in Figure 11.10.

Initially, the learner may not accept the idea that a collie is a dog, saying, "No, it's not a dog. It's a collie." The teacher should respond to this objection by saying, "It's

Figure 11.10

Example	Teacher Wording
1	This is not a dog.
2	This is not a dog.
3	This is a dog.
4	This is a dog.
5	Is this a dog?
6	Is this a dog?
7	Is this a dog?
8	Is this a dog?
9	Is this a dog?
10	Is this a dog?

a dog," and repeating the task. (Long explanations will not help.)

Note that **collie** is not the first positive that is presented. The reason is that the sequence must establish a basis for grouping **collie** with other dogs on the basis of common features. By first presenting two other dogs that are obviously not collies, the sequence makes the basis for giving **collie** a new name more obvious.

After the learner has successfully responded to all examples in the higher-order sequence, **collie** is introduced as a type of dog. The teacher points to the collie and asks, "Is this a dog?" ("Yes.") "You already know what kind of dog this is. This dog is a collie. What kind of dog is this?" Following this step, the teacher would proceed to introduce names of other dogs using noun sequences for each.

Collie is not taught through a sequence. The teaching occurs as the last part of the initial teaching for the higher-order category. A variation of this procedure would be used if the learner knew names of more than one member.

Other Hierarchical Classes

Variations of the procedures outlined above can be used to teach any higher-order relationships. To teach **successive** and **simultaneous events**, begin with the higher-order class **events**. (See Figure 11.11.)

Figure 11.11

Example	Teacher Wording
A ride on a pony	Is that an event? Yes.
Sitting on a pony	Is that an event? Yes.
A pony	Is than an event? No.
A room	Is that an event?
Walking through a room	Is that an event?
A room	Is that an event?
A party	Is that an event?
A party hat	Is that an event?
A walk in the park	Is that an event?
A park near the river	Is that an event?
A bullet and a piece of wood	Is that an event?
A bullet going through a piece of wood	Is that an event?

After the learner has mastered the higher-order discrimination of **event, not-event**, the lower-order members (**successive** and **simultaneous events**) would be introduced. Figure 11.12 gives a sequence for **successive events**.

The next sequence would teach **simultaneous events**. The sequence could present the discrimination as a correlated feature ("If the events are not successive, they are simultaneous"). Figure 11.13 gives the beginning of a possible sequence. Or it could begin with an explanation of the relationship followed by a set of examples.

Figure 11.14 shows a possible sequence preceded by an explanation.

Teaching the lower-order members **successive** and **simultaneous** involves less teaching because there are only two possible lower-class members. Therefore if a member is not one type, it must be the other. The learner is not required to look for new features to identify the second type; merely to substitute the designation "not-successive" for the new word, "simultaneous." For this

Figure 11.12

Example	Teacher Wording
A man presses on the brake. Then the car stops.	Those are successive events.
A woman runs and then jumps over the fence.	Those are successive events.
A stone goes up and then comes down.	Those are successive events.
The woman presses on the brake. At the same time, she hits the horn.	Tell me about those events.
As the sun moved one way, her shadow moved the other way.	Tell me about those events.
Before he moved to the city, he bought five hats.	Tell me about those events.
While standing on one foot, she scratched her nose.	Tell me about those events.
He sneezed and blinked at the same time.	Tell me about those events.
After carrying the refrigerator down the stairs, he collapsed.	Tell me about those events.

Figure 11.13

Example	Teacher Wording
	Events that are not successive are simultaneous. They happen at the same time.
The woman shouts and claps at the same time.	What kind of events?
The top was spinning and moving at the same time.	What kind of events?
The man stood up and then stretched.	What kind of events?
They sang the words at exactly the same time.	What kind of events?

Figure 11.14

Example	Teacher Wording
She fell, then skidded 6 meters.	These events are successive. How do I know? One event followed the other.
He talked as he ate.	These events are not successive. How do I know? One event does not follow the other.

introduction to be effective, the learner must be quite firm on **successive, not-successive**. If the learner is weak on this discrimination, serious problems will arise when **simultaneous** is taught. Figure 11.15 gives a schedule.

Note the large gap between the teaching of **successive** and **simultaneous**.

Figure 11.15

	1	2	3	4	5	6	7
A Event, not-event	A	A					
B Successive event	B	B					
C Simultaneous event					C	C	
Expansion activities			AB	AB	AB	C	
Cumulative Review							BC

Successive events and **simultaneous events** are treated as minimally different members. According to the rules for ordering members, these members cannot be juxtaposed in the introduction. A gap in the sequence following the introduction of **successive events** prevents them from being closely juxtaposed. During this gap, the learner practices the **successive-event** discrimination through expansion activities. On lesson 5, **simultaneous events** is taught.

Coordinate Higher-Order Classes

When we teach different higher-order classes, we frequently find ourselves teaching two coordinate higher-order classes, such as **gymnosperms** and **angiosperms**, or **vehicles** and **clothing**, or **nouns** and **adjectives**. Even if the learner knows the names of members of the classes, there may be some question about whether the learner can correctly classify trees as **gymnosperm trees** or **angiosperm trees**.

To firm the higher-order classes, we introduce a sequence after two *classes* have been taught and the learner has practiced working with each. (A class would include the higher-order label and the names of members.) The sequence takes the form of a cumulative-review sequence (no examples are modeled). Different trees are presented in an unpredictable order. The learner indicates the class to which each belongs.

Figure 11.16 gives the first part of a possible sequence that could be presented after the learner has been taught **vehicles** and **clothing**.

If the learner has been taught correlated features for the different classes, the firming sequence for the higher-order discrimination would be modeled after a correlated-features test segment (see Figure 11.17).

Figure 11.16

Example	Teacher Wording
	I'll show you things that are either in the class of clothing or the class of vehicles.
(shirt)	What class is this in?
(car)	What class is this in?
(motorcycle)	What class is this in?
	Etc.

Figure 11.17

Example	Teacher Wording
	I'll show you seeds from gymnosperm trees and angiosperm trees.
(White spruce)	What type of tree? How do you know? (Because the seeds are naked.)
(Beech)	What type of tree? How do you know? (Because the seeds are not naked.)
Etc.	

Variations of this higher-order firming sequence would be repeated after three coordinate classes have been introduced, and after each subsequent higher-order class has been taught.

Variations of the basic higher-order discrimination sequence are possible, such as a "fooler." (Fooler procedures are more fully discussed in Chapter 15.) Figure 11.18 shows an example of how a fooler would be used after the learner had been taught **vehicles, appliances, clothing,** and **containers**.

If **vehicles** had been the last-taught class, the sequence above would be well-designed to firm the higher-order discriminations. If the last-taught class had been **containers**, the format should change to: "I'll name some containers. When you hear me make a mistake, say 'stop.'"

The schedule in Figure 11.19 shows the pattern for higher-order firmings. Note that the schedule does not show all the sequences used to teach the members of the various classes and does not show the time interval between the various higher-order introductions.

Figure 11.18

Example	Teacher Wording
	My turn to name some vehicles. When you hear me make a mistake, say "stop." Here I go, naming vehicles.
Truck…car…motorboat …washing machine	Why did you say stop? (Because a washing machine is not a vehicle.) What is a washing machine? (An appliance.)
Motorboat… motorcycle…shirt	Why did you say stop? What is a shirt?
Motor home…car… truck…suitcase	Why did you say stop? What is a suitcase?
Blender	Why did you say stop? What is a blender?

(Possibly, 15 intervene between the firming of **appliances** and the firming of **containers**.)

Figure 11.19

Skills	Lessons				
A Vehicles	X				
B Clothing		X			
C Appliances			X		
D Containers				X	
Higher-Order Firming			AB	ABC	ABCD

The schedule shows that the firming activities first appear after the learner has completed the second class (higher-order label and members). The higher-order firming could begin as the class is still being taught. This decision and the frequency of the higher-order firming activities depend on other applications that are presented to the learner. Once taught, however, a discrimination should be used.

Alternative Approaches to Teaching Higher-Order Relationships

The procedures presented for teaching higher-order relationships is quite thorough. It assumes that the new members and the higher-order discriminations must be taught carefully. In many cases, this caution is not needed. The learner could easily learn the information about **simultaneous events** or **gymnosperms** far faster than the procedures we have presented would permit. For the sophisticated learner, the discriminations can be described and the description can even tell about the variation of features observed in the examples. The goal of instruction for these learners is not so much to teach the discriminations as it is to teach the various labels and the relationships of the parts within the higher-order system. Procedures that are appropriate for these situations are specified in Chapter 14 (Programs for Teaching Fact Systems).

Summary

If the goal is to provide complete teaching for a hierarchical or higher-order relationship, a program is needed. The program for the members follows the same rules as the program for introducing coordinate members to a set. In addition, a sequence for the higher-order class name is needed.

Follow these steps:

1. Begin the program with the sequence for the higher-order name.
    - Use a higher-order noun sequence (test question: "Is this a ___?").
    - Present non-continuous examples.
    - Use minimum-difference negatives that are *safe*.

2. Follow the teaching of the higher-order class name with a sequence for the first lower-order member.
    - Use a higher-order noun sequence, non-continuous examples, and minimum-differences selected from the set of members that will be taught later.
    - The test question is: "Is this (higher-order noun) a (lower-order noun)?"

3. Follow the first member with noun sequences for the teaching of each subsequent member. (The test task is: "What kind of ___ is this?" or, "Tell me about this ___.")

4. Process each member through an initial-teaching sequence, expansion activities, and cumulative review.

5. If more than one class is introduced, present a *higher-order firming* sequence that requires the learner to identify examples from different classes by their higher-order name. ("Tell me vehicle or clothing.")

6. For the more facile learner, use correlated-feature sequences to express the basis or rule for classifying members in a particular class.

Chapter 12
Programs Derived from Tasks

The most elementary program is one that simply introduces members into the set. A variation of this program is the higher-order class program that is more complicated because it teaches both higher-order discriminations and discriminations for various members. This chapter presents a third basic program. It derives from *a task*. A *task* consists of some sort of directions to the learner and some requirement for the learner to respond. "Put the ball on the table," is a task. So is "Write the answers to all questions on Part 1 of your worksheet." This is *not* a task: "The learner will respond to questions that involve prepositions." It is not a task because we do not know the words that occur in these questions. Unless we have the exact instruction that the learner is to follow and the exact behavior that the learner is to produce, we do not have a task. Conversely, any specific instruction to the learner (any question or direction) for which a specific response (or set of responses) is called for, is a task.

Programs that derive from tasks share many features with the other programs. The major difference has to do with the procedures by which the members or component discriminations to be taught are identified. Programs that derive from tasks are the product of *task analysis*. The process of task analysis consists of identifying the *component* discriminations and responses that appear in the task. Some components do not have to be taught at all, because they do not imply any new or difficult behavior on the part of the learner. Most components, however, should be pretaught, before the complete task is taught. These components are treated as *members* that we must introduce into a set. We follow the same rules for processing these members that we used for members in the other basic programs—the rules about separating members that are minimally different and separating introductions that involve minimum-difference discriminations. We cycle each member through these phases: initial teaching, expansion, and cumulative review.

Task Analysis

A task analysis includes three steps:

1. **Identifying the component discriminations of a task that should be pretaught.** The test for preteaching is: Could the learner who does not understand a discrimination that appears in the task *possibly* fail the task because of this deficiency? If the answer is "Yes," the component discrimination should be pretaught.

2. **Classifying each component discrimination identified for preteaching.** A discrimination is classified as either a single-dimension concept, a noun, a transformation, or a correlated-feature concept. This classification indicates how we would teach each discrimination identified.

3. **Scheduling the component discriminations.** Each discrimination is treated as a member of a set to be scheduled for initial teaching, expansion, and cumulative review. As noted earlier, the scheduling is governed by the basic rules for introducing members to a set.

Strict Task Analysis

A strict task analysis does not look beyond a specific task. It does not take into account the fact that the learner will be expected to do things that are closely related to those specified by the task. The analysis assumes only that the task is to be taught and that the components of the task can be identified and pretaught.

Let's say that we conducted a strict analysis on the task: "Put the ball on the table." By inspecting the task, we identify the components: **ball, table,** and **put** (or **put the ball**). By performing the first steps suggested for the task analysis, we arrive at judgments about the necessity of preteaching these components. We do not have to preteach the components *if our objective is to teach the task and only that task*. If the learner is simply going to *put the ball on the table* in response to repeated presentations of the direction, "Put the ball on the table," no preteaching is necessary because **ball** is not discriminated from any other objects that could be put on the table, and **table** is not discriminated from any other object that could receive the ball. Therefore, the learner does *not have to attend to these words*. After a naive learner has performed on the task a dozen times, the teacher could say, "Blop the tober umuck an elephant," and the learner would produce the behavior of *putting the ball on the table*.

This situation points out a serious problem with a strict task analysis. The analysis is not appropriate for cognitive skills because it creates generalization problems. The strict analysis is more appropriate for physical skills (shoe-tying, teeth brushing, downhill skiing, etc.). But even for these tasks, we are faced with the problem of specifying the task so that the teaching will account for generalization, not merely for performance on a single task.

Transformed-Task Analysis

The analysis of cognitive skills is more reasonable if we deal not only with the task that is presented, but also with a *set of related tasks* or with a *transformed task*. The transformed task is created by indicating substitutions for parts of the task. The task, "Put the ball on the table," is a member of the set, "Put the **A** on the **B**," with the letters referring to any familiar objects. By transforming the task in this way, we indicate the *generalizations* that are to be taught. Now the teaching of various components that we identify becomes functional because the learner must discriminate the names of different objects. (The learner must discriminate between "Put the book on the table," and "Put the ball on the book.") Note that we could transform the task even more by creating the transformed task, "Put **A** (position) **B**."

The component skills also change when we use a transformed-task analysis. Now it is important to teach components because the learner could possibly fail the original task by not knowing the component names.

The teaching of components for "Put **A** on **B**" is fairly straightforward. We teach a *set* of objects (or we assume that the learner has been taught a set of objects). We assure that **table** and **ball** are in the set before they are named in the original task; however, we do not limit the set to these objects. We then teach the discrimination on using a non-comparative sequence. Next we present a series of tasks that are described by our transformed objective, "Put **A** on **B**." These tasks would include: "Put the ball on the table," "Put the ball on the floor," "Put the spoon on the ball," and so forth. Note that the program is designed to include the original task ("Put the ball on the table"); however, it is not limited to this task. It includes a range of tasks that have the same form ("Put **A** on **B**").

Correlated-Feature Sentences

In later chapters, we will use transformed-task analysis to derive programs for a variety of skills, such as routines for solving column multiplication problems. The applications that we will present in the remainder of this chapter, however, involve simpler tasks and simpler programs. These tasks are simpler because they have already been transformed. All take this form: "The learner will respond appropriately to applications of this rule: 'When air gets hotter, it expands.'" The responses the learner will produce are not specified. The specific tasks that will be presented are not specified. However, the transformed task indicates that we must provide a good test of the learner's ability to handle applications that derive from the rule, "When air gets hotter, it expands." The sentence expresses a correlated-feature relationship; therefore, we would teach the relationship through a correlated-features sequence. This sequence would provide us with the specification of responses the learner is to produce. Most important for our present purpose, the sentence itself serves as a part of the task sequence that is given. If the learner is to deal with applications based on the sentence, we must teach any component discriminations named in the sentence that would serve as possible causes of confusion for the naive learner.

For the remainder of this chapter, we will deal only with sentences that express correlated-feature relationships. We will identify the component skills expressed in the sentences. We will indicate how the component skills could be taught and scheduled.

Correlated-feature sentences are well suited to an analysis of component skills because they express one particular meaning of the words and they admit to a relatively straightforward analysis.

Meanings and Words

Different sentences generate different meanings of words. "This picture should be hung on the west wall," uses the any-surface meaning of **on**. "Pillows belong on the bed," assumes a different meaning of **on**. *The particular* *meaning that we will teach depends on the sentence we start with.* When analyzing components of sentences, we are concerned with only that meaning. (Without this stipulation, the designer's quest becomes one of trying to teach all meanings. The task does not require the learner to know every meaning of a word like **on**.)

Wording. A task indicates the meaning of specific words that are to be taught and specifies the wording that must be used to teach particular discriminations. If the task that we begin with contains the words **in contact with**, we would use these words and only these words in teaching the idea **in contact with**. We would not substitute the words **in contact with** for **on**. Similarly, if the task refers to a *living organism*, we would design sequences that teach the idea expressed by this component in the task, and we would use the words **living organism** (and only these words) when we taught this component.

In summary, the task provides specific directions for both the meaning that is to be taught and the exact wording to be used in conveying the meaning.

Analysis of Sentences

The sentence we start with specifies an entity and then tells about one feature correlated with that entity. Since the sentence is divided into two parts (the specifying of the entity and the telling of the correlated feature), *the sentence contains at least two component discriminations.* The naming of the entity (the first part of the statement) may be made up of component discriminations. The second part of the statement may also contain component discriminations. In a careful program, components of each part would be taught first, the entire part would be taught next, and the correlated-feature relationship would be taught last.

Figure 12.1 shows a diagram of how the teaching might occur for a sentence made up of two parts, each of which contains three component discriminations (labeled **A** through **F**).

Figure 12.1
Sentence: ABC/DEF

1. First taught: components of parts. → A B C   D E F
2. Next taught: parts. → ABC   DEF
3. Last taught: correlated-feature relationship. → ABC/DEF

For some sentences, the pattern might look quite different because all the discriminations that must be pretaught would be in the first part of the sentence. For other sentences, some discriminations occur in the first part and perhaps one occurs in the second. Regardless of the pattern, the general strategy is suggested by the diagram above. First the components are taught—one at a time. Then these are integrated to form parts of the sentence. The last step is the correlated-feature relationship.

The Program

Suppose we start with a correlated-feature relationship expressed by the sentence: *If the leaf is pinnately venated and has pointed lobes, it is a black oak leaf.* The first part tells the conditions that must be met for the oak leaf to be a black oak leaf. The second part specifies the label that we will use to refer to objects that meet the conditions.

Identifying components. The discriminations that should be pretaught appear in the first part of the sentence: **leaf**, **pinnately venated**, and **pointed lobes**. Although we can test the learner with a sequence that involves **leaf**, **not-leaf**, we can combine the teaching of this discrimination with that of other components.

Classifying components. To teach **pinnately venated**, use a non-comparative sequence. To teach **pointed**, use a non-comparative sequence. The correlated-feature sequence would be used to teach the relationship expressed in the sentence.

Schedule. Figure 12.2 shows a possible schedule for the components.

Figure 12.2				
Components	Days			
	1	2	3	4
A. Pinnately venated	X			
B. Pointed lobes		X		
C. Correlated-feature sequence			X	X
Expansion				C
Review		AB		

Note that the initial teaching is presented on only one day for each component. The correlated-features sequence appears on two days. On the first day it appears, it would be the last teaching event, occurring after the review and work on pointed lobes.

Figure 12.3 shows a sequence for teaching **pinnate, not-pinnate**.

Figure 12.3		
Example		Teacher Wording
	(leaf)	Here's a leaf with no vein pattern on it. I'll put a pattern on it and tell you if it's a pinnately-venated pattern.
1	(leaf)	This pattern is not pinnately venated.
2	(leaf)	This pattern is pinnately venated.
3	(leaf)	Tell me about this pattern.
4	(leaf)	Tell me about this pattern.

The various patterns could be created by placing two different transparencies over the leaf. One would show the pinnately venated pattern; the other would show the other vein pattern. If the teacher were dealing with sophisticated learners, the teacher could require labels for both patterns. In this case, the introduction would be changed to: "Here's a leaf with no vein pattern on it. I'll put patterns on and tell you if the pattern is a **pinnately-venated** pattern or a **palmately-venated** pattern." The teacher might require the learner to repeat the names before proceeding. The sequences could also call attention to the difference between the patterns. "If the veins don't come together at one point, the pattern is pinnately venated." The essential aspects of the sequence are the presentation of positive and negative examples and the use of the label that will be used in the correlated-feature sequence. The directions for each test example, "Tell me about this pattern," require the learner to say the word rather than responding by saying "Yes" or "No."

The next discrimination to be taught is **pointed lobes** (**B**). We may decide first to teach **lobes**, then **pointed lobes**. Decisions of this type are frequently required when we analyze sentences for component discriminations. It is usually safe to deal with the conjunctive concept (**pointed lobes**) because the negative examples that are implied by the sentence are lobes that are *not* pointed. (The leaves that are most similar to black oak leaves have lobes. Whether the lobes are pointed becomes the critical basis for discriminating black oaks from these leaves.) As a general rule, you can deal with the larger phrases that appear in a sentence.

Figure 12.4 shows a possible sequence for teaching **pointed lobes**.

Figure 12.4		
Example		Teacher Wording
	(leaf)	Here's an outline of a leaf with no lobes on it. I'll put lobes on it. Tell me if the lobes are pointed or not pointed.
1	(leaf)	Tell me about the lobes.
2	(leaf)	Tell me about the lobes.
3	(leaf)	Tell me about the lobes.
4	(leaf)	Tell me about the lobes.

The examples above could be created by placing transparent overlays over the original leaf form. No models are presented in this sequence because we assume that the learner already knows the difference between **pointed** and **not-pointed**. We could expand the sequence by introducing a wider variety of lobe examples. We could also change the test instructions so that the learner responded by saying "pointed lobes" or "rounded lobes."

After we have taught the discrimination of pinnately-venated and pointed lobes, we are ready to teach the correlated-feature relationship: "If the leaf is pinnately venated and has pointed lobes, it is a black oak leaf." The sequence will show what is mentioned first in the sentence-leaves that have (or do not have) pinnately venated patterns and pointed lobes. The learner will respond by identifying it either as a black oak or a not-black oak. A second question will ask, "How do you know?" Figure 12.5 shows the sequence.

Figure 12.5		
Example		Teacher Wording
1		This is a black oak leaf. How do I know? Because it is pinnately venated and it has pointed lobes.
2		Your turn: Tell me black oak or not-black oak. How do you know?
3		Tell me black oak or not-black oak. How do you know?
4		Tell me black oak or not-black oak. How do you know?
5		Tell me black oak or not-black oak. How do you know?
6		Tell me black oak or not-black oak. How do you know?

The sequence of examples shows the following variations:

pinnately venated and pointed lobes

pinnately venated and not-pointed lobes

not-pinnately venated and not-pointed lobes

not-pinnately venated and pointed lobes

We could construct a sequence that has a larger number of examples; however, the crucial aspects of any acceptable sequence are that it must show minimum negatives and that it must require the learner to conclude whether or not each example meets the criterion for **black oak**.

The program above derives from a sentence that is complicated; however, there is nothing really new in the program. It is a simple extension of the sequences and rules presented in the preceding chapters.

Validity. There is always the question of truth or validity of the statement that is being taught. The statement about black oak leaves would not permit the learner to discriminate between black oak and all other leaves. A qualification could be presented to resolve the problem. "I'll show you leaves that are black oak leaves and leaves that are not-black oak leaves." This qualification permits us to use the sequence.

Illustration

Here's a different correlated-feature sequence that could serve as the objective for a task-analysis program: *When solids are heated enough, they turn into liquids.*

Component discriminations. The discriminations are **solids**, **heated**, and **liquids**. All these discriminations would be taught before the correlated-feature relationship is taught. **Heated** is a comparative (getting hotter). **Solid** and **liquid** are coordinate members of the same set. They would be taught as members of a set with the first member taught through a higher-order noun sequence that presents the liquids as minimum-difference negatives. The sequence for the second member is a regular noun sequence.

The schedule in Figure 12.6 shows a fast introduction. No problems would result if the discriminations were presented with time gaps between them, so long as the reviews were adequate.

Figure 12.6				
Components	Days			
	1	2	3	4
A. Solid	X			
B. Heated	X	X		
C. Liquid			X	
D. Correlated-features			X	X
Review		A	A	

For the teaching of **solids**, the negative examples would be liquids and possibly gases. The range of solids includes things that are pliable, such as cloth, and those that are stiff, such as ice. Figure 12.7 shows a possible sequence.

The sequence is a higher-order noun sequence that opens with three positives followed by a minimum difference and mix of positives and negatives. The learner identifies each example as "solid" or "not-solid."

Heated is a comparative. To teach **heated** as a basic sensory quality, we could present the learner with water from a mixer faucet. Note that we would teach the wording **heated** if that wording appeared in the sentence that was to be taught. If the sentence referred to **getting hotter**, we would use the same basic sequence of examples with the wording "getting hotter."

Figure 12.7	
Example	Teacher Wording
Ice cube	This is a solid.
Plastic bag	This is a solid.
Paper bag	This is a solid.
Plastic bag	Tell me solid or not-solid.
Brown rock	What's this?
Molasses	What's this?
Water	What's this?
Wood chips	What's this?
Ice cream frozen	What's this?
Block of glass	What's this?
Melted ice cream	What's this?
Blanket	What's this?

Figure 12.8 shows a sequence that is created by referring to degrees. This sequence assumes that the learner has already been taught the basic *sensory* discrimination **heated**.

Figure 12.8	
Example	Teacher Wording
	Let's say an object is 30 degrees. I'll tell you if it gets heated.
Temperature changes to 31°.	Did it get heated? Yes.
Temperature changes to 85°.	Did it get heated? Yes.
Temperature changes to 84°.	Did it get heated? No.
Temperature changes to 83°.	Did it get heated?
Temperature changes to 84°.	Did it get heated?
Temperature changes to 12°.	Did it get heated?
Temperature changes to 15°.	Did it get heated?
Temperature changes to -15°.	Did it get heated?
Temperature changes to 2081°.	Did it get heated?
Temperature changes to 2029°.	Did it get heated?
Temperature changes to 5°.	Did it get heated?
Temperature changes to 28°.	Did it get heated?
Temperature changes to -3°.	Did it get heated?
Temperature changes to 11°.	Did it get heated?

Examples are created verbally in this sequence. The sequence is non-continuous. It follows the juxtaposition pattern for the comparative sequence. It begins with a starting point example, followed by two positives, two negatives, and a series of unpredictable examples. There are no no-change negatives in the sequence.

The third component of the task is **liquids** (see Figure 12.9).

Figure 12.9	
Example	Teacher Wording
Water	My turn: This is a liquid.
Molasses	This is a liquid.
Water	What's this?
Ice	What's this?
Brown rock	What's this?
Gasoline	What's this?
Plastic bag	What's this?
Mercury	What's this?
Wood	What's this?

Two positives are followed by an **E1** test and then an **E2** test. The learner responds to the test examples by saying either "liquid" or "solid."

After the learner has been taught the concepts **solid**, **heated**, and **liquid**, the correlated-feature relationship is taught. We present examples referred to in the first part of the sentence (solids being heated or not-being heated), and the learner tells whether this change would make the solid into a liquid. (See Figure 12.10.)

Figure 12.10	
Example	Teacher Wording
Here's what happens. A solid object goes from 45° to 46°.	What's going to happen if this change keeps going? The solid will turn into a liquid. How do I know? Because the solid is being heated.
Now it goes to 312°.	My turn: What's going to happen if this change keeps going? The solid will turn into liquid. How do I know? Because the solid is being heated.
Now it goes to 311°.	What's going to happen if this change keeps going? How do you know?
Now it goes to 56°.	What's going to happen if this change keeps going? How do you know?
Now it goes to 300°.	What's going to happen if this change keeps going? How do you know?

Note that the correlated feature expressed in this sequence is not the strongest one possible. However, if it is the one selected for instruction, it serves as a task that implies the component sequences (or their equivalent as preskills).

Illustration

A final example is the sentence: *If the word ends in* **CVC** *(consonant-vowel-consonant), and the next part begins with a* **V** *(vowel), you double the last* **C** *(consonant)*.

Components. The learner should be taught whether letters are **C** (consonant letters) or **V** (vowel letters). The learner should discriminate whether a word ends in **CVC**. The learner should discriminate whether the next part begins with a **V**.

Sequences. The discrimination of **vowel** would be taught first. The strategy would be to teach the members that are vowels: "Name the vowels." This is a memorization task. After it has been taught, the learner would be presented with different examples of letters. The learner would identify each as either "vowel" or "not-vowel." The sequence would be a higher-order noun sequence.

The discrimination **consonant** would be taught through a noun sequence. Those letters that are not vowels are consonants. The learner identifies each example as "vowel" or "consonant."

The discrimination **ends in CVC** implies a non-comparative sequence or a transformation. The discrimination, **next part begins with a vowel** implies a non-comparative sequence or transformation. Figure 12.11 shows a possible program schedule.

Figure 12.11												
Components	Days										
	1	2	3	4	5	6	7	8	9	10	11
A. Vowel	X	X	X								
B. Consonant					X	X					
C. Ends CVC								X	X		
D. Part begins V								X	X		
E. Correlated-feature										X	X
Review and expansion		A	A	A	A	AB	AB	AB		AB	

After vowels have been taught, the teacher might list them, then present a sequence that requires the learner to identify whether each letter is a vowel or a not-vowel (lesson 5). Figure 12.12 shows the first part of a possible sequence.

Figure 12.12	
Example	Teacher Wording
	Letters that are not vowels are consonants.
c	My turn: What's this? A consonant.
d	My turn: What's this? A consonant.
v	My turn: What's this? A consonant.
d	Your turn: What's this?
h	What's this?
a	What's this?
j	What's this?
r	What's this?
p	What's this?
e	What's this?

The sequence begins with a rule. Note that the discrimination could be taught without this rule; however, the use of the rule makes the discrimination more obvious to the learner.

After the learner has been taught to discriminate consonants and vowels, we would teach the learner to discriminate what words **end in**. Perhaps the best sequence for this teaching is a single-transformation sequence (see Figure 12.13). The single-transformation juxtapositions permit a precise demonstration of how each word ends.

Figure 12.13	
Example	Teacher Wording
	I'm going to call any vowel **V** and any consonant **C**.
band	My turn: What type are the last three letters in this word: **VCC**.
ban	My turn: What type are the last three letters? **CVC**.
bran	Your turn: What type are the last three letters?
brad	What type are the last three letters?
beak	What type are the last three letters?
smoke	What type are the last three letters?
tree	What type are the last three letters?
sent	What type are the last three letters?
rot	What type are the last three letters?
strip	What type are the last three letters?
Etc.	What type are the last three letters?

The sequence follows the pattern of other single-transformation sequences. A series of progressive minimum-difference examples is followed by greater-difference examples.

A similar sequence would be used to teach the **beginning of parts**. Figure 12.14 shows some test examples.

Figure 12.14	
Example	Teacher Wording
er	This part begins with a vowel (**V**).
ed	What type of letter does this part begin with?
red	What type of letter does this part begin with?
s	What type of letter does this part begin with?
ing	What type of letter does this part begin with?

Only one example is modeled because the learner already can identify vowels and consonants. We assume that the learner also knows **word** (or **part**), **beginning** and **end**. (If the learner does not know **beginning** or **end**, these would be taught through a non-comparative sequence. The teacher would say, "I'll touch a part of a word. I'll tell you if it's the beginning." The teacher would then touch either the beginning or end. The teacher would model several examples and then test on others. Only one discrimination would be taught initially, either **beginning, not-beginning**; or **end, not-end**.)

To teach the discrimination **double the last C**, we could present a single-transformation sequence. Figure 12.15 shows the first part of such a sequence.

Figure 12.15	
Example	Teacher Wording
bent	My turn to double the last **C** in this word: **t, t**.
bend	Your turn: Double the last **C**.
bena	Double the last **C**.

After the learner has been taught to identify the last three letters of a word, whether a part begins with a vowel or a consonant, and how to double the last **C**, the final relationship would be taught through a correlated-feature sequence. The relationship being taught is: If the word ends in **CVC** and the next part begins with a vowel, you double the last **C** (see Figure 12.16).

The rule is complicated, on the verge of being unmanageable. To make it more manageable, we might make more of the steps overt. However, the same basic relationship shown in the sequence above would remain in the more overtized procedure. There would be a series of examples, at first those that show minimum difference, then those that show greater difference.

Figure 12.16	
Example	Teacher Wording
sit + ing	My turn: Do I double the last **C** in sit? Yes. How do I know? Because sit ends in **CVC** and the last part begins with a vowel.
sit + s	My turn: Do I double the last **C** in sit? No. How do I know? The last part doesn't begin with a vowel.
sleep + ing	My turn: Do I double the last **C** in sleep? No. How do I know? Because sleep does not end in **CVC**.
slip + ing	Your turn: Do you double the last **C** in slip? How do you know?
drop + s	Do you double the last **C** in drop? How do you know?
drift + ing	Do you double the last **C** in drift? How do you know?
slip + s	Do you double the last **C** in slip? How do you know?
treat + ing	Do you double the last **C** in treat? How do you know?
look + ing	Do you double the last **C** in look? How do you know?
ask + er	Do you double the last **C** in ask? How do you know?
flat + en	Do you double the last **C** in flat? How do you know?
slit + s	Do you double the last **C** in slit? How do you know?

This description of the program for the **CVC** rule is quite incomplete. The point, however, is not to articulate the development of the program, but to show that even very complicated rules are composed totally of sensory discriminations, correlated-feature relationships, and transformations. These components are contained in the facts that serve as tasks for analysis. The facts provide the specific wording for all the necessary discriminations and relationships. Also, the facts provide the precise meanings that are to be taught.

Analyzing Preskills Contained in Facts

We do not have to preteach all discriminations presented in a correlated feature sentence—merely those that pose possible confusion. Sometimes it is easier to see what should be taught by rephrasing the sentence as an **if-then** sentence. Here are some rephrased items:

- The faster something moves, the more inertia it has.

  Rephrased: If it goes faster, it has more inertia.

- Sedimentary rocks include limestone, sandstone, and shale.

  Rephrased: If the rock is limestone, sandstone, or shale, it is a sedimentary rock.

- Ornithischian dinosaurs have a pelvis structure like birds'.

  Rephrased: If the dinosaur has a pelvic structure like a bird's, the dinosaur is an ornithischian dinosaur.

- Heated objects expand.

  Rephrased: If the object is heated, it expands.

- Indolent means lazy.

  Rephrased: If a person is lazy, a person is indolent.

When the sentences are set up this way, the first part of the sentence contains names that must be pretaught. Perhaps the last part does, too. However, you must decide whether the last part tells about something that will *also happen* or simply provides a new name for the events described in the first part of the sentence. The sentence: **If the animal has a backbone, the animal is a vertebrate,** does not mean that the animal changes into a vertebrate. It means that if the animal meets the classification criterion of having a backbone, the animal is *called* a vertebrate. The situation is quite different from this sentence: **If the object is heated, it expands**. **Expanding** is not simply another way of saying that the object is heated.

One test of whether the last-mentioned words should be pretaught is this: if you can add the word **called** to the rule, you are dealing with an equivalent-meaning sentence, and you should not teach the last-mentioned words. The word **called** has been added to the following sentences:

- If the pubis bone of a dinosaur's pelvis is forward, the dinosaur is *called* saurischian.

- If the organism lives in an environment that has no free oxygen, the organism is *called* anaerobic.

- If someone tends to be irritable, that person is *called* irascible.

For all these sentences of equivalent meaning, we would not preteach the new word. The correlated-feature sequence would provide that teaching.

If the word **called** cannot be added, the discrimination referred to in the last part of the sentence should be pretaught.

For the sentence, **If molecules are heated, they move faster; molecules, heated**, and **moving faster** should be pretaught.

For the sentence, **If something moves farther from the surface of the earth, it weighs less; moving farther from, the surface of the earth**, and **weighing less** should be pretaught.

These and similar sentences tell about the relationship of one event to another.

Prescriptive Applications of Programs

The basic task-analysis procedure applies to prescriptive, or remedial instruction. In these situations, learners have trouble because they have not been taught some necessary prerequisite skills or discriminations.

This situation is very common. The teacher tries to teach how rain is formed, the difference between adjectives and adverbs, the spelling of a particular class of words, or how expansion works. Often, students do not understand what the teacher is trying to communicate.

Instead of providing an entire program, the remedy involves *probing* (to determine precisely what the students do know) and determining an appropriate sequence of skills. The procedure for probing is not the random exploration that is sometimes called probing. It is the identification and testing of the component basic discriminations that are implied by the correlated-feature relationship. The teaching of those skills follows from the probe.

Testing Skills

We begin with the test of the correlated-feature relationship. Let's say that the teacher is trying to teach students how rain is formed. As part of the instruction, the teacher explains that "When the water-laden air rises over the mountains, it cools and can no longer hold all the water. The result is rain." We suspect that the students do not understand the explanation. This assumption is reasonable, because the explanation is mystical, suggesting that the inability of the cooler air to hold water is related to mountains. Also, the sentence contains far too much information. The critical relationship is: "When air rises, it can't hold as much water." Figure 12.17 illustrates a test.

Figure 12.17	
Example	Teacher Wording
	(Teacher touches spot on chalkboard.) Pretend that my finger is a mass of air. Watch what the air does and tell me about the amount of water it can hold.
Finger goes up one foot.	Can it hold more water now, or less water? How do you know?
Finger goes down six inches.	Can it hold more water now, or less water? How do you know?
Finger goes up slightly.	Can it hold more water now, or less water? How do you know?
Finger goes way up.	Can it hold more water now, or less water? How do you know?

Another correlated-feature probe could be used to test the learner's understanding of the temperature of the air as illustrated in Figure 12.18.

Figure 12.18	
Example	Teacher Wording
	This time, I want you to tell me whether the air cools or becomes hotter. Watch my finger.
Finger goes up a few inches.	Tell me what happens to the temperature...How do you know?
Finger goes up a foot.	Tell me about the temperature...How do you know?
Finger goes down a few inches.	Tell me about the temperature...How do you know?

If the learners performed well on the sequences, the teacher could proceed with the original explanation and could ask questions that require students to predict what will happen.

"The air moves up the mountain. Is this air rising or falling? . . . So what's going to happen to the temperature of the air? . . . And what's going to happen to the amount of water the air can hold? . . . If the air can't hold the water, where will the water go? . . . And that's how rain is formed."

In later chapters, we will provide more information about how to construct applications and how to test preskills.

Summary

The programs formulated in this chapter derive from a *task analysis*. There are two basic approaches to task analysis. The first is to adhere rigidly to the wording and behaviors that are called for in the task. This approach is more reasonable when the instruction involves teaching motor behavior rather than discriminations. The second type of task analysis begins by *transforming* the original task into a form that suggests the range of discriminations the learner is to make when dealing with the tasks of that type. The transformed task indicates the substitutions that can be made to create the crucial discriminations.

Task analysis applies to any complex task. This chapter applied the analysis to sentences of correlated-feature relationships. These sentences are usually good starting points for developing small programs because they usually do not require transformations.

Deriving a program from a correlated-feature sentence (or from other tasks) involves three steps:

1. Identifying the component discriminations presented in the task.

2. Classifying each component discrimination in a way that indicates how to teach the discrimination.

3. Scheduling the components that are to be included in the program.

When we use the task analysis, we assume that the task is given. That means the wording in the task is accepted as the wording that the learner will respond to. It also means that the particular meaning of a word or phrase presented in the sentence is the meaning that we accept for the program.

- The sentence contains the wording that should be used in the program for teaching component skills.

- The sentence contains the *meanings* that should be used with each component.

- Each sentence consists of two major discriminations: the entity named first in the sentence and the features attributed to the entity.
- Possibly, both the entity and the feature can be broken into component discriminations.
- The test of whether a discrimination should be taught is: Would it be possible for the learner to fail to understand the relationship expressed by the sentence without knowledge of individual components?
- As a rule, the most relevant components are composed of a group of words. If you are in doubt, however, teach some of the smaller components.
- Classify each component as a single-dimension discrimination, a noun, or as one of the joining forms. This classification suggests how we will teach the component.
- The scheduling of components follows the procedures for introducing members to a set.
- Highly similar discriminations are separated in time. So are introductions that involve minimum-differences.

The biggest point this chapter makes is that if we accept a task, such as a correlated-feature sentence, we can identify the preskills that the learner should be taught.

Section VI will show how the analysis applies to complex cognitive routines, tasks far more complicated than sentences. Although the task analysis is more complicated when applied to these routines, it involves the same procedures outlined in this chapter—identifying the component discriminations and specifying the sequences and examples needed to teach each discrimination. The building blocks, or component discriminations, always imply sequences for teaching comparatives, non-comparatives, nouns, transformations, or correlated features. The wording and meaning presented in the complex task directs which sequences, which wording, and which meaning are implied for each discrimination.

Chapter 13
Double Transformation Programs

Although the structure of the double-transformation relationship is complicated, the strategy for the double-transformation program is not. The double-transformation relationship always involves two sets of single-transformation examples that share some relevant features. The strategy for teaching the relationship involves first teaching one set using the standard procedures for introducing single-transformations. The second set, however, is taught in a new way. The learner is shown the *difference* between the first and second sets. Since the learner is required to learn only the difference, the learning demands are substantially reduced for the second set; therefore, the amount of teaching time is decreased. If we arbitrarily say that concept **X** and concept **Y** each have ten features, and eight of these are common to both discriminations, we could reduce the amount of teaching for **Y** by eight features if we showed **Y** as being a variation of **X**. In effect, teaching the difference is designed to induce this type of awareness for the new concept, "Oh, that's just like **X** except that it . . ."

The strategy for teaching a double-transformation relationship has two advantages:

1. It achieves savings in teaching time.
2. It assures that the learner will learn the relationship between discriminations that are related in significant ways.

We have used a variation of this strategy for the teaching of polars. We do not try to teach the polars **hot** and **cold** at the same time. Instead, we teach one of the discriminations (**hot, not-hot**). Later, when the learner has mastered this discrimination, we teach the difference between **not-hot** and **cold**. (The only difference is the label.)

The double transformation relationship is more complicated than the relationship between **not-hot** and **cold**; however, the strategy is basically the same.

Double-Transformation Structure

Every double-transformation relationship involves two single-transformation sets of examples. Arithmetic provides many examples of double-transformation sets; however, the double-transformation relationship is not limited to arithmetic. To find a double-transformation relationship, start with a set of single-transformation examples. For instance, start with the arithmetic facts 0+1 through 19+1.

Now think of a set of examples that "parallels" the plus-one set. *This second set parallels the plus-one set if you can create all members of the second set by applying the same transformation to any member of the first set.* A parallel set would be *plus-ten facts*. For every plus-one fact, a corresponding plus-ten fact is created by applying exactly the same transformation (adding a zero to each numeral): 4+1=5 changes into 40+10=50; 5+1=6 changes to 50+10=60; etc. By following the same transformation rule, we can create all members of the plus-ten set.

The plus-ten set is not the only set that bears a double transformation relationship with the plus-one set. For every member of the plus-one set, there is a member of the minus-one set. Every member of the minus-one can be created by applying the same transformation to a member of the plus-one set. By applying the transformation to 4+1=5, we create 4−1=3. By applying the transformation to 19+1=20, we create 19−1=18, and so forth.

Still another set that bears a double transformation relationship with the plus-one set is the plus-two set. By applying the same transformation to different members of the plus-one set, we change 7+1=8 into 7+2=9, and change 4+1=5 into 4+2=6, etc.

Figure 13.1 shows the double-transformation associated with plus-one facts and corresponding plus-two facts. The left column shows the plus-one set. There are minimal differences *within* the plus-one set (the plus-one column). The horizontal arrows show that the same transformation converts any plus-one problem into a corresponding plus-two problem. The right column

Figure 13.1

Plus-One Set	Standard Transformation	Plus-Two Set
6 + 1	Add 1 more to second number →	6 + 2
5 + 1	Add 1 more to second number →	5 + 2
4 + 1	Add 1 more to second number →	4 + 2

(Minimum differences shown on both sides)

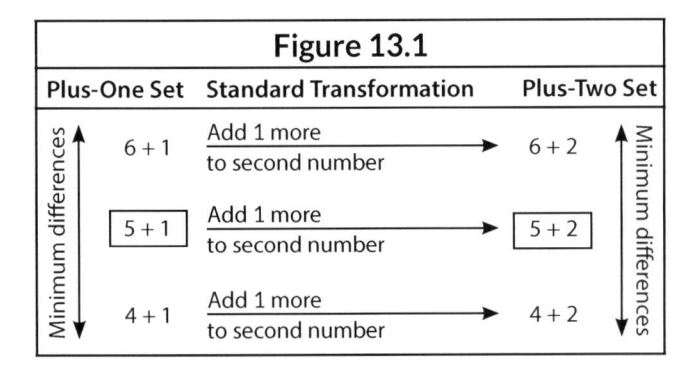

shows the corresponding minimum differences that are generated within the plus-two set.

Note that the same transformation (horizontal arrows) accounts for the creation of every example in the plus-two set.

Criteria for Double Transformations

The test of whether a concept has double-transformation features involves two questions. If the answer to both questions is "Yes," the concept is a double-transformation concept.

1. Are different within-set responses created by applying the *same operation* to different examples? For example, different examples of words said loudly are created by applying the same operation—"Say it loud"—to different words of two syllables. "Meeting. Say it loud." "Funny. Say it loud." Etc.

2. Can you create a corresponding member of another set by applying the *same* transformation to *any member of the original set*? We can convert any member of the set of words that is said loudly into a word that has only the last part pronounced loudly. We apply the same transformation to every word in the said-loudly set. This transformation generates all members of the second set we refer to and is therefore the standard transformation of the across-set transformation.[1]

---

[1] We frequently do not have a tidy vocabulary that expresses these across-set transformations. Most of our standard vocabulary focuses on within-set features. We can take any word and "say it louder" or "say it faster." But we may have trouble describing precisely how to change some word to make it "louder" or make it "faster." An explanation is possible. However, it would be very elaborate and technical.

Criterion 1 is the test for within-set differences. If the learner produces different responses while the same instructions are presented with various examples, the set has the essential features of a single-transformation concept. Criterion 2 indicates whether a double-transformation is involved. If it is possible to convert every member of the single-transformation set into a member of another set by performing a standard transformation, the concept is a double transformation.

There are two kinds of double transformations. One involves a difference in the *examples* (with the same instructions used for both sets); the other involves changes in the *instructions* (with the same examples used for both sets). The second type is the easiest to recognize. If we change the instructions so that a different instruction *creates* all members of the transformed set ("Say it in a whisper," "Tell the percent the fraction equals," "Reverse the notation"), we are dealing with a double transformation. The instructions indicate that a variation of a familiar operation is to be performed. The type of double-transformation that involves the same instructions, but different examples, is more difficult to recognize and is more arbitrary. For instance, we can identify many subsets of written words that are irregular from a decoding standpoint. For instance, words that contain **al** (**tall, malt, also**, etc.) form such a subset. The set could be taught as a double-transformation set. The examples in this set are different from words in which the **a** sound is "regular" (**at, man, back**, etc.); however, the instructions for reading **al** words is the same as that for reading any other word: "Read it." Theoretically, any large subtype of examples (examples that require a variation of the operation used for other examples) can be treated as a double-transformation set.

In summary, the two types of double-transformation sets are:

- Those in which there are different instructions for the same example that had been processed with a familiar operation.

- Those in which the instructions are the same, but the examples are a subset requiring a different operation.

Note that if the examples are the same for the familiar set of examples and for the transformed set, the instructions are different. If the examples are different for the transformed set, the instructions are the same.

Juxtapositions

Our objective for the double-transformation program is the same as the objective for more basic sequences—to go from the simplest juxtapositions to the most difficult or unpredictable ones.

Below are four examples of word-saying tasks (two from the familiar set and their counterparts from the transformed set).

1. Map. Say it in a whisper.
2. Alligator. Say it in a whisper.
3. Map. Say it loud.
4. Alligator. Say it loud.

The juxtaposition of 1 and 2 is the easiest juxtaposition *because it permits the learner to do the same thing with juxtaposed examples.*

The 1, 3 juxtaposition is an across-set difference. The same example is presented with different instructions. *Only two examples of this type can be juxtaposed at a time*; therefore, the learner does not receive the opportunity to work on a series of examples in which the instructions are different, but the examples are the same. This type of juxtaposition is more difficult than the 1, 2 juxtaposition because it does not provide *a series* of examples of the same type.

The juxtaposition of 1, 4 is the most difficult type because it calls for the greatest difference between examples. The example changes (from **map** to **alligator**). The instructions change (from "Say it in a whisper," to "Say it loud"). The amount of processing involved is therefore greater than that required by the other juxtapositions.

Based on the relative difficulty of the patterns, the double-transformation program will proceed from 1, 2 juxtapositions (within-set) to 1, 3 (across-set minimum differences) to 1, 4 (mix of the two sets).

The Double-Transformation Program

The double transformation involves two sets of examples: examples that are in the *familiar set*, and examples that are in the *transformed set*. The familiar set has therefore been taught. If the learner knows plus-one facts, selected plus-one examples comprise the familiar set. The transformed set would consist of the plus-two counterpart for each member of the familiar set presented in the program. (If 7+1 is a member of the familiar plus-one set, 7+2 would be a member of the transformed, plus-two set.) The transformed set is the one we teach through the double-transformation program.

No within-set minimum difference examples are used in the program. *The only minimum-difference juxtapositions are across-set differences, achieved by juxtapositioning a member of the familiar set with a corresponding member of the transformed set.* (7+1 juxtaposed with 7+2, for instance.)

We will describe the double-transformation program as a very elaborate *sequence*, although we probably would not present the entire sequence at one time. (The relationships among examples are more apparent when the program is viewed as a sequence.) After we have discussed these relationships, we will examine ways of distributing parts of the elaborate sequence to make a variety of possible programs.

The examples in a double-transformation program are grouped into four parts or cycles.

1. Familiar Set

The double-transformation begins with a set of four or five members of the familiar set that are sequenced to show *sameness*. (Juxtaposed examples are different from each other.) The familiar-set examples appear first to assure that the learner is firm on what has already been taught. We refer to the familiar-set members as examples 1, 2, 3, 4, 5.

2. Transformed Set (Within-Set Juxtapositions)

Immediately following example 5 of the familiar set, we present *corresponding* members of the transformation set, sequenced in an order different from that of the familiar set. The transformed set is sequenced so that the last member of the familiar set (5) is juxtaposed to a minimally different member of the transformed set (5'). The transformed-set members are referred to as 1', 2', 3', 4', and 5'.

$$\text{Thus: } 1, 2, 3, 4, 5, 5', 3', 1', 4', 2'$$

The juxtapositions presented so far in the sequence are: sameness juxtapositions for the familiar set (1, 2, 3, 4, 5); minimum difference juxtaposition across-set (5, 5'), sameness juxtapositions for transformed set (5', 3', 1', 4', 2').

3. Partial Cycle (Across-Set Juxtapositions)

The presentation of the familiar set followed by the transformed set constitutes a *full cycle*. Following this full cycle is a partial cycle. *Only two familiar and two transformed members are included in the partial cycle.*

```
       Full Cycle              Partial Cycle
┌─────────────────────┐      ┌───────────┐
1, 2, 3, 4, 5, 5', 3', 1', 4', 2'      2, 1, 1', 3'
```

The partial cycle has two familiar-set examples and two transformed-set examples. The partial cycle involves two minimum-difference across-set juxtapositions (2' and 2, 1 and 1').

The full cycle emphasizes the within-set sameness of the transformed-set members. The learner does the same thing with five juxtaposed examples of the transformed set (within-set juxtapositions). The partial cycle does not stress the sameness of the transformed set members, but rather *the difference between transformed-set members and familiar-set members.* This change in emphasis is achieved by using more frequent across-set juxtapositions. By the time the learner has completed the partial cycle, across-set juxtaposition have been provided for three of the five pairs of examples. (5, 5', 2, 2', 1, 1').

4. Integration of Familiar Set and Transformed Set

Following the partial cycle are unpredictably ordered examples. The examples in this part include:

- All familiar-set members 1-5.
- All transformed-set members 1'-5'.
- Additional transformed-set members 6'-8'.

The juxtaposition of examples is unpredictable with the familiar set and the transformed-set items "mixed up."

```
  Full Cycle         Partial         Integration
                      Cycle
┌───────────────┐   ┌───────┐   ┌───────────────────┐
1 2 3 4 5 5' 3' 1' 4' 2'   2 1 1' 3'   5 4' 2' 3 5' 6' 1 4 7' 1' 2 8' 3'
```

Note the integration segment presents the most difficult juxtapositions. Juxtaposed examples differ in both within-set and across-set features. Example 5' is not juxtaposed to either 4' or 5. It is juxtaposed to 3. The difference between 3 and 5' is a combination of within-set and across-set differences.[2] Also the integration segment introduces new examples of the transformed set (6', 7', and 8').

Illustration 1

Figure 13.2 shows the double transformation sequence that conveys the relationship of plus-one facts and plus-two facts. The familiar set consists of plus-one problems. (The learner is assumed to know a wide variety of these.) The transformed set consists of plus-two problems. (These are not known to the learner.) Note that there is no difference in test wording in the familiar set and the transformed set. The same question ("What's the answer?") is presented for all test examples. The only change from the familiar set to the transformed set, therefore, is a change in example—not in wording.

Illustration 2

Figure 13.3 shows the double-transformation sequence applied to the relationship between reading words spelled with **all** and their counterparts spelled with **ar**.

Like the illustration of the relationship between plus-one and plus-two problems, the **all-ar** sequence uses the same test wording for members of both sets. The difference between the familiar set (words that end in **all**) and the transformed set (words that end in **ar**) has to do with the type of examples.

Teacher Models

In the double-transformations that we have shown, test wording is presented on all examples except the first two members of the transformed set (5', 3'). The teacher models these items and then tests on the remaining items. Other modeling conventions could be used for transformations that are more difficult to demonstrate or that involve responses that are more difficult. The teacher may model the first two examples and then test *on these examples* before testing on the remaining items in

---

[2] The integration segment also provides the least specific diagnostic information about the specific causes of errors. If the learner makes a mistake on an item that is the same as the preceding item except for a single detail, we know that the learner is not processing that detail. The cause of failure is quite specific. If the learner makes a mistake on an item that differs from the preceding item in many ways, however, the error provides us with very little specific information about the cause of the error. We know only that when the task that was failed is presented in the context in which it appeared, the learner cannot process it.

Figure 13.2

		Example		Teacher Wording
Familiar Set	1	3 + 1		What's the answer?
	2	15 + 1		What's the answer?
	3	6 + 1		What's the answer?
	4	1 + 1		What's the answer?
	5	37 + 1	Across-set minimum difference	What's the answer?
Transformed Set	5'	37 + 2		My turn: What's the answer? Thirty-nine.
	3'	6 + 2		My turn: What's the answer? Eight.
	1'	3 + 2		Your turn: What's the answer?
	4'	1 + 2		What's the answer?
	2'	15 + 2	Across-set minimum difference	What's the answer?
Partial Cycle	2	15 + 1		What's the answer?
	1	3 + 1	Across-set minimum difference.	What's the answer?
	1'	3 + 2		What's the answer?
	3'	6 + 2		What's the answer?
Integration	5	37 + 1		What's the answer?
	4'	15 + 2		What's the answer?
	3	6 + 1		What's the answer?
	2'	15 + 2		What's the answer?
	3	6 + 1		What's the answer?
	4'	1 + 2		What's the answer?
	6'	72 + 2		What's the answer?
	1	3 + 1		What's the answer?
	5'	37 + 2		What's the answer?
	4	1 + 1		What's the answer?
	7'	100 + 2		What's the answer?
	1'	3 + 2		What's the answer?
	2	15 + 1		What's the answer?
	8'	24 + 2		What's the answer?
	3'	6 + 2		What's the answer?

the transformed set (modeling examples 5' and 3', then testing on 5', 3', 1', 4', 2', etc.). The teacher may model *all* examples of the transformed set, then return to the beginning of the transformed set and test on all examples. This approach is justified if each example is elaborate. For instance, if the double transformation presents the relationship between predicates in regular-order statements and predicates in their inverted counterparts ("He *went to the store after supper; After supper* he *went to the store*"), the teacher might model all five transformed-set items. Figure 13.4 illustrates the transformed set that would follow the familiar set.

Usually, two models of the transformed set are sufficient to prompt the operation that is common to all transformed-set members.

One-Difference Across Sets

An important feature of appropriately designed double-transformation sequences is that there is *only one difference* between any member of the familiar set and the

Section IV | Programs

Figure 13.3

		Example		Teacher Wording
Familiar Set	1	call		What word?
	2	ball		What word?
	3	fall		What word?
	4	mall		What word?
	5	tall	Minimum-difference	What word?
Transformed Set	5′	tar		My turn: What word? Tar.
	3′	far		My turn again: What word? Far.
	1′	car		Your turn: What word?
	4′	mar		What word?
	2′	bar	Minimum-difference	What word?
Partial Cycle	2	ball		What word?
	1	call	Minimum-difference.	What word?
	1′	car		What word?
	3′	far		What word?
Integration	5	tall		What word?
	2′	bar		What word?
	3	fall		What word?
	4′	mar		What word?
	6′	par		What word?
	1	call		What word?
	5′	tar		What word?
	4	mall		What word?
	7′	jar		What word?
	1′	car		What word?
	2	ball		What word?
	8′	star		What word?
	3′	far		What word?

corresponding member of the transformed set. As noted earlier, that difference can either be *a feature of the instructions or of the example presented—but not of both*. Let's say that this is the familiar-set item:

Example	Teacher Wording
mat	Read it.

A transformed-set counterpart has the same examples or the same wording. Here's an illustration of an item that involves the same example, but different wording:

Example	Teacher Wording
mat	Read it. (Familiar item)
mat	Spell it. (Transformed to spelling instructions)

Here's an illustration of an item that involves different examples, but the same wording as the familiar item:

Example	Teacher Wording
mat	Read it. (Familiar item)
mate	Read it. (Transformed to a long-**a** example)

If there is a difference in both wording and in the example, the learner may perform on the sequence

Figure 13.4

Example	Teacher Wording
To get to the roof, she climbed the gutter.	My turn: What's the predicate? Climbed the gutter to get to the roof.
When the game was finished, the crowd cheered.	My turn: What's the predicate? Cheered when the game was over.
Next to the large box, a leaf nestled.	My turn: What's the predicate? Nestled near a large box.
Shortly before noon, the train started to move.	My turn: What's the predicate? Started to move shortly before noon.
Just so he could boast, Henry climbed the oak.	My turn: What's the predicate? Climbed the oak just so he could boast.
To get to the roof, she climbed the gutter.	Your turn: What's the predicate?
Etc.	

without attending to relevant details of the examples or the instructions.

The following is the first part of an inappropriate sequence of items that presents differences in both the example and the wording.

Example	Teacher Wording
mat	Read it.
fat	Read it.
hat	Read it.
hate	Spell it.
mate	Spell it.
fate	Spell it.

The presentation generates two serious misrules:

- If the word does not end in **e**, read it.
- If the word ends in **e**, spell it.

The misrules are serious because the learner can correctly respond to all examples without attending to the instructions.

To avoid the misrules, we must design the sets so there is only one difference between the familiar and the transformed sets.

Here are two ways to correct the sequence. Part of the full cycle is shown for each sequence. The first sequence shows the difference between reading and spelling. The examples are the same across sets, while the instructions vary across sets.

Example	Teacher Wording
mat	Read it.
fat	Read it.
hat	Read it.
hat	Spell it.
mat	Spell it.
fat	Spell it.

The next sequence shows the difference between short-**a** words and their long-**a** counterparts. The instructions are the same for all examples.

Example	Teacher Wording
mat	Read it.
fat	Read it.
hat	Read it.
hate	Read it.
mate	Read it.
fate	Read it.

Across-Set Differences in Wording

The two full, double-transformation sequences that we presented use the same wording for the familiar and transformed sets. The across-set difference is a change in the examples. Figure 13.5 shows a full sequence of a different type. The only across-set difference is in the wording. The same set of examples is presented for the familiar and the transformed set.

The progression of juxtaposition follows the same pattern as that for transformations that involve the same wording for both sets.

During the full cycle of the transformed set, the learner does not have to attend to the instructions about "active" or "passive" because the learner can follow the model provided by the teacher at the beginning of the transformed set.

The difficulty in the partial cycle increases because the learner must now attend to the words **active** and **passive**.

In the integration segment, the difficulty is further increased because the learner must now: (1) listen to the instructions, and (2) attend to the relevant details of each picture. Also, the learner must apply knowledge of passive-voice constructions to new sentences (6', 7', and

Figure 13.5

		Example	Teacher Wording
			You are going to make up sentences about the person in each picture.
Familiar Set	1	Picture of boy climbing tree	Make up an active voice sentence.
	2	Picture of boy washing car	Make up an active voice sentence.
	3	Picture of boy brushing his teeth	Make up an active voice sentence.
	4	Picture of boy kissing a girl	Make up an active voice sentence.
	5	Picture of boy eating a hamburger	Make up an active voice sentence.
Transformed Set	5'	Picture of boy eating a hamburger	My turn: Make up a passive voice sentence. The hamburger is being eaten by the boy. Say that passive-voice sentence.
	3'	Picture of boy brushing his teeth	My turn: Make up a passive voice sentence. The boy's teeth are being brushed by the boy. Say that passive-voice sentence.
	1'	Picture of boy climbing tree	Make up a passive voice sentence.
	4'	Picture of boy kissing girl	Make up a passive voice sentence.
	2'	Picture of boy washing car	Make up a passive voice sentence.
Partial Cycle	2	Picture of boy washing car	Make up an active voice sentence.
	1	Picture of boy climbing tree	Make up an active voice sentence.
	1'	Picture of boy climbing tree	Make up a passive voice sentence.
	3'	Picture of boy brushing his teeth	Make up a passive voice sentence.
Integration	5	Picture of boy eating hamburger	Make up an active voice sentence.
	2'	Picture of boy washing car	Make up a passive voice sentence.
	3	Picture of boy brushing teeth	Make up an active voice sentence.
	4'	Picture of boy kissing girl	Make up a passive voice sentence.
	6'	Picture of boy riding a horse	Make up a passive voice sentence.
	5'	Picture of boy eating hamburger	Make up a passive voice sentence.
	4	Picture of boy kissing girl	Make up an active voice sentence.
	7'	Picture of girl throwing ball	Make up a passive voice sentence.
	1'	Picture of boy climbing tree	Make up a passive voice sentence.
	2	Picture of boy washing a car	Make up an active voice sentence.
	8'	Picture of girl sitting on a fence	Make up a passive voice sentence.
	3'	Picture of boy brushing teeth	Make up a passive voice sentence.

8'). Two of these involve a new actor, which means that the items are more difficult than those involving "the boy." The addition of these new examples should not be too difficult for the learner, if the learner has successfully performed in the sequence to the point at which they are introduced. If the learner understands a wide range of examples from the familiar set and if the learner has learned the standard transformation for the transformed members presented in the full cycle, the learner should be able to apply the standard transformation to other members of the familiar set.

Other Applications

1. If we wanted the learner to respond with percent notations for the familiar-set examples and with decimal notations for the transformed set, we could use an across-set difference in wording. We could present the learner with a set of fractions that have 100 as the denominator. The same examples would be presented for both the familiar set and the transformed set. The instructions would differ across sets, however. The learner would

be instructed to "Tell me the percent" for the familiar-set items, and to "Tell me the decimal" for the transformed-set items.

2. If the learner knows *consonants*, we could show their relationship to vowels by presenting the learner with short, written words. For the familiar-set items, the learner would be told to "Name all the consonants." For the transformed set the instruction would be, "Name all the vowels."

3. By creating across-set difference in instructions we can firm the learner's understanding of item types that are often confused. (See Figure 13.6.)

Figure 13.6	
Example	Teacher Wording
53 75 81	Read the digits in the ones column. (Familiar)
53 75 81	Read the digits in the tens column. (Transformed)
Example	Teacher Wording
The girl said, "Let's go."	Say the sentence. (Familiar)
The girl said, "Let's go."	Say what the girl said. (Transformed)

The two pairings in Figure 13.6 present instructions that the learner may confuse. By first firming one of the sets (so that it becomes familiar) and then processing the discrimination through the double-transformation program, the learner will be shown the difference between the two instructions. As a rule, if the learner is confused on instructions, we create a sequence in which the only difference between sets is a change in instructions.

Designing the Double-Transformation Program

We usually present the double-transformation relationship in three different parts or sections. The first establishes the familiar set. The second introduces the transformed set. The third integrates familiar and transformed sets.

The Familiar Set

The double-transformation relationship assumes that one single-transformation discrimination has been taught. Once the initial single-transformation discrimination has been identified, it is taught through initial-teaching sequences. These are followed by expansion activities.

The transformed set does not have to be introduced soon after the teaching of the familiar-set concept. The learner will not learn serious misrules if the transformed set is delayed.

Rather, a firm knowledge of the familiar-set discrimination facilitates mastery of the transformed set, because it reduces the possibility of the learner confusing transformed-set items or instructions with the familiar-set counterparts.

The initial teaching of the familiar set is achieved through a single-transformation sequence. The expansion and review activities continue until the transformed set is introduced. (See Figure 13.7.)

The number of days specified on the schedule is arbitrary. In calendar time, the familiar set illustrated above would be introduced about one month before the transformed set begins. The procedures for the initial teaching are those used for single-transformation concepts (Chapter 10). The expansion activities require the learner to use the discrimination in new settings and contexts. The schedule show more expansions than reviews, because

Figure 13.7																				
Components	Familiar Set Lessons																			Transformed Set Begins
	1	2	3	4	5	6	7	8	9	10	11	12	13	14	15	16	17	18	19	
Initial Teaching	X	X																		
Expansion			X	X		X						X		X	X			X	X	
Review							X			X	X									

the expansions permit the learner to use the discrimination in relevant applications.

As a rule of thumb, the learner should work with the familiar-set items for a minimum of six to ten days before the transformed set is introduced. This period is usually enough to assure that the familiar discriminations are familiar. For many discriminations, however, the transformed set may not be introduced for months after the familiar set has been introduced. This situation presents no problem so long as the learner is not engaged in any activities that require the transformed-set discrimination.

The Transformed Set

There are two approaches to the introduction of the transformed set. The first approach is to introduce it in the way suggested by the double-transformation sequence. The other, called the *separate-set approach*, is to teach the transformed set apart from the familiar set, then integrate it with items from the familiar set. The schedule in Figure 13.8 shows the strategy for introducing the transformed set that is based on the events of the double-transformation sequence.

Figure 13.8								
Components	Transformed-Set Lessons							
	1	2	3	4	5	6	7	8
Familiar Set	X	X						
Transformed Set	X	X	X	X				
Partial Cycle		X	X	X				
Integration			X	X	X	X		X
Expansion	X	X	X				X	

On the first lesson, the full cycle is presented (the familiar and transformed set presented in sequence). On lesson 2, the same sequence is presented, and the *partial cycle* is added to the sequence. On lessons 3 and 4, the familiar set is dropped; only the transformed set and partial cycles are presented. The assumption is that the learner is familiar with the familiar-set discrimination. Also, the partial cycle and the integration require the learner to use familiar-set discriminations. The integration continues after lesson 4. It functions as a cumulative review, testing the learner on the familiar and the transformed discriminations.

The expansion activities that occur on the first three lessons involve *only* the transformed-set discrimination.

(They require only the within-set understanding of the concept, not an ability to discriminate between transformed-set items and familiar-set items.) The idea is to give the learner some familiarity with the transformed-set examples before the learner is required to discriminate between these and their familiar-set counterparts. The expansion on lesson 7 involves both sets.

The rate of introduction for the different parts of the program can be modified substantially, depending on the difficulty of the discrimination being taught. Possibly, lesson 1 could be eliminated from the introduction. If the learner is quite facile, the entire sequence (full cycle, partial cycle, and integration) can be presented in the first lesson, repeated on the second lesson, and reviewed on a few subsequent lessons. If the learner is not as facile, a more careful introduction is needed. Think of the difficulty of this introduction in terms of the types of juxtapositions that are presented. Lesson 1 presents the easiest juxtaposition (within-set juxtapositions for the transformed set). Lesson 2 adds a more difficult type of juxtaposition (across-set juxtapositions). Lessons 3 and 4 add a still more difficult type—within-set and across-set discriminations. The remainder of the program presents additional reviews of the difficult juxtaposition. Without changing the general direction of the program, we can introduce variation in the rate at which the different juxtapositions are introduced.

Separate Sets

The strategy above is a phased introduction of the double-transformation sequence. This strategy is appropriate for most discriminations. However, if the *responses* involved in the program are difficult for the learner, the separate-sets strategy should be employed. This strategy assures greater practice with the transformed-set responses before they are presented in the same context as the familiar-set responses.

The separated-sets strategy involves *first working on the within-set discrimination for the transformed set, then teaching the relationship.*

This strategy potentially increases the danger of stipulation; however, the strategy frequently is desirable, particularly when the discriminations involve difficult responses. The schedule in Figure 13.9 shows the separate-sets strategy. Note that this schedule begins after the familiar set has been taught.

Figure 13.9

Components	Separate-Sets Lessons																		
	1	2	3	4	5	6	7	8	9	10	11	12	13	14	15	16	17	18	19
Familiar Set A									X	X									
Transformed Set B	X	X	X						X	X	X	X							
Partial Cycle										X	X	X							
Integration												X	X	X		X	X		X
Expansion & Review	A	A	B	B	A	B	AB	AB	A	B	A	B	B	B	A	B			

The transformed set is taught for three lessons. The teaching of the transformed set follows juxtaposition rules for introducing single-transformation concepts. *The number of items introduced is not limited to five.* The same type of minimum-difference juxtapositions used for teaching the familiar set is used for teaching the transformed set. The transformed set is expanded starting with the third lesson. Note that expansion activities for the familiar set (**A**) occur on lessons 1 and 2. These activities would not be juxtaposed to the initial teaching of the transformed set in the lesson. They would occur at some other time. Review and expansion continue on lessons 4, 5 and 6.

Starting with lesson 7, both the familiar set and the transformed set are reviewed. This review consists of examples of each set *that are fairly different from each other* (the same type of examples that will be used in the sequence). Presentation of these sets would not be juxtaposed in the lesson. The idea is to make the learner facile with each discrimination, but not to require the learner to discriminate *between* the sets. Starting with lesson 9, the parts of the full cycle are juxtaposed as they are in the double-transformation sequence. First, the familiar-set items are presented, followed by the transformed set. There are five items in each set, and the sets are designed according to the specifications of the double-transformation sequence. The teacher models the first two examples of the transformed set (as in presenting the double-transformation for the first time).

On lesson 10, the parts are again juxtaposed, with the partial cycle following the transformed set. The remainder of the schedule is similar to that for the program based on the parts of the double-transformation sequences; however, there is a more careful scheduling of expansion activities. The reason for this elaboration is that the responses are relatively difficult for the learner (either because the learner is relatively naive, or the responses are difficult even for a sophisticated learner).

Think of the separate-sets program as two sets that remain separate in time until both are firm. They are separated in time, but both receive attention. Lessons 1-8 of the program teach the within-set discriminations for the transformed set and assure that the learner also retains the within-set discriminations for the familiar set. Starting with lesson 9, the teaching begins for the across-set discrimination. The first step in this teaching involves bringing the sets closer together in time. The next steps are identical to those in the sequence-derived program.

Illustration

Arithmetic skills often require the separate-set approach. Assume that the learner has been taught multiplication (familiar set) and is to be taught algebra multiplication (transformed set).

Figure 13.10

Example	Teacher Wording
5 × ☐ = 20	My turn: Five times how many equals twenty? Five times four equals twenty.
5 × ☐ = 15	My turn: Five times how many equals fifteen? Five times three equals fifteen.
5 × ☐ = 25	Your turn: Five times how many equals twenty-five?
5 × ☐ = 5	Five times how many equals five?
5 × ☐ = 30	Five times how many equals thirty?
5 × ☐ = 45	Five times how many equals forty-five?
5 × ☐ = 15	Five times how many equals fifteen?
5 × ☐ = 50	Five times how many equals fifty?

The teaching for the transformed set begins when the learner is firm on the familiar-set examples. For three days, the learner works on transformed set problems while engaging in review activities that involve the familiar set. Figure 13.10 shows a possible sequence for lesson 1.

The teacher may present more information about how to figure out the answer to each problem. (Strategies for such routines are specified in Section VI.)

Starting with lesson 7, the teacher would present review examples of algebra multiplication at one time during the lesson and review examples involving regular multiplication at another. The juxtaposition of problems of the same type serves as a prompt to the learner to do the same thing on juxtaposed examples. The following is a possible group of transformed-set problems that might be presented on lesson 7.

$$5 \times \square = 15$$
$$5 \times \square = 30$$
$$5 \times \square = 0$$
$$5 \times \square = 20$$
$$5 \times \square = 45$$
$$5 \times \square = 10$$
$$5 \times \square = 50$$
$$5 \times \square = 25$$
$$5 \times \square = 5$$

Note that the juxtaposed examples in the sequence are quite different from each other, forcing the learner to deal with the sameness of the transformed-set members. This juxtaposition is the same type that will be used on lesson 9 when the familiar and transformed sets are linked together to form the first part of the sequence.

Figure 13.11 shows the examples that might be presented on lesson 9. The familiar and transformed sets are juxtaposed to form a full cycle. Note that the set of examples is not the same as the set presented on preceding lessons.

On subsequent lessons, the teaching at the beginning of the transformed set is dropped. Note that the sequence above presents very abbreviated wording. To reduce the possibility that the learner's errors are caused by misreading the problem, the teacher could present two tasks with each problem that is tested: "Read it . . . What's the answer?" The introduction of the first question would make the learner's perception of the problem overt. At the same time, the presentation of the first question does not create a misrule because the same wording is used for each example.

Figure 13.11

		Examples	Teacher Wording
Familiar Set	1	$5 \times 2 = \square$	What's the answer?
	2	$5 \times 10 = \square$	What's the answer?
	3	$5 \times 7 = \square$	What's the answer?
	4	$5 \times 4 = \square$	What's the answer?
	5	$5 \times 3 = \square$	What's the answer?
Transformed Set	5'	$5 \times \square = 15$	My turn: What's the answer? Three.
	2'	$5 \times \square = 50$	My turn: What's the answer? Ten.
	1'	$5 \times \square = 10$	Your turn: What's the answer?
	3'	$5 \times \square = 35$	What's the answer?
	4'	$5 \times \square = 20$	What's the answer?

Lessons 13 through 19 assure that the learner practices the integration part of the sequence with different examples. This part presents the most difficult discriminations. There are no juxtaposition prompts to tell the learner whether the next example will be from the familiar or from the transformed set. Figure 13.12 shows a possible integration sequence.

Figure 13.12

Example	Teacher Wording
$5 \times \square = 35$	Read it. What's the answer?
$5 \times 1 = \square$	Read it. What's the answer?
$5 \times 6 = \square$	Read it. What's the answer?
$5 \times \square = 0$	Read it. What's the answer?
$5 \times \square = 30$	Read it. What's the answer?
$5 \times 2 = \square$	Read it. What's the answer?
$5 \times \square = 15$	Read it. What's the answer?
$5 \times 9 = \square$	Read it. What's the answer?
$5 \times \square = 20$	Read it. What's the answer?

Summary

To identify double transformation items, we start with a series of single-transformation tasks, such as those involving the directions, "Add those numbers." We ask, "Can you create a parallel set by changing either the examples or the instructions?" If we can, we are dealing with a double-transformation relationship.

The change may be in the examples:

	Examples	Wording
Familiar Set:	4 + 2	Add these numbers.
Transformed Set:	400 + 200	Add these numbers.

The change may be in instructions.

	Examples	Wording
Familiar Set:	4 2	Add.
Transformed Set:	4 2	Subtract.

The double-transformation program consists of four parts:

1. **The familiar set:** five familiar examples that come from different subsets and are ordered to communicate sameness.
2. **The transformed set:** five counterparts for each of the familiar-set examples.
3. **The partial cycle:** juxtapositions that show across-set differences.
4. **The integration:** a near-random juxtaposition of items from either set, and additional items for the transformed set.

The program teaches both the transformed set and the relationship between the familiar and transformed sets.

As a *sequence*, the double-transformation is long; therefore, the probability is great that the learner will become confused, will forget, and will make errors if the entire sequence is presented at one time. To avoid these possibilities, we expand double-transformation *sequences* into double-transformation *programs*.

There are two basic types of double-transformation programs. *The sequence-derived program* introduces the parts of the program in roughly the same order they occur in the double-transformation sequence. This order of introduction quickly teaches both the within-set discrimination for the transformed set and the across-set difference between sets.

The other approach is the *separate-sets program*, which first teaches the within-set discrimination for the transformed set, while reviewing the within-set discrimination for the familiar set. After both sets have been mastered in isolation (or in blocks of items), the across-set discrimination is taught through a series of events modeled after the double-transformation sequence.

The assumption behind both double-transformation programs is that the work of the transformed set does not begin until the familiar set has been thoroughly mastered. However, the learner may have trouble with the "familiar" items when they become juxtaposed with the transformed-set items. The familiar items were firm *in one context*; however, the context presented by the double-transformation sequence implies attention to a much wider range of detail than the earlier contexts required.

The same expansion-review procedures used for other programs are employed in the double-transformation programs. Many details of a schedule for introducing a double-transformation concept are arbitrary. The non-arbitrary aspects of the program are that the learner must work on newly-taught skills for at least two consecutive lessons, must review skills periodically, and must use newly-taught skills in a context other than those provided by the review activities.

Chapter 14
Programs for Teaching Fact Systems

In the teaching sequences that we have dealt with, the same response dimension is involved in juxtaposed examples. If the sequence deals with words that rhyme with **at**, all items deal with the same response dimension, rhyming with **at**. If the sequence deals with **getting hotter**, all examples deal with whether the objects gets hotter. Some double-transformation programs use two different response dimensions (indicated by the two different directions presented in the sequence); however, the double-transformation program presents two sets of discriminations that are related through a single transformation.

The programs that we will examine in this chapter are completely different. Each fact-system program calls for *a variety of different responses*. The various response dimensions of the fact system are the *features* of the system, the details that distinguish the system from other systems. The juxtaposed items for this type of program virtually never deal with the same response dimension. Furthermore, the goal of the instruction is *not* to teach a particular response dimension and how it works (which is the goal of the preceding programs). Rather, the goal is to teach a complex system by teaching the various features of the system. The communication that teaches the system is a *complex* communication because it must convey information about various features of the system, each of which involves a different fact or response dimension.

The common characteristic of these programs is that they present a *visual-spatial display* of some type. The display shows the *whole* or the *system* that is to be learned. Parts of the system are also shown or labeled. These details provide information about particular aspects of the whole and about relationships among the parts.

Fact systems that can be presented as visual-spatial displays include virtually any topic that can be outlined or diagrammed, including:

- John Stuart Mill's views on personal liberty.
- The classification of cherries.
- The workings of an internal combustion engine.
- The human circulatory system.

Types of Fact Systems

There are three different types of fact systems.

1. The Natural-Part, Natural-Whole System

This type of system is a representation of something that can be found in the environment. The fact system shows the parts and relationships of the object. For instance, a cut-away view of a volcano is something that would be observed if we could make a vertical slice to create a cross-section of a volcano. Similarly, a diagram of the human's breathing apparatus, the workings of a carburetor, the parts of a typewriter—all are systems that may be found in the environment. The presentation may make some parts more prominent than they would be in reality; however, the presentation deals with something that exists in basically the same form that it appears in the fact system. The parts are "natural" parts (the core of the volcano, for instance) and the whole is a "natural whole" (the entire volcano).

2. The Natural-Part, Created-Whole System

For this type of system, the parts exist in nature or in the environment; however, the parts do not occur in the type of "whole" or organization presented by the fact system. For example, the game birds of North America is a system that is made up of parts. The parts—pictures of various game birds—are representations of things that exist in nature. The whole, or system that is created when these birds are organized and displayed, however, does not exist in nature. It would be highly unusual if one observed a quail next to a ringneck pheasant, next to the various ducks and geese, etc. A chart showing various landforms is also made up of parts that exist in the environment; however, the organization does not exist in nature. Another example of this type would be a classification of currency. The particular arrangement shows the relationship of the various bills and coins. Although this arrangement is a fabrication designed to communicate the system, the parts—the coins and bills—exist in the environment.

3. The Created-Part, Created-Whole System

Both the parts and the whole of this system are representations that do not actually occur in the environment. If we showed the organization of a business, with the president, the various vice-presidents, etc., we would represent the positions by *words* such as "director of marketing." The diagram would not show a picture of a director. Neither would it show a system of relationships that exists physically. The relationships would be visual representations of a hierarchy. Other fact systems of the created-part, created-whole form include all the systems that could be put into an "outline." Descartes' argument about the existence of God, the history of events in Napoleon Bonaparte's career, etc. Systems of this type also include things that are diagrammed or symbolized, such as the horsepower and torque curves for an engine at different speeds.

The distinction of the three types becomes important when we consider what kind of prompts the display should give them. However, the general rules for presentation and design hold for all three types of systems.

Fact System Teaching

To teach a learner the fact system, *we must convey the individual facts and relationships.* Note that within the system, the facts (and their arrangement) are the features that distinguish the system from other possible fact systems. The primary objective of the instruction is not to teach the *meaning* of individual facts, but to teach the particular fact system as the sum of the component facts.

For showing the relationship between the facts we will use *codes.* For example, if something is coordinate with another thing, we will show the two things occupying the coordinate space. If something happens before something else, we will show a linear relationship, with the events arranged spatially. If something includes something else, we will show the larger thing as if it physically includes the smaller thing.

The conventions that we use for designing a fact system suggest whether we would use a specific program with a given learner. For the learner to qualify for entry, the learner must possess generalized understanding of the coding that we will use to create the event. Our system may consist of words and spatial relationships to show exclusion, coordination, seriation, or temporal relationships. It may contain arrows, diagrams, and other symbols. If the learner does not understand each of these code functions, the system should not be presented through a visual-spatial display. If the learner cannot read, the learner should not be exposed to a system that contains words. If the learner does not know that things occurring before other things are positioned to the left of other things, the system that assumes this knowledge should not be presented.

The learner, in other words, should know enough that misrules are not implied by the presentation of the fact system. (We do not want the learner to think that the boxes on a diagram exist in nature.)

The Presentation Format

Although there are many ways to convey the information presented on a visual-spatial display, we will deal with a three-step format:

1. **Prompted chart and script.** The teacher presents a visual-spatial display and rehearses the learner on the words that go in the various cells of the display. The teacher reads a script that refers to the parts of the chart and also possibly refers to information not directly displayed.

2. **The unprompted chart and test.** The teacher presents an unprompted version of the chart. *This chart does not have the words written in the various cells.* The learner must identify what words go in the cells.

3. **The game.** A group of learners play a game in which they roll dice and answer the question that corresponds to the number on the dice. Most of the questions ask about the wording in various cells of the visual-spatial display.

The three phases of the presentation correspond roughly with the progression of events in the initial-teaching sequences we have examined. The first step is the teaching, the communication of information that will be called on for the test step.

The second step tests what was demonstrated in step 1, using a direct, unembellished test.

The third step functions as an expansion activity, permitting the learner to perform in a different context, to tasks that are somewhat different from those presented in the test. At the same time, the game (third step) provides for sufficient repetition to firm the information (in a reinforcing manner).

Illustration

Figure 14.1 gives a complete presentation for a visual-spatial fact system dealing with basic information about teeth. The display is a natural-part, natural-whole type, with the different types of teeth labeled as *parts* and a diagram of the teeth showing the *whole*.

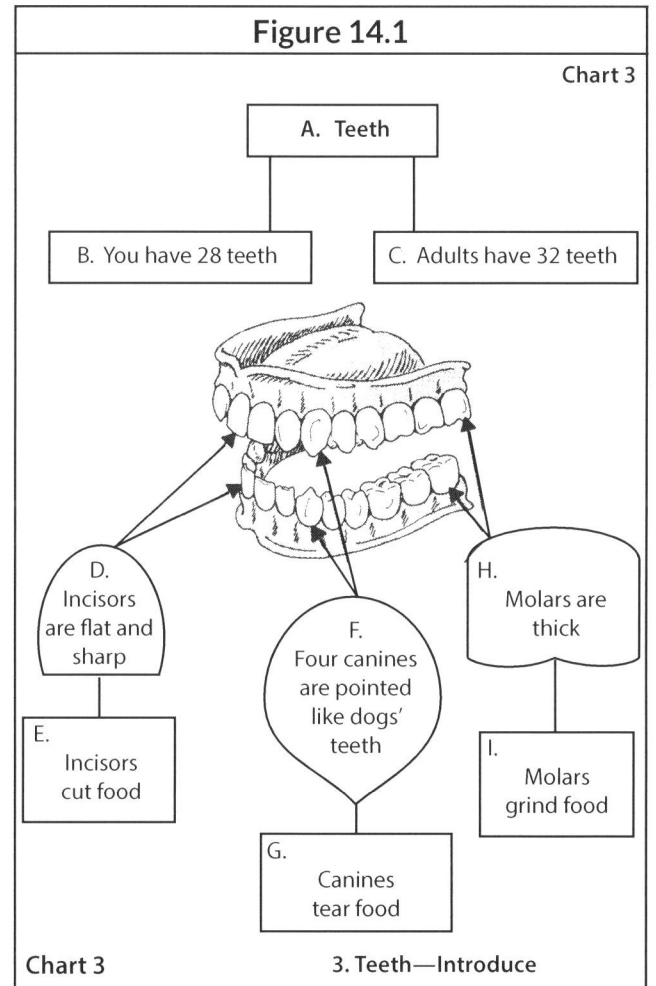

Figure 14.1

Chart 3

- A. Teeth
  - B. You have 28 teeth
  - C. Adults have 32 teeth
  - D. Incisors are flat and sharp
    - E. Incisors cut food
  - F. Four canines are pointed like dogs' teeth
    - G. Canines tear food
  - H. Molars are thick
    - I. Molars grind food

Chart 3   **3. Teeth—Introduce**

1. Everybody, open your student book to page 3. *Check.* Remember the exact wording for each space.
2. Everybody, touch A. *Wait.* Teeth. Say it. *Signal.* "Teeth."

    I'm going to tell you about teeth. You have different kinds of teeth to do different jobs. Remember, teeth.

3. Everybody, touch B. *Wait.* You have 28 teeth. Say it. *Signal.* "You have 28 teeth."

    You don't have all your teeth yet. You'll get more as you get older. Remember, you have 28 teeth.

4. Everybody, touch C. *Wait.* Adults have 32 teeth. Say it. *Signal.* "Adults have 32 teeth."

    Adults have four more teeth than you have. These teeth are in the back of their mouth. Remember, adults have 32 teeth.

5. Everybody, touch D. *Wait.* Incisors are flat and sharp. Say it. *Signal.* "Incisors are flat and sharp."

    Incisors are in the front of your mouth.

    Everybody, touch an incisor on the top of your mouth. *Check.*

    Now touch an incisor on the bottom of your mouth. *Check.*

    You can feel the edge of your incisors. Remember, incisors are flat and sharp.

6. Everybody, touch E. *Wait.* Incisors cut food. Say it. *Signal.* "Incisors cut food."

    Remember, incisors cut food.

7. Everybody, touch F. *Wait.* Four canines are pointed like dogs' teeth. Say it. *Signal.* "Four canines are pointed like dogs's teeth."

    Your canines are next to the incisors. You have four canines—two on the top and two on the bottom.

    Everybody, touch a canine on the bottom of your mouth. *Check.*

    Everybody, touch a canine on the top of your mouth. *Check.*

    Remember, four canines are pointed like dogs' teeth.

8. Everybody, touch G. *Wait.* Canines tear food. Say it. *Signal.* "Canines tear food."

    Remember, canines tear food.

9. Everybody, touch H. *Wait.* Molars are thick. Say it. *Signal.* "Molars are thick."

    Molars are in the back of your mouth.

    Everybody, touch a molar on the bottom of your mouth. *Check.*

    Everybody, touch a molar on the top of your mouth. *Check.*

    You'll get four more molars when you get older. Remember, molars are thick.

10. Everybody, touch I. *Wait.* Molars grind food. Say it. *Signal.* "Molars grind food."

    Remember, molars grind food.

11. Let's go over the facts about teeth one more time.

12. Everybody, touch A. *Wait.* Tell me the words. *Signal.* (Students respond.)

13. *Repeat step 12 with B, C, D, E, F, G, H, I.*

3. Teeth—Firm-up

1. Everybody, open your student book to page 28. *Check.*

Section IV | Programs

The spaces are empty on this chart. Get ready to tell me the exact words that go in each space.

2. Everybody, touch A. *Wait.* Tell me the words. *Signal.* (Students respond.)

3. *Repeat step 2 with B, C, D, E, F, G, H, I.*

3. Teeth—Starter's Game Preparation

1. Now you're ready to play the starter's game for Teeth.

   I'll tell you who the monitors are for today. *Identify a monitor for each group.* Monitors, open your student book to answer sheet 3 for Teeth on page 60. *Check.*

   Monitors, give out a scorecard to each player, including yourself. *Wait.*

2. *Write on board: 3. Teeth.*

   Everybody, write your name and the name of this game at the top of your scorecard. *Check.*

3. Remember the rules: You read each question out loud. Then tell the exact words. Remember, you must say the exact words for each space to get a point. Also, if you argue with the monitor, you lose one turn. If you argue again with the monitor, you're out of the game. If you're a monitor, you have to be careful not to show anybody the answers. Keep the game moving quickly. But don't let the players roll the dice before the last player has answered the question.

4. *Tell the monitors to start the game. Note the time. The game is to continue for ten minutes. Observe games. Give feedback to groups that are playing well.*

5. *After players have played for ten minutes, stop the games.*

   Monitors, give yourselves twenty points for monitoring.

   For each game that ran smoothly, tell the monitors to award five bonus points to themselves and the players.

6. *Instruct students to return their scorecard to their notebook or folder.*

The game. When students play the game, they use the score card illustrated in Figure 14.2. The scorecard displays a picture of the unprompted display. The student rolls the dice, orally reads the question that corresponds to the number shown on the dice, and answers the question. If the answer is correct, the monitor makes a check mark in one box.

Figure 14.2

2. What words go in space B?
3. What words go in space E?
4. What words go in space D?
5. What words go in space H?
6. Which teeth can cut food?
7. What words go in space F?
8. Which teeth grind food?
9. What words go in space I?
10. What words go in space C?
11. What words go in space G?
12. What words go in space A?

Chart 3

Name _____
Scorecard _____
Starter's Scorebox
Superstar Scorebox
Expert's Game _____
Better's Scorebox
★★★★★★★★★
Here's How Much I Bet
Here's How Much I Won

Game Points
Starter's _____
Superstar _____
Better's _____
Challenge _____

Challenge Box
| 30 | 15 | c.o. |

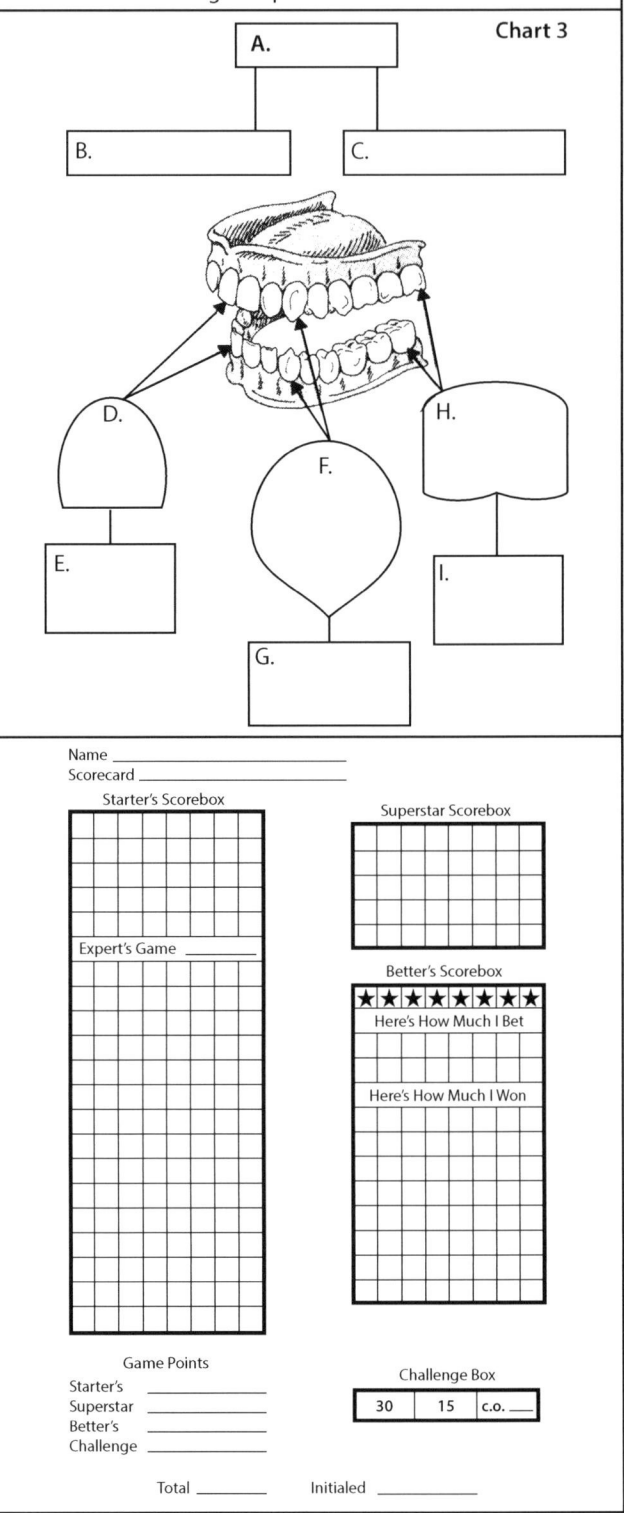

Total _____   Initialed _____

Note that the game is played on more than one day. On subsequent lessons, the teacher provides either a brief review of the chart or no review before the game begins.
The teaching. As the script given as part of Figure 14.1 indicates, the teacher teaches new names and new facts. The initial teaching for **incisors, canines**, and **molars** is presented through the visual-spatial presentation. The script also introduces the facts about each type of tooth (how they look, where they are, and what they do) and the facts about the number of teeth children and adults have.

Although a great deal of teaching is presented through a single communication, the teaching is not extremely difficult because:

1. The visual-spatial display provides prompts about the position of each fact.
2. The new names are incorporated in sentences that provide information about the names.
3. No serious discrimination problems are involved for the learner who is sophisticated enough to qualify for a visual-spatial presentation.

If the learner learns the fact statements about **molars** ("molars are thick"), the learner is provided with a mnemonic for remembering **molars**. The primary communication problem for teaching **molars** is not to teach subtle differences between examples of molars and other teeth. These are the teeth that are quite familiar to the learner as teeth in the back of the mouth. The learner must learn the name for these teeth and have some method of associating the name with information about function, shape, and position. The wording in the cell provides information about the relationship of name and function. The visual display shows the relationship of position and name. Therefore, the display nicely provides the essential information that the more sophisticated learner would need to understand molars as part of the system of teeth.

The contrast of the visual-spatial display approach to teaching fact systems with traditional procedures is instructive. Traditional procedures that are supposed to teach fact systems usually require the learner to extract the information from material that is read. The learner's first exposure to **molars** may be in a health book. The assumption of the book is that the explanations, which are frequently elaborate, will induce knowledge of the discrimination and knowledge of the word. This assumption is unfounded. For the student to become firm on the facts presented on the teeth display, the students would have to practice these names in an unprompted setting. No such practice is provided. An even more serious problem is that a chapter of the student text typically deals with far more information than the display of teeth presents. The overload of information is typically so great that the student learns very little from reading the text. After reading the text, the teacher may explain what the student has read. This juxtaposition of events suggests that the text is not a purveyor of information. A far more reasonable order of events would introduce the basic facts first (through a visual-spatial display). Following the firming on the basic facts, the student reads the text. Now the text is perfectly comprehensible, even if it introduces some information that is not related to the facts presented on the visual-spatial display. The reason is that the student has well-grounded facts to which the new information relates. Without the well-grounded facts, however, the new information is unrelated, difficult to classify or associate, and therefore difficult to remember.

Designing Displays

It would certainly be possible to include more information in a display than the example in Figure 14.1 provides. As a rule, the learner should easily be able to handle a display with 11 cells, but not more than 16. (Figure 14.1 has only 9.)

Note that in the teeth display, coordinate wording is contained in cells that are spatially coordinate. Cells **B** and **C** are spatially coordinate. The wording in these cells is coordinate. "You have 28," "Adults have 32." Both cell **B** and **C** are subordinated to cell **A**.

The other cells occur in pairs. The top cell in the pair tells: (1) the name of the tooth, and (2) how it looks. The bottom cell tells what the tooth does (cuts food, tears food, grinds food).

One important consideration in designing a display is the configuration and content of the other displays the learner is being taught. Each display is a member of a set. If the learner is presented with a series of visual-spatial displays, highly similar members should not be juxtaposed, which means that displays that are highly similar in either content or form should be separated in their order of introduction.

We have many options in designing a display so that it is highly dissimilar from the preceding display. We can make a given organization linear, round, or angular. We can make the cells boxes, circles, or some other shape. Therefore, if the preceding display is angular, we can make one that is vertical or round. Figure 14.3 presents a few options that are available for showing the higher-order relationship of five vehicles. Note that on all displays, the higher-order label (**vehicles**) is treated differently from the other labels; however, each of the lower-order cells is related in the same way to the higher-order label. All five displays treat the information as a created-part, created-whole system (although it would be possible to treat it as a natural-part, created-whole system by showing pictures of the various vehicles).

Designing Individual Cells

The basic rule for designing cells for coordinate cells is that there should not be more than *four* coordinate cells that are the same, unless the cells are always approached in the same order. According to this criterion, the arrangement of coordinate cells for both the vertical display and one horizontal display above are inappropriate. The reason is that if all cells are empty, they are hard to discriminate. We will easily remember the end cells and possibly some of the others, but the coordinate cells in the middle share too many features.

There are three solutions to this problem:

1. Remove at least one of the cells.
2. Change the shape of at least one coordinate cell (preferably the middle cell).
3. Always require the learner to respond to the coordinate cells in the same order.

One horizontal display presents a unique shape for the middle cell (**truck**). Some of the other displays adequately deal with this problem in different ways. For instance, the round display presents different shapes for each cell.

Another way to make the cells more distinguishable is to change the display so that it is a natural-part, created-whole type. When the actual pictures (or representations of the different vehicles) are presented in each cell, the coordinate cells are no longer similar.

For other situations in which there are more than four coordinate cells, one of the other solutions may be reasonable—removing a cell or always presenting the cells in the same order.

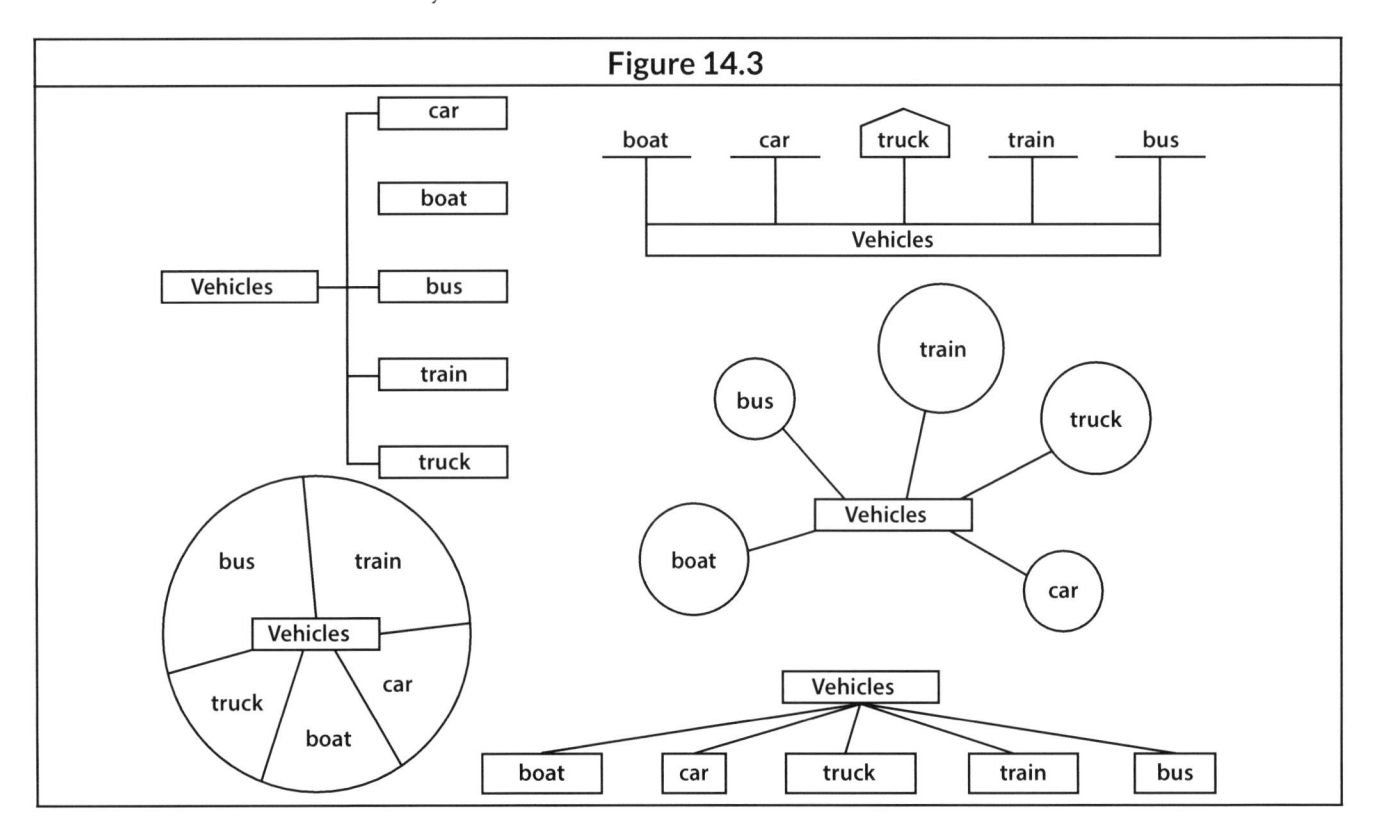

Figure 14.3

If we were teaching the five types of vertebrates, we might arrange the five highly similar cells in order:

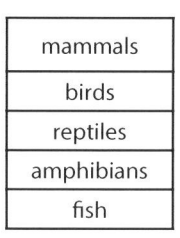

| mammals |
| amphibians |
| reptiles |
| amphibians |
| fish |

And we might always refer to the cells in order, starting with **fish**. The rationale for this approach is that the arrangement of vertebrates corresponds to their appearance geologically. By presenting the cells in the same order, we prompt the learner to understand the evolutionary changes in vertebrates. Later, we can add geological information:

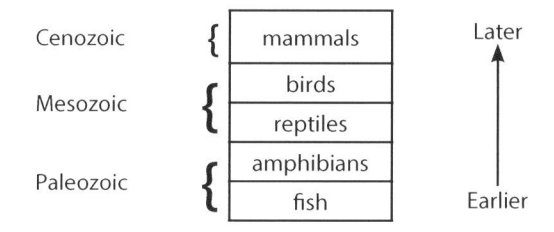

Cenozoic { mammals } Later
Mesozoic { birds / reptiles }
Paleozoic { amphibians / fish } Earlier

We now have a timeline that corresponds to rock strata, evolutionary development, and to geological eras. The potential economy of this approach justifies the use of five cells that are highly similar, although it could be possible to modify the shape of the middle cell, perhaps by making a heavy outline around it.

Spurious Prompts

A prompt is spurious if it permits the learner to produce the appropriate response for the wrong reason. If the learner is able to tell that the next example in a teaching sequence is positive because the examples alternate from positive to negative to positive, the alternation serves as a spurious prompt for the correct response. Here are rules for avoiding spurious prompts in a visual-spatial display:

1. The shape of the cell should never be designed to give the learner "decoding" information about how to pronounce the name. If the response for a cell is "mammal," and the cell is shaped like an **M**, the shape of the cell provides a spurious prompt.

2. If the learner is expected to learn a group of cells in a particular *order*, the cells should be as similar as it is practical to make them. The cells for the five classes of vertebrates are identical. Figure 14.4 shows spuriously-prompted cells for vertebrates. Although the cells are not in the appropriate order, the learner is able to respond appropriately to every name (**mammal, fish, reptile, amphibian,** and **bird**). The learner is not required to learn a particular order because the features of the individual cells provide information about the responses for each cell. Therefore, the learner may attend to the individual features of the cells, regardless of their order.

3. Closely related to rule 2 above, if the learner is expected to learn a particular spatial arrangement of parts, the display should be designed so that the learner must attend to the spatial details of the display. If individual cells are designed to "tell" the learner what to say, the cell does not reinforce attention to the spatial arrangement.

4. If *familiar names* are called for by cells, the shape of the cell should not be designed to prompt the name. The spurious display in Figure 14.4 shows an outline of a fish and a bird. The responses "fish" and "bird" are familiar responses of the learner. The pictures, therefore, prompt these names spuriously. The outline of the frog is not particularly spurious, however, because the name "amphibian" is called for, a name that may not be familiar to the learner.

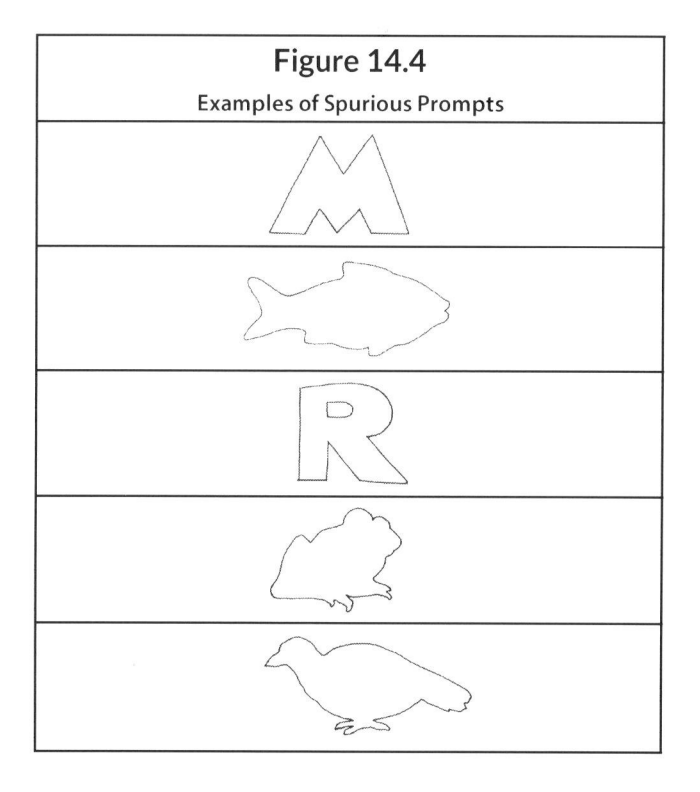

Figure 14.4
Examples of Spurious Prompts

Section IV | Programs

As a general guideline, a created-part, created-whole display should not prompt *responses* for the individual cells. For this type of display, the learner is expected to learn both what goes in the cells and the organization of cells. The objective is most easily achieved if the learner must respond to where the cell is, not to its shape or to features that "tell" the learner what to say. The test for cells of a created-part, created-whole display is: If the learner could respond to a cell no matter where we might move it, the cells are probably providing some spurious cues.

For the natural-part, natural-whole display, the organization of parts is not a spurious problem, because the organization is already given. We simply require the learner to label the parts and label the whole (such as the parts of the respiratory system).

The natural-part, created-whole display presents the most serious problems because it is an organization of natural parts. If we want the learner to respond to the *organization*, however, we should not prompt the individual cells by presenting pictures in them. If we want the learner to identify the various parts, however (and if this learning is new for the learner), we should present the pictures that are to be identified. The solution to the problem of the natural-part, created-whole display is to present pictures and to *add questions* that require the learner to respond to the organization of the parts. We can illustrate both the problem and the solution with a display designed to teach **birds of prey**. First we must decide whether we should present the information through a natural-part or a created-part display.

If the learner can already identify all the birds, we could teach the organization of the various names through a created-part, created-whole presentation. If the learner knows only some individual birds but not others and does not know the organization, we could present a natural-part, created-whole display, such as the one in Figure 14.5.

After the information has been introduced, the learner is tested on a variation of the chart that is identical to the one in Figure 14.5 except that all wording is removed. The pictures remain. This test display is relatively weak at teaching the coordinate names because the names are always prompted by pictures. (The learner can look at

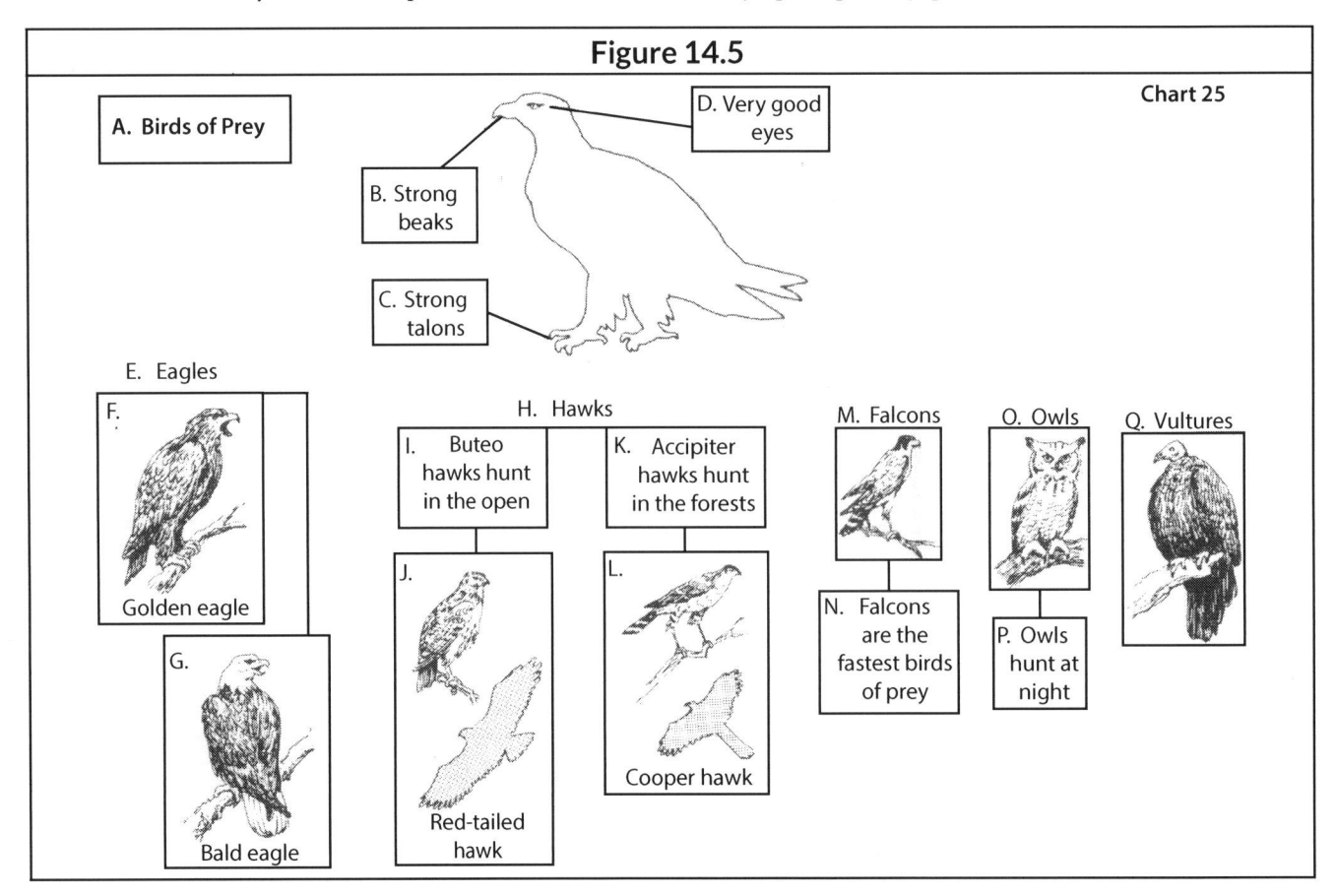

Figure 14.5

Chart 25

A. Birds of Prey
B. Strong beaks
C. Strong talons
D. Very good eyes

E. Eagles
F. Golden eagle
G. Bald eagle

H. Hawks
I. Buteo hawks hunt in the open
J. Red-tailed hawk
K. Accipiter hawks hunt in the forests
L. Cooper hawk

M. Falcons
N. Falcons are the fastest birds of prey

O. Owls
P. Owls hunt at night

Q. Vultures

Theory of Instruction: Principles and Applications

the pictures of the eagles, for example, and identify E as "eagles.")

The possible shortcomings of this display does not imply that the display is unreasonable. The display teaches the learner to identify the various birds. It also teaches the information in cells B, C, D, I, K, N and P. It requires the earning of distinguishing features and new names (particularly in the hawk family). It is simply relatively weak in not requiring the learner to "list" the various types of birds of prey without operating from picture prompts (or to name the two types of eagles without looking at the pictures). To compensate for these possible weaknesses, we could simply add activities to the game that follows the presentation of the display. One item might instruct the learner to: "Name the five types of birds of prey without looking at the picture." Another might be: "Name the two hawk families without looking at the pictures." The learner would not be required to name the entries in a particular order, but merely list them.

In summary, visual-spatial displays that retain pictures tend to provide prompts that *may be* spurious, depending on what kind of organizational information we expect the learner to remember. The displays that are most susceptible to this problem are the natural-part, created-whole displays because we are creating an organization. The extent to which we expect the learner to remember this organization determines the extent to which we supplement the display with questions that require the learner to respond to organizational features without looking at the pictures on the chart.

Choice of Displays

Different fact systems are appropriate for different objectives. If the system to be tested is a natural-whole system, such as a carburetor, teeth, a mountain, or a window and its frame, the natural-part, natural-whole display is clearly implied. The reason is that the learner will always encounter the parts within the context of the whole; therefore, the objective of instruction should be simply to teach the learner to label the parts and the whole.

For many systems, the same information that can be presented in a created-part, created-whole display can also be incorporated into a *natural-part*, created-whole display. The choice of displays depends on whether the primary objective is to teach *new parts* or the system of organizing familiar parts into a new system. If the objective is to teach new parts, the natural-part, created-whole display is most appropriate. This display *shows* the parts that are to be identified. If the objective is to teach a system of organizing familiar parts, the created-part, created-whole display is most appropriate.

Decisions about created-whole displays are not as easy to make as those about natural-whole systems. The reason is that the learner will never see the created-whole in the environment. If the parts are presented as unprompted cells with wording in them, the learner will be forced to learn the whole or the system of relationships between the parts because these relationships provide the only clues about which wording goes in which cell. To teach any *system* of classification, the created-part, created-whole display is the strongest.

If the learner does not know the parts, the presentation of a created-part, created-whole display would be a word game. If we change the display into a natural-part, created-whole display, however, the communication is not as emphatic in requiring the learner to learn the whole, because *the parts* are clearly identifiable. The display reinforces more attention to the individual differences in the cells, and not as much to their arrangement.

Logical Interpolation or Extrapolation

If designed properly, the visual-spatial display will prompt interpolation or extrapolation. For example, if we present the display of information about metals shown in Figure 14.6, we prompt the learner to organize the metals according to their weight.

The display uses two devices to assure interpolation and extrapolation:

- The left-to-right arrangement, with the heavier metals to the left of the lighter ones.
- The length of the stems, with longer stems on heavier metals.

Neither prompt is spurious. Together, they prompt an organization of metals in a seriated arrangement. With the understanding of this arrangement, the learner can interpolate new metals and can also extrapolate.

At some later time, we may be able to add new entries by relating them to entries already on the display. To do this, we would describe the relative weight of each new entry. For instance, we present a test chart (no wording

Section IV | Programs

Figure 14.6

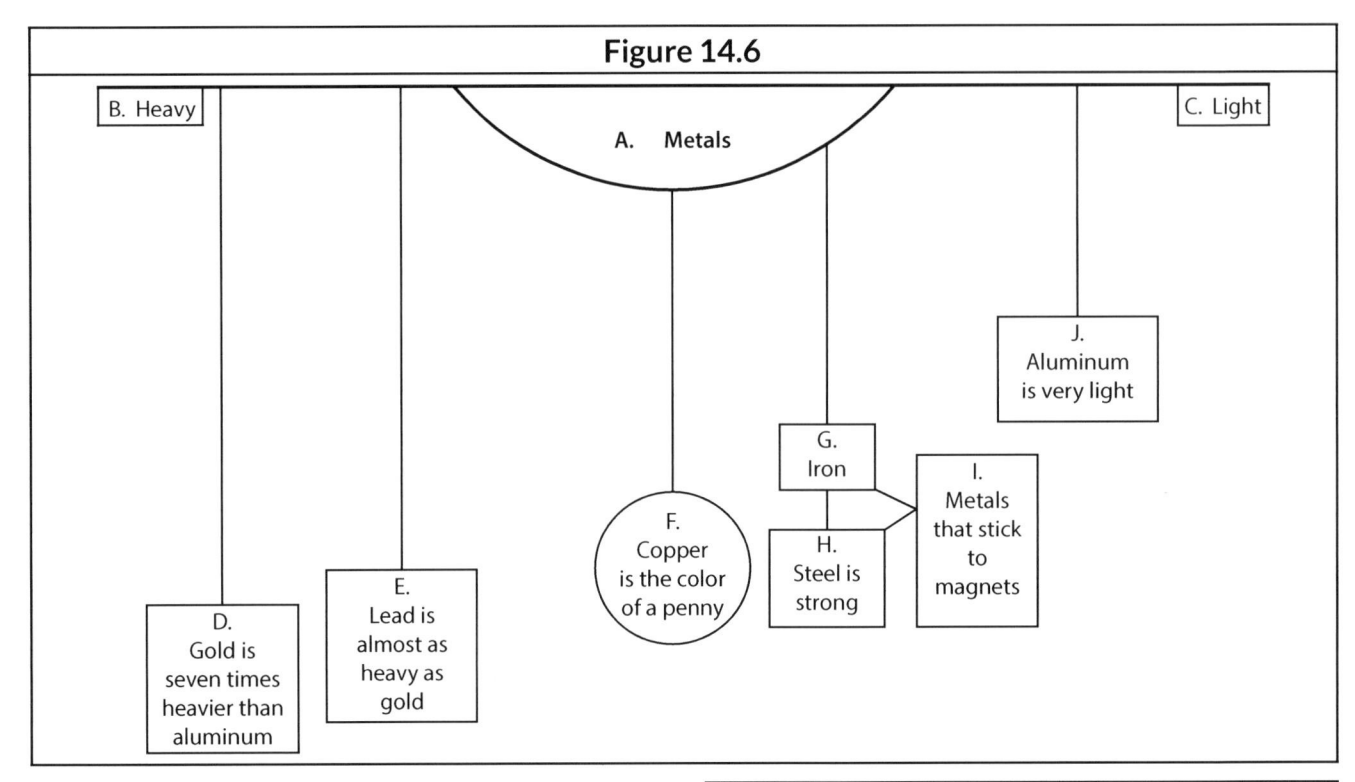

- A. Metals
  - B. Heavy
    - D. Gold is seven times heavier than aluminum
    - E. Lead is almost as heavy as gold
  - F. Copper is the color of a penny
  - G. Iron
    - H. Steel is strong
  - I. Metals that stick to magnets
  - C. Light
    - J. Aluminum is very light

in the cells) and describe a new metal this way: "Mercury is heavier than lead, but not as heavy as gold. Show me where mercury would go on the chart." "Magnesium is lighter than aluminum. Show me where it goes on the chart."

Add-On Information

The design of visual-spatial displays should be approached with the understanding that it is not necessary to teach everything through a single chart. If charts are properly designed, we can later add on additional information.

The strategy for add-on information should be that what had been taught earlier remains intact. For instance, information about **geological time** can be added on to the simple display of the five types of vertebrates. The illustration in Figure 14.7 shows five vertebrates with a different type of add-on information.

Information about **fish** is added to the basic five-cell display for vertebrates. Additional add-ons can be made for each of the other vertebrates. These add-ons would be positioned to the left of the basic display.

Add-on displays are presented one at a time. Each add-on would involve between 8 to 16 cells. Each would be firmed and reviewed in the same manner as the

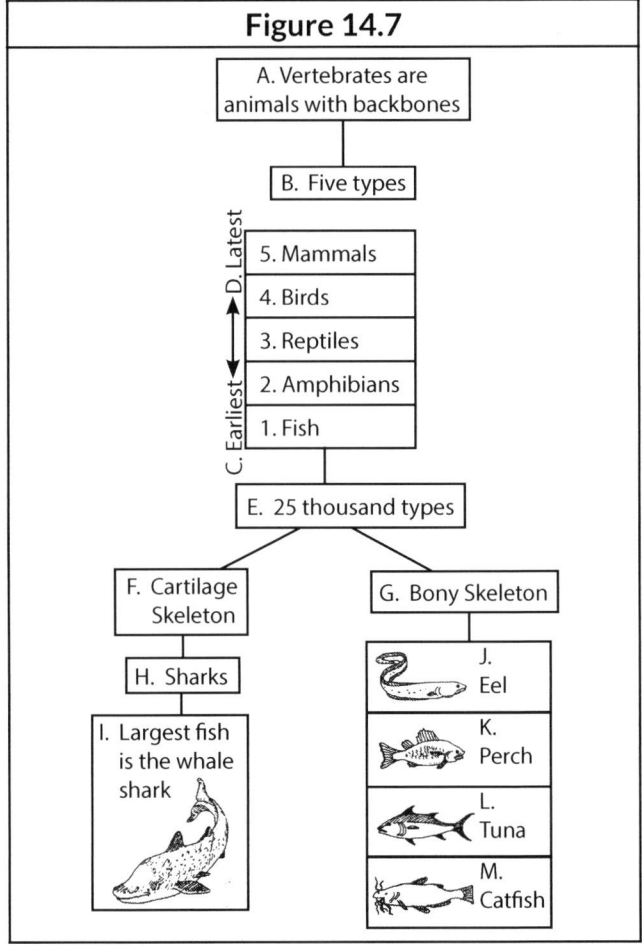

Figure 14.7

- A. Vertebrates are animals with backbones
  - B. Five types
    - D. Latest ↑
      - 5. Mammals
      - 4. Birds
      - 3. Reptiles
      - 2. Amphibians
      - 1. Fish
    - C. Earliest ↓
  - E. 25 thousand types
    - F. Cartilage Skeleton
      - H. Sharks
        - I. Largest fish is the whale shark
    - G. Bony Skeleton
      - J. Eel
      - K. Perch
      - L. Tuna
      - M. Catfish

Theory of Instruction: Principles and Applications

original display is introduced and reviewed. A cumulative review would follow in the form of a "super display," showing both the original and all add-on displays. The students would play a game that requires identifying the wording for all empty cells in this super display.

Showing Variation in Coordinate Entries

If there are four coordinate entries and one of these differs from the others *with respect to an important feature*, we can visually show both that the variant entry is coordinate with the others and that it is different. The display in Figure 14.8 illustrates the procedure. Four western cedar trees are presented. The fact that they are coordinate is shown by the fact that all are subordinated under the same heading. One cedar is visually different from the others, however. The Alaskan cedar occupies a unique position. This position is intended to reflect the fact that the leaves of the Alaskan cedar are different from those of the other cedars. The leaves of all others have stomata patterns (distinctive patterns of white lines) on the underside. The Alaskan cedar leaf has no stomata pattern.

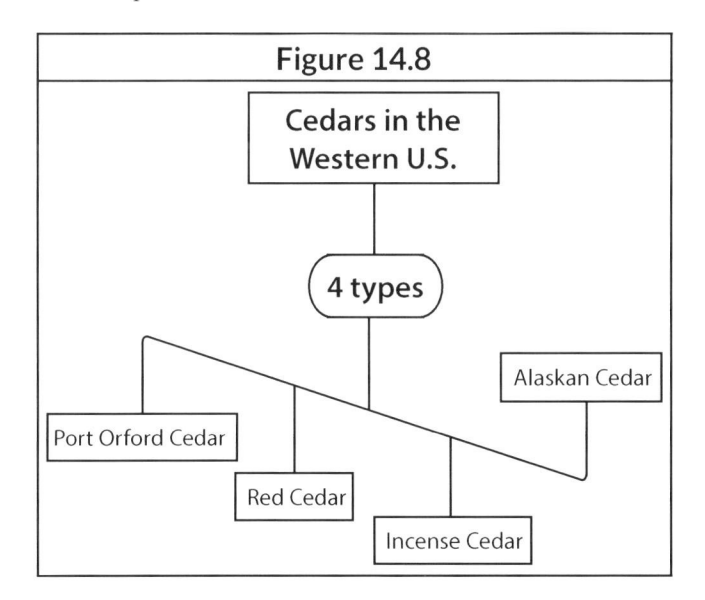

Figure 14.8

Cedars in the Western U.S. — 4 types: Port Orford Cedar, Red Cedar, Incense Cedar, Alaskan Cedar

This technique is appropriate if only one entry is different from all others in an important way. It is not appropriate to show that each coordinate entry has some unique feature. If all coordinate cells are different from the others, the fact that they are coordinate becomes obscured.

In summary, if only one cell is different from other coordinate members, show: (1) that it is coordinate by giving it coordinate position or coordinate shape, or other features that are possessed by the coordinate members; and (2) that it is different by creating a salient (obvious) difference between it and any other coordinate member.

Do not use this technique if there are only two coordinate entries or if each coordinate entry in a larger group has an important distinguishing feature. For the latter situation, add a cell below each entry that *tells* about the feature.

Selecting Information for Displays

The amount of information included on the display should not exceed 16 cells, with each cell containing either a single label, phrase or sentence. Selecting information is easy for some displays. If we are dealing with a simple higher-order classification system such as **vehicles** or **types of trees**, the information that goes on the visual display has been clearly specified and ordered for us. We simply translate it into visual relationships that show which classes are higher and which are lower.

When we deal with more complex events, however, the design becomes less clear. A recurring guideline in a logical approach to instructional design is that we should not attenuate what we teach, but we should teach no more than is necessary. When we teach a noun, such as **shoe**, we do not try to find the most precise "definition" of **shoe**. We teach the discriminations that are suggested by what the learner already knows. Similarly, when we select information to include on a visual-spatial display, we select only the most salient information. We do not try to exhaust the subject, but merely to provide the learner with information needed for the immediate applications. The amount of information that should be provided for a learner will vary from one learning situation to another, just as the specificity of a noun changes from situation to situation, depending on the context in which the noun is to be used. Here are procedures for selecting information:

1. Include the information that would be included in a good outline of the topic. An outline specifies the main ideas and provides some supporting detail. The outline is not exhaustive with respect to the supporting detail; however, the main ideas imply how supporting detail that is not mentioned *would* be included in the outline. For instance, an outline of general tree classifications might mention **oaks** and **maples** as shade trees (the entries for the tree-classification chart). Although other shade trees are not named (**sycamore, cottonwoods,**

etc.), these are implied by the outline (given that the learner has information about how these trees look). By following the same basic conventions for developing a good outline, we can create a visual display far more powerful than the outline because it is not limited to words. The various relationships can be shown through visual analogues, instead of mere indentations under a heading or through parallel structure.

2. Design the wording of cells so the wording for coordinate cells is parallel. If we use a sentence in one cell of a particular type, we use a sentence in other coordinate cells. This requirement may seem trivial, but it is quite important. When the teacher asks a group of students which words go in various cells, the activity will quickly reduce to frustration if the wording for one cell is a phrase and the wording in a coordinate cell is a sentence. The strong tendency of the students will be to say phrases for both cells or to say sentences for both. Much hardship may be avoided by designing the cells so that parallel structure suggests parallel wording.

3. Try to limit information to that which is relevant. Many facts about a particular topic are not relevant to the understanding of it. The history of the internal combustion engine is not relevant to how the engine works. If the goal of the topic is to provide information about how the engine works, the display should be limited to information about how it works. If the topic is the history of the internal combustion engine, on the other hand, the decisions about which information to include become far more difficult. We do not know the value of various contributions unless we understand how the machine works. Ideally, our approach to history would be to frame *specific problems* and then present solutions. For instance, a problem would be that starting cars by cranking was bothersome and sometimes dangerous (broken arms). The solution: Kettering invents the electric starter. If a topic is new for the learner and presents many new names, try to limit the information to 11 cells with the understanding that subsequent add-ons may be introduced.

Designing the Script

The script is designed by: (1) expanding the information in the cells of the visual-spatial display; and (2) adding information that *is related to some cells*.

The spatial relationships of the cells imply statements that should appear in the script. The words that appear in each cell should also appear in the script. The script should present the displayed information in systematic order, referring to the more general categories first and the more specific ones later.

In addition to conveying information provided by the various cells of the display, the script should contain other information. This script information includes anecdotes, information that is unusual or unexpected, and facts about entries on the display. As a rule of thumb, about 25 percent of the total scripted information should consist of information that is not directly shown on the display.

The criteria for constructing a script serves as a basis for testing whether the script is adequate. If the script is adequately designed, the answer to each question below should be, "Yes."

- Does the script contain statements about every cell and about "connections" shown on the display?
- Does the script present this information in a logical order, starting with the general information?
- Does the script contain information that is not contained on the chart?
- Does each bit of secondary information relate to specific cells or spatial relationship cells on the chart?
- Does the secondary information comprise about 25 percent of the total information presented in the script?

Analysis of Preskills

Once designed, the display serves as a *task*. We can analyze the task as we can any other task. Ideally, we would use a transformed-task approach. Our objective would be to assure that the learner understands all the prerequisite concepts that are needed before the chart is presented. However, the display is usually capable of teaching most new names.

Here are the entries that might appear on a chart dealing with cedar tree identification:

stomata—white lines

Port Orford Cedar—**X**'s on the underside

For the first entry, we would not preteach the meaning of stomata. The entry itself provides a description that is adequate for the purpose of identifying leaves of cedar trees. Stomata are the white, powdery lines that appear on some leaves. If preteaching were necessary, it would involve teaching the meaning of white lines. The probability, however, is great that the learner already understands this discrimination.

The entry, *Port Orford cedar—**X**'s on the underside*, assumes that the learner understands what **X**'s and **underside** mean. If the learner does, no further preteaching is required. The entry itself is capable of teaching the relationship about the identifying feature of the Port Orford leaf. (It has **X**'s on the underside.) The script presented with the display could amplify this point: "If you look on the underside of Port Orford cedar leaves, you'll see a line of **X**'s on top of each other. The **X**'s will be in white stomata. Remember, Port Orford cedar—**X**'s on underside."

Often, the sentences that define words do not imply preteaching for these reasons:

1. The facts that are presented often have very little generalizability and therefore do not imply heavy discrimination teaching.

2. The type of test that is provided in connection with the visual-spatial display is usually adequate to assure that the learner is discriminating highly similar members (such as Port Orford with its **X**'s, incense cedar with its stomata pattern of wine glasses, and western red with its stomata butterflies).

3. The phrases or sentences used to describe new words are usually familiar to the learner. (Describing stomata in terms of plant physiology would result in an item that would require extensive preteaching. Not only would the learner be unaware of the meaning of **stomata**, but also the learner would probably have to learn components of the physiological explanation. Typically, however, sentences that explain new words *phrase the explanation in words familiar to the learner.*)

4. The script can be used to amplify or clarify meanings that may not be obvious.

Some entries on a visual-spatial display imply preteaching. Although it is possible to explain the four strokes of an internal combustion engine without referring to anything beyond the engine, the transformed-task analysis would suggest that the learner should have a generalized understanding of **compression, exhaust**, and **intake**. To achieve this teaching, we would teach **compression** (possibly teaching it as a comparative—more compressed versus not-more compressed). (We might press against a spring.) For **exhaust** and **intake**, we could use **breathing in** and **breathing out**, with the learner labeling each example as **intake** and **exhaust**.

In summary, those entries that are defined or described on the chart usually need no preteaching if the explanation presents a familiar idea and familiar words. Some entries, however, assume an understanding not provided by the display. Preteaching for such entries is desirable if not necessary.

Scheduling Different Displays

The rules for ordering the displays are the same as those for other members. Each display is a member. Displays that are minimally different should be separated in the order of introduction. If an introduction is difficult (involving many new words or minimum-difference discriminations), the next display should not be as difficult.

The juxtaposed displays should look as different from each other as possible and the topics should be as different as possible. Often, great difference in topic is not possible if the various charts are designed to develop a particular subject. For example, if we are developing the subject of vertebrates, each display will deal with the same general topics; however, as much as possible, the juxtaposed displays should deal with different aspects of the topic. One display might deal with characteristics of fish, while the next deals with mammals. The two types of vertebrates are not easily confused. The next display might deal with reptiles, followed by birds, followed by amphibians. The highly similar members—reptiles and amphibians, and possibly fish, are separated in this order of introduction. Greater separation of these members is possible if we intersperse displays that deal with geological information between those that deal with types of vertebrates.

The juxtaposed displays should not be similar in form. As we mentioned earlier, the displays should be ordered so that each is unique—ideally not highly similar to any of the others in the group that is to be presented. The extent to which each display is unique is the extent to which the learner will not confuse elements or parts of different displays. If charts are similar in shape or structure, they should deal with different information. (Two circular charts should not be used for the same topic.)

Add-ons should be designed both so that the add-on part is unique in structure and so the total display (original and add-on) is not highly similar to any other display.

Summary

Programs that use visual-spatial displays are effective for teaching the structure of topics for a wide range of content.

The goal of a display is to teach a system of facts that are relevant to a topic. The learner understands the topic if the learner understands the individual facts and their relationship. The visual-spatial display provides a framework for inducing this understanding.

Although the goal is to teach only one thing (one topic) through a display, the teaching is complex because the topic is composed of facts. The facts and their relationships are the *features of the topic*. The teaching therefore firms the learner's understanding of the facts.

The visual-spatial display uses codes for indicating information in various cells and codes for showing relationships between cells.

The display should therefore not be used with learners who do not understand these codes and who may assume that what is being shown is a real thing of some sort (rather than a representation of a system).

For the more sophisticated learner, the visual-spatial display is an extremely efficient way to learn about systems. The spatial arrangement of elements provides visual prompts for retrieving any particular entry from memory. (By remembering what is next to the cell, what above the cell, or what the shape of the cell is, the learner may be prompted to retrieve the information for a particular cell.) Also, the wording presented for each cell provides a logical basis for retrieving the information.

Accompanying the display is a script that deals with the wording of each cell, amplifies what is said in each cell, and provides perhaps 25% additional information that is not provided by the visual display.

Following the presentation of the display with words in the cells, the learner is tested on a blank-cell version of the display, then engages in expansion activities that usually take the form of a game.

There are three types of visual-spatial displays: the natural-part, natural-whole; the natural-part, created whole; and the created-part, created-whole. Often information that involves a created-whole or classification system can be presented as either a natural-part, created-whole, or a created-part, created-whole presentation.

If the new teaching focuses primarily on the organization, the created-part display is preferable. New words may be introduced, but they should be "defined" with familiar words.

If the learner is to learn to identify parts that cannot be described with familiar words (such as game birds), the natural-part display is preferable.

The general rules for designing the visual-spatial display are:

- Limit the information to 16 cells with only one "idea" presented by each cell.
- Use coordinate wording for cells that are coordinate in structure (visually coordinate).
- Show subordination by using lines or cell design. If three things are subordinated under a particular cell, all will have lines leading to that cell or all will be included in a larger cell.
- Show that members are coordinate by lines and form. If cells are coordinate, they should occupy the same relative position and they should be visually the same.
- If one of the group of coordinate entries is different from the others in an important way, we can show the difference by adding a visual clue to the cell of the different member.
- Avoid spurious cues. A cue is spurious if it is designed to prompt a name that is familiar to the learner. The cell may be in the shape of a letter or the shape of the familiar object.

Apply a transformed-task analysis to the display and identify any preskills that are to be taught. As a rule, sentences or phrases that appear on the display do not imply preskill teaching. The explanation of the new word is usually expressed in terms the learner can understand. Some labels imply preteaching. These are labels that are not adequately taught through the display and that are important to the understanding of the displayed information.

To present a series of visual-spatial displays, use the procedures specified for introducing members to a set. Each display is a member. No display should be juxtaposed to a display that is highly similar in shape or highly similar in content.

Add-ons may be used when a topic is extensive (more than 16 cells). Two types of add-ons are possible. One type adds individual cells as interpolated or extrapolated members. These add-ons are possible when the cells are arranged according to some generic ordering rule (such as weight, size, number, or other feature that admits to a clear presentation on a continuum). By teaching the original display, information points on the continuum are provided. These become the basis for possible interpolation or extrapolation.

The other add-on is a *unit* or group of cells that is added to the appropriate entry of an earlier chart. The procedure is first to teach the original display, then (after the learner has had an opportunity to work with this display and learn it thoroughly) introduce the add-on. The presentation of the add-on should not be juxtaposed with the presentation of the original display. The add-on should be unique in shape. The display that results when the add-on is included should be unique in form.

If more than one display is introduced to the learner, each display is a member of a set. Following the rules for members, juxtaposed displays should be as maximally dissimilar as possible.

SECTION V
COMPLETE TEACHING

The sequences presented in Section II and Section III are *initial teaching sequences*. They communicate with the learner in the most straightforward manner possible, showing what controls the discrimination response and how changes in the features of the examples relate to possible changes in the responses. The initial teaching sequences, however, do not provide for complete teaching. They do not show the learner the range of application for the discrimination. And, they do not provide practice in which the discrimination is juxtaposed with *different discriminations*. Solving the problems of stipulation and juxtaposition prompting is the goal of complete teaching.

The Problem of Stipulation

The initial-teaching sequences are guilty of two types of stipulation: (1) they stipulate the range of examples, and (2) they stipulate the responses that are called for. Following a presentation of the concept **farther apart** demonstrated with the teacher's hands, one learner may think that **farther apart** applies only to the hands; another may think that it applies only to humans; another may think that it applies to any physical thing. All interpretations are consistent with the presentation, which means that the presentation has done nothing to confirm or reject any of these speculations about the range of application. *The longer the teacher works on a limited range of examples or a particular response, the greater the amount of stipulation that results.* If a teacher repeated a demonstration of **farther apart** on ten different occasions and never showed that **farther apart** applies to anything but hands, naive learners would tend to learn the stipulation much more than they would if the teacher presented the sequence only once or twice.

To solve the problem of stipulation, we:

1. Work on the initial-teaching sequence no longer than necessary.

2. Immediately follow the sequence with applications of the discrimination that use *new examples* and that require *new responses*.

The Problem of Juxtaposition Prompting

Juxtaposition prompting occurs in most initial teaching sequences because tasks in the sequence teach within-set discriminations, which means that the learner attends to the same instructions and responds to juxtaposed tasks that involve the same response dimension. This pattern of juxtapositions prompts attention to particular features of the examples and is relatively easy for the learner because it involves less memory of what to attend to and which label goes with an observed change or feature. *Our goal, however, is to teach the learner to deal with situations in which the discrimination is not prompted by being preceded by a task that involves the same discrimination.*

To "shape" the learner's memory for the discrimination's details and its label, *we shape the context or the pattern of juxtapositions*. To do this, we sandwich different tasks between tasks that involve the newly-taught discrimination. Think of interspersed activities as interference. In the initial teaching sequence, there is no interference. Immediately after operating on one example in a specified way, the learner operates on another example in basically the same way. No interference occurs between trials. By interspersing other activities between the trials with the target discrimination, we increase the interference. We increase the demands on the learner's memory (and demonstrate that we expect the learner to remember the label and the details of the examples). We increase the difficulty of dealing with the new discrimination in stages, not in one leap from the initial teaching situation to situations that contain no juxtaposition prompting, but through stages that increase the amount of interference.

General Directions for Expanded Teaching

We will look at a number of specific techniques for expanded teaching. All are effective in overcoming the problems of stipulation and juxtaposition prompting. However, expansion activities are very natural and easy to construct if the initial teaching is effective. The most frequently encountered problem observed in teaching situations is that the learner has not been taught a discrimination, but adequate expansion activities are provided.

The simplest strategy for dealing with the problem of expanding what has been taught is to teach it and immediately apply it in a significant way. When we follow the simple strategy of teaching what is to be used and using what is taught, we eliminate many problems of "keeping discriminations alive" through techniques such as the expansion activities described in this section.

Chapter 15 presents various expansion tasks that do not involve worksheets. Chapter 16 explains worksheet strategies.

Chapter 15
Expanded Teaching

The activities that we will deal with in this chapter are presented after the initial-teaching sequence. Their purpose is to show the learner that the newly-learned discrimination applies to examples and tasks beyond those shown in the initial teaching setup.

The five primary types of expansion activities are:

1. Manipulative tasks for basic-form and correlated-feature concepts.
2. Implied conclusion tasks for all concepts.
3. Divergent tasks for single and double transformation concepts.
4. Fooler games for all concepts.
5. Event-centered task series for all concepts.

Manipulative Tasks

A manipulative task calls for a *production response*. The learner is told to produce an example of the concept. Instead of calling for a verbal or symbolic response, however, the manipulative task calls for a non-verbal response. Manipulative tasks may be presented immediately after the learner has successfully performed on the initial-teaching sequence for any basic discrimination and for many correlated-feature relationships. Here are several tasks that could follow the presentation of the positional concept **over**.

> "Your turn: Take the block and hold it **over** this table…"
> "Now put it so that it is **not over** the table…"
> "Now hold it **over** the table again…"

Possibly, the teacher could introduce different objects for the child to hold the object over:

> "I'll name things. You hold the block over them.
> Hold it over the table.
> Hold it over the chair.
> Hold it over the floor."

Manipulative tasks may be presented to a group. For instance, the teacher puts his hand on his knee:

> "Put your hand like this." He prompts children to put their hand on their knee.
> "Your hand is not **over** your knee. When I clap, put your hand **over** your knee." Teacher claps. "Good."
> "When I clap again, hold your hand so that it is not-over your knee." Teacher claps. "Good."
> "When I clap again, hold your hand so that it is way over your knee." Teacher claps.

Many variations of manipulative tasks are possible. To construct them, follow these rules:

1. Design the tasks so they do not involve much that is new, particularly new instruction forms.
2. Use the same setup for more than one positive example.

The illustrations just presented introduce some new wording. The choice-response sequence teaches **over–not over** without naming the second object. ("The eraser is over," not, "The eraser is over *the table*.") The use of manipulative tasks makes it fairly easy for the learner to respond to these new instructions. If the learner understands **over**, the first series of tasks is obvious because all tasks involve "this table," pointed to by the teacher. The task involving "the knees" is of the same form. The tasks involving different objects involve the same block, so mistakes are improbable.

Manipulative tasks can be designed so they go beyond what had been taught in the initial-teaching sequence; however, the gap between the manipulative task setup and the initial-teaching setup should not be too great initially. If it is, the learner's responses will probably provide us with feedback that we have made the task too difficult.

Manipulative tasks are easily designed to expand comparatives. Here is a possible sequence of manipulative tasks that might follow the presentation of **higher**.

"Everybody, hold your hand out like this…When I clap, move it a little higher." Teacher claps. "Good."

"Let's do it again. Hold your hand out like this…When I clap, move it a lot higher." Teacher claps.

Variations of this kind of manipulation are appropriate for most comparatives. A similar variation is possible for correlated-feature relationships that involve comparatives. The following are some manipulative tasks that could follow the presentation of the relationship: **The hotter it gets, the higher the line in a thermometer.**

"Your turn: Hold your hand in front of you, like this…Your finger is the top of the line in a thermometer. I'll tell you what happens to the temperature. When I clap, you show me how the line moves."

"The air gets a little hotter…" Teacher claps.

"The air gets a lot hotter…" Teacher claps.

"The air stays the same temperature…" Teacher claps.

"The air cools a little tiny bit…" Teacher claps.

"The air gets a little bit hotter…" Teacher claps.

"The air gets a little hotter…" Teacher claps.

The teacher could add a second question to each example:

"The air gets a little hotter…Why did you move up a little bit?…Yes, because the air got a little hotter, so the line moved up a little bit."

This type of expansion activity is well-designed for work with a group because it provides clear feedback on the understanding of individual group members. Many trials can be juxtaposed and the teacher can readily observe problems.

Manipulative tasks can be designed so they test the discrimination or so that they do not actually test it. If the learner does not actually produce an example of the discrimination being taught, the task is not actually testing the discrimination. Here are manipulative tasks that do not test the discrimination being taught:

"There's a rabbit in this room. And that rabbit is going to hide under different things. I'll tell you where the rabbit is hiding. You point to the place the rabbit is…"

"The rabbit runs under the table…"

"Now the rabbit goes under the window…"

"Now the rabbit is under Janey's desk…"

"Now the rabbit is under my desk…"

If this sequence is presented to a group of children, we could not actually tell whether each child was pointing under the various objects. Possibly some children simply point at the objects named. We could change the response so that the children clearly produce positive examples of **under**. "Touch the place the rabbit is . . ." Now, however, the task becomes perfectly unmanageable with children tumbling about the room, making a game of the touching, and making it impossible for the teacher to maintain any sort of reasonable pacing from one task to another.

The pointing task above may easily be justified on the ground that although it does not clearly require the learner to produce positive examples, it does acquaint the learner with the idea that the concept **under** can be used in connection with a variety of objects.

By changing the task somewhat, we could make it manageable.

"There are many rabbits in the room. One of them is on your chair. Touch the place that rabbit is."

"Now that rabbit is under your chair. Touch the place that rabbit is…"

In summary, the manipulative task consists of instructions for the learner to produce a non-verbal response. Ideally, the task should be designed so that the learner produces examples of the concept. The manipulative task can be used to expand any basic concept and for many correlated-feature relationships. It may be introduced as soon as the learner performs successfully on an initial teaching sequence, even as the final task in the series (following the test segment).

Manipulative tasks are most manageably presented as a series that involve a common setup. For example:

1. The teacher begins with general instructions, telling: (a) what the teacher will do, and (b) how the learner is to respond.

2. The teacher then presents 3 to 6 examples.

3. Although some new information may be introduced through these examples, the tasks should not be drastically different from those presented in the initial-teaching sequence.

Implied-Conclusion Tasks

The initial teaching sequences are direct. They show examples of the discrimination being taught and they ask questions about that discrimination. They do not ask about other discriminations. For instance, the learner is asked about **bigger**. The learner is not asked to *name the object that gets bigger*, to *respond to the position of the object that gets bigger*, or to *label anything other than the discrimination being taught*. The learner's responses change in a way that parallels changes in the example, so the most direct relationship possible exists between the examples and the response.

Once the learner has performed on an initial-teaching sequence, we can introduce tasks of a different nature: *implied-conclusion tasks*. For these, the learner *uses* the discrimination that was taught to draw a conclusion. The learner will not produce overt responses of "bigger" and "not-bigger" for the implied-conclusion tasks; however, the learner will *use* the discrimination **bigger–not-bigger** in responding to these tasks.

Here is an example. The teacher presents three familiar objects: a dog, a horse, and a man. The teacher says, "One of these objects is bigger than the others. Which object is bigger?"

The response: "The horse."

Note that the learner is required to use the concept **bigger**. But instead of saying "bigger," the learner was required to name the thing that was bigger.

The teacher could have asked a variety of other questions, such as: "Is the bigger object sitting or standing?" "What color is the bigger object?" "Where is the bigger object?" "What is the bigger object doing?" Note that the teacher would present one of these tasks, not the series. For each of these tasks, the learner must: (1) *first find the object that is bigger*, and (2) *follow the response conventions called for by the questions*.

Designing Implied-Conclusion Tasks

The easiest way to figure out how to construct implied-conclusion tasks is to make up a statement that names the newly-taught discrimination in a fact. Then create a display consistent with the fact and that requires the learner to discriminate. If the newly-taught discrimination is **gymnosperm**, the statement might be: "A girl sat under the gymnosperm." If the newly-taught discrimination is **bigger**, the statement might be: "The red object is bigger than the other objects." If the newly-taught discrimination is **rhyming**, the statement might be: "John rhymed with the word **am**."

Each fact tells about a possible implied-conclusion display. Consider the sentence, "The red object is bigger than the other objects." We can create a display that is consistent with this fact. The display would show a group of colored objects. The red object would be bigger than the others.

For the fact, "A girl sat under the gymnosperm," we would show a girl sitting under a gymnosperm tree.

We now adjust the display to make sure that the learner discriminates. To do this, we add other objects to each display.

For the display that shows the red object bigger than the others, we could ask, "*What color* is the bigger object?" Or we could ask, "Is the bigger object yellow? . . . Is the bigger object blue? . . . Is the bigger object red?" Or we ask, "*Where* is the biggest object?"

To answer the question, "What color is the biggest object?" the learner must first find the object that is biggest, then respond to the color of that object. We design the display so that the learner must find the bigger object to answer the question. (Only one object is red.)

For the display of John rhyming with **am**, we could ask: "Who is rhyming with **am**?" or, "Is Terry rhyming with **am**? . . . Is John rhyming with **am**? . . . Is Martha rhyming with **am**?"

The task does not require the learner to rhyme with **am** (which is what the initial teaching sequence teaches). However, to respond correctly, the learner must first attend to what John is rhyming with, then respond to the task that is presented.

If John is the only person rhyming, the learner could respond to the task, "Who is rhyming with **am**?" by simply naming the only person who is rhyming. Therefore, the display would show not only John, but also the other people, each of whom would rhyme with words other than **am**.

For the display that shows a girl sitting under the gymnosperm, we could ask the following questions: "Who is sitting under the gymnosperm?" "What is the person under the gymnosperm doing?" "Is there a girl under the gymnosperm?" "Is there a boy under the gymnosperm?"

To assure that the learner uses the discrimination **gymnosperm** in answering these questions, we would make sure that there is more than one person in the picture (ideally someone under an angiosperm tree). This person would not be sitting if we ask the question, "What is the person under the gymnosperm doing?" We would make sure that the person under the angiosperm is not a girl, if the learner is asked, "Is there a boy under the gymnosperm?"

The following is a summary of the steps for constructing implied-conclusion tasks:

1. Construct different facts that include the name or label of the discrimination that had been taught. Underline the discrimination in each sentence. "Martha constructed a fraction equivalent to two-thirds."

2. Make up a display that shows what the fact says. For the fact, "Martha constructed a fraction equivalent to two-thirds," we would show a girl (labeled **Martha**) holding a fraction that is equivalent to two-thirds (e.g., 4/6). For the fact, "Five of the eight fractions were equivalent to two-thirds," we would show eight fractions, five of which are equivalent to two-thirds.

3. Present a task that does not call for the label or name of the discrimination. For the displays involving fractions, the tasks could be: "Tell *who* constructed a fraction that is equivalent to two-thirds," and "Name all the fractions that are equivalent to two-thirds.

4. Make sure that the learner is not able to respond correctly without using the discrimination. Add negatives to the display that share features with the positives. Show people other than Martha holding up fractions.

Divergent Activities for Transformation Concepts

Divergent tasks are most appropriate for single-transformation and double transformation concepts. It is usually possible to construct manipulative tasks for the transformation concepts. We could require the learner to "Touch the word that rhymes with **am**," which would satisfy the requirement for manipulative tasks. The learner creates an example of rhyming with **am** and the response is non-verbal. It is also usually possible to construct implied-conclusion tasks for transformation concepts. ("*Who* is rhyming with **am**?") Often, however, the best expansion tasks for transformation concepts are divergent tasks. "Say some words that rhyme with **am**."

The difference between divergent tasks and the type presented in the initial-teaching sequence is that *there is a range of correct responses for the divergent task.*

If the learner has been taught to construct predicates through a single-transformation sequence, we can construct divergent tasks that require the learner to make up predicates. If the learner has been taught to tell **where** something is through a single-transformation sequence, we can design divergent tasks that require the learner to tell where different things are. "Make up sentences that tell where the things in this room are." Like other expanded activities, the divergent tasks can be presented as soon as the learner has mastered the initial-teaching sequence.

Here is a possible sequence of divergent tasks that might follow the teaching of predicates:

Teacher: "My turn to make up predicates for sentences that start out with the subject, **the girl**. The girl" (pause) "went to school. The girl" (pause) "liked ice cream." Your turn. Make up predicates for sentences that start out with the subject, **the girl**."

After teaching rhyming, the teacher could present this divergent sequence:

"I'm going to rhyme with **am**. Ram...Sam...Your turn: Make up some new words that rhyme with **am**."

After teaching simple addition facts, the teacher might present this sequence:

"I'm going to say addition statements with numbers that add up to four. Listen: Four plus zero equals four. Your turn: See if you can make up more statements that add up to four."

After teaching simple spelling of words that end in the letters **a-n**:

"I'll spell some words that end with the letters **a-n**. Listen: **C-a-n** spells **can**. **M-a-n** spells **man**. Your turn: Make up some words that end with the letters **a-n**."

To design divergent tasks:

1. Select a task for which at least five answers are correct and available to the learner.
2. Model one or two responses.
3. Require the learner to make up at least two more examples.
4. Reinforce acceptable responses.

Reinforcing Divergent Responses

Although the illustrations above do not specify teacher reinforcement, reinforcement is very important for success in divergent activities because these activities involve varying degrees of "risk taking." Unless there is some potential payoff for taking risks, the learner will be reluctant to produce more than very safe responses. Also, if there is a great penalty for creating an unacceptable example, the learner will not be very adventurous.

If the teacher is working with more than one learner, the teacher can show the kind of responses that are worthy of "ooos and aaahhs" by responding with obvious admiration to learners that produce examples somewhat different from those modeled by the teacher. If no student produces these, the teacher can model a couple of them and brag about how smart she is. If the teacher is a good actor, the students will usually work very hard to emulate her model. As a rule, however, divergent tasks are far less manageable than other tasks, particularly within the group setting. Often this setting gives the impression of great discovery and application because many of the students may be performing. If the goal is to teach **all**, however, the teacher must have systematic procedures both for monitoring all the students and for providing those who do not perform with prompting and reinforcement.

One possible solution to the problem of reinforcing divergent responses in a group is to use a "gamble" format. Everybody in the group receives a desirable reward if the work of a randomly-selected learner meets specified criteria. For instance, students write down four words that rhyme with **at**. The teacher secretly selects the work of one student. If all of the student's responses are correct, the teacher rewards *everybody* in the group. If the student's responses are not correct, the teacher does not disclose the student's name, but does not give any member of the group the reward.

All other solutions to the problem of reinforcing divergent responses in a group setting are similar to the one above in that they require the teacher to "sample" the work of each student frequently enough to provide feedback and encouragement.

Fooler Games

Foolers are expansion activities that can be used after nearly any initial teaching sequence. The details of various foolers differ; however, all are based on the idea that the teacher will make some mistakes and the learner will be able to catch those mistakes if the learner uses knowledge of the newly-taught concept. If the learner has been taught **bigger**, the teacher may present different pairs of discs. One disc in each pair is bigger than the other.

> Teacher: "I'm going to try to fool you. If you see me make a mistake, say: 'You didn't touch the bigger disc.' What are you going to say if I make a mistake?"
>
> "Here I go." Teacher touches bigger disc. "I touched the bigger disc."
>
> Teach replaces one disc, touches bigger disc. "I touched the bigger disc."
>
> Teacher replaces one disc, touches smaller disc. "I touched the bigger disc…Show me what I should have done…Oh, that's the bigger disc."

The fooler game has the potential of being challenging to the learner, because the learner has the opportunity to correct the teacher by using knowledge of *bigger*.

Many variations of the fooler game can be created. Instead of using different pairs, the teacher could present a group of five discs that vary in size. By adding a disc or taking one away, the teacher could create a series of examples for the game. "One disc is bigger than any other disc. I'll touch that disc." After touching a disc, the teacher says: "I touched the disc that is bigger." The children respond to examples in which the teacher is wrong by saying, "You didn't touch the disc that is bigger." The rest of the procedures are the same as those for the original fooler game.

The fooler game above calls for three different types of responses:

1. Responses to correct teacher assertions (by saying nothing).

2. Responses to incorrect teacher assertions (by using the label for the new discrimination, "You did not touch the *bigger* disc").

3. Manipulation responses. (In response to, "Show me what I should have done.")

A similar fooler format can be used with transformation concepts. For example, after the learner has been taught to rhyme, the teacher may present this type of fooler:

> "See if I can fool you. I'll say words that rhyme with **am**. When you hear me make a mistake, tell me to stop. **am, bam, jam, jack**...Starting over: **ram, ham, hat**...Starting over: **ran, cat**..."

A powerful fooler might be used after the learner has been taught to read simple words.

> "Follow along as I read. See if I can fool you. When I make a mistake, tell me to stop. That...dog...can...ran...What should I say? Yes, **run**. Starting over: That...dog...can...run...with...me...What should I say? Yes, **us**. Starting over: That...dog...can...run...with...us...We...have...What should I say? Yes, **had**."

Here is a fooler that might be presented after the learner has been taught to identify the subject of simple sentences:

> Teacher shows a list of sentences. "Let's see if I can fool you. I'll say the subject of each sentence. If I say it wrong, tell me to stop. *The boy went to the lake.* The subject is: *the boy.*
>
> "*The boy and a dog went to the lake.* The subject is: *the boy...* What is the subject?
>
> "*My mother was sitting on the grass.* The subject is: *my mother was...* What is the subject?

Here is a fooler that might be presented following the initial teaching sequence for the relationship: **The steeper the grade, the faster the stream flows.**

> "I'll tell you a story about a woman who is paddling down a river. See if I can fool you. When you hear me make a mistake, say 'stop.' The woman started out going down a very steep grade. The water was moving very fast. Then the stream leveled off a bit and the stream slowed down. Then the stream leveled off more and the stream moved faster... What's wrong?...What should have happened?...How do you know?...Then the grade became really steep and she had to paddle to keep the canoe moving...What's wrong?...How do you know?...What should have happened?...How do you know?...Then the grade flattened out completely and she had to paddle to keep the canoe moving..."

To construct the fooler game:

1. Design a setup or story line that will permit you to present at least six examples.

2. Make about one third of the examples foolers.

3. Precede the series with general instructions to indicate what you will tell the learner and what the learner is to do if a mistake occurs.

4. If practical, ask the learner what you should have said instead of what you did say when you made a mistake.

Event-Centered Tasks

Event-centered tasks can be used to expand any newly-taught discrimination. An event-centered series is created when the teacher presents a single object or example and asks different questions about that object, including questions that call for the newly-taught discrimination.

All questions asked about the object involve skills that have been taught to the learner.

Let's say that the learner has been taught names of common objects, basic color names, position names: **round, slanted**, and **smooth**. The most recently taught concept is the classification of **vehicles**.

> Teacher presents a blue truck to the learner. "What color is this object?...Touch a part of the object that is round...Is this object a vehicle?...What kind of vehicle is it?...What are trucks used for?...What kind of things would a truck like this carry?...Do you know that a truck like this could carry all the furniture that you would find in three houses?"

Ideally, the series of questions should be designed so that:

1. The newly-taught skill (in this case, **vehicle** and **truck**) is juxtaposed with the other discriminations associated with a particular object. This juxtaposition assures that the learner becomes familiar with the more common "associations" for a newly-taught discrimination.

2. A variety of tasks is presented. In the sequence above, there is a manipulative task, a yes-no task, a divergent-response task, and a rhetorical question.

3. The target tasks (those dealing with **vehicle** and **truck**) do not appear at the beginning of the series.

Ideally, they should occur after two or three other tasks have been presented.

4. Not all tasks are necessarily pretaught. For instance, the task about what kinds of things the truck might carry might not be pretaught.
5. Included in the series is some additional information. To make the presentation interesting to the learner, the teacher should tell something about the object. In the series above, the telling takes the form of the last question.

The event-centered series is perhaps the easiest for traditional teachers to construct because it involves the variety of tasks that are typically presented when an object, event, or picture is analyzed (an activity historically referred to as an *object lesson*). The teacher asks about specific details of the presentation. The teacher also asks questions of the form, "What do you think?..." And the teacher presents some new interesting information about the object or part of the object.

Event-centered tasks are very effective for removing what had been taught from the juxtaposition context of the initial teaching series.

Using Expanded Activities in Programs

To expand a newly-taught discrimination, you may use any combination of the five expansion activities—manipulative tasks, implied conclusion tasks, divergent tasks, fooler games, and event-centered series. Not all expansion activities are perfectly appropriate or manageable for every discrimination, and some activities are generally more useful than others. The most widely-applicable activities are: implied conclusion tasks, fooler games, and event-centered series. The event-centered series may include manipulative tasks, so there is often no need to present additional manipulative activities. Divergent tasks are very good; however, they are not manageable for many concepts. Also, it is possible to incorporate divergent tasks in an event-centered sequence.

The schedule in Figure 15.1 shows how the various expanded activities might be used in connection with the teaching of the concepts **on** and **over** and **between**.

The initial teaching of new discriminations is repeated (on two consecutive lessons in the schedule). After the second member (**over**) has been introduced, a cumulative review is presented. Between lessons 6 and 11, the discriminations **on** and **over** are reviewed and expanded. Another cumulative review occurs on the second initial teaching lesson for **between** (lesson 12). The assignment of particular activities on different days is arbitrary. The general pattern is for two activities to be presented as part of the expansion—one to deal with the most recently taught discrimination, and the other to deal with the earlier-taught concepts.

Figure 15.2 shows the expansion activities for lesson 1.

Figure 15.3 shows the activity that is presented as part of lesson 13. Note that the single activity presents event-centered tasks involving **on**, **over**, and **between**. It also presents implied conclusion tasks for **on**, **over**, and **between**.

The series contains some tasks that have nothing to do with **on, over**, and **between**.

The schedule of expanded activities for the prepositions assumes no other applications of the concept are provided for the learner, which means that all expansion must occur through the activities specified in the

Figure 15.1
An Expanded Activities Program

Components	Lessons													
	1	2	3	4	5	6	7	8	9	10	11	12	13	14
1. on	X	X												
2. over				X	X									
3. between											X	X		
Expansion		F1	I1	E1	F2 E1,2	I 1,2	E1 I2	F1 E2		I1 F2	F2 E1,2		E1,2,3 I1,2,3	I2,3 F3
Cumulative Review						1, 2			1, 2			1, 2, 3		
I = Implied conclusion						F = Fooler							E = Event-centered	

teaching schedule. Hopefully, this situation does not occur frequently. In more typical situations, fewer expansion activities are needed because the learner uses what has been taught. For instance, the learner engages in a "building project" that utilizes prepositional concepts as soon as they are taught. When engaged in this activity, the learner receives instructions that refer to prepositions, and the learner gives instructions to others. The building activity serves as the primary expansion. It provides an ongoing, "cumulative review," and it automatically provides for a variety of tasks.

Figure 15.2
Expansion Activities for Lesson 1

Example	Teacher Wording
Teacher places objects on, under, and above a table.	I'm going to try to fool you. If you hear me make a mistake say, "stop."
Touches object on table.	This object is on the table.
Touches object above table.	This object is on the table. Show me an object I should have touched.
Touches object on table.	This object is on the table.
Touches object on table.	This object is on the table.
Touches object on table.	This object is on the table.
Touches object above table.	This object is on the table. Move it so that it is on the table.

With such an activity scheduled on a regular basis, the number and type of expansion activities (and review activities) can be reduced (see Figure 15.4).

Note that the rate of introduction for prepositions is faster. The reason is that the building activity is a better vehicle for consolidating these concepts. The learner works for longer periods of time and receives stronger associations for using the newly-taught concepts.

Expansion for Advanced Applications

For the advanced learner, the problem of stipulation is not severe; however, expansion activities of some sort reduce possible juxtaposition prompting and shape the learner's memory of the discrimination. Part of the expansion for the advanced learner may take the form of worksheet activities (Chapter 16). Therefore, only infrequent expansion tasks may be needed for advanced applications. The activities that are generally most useful are the same as the most useful ones for the fairly naive learners–foolers, implied conclusions, and event-centered series.

Figure 15.5 shows a variety of a fooler game that might be presented after the learner has learned to discriminate between white oak, red oak, and sycamore leaves. The teacher presents a variety of leaves.

Figure 15.3

Teacher touches the horse. What kind of animal is this?
What kind of animal is over the tree?
Touch the animal that is climbing something.
What kind of animal is that?
Where is the chicken?
What is between the two clouds?
What is the horse on?
Which animal is on the tree?
What are those white things in the sky called?
Why do you think that cat is climbing the tree?
What do cats like to hunt?
What object is right over the house with the chicken on it?
Which animal is between two trees?
Where is the flying bird?
Name the animals the cat is between.

Figure 15.4
A Reduced Expanded Activities Program

Components	Lessons									
	1	2	3	4	5	6	7	8	9	10
1. on	X	X								
2. over				X	X					
3. between							X	X		
Expansion		F1		E1,2			F1,2			
Building		1	1	1,2	1,2	1,2		1,2,3	1,2,3	1,2,3

F = Fooler   E = Event-centered

Figure 15.5
Expansion Activities for Advanced Applications

Example	Teacher Wording
	I'll point to each leaf and tell you what kind it is. Correct me if I make a mistake.
Points to black oak	This is a black oak…
Points to white oak	This is a black oak…How do you know it's not a black oak?…What is it?
Point to sycamore	This is a sycamore.
Points to black oak	This is a sycamore…How do you know it's not a sycamore?…What is it?
Points to white oak	This is a white oak.
Points to sycamore	This is a black oak…How od you know it's not a black oak?…What is it?

As a rule, expansion activities are appropriate for the sophisticated learner if no worksheet activities are presented, and if there is no ongoing application that requires the discrimination. The schedule of expansion activities, however, is more sparse than that used for the naive learner. Whether we work with the naive learner or the sophisticated learner, what is taught must be used and it must be applied to new contexts. If this requirement is not met through worksheets and other ongoing activities, it must be met through expansion activities. Conversely, if the expansion functions are effectively handled through activities for which the discriminations were needed in the first place, the formal expansion activities can be reduced drastically or even eliminated.

Summary

Expanded activities are designed to amplify the learner's understanding of the discrimination that is taught through the initial-teaching sequences. The expanded activities follow immediately after the completion of the initial-teaching sequence (either following the first appearance of the sequence or following the second appearance). Expanded activities consist of a group of tasks, as few as three and possibly as many as twelve.

The five types of expanded activities are:

1. Manipulative tasks
2. Implied-conclusion tasks
3. Divergent tasks
4. Fooler games
5. Event-centered series

The most useful types are the implied-conclusion tasks, fooler games, and event-centered series. These types can be used for nearly all discriminations.

Manipulative tasks are well-designed to amplify the teaching of basic-form concepts and correlated-feature relationships. They permit the teacher to monitor responses of various individuals within a group.

Implied conclusion tasks are appropriate for all discriminations. When presented with an implied conclusion task, the learner must use the newly-taught discriminations to figure out which example is referred to. The response that the learner produces, however, is different from the one used in the initial-teaching sequence. (Instead of identifying the color of a circle the learner might answer a question such as, "What shape is the orange object?")

Divergent tasks are appropriate for single-transformation and double-transformation concepts. The teacher models one or two examples; the learner makes up some examples of the same type.

Fooler games are appropriate for any discrimination. The teacher presents positive examples and negative examples of the discrimination. The learner responds to the negative examples by indicating that they are wrong and by telling either why they are wrong or what should be done to them to make them right.

Event-centered series present the newly-taught discrimination in the context of other tasks and skills that have been taught. The sequence provides assurance that the new discrimination is recognized in this context. A variety of tasks may be included in the sequence—implied-conclusion tasks, manipulative tasks, and tasks that are not related to the new discrimination. The use of different types of expansion activities assures that the discrimination is processed in different contexts.

Discriminations taught to naive learners generally need more careful expansion than those presented to advanced learners. One reason is that the problems of stipulation may not be as great with advanced learners. Effective expansion for both naive and sophisticated learners coordinates activities with cumulative review exercises to assure that the new learning is thoroughly integrated with familiar concepts and skills.

Chapter 16
Worksheet Items

The three primary advantages of worksheet items are:

1. They provide independent practice.
2. They are good vehicles for reducing juxtaposition prompting.
3. They are good for introducing a variety of new task forms.

The major disadvantage of worksheet items is that they do not provide corrective feedback.

Their use, therefore, should be limited to situations in which the probability of errors is low. The strategy that we will use with worksheets involves:

1. First teaching the learner a discrimination through initial teaching sequences.
2. Possibly expanding the discrimination through expansion activities and oral review activities.
3. Presenting worksheet items as part of the expansion and review.
4. Providing a workcheck to assure that the learner's worksheet performance is promptly checked and the learner is provided with corrective feedback.

Worksheet Items for Different Jobs

Some worksheet items are better suited than others for particular jobs. Some require strong responses; others do not. Some are more manageable for particular discriminations. Some can be used as an extension of the initial-teaching sequence for hard-to-teach concepts that may require a very careful transition; others are not well-suited for this job.

A summary of the various types of worksheet items and an indication of their strength is given in Table 16.1. As the classification system suggests, there is more to worksheet items than multiple-choice items, and even within the domain of multiple-choice items, some are better-suited than others to achieve certain instructional objectives. This classification does not suggest that we must use a particular type if we wish to achieve specific objectives. The classification merely suggests options and alerts us to possible problems. There is no exact formula for using the types.

> **Table 16.1**
> **Types of Worksheet Items**
>
> **Choice Items**
>
> 1. *Choice of examples*. Items consist of single label and different examples. Items are good for strengthening the *discrimination of features and examples*—the discrimination taught through the initial-teaching sequence.
> 2. *Choice of label*. Items consist of a single example and different labels. Items are good for strengthening *discriminations of labels*.
> 3. *Matching labels and examples*. Items consist of different labels and different examples. These are space-efficient items that reinforce *discrimination of label and of example*.
>
> **Production Items**
>
> 4. *Production of label*. Items consist of an example that the learner labels (or answers questions about). Items are good for strengthening *production responses* used in transformation, noun sequences, or correlated-feature sequences.
> 5. *Production of example*. Items consist of label. Learner creates example to fit label. Items are good for strengthening *discriminations taught through any sequence*.

Just as it is possible to create choice-response sequences for any concept, *it is possible to create choice-response worksheet items for any concept*. They are generally easy to manage and they are usually unambiguous. Their weakness is that they lead to fairly weak responses and often responses that are artificial. For example, the type of item that presents a passage and requires the learner to choose the appropriate main idea is artificial with respect to real-life applications. Rarely would one be in a position of listening to an argument or proposal and then receiving the instructions, "What was the main idea of the argument? Indicate choice **A**, **B**, or **C**." Obviously, the response is weak.

While the production-response items require stronger responses than choice-response items, they are often more unmanageable and are mechanically hard to "grade." They also introduce a variable that may not be present in choice items. The learner who is able to read the item, understand it, and understand the discrimination, may fail the production-response item if the learner cannot produce the response called for by the item. For example, the learner may not be able to make up a reasonable main-idea sentence even though the learner understands what that sentence should be and would be able to discrimination between a choice of sentences. Also, the learner may not draw acceptable pictures of an oak tree, although the learner understands the item and can discriminate between oak trees and others.

Illustration of Five Worksheet Item-Types

We will illustrate the five different items and then discuss how to design items for various purposes. The illustration of the item types (Figure 16.1) provides an overview of the range of skill expansion that is possible through worksheet applications.

Figure 16.1
Five Worksheet Item Types

1. Choice of Examples

The choice-of-examples form presents positive and negative examples of the discrimination and a single label.

a. [tree] [cup] [vase] [mug]

Circle the **CUPS**.

b. $\frac{100}{101}$ $\frac{7}{5}$ $\frac{1}{1}$ $\frac{6}{6}$ $\frac{a+1}{a+0}$ $\frac{5}{6}$ $\frac{6}{5}$ $\frac{a-1}{a+1}$ $\frac{4}{3}$

Circle the fractions that are equal to more than 1.

c. Cross out every adjective in this passage:

The oldest boy-wonder in the history of funambulistic gyrations was Ron ("Lizard") Torpy, who, at the ripe old age of 14, was already a 45-year-old person.

2. Choice-of-Labels

The choice-of-labels form presents one example and a choice of labels.

a. Circle the correct label.

Tree
Bottle
Cup
Dish

Figure 16.1 (Continued)

b. Circle the correct label.

More than 1
Less than 1 $\frac{2}{2}$
More than 2
Less than 2

c. The underlined word is:

adjective   noun   pronoun   adverb

He turned <u>around</u>.

3. Match of Labels and Examples

This form presents more than one example and more than one label.

a. Girl •   • [cup]
   Dog •   • [dog]
   Cup •   • [tree]
   Tree •   • [girl]

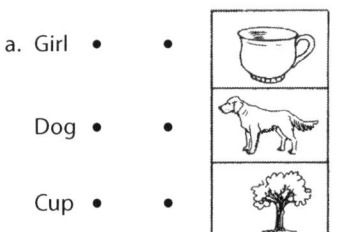

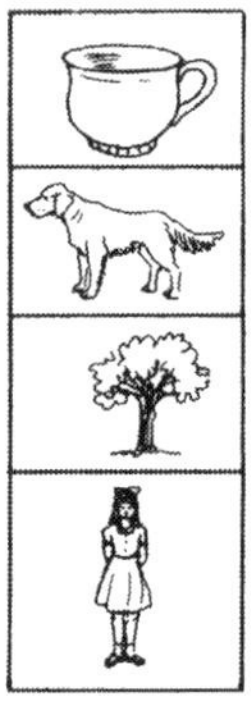

b. More than 1 •   • $\frac{1}{5}$
   Less than 1 •   • $\frac{5}{1}$
   Equals 1 •   • $\frac{5}{5}$

c. Adjective •   • Why **should** we go?
   Adverb •   • That ship went **under**.
   Pronoun •   • Where is **she**?
   Verb •   • Why should we **go**?
   Noun •   • **Running** is tiring.

4. Production of Labels

This item form presents an example that is to be "described" by the learner.

a. What kind of animal is this?

b. How many people are illustrated?
   How many legs are illustrated?
   How many smiles are illustrated?

> **Figure 16.1 (Continued)**
>
> c. What is happening in this picture sequence? 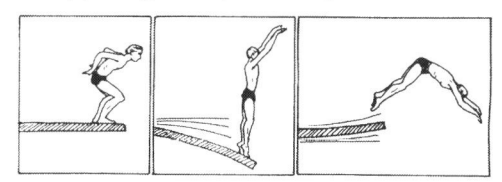
>
> d. Solve this problem: $\frac{2}{3} R = 5$
> $R = \square$
>
> e. Read the passage on page 112 and state the main idea.
>
> **5. Production of Examples**
>
> Instructions direct the learner to create or complete the example.
>
> a. Complete this sequence. 
>
>   □ ○ △   □ ○ △   □
>
> b. Draw the shadow of the girl. 
>
> c. Make leaf 1 a black oak, and leaf 2 a white oak.
>
>   1.   2.
>
> d. Make up four fractions so that each is equivalent to $\frac{7}{8}$.
>
> e. Make up a paragraph for this main idea: **The railroads opened the West**.

Designing Worksheet Items

Here are the general strategies for item design:

1. Use production-response items if possible, to create items that are manageable and unambiguous.

2. If the discrimination cannot be adequately controlled as a production-response item, present it as a choice-response item.

3. If the discrimination is difficult (involving either a complicated discrimination or difficult responses), present it first as a choice-response (easier item) and then as a production-response (more difficult item).

Using Choice-of-Example Items

A series of these items may be patterned after initial-teaching sequences. The series can be used to help firm the learner on attending to *features of the examples*. This item type is not particularly useful in reinforcing the *use of the label* because the same response dimension is used with juxtaposed examples. Item order and form may be modeled after those in the initial-teaching sequence.

If the learner has been recently taught **slanted, not-slanted**, we could introduce the following choice-of-examples worksheet items.

Circle every slanted line.

The choice-of-example item is well designed for the non-reader because only one response dimension is used. The teacher can therefore present the instructions verbally.

A variety of response conventions are available for a series. The instructions for the example above direct the learner to circle the positive examples. A similar sequence could be presented with the instructions: "Cross out every line that is not slanted," or, "Make a box around every slanted line."

Using Choice-of-Label Items

These items serve well as review items. Since they present a single example and a choice of labels, they help firm the learner on the *use of different labels*. A single item serves as an event-centered series. Let's say that the learner has been taught the discriminations **in front of, under**, and **in back of**. Choice-of-labels items could be used to firm the different labels.

Section V | Complete Teaching

- The girl is on the chair.
- The girl is under the chair.
- The girl is in front of the chair.
- The girl is in back of the chair.

Note that different labels are juxtaposed; therefore, the item type firms the discrimination of the labels. The choice-of-label items are most appropriate for learners who can read. If the learner cannot read well, the reliability of these items drops and the mechanical problems associated with presenting the items increase.

A variation of the choice-of-labels items can be created for basic discriminations. Each item presents two choices as in the next illustration (positive label and negative label).

Circle the right words.

Slanted	———	not-slanted
Slanted	\\	not-slanted
Slanted	/	not-slanted

If the learner has been taught names that are similar or that describe members of the same class, use choice-of-label items to firm the learner's understanding of the names. Choice-of-label items are well-suited for reviewing nouns, hierarchical classes, and other systems of names (color names, names of position or orientation, and names of parts of speech).

Using Match-of-Label-and-Examples Items

These items are space-efficient and provide for firming of both the labels and the features of the examples. If the learner has been taught the following concepts: **slanted**, **vertical**, and **horizontal** and has been firmed on these concepts in simpler worksheets, we could use the matching format to review the concept:

Connect each word with the right line.

Horizontal •   • /
Vertical •   • ———
Slanted •   • |

Variations of this item may be created so that more than one example of each type of line is presented.

The following is a possible item that could be presented after the learner has been taught the names of four vehicles:

Connect the words with the pictures.

Boat •   • [car]
Truck •   • [truck]
Car •   • [train]
Train •   • [sailboat]

Figure 16.2

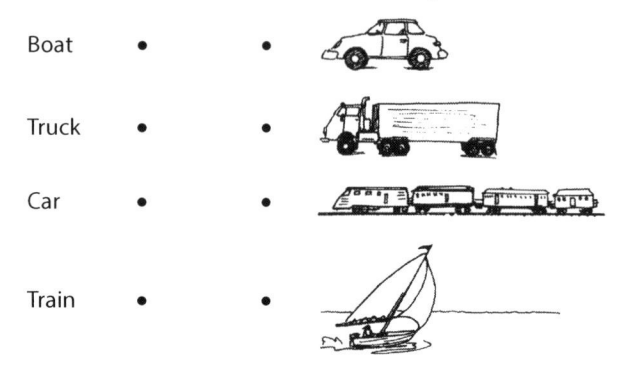

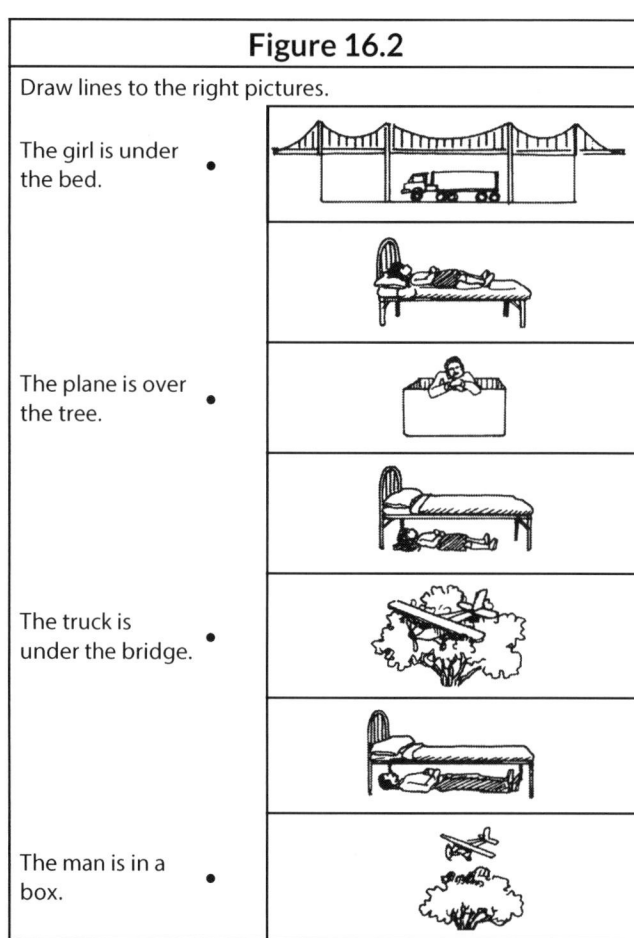

Draw lines to the right pictures.

The girl is under the bed. •	[bridge with truck under it]
	[bed with person on it]
The plane is over the tree. •	[person in box]
	[person under bed]
The truck is under the bridge. •	[plane in tree]
	[person on bed]
The man is in a box. •	[plane over tree]

Figure 16.2 illustrates a match-of-labels-and-examples item that includes some "left-over" pictures. Variations in which there are left-over labels or left-over pictures

are better than those that call for one-to-one matching because they tend to discourage the learner from using an "elimination" strategy. With one-to-one matching, the learner can skip uncertain items. By eliminating the various items, the learner is often able to respond correctly to one or more uncertain items.

If we wished to teach the learner an elimination strategy, however, the one-to-one matching item is ideal. For instance, we might present this item:

Draw a line from each word to the meaning.
Then write a sentence using the word **indolent**.

store	•	•	Something that lets you talk to people far away.
telephone	•	•	Lazy
swim	•	•	A place where you buy things.
happy	•	•	What you do when you move in water.
indolent	•	•	How you feel when things go well.

By figuring out the known words, the learner discovers the meaning of **indolent**.

Match-of-labels-and-examples items can be used in situations for which choice-of-labels items are appropriate. Generally, match-of-labels-and-examples items are more difficult than choice-of-label or choice-of-example items.

Using Production-of-Label Items

These items ask about the example. Either a single question or a series is asked. This item form can serve as a worksheet version of an event-centered series of tasks.

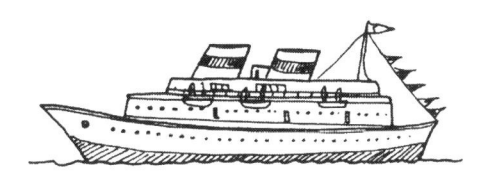

What small class is this object in?
What larger class is it in?
How many stacks does it have?
What's another name for its front?

It is possible to test comparatives by presenting a picture of more than one object and using a production-of-label form.

Which person is taller?

Jane   Jill

Here's a more sophisticated item:

What element is the left atom?
What element is the right atom?
Which atom is heavier?
Which atom would not enter into a chemical reaction?
How do you know?

A variation of the production-of-label item can be used when no actual object is present. Possible questions are: "In what year did Columbus discover America?" "How many trucks were in the school yard this morning?" These questions ask about factual relationships.

Using Production-of-Example Items

These items are useful in reviews. The items name things that had been taught; the learner creates or completes the examples.

1. Draw a white oak leaf.
2. Make an acute angle.
3. Show particles in a rhombic formation.
4. Draw four more weights on the scale so that the scale balances.

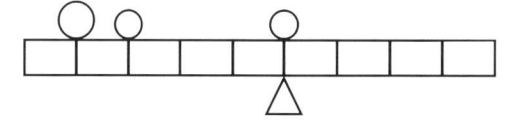

5. Draw a shape that is more elliptical than the one shown.

6.

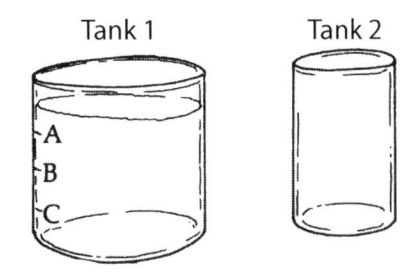

Tank 1   Tank 2

- Draw the water level in tank 2 so that the pressure at the bottom of that tank is the same as at the bottom of tank 1.
- Place an **O** in tank 1 so that the **O** has more pressure than **A** or **B**.
- Place an **X** in tank 1 so that it has more pressure than **A** but less than **B**.
- Place a **V** in tank 2 so it has as much pressure as **B**.

Production-of-example items are very good for firming the learner on following instructions. The most efficient instructions are "low-probability" items, which means that the response is not apparent unless the instructions are read. Here are examples:

- Make a box on the left end of the line.
- Make a circle just below the right end of the line.
- In the middle of the line, make a right-angled triangle.

In summary, choice-response items offer control. They permit testing a variety of skills. They are particularly useful for giving the learner practice in discriminating different labels that are introduced (choice-of-labels, and match-of-labels-and-examples). The choice items usually test the concept directly. The reason is that the items vary along a single response dimension. Therefore, the choice items are best for immediate, direct testing of a newly-taught concept.

The production-response forms permit activities that parallel the verbal expansion activities presented in Chapter 15. Implied conclusion tasks can be created, as well as event-centered series that incorporate a variety of different questions. The production forms are good for testing the learner on labels that have been taught, for providing practice with transformations, for reinforcing the skill of following directions, for testing applications of rule-related information, and for reducing the prompts associated with the initial presentation of the concept.

Using Worksheet Items in Programs

There are three basic uses of worksheet items: review, expansion, and integration.

For a given discrimination or set of discriminations, you may use worksheets to achieve one or more than one of these functions.

Review Functions

The general strategy for using the worksheet items as a review is to substitute worksheet items for oral cumulative review exercises. Note that such substitution is not possible for all concepts.

To design a review block, use item forms that provide a fairly direct test of the material that is being reviewed. Include enough items to provide a reasonable test.

Here is a possible review item for the discriminations **gymnosperm-angiosperm**.

Circle the correct class name for each tree.

Dawns redwood	Red cedar
gymnosperm	gymnosperm
angiosperm	angiosperm
Hemlock	**Live oak**
gymnosperm	gymnosperm
angiosperm	angiosperm
Pacific yew	**Vine maple**
gymnosperm	gymnosperm
angiosperm	angiosperm

The review block consists of six items. It provides a test of the higher-order class names. The items are choice-of-label items.

The best forms for reviewing lower-order members is match-of-label-and-examples items or production-response items that involve a non-symbolic referent.

Figure 16.3 shows two possible blocks.

Many other review blocks are possible. Remember, review is necessary when different coordinate members have been introduced into the set. The learner may confuse these members either because they are similar in appearance, similar in label, or similar in both appearance and label. A review block should require the learner to use labels that may be confused.

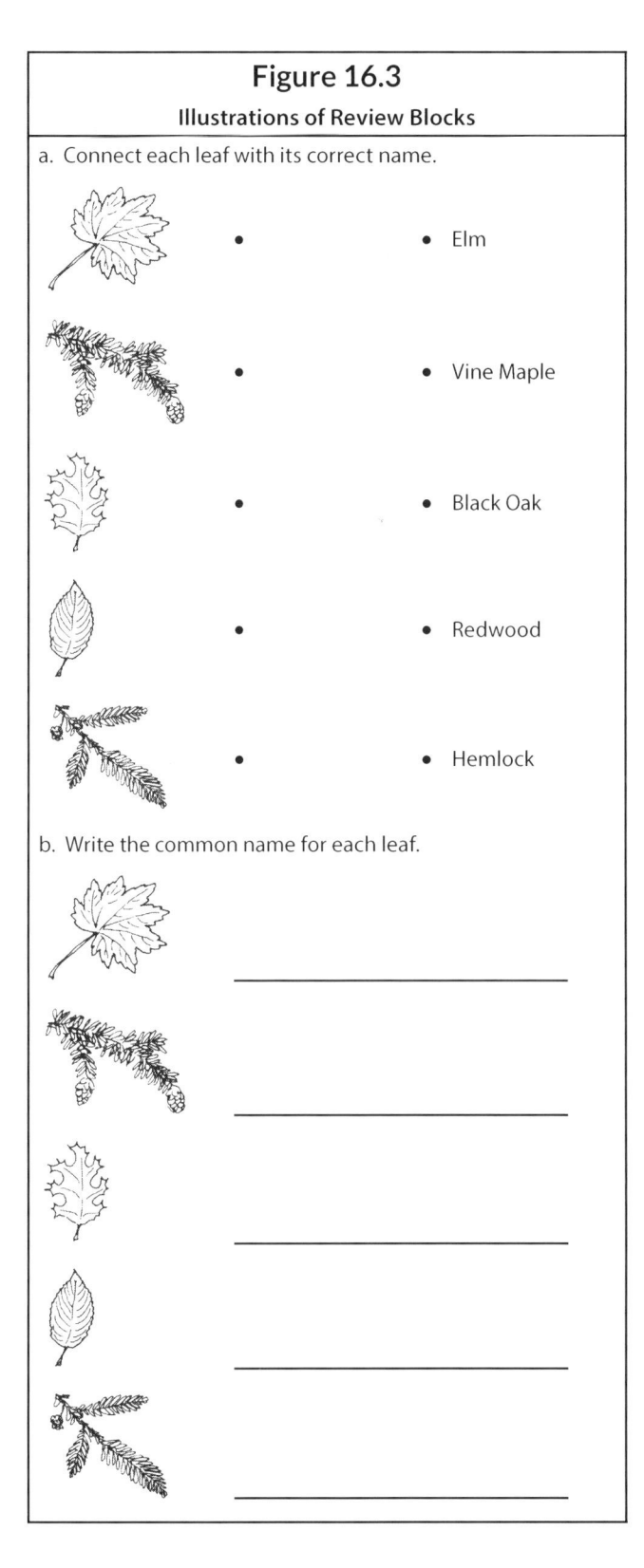

Figure 16.3
Illustrations of Review Blocks

a. Connect each leaf with its correct name.

- • Elm
- • Vine Maple
- • Black Oak
- • Redwood
- • Hemlock

b. Write the common name for each leaf.

_____
_____
_____
_____
_____

One way to present review blocks is to use a structured presentation with learners before having them work the items independently. This *precorrection* approach assures that the students will first reach an acceptable criterion of performance on the various tasks before working independently. It reduces the need for immediate feedback following the independent work.

For the structured presentation, the teacher would simply go through each worksheet item:

> "Don't write anything. Look at the leaves in part 3 of your worksheet.
>
> The first leaf: what kind? Next leaf: what kind?"

Ideally, the teacher would engage the students in several intervening activities before instructing them to do the written items. To succeed, the students must remember the various items. The prompt of going over the items before the independent work can be dropped after the students have performed successfully on a similar review block.

Expansion Functions

When items are used to expand a discrimination, *they do not necessarily occur in a block of items of the same type.* These items would introduce new response forms or extend the range of examples that had been presented. Production-response items are generally the best for expanding.

By using the same procedures used to create verbal implied-conclusion tasks, we can create good worksheet tasks that expand a newly-taught concept. We start with a statement that uses the discrimination taught. For the concept **rate increase**, we create an item by starting with a sentence that uses the discrimination, "The boy's heart **rate increased**." We use this sentence to design an item:

Which activity caused an increase in the boy's heart rate?

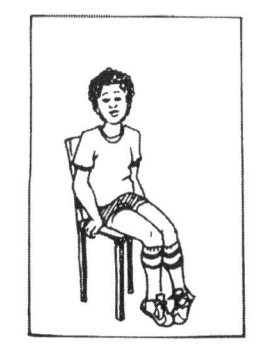

Other items are possible, such as, "If his heart rate is 72 when sitting, what do you know about the rate when he is running?"

Another good expansion activity is one that presents an event-centered series of tasks.

Here is a statement:

The boy got up from his desk and began to walk briskly, then run.

What happened to the boy's heart rate during the second activity and the third activity?

What is a "normal" rate of heartbeat?

If the boy is an athlete, how would his rate of heartbeat compare to that of a non-athlete?

Scheduling expansion activities. Figure 16.4 shows a schedule for worksheet activities that serve both review and expansion functions.

Note the pattern that occurs with discrimination **C**. First it is verbally expanded. On the following day, choice-of-label worksheet exercises are introduced. These require the learner to discriminate the newly-taught label (**C**) from the familiar labels (**A** and **B**). On the third day of **C**, a matching task is introduced (involving **A**, **B**, and **C**). Finally, a production-response expansion activity is presented on lesson 10. This activity requires the learner to apply knowledge of labels and examples to production-response worksheet items.

Integration Functions

When we deal with single-transformation and double-transformation items, we can use blocks of items to firm and even teach relationships. This type of integration is modeled after the double-transformation program.

- First the block of new items is separated from the block of familiar items.
- Then items from both blocks are mixed.

Figure 16.5 shows a single list of worksheet items that follows this general pattern. The new subtype being taught is the algebra-addition form of $2 + [6] = 8$; $3 + [5] = 8$; $7 + [1] = 8$. The familiar type is the regular addition form.

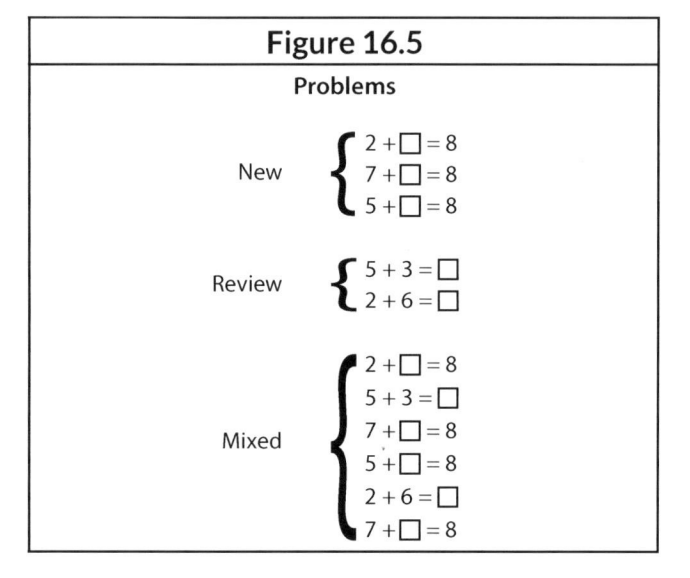

Figure 16.5
Problems

New	$\begin{cases} 2 + \square = 8 \\ 7 + \square = 8 \\ 5 + \square = 8 \end{cases}$
Review	$\begin{cases} 5 + 3 = \square \\ 2 + 6 = \square \end{cases}$
Mixed	$\begin{cases} 2 + \square = 8 \\ 5 + 3 = \square \\ 7 + \square = 8 \\ 5 + \square = 8 \\ 2 + 6 = \square \\ 7 + \square = 8 \end{cases}$

The transformation form may be used to firm weak discriminations. The three facts that are checked in Figure 16.6 have been missed four or more times. We can treat these facts *as members of a new or unfamiliar set.* The other facts become the familiar facts in a shortened version of the standard transformation sequence.

Figure 16.7 shows a sequence that integrates the unfamiliar and familiar facts.

Figure 16.4										
Components	Lessons										
	1	2	3	4	5	6	7	8	9	10
Discrimination A	X	X								
Discrimination B			X	X						
Discrimination C							X	X		
Expansion Activities		A	A	B			C			
Worksheet Activities*		1 A		2 A	3 AB	4 AB	4 AB	2 ABC	3 ABC	4 ABC
*1. Choice of example 2. Choice of label 3. Match of labels and examples 4. Production-response responses										

Figure 16.6

Problem	Errors
7 + 1	2
9 + 1	1
4 + 1 √	4
8 + 1 √	5
6 + 1	2
2 + 1	2
7 + 1	0
5 + 1	1
3 + 1 √	5
6 + 1	2
8 + 1	2
2 + 1	1

Figure 16.7

New
$\begin{cases} 4 + 1 \\ 8 + 1 \\ 3 + 1 \end{cases}$

Familiar
$\begin{cases} 2 + 1 \\ 7 + 1 \end{cases}$

Mixed
$\begin{cases} 8 + 1 \\ 3 + 1 \\ 4 + 1 \\ 9 + 1 \end{cases}$

Mixed
$\begin{cases} 2 + 1 \\ 8 + 1 \\ 1 + 1 \\ 3 + 1 \\ 6 + 1 \\ 4 + 1 \\ 7 + 1 \\ 9 + 1 \\ 8 + 1 \end{cases}$

This worksheet can be used to firm any subtype that the learner has trouble with. A good procedure is to use structured teaching with the new set before the learner works independently. The teacher tests the learner on the first three items. The learner responds orally. Later the learner works all the items independently. (If the learner performed quite poorly on the oral activity, the teacher could provide oral practice on all items in the sequence before permitting the learner to work the items independently.)

The scheduling strategy for the integration parallels that of the double-transformation program. Figure 16.8 shows the kind of schedule that would be appropriate for difficult discriminations. At first the worksheets present only the *blocks* of familiar and *blocks* of transformed items. Later, the juxtapositions shift, so that the mixed part of the double-transformation program is presented. The mixed items continue until the learner is firm on the various items within the context of the mixed block. Finally, the individual items from the sequence are dispersed throughout the worksheet. The steps in this program proceed from blocks that provide a great deal of juxtaposition prompting to contexts in which there is no prompting for the individual items.

For integrations that require less careful scheduling, the same strategy would be followed (from pure blocks to dispersed items); however, the procedure would be accelerated, requiring perhaps no more than three or four lessons for relatively easy integrations.

Transformation worksheets. Specific worksheet forms are well-designed for integrating transformation concepts. More forms clearly show the across-set relationships. Let's say that the learner has been taught the relationship between words that end in consonant-**y**, and the same words with the ending **iest**. Here is a possible sequence:

Write the words in each blank.

funny   funniest

_____   happiest

Figure 16.8

Components	Lessons																			
	1	2	3	4	5	6	7	8	9	10	11	12	13	14	15	16	17	18	19	20
A	√	√	√	√																
B	√	√	√	√	√															
C			√	√	√	√	√	√	√											
A¹ B¹										√	√	√		√	√				√	√

A Familiar set items (blocked).
B Transformed or subset items (blocked)
C Mixed set of familiar and transformed (blocked).
A¹ B¹ Familiar and transformed items (distributed throughout parts of worksheet).

lonely	_____
hardy	_____
_____	clammiest
stingy	_____

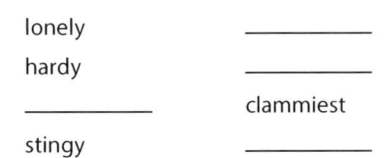

The layout makes the relationship obvious, a prompt that helps the learner who is beginning to work with the transformation.

If the learner has been taught the relationship between percent, fractions with a denominator of 100, and decimals, a three-column variation can be designed:

Fill in the blanks.

$\frac{50}{100}$	50%	.50
$\frac{27}{100}$	_____	_____
_____	4%	_____
_____	_____	3.50
_____	58%	_____
$\frac{475}{100}$	_____	_____
_____	_____	.40
$\frac{15}{100}$	_____	_____
_____	152%	_____
_____	_____	.09

The transformation worksheet form shows the range of variation for each set (column) because the juxtaposed examples differ greatly from each other. The across-set relationship (rows) make the transformation relationship clear because the row items are minimally different.

The transformation worksheet form provides a great deal of prompting. Therefore, after items have appeared in the transformation worksheet form, they should be moved into some other form. Remember, the transformation form prompts across-set understanding. Once this understanding has been demonstrated by the learner, more difficult, less prompted worksheet item forms should be presented.

In summary, the integration procedures are modeled after the double-transformation program. The basic procedures can be used for three purposes:

- To integrate a set of new members or facts with familiar facts.
- To teach a particular subtype.
- To firm particular items or facts that give the learner problems.

The transformation worksheet involves blocks or sets of items—a large block for the new set of discriminations, a smaller block for the familiar discriminations, and a block that mixes the new with the familiar. As the learner masters the transformation, the learner works on separate blocks. Each block contains only familiar or only transformed items. Next, the mixed-item block is introduced. The mixed-item block continues until the learner is firm on items in this context.

Summary

Worksheet items serve review, expansion, and integration functions. They are effectively used to reduce juxtaposition prompting and stipulation caused by the initial teaching sequence.

Different worksheet item-types are better-suited for different jobs.

The choice-of-example worksheet firms a discrimination. It is a worksheet parallel of the initial-teaching sequence, with the same response dimension (instructions) presented for a series of juxtaposed items.

The choice-of-label worksheet firms the label. This item form presents a choice of labels for a single example. The learner must attend to the differences in labels to perform adequately. This worksheet form, therefore, serves as a good review item.

The match-of-examples-and-labels form is a space-efficient means of providing practice both on the features of the examples and on the features of different labels. The learner matches labels with names, a procedure that focuses attention on both labels and names.

The production-of-label form is one that requires the learner to use an example as the basis for answering a question. The example may be a picture, a passage, or a fact. These items do not provide the degree of control that choice items do; however, they are very effective at firming labels. The reason is that they require the learner to produce the label, not merely choose it from a group of candidates.

The production-of-example form requires the learner to create or complete an example. These items provide a good test of the learner's understanding of the features of the examples. However, they may call for responses that are difficult or may create situations that are not manageable.

As a general rule, production-response items are better than choice-items for testing the learner's understanding; however, choice items are more manageable than production items.

When used as part of a program, worksheets augment other review and expansion activities. If there is a need for a careful progression of item difficulty with the worksheet items, the schedule would first call for choice items, and later for production items. The most efficient choice items are those that require matching. They are efficient because they test a large number of labels and examples in a relatively small space.

A variation of the double transformation program may be used for integrating new subtypes or new transformations that are taught. The strategy involves creating item blocks that correspond to the three parts of the double-transformation program—one block for the familiar set, one of the transformed set (or new subtype), and one for the mix of the two sets.

To integrate a transformation, first present the isolated blocks. When the learner performs acceptably, introduce the block of mixed items, and drop the other blocks. Finally, disperse individual items throughout the worksheet.

A special worksheet form makes the across-set differences apparent for transformations. This form presents the familiar-set items in one column and the transformed-set items in the next. The rows show how each item of the familiar set is modified to create a corresponding member of the transformed set.

This form is space-efficient and instructive; however, it provides very strong prompts about how to create items. Following the learner's successful performance on it, it should be replaced by worksheet forms that do not provide as much prompting.

We have many options when designing worksheet items. There is no exact formula for using them, except that they should not be introduced unless there is reason to believe that the learner will perform well on them. Also, the instructional effort should be designed to provide feedback soon after the learner has completed the worksheet. This requirement is necessary when the learner first works with items that introduce a new discrimination. The need for feedback diminishes as the learner's performance improves.

SECTION VI
CONSTRUCTING COGNITIVE ROUTINES

Chapters 17, 18, and 19 present procedures for developing and sequencing cognitive routines. These routines are designed to show the learner how to handle complex cognitive operations, such as solving fraction problems or extracting the main idea from a passage. The philosophy of designing such routines or "algorithms" is the opposite of "discovery-learning" philosophy. The structured-communication philosophy holds that using algorithms or guides for solving cognitive problems will not stifle the learner, will not inhibit generalizations, and will not make the learner a passive receiver of information rather than an active seeker of information.

A logical analysis of any discovery situation reveals why it is far inferior to a more structured format for communicating a particular concept to the learner. The learner in a discovery situation is expected to discover some sameness from exposure to concrete situations. The concrete situations have many features. Therefore, any observed sameness across these situations: (1) may involve features that are irrelevant to the discrimination or concept; (2) may be associated *only with a particular subset of the examples*, not with the full range for which the discrimination holds.

The first possibility above suggests that the presentation is capable of generating *misrules*. The second possibility implies *stipulation* problems.

Consider the situation in which the child is using rods of different colors and lengths to solve "arithmetic" problems. The teacher presents a green rod (10 units long). Next to it, the learner places two yellows (each 5 units long). With the two yellow sticks positioned end to end, they are as long as the green rod. By repeating similar "matching" exercises, the learner becomes facile at making strings of rods that are as long as the pattern presented by the teacher.

A perfectly credulous interpretation of this situation is that the learner has learned the various numerical equivalences. The learner has responded to the teacher's instructions, "Show me how many fives it takes to equal ten," by placing two yellows next to the green.

There is no question about what the learner *does*. The question is whether it is possible for the learner to respond in the manner observed *without attending to numerical features of the examples*. Stated differently, if the presentation is consistent with more than one possible interpretation, the learner could learn misrules. For example, it is quite possible for the learner to perform in the observed manner by attending to *length*–not number. (We do not have to count to judge things the same length.) Once shown that the activity is a matching game, the learner may ignore the instructions and make rows as long as the one presented by the teacher.

Even if the learner had the idea that the rods were associated with "number" (the idea that all fives are the same color and length), the learner might suppose that the relationship holds only for measuring *length*, or that there is some sort of special relationship between a color (yellow) and a number value (five). (Perhaps only yellow things can have a value of five. Perhaps five refers to a comparative relationship–with the smaller object always yellow.)

To correct the logical communication problems of the discovery situation, we would have to make the learning consistent with a single interpretation. For instance, we would have to show the learner how *all* examples of two-fives-equal-ten are the same.

If we consider what relevant sameness obtains for all possible applications of two-fives-equal-ten, we discover that it is the numerical operation, expressed as: 5+5=10, or 5x2=10. *If this feature is the irreducible sameness possessed by the various examples of the two-fives-equals-ten, this feature is the one we must teach–not color, position, or "matching."*

The routine that we design to achieve this teaching must have the following properties:

1. It must permit the learner to handle any application of two-fives-equals-ten by responding in the same way.
2. It must require responses that are unambiguously directed at the *numerical* features of the examples, not at irrelevant aspects of the examples.
3. It must provide a behavioral sameness for every relevant sameness in the examples.

For efficiency in teaching an operation a well-designed routine will prove to be far superior to discovery because of the inherent communication clarity provided by the routine.

If the goal of instruction is to teach the learner *to discover* a particular relationship, actual practice in discovery is imperative. Such practice can be provided through a cognitive routine, however. The routine is demonstrated with some examples. The learner then applies the routine to other examples. By encouraging the learner to make up problems that may be solved by the routine and then testing them to see if the routine works, we provide the learner with *a framework for discovery*. The idea is to find examples that do not work. If the learner is not able to find any, the discovery validates the routine. If some are found, the limits of the routine are clarified.

Before leaving the question of discovery, we should emphasize one point. The learner becomes practiced in discovery only through discovering. Therefore, any program that is designed to develop specific discovery skills must have provisions for adequate practice. If the practice is reasonably well-designed, it will make the learner increasingly proficient in discovering relationships.

As noted earlier, although the learner may benefit from unguided practice of physical skills, unguided practice of cognitive skills cannot lead to the same types of benefits. The reason is that the physical environment provides feedback on attempts to perform physical acts; however, the physical environment does not provide feedback about cognitive acts.

The following are properties of any physical operation, such as throwing stones, opening a door, tying a shoe, doing a backward somersault, performing a specific shot on a pool table, and any other physical operation.

1. All attempts that lead to the successful outcome of the operation have common, observable features which are overt behaviors.
2. The overt behaviors completely account for the outcome of the operation.
3. The learner is prevented by the physical environment from achieving the desired outcome unless the learner performs the necessary set of overt behaviors in the appropriate sequence.
4. Since the learner achieves the outcome only if an adequate sequence of behavior is produced, the physical environment provides feedback on every trial—information that a set of overt behaviors are inadequate for successful trials.
5. The learner may successfully practice the physical skill independently so long as the learner understands the goal of the physical operation (for example, understanding that the ball is to go into the corner pocket, that the pieces of the puzzle should fit together with none left over, etc.).

None of the five statements above apply to any cognitive skill. Consider reading or any arithmetic skill, such as working a story problem.

1. **For any cognitive operation, there is no common set of overt behaviors.** One learner may read a word out loud. Another may read the same word covertly. One learner may solve a story problem by writing many numbers and signs on paper. Another learner may frown for a moment and say the answer to the question. For all instances of a particular physical operation, a common set of overt behaviors is observed.

2. Since there is no necessary overt behavior associated with cognitive operations, **the overt behaviors cannot account for the successful outcome of the operation.** When the learner throws a stone (a physical operation), we can see that the outcome is *completely* explained in terms of the behaviors that we observe. Furthermore, it is impossible for a learner to successfully throw the stone without producing observable behaviors that completely account for the outcome. When we observe the learner who frowns before giving the answer to a story problem, we would be ill-advised to use the observable behavior as the basis for explaining the outcome. It is theoretically possible for any cognitive operation to be performed covertly, with a minimum of overt behavior; therefore, the overt behavior cannot explain the outcome.

3. **The physical environment does not prevent the learner from producing inappropriate responses for a cognitive operation.** The physical environment prevents the learner from achieving the outcome for a physical operation unless the necessary set of steps is produced in the appropriate sequence. The learner who does not produce the response of hitting the 5-ball in the correct spot will not achieve the goal of sinking the 5-ball in the corner pocket. The physical environment exercises no such control over cognitive operations. If the learner misreads a word, the physical environment does not prevent the learner from saying the wrong word and does not give the learner the slightest clue that the response is wrong. Similarly, the environment does not respond to the learner's wrong answer to the story problem, or to any other cognitive problem.

4. **The physical environment cannot provide feedback on cognitive operations.** The environment provides feedback on every trial of a physical operation. If the ball did not go in the pocket, the behaviors that led to this outcome were wrong. If the ball did go in the pocket, the learner received information that the behaviors leading to the outcome were appropriate. No such corrections or reinforcement are provided for cognitive operations. If the learner misreads a word, the physical environment does not "correct" the response and may not even imply that it is wrong. Correctly reading the word does not lead to different reinforcement.

5. **Independent practice on new cognitive operations does not necessarily imply that the skills will improve.** The learner who understands the objective of a physical skill may safely practice the skill independently because the learner is never really "alone." The physical environment provides feedback on every trial and this feedback has the potential for shaping the learner's behaviors. The cognitive operation does not run a parallel course. The learner may practice superstitious behavior, misrules, or inadequate strategies, but the physical environment will not provide direct feedback and therefore cannot shape the learner's understanding.

Because cognitive operations do not parallel physical operations, we must create *routines* so that they have the important properties of physical operations.

1. We make all necessary steps that lead to the desired outcome *overt* so that by producing the overt steps, the learner would achieve the outcome.

2. We design these steps so that the set of steps works for every example that is to be processed by the cognitive operation.

3. When the learner produces the behaviors that lead to the outcome, *we* provide feedback–corrections for incorrect behaviors and reinforcement for appropriate behaviors.

By following these design requirements, we can create routines that communicate as effectively as physical operations.

There are two tests for whether it is reasonable to design a cognitive routine for teaching a particular discrimination:

1. Can the operation be expressed as a series of steps that holds for all instances of the operation?

2. Would less teaching be involved in teaching the various steps or in teaching the operation in some other way–perhaps as a basic discrimination?

Chapter 17
Cognitive Routines

Cognitive routines grow from a need for the presentation to be consistent with a single interpretation. For most of the concepts we have dealt with, we can achieve a single interpretation if we simply *show* how changes in the example lead to corresponding changes in the responses. The relationship between features of the example and changes in the responses is not obvious for some concepts, which means that if we simply show changes in the examples and corresponding changes in the response, our presentation may not be consistent with a single interpretation. We can illustrate the problem with the following sequence.

Teacher Wording

50 is not a grommel.
49 is not a grommel.
48 is a grommel.
24 is a grommel.
80 is a grommel.
Is 81 a grommel? (No.)
Is 12 a grommel? (No.)
Is 8 a grommel? (Yes.)
Is 16 a grommel? (No.)
Is 15 a grommel? (Yes.)
Is 35 a grommel? (Yes.)
Etc.

Note that the sequence follows the basic format for choice-response discriminations. Minimum differences are provided. So is a range of positives.

If we presented enough examples, we would certainly make it possible for the learner to discover what grommels are. The presentation above, however, falls far short of making the meaning clear.

A correlated-feature sequence, such as the one that follows, makes the critical features of the discrimination clear.

My turn:
Is 24 a grommel?   Yes.
How do I know?   Because there is a difference of 2 between the numbers multiplied together.

Your turn:
Is 15 a grommel?   (Yes.)
How do you know?   (There's a difference of 2 between the numbers multiplied together.)
Is 16 a grommel?   (No.)
How do you know?   (There is not a difference of 2 between the numbers multiplied together.)
Is 35 a grommel?   (Yes.)
How do you know?   There's a difference of 2 between the numbers multiplied together.)

The clarity of **grommel** comes from the answer to, "How do you know?" The answer discloses that: (1) the arithmetic operation of multiplication is involved in determining whether the example is a **grommel**; and (2) the relationship between the size of the numbers multiplied is relevant to whether the example is a **grommel**.

Grommel is different from discriminations we have dealt with because the labeling of **grommel** depends less on the *immediately-observable features of the examples than on the procedure for creating* **grommels**. A particular number can be reached through an incredible variety of procedures. It is therefore necessary to specify the procedure used and the steps that were taken.

The correlated-feature sequence does not fully satisfy our requirements for creating a presentation of **grommel** that is consistent with only one interpretation. When the learner answers the questions, "How do you know?" in sequences above, the learner *describes* the operation, but we do not know that the learner has actually *applied* the operation and determined the numbers. The solution to the ambiguity problem is to add a question to the pair of questions used in the correlated-feature items.

My turn:

Is 24 a grommel?	Yes.
How do I know?	Because there is a difference of 2 between the numbers multiplied together.
What are those numbers?	Six and four.

Your turn:

Is 15 a grommel?

How do you know?

What are those two numbers?

Is 16 a grommel?

How do you know?

What are those two numbers?

Is 35 a grommel?

How do you know?

What are those two numbers?

By satisfying any doubts about whether the learner is attending to the relevant details of **grommel**, we have created a *cognitive routine—a series of steps that solves any problem of a given type.* Although the cognitive routine for **grommel** above may not be the best designed one that we could create, it has the properties of cognitive routines.

1. The routine consists of a series of more than two steps, which means that the learner is asked a series of more than two questions or is given a series of more than two instructions each time the routine is applied to a positive example of *grommel.*

2. The routine requires the learner to produce overt responses and these responses tell us whether the learner is approaching each example appropriately.

These features of a cognitive routine imply its weakness and strength. The primary weakness is that *the juxtaposition pattern is not well-designed to teach component discriminations.* The juxtaposition pattern of component discriminations that is easiest for the learner is one that requires the learner to do the same thing on juxtaposed examples. After successfully responding to question 1 in the routine, the learner must respond to questions 2 and 3 before having another opportunity to respond to a new example of question 1. Questions 2 and 3 function as interference, pulling the learner's attention from those variables associated with question 1. Because this juxtaposition pattern is not well-designed for initial teaching, the component discriminations involved in a cognitive routine should be pretaught before the routine is introduced.

The routine's principle strength is that *the routine is a good vehicle for* teaching the learner to solve a problem by chaining a series of steps together. The cognitive routine is well-designed to teach the learner the chain of steps because the routine *stipulates the same series of steps for all positive examples.*

As the **grommel** illustration points out, the cognitive routine assures that the learner attends to the appropriate features of the examples. If all **grommels** are characterized by a multiplication relationship, the learner must attend to this feature of the example and not to irrelevant features. We know that the learner is attending to the appropriate features if the learner produces a series of responses. The series would be virtually impossible to produce if the learner attended to irrelevant features.

Designing Cognitive Routines

Designing cognitive routines is difficult. The guidelines that we present for designing cognitive routines provide the criteria for determining that one is well-designed. These general guidelines, however, do not lead to the same degree of rigor that is possible with the component discriminations. The reason is that there are many decisions that must be made in designing these routines. And at each decision point, there is more than one acceptable solution.

Throughout the process of designing the routine, we must consider the routine in the perspective of other routines. The routine we design is not an island. Rather, it will exist in the context of other routines and the *parts* of the routine we design will often appear in other routines. The equal sign in addition problems has the same function as the equal sign in subtraction and multiplication problems. We must honor this sameness. If the parts are the same in related operations, we should treat these parts the same way in these operations, thereby demonstrating that they are the same.

There are four steps that we follow to design a cognitive routine.

1. Specify the range of examples for which the operation will work.

2. Make up a *descriptive rule* that tells exactly what the learner must do to attack every example within that range. (The same rule must hold for all examples.)

3. Design a task that tests each component discrimination mentioned in the descriptive rule.

4. Construct a chain composed of tasks that test the component skills or the "steps" in the operation.

Before presenting details of how to perform each of these design steps, we will illustrate the procedure with two examples.

Illustration 1: Stop-Sound-First Words

The illustration deals with teaching the learner to read regularly-spelled words that begin with stop sounds (**can, bad, pin, top, prod**, etc.).

Specify the range of examples. The range we will deal with is regularly-spelled words of not more than four sounds (at least for the initial teaching of the routine).

Make up a descriptive rule that tells what the learner must do to attack every example. To read these words, the learner first sounds out and identifies the part of the word that includes all but the first sound; then the learner identifies the entire word by rhyming with the part that has been identified.

Design specific tasks for every component mentioned in the descriptive rule. We will illustrate the tasks by referring to the teaching sequences in which the tasks would be used.

  a. The descriptive rule refers to *sounding out the word*. Sounding out could be taught through a series of verbal activities such as: "Sound out this word: **op**. Sound out this word: **ip**," etc. The same procedure could be used with written words (**op, ip**, etc.)

  b. *Identifying the word part* could be initially taught as a verbal discrimination. "Listen: aaammm. Say it fast. Listen: aaaat. Say it fast," etc. Later, the learner could produce the same responses with written words instead of oral words.

  c. The descriptive rule refers to *rhyming with the word part that had been identified*. If the word is **pat**, for instance, the learner would rhyme with **at**. The discrimination could initially be presented as a task that presents written symbols.

    f   Rhyme with **at** (fat)

    t   Rhyme with **at** (tat)

    p   Rhyme with **at** (pat)

Note that all the discriminations *named* in the descriptive rule *have now been translated into discriminations* that can be taught through specific tasks.

Construct a chain composed of tasks used to test the component skills. Here is a possible routine that is composed of the component skills and that incorporates the same wording as that used with the component skills.

> **Example: pat**
>
> Teacher covers **p** and points to **at**. "Sound out this part."
>
> Teacher touches under **a** and **t** as learner says: "aaat."
>
> Teacher: "Say it fast."
>
> Learner: "at."
>
> Teacher uncovers **p**. "This word rhymes with at."
>
> Teacher touches under **p**.
>
> Learner: "pat."

The routine provides overt behavior for every discrimination that is mentioned in the descriptive rule. The routine, in other words, translates the descriptive rule into a chain of behaviors, which shows that the learner is producing the discriminations named in the descriptive rule.

Illustration 2: Factoring Any Number From an Expression

Specify the range of examples. Any expression involving numerals or letters.

Make up a descriptive rule. To factor any value from an expression, create a fraction equal to one, with the *desired value* in the numerator and denominator of the fraction. Rewrite the initial expression so that it is multiplied by this fraction of 1. Then rewrite the fraction so the denominator of the fraction is distributed.

Design tasks for each component discrimination. The rule refers to creating a fraction equal to one with the desired value in the numerator and denominator. Here is the discrimination:

> Make up a fraction of one that has six in the denominator (six sixths).
>
> Make up a fraction of one that has six j in the numerator (six j over six j).
>
> Etc.

The rule also refers to *rewriting an expression* so that it is multiplied by a fraction of one. Here is the beginning of a possible sequence:

Example	Teacher Wording
3 – 4j	My turn to show how to rewrite 3 – 4j when we multiply by four-fourths: $\frac{4}{4}(3-4j)$
3 – 4j	Your turn: Show how to rewrite 3 – 4j when we multiply by 4N over 4N. $\frac{4N}{4N}(3-4j)$

Finally, the descriptive rule specifies that the fraction of one is to be "distributed."

Example	Teacher Wording
$\frac{4}{4}(3+2-5+1)$	Here's how to rewrite the four-fourths: $4(\frac{3}{4}+\frac{2}{4}-\frac{5}{4}+\frac{1}{4})$
$\frac{6}{6}(3+2-5+1)$	Here's how to rewrite six-sixths: $6(\frac{3}{6}+\frac{2}{6}-\frac{5}{6}+\frac{1}{6})$

Construct a chain composed of tasks used to test component skills.

Example: 3 + 2 – 5 + 1

Teacher: We're going to factor 7 from this expression. The first thing we do is make up a fraction of 1 that has 7 in the numerator. What fraction? (Signal.) $\frac{7}{7}$

Teacher: $\frac{7}{7}(3+2-5+1)$
Now we rewrite the fraction. Do it.

Learner: $7(\frac{3}{7}+\frac{2}{7}-\frac{5}{7}+\frac{1}{7})$

Teacher: You factored seven from the expression.

The routine above could be changed after one or two examples have been processed. The changes would require the learner to do more of the operation. For instance:

> We're going to factor 7 from this expression. So what's the first thing we do? (Signal.) "Make up a fraction that has seven in the numerator."
> What fraction? (Signal.) "Seven-sevenths."
> Now what do we do? (Signal.) "Multiply the expression by seven-sevenths."
> Do it. (Learner multiplies.)
> Now we rewrite the fraction. Do it.
> (Learner writes.)

The two routines we have illustrated for rhyming differ in many respects from the fraction routine. The rhyming routine is designed for a relatively small range of words. The factoring example applies to *any expression*, not merely those that contain multiples of the number that is to be factored. The rhyming routine directs the learner to produce sounds. The routine for factoring directs the learner to answer questions and to write responses.

Despite their differences, the routines are the same from a construction standpoint. The starting point is a descriptive rule that tells about the essential steps needed to attack all examples that are to be processed through the routine. If the descriptive rule is accurate, the resulting routine should provide behavioral steps for each discrimination named in the descriptive rule.

Identifying the Range of Examples and the Descriptive Rule

The simplest procedure for determining the range of examples to be covered by the routine and the descriptive rule is to begin with the broadest possible range of concrete examples that could possibly be dealt with by a single operation, and then use the examples to determine the descriptive rule. Following are the steps involved in this procedure. (Note that the procedure is similar to the subtype analysis described in Chapter 10. The difference between the two procedures is that the present one is designed to identify what is the same about all the examples within the range.)

1. Arrange a series of examples in a way that would communicate *sameness*. Juxtapose examples that differ greatly and that cover the full range of possible variation for an operation. Try to include all subtypes of the operation.

2. Make a list of operational samenesses that are shared by all concrete examples in the list. An operational sameness would refer to a common detail of all examples that must be responded to in a specific way. For instance, "All problems have denominators."

3. Evaluate the list of samenesses. If there is a statement of sameness for every detail of each example that would logically have to be processed to solve the problem, the list of samenesses provides a basis for an adequate descriptive rule. If important details for some examples are not referred

to by the statement of sameness, the basis for an adequate descriptive rule does not exist.

4. Adjust the set of examples if the statements of sameness do not include all examples. The simplest adjustment is to eliminate the examples that are not sufficiently described by the statements of sameness.

5. Make up a descriptive rule that is based on the statements of sameness.

Illustration: Sounding out simple words. If we follow the steps above for dealing with sounding-out beginning reading words, we would start by juxtaposing beginning words in a way that implies sameness. For our present purpose, we will limit the words to those having no more than four letters. This is a sample of possible words we might start with: **from, me, and, belt, if, meet, ate, any, then**.

We now make up a list of operational samenesses:

- All have letters.
- The sounds for the letters roughly correspond to the left-to-right arrangement of letters.
- For each letter or pair of letters, some sound is called for.

This set of samenesses does not imply a descriptive rule that would deal with every critical feature of *each* word. Therefore, we must either modify some of the examples or eliminate them from the set.

If we eliminate the two-letter combinations that make a single sound (**ee** and **th**), and eliminate those words that do not have a standardized relationship between the sound that is pronounced for a given letter (**from, me, any, ate**), we have a much smaller range of variation. The convention that we will arbitrarily adopt is that of using only short-vowel words, e.g.: **and, belt, if**.

We can add more words of this general type to the set. However, even if we do not, we are now able to make a more precise set of sameness statements.

- All words have a standard sound for each symbol.
- All sounds are produced in order, starting with the sound for the left letter.

These two statements of sameness imply a descriptive rule for sounding out that will account for all important details of each word:

To sound out the word, start with the left letter and say the specified sound for each letter in order.

If we wish the learner to *hold* every sound of the word before going on to the next sound, we have to modify the set further. The reason is that it is impossible to hold sounds like **b**. We would therefore have to eliminate **belt** from the set (and any other word that begins with **b, c, d, g, h, j, k, p, q, t**).

The set would now consist of two-letter, three-letter, and four-letter words that begin with continuous sounds only (**a, e, f, i, l, m, n, o, r, s, u, v, w, y, z**), and that do not have stop sounds except as the last letter of the word. The examples in this set have an additional sameness: *All sounds except possibly the last sound can be held.*

We can now modify the sounding-out operation:

To sound out the word, start with the left letter, hold the specified sound for that letter, and repeat the procedure for each remaining letter in the word except possibly the last letter (which may not be held).

The rule now describes an operation that deals with all relevant aspects of each example. The operation that would be used for the last set of words eliminated from the larger set (those that begin with stop sounds) could be processed through the rhyming operation.

Illustration: Factoring. By following the same procedure for determining an operation for factoring, we begin with a list of examples sequenced to show sameness:

a. $¼ + ½ + ¾$

b. $A^2 + 2Ab + b^2$

c. $12 - 9 + 3 - 6$

d. $-5 - 6J$

e. $1⅔B + 5 - ½J - 6R$

Next we make up a list of statements that hold for all examples:

- Each expression can be written as the product of a fraction of one times the original expression.
- The denominator of the fraction can be distributed so that it appears in the denominator of each term.

These statements of sameness imply an adequate descriptive rule: To factor a number value, first write the expression as a product of a fraction of one and the original expression. Then distribute the denominator.

Since this operation will apply to all expressions from which a single value is to be factored, we do not have to eliminate any example types from the original set.

The preceding illustrations point out some important facts about designing cognitive routines. *A cognitive routine works only for examples that share a common set of features.* The routine may cover a very broad range of examples or a narrow one. We can design a routine for rewriting fractions and decimals that involves only positive numbers or that involves positives and negatives. We can design a routine for decoding words that applies to *all* English words, one that applies to a specified set of words, one that applies to all simple regularly-spelled words, or one that applies to some other set of words.

When initially designing cognitive routines, we should try to identify the broadest possible range of application for the routine.

The rule should contain two sections. The first tells about the goal of the rule. The second tells about the overt behavior that the learner must engage in to process every example. Start the rule by referring to the goal:

To decode all regularly-spelled simple words . . .

To convert fractions into decimals . . .

To find the angle of reflection . . .

The second part of the rule should specify at least two overt things that the learner must do. Initially, you may write the rule in a way that describes only one thing that is done, such as: To make a **grommel**, multiply two numbers that have a difference of two. Certainly this rule implies that you must identify the numbers before you multiply them. To make it easier to design a routine, recast the rule so that it expresses at least two steps:

To make a **grommel**:

1. Select a pair of numbers that have a difference of two.
2. Multiply them together.

The requirement that the rule must specify at least two overt behaviors is a logical one. If you can specify only one behavior that is needed for all examples ("To read a word, you say it"). The skill is most properly taught as a discrimination, not as something processed through a cognitive routine.

The descriptive rule does not necessarily contain the words that the learner will encounter. The rule is for the instructional designer. It provides a clear list of skills that we must teach. For example, a descriptive rule for reading regularly-spelled words may refer to "beginning with the left letter of a word." This phrase does not imply that you teach labels, "begin," "left," "letter," and "word," to the learner. However, the routine must account for overt responses that show whether the learner is beginning with the left letter of a word. The wording in the routine may be, "Touch the *starting point.*" The learner touches the left letter. The wording may be: "Touch the *beginning of the word*," or "Name the letter that is at the *beginning of the word*," or "Tell me the sound of the *left letter.*" All are acceptable, because all satisfy the requirement of providing the learner with a clear signal to respond to the left letter, and all lead to a response that leaves little doubt about whether the learner understands the discrimination of "the left letter."

Constructing a Routine for a Set of Examples

Perhaps the greatest mistake that designers make when trying to design routines is to start with some sort of *task* that is to be analyzed. Although it is possible that somebody has worked out the best possible procedure for solving problems, we should not begin with this assumption. We should recognize that cognitive operations are not like physical ones, that the procedures people have developed for solving different types of problems are not necessarily the only ones possible, and that even behaviors that may seem perfectly essential may not be essential if we change the operation. For example, the process of "borrowing" seems to be necessary for solving column subtraction problems like:

$$\begin{array}{r} 52013 \\ -31425 \end{array}$$

The following is a method for solving the problem that does not involve borrowing. The method is "the mirror" method.

```
           522        = 588
         52013
         −31425
           20
        (Answer)      = 20588
```

Solving the problem through the mirror method involves subtracting one value from another in each column, writing the answer *nearest (above or below) the smaller number in that column*, adding 1 to the bottom number of the next column if the answer for the preceding column is written above, and converting the mirrors on top to the corresponding values on the bottom, Subtract 3 from 5 in the one's column and write it above the 3. Then add one to the bottom number of the tens column, making the value 3. Now do the same thing in the tens column, starting with 3 and subtracting 1, and writing the answer closest to the 1. After all numbers have been computed, convert all mirrored numbers on top to their real value. 9 is the mirror of 1; 8 is the mirror of 2; 7 is the mirror of 3; etc.

The operation requires carrying, not borrowing. Whether or not we would judge it superior to some other operation depends on how well it fits in with other skills we teach. Possibly, this method would never be recommended. The point, however, is that we cannot start out by accepting conventional borrowing as a *given operation*. The various methods of borrowing are merely algorithms for converting a very difficult discrimination (saying the answer to the problem) into a series of overt behavior steps that yield the answer.

Designing Tasks for Components Named in a Descriptive Rule

Once we have developed a descriptive rule that seems adequate, we must transform the rule into a series of behaviors. The rule tells us what the learner is to do. In translating the rule into behavior, we can either try to design the cognitive routine and then identify the components, or we can first determine how we might teach the various components named in the rule. If we first specify the tasks for teaching the components, we create specific wording that will then be used in the routine we create. Designing the final routine involves simply "chaining" the component descriptions together. Although the approach of identifying components first and then chaining them may be somewhat mechanical, it is reliable.

To use this approach, we translate every discrimination named in the descriptive rule into a task that tests the discrimination. Each task calls for an overt response that leaves little doubt that the learner is appropriately attending to relevant details of the example and operating on them in the prescribed manner.

Responses. When we design specific tasks for the components of the descriptive rule, we should try to use strong responses. The strongest responses are those that actually require the learner *to do something* rather than describe it. For verbal responses, production-responses are stronger than choice-responses.

Choice responses. These responses are the weakest verbal responses because:

1. The probability is higher that the learner will answer correctly by guessing, since the number of choices is severely limited.

2. Spurious transformations are prompted since the same task leads to answers that may be minimally different (e.g., reversals). (For example, the task, "Tell me when I touch the left of the word," may create reversals because the only difference in examples is where the teacher touches. The task, "Touch the left of the word," stipulates the correct behavior and reduces the possibility of spurious transformations.)

The great single advantage of the choice-response item is that it is manageable and frequently unambiguous. Here is a production-response item presented in working a long-division problem. "Where do I write the 3?" The answers range from "right there," to "under the 7." When working with a group, this range of response variation creates management problems. The problems can be reduced by several techniques, such as a more precise production-response task. "Under which number do I write the 3?" A choice response alternative–but not necessarily the most desirable–might be, "Tell me where to write the 3, under the 7 or under the 0."

Another possible advantage of choice-response tasks is that we can construct a **yes-no** choice for any discrimination or relationship. Therefore, if we have trouble figuring out how to ask about a particular discrimination, we can construct a **yes-no** task or a choice-task as a last resort.

In summary, the advantages of choice-response tasks are that the tasks are manageable, they can be designed so they are clear, and they are possible options for any discrimination or relationship.

Production-responses. The advantages of production responses are that they do not promote spurious transformations; they provide for very "strong" responses (because they require the learner to create either the label that is being taught or an example for the label); and they are logically capable of testing more information with fewer examples. If we were to test the learner's understanding of rhyming through **yes-no** tasks, we would first have to test on words that rhyme with one ending, then on words that rhyme with another, and so forth. To test each ending would require at least three items. If we used production responses, a single item for each ending would provide much information. ("Rhyme with **am** and start with the sound **ssss** . . . Rhyme with **at** and start with **sss** . . ." etc.)

The most serious problem with production responses within the context of a cognitive routine is that the learner may not be able to produce them quickly. Responses to "Write it," "Draw it," "Do it," "Say it," "Tell where," "Tell how," and other production-response items may require five seconds or more. This pause seriously affects the flow of the cognitive routine. During the time that the learner "Writes it," the link of the writing step with the rest of the routine may have been lost. If the learner is to learn a chain of behaviors, these behaviors should occur in an obvious sequence. The sequence becomes less obvious if the individual responses are long or require firming by the teacher. The problem of the long production response is less serious if the routine has only three steps. If it is a relatively long routine, long responses become increasingly troublesome.

Guidelines for using the names that appear in the descriptive rule. If we were to make up a cognitive routine for determining whether a fraction is more than one whole, we might state the rule so that it refers to **numerator** and **denominator**. *If the learner is not required to use these words in other contexts, there is no particular reason to teach them.* The learner can learn the discrimination about the fractions by referring to the **top number** and the **bottom number**–familiar terms. The introduction of new vocabulary simply lengthens the amount of teaching that is required for the discrimination. It also introduces another possible source of error. Unless the new words are thoroughly taught, the learner may begin to reverse them, a problem that will not exist if the familiar terms **top** and **bottom** are used in the task.

Sometimes new vocabulary may be necessary. For example, if our rule had to do with teaching the learner to express fractions such as:

$$\frac{A \times A \times A}{A} = A^2$$

we might find it necessary to refer to the **base number** and the **exponent**. If we try to refer to the base number as the "big number" and the exponent as the "little number" we may create confusion when the base number is smaller than the exponent (e.g., 4^5). If we try calling the base number the "lower number," we may have trouble communicating with the learner when we introduce problems that have bases above and below the fraction line:

$$\frac{2^3}{3^4}$$

(The 3 is an upper and a lower). Granted, there may be solutions to these problems. However, if these solutions seriously limit the range of examples presented, require new teaching, or lead to contrived wording that will later have to be dropped, the conventional terms **base** and **exponent** may present the most straightforward solution.

In summary, if it is possible to design discrimination teaching that uses only familiar names, do so. If communication problems result or if the teaching become contrived, teach the words that are in your descriptive rule. Note, however, that the determination about using words does not come from a reference book or from an examination of how the operation is traditionally taught. It comes from trying out the *simplest wordings* and noting the problems that result. The problems encountered suggest whether more precise terms should be introduced.

Responses that Describe Behavior. Here is a task that calls for a description of behavior:

Teacher: What do you do first when reading a word?
Student: Start with the left letter of the word.

Although the response was correct, we have no compelling reason to believe that the learner carries out this response when reading a word. The task provides only a verbal response. A more convincing demonstration would be provided if the learner showed the starting point. Furthermore, if the learner produced this response, there might be no reason for the learner first describing what to do.

For some situations, we may want the learner to produce descriptive responses like the one above. As a general procedure, we would avoid descriptive responses unless they set the stage for steps the learner is to carry out when working independently. If we decide to include descriptive responses, *an additional step must follow*, in which the learner carries out the behavior described.

 Teacher: What do you do first when reading a word?
 Student: Start with the left letter of the word.
 Teacher: Do it.
 (Student touches left letter of word.)

Constructing tasks for component discriminations. The wording that will direct the learner in each step or task determines how each component discrimination is to be pretaught. If we refer to the top of the fraction and the learner is to respond to the top of the fraction, we can require the learner either to identify the top or touch the top. "Tell me the part of the fraction I touch . . ." This task could imply a choice-response sequence. If the descriptive rule says that the learner is to make fractions of one with specific values in the denominator, we could present a single-transformation sequence. "I'll show you numbers that are on the bottom of fractions that equal one. You tell me the fraction of one for each bottom number."

The descriptive rule for the mirror-method of borrowing suggests that the learner finds the final answer by converting mirror numbers into "regular" numbers. We are not required to refer to "mirror numbers." We can call them anything we wish. A good name is one that prompts their relationship to regular members. We may decide to call them *wrong-way numbers*, because this name suggests that they are not "right" in their present form.

Once we decide on the wording for the task, we can create a sequence for preteaching the relationship between wrong-way numbers and their counterparts. One procedure would be to make a "folding" number line with 5 in the middle. When folded, the 9 would be under the 1, the 8 under the 2, the 7 under the 3, the 6 under the 4, and nothing under the 5. The dotted segment shows the number line when it is unfolded. The arrow shows the direction this part moves when folding.

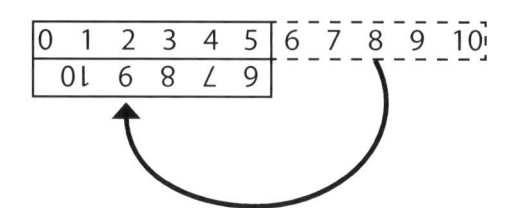

Teacher presents the folded number line.
 Teacher: The wrong-way numbers are those that are under the other numbers.
     My turn: What's the wrong-way number for 3? 7.
     What's the wrong-way number for 2? 8.
     Your turn: What's the wrong-way number for 9?
     What's the wrong-way number for 5?
     Etc.

The sequence above presents the relationship through a single-transformation sequence. Another option is a correlated-feature sequence. This sequence adds a question.

 Teacher: My turn: What's the wrong-way number for 3? 7.
     How do I know? Because 3 is over 7.
     My turn again: What's the wrong-way number for 4? 6.
     How do I know? Because 4 is over 6.
     Your turn: What's the wrong-way number for 6?
     How do you know?
     Etc.

Following the introduction, the learner would be required to perform when the number line is unfolded. For corrections, the teacher would fold the line and show the answer.

There are different ways of presenting the wrong-way discrimination. A possible approach is this:

 0 1 2 3 4 5 6 7 8 9 0

 Teacher: (Touches under 5 with chalk and draws a line that loops under 4 and ends at 3.)

 0 1 2 3 4 5 6 7 8 9 0

 My turn: What's the wrong-way number for 3?

(Draws loop from 5 to 6 to 7.) 7 is the wrong-way number.

0 1 2 3 4 5 6 7 8 9 0

(Draws one more loop to 2.) My turn: What's the wrong-way number for 2? (Adds one loop to right.) 8.

Your turn: What's the wrong-way number for 8? (Signal.) 2.

(Loops from 5 to 4.) What's the wrong-way number for 4? (Signal.)

The wording of the task could be changed to be more consistent with what the learner will do in the subtraction problems, which is to convert wrong-way numbers into right-way numbers. The wording might therefore be, "If 4 is a wrong-way number, what's the right-way number?" Regardless of the specific wording, the product of translating a discrimination that is named in a descriptive rule is a step for a cognitive routine. That step will have the same wording as the task that is created to teach the discrimination named in the descriptive rule.

Component skills that are modified. Sometimes, the descriptive rule specifies behaviors that are not well-designed for an introductory cognitive routine. As noted above, the steps in a cognitive routine should be chained without interruption, particularly if the routine is relatively long. Responses that interrupt the chaining should be eliminated from initial routines.

The descriptive rule for mirror numbers indicates that the learner will convert wrong-way numbers *by writing their right-way counterparts*. The writing is probably not desirable for the initial teaching; however, we should try to make the component that deals with converting the wrong-way numbers as similar as possible to the component that will appear in the final routine. Here's a possible setup:

2 6 9 1 0 5 3
_____

Teacher: The numbers above the lines are wrong-way numbers. For each wrong-way number, *tell me* the right-way number that goes below the line.

After the learner responds to each number, the teacher writes it below the bottom line. The pacing is maintained. The learner receives models of where the numbers will be written. And the tasks are presented in the same context that will be presented by the cognitive routine.

When the routine for wrong-way numbers first appears, the learner will tell and the teacher will write. Later, the learner will write the converted numbers.

Chaining the Discriminations Together

Usually, all discriminations referred to in the descriptive rule should be pretaught, then chained together in a routine.

1. The wording used in the cognitive routine should be as close as possible to the wording used in the teaching of the component discriminations.

2. The set of steps designed from the descriptive rule should provide a good test:

   a. Some items should test on the mechanical details that might interfere with the learner's performance.

   b. Some items should test whether the learner attends to the appropriate features of example and responds appropriately.

   c. All items should provide "strong" responses (*doing* rather than choosing or describing) if possible.

Wording. If the wording used to teach **numerator** is "top number," the same wording would be used in the cognitive routine. If mirrored numbers are referred to as "wrong-way numbers" they would retain this designation in preteaching and in the routine. If the discrimination of beginning at the left has been labeled "touching the starting point," the same wording would be used in the cognitive routine.

If we discover that the wording is ambiguous, awkward, or inaccurate when it is used in the routine, we change it both in the routine and in the teaching of the component discriminations.

Order of steps. After the component skills have been taught, the idea is to arrange steps into an order that will permit the learner to move through various examples smoothly.

1. Ideally, the first steps should deal with mechanical details.

2. The remaining steps should reflect the order of events suggested by the descriptive rule.

When we put mechanical details first, we first require the learner *to read the problem or identify symbols that are involved in the routine.* By dealing with mechanical details first, we reduce the possible causes of failure on later steps in the routine. We therefore increase the potential for diagnosing the learner's specific problems if the learner does not perform in parts of the routine. When we know that the learner is accurately decoding the problem, we know that misidentifying the symbols cannot contribute to failure in working the problem. If we are not sure whether the learner is accurately decoding the problem, we cannot tell whether failure on later steps results from misidentification, from faulty understanding of an operation, or from a combination of problems. If we are reasonably sure that the learner is firm on mechanical details, we should not begin the routine with such detail.

Ideally, we should design the remaining steps (those that deal with the procedure) so they form a kind of acting-out of the descriptive rule.

Let's say that we have designed the descriptive rule: "To find out if the fraction reduces to a whole number, count by the bottom number. If you say the top number, the fraction reduces."

Assume we have taught counting by different numbers, identifying the bottom number and identifying the top number of fractions. Now we must chain the components together to achieve the operation called for by the rule. We start with mechanical details.

Here is a possible beginning of the cognitive routine:

Example	Teacher Wording
$\frac{24}{6}$	What's the bottom number?
	What's the top number?

Now the operation follows. According to the descriptive rule, we want the learner to count by the bottom number and determine whether the top number is said in the process. The top number is critical, because the learner must compare it with the numbers said when counting by 6. Therefore, we could name the top number in our instructions to prompt the learner. "Count by the bottom number and see if you say 24. Get ready . . ."

The rest of the routine will involve drawing a conclusion about whether the fraction reduces.

"What do you know about the fraction?" (It reduces to a whole number.)

"How do you know it reduces to a whole number?" (Because I said the top number.)

A variation of this routine can be used with various fractions. Here is the entire routine with italicized parts indicating words that change when different examples are introduced.

1. What's the bottom number?

2. What's the top number?

3. Count by the bottom number and see if you say *24.* Get ready.

4. What do you know about the fraction?

5. How do you know it *reduces* to a whole number?

The 24 is italicized because any number could be used as the top number of the fraction. Also, the *reduces* in step 5 is italicized because this step might say, "How do you know it *does not reduce* to a whole number?"

Although the routine could be used with any number, it is not as smooth as it might be. The question, "What do you know about the fraction?" is possibly vague. Furthermore, the routine does not contain very good provisions for teaching the correlated-feature relationship between the top number of the fraction and whether the fraction reduces. To correct these problems, we may add a step to the beginning of the routine.

1. *If you say the top number when counting by the bottom number, what do you know about the fraction?* (It reduces to a whole number.)

2. What's the bottom number of this fraction? (Six.)

3. What's the top number of this fraction? (Twenty-four.)

4. Tell me the number you're counting by.

5. Count by that number and see if you say 24. Get ready . . . (6, 12, 18, 24)

6. What do you know about the fraction? (It reduces to a whole number.)

7. How do you know it reduces? (Because I said 24.)

Step 6 would be easier if it were changed to a choice-response task: "So does this fraction reduce or not reduce?"

Comparing the Routine with the Components

Now that the routine has been designed, we have a final check on the various component skills that should be pretaught. We see that step 1 is a question about correlated features. Step 2 and step 3 involve numeral identification (which skill would be taught through noun sequences that introduce the various numerals). Step 4 is a correlated-feature relationship that is not stated. "If the number is on the bottom, you count by it." Step 5 calls for another correlated-feature response. Steps 6 and 7 present a correlated-feature relationship.

The general order of events in this routine divides into two parts. The first is the mechanical (steps 1 through 3). The second part is the application (steps 4 through 7). In the first part, the learner describes the criterion used for determining whether a fraction reduces and identifies the numerals involved in the particular problem. In the second part, the learner applies the descriptions and the identification to determine whether the fraction reduces.

The relationship that we added as step 1 of the routine implies possible preteaching. The relationship might be taught through a series of sequences, each showing how the counting operation applies to fractions with a particular denominator.

Example	Teacher
$\frac{19}{6}$	I'll tell you about fractions that have the bottom number of 6.
	My turn: When you count by the bottom number 6, you don't say 19.
	So what do I know about the fraction 19 over 6? It doesn't reduce to a whole number. How do I know? Because you don't say 19 when counting by 6.
$\frac{18}{6}$	My turn: When you count by the bottom number 6, you say 18.
	So what do I know about the fraction 18 over 6? It reduces to a whole number. How do I know? Because you say 18 when counting by 6.
$\frac{20}{6}$	Your turn: When you count by the bottom number 6, you don't say 20.
	What do you know about the fraction 20 over 6?
	How do you know?
	Etc.

The same type of correlated-feature sequence would be repeated with fractions having denominators of 4, 9, 5, and other numbers the learner can count by.

Testing the Learners Understanding

If the cognitive routine is adequately designed, it provides overt responses for the key discriminations named in the descriptive rule. By observing how the learner performs these overt steps, there would be little doubt about whether the learner was attending to relevant details of that example. If we observed the learner performing on an example of a fraction that reduces to a whole number, for example, we might be tempted to conclude that the learner understands the operation; however, the learner's performance does not suggest how the learner would perform when presented with a fraction that does not reduce. We need a test of more than one application.

The series of examples that we use to test a routine should parallel the series of examples used to test simpler discriminations.

We test the learner's understanding of simple discriminations by requiring the learner to respond to a variety of examples, arranged so that there is no predictable relationship between examples. (These examples are designed to test sameness across a range of possible variation.) If the learner performs appropriately on the set, we judge that the learner understands the discrimination.

In following the same procedure for the cognitive routine, we test the learner by requiring the learner to perform on a variety of examples. These are ordered so that there is no predictable relationship from example to example. The learner carries out the same steps of the routine on different examples. Successful performance implies that the learner understands the concept.

Summary

A cognitive routine is a creation designed to make problem-solving easier for the learner.

Cognitive routines deal with discriminations; therefore, anything presented through a cognitive routine could be presented as a simple discrimination. The communication will be better, however, if the problem-solving is designed as a series of overt steps that lead to the solution.

Our guide is physical operations. We construct the routines so they incorporate the three primary features of these operations–the functional nature of the various steps, the essential overtness of steps, and the feedback on every application. We try to design the steps so that each leads us closer to the outcome, and so that each is overt.

The steps for designing a cognitive routine are:

1. Specify the range of application for the routine.
2. Construct a descriptive rule that indicates what the learner is to do.
3. Indicate a task that tests each discrimination named in the descriptive rule.
4. Chain the tasks designed into a routine.

Start the chain with mechanical details. Then present the events that parallel those described by the rule.

The easiest way to evaluate the overtness of the routine is to play devil's advocate. Ask, "Would the learner's successful performance on examples of that routine convince me that the learner is attending to the appropriate details of the example and is operating on them in a way that is called for by all examples of the routine?" If the answer is "Yes," the routine is adequate. If the answer is "No," the routine must be redesigned to show which details the learner is processing and to show what the learner does to create a solution to the problem.

If we cannot specify tasks for parts of the rule that we have constructed, either we do not understand the discrimination, or there *is* no discrimination. The intent of specifying the tasks for everything named in the descriptive rule is not so much to articulate the tasks involved in the preteaching as it is to force us to specify each discrimination as a task. That task must either be a basic form or a joining form.

The great strength of the cognitive routine is that it stipulates a series of steps that, if followed, will appropriately process all examples of a given type.

The routine's greatest weakness is that it is not well-designed for initial teaching, because the pattern is juxtaposed if the routine consists of different steps. This weakness suggests that the component skills that are to appear in a cognitive routine should be pretaught, according to the general rules for introducing discriminations into a set.

Chapter 18
Illustrations of Cognitive Routines

Chapter 17 presented a general procedure for designing cognitive routines: start by specifying the range of examples; specify a descriptive rule that accommodates any application within this range; design tasks for the component skills named in the rule; and construct a routine composed of the component tasks. Chapter 17 demonstrated the procedure with several routines, but it did not show the range of variation in routines. The purpose of this chapter is to demonstrate the range. We will look at some routines that involve the prediction of physical outcomes and the verification of these outcomes. We will deal with routines that are designed for the sophisticated learner who has reasonable verbal understanding and the motor skills that are involved in the routine. The focus of these routines is on providing a list of things the learner is to do, not on providing actual teaching for the component behaviors. The words that appear in the descriptive rule often appear in the routine that we design for the sophisticated learner. At the other end of the continuum is the unsophisticated learner, who has neither a great deal of verbal knowledge nor the motor skills called for by the routine. The emphasis for this learner is on communicating the actual behavior. The routine probably will not contain the language that appears in the descriptive rule.

This chapter also illustrates that although some descriptive rules are very complicated, the resulting routine may be fairly simple. In contrast, other descriptive rules may be relatively simple, but the routine that is called for may be quite elaborate—so elaborate that it may have to be presented a part at a time.

Routines Based on Rules that Predict Physical Outcomes

The rule, *Objects fall at the same rate*, predicts that two objects quite different in size and weight will fall at the same rate. Other rules of science and of arithmetic are the same in that they predict particular outcomes. When we work with these rules, we should try to design them according to an ideal formula.

1. The learner takes the steps necessary to arrive at the appropriate answer.
2. A confirmation occurs *after* these overt steps have been taken.
3. The confirmation takes the form of an observation of something familiar to the learner.

For some routines, the confirmation may not take the form of a physical outcome, but of verbal confirmation by the teacher. This confirmation is usually not as desirable, but is often far more practical than observation of a physical outcome. (Confirmation for the rule about falling objects would provide the learner with a demonstration that two dissimilar objects, such as a feather and a lead ball, fall at the same rate. A verbal confirmation would simply be a verbal statement that the objects fall at the same rate.)

Illustration 1: Angle of Incidence and Angle of Reflection

The *setup* for the routine is very important. It is a format or structure that permits us to *process a range of examples by conducting the same series of steps*. The setup is a device that makes the sameness of the various examples obvious, because it shows that each example is processed in the same way.

We want to teach this idea: *The angle of reflection equals the angle of incidence.* The rule applies to the reflection of light, ricocheting of balls, etc. Here is a possible descriptive rule based on the idea: *To figure the angle of reflection, you first figure the angle of incidence and then mark off the same angle for the reflection.*

Identifying components. How do we show that two angles are the same? The temptation is to deal with numbers, perhaps constructing tasks such as, "What's the same angle as forty-five degrees?" The answer would not convince us that the learner would be able to recognize angles that are the same. A far more convincing task would require the learner to *construct* angles that are the same.

Section VI | Constructing Cognitive Routines

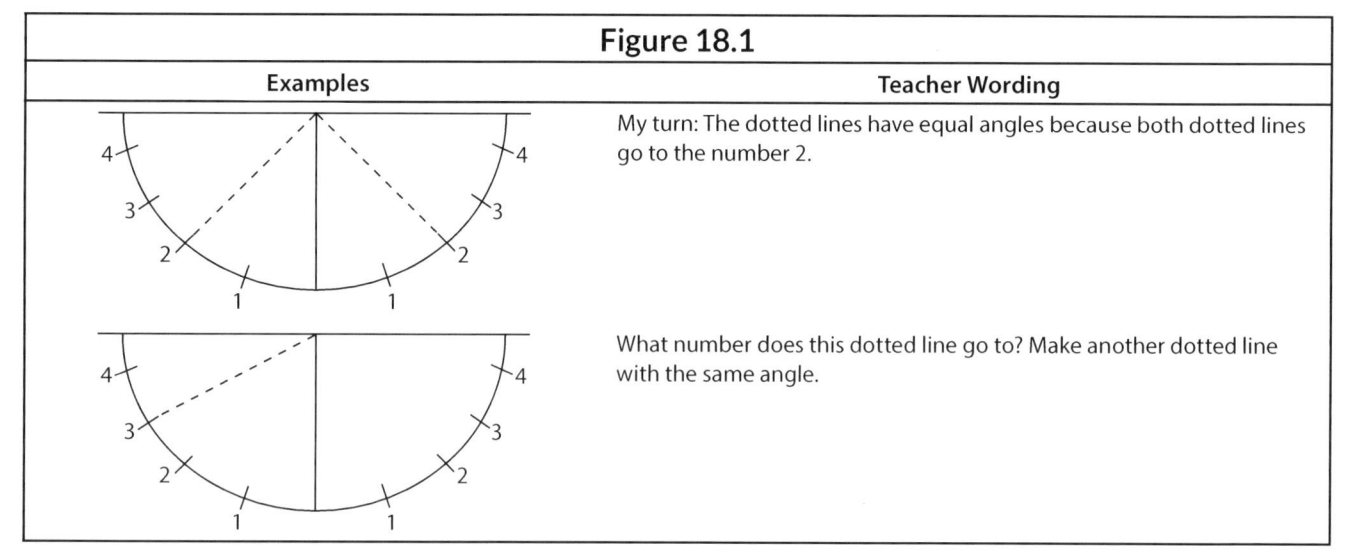

Figure 18.1	
Examples	Teacher Wording
[diagram: semicircle with marks 1-4 on each side, dotted lines from center to mark 2 on both sides]	My turn: The dotted lines have equal angles because both dotted lines go to the number 2.
[diagram: semicircle with marks 1-4 on each side, dotted line from center to mark 3 on left side]	What number does this dotted line go to? Make another dotted line with the same angle.

Figure 18.1 shows the beginning of a possible task series for teaching **same angle**. These tasks are presented as worksheet items. This preskill actually teaches the same basic discrimination that is involved in the angle of reflection.

The setup for the routine. Figure 18.2 shows a diagram of a physical *setup* that permits verification that the correct angle has been constructed. Note that it is quite similar to the worksheet items the learner works for figuring equal angles. This setup involves actual objects. A small mirror is attached to the wall. A center line marks the 0 angle. A semi-circular chalk line on the floor shows the path that is used for figuring the "same angle." The basic game is for a person to figure out where to stand to see an object. Confirmation is possible by standing in the specified place and looking into the mirror.

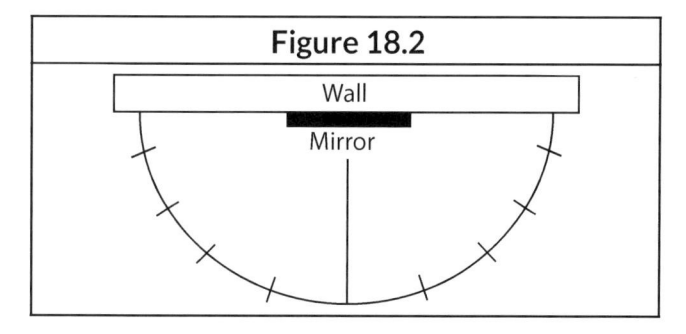

Figure 18.2
[diagram showing Wall with Mirror attached, and a semicircle on floor with tick marks on both sides and a center line]

The new descriptive rule. Now that we have designed the setup, we can construct a rule that is more precise than the original descriptive rule.

> To see a target in the mirror (to predict the angle of reflection), first see how many marks the target is from the center line, then mark off the same number of places on the other side.

This new rule suggests the preskills of judging how many places from the center line a target is, marking off the same number of places on the other side. If the learner did not have these preskills, we would design teaching for them.

The routine. The following routine begins with the mirror covered.

1. Teacher: If you want to see me in the mirror, you have to make the same angle on the other side. I start in the center and then I move to the third mark. Which mark did I move to?
   Learner: The third mark.
2. Teacher: (Moves to the third mark on the left.) If you want to see me in the mirror, which mark do you have to move to on the other side?
   Learner: The third mark.
3. Teacher: Do it.
   Learner: (Moves three marks from the center line.)
4. Teacher: You made the same angle on the other side. So will you be able to see me in the mirror?
   Learner: Yes.
5. Teacher: How do you know?
   Learner: Because I made the same angle on the other side.
6. Teacher: (Uncovers mirror.)

Note that the verification *comes after* the learner has carried out the steps. This point is important. The verification is a contingency, so that the verification functions in the same way that a successful outcome functions when the learner is engaged in a physical operation, such as throwing a ball at a target. *Unless the routine places*

246   Theory of Instruction: Principles and Applications

emphasis on the steps that lead to the verification, the routine will be weak. If we had designed the routine so the learner merely walked around the semi-circle until the teacher was visible in the mirror, there would be no compelling reason for the learner to learn the relationship between the angles on either side of the center line. The learner could simply attend to seeing the teacher in the mirror, not to first figuring out where to stand to see the teacher. The teacher's explanations of *why* she is visible in the mirror would be after-the-fact explanations that do not require the learner to attend to the angles.

If the routine is designed so the learner must take certain steps and figure out the answer before receiving verification of the answer, the routine works like a physical operation. The outcome depends on the successful performance of certain steps.

Illustration 2: Finding the Number You Multiply By

The idea that we start with is: *You can change any number into any other number by multiplying. The number you multiply by is simply that value that is needed to make the sides of the equation equal. The number is always expressed in terms of the other two numbers.*

In a general way, we can express the rule as:

$$\frac{a}{b}\left(\frac{bc}{ad}\right) = \frac{c}{d}$$

The value that is in parentheses is what we multiply a/b by to change it into c/d. We can show that the value in parentheses is correct by analyzing how many are on each side of the equation. The first two fractions on the left side:

$$\frac{a}{b} \times \frac{b}{a} \text{ equals one } \left(\frac{ab}{ab}\right)$$

because the top and bottom numbers are the same. What remains on the left side of the equation is c/d. The same value is on the right side of the equal sign. Since c/d=c/d, the value inside the parentheses must be correct.

The objective of our routine is to teach the learner how to figure out what goes into the parentheses for any problem such as:

$$4\ (\ ) = 6$$
$$\frac{a}{3}\ (\ ) = \frac{1}{b}$$
$$\frac{9}{3}\ (\ ) = \frac{4R}{7}$$

Figure 18.3

Example: 3( )=6
3( )=6

1. **Teacher:** You know the answer to this problem. But we're going to work it a new way and see if we get the right answer. Three times some number equals six. What number?
   Learner: Two.
   Teacher writes 2 in top problem: 3(2)=6.

2. **Teacher:** Now let's work the same problem another way. I'll pretend that I don't know what to multiply three by to change it into six, but I do know what to multiply one by. So first I multiply to change three into one. What do I multiply by?
   Leaner: One-third.
   Teacher writes: 3($\frac{1}{3}$)=6

3. **Teacher:** Are the sides of the equation equal now?
   Learner: No.

4. **Teacher points left:** How many are on this side?
   Learner: One.

5. **Teacher points right:** How many are on this side?
   Learner: Six.

6. **Teacher:** So we multiply by six inside the parentheses.
   Teacher writes: 3($\frac{1}{3} \times \frac{6}{1}$)=6

7. **Teacher:** Multiply and tell me the fraction that is in the parentheses.
   Learner: Six-thirds.

8. **Teacher:** What does six-thirds reduce to?
   Learner: Two.

9. **Teacher:** How do you know?
   Learner: Because the top is two times bigger than the bottom.

10. **Teacher:** We ended with the right number when we worked the problem this way.

The rule and the setup. As with the routine for the angle of reflection, the learner should go through the steps that will lead to the correct answer. Then the learner should receive some form of verification that the answer is correct (possibly a compelling observation). The routine in Figure 18.3 assumes that the learner can reduce fractions to whole numbers and that the learner understands whether fractions equal one whole.

There are two important points about this routine.

1. The attack is logical. First we make the left side equal to one. Then we multiply by whatever is needed to make the left side equal to the right. This basic procedure is logically compelling.

2. The validation comes from applying a familiar reducing procedure that is assumed to be valid.

Figure 18.4

Example: $\frac{4}{3}(\quad) = \frac{7}{8}$

1. **Teacher:** I don't know what to multiply four-thirds by to change it into seven-eighths, but I do know what to multiply some number by. What number?
   Learner: One.
2. **Teacher:** So what do I multiply by first?
   Learner: Three-fourths.
   Teacher writes: $\frac{4}{3}\left(\frac{3}{4}\right) = \frac{7}{8}$
3. **Teacher:** How many are on the side now?
   Learner: One.
4. **Teacher:** So what do I do to make the sides equal?
   Learner: Multiply by seven-eighths.
5. **Teacher:** What fraction is inside the parenthesis?
   Learner: Twenty-one thirty-seconds.
   Teacher writes: $\frac{4}{3}\left(\frac{3}{4} \times \frac{7}{8}\right) = \frac{7}{8}$
6. **Teacher:** That is the answer.

Instead of designing the initial routine so that it deals with examples that are not readily verifiable, such as 4/3( )=2/8, we present an example that reduces to a whole number. This procedure validates the routine. If the routine works with different values that can be verified through reduction, the routine should work for other values. Once the validity of the routine has been established, a variation that involves no validation is applied to a full range of examples. The routine in Figure 18.4 is changed slightly so that it provides less prompting. The same routine will work for any value.

Illustration 3: Rewriting Numbers That Have Exponents

This illustration involves a descriptive rule that is quite complicated; however, the resulting routine is not very complicated. This relationship is observed in many skills.

The goal of the teaching is to show the learner how to write exponents such as N^4 or N^{-4} as $N \times N \times N \times N$ and $\frac{1}{N \times N \times N \times N}$. For this teaching, we do not encounter the problem that we encountered in the preceding illustrations. For these problems, we had to design a setup. For the exponent routine, we are going to use the conventional setup or notation system and simply teach the learner how it works. Our major concern is that of dealing with a complicated descriptive rule:

> To write numbers that have exponents as fractions that show repeated multiplication, multiply the base the number of times the exponent indicates; use the sign of the exponent to determine where the multiplication occurs—with the multiplication occurring where the exponent is shown if the exponent is positive and the multiplication occurring in the opposite part of the fraction if the exponent is negative.

The exponent is written on either the top of the fraction or on the bottom: N^2 or $\frac{1}{N^2}$. If the exponent is positive (+), the multiplication occurs in the same place the exponent appears (top or bottom). If the exponent is negative (N^{-2} or $1/N^{-2}$), the multiplication occurs in the opposite part of the fraction (on the bottom for N^{-2} and on the top for $1/N^{-2}$).

We next translate each component discrimination into a task that tests the discrimination. The discrimination named first in the descriptive rule is: "The base number is multiplied." The task could be "Which number is multiplied?" We could use a single-transformation sequence to teach this skill as in Figure 18.5.

To teach the discrimination that the exponent tells how many times the base is multiplied, we could use a pair of correlated-features tasks (illustrated in Figure 18.6).

We may have some problems with the next idea expressed by our descriptive rule. The idea is that the sign of the exponent tells whether the multiplication occurs

Figure 18.5

Example	Teacher Wording
4^6	My turn: Which number is multiplied? Four.
6^4	Your turn: Which number is multiplied?
6^5	Which number is multiplied?
5^6	Which number is multiplied?
N^4	Which number is multiplied?
21^{-7}	Which number is multiplied?

Figure 18.6

Example	Teacher Wording
N^5	My turn: How many times is the base number multiplied? (Five.) How do you know? (Because the exponent is five.)
N^{15}	My turn again: How many times is the base multiplied? (Fifteen.) How do you know? (Because the exponent is fifteen.)
$5N^{15}$	Your turn: How many times is the base multiplied? (Fifteen.) How do you know? (Because the exponent is fifteen.)
Etc.	

on the same part of the fraction as the exponent. We should probably use correlated-feature tasks for this discrimination.

Figure 18.7 shows the test wording of four examples that teaches the relationship.

Figure 18.7

Example	Teacher Wording
$\frac{N^{-5}}{1}$	Where is the base multiplied? (Away from the exponent.) How do you know? (Because the exponent is negative.)
$\frac{N^5}{1}$	Where is the base multiplied? (Where the exponent is.) How do you know? (Because the exponent is positive.)
$\frac{1}{N^5}$	Where is the base multiplied? (Where the exponent is.) How do you know? (Because the exponent is positive.)
$\frac{1}{N^{-5}}$	Where is the base multiplied? (Away from the exponent.) How do you know? (Because the exponent is negative.)

The final routine requires the learner to tell us how to rewrite different numbers that have exponents. The routine is created by chaining the various tasks that teach the component skills. We simply add steps that require the learner to carry out the multiplication. See Figure 18.8.

Figure 18.8

Example	Teacher Wording
$\frac{N^{-5}}{1}$	1. What's the base? (N)
	2. What's the exponent? (Minus five.)
	3. How many times is the base multiplied? (Five times.)
	4. How do you know? (Because the exponent is five.)
	5. Where is the base multiplied? (Away from the exponent.)
	6. How do you know? (Because the exponent is negative.)
	7. What's another way of saying: "N to the minus five over one?" (One over N x N x N x N x N.)

Although the descriptive rule from which we started is quite complicated, the resulting routine is simple. The learner first responds to two mechanical questions. The bulk of the routine consists of two correlated-feature relationships.

To firm the concept of multiplying away from where the base is and multiplying where the base is, we would present minimally different applications of the routine as illustrated in Figure 18.9.

Figure 18.9

Example	Teacher Wording
$\frac{1}{N^5}$	1. What's the base? (N)
	2. What's the exponent? (Five.)
	3. How many times is the base multiplied? (Five times.)
	4. How do you know? (Because the exponent is five.)
	5. Where is the base multiplied? (Where the exponent is.)
	6. How do you know? (Because the exponent is positive.)
	7. What's another way of saying: "One over N to the five?" (One over N x N x N x N x N.)

Illustration 4: Column Addition

Some complex descriptive rules imply a series of routines or a variation of the basic routine. Column addition illustrates this type.

Let's say that the idea is to teach procedures for column addition problems that do not involve carrying. The problems would include different types:

$$\begin{array}{r}203\\55\\+\ 320\end{array} \qquad \begin{array}{r}41\\57\\+\ 92\end{array} \qquad \begin{array}{r}41\\34\\+\ 2\end{array}$$

Before we can design a descriptive rule, we must determine a procedure that we will use to achieve the addition. (No single procedure holds for all column-addition problems because some later problems will require carrying.) If we used a conventional approach, the rule for non-carrying problems could be expressed:

> To solve the problem, first add the numbers in the ones column and write the answer. Then add the numbers in the tens column and write the answer.

To design a non-carrying routine, we first specify tasks for the various parts of the descriptive rule.

The rule requires the learner to discriminate ones column and tens column.

We should teach the learner to operate first in the ones column, but we should try to avoid teaching a discrimination (ones column vs. tens column) that would prompt possible reversals (spurious transformations). (See Figure 18.10.)

Figure 18.10

Example	Teacher Wording
	We always start adding in the ones column. That's the last column.
A. $\begin{array}{r}24\\+\ 31\end{array}$	Touch the ones column for problem A.
B. $\begin{array}{r}340\\+\ 246\end{array}$	Touch the ones column for problem B.
C. $\begin{array}{r}798\\101\\3\\+\ 52\end{array}$	Touch the ones column for problem C.

By touching only the correct column, the learner is not required to discriminate between the two labels and the two columns, merely to learn which column is the one you start with. The task, "Touch the ones column," becomes a component or step in the routine.

Now we teach the routine for solving the problem in the ones column. The routine stipulates the first behaviors involved in solving all problems. (See Figure 18.11.)

Figure 18.11

Example	Teacher Wording
$\begin{array}{r}20\\15\\+\ 23\end{array}$	Read problem A. (Learner reads.) Touch the column you start adding in. (Learner touches ones column.) Which column did you touch? (Ones column.)
	Write the answer for the ones column. (Learner writes.)

By presenting this routine with juxtaposed examples, we show the learner that the same steps apply to all problems.

To assure that the learner writes the answer in the appropriate place (directly under the ones column), we could make answer boxes under the ones column and under the tens column. (Note that if we placed an answer box only under the ones column, the box would serve as a spurious prompt about where to add first.)

After the routine of starting problems in the ones column has been applied to perhaps a dozen problems, we could introduce an entire routine for dealing with the ones column and the tens column. (See Figure 18.12.)

Figure 18.12

Example	Teacher Wording
$\begin{array}{r}30\\15\\+\ 23\end{array}$	Read problem A. (Learner reads.)
	Touch the column you start adding in. (Learner touches ones column.)
	Read the problems in the ones column. (Learner reads.)
	Write the answer for the ones column. (Learner writes 8.)
	Now read the problem in the tens column. (Learner reads.)
	Add the tens and write the answer below the tens column. (Learner writes 6.)
	How many tens are in the tens column? ("Six.")
	When you add 30 and 15 and 23, how many do you end up with? ("Sixty-eight.")

The questions that the teacher presents require the learner to discriminate between the ones column and the tens column, the total for the ones column, the total for the tens column, and the total for the whole problem.

The questions are presented so that they minimize reversal problems. The reason is that the routine presents a chain of behaviors that always occur in the same order.

An alternative routine that would provide better juxtaposition of examples for the tens column could be introduced after the learner has practiced working with the ones column only. This intermediate routine would be introduced before the total routine is presented. (See Figure 18.13.)

	Figure 18.13
Example	Teacher Wording
20 56 + 13	Touch the column you start adding in. (Learner responds.) The answer is nine. Write the answer in the ones column. (Learner writes.) Read everything in tens column. (Learner reads.) How many tens is two tens, five tens and one tens? Write the numbers of tens in the tens column.

The juxtaposition of examples is improved because the learner does not have to work the ones column, merely touch the column and write the answer. After the learner has worked 5 to 10 problems with this routine, the total routine could be introduced.

In summary, the descriptive rule for these addition problems implied a *program*, a sequence of more than one routine. Certainly we could have started with the final routine; however, the juxtapositions would have been very poor. The central thrust of the program is to stipulate the first behavior that the learner is to perform when working the column-addition problems. This starting behavior is critical, because after it is established, the remaining steps tend to follow naturally. Perhaps the best way to demonstrate this feature is to compare the final routine with one that has weak beginning steps and nonfunctional discrimination tasks (Figure 18.14). Note the choice.

Although this routine is not a perfect disaster (and would certainly work with most learners), it is relatively weak because it does not strongly prompt the starting steps and it does not stipulate these steps in a way that makes them *different* from other steps. The routine presents two questions about choosing the ones column or the tens column. Although the learner may respond correctly

Figure 18.14
Teacher Wording
When you start adding, do you begin in the tens column or the ones column?
Read the problem in that column.
Do you write the answer to that column under the tens column or under the ones column?
Do it. (Check.)
Which column do you add next?
Read the problem in that column.
Do you write the answer to that column under the tens column or under the ones column?
Do it. (Check.)

to step 1 of the routine, the learner may start to read the problem incorrectly in step 2 because *the routine does not provide us with a strong indication that the learner knows which column is the ones column.* The second question about where the answer is written is not functional. If the learner has already written an answer under the ones column, where could the answer for the tens column go, except under the tens column?

Illustration 5: Routines that Call for Descriptive Responses

Earlier, we cautioned against the use of descriptive responses. We noted that if a descriptive response is used, the learner should be required to actually perform the step described. In some situations, descriptive steps are both reasonable and efficient, even if they are not followed by behavioral demonstrations. These steps are used extensively in procedures that direct adults and sophisticated learners to perform physical manipulations—such as achieving a high-brace turn in a canoe, tying a square knot, hypnotizing yourself, preparing egg salad, etc.

These routines are justified if they clearly specify the intended behaviors *and if the learner is capable of translating the descriptive steps into appropriate behavior.* For these situations, the descriptive steps of the routine are not intended to teach *actual behavior*, but to teach discriminations or facts. Consider operations such as fixing an omelet, repairing a tire, dressing to look slim, or bathing a dog. If we were to teach the behaviors, we would begin with the component skills. We would then introduce the routine and teach it. In many situations, however, we cannot take responsibility for the entire teaching.

Furthermore, we assume that it has been taught. We therefore may decide to design routines that concentrate only on the *learner's symbolic understanding of the situation, not on the actual behavior*. These routines provide information necessary to chain known behaviors together–however, they do not teach the actual behaviors.

Let's say that we wanted to teach the learner a procedure for remaking a garment to get rid of wrinkles in the sleeves.

The descriptive rule. To get rid of wrinkles in a sleeve of a garment that is being made, increase the sleeve seam and taper the seam from under the arm to the cuff.

The descriptive rule not only describes the discrimination that we must teach; it probably also contains the language and the order of events.

Increase the seam. We will say that the seam is increased if no part of it is smaller than it had been. We use a variation of a non-comparative sequence (see Figure 18.15).

Figure 18.15

Example	Teacher Wording
	The solid lines show the original seam. The dotted lines show the new seam.
	Is this seam increased? Yes.
	Your turn: Is this seam increased? Yes.
	Is this seam increased? Yes. Etc.

Tapering from the shoulder to the neck. This discrimination is best taught as a non-comparative. Figure 18.16 shows the first part of a possible sequence.

The final routine is simply a correlated-feature sequence that expresses the two things that are done to *get rid of wrinkles* (Figure 18.17). Because the final routine is verbal and does not involve actually doing the operation, it begins by expressing the two things that must be done to get rid of the wrinkles. Following the mechanical test on this information are applications. The applications are simply correlated-feature examples.

Figure 18.16

Example	Teacher Wording
UA — C	My turn: How does this seam taper? It doesn't.
UA — C	How does this seam taper? From the cuff to under the arm.
UA — C	How does this seam taper? From under the arm to the cuff.
	Your turn: How does this seam taper? Etc.

Figure 18.17

Example	Teacher Wording
	To get rid of the wrinkle, you do two things. You have to increase the sleeve seam, and taper it from under the arm to the cuff. What are the two things?
Shows increased seam tapers from under the arm to the cuff.	My turn: Could this get rid of the wrinkle? Yes. How do I know? The seam increased and is tapered from under the arm to the cuff.
Shows seam not increased.	Your turn: Could this get rid of the wrinkle? (No.) How do you know? (The seam is not increased.)
Shows seam not tapered.	Could this get rid of the wrinkle? (No.) How do you know? (The seam does not taper from under the arm to the cuff.)

Note that the routine begins with a positive to assure that both criteria are presented to the learner as quickly as possible.

Following the routine above could be applications that require the learner to perform the operation. The routine for the application is quite simple.

Teacher: What are the two things you do to get rid of a wrinkle in the sleeve?

(Learner responds.) Do it.

Although the final routine requires the learner to "do it," the teacher emphasis is on the *description* of what is to be done.

Illustration 6: The Concept of Specific Gravity

This illustration points out that the procedures specified for designing cognitive routines work for any concept that can be treated as a problem-solving routine. The concept of specific gravity is one that is sometimes used as a developmental marker and one that is not frequently taught in a direct manner. We can create a descriptive rule that satisfies the requirements for describing specific gravity; therefore, we can design a routine for teaching the concept.

The descriptive rule. To determine whether an object sinks or floats in a medium, the learner receives information about the weight of the object as it compares to the weight of the medium in which the object is to be placed. The learner then concludes that: (a) the object will float (if lighter than an equal volume of the medium); or (b) the object will sink (if heavier than an equal volume of the medium).

Before we can design the routine, we have to make a decision about how the learner receives the information about the density of the object, and of the medium. The information could be provided through verbal statements of fact or through some sort of physical demonstration that involves weighing the object and the medium. Unless we make some decisions about how the learner will receive this information, we do not know what kind of setup to create for the routine.

Let's say that the learner receives density information by weighing *part* of the medium and an equal-size *part* of the object. One possible setup consists of an object that is composed of blocks. To determine the relative weight of the medium and object, the learner selects part of the object and fills a container the same size as the block with the medium. Both are weighed on a balance scale. The learner then predicts whether the object will float or sink in the medium. (See Figure 18.18.)

Because of the large number of component discriminations, we will present the routine first (Figure 18.19), then show the component skills. Note, however, that if we were designing the routine, we would start with identifying the various discriminations referred to in the descriptive rule.

The learner first predicts what will happen, then receives confirmation in the form of an observation. The confirmation serves as reinforcement for working the problem and predicting correctly.

Figure 18.18

Object

Part of object

Container for weighing medium

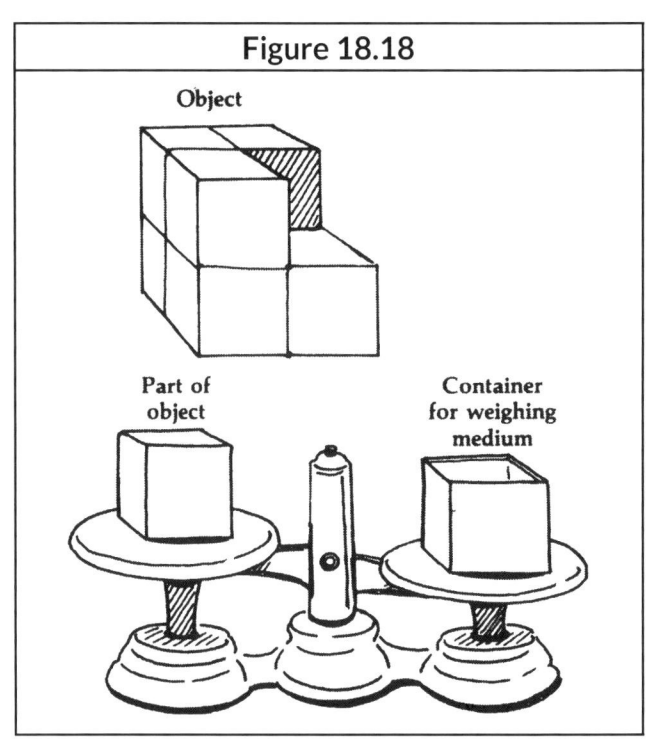

Figure 18.19

Teacher Wording	Learner's Response
(Presents object.) What do you do to figure out whether the blocks will float or sink in the medium?	Weigh a block and weigh a piece of the medium the same size.
Do it.	(Detaches one block from object, fills second block with water from the tank, and places one object on either side of the balance scale. The block from the object goes up.)
What did the object do on the scale?	Went up.
So what will the object do in the medium?	Float.
How do you know?	Because it's lighter than a piece of medium the same size.
Let's see if you're right. (Places object on the medium.) What's it doing?	Floating.

Let's assume the learner has to be pretaught **float** and **sink**.

   Teacher: Listen. Another way of saying that an object goes down in air is this: An object sinks in air.

What's another way of saying an object goes down in water?

What's another way of saying an object goes down to the bottom of the lake?

What's another way of saying an object does not go down in gasoline?

etc.

The purpose of this wording is to show what is the same about **floating** and **sinking** in *any* medium. By making the wording the same for different media, we prompt the sameness.

To teach the discrimination of **medium**, we could do another transformation sequence (Figure 18.20).

Figure 18.20	
Example	Teacher Wording
	An object is always in a medium
(Holds egg in air.)	What medium is the egg in now?
(Holds egg in sand.)	What medium is the egg in now?
(Holds egg in water.)	What medium is the egg in now?
Etc.	

To teach **the same size**, we would use a correlated-feature relationship. For this series, the teacher pours sand from the one container into containers of different shapes and sizes (Figure 18.21).

Figure 18.21	
Example	Teacher Wording
Teacher presents sand in flat container.	Here's a rule: If things hold the same amount, they are the same size.
Teacher pours sand into round container of same size.	Are the containers the same size? (Yes.) How do you know? (They hold the same amount.)
Teacher pours sand into rectangular container same size.	Are the containers the same size? How do you know?
Teacher pours sand into rectangular container not the same size.	Are they the same size? How do you know?
Etc.	

In addition to the single-transformation sequence for **floating**, the learner would be tested on concrete applications that require the learner to tell whether the object sinks or floats, and to identify the medium (Figure 18.22).

Figure 18.22	
Example	Teacher Wording
Object sinks in water.	What did the object do? What did it sink in?
Object floats in water.	What did the object do? What did it float in?
Object floats in air.	What did the object do? What did it float in?

Another skill would be to determine which object is lighter. To teach this skill, the balance scale would be used. The concept is a correlated-features relationship.

Teacher: Which is lighter, the block or the egg?
Learner: The block.
Teacher: How do you know the block is lighter?
Learner: The block went up on the scale.

We could also teach the relationship between the behavior of objects on the scale to their floating and sinking behavior (Figure 18.23).

Figure 18.23	
Example	Teacher Wording
Teacher presents two objects, A and B.	(Point to A.) This is the object. (Point to B.) This is part of the medium we will put the object in. The object and the medium are the same size. How do I know that? (They hold the same amount.)
Teacher places object and medium on a scale.	What did the object do on the scale? That's what it will do in the medium.
Object goes up on scale.	What will this object do in the medium? How do you know?
Object goes up on scale.	What will this object do in the medium? How do you know?
Object goes down on scale.	What will this object do in the medium? How do you know?
Etc.	

This sequence is possibly weak because the learner should understand that the objects must be the same "size" or volume. This discrimination is not required by the tasks, however. We would correct this problem by requiring the learner to produce "stronger" responses (Figure 18.24).

Figure 18.24

Example	Teacher Wording
Object goes up on scale.	What will the object do in the medium? (Float.) How do you know? (It's lighter than a piece of medium the same size.)
Object goes down on scale.	What will the object do in the medium? (Sink.) How do you know? (It's heavier than a piece of medium the same size.)

The routine that appears on the previous page is a chaining of the various skills that would have been pretaught. Like the other cognitive routines, it serves as a model that prompts a complex discrimination. In this case, the routine must prompt the idea that for homogeneous objects the whole object sinks if any part of the object sinks. After demonstrating with the routine that the whole object floats, the teacher might say, "Listen. If each part of the object is lighter than a piece of the medium the same size, each part will float." This step expresses the idea that there is a constant ratio of object-to-medium of the same size. If the routine prompts this notion, it communicates the essence of the concept of **specific gravity**.

Although the concept of **specific gravity** is seen by some cognitive psychologists as something that operates within the learner's mind and that evolves through unspecified development, it can be taught if we formulate a descriptive rule that expresses what behaviors would be accepted as evidence that the learner has the concept. The routine that would succeed in teaching this concept to learners has the same properties as the routine for teaching angle of incidence, beginning decoding, or any other cognitive skill. Overt behaviors are designed for the various component discriminations named in the descriptive rule. These discriminations are then chained together in a routine that can be used for *all* examples of the cognitive skill (in any medium and with any object.)

Summary

There is no right way to construct cognitive routines. Rather, there are strategies that are acceptable and some that are better than others.

When we deal with rules about the physical world, we want the learner to understand that the routine is actually a vehicle for predicting outcomes. We therefore design the routine so that the observation of the predicted outcome comes *only after the learner has taken the appropriate steps*. The observation is treated as "reinforcement" for solving the problem. It serves as an analogue to a successful trial with a physical operation.

Some routines simply list the various steps the learner is to perform. The emphasis is placed not so much on the actual skills, but on the cognitive discriminations. The idea is to prepare the learner with *understanding* of how the operation should work, not necessarily with the motor skills of doing it. For such routines, conventional wording is usually acceptable (the wording that appears in the descriptive rule).

The opposite situation occurs if new, difficult responses are called for by the routine. The wording that is used by the teacher becomes arbitrary. The focus of the routine is on *doing*. This routine is designed to prompt the actual behavior—not merely to serve as a checklist.

Some routines deal with skills that are not conventionally taught (such as **specific gravity**). The procedure is basically the same for these routines so long as we can express a rule that describes the things that a learner must do to solve the problem.

When routines do not involve a conventional setup, we must design one. For many problems, we accept the conventional setup (such as the conventional symbol system for numbers). However, we may decide to reject the conventional setup, or we may have to create one if it does not exist.

Some descriptive rules need more than one routine. These are usually rules that involve long strings of behavior. If we introduce one routine that contains all the behavior, the juxtaposition of steps is not well-designed to stipulate a chain of behaviors, particularly the very important first steps. Therefore, we create one routine that deals with the starting behavior, then another that presents the starting behavior and additional behavior.

Although there is an incredible variation of routines, all are designed to provide a series of overt steps that lead to solutions to a class of problems. And all are composed entirely of components that can be identified and pretaught.

Chapter 19
Scheduling Routines and Their Examples

This chapter deals with three issues of coordinating routines:

1. How do we schedule examples *for the different components* of a routine?
2. How do we schedule *the examples* that are to be processed by a complete routine?
3. How do we schedule *conditional parts* of routines?

Scheduling Components

Once the routine has been tentatively designed, the components have been identified. The routine functions as a "format." By substituting different instances, we create a range of applications (examples) for the routine. The various components of the routine are members. The procedures for introducing the members are those that we follow for all *members*. We separate highly similar members. We avoid juxtaposing introductions that involve minimum-differences, and we provide for the firming of each component skill. Each skill must be:

1. Introduced through an initial teaching sequence.
2. Expanded in activities that require responses and contexts different from those in the initial-teaching sequence.
3. Reviewed until the component is used in the routine (or in some other application).

The order in which the components are introduced for a particular routine *does not necessarily reflect the order in which the skill appears in the routine*. Decisions about the order of introduction are based on: (1) features of the components; and (2) the complexity of the components (with more practice time allotted to components that require difficult discriminations and difficult responses).

Minimum-Time Schedules

In its purest form, the schedule for the components of a particular routine would be specified in much the same way as those for other programs that derive from tasks. In practice, some components would have been pretaught to achieve objectives that are not related to the routine. The schedule for the components of a particular routine would therefore show some components being taught months, perhaps years, before the introduction routine. If we assume that none of the components involved in the routine have been pretaught, we design a *minimum-time schedule*. This schedule provides a careful introduction and shows the best estimate of the minimum time that would be required for the introduction.

Illustration: Beginning word reading. To teach the reading of regular words, we must teach some letters that can be identified as sounds and we must teach oral blending. For the schedule in Figure 19.1, sounds are introduced at the average rate of one new sound every three days. On the first few days, however, the rate is somewhat higher because the discriminations are relatively easier. (Note that the letter **e** is pronounced "ee," not the short sound.) Oral blending exercises begin on lesson 1 and continue through lesson 22. The sound review begins on

Figure 19.1

Components	Lessons																								
	1	2	3	4	5	6	7	8	9	10	11	12	13	14	15	16	17	18	19	20	21	22	23	24	25
Sounds	a,r	a,r	s	s	m	m	e	e	d	d		u	u		l	l	o	o	g	g		t	t		
Review			X	X	X	X	X	X	X	X	X	X	X	X	X	X	X	X	X	X	X	X	X	X	X
Oral Blending	X	X	X	X	X	X	X	X	X	X	X	X	X	X	X	X	X	X	X	X	X	X			
Word-Reading Routine							X	X	X	X	X	X	X	X	X	X	X	X	X	X	X	X	X	X	X

lesson 3 after three sounds have been introduced. The word-reading routine starts on lesson 9. At this time, the learner has been introduced to the sounds for *r, a, s, m,* and *e.* The routine continues on every lesson.

The routine processes only those sounds that are firm, which means that the learner has worked with them for at least two lessons. The routine can safely be introduced nine lessons after the program begins. *This is the minimum schedule that is required for a careful introduction.* Information about specific problems the learner encounters or that the teachers experience in presenting the tasks may lead to modification of what we consider a minimum schedule. Also, if learners are sophisticated (which means that they have learned some of the specific skills demanded by the program and a general "learning strategy"), we may accelerate the rate of introduction. Possibly, the learner has already learned sounds for some of the letters. Possibly, the learner already knows the names of the letters and therefore requires less instruction to master the sounds. For this learner, the introduction of the cognitive routine would appear on lesson 3 or 4; however, the 9-lesson presentation would be safe for most learners who have received no appreciable preteaching.

Illustration: Getting rid of wrinkles in a sleeve. This routine involves two discrimination components ("Is the seam increased?" and "How does this seam taper?"), a correlated-feature sequence, and a routine that combines the components. Figure 19.2 shows a possible schedule.

Figure 19.2			
Components	Lessons		
	1	2	3
Discrimination: Is the seam increased?	X	X	
Discrimination: How does this seam taper?	X	X	
Correlated feature relationship	X	X	
Routine		X	X

Note that this sequence assumes that the learner is fairly sophisticated and that the skills are introduced for the first time. Each skill appears on two consecutive lessons, with the preskills for the routine preceding the introduction of the routine by one lesson.

In most situations, the information about increasing the seam and tapering a seam would not be delayed until we teach about removing wrinkles. These skills would play a role in many more elementary tasks; therefore, they would be introduced long before the correlated-feature relationship and the routine. A more reasonable program for removing the wrinkles would assume that the only skills directly implied by the routine are the correlated-features relationship and the routine (Figure 19.3).

Figure 19.3		
Components	Lessons	
	1	2
Correlated-feature relationship	X	X
Routine	X	X

This schedule presents both the correlated-feature relationship and the routine on the same lessons. (The reason is that this program introduces less that is new to the learner.) The correlated-feature relationship deals with discriminations familiar to the learner; therefore, the application (the routine) may immediately follow the verbal training (the correlated-feature sequence).

Scheduling Clusters

Some routines have many steps. Routines that involve long division or similar long arithmetic operations may have as many as 30 steps. If we follow the basic procedure of teaching each component individually and then combining them into the routine, we create a rather rough transition. We observed earlier that the pattern of juxtaposition for long routines makes it difficult for the learner to remember the sequence of steps. To make the transition easier, we introduce an intermediate step. Instead of proceeding directly from individual components to the cognitive routine, *we proceed from the individual components to small groups or "clusters" of components.* The schedule in Figure 19.4 shows the strategy. Note that a cluster is composed of juxtaposed steps; however, the steps are not necessarily scheduled according to their occurrence in the routine (with **AB** first, **BC** next, etc.). In the schedule, **AB** and **GH** are scheduled at the same time.

The pattern shown in Figure 19.4 groups the component skills into pairs. These pairs would be two consecutive steps in the final routine. Not all skills can be grouped gracefully into pairs. For some routines, a more logical grouping might involve one cluster composed of four steps and perhaps another composed of two. The goal,

Figure 19.4

Components	Lessons									
	1	2	3	4	5	6	7	8	9	10
Skills: A	•	•								
B		•	AB	AB			AB			
C				•	•					
D					•	CD	CD			
E				•	•					
F						•	EF	EF		
G	•	•								
H		•	GH	GH			GH			
Routine								A-H	A-H	A-H

however, is to present subparts of the routine as intact clusters. When the learner practices a cluster, the transition from clusters to routine is easier because less new learning is involved. Instead of being faced with a series of familiar independent steps that are brought together in an unfamiliar chain, the learner simply chains two or three smaller chains or clusters together.

Figure 19.5

Example	Teacher Wording
$\frac{24}{6}$	1. If you say the top number when counting by the bottom number, what do you know about the fraction? (It reduces to a whole number.)
	2. What's the bottom number of this fraction? (Six.)
	3. What's the top number of this fraction? (Twenty-four.)
	4. Touch the number you're going to count by. (Learner touches 6.)
	5. Count by that number and see if you say twenty-four. Get ready… (6, 12, 18, 24.)
	6. What do you know about the fraction? (It reduces to a whole number.)
	7. How do you know it reduces? (Because I said the top number.)

We can illustrate the cluster strategy with the 7-step routine in Figure 19.5. This routine is designed to teach the procedure for determining whether a fraction reduces to a whole number. Steps 1, 2 and 3 deal with the mechanical details of the routine. Steps 4, 5, 6 and 7 analyze the fraction. We could create various clusters from this routine. For instance, steps 2 and 3 should go together as a cluster. Possibly, 2, 3 and 4 could go together as a cluster. Possibly 1, 6, and 7 (or a slight variation of these steps) could go together in a correlated-feature sequence.

The following is a brief description of how we might achieve major clusters, one composed of steps 2, 3, 4; another composed of steps 1, 6, 7; and a third made up of steps 4 and 5.

We would introduce steps 2 and 3 initially as a test. We would present various fractions and tell the learner, "Touch the bottom number . . . Touch the top number." We would present the tasks in the reverse order for some fractions.

As soon as the learner is firm on steps 2 and 3, we would add step 4, creating the first cluster. Step 4 could be introduced as a separate step before being incorporated into the cluster of 2, 3, and 4.

Teacher: I'll show you fractions you're going to reduce later. When you reduce fractions, you count by the bottom number.

    a. What's the bottom number of this fraction?
    b. What's the top number of this fraction?
    c. Touch the number you're going to count by.

Another cluster is formed from steps 1, 6, and 7. Although step 1 is not juxtaposed with step 6 in the complete routine, it is needed to make 6 and 7 clear. Step 1 is a rule that precedes a correlated-feature sequence:

Teacher: Listen. If you can say the top number when counting by the bottom number, the fraction reduced to a whole number.

Listen again: If you say the top number when counting by the bottom number, what do you know about the fraction?

After the learner is firm on the rule, the teacher presents a series of correlated-feature examples (Figure 19.6). The sequence contains the exact wording of steps 6 and 7. And the learner's responses are the same as those called for by steps 6 and 7.

Figure 19.6	
Example	Teacher Wording
	I'll tell you about each of these fractions. You tell me if the fractions reduce to whole number.
$\frac{25}{6}$	You don't say the top number of this fraction when counting by the bottom number. So what do you know about this fraction?...How do you know it doesn't reduce?
$\frac{24}{6}$	You say the top number of this fraction when counting by the bottom number. So what do you know about this fraction?...How do you know it reduces?
Etc.	

To make sure that the learner counts by different numbers, we may introduce a cluster that involves step 4 and 5. ("Touch the number you're going to count by . . . Count by that number and see if you say twenty-four.") We assume that the learner already has the counting skills and the skill of telling whether or not a particular number was said when counting.

Figure 19.7 gives a possible schedule that shows the different clusters.

For this routine, only two steps are taught as single-step tasks–steps 1 and 4. The teaching for each occurs on only one lesson. Following that lesson, the skill is incorporated into a cluster.

This pattern of introduction is only one of many possible patterns. However, it illustrates the common strategy, which is to create clusters of *juxtaposed steps* that are the same, (or nearly the same) as the steps that will appear in the final routine. We should create clusters for long routines, usually those with more than six steps. In some cases, we may not be able to use the exact wording that appears in the final routine. In other cases, we may

Figure 19.7						
Components	Lessons					
	1	2	3	4	5	6
Steps 1	X					
2						
3						
4		X				
5						
6						
7						
Cluster	2,3	2,3	2,3,4			
Cluster		1,6,7	1,6,7			
Cluster		5	4,5			
Routine				X	X	X

decide to create a cluster that consists of steps that will not be juxtaposed in the final routine (as we did with 1, 6 and 7). If we make the latter decision, we should have strong logical grounds for creating the cluster. Also, the cluster should contain *at least two steps that will be juxtaposed in the routine.*

Scheduling Examples In The Routine

The routine, or a cluster that presents part of the routine, is an initial-teaching tool. Like other initial-teaching tools, it processes examples.

1. The set of examples must show the *range of variation* that the learner is expected to understand, and show how all applications of the routine within this range are the *same*.

2. The set of examples must show how *differences* in the examples cause differences in the outcome or responses.

3. The set of examples must provide an adequate *test* of the learner's mastery of the operation that is being taught.

Another parallel exists between the cognitive routine and other initial-teaching sequences. Since routines are designed to establish initial teaching, they present a context that is very controlled–one that provides minimum noise and maximum direction. Routines are therefore susceptible to the same problems we observe in other initial teaching procedures. If the routine is retained too long, stipulation misrules may result. The learner may become too dependent on the teacher's direction for initiating the steps. The routine, therefore, must be dropped or changed as soon as it has done its job. The routine should not be dropped, however, until an appropriate range of examples has been processed.

Below are the five procedural rules for ordering and designing the examples of a routine:

1. We generally construct the *same sequence of examples* that would be presented through basic teaching sequences.

2. We present examples that could be failed because of difficult responses near the end of the sequence of examples.

3. We show subtypes (the range of variation within the positive examples) as early in the sequence as possible.

4. We process minor "exceptions" through the routine if such processing violates conventions or idioms, but does not affect the operation or discrimination.

5. If there are major subtypes that cannot be processed through the routine, we introduce examples of the subtype early, possibly as negative examples.

Samenesses and Differences

Cognitive routines show differences and samenesses. To show differences, we follow the same rule of juxtaposition that we use when dealing with discriminations: juxtapose examples that are minimally different and respond to them differently. Similarly, the routine must convey information about sameness. To show this sameness, we follow the rule of juxtaposing examples that differ greatly. *By using the same steps to approach each example, we treat examples in the same way.* When greatly different examples are juxtaposed, we show that we treat them in the same way, thereby showing that the examples are the same.

Since we have the same basic concerns with the examples processed through a routine or cluster that we have for examples processed through a discrimination sequence, we pattern the sequence of examples for a routine after the sequences for more basic forms. Most routines are single-transformation discriminations, in that the learner produces different "answers" for different examples. (The learner reads different words, or figures out different answers, in response to the same basic set of steps.) Therefore, the most frequent patterns of ordering examples for a routine require starting with mid-range examples and introducing progressively arranged minimum differences at the beginning of the sequence, followed by larger differences near the end of the sequence.

Some routines have conditional parts. The specific steps the learner takes depends on a choice-response discrimination. If one outcome occurs, the learner proceeds one way. If another outcome occurs, a different set of steps follows. For these routines, the choice-response pattern of juxtaposition is generally most appropriate. One contingency is treated as the "positive" outcome; the other becomes the "negative." The sequence of examples follows the familiar form used for comparatives and non-comparatives: NNPPPN or PPPNNP with minimum difference negatives and a range of positive variation.

Following the examples that show sameness and difference is a set of examples that test the learner. The test juxtaposition used for the basic discrimination sequences is appropriate for routines. Examples are juxtaposed so that no relationship is obvious from one example to the next. The examples require the learner to use the information provided through the earlier examples. A set of examples for a routine provides an adequate test if the set requires the learner to work juxtaposed examples that differ greatly from each other.

As a general rule, 12 to 14 examples of the routine are needed to teach the procedure and to provide an adequate test. For more sophisticated learners and for routines that have relatively few steps, as few as 5 or 6 examples may be adequate. For routines that require a large number of steps or responses that are elaborate, as many as 30 or 40 examples may be needed. Also, a large number of examples is needed if only a few applications of a routine are presented during a session. Generally, however, the learner should be considered firm after performing successfully on 3 or 4 consecutive applications. The test segment should, therefore, be 5 to 7 examples long.

Examples with Difficult Responses

In a production-response sequence, examples that call for difficult responses are presented near the end of the sequence. The sequence first permits the learner to concentrate on the features that control the discrimination in a relatively easy context. After the learner has performed in this context, the context is made more difficult by introducing examples that demand more difficult responses. If the learner fails these examples after performing successfully on examples that present only modest response difficulty, we know that the learner's problem has to do with the response production, and we work on response production—not on the discrimination. If the responses that call for difficult responses are placed earlier in the sequence, however (before we have received a demonstration that the learner can handle relatively easy examples), we do not know how to interpret the failure of a learner. Perhaps the learner has trouble producing the response. Perhaps the learner does not understand the discrimination being taught.

Cognitive routines are governed by the same considerations as the sequence. By placing the difficult-response examples near the end of the sequence, after the learner has performed on a series of examples that involve relatively simple responses, we limit what the learner has to learn when working on these difficult-responses and we increase the information that we receive about the learner's performance.

A routine for figuring out how many minutes after the hour the clock shows requires the learner to start at zero and count by fives for each number until reaching the minute hand. The response for figuring out 55 minutes after the hour is far more elaborate than the response for determining 20 minutes after the hour. We would therefore sequence the examples so that the learner dealt with a range of examples not much more difficult than 20 minutes after (15 minutes, 25 minutes, 10) before we introduced examples that were as difficult as 55 minutes after. Similarly, if we were teaching single-syllable words that ended in consonant-vowel-consonant, we would not include **splat** or **strip** at the beginning of the sequence, because the initial consonant combinations in these words make the decoding far more difficult than that for words like **lat** and **rip**. The less elaborate words would therefore occur early in the sequence and **splat** and **strip** would occur near the end, after the learner had demonstrated ability to handle words that involved easier responses.

The Range

We want to show the range of variation as early as possible in the sequence of examples; however, this procedure must be considered in connection with placing the difficult responses at the end of the sequence. The examples that *do not involve difficult responses* should be designed so that they show a fair range of variation early in the sequence. If the routine deals with fractions, the early examples should include those that involve single-digit numbers, letters, and combinations of letters and numbers. If simple, regular words are introduced, early examples should include vowel-consonant words, consonant-vowel-consonant words, consonant-vowel words, and possibly consonant-vowel-consonant-consonant words.

It is not always necessary to show every subtype of example that is to be taught. If the examples include a fair variety of types that can be processed through the routine, the set of examples *implies* that types not shown may also be processed through the same routine. Let's say that this set of examples is presented to teach carrying:

```
   23         24                      67
    4          4         23            1
 + 17       + 17       + 17          + 4
```

```
              781       5234          28
   236          9        432          34
 + 918      + 505      + 306        + 44
```

All problems involve carrying to the tens column only. Therefore, the routine used to process these problems should not run too long. However, if we were to specify every type of problem in which carrying occurs in the ones column, we would find that the set shows only a few of the possible types. The set does not show problems that involve adding four numbers, five numbers, six numbers, twenty numbers, and so forth. However, the range of variation is sufficient to imply a generalization to types not shown because they are not generically different from the types shown. We can state this sort of extrapolation as a general rule: *If* the same operation is contingent on a feature of the examples, and *if* the feature is demonstrated across a set of examples that shows some variation, the operation is implied for the full range of examples.

This rule is a restatement of the double-transformation principle. We do not have to teach the entire transformed set. The carrying operation is the standard transformation. The familiar set is the non-carrying problems the learner has worked. If we show the "transformation" with a fair range of examples, we assure generalization. The procedure that we should follow is to show as much variation in examples as we can reasonably process through the routine without violating the constraints imposed by showing samenesses and differences and by withholding examples that call for difficult responses.

Scheduling Limited Generalizations

We have referred to the teaching of irregular words and irregular notations for decoding numerals. Irregulars occur in other areas that involve sets of symbols. From the standpoint of teaching, irregulars imply that *the generalizations the learner is taught must be limited to some arbitrarily designated members.* For an arbitrary reason, **14** is pronounced "fourteen," but **11** is not pronounced "oneteen." The word that is spelled **chef** is pronounced as if it is spelled **shef**. Despite these limiting examples, a generalization is possible for most of the teen numbers and a different generalization is possible for most words spelled with the letters *ch*.

Three instructional design problems are associated with limited generalizations:

1. Teaching the generalization for the *large set* (the regularly-spelled words or the regularly-pronounced numerals).

2. *Teaching the negative examples for this large-set generalization* (irregulars).

3. Teaching negatives early enough to alert the learner to the fact that the generalization for the larger set does *not* apply to all examples.

If we introduce the negatives of the generalizations early, they serve as advance organizers that alert the learner to the fact that the generalization is not universal. For the decoding of irregularly-spelled words like **was**, the strategy would be to apply the routine for 15 to 40 regularly-spelled words and then introduce a new routine for irregularly-spelled words.

For other limited generalizations, however, we can introduce the negatives for the limited generalizations earlier, even before the routine for the limited generalization is introduced. Our guide for introducing the negatives is the similarity of the routines for processing the positives and negatives. If the routine for the negatives is not highly similar to that for the positives, the negatives can be introduced even before the positives. If the routine for handling negatives is highly similar to that for positives, a range of positives should be introduced through the routine before the negatives are introduced through its routine. The latter situation occurs with decoding, which is why the routine for regular words is presented before the routine for irregulars. The routine for irregulars involves many of the same steps involved in decoding regularly-spelled words. The learner sounds out the word and says something fast. The difference is that what the learner says fast is not the sum of the regular letter sounds. The sounds are transformed somewhat (which is the only difference between regularly-spelled words and irregularly-spelled words).

It might seem that decoding irregular words could be introduced before regulars if we make the routines different. The regulars would be "sounded out" while the irregulars might be introduced as "sight words." The problem with this analysis is that the learner has *no direct way of knowing whether a word is a sight word.* Every word is a group of letters. If the learner knows how a particular word *is pronounced*, the learner knows whether or not it is irregular. But the learner is not given information about how to pronounce the word. The learner is simply presented with a group of letters. The decision about how to pronounce the word must therefore be based on the arrangement of these letters. And it is impossible for the learner to identify whether the word is irregular until after the learner attends to the arrangement of the letters. (The only difference between *said*, which is irregular, and *sad*, which is regular, is a difference in a single letter.) Unless the routine for irregulars points out the arrangement of letters, the routine will not convey information about the features that distinguish a particular irregular from other words. However, if the routine for irregulars deals with the individual letters in a word and their order, the routine will be highly similar to the routine for regular words. This routine should be delayed until the learner has mastered the routines for regulars.

Spelling words with e-a. Spelling words presents a situation quite different from that of decoding words. Negatives for limited generalizations can frequently be introduced very early because they can be processed through a routine not highly similar to that for the positives. To avoid confusing spelling problems with decoding problems, we must remain sensitive to the context of spelling. The learner is presented with a *verbal word* and indicates the symbols for that particular sound pattern. Generalizations are often possible because a particular sound (such as the **f** sound) may reliably signal a particular spelling. The generalization that is possible for some other sounds is more limited. For instance, the /ĕ/ sound that occurs in words like **head** is spelled with the letters **e-a**. The /ĕ/ sound in other words, however, is spelled with a single **e** (**red**). The two groups of words present the same /ĕ/ sound but call for different behavior.

A second problem exists because the *response of spelling with the letter **e** or with the letters **ea** is not limited to words that have the sound /ĕ/*. Words like **meal** and **me** are spelled with the same letters that occur in the spellings for /ĕ/ words (**head** and **met**).

Here is a summary of the major subtypes associated with the short-**e** sound:

- For some words, the sound /ĕ/ leads to spelling with **e**.
- For some words, the sound /ĕ/ leads to spelling with **ea**.
- For some words, the sound /not-ĕ/ leads to spelling with **e**.
- For some words, the sound /not-ĕ/ leads to spelling with **ea**.

The generalization problem is complicated, but is basically the same as that for decoding examples. If we wait too long before alerting the learner that the four possibilities exist, we may induce serious misgeneralizations. The learner *may* come to believe that any word with the sound /ĕ/ spelled **ea**, and that no word with a /not-ĕ/ sound is spelled **ea**.

We can introduce some negatives before we introduce the generalization for spelling /ĕ/ words with **ea** because we can present a unique context for the negatives. Let's say that we wish to teach the spelling of words like **head, instead, bread, tread**, etc. Before we present the routine for spelling these words, we introduce several words that contain the sound /ĕ/, but that are spelled differently (**bed, met, send**, etc.) We also introduce words spelled with **ea** that do not make the sound /ĕ/ (**meat, seal**). We teach these token negatives in a sentence such as: *Her letter was ten years late.* By memorizing the spelling of words in this sentence, the learner learns that the sound /ĕ/ can be spelled with the single letter (in the words **letter** and **ten**); that the letter **e** does not always produce the sound /ĕ/ (**late** and **her**); and that the letters **ea** may be pronounced as /ē/ (**years**). After the sentence has been memorized, we can introduce the routine for processing words that make the sound /ĕ/ spelled with **ea**.

Although we do not introduce many negatives, we introduce enough to assure that the learner will approach the words **bread, instead**, etc., with a perspective about their sounds and spelling. Furthermore, the sentence presents a context that is different enough to militate against confusion. The sentence is treated as an event. The words occur only in the context of this event until the spelling has been highly stipulated. Then the words are integrated with other words that have been taught.

In summary, it is possible to inform the learner about the limits of generalizations before serious misrules have been induced. If a generalization is limited, some negatives (perhaps only a few "token" negatives), should be introduced as early as possible. If the routine for processing the negatives is highly similar to that for positives, the positives should be firmed first. If there is a reasonable way of presenting the negatives through a routine that is quite different from the routine for the positives, the negatives can be introduced quite early, perhaps before the positives are presented.

The test for sets that involve limited generalizations involves two questions:

1. Does the same symbol or feature call for one type of response in some examples and another type of response in other examples?

2. Does a different symbol or feature call for the *response* associated with the symbol or feature under consideration?

If the answer to either question is "Yes," negatives for the generalization are implied. We should try to design the routines for these negatives at the same time we design the routine for the positives. If there is doubt about the extent to which the very early introduction of negatives may interfere with the teaching for the positives, we can delay the introduction of the negatives until at least some positives are firm. Another possibility, that of regularizing the examples through prompts, is presented in Chapter 20.

Scheduling Routines with Conditional Parts

Special identification and sequencing problems occur when routines have conditional parts. As the name suggests, a conditional part is a part that occurs only under certain conditions. The part of a routine that deals with the carrying operation occurs only under certain conditions–the total of a column adding up to more than 9. Similarly, steps that follow when the trial answer in a division problem is too large occur only under certain conditions (the answer being tried is too large).

Applications that involve conditional parts are a subtype of all the applications for the routine. The conditional-part routine is not totally different from the non-conditional routine. In fact, the routines are identical until they reach the point where the conditional outcome occurs.

If we tried to introduce both the conditional-part routine and the non-conditional-part routine at the same time, the schedule might not be well-designed to teach either the non-conditional or the conditional operation. Therefore, we firm the non-conditional routine first, then introduce the conditional part. We try to schedule examples so that we do not induce stipulation by working too long on the non-conditional routine and so that the learner is reasonably firm on the non-conditional routine before the conditional routine is introduced.

Structure of Conditional Parts

All conditional parts work in the same way. A key discrimination determines whether or not the conditional steps are to be taken. If a specific condition occurs, the conditional operation is performed. If it does not occur, the non-conditional operation is followed.

In dealing with the conditional parts, we answer two questions:

1. What detail or feature of the problem tells us that the learner must take the conditional steps?
2. What are these conditional steps?

The first question involves a discrimination. Often, the discrimination can be communicated to the learner as a correlated-feature relationship: If **X** happens, you do **Y**. The second question implies a descriptive rule, derived by the same procedure used for other cognitive operations.

The most efficient strategy for introducing contingent parts is to: (1) work on the discrimination that keys the conditional part, and (2) chain a *shortened version* of the original routine with the discrimination *and the contingent part.*

Illustration. Let's say that we have already taught the learner column-addition problems involving no-carrying. We now introduce the *discrimination* for **carrying** (if the answer in a column is more than 9, you carry the tens). The discrimination is expressed as a correlated-feature relationship. Figure 19.8 illustrates a possible sequence.

Figure 19.8	
Example	Teacher Wording
35 + 24	What's the answer in the ones column? (9) My turn: Do we carry? No. How do I know? Because the answer is not more than 9.
35 + 25	What's the answer in the ones column? (10) My turn: Do we carry? Yes. How do I know? Because the answer is more than 9.
35 + 29	What's the answer in the ones column? (14) Your turn: Do you carry? (Yes.) How do you know? (Because the answer is more than 9.)
39 + 29	What's the answer in the ones column? (18) Do you carry? (Yes.) How do you know? (Because the answer is more than 9.
39 + 20	What's the answer in the ones column? (9) Do you carry? (No.) How do you know? (Because the answer is not more than 9.)

The question, "What's the answer?" is added to the two correlated-feature questions to assure that the learner produces the correct answer. The examples are designed after the negative-first choice-response sequence.

The sequence in Figure 19.9 deals with the mechanical problems of writing an answer to the ones column that is more than nine. The steps that take place before the carrying operation are minimized.

Additional examples involving teen answers would probably be needed because the name of these numbers does not indicate how many tens they contain.

Also, examples that involve no-carrying could be presented through the routine shown in Figure 19.10.

Section VI | Constructing Cognitive Routines

Figure 19.9

Example	Teacher Wording
38 46 + 29	The answer in the ones column is 23. How many tens in 23? So we write 2 in the tens column and 3 in the ones column (teacher demonstrates).
39 46 + 29	The answer in the ones column is 24. How many tens in 24? So what do you write in the tens column? And what do you write in the ones column?…Do it.
39 46 + 20	The answer in the ones column is 15. How many tens in 15? So what do you write in the tens column?…Do it.
9 39 49 + 29	The answer in the ones column is 36. How many tens in 36? So what do you write in the tens column?…And what do you write in the ones column?…Do it.

Figure 19.10

Example	Teacher Wording
37 41 + 24	The answer in the ones column is 8. How many tens in 8? (None.) So what do you write in the tens column? (Nothing.) And what do you write in the ones column? (Eight.)

Following the teaching of the discrimination and of the routine for the conditional part, we could introduce a routine that involves application of the discrimination and the new step. For this routine, the learner performs the *discrimination* in all problems, but works only the problems that involve carrying (Figure 19.11).

Figure 19.11

Example	Teacher Wording
29 + 48	You'll work only the problems that involve carrying. What's the answer in the ones column? Do you carry? How do you know? Write the answer in the tens column and the ones column.
69 + 99	What's the answer in the ones column? Do you carry? How do you know? Write the answer in the tens column and the ones column.

Once the learner has successfully performed on the discrimination and on the procedures for writing an answer that is more than ten, very little additional teaching remains for the contingent part. The learner must be reminded to "Add everything in the tens column, starting with the one ten that you carried." However, beyond this prompt the remaining steps are the same as those for the regular addition problem.

The schedule in Figure 19.12 shows the different activities for carrying.

Figure 19.12

Components	Lessons								
	1	2	3	4	5	6	7	8
1. No carrying routine								
2. Discrimination (Carrying, no carrying)	X	X						
3. Steps for carrying		X	X					
4. Combination discriminations and carrying				X	X			
Worksheet applications for	1	1 2	1 2	3 2	4	4	1-4	1-4

This schedule does not show the teaching of the no-carrying routine (1). This routine had been taught earlier and is reviewed through worksheet applications on lessons 1, 2 and 3. Note that the discrimination (2) appears on worksheets starting with lesson 2 and continues through lesson 4. The routine for determining whether carrying is involved and for carrying out the operation is presented on lessons 4 and 5.

The rate of introduction for the conditional part could be accelerated. However, the same progression would be followed. This discrimination would come first, followed by the operation. The worksheet exercise would be introduced early and would continue until the learner was quite proficient at using the routine.

A schedule similar to the one for carrying is appropriate for different conditional-part routines. First, the original routine is firmed. Then the conditional part is taught (discrimination and procedures) and the non-conditional operation is applied to worksheet exercises or to review items. When the learner is firm on the conditional operation, the types are integrated in a way that is modeled after a double transformation program (see Chapter 13). The final integration is a mix of problems with non-conditional parts and problems with conditional parts.

(In the schedule above, this integration is referred to as worksheet applications 1-4 on lessons 7 and 8.)

Illustration: Over-estimating answers in long division. One conditional part in a long division routine deals with a trial number in the answer that is too large. The discrimination is based on details of the partially-worked problem.

$$33 \overline{)211} \begin{array}{c} 7 \\ \hline 231 \end{array}$$

The number in the answer is too large because 231 is larger than the number above it (211).

The discrimination can be expressed as a correlated-feature relationship: If the number subtracted is bigger than the number above it, the number in the answer is too large. This rule is involved, but manageable. (See Figure 19.13.)

Figure 19.13	
Example	Teacher Wording
$30\overline{)211} \begin{array}{c} 7 \\ \hline -210 \end{array}$	The 7 in the answer is not too big. How do I know? Because 7 x 30 is *not* more than 211.
$31\overline{)211} \begin{array}{c} 7 \\ \hline -217 \end{array}$	The 7 in the answer is too big. How do I know? Because 7 x 31 *is* more than 211.
$57\overline{)211} \begin{array}{c} 4 \\ \hline -228 \end{array}$	The 4 in the answer is too big. How do I know
Etc.	
Additional steps may be included in the routine to make sure that the learner knows how much 4 x 57 or 7 x 31 equal.	
$57\overline{)211} \begin{array}{c} 4 \\ \hline -228 \end{array}$	What number is the answer? (4) What does 4 x 57 equal? (228) Is the 4 in the answer too big? (Yes.) How do you know? (228 is bigger than 211.)

The steps for the conditional part involve making the number in the answer smaller and multiplying it to see if the smaller number works. Figure 19.14 shows a routine for the conditional part.

The routine in Figure 19.14 does not deal with the discrimination of whether the answer is too big–merely with the steps involved in the conditional part. We would next present a routine that involves the discrimination *and* the steps for carrying out the contingent part if the answer is too large. A possible strategy would require the learner to work a series of problems in which the

Figure 19.14	
Example	Teacher Wording
$31\overline{)216} \begin{array}{c} 7 \\ \hline -217 \end{array}$	The number in the answer is too big, so we erase the number we are subtracting and the number in the answer. We write a number that is smaller in the answer, then we multiply. (Teacher demonstrates):
$31\overline{)216} \begin{array}{c} 6 \\ \hline 186 \\ \hline 30 \end{array}$	
$31\overline{)216} \begin{array}{c} 7 \\ \hline 217 \end{array}$	(Teacher returns to original problem.) Your turn: The number in the answer is too big. So what do you erase? And what number do you write in the answer? Do it. Now what do you do? (Multiply.) Do it.

answers would follow the positives-first pattern: P, P, P, N, N, P. The first five problems might be:

$$29\overline{)568} \begin{array}{c}2\\ \hline -58\end{array} \quad 31\overline{)188} \begin{array}{c}6\\ \hline -186\end{array} \quad 56\overline{)505} \begin{array}{c}9\\ \hline -504\end{array} \quad 56\overline{)503} \begin{array}{c}9\\ \hline -504\end{array} \quad 31\overline{)180} \begin{array}{c}6\\ \hline -186\end{array}$$

Following the variation above, a similar sequence of problems that give only the answer could be presented:

Example	Teacher Wording
$56\overline{)505} \begin{array}{c} 9 \end{array}$	Is the number in the answer too big? How do you know? (If it is too big:) What do you do? Do it.

We could use a variation that requires the learner to, "First circle all the problems with answers that are too big." After the learner has circled these problems, we ask, "How do you know the answer is too big in this problem? . . . So what do you do? . . ." The learner then works these problems. When this procedure is used, the spatial juxtaposition of the problems is not as important as it is for the other procedure. The reason is that the learner "groups" the positive examples of over-estimated numbers by circling all examples. Regardless of their positioning on the page, these problems are juxtaposed when they are worked.

Figure 19.15 shows a schedule for the activities involved in teaching the conditional part.

The answer is written for each worksheet problem. When working independently, the learner marks or indicates problems in which the number in the answer is too large. The learner works on the conditional part by crossing out the number in the answer and the number subtracted. The learner then replaces the number in the answer, multiplies by the new number, and subtracts to verify that the new number is not too big.

Figure 19.15					
Components	Lessons				
	1	2	3	4	5
A. Problems that do not involve over-estimation					
B. Discrimination	X	X			
C. Contingent part			X	X	
D. Combination				X	X
E. Worksheet	A	A,B	C	A,D	D

The development of conditional parts presents nothing that is generically new. Some particular feature or detail of the problem keys the contingent behavior. We can identify that detail and we can design a communication that teaches it. Furthermore, we can design the communication so that we achieve relatively efficient juxtaposition of events. Juxtapositions are more efficient if we can shorten the chain of behavior and give the learner repeated practice on "doing the same thing." This axiom translates into abbreviated routines. First, we work with the discrimination that keys the conditional part. Then we chain the discrimination to the routine for the conditional part, requiring the learner to identify whether the conditional routine is called for and to work problems that require the conditional routine. When the learner is facile with this abbreviated routine, we can introduce the entire routine and require the learner to work all problems. We integrate the types (the conditional-part routine and the non-conditional part routine). First we block examples; then we disperse examples of the two types. Now the discrimination is both firm and integrated within the context of the problem types that call for the discrimination.

Summary

Strategies for scheduling of component skills, for presenting examples of cognitive routines, and for dealing with conditional parts of routines can be largely explained with reference to basic instructional-design procedures.

Component skills that are brought together in a routine can be viewed as members of a set and scheduled accordingly. They are introduced through an initial teaching sequence, reviewed, and integrated with other skills that have been taught.

The routine is an initial teaching tool, designed to acquaint the learner with a procedure that is to be applied to a range of examples. Sequencing examples of a routine initial teaching sequence for basic-form discriminations.

Examples should show the range of variation, should show how differences in the examples lead to specific differences in the response, and should provide an adequate test. Examples that require difficult responses should either be eliminated from the initial presentations or should be included at the end of the example sequence—appearing after the learner has demonstrated mastery of the routine with simpler examples.

To avoid stipulation for routines that deal with "limited generalizations," the negative examples should be introduced early. (Irregulars should be presented early enough to assure that the learner does not overgeneralize that all examples will be regular.)

The procedures for dealing with conditional parts of routines derive primarily from concerns over juxtaposition of steps. We encounter the same problem with long routines. If the routine is very long, it is not well-designed to stipulate the various steps or to provide practice for those steps that may be troublesome. We first teach the non-conditional routine. Teaching the conditional part involves introducing: (1) a discrimination, and (2) a conditional routine.

The schedule of events for the conditional routine first introduces the discrimination that triggers the contingent steps, then introduces the steps for dealing with the conditional part.

Conditional parts present one of the most elaborate programming forms that we use in communicating with the learner. The conditional part must be coordinated with the non-conditional routine.

Despite the complexity of the routine with conditional parts, this design problem presents very little that is new. The types of discriminations processed through these routines admit to the same analysis that serves us in other design situations. The procedures for introducing members to a set, providing initial teaching, reviewing discriminations, and expanding them, are common to the procedures used for many more basic communication forms.

Chapter 20
Prompting Examples

A prompt of an example is a detail that is added to an *example* so that relevant features of the example are more obvious than they are in the unprompted example. A prompt is used only for initial teaching and is then removed. (Verbal instructions are not prompts of the examples as we use the term.)

The form of a routine depends on whether the examples are prompted. If the word-reading examples are prompted with an arrow that runs under each word, showing the direction in which the word is to be decoded, the routine can refer to the arrow. If no arrow exists, the routine must change. The routine could still refer to the "starting point" of the word, because the word still possesses the feature of having a "left letter" or the one that produces the first sound. The arrow simply adds details that make the starting point more obvious.

All prompted examples work in basically the same way as the arrow. They provide details that increase differences. Both ends of a word may look the same to the naive learner. With the addition of the arrow, however, one end looks discriminably different from the other:

$$\bullet\text{-}\text{-}\underline{if}\text{-}\text{-}\rightarrow$$

The letters **b** and **d** are highly similar because they are the same object with different orientations. A prompt can create additional discriminable differences between the letters.

b d **b d**

unprompted one-feature difference   prompted four-feature difference

The two basic assumptions underlying prompting are:

1. Prompted examples are easier because they make the relevant features of the prompted example more obvious (increasing the probability that the learner will attend to some relevant detail of the prompted example.)
2. After prompts have been removed, the learner will perform with the unprompted example.

Difference Prompts and Sameness Prompts

There are two generically different types of situations in which prompting is appropriate. One deals with *difference* between examples of a particular type and examples that are minimally different. (The **b-d** discrimination is an illustration of this type.) The other type deals with *sameness*. The purpose of the sameness prompt is to show the learner something that is the same (but possibly not obvious) about all the examples that will be dealt with. The arrow under the word illustrates this type of prompt. All words are read from left to right, and the arrow prompts this common feature. Different procedures are used for analyzing, designing, and fading the two types of prompts.

Difference Prompts

These prompts are used to create a greater difference between minimally different examples. As the description of the **b-d** examples indicates, the prompt increases the number of features that are different. Therefore, the prompt increases the probability that the learner will attend to *some* difference between the examples. If there is only one difference between the positives and negatives, the learner must attend to that difference. If four differences are present, the learner may reliably discriminate between the examples by attending to any of the four differences or any combination of the differences.

For difference prompting, we prompt only those features of the example that are relevant to the *discrimination*. The features that are relevant to the discrimination are those that are different between the positive examples and the negative examples. To determine which features are different, we juxtapose a positive example (for which a prompt is being considered) with a negative that is minimally different. The difference between the two examples is the only feature that should be prompted.

If we were interested in designing a prompt for adding fractions that would alert the learner not to add the bottom numbers, we would create an example of a fraction-addition problem and juxtapose it with a fraction multiplication problem that has the same numbers. These examples are minimally different.

$$\frac{4}{3} + \frac{6}{3} =$$

$$\frac{4}{3} \times \frac{6}{3} =$$

The features that are *different* across these two examples *are the features that are relevant to the discrimination of addition and multiplication of fractions.* The only difference is the sign; therefore, the only element that should be prompted is the sign.

If we modify the signs so they are more greatly different from each other, we create no misrule problem. If we prompt any other elements of the problem, however, *we create a situation in which the learner can solve the problem by attending to the irrelevant details of the problem, not the relevant ones.* We could create an inappropriate prompt for the discrimination of addition and multiplication by using two types of numerals as prompts:

$$\frac{4}{3} + \frac{6}{3} =$$

$$\frac{4}{3} \times \frac{6}{3} =$$

Only the top numbers in the addition problem are italic. Therefore, the learner operates only on the top (by adding).

Both top and bottom numbers in the multiplication problem are italic. Therefore, the learner operates on both the top and the bottom of this problem (by multiplying across the top and multiplying across the bottom).

The spurious nature of the prompt can be determined by simply answering the question, "Would it be possible for the learner to discriminate between prompted multiplication and addition problems without ever attending to the detail of the example that is relevant to the discrimination (the signs)?" The answer is "Yes." The learner could develop the strategy of simply finding the bold numerals and operating on these numerals. In this case, the prompt is a success if we look only at the learner's performance on the prompted examples. When we remove the prompts, however, we will certainly find that some learners will be unable to perform, because they were never required to attend to the relevant difference between the two types of problems. A number of appropriate prompts are possible with the signs of the problem. Below is a pair of prompted signs.

$$\frac{4}{3} \uparrow\!\!\!\!\!\rightarrow \frac{3}{3} =$$

$$\frac{4}{3} \times\!\!\!\!\nearrow \frac{3}{3} =$$

The addition sign shows that you operate only on the top. The multiplication sign points to the top and to the bottom, indicating that you must multiply on both top and bottom. These signs are simple modifications of the already-existing signs. Some features have been added to direct the learner. The learner, however, *must look at the sign to find the prompt.* The learner is therefore attending to the element that is relevant to the discrimination. After the prompts have been removed, the unprompted element still provides hints that were made more salient by the prompted signs. The unprompted addition sign has only one bar that points to the following fraction, while the times sign has bars that point to top and bottom. This prompt, while not essential to teach the discrimination of multiplication and addition of fractions, is not as potentially dangerous as a prompt that makes the *irrelevant* features of the example more salient or discriminable.

Spurious prompts may be created for many types of cognitive knowledge. We could prompt the naive, non-reading learner to read color words by printing each word in the color that the word names (presenting the word **red** in red, the word **yellow** in yellow, etc.). A comparison of the word **yellow** and any word that is minimally different discloses that the relevant difference between the word has to do with the letters:

yellow

yeller

The color prompt, therefore, permits the learner to identify the word by attending to features that are irrelevant to the discrimination of **yellow** and any other word. Just as the learner who is provided with the irrelevant prompt for adding fractions might work every problem correctly without attending to the part of the example that is relevant to the discrimination, the naive reader is provided with the option of "reading" every word correctly without attending to the details of the word that are relevant to the discrimination. (Even if we "fade" the prompt out, so that a word like **yellow** is primarily black with only tiny flecks of yellow, the learner is still provided with an irrelevant prompt.) When we remove all prompts, the prediction would be that a fair percentage of naive readers would call every color word, "black."

The procedure for analyzing discriminated features that may be prompted is to juxtapose examples of the type that is to be discriminated with minimally-different negative examples. The difference between the positives and negatives indicates the features that may be prompted.

The assumption of prompting or exaggerating the difference is that once appropriate behavior has been established with the prompted example, the learner will attend to other features, including the features that are relevant to the unprompted examples. Therefore:

1. The relevant features of the unprompted examples must be present in the prompted counterpart.

2. The teaching of the prompted examples must be designed so that the learner attends to the features that are relevant to the unprompted example.

3. The transition from prompted to unprompted examples must be executed to assure that the learner attends to relevant features.

Difference prompts must take the form of additions or simple transformations, not substitutions. We cannot replace **d** with a symbol such as ♂. While the learner may have little difficulty discriminating between **b** and ♂, the new symbol is not a variation of **d** and does not have the features of **d**; therefore, the symbol does not serve well as a prompt. It requires initial learning (identifying the symbol) which proves to be dead-end learning when the transition occurs and the symbol **d** is introduced. The prompted example **ď** has all the parts of the unprompted example. The shape has simply been transformed somewhat to create difference.

Teaching with prompted examples. If the learner does not attend to the features of the example that will be present when the example is no longer prompted, the learner will not recognize the unprompted example. We must assure that this does not happen. One teaching procedure that requires attention to the features of examples that will remain relevant involves *pairing* juxtaposed prompted and unprompted examples. For instance, the learner may be required to trace sentences that do not use the prompted letter **d**.

his dad dug

Note that the dotted letters show the conventional **d**. The learner first reads the sentence above (with prompted **d**'s), then traces the sentence and *reads* the traced sentence. When performing this last step, *the learner is actually reading unprompted orthography.*

Other discrimination tasks could include:

d d **d** d **d** d

Teacher: "Look at the **d**'s. Two of them look more like **b**'s. Circle those **d**'s."

This task alerts the learner to the idea that although the objects are still labeled **d**, they differ somewhat from those with which the learner is familiar. The task can be dangerous for low performers because it calls attention to **b** and possibly prompts a spurious transformation. This problem could be avoided if the teacher circled one of the conventional **d**'s and told the learner, "Circle all the **d**'s that look like this **d**."

Transition to unprompted examples. The transition for a difference prompt should occur: (1) after the learner has developed some fluency using the prompted examples, but (2) before the prompted examples become so heavily stipulated that the learner has trouble with the unprompted examples.

As a rule, the difference prompts should be retained until the learner has become reasonably facile with the prompted examples, but has not attained a "high" criterion of performance. As soon as the behavior has been reliably established, we should provide a transition to unprompted examples.

Sameness Prompts

The prompting procedures that we have outlined apply to types of examples that are to be discriminated from other types. In some cases, however, we are interested in prompting common features, not those that are different. Both the analysis of sameness features and the procedures for prompting them are different from those used for discriminated features.

If the feature is the *same* across all examples the learner will encounter, the feature may be prompted by *creating a detail that has no counterpart in the unprompted examples.* As noted earlier, a common feature of all examples of reading words is the left-to-right progression. There are no examples in which the learner reads from right to left. Since this left-to-right orientation is common to all examples the learner will work with, we may create a prompt that has no counterpart in the unprompted examples. For instance, we may create an arrow under the word:

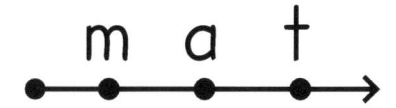

$$\underset{\bullet\quad\bullet\quad\bullet\quad\bullet\rightarrow}{m\ a\ t}$$

This prompt provides the learner with a basis for approaching any word. Because the learner's behavior is the same for every word with respect to starting left and proceeding right, the prompt creates no serious problem. After the behavior has been established and is stipulated through many practice trials, the prompt is removed and the behavior will remain (because of the stipulation).

This situation is greatly different from the one in which we prompted the signs in the fraction problems. In creating prompts for the fraction problems, we had to modify each sign so that it was a clear variation of the sign that would occur in the unprompted examples. We were permitted to prompt only the sign because only the sign discriminates the addition and multiplication operations. The word-reading example, on the other hand, involves a feature of the examples that is common to all examples. The function of the prompt is not to call attention to a detail that may be confused with some other detail. Rather, the function is to *stipulate* the common behavior.

Consider working column problems of addition, subtraction, or multiplication. The learner always begins with the ones column. Therefore, it would be perfectly reasonable to create a prompt that makes the ones column different from the other columns.

$$\begin{array}{r} 23 \\ +\ 16 \end{array}$$

Although an analogous prompt (bold digits) would be spurious for prompting the *difference* between adding fractions and multiplying fractions, it is not spurious for the problem above because it deals with an operational feature common to all column problems. We could therefore introduce the bold-digit prompt without running the risk that the learner will develop a misrule. It is not possible for the learner to attend to the prompt without attending to a feature of the example that is relevant to the operation.

Because we are prompting something that is the same for all examples, we are permitted to introduce details that will not appear in the unprompted examples. Therefore, we could use this prompt for the column problems:

$$\begin{array}{r} \downarrow \\ 23 \\ \downarrow \\ +\ 16 \end{array}$$

No serious misrule problem is created.

Teaching with sameness prompts. A general procedure for teaching with sameness prompts involves pointing out the prompt and interpreting it to the learner. When introducing the column problems, the teacher would point out the bold numbers and present this rule: "*You always start with these heavy numbers.* Then you add the other numbers." The fact that the learner performs the operation provides sufficient evidence that the learner is attending to some relevant details of the problems.

Transition to unprompted examples. If the goal of the prompt is to direct the learner to perform some operational step that is the same for all problems, the problem of stipulation is not serious. Therefore, the prompt may be retained longer than a prompt for demonstrating difference between minimally different examples. As a rule, we can retain the sameness prompts until the learner becomes quite facile; however, we may remove them as soon as the learner becomes reliable in performing the operation.

Summary of Prompting Procedures

Prompts may be used to show differences between minimally different examples or used to show operational sameness. The simplest procedure for determining the type of prompt that is appropriate is to juxtapose minimally-different examples. The features that are different between these examples are features that may be prompted through difference prompts. The features that are common to the examples are features that may be prompted with sameness prompts. If the equal sign is a common feature that is relevant to both examples, the equal sign may be prompted in both examples (a sameness prompt). If the two problems have different signs and if this difference is relevant to the operation, the signs may be prompted differentially (a difference prompt).

For difference prompts, we may only modify the unprompted example.

For sameness prompts, we may modify the unprompted example or create a new addition or detail to the example.

For difference prompts, the transition to the unprompted examples must occur as soon as we can practically engineer it.

For sameness prompts, the transition may occur early or may be delayed. The delay will not create a serious stipulation problem.

Prompts and Cognitive Routines

The context in which prompts become most important is the cognitive routine. There are two reasons:

1. Prompts may be used to facilitate the creation of unambiguous overt responses.
2. Prompts may be used to reduce irregular examples.

A cognitive routine works only for examples that have a fixed value and that work in the same way as the other examples processed by the routine. For instance, we can use this routine: "Say the sounds . . . Now say the sounds fast," for decoding words such as **met** and **top**, but not for words such as **me**, and **so**. The letters **e** and **o** make different sounds in the different words.

The solution to this problem that we offered in Chapter 17 involved adjusting the range of application and the descriptive rule until:

1. There was a sufficient amount of overt behavior for the routine.
2. The same behavior worked for every application in the specified range.

If we applied this solution, we would make up a routine that did not apply to words like **go** and **me**. A variant routine would be needed for these examples. The original routine would be retained for words like **met**, **got**, and other short-vowel words.

Another possible solution to the problem of irregular examples is to *use prompts to regularize the symbols*. This solution involves creating new symbols that are prompted. According to the basic procedure for creating prompted elements for differences, we would design them so they are obvious variations of their unprompted counterparts. The letter **e** is the unprompted symbol that will appear in words like **me**. Therefore, the prompted counterpart that we create must be an obvious variation of the unprompted symbol. At the same time, the prompted variations must be clearly different from the unprompted counterparts. For instance, we could create these symbols: **ē** and **ō**. Each would signal the long vowel sound (and only this sound). By adding these symbols to the set, we can use one routine ("Say the sounds . . . Say the sounds fast . . .") for all examples that have long vowels and all examples that have short vowels. Here is the orthography for some words: **gō, sō, mē, bē, met, bell, got, mom**.

We refer to this solution as *regularizing the examples* by creating new prompted examples that will later be dropped.

A problem similar to the decoding problem occurs with numerals. The symbol **1** does not always stand for a value of one. In **103**, it stands for one hundred, while in **310**, it has a value of ten. The value is not obvious from inspection of the symbol. Just as we can assign prompts to make perceptible differences between the various **e**'s we can assign prompts to make perceptible differences between the various **1**'s. By writing **10** in this manner: 1^0, and **100** in this manner: 1^{00}; we can use these symbols when the fixed value **10** or **100** is called for in a problem. We would write **18** as $1^0 8$ and **108** as $1^{00} 8$. The regularized set includes the symbol **1** and these other symbol variations. All prompted **1**'s are highly similar to **1**. Each numeral in the prompted set has a fixed value and always retains this value. The symbol **1⁰** always has the value of ten in the regularized set, never any deviant value.

There are other solutions to the regularizing problem. We could introduce a routine that requires the learner to indicate the number of places and then identify whether the unprompted **1** in the numeral tells about one, one ten, one hundred, etc. For some situations, this solution would be a better choice. For others (particularly those that are designed for relatively naive learners), the prompted variations would present the most efficient solution. In any case, the prompt serves as an alternative approach to dealing with symbolic matter that is not perfectly regular. We can create new examples that are prompted and that may be processed through the same routine that processes the unprompted examples.

In summary, the prompts used with symbol systems:

1. Permit the use of a particular cognitive routine across a much broader range of applications.
2. Eliminate or reduce the number of irregular examples.
3. Create a perceptible variation in an element or a symbol for each response.

The process of making up regularized (or partially regularized sets) follows these three rules:

1. All elements (symbols or objects) that appear in the conventional set *must* appear in the regularized set.
2. All elements in the regularized set must have a fixed value from application to application (always calling for the same response).
3. All *new* elements created for the regularized set must be obvious variations of the corresponding elements in the conventional set.

Stipulation

Like all techniques that make the communication more articulate, the completely regularized set involves trade-offs, the greatest of which is the possible stipulation that occurs if the learner is exposed to only "regular" examples. *This teaching stipulates that there are no exceptions and does not adequately prepare the learner for the strategies required when the prompts are removed.* Also, the transition from the regularized set of symbols to the conventional set may be difficult. The more completely the set has been regularized, the more involved the transition becomes. The longer the learner has worked with the regularized examples, the greater the probability that the learner will have trouble with the transition.

Regularized Symbols for Decoding

According to the three rules for regularizing a set, we would include all conventional letters in the regularized words (rule 1). Only one response would be produced for any element in the regularized set (rule 2). Any new element we created must be an obvious variation of the corresponding element in the conventional set (rule 3).

If we apply the prompting procedures to letters like **t**, we must create a prompted variation that applies to the **th** sound. It must look like a **t**, but should be linked with the **h** and should look different from the **t** that signals the regular **t** sound. Here are three possible conventions:

math math math

If we use the underlining convention, the underlined letters have one fixed value. Letters not underlined have another. Although the **t** and the **h** are quite visible in the underlined variation, the underlining provides a cue that a different response is called for by the underlined **t**. The other prompts function in the same way as the underlined **th** functions. To transition from the regularized set to the conventional set, we simply eliminate the prompt. In the meantime, the learner reads the regularized elements, a skill that should easily transfer to the conventional orthography.

A similar regularizing problem exists with respect to silent letters. In the word **have**, the final **e** does not make a sound. According to the three criteria for creating a regularized set, we must somehow retain the letter for the silent **e**, create a discriminable difference between a silent letter and one that is not silent, and design a silent letter so that it is a recognizable variation of **e**.

Below are three conventions for creating regularized silent **e**.

hav_e_ hav⬚e⬚ have

Each convention satisfies the requirements for

regularized elements. If we use the convention of making silent **e** smaller, every smaller **e** has a fixed value (it is silent or not read). The learner can easily discriminate between a normal-sized **e** and a smaller **e**. The conventions adopted for regularizing silent **e**'s could be used for other silent letters, such as the **a** in **breath**, or the **i** in **paint**.

The orthographic illustrations of prompting are not intended to be exhaustive. They merely point out some options that are available. There is no prompt that is "correct." A prompt serves a need. If it is constructed according to the appropriate procedures, it will serve the need.

Illustration: Telling Time

Just as the set of symbols used in beginning reading and those used in beginning arithmetic may benefit from regularization, the set of examples used in initial time-telling may benefit from regularization.

The hands on a clock are minimally different in features; however, each hand signals a different operation. The hour-hand signals the learner to *read* a number on the clock face. The minute hand signals the learner to multiply the number on the clock face by five. Although it is possible to teach the differences between the hands and teach which hand signals us to count by five (rather than to read), the elements can be regularized to *show* when counting is called for.

On the clock face in Figure 20.1, the long hand (minute hand) terminates in a large stylized 5. It points to the number that is to be reached through counting by fives. The shorter hand has an arrow. It points to the number to be read.

Semi-Specific Prompts

The prompts that we have been using are specific. One prompt is used for one subtype of example. All subtypes of long-vowel sound receive the same prompt (i.e., a line). All subtypes of silent letters receive the same prompt (a smaller letter). And so forth. When we use a semi-specific prompt, we use the same prompt for a *group of subtypes*. For instance, we might use a line over any pair of letters in a word that makes an irregular sound in that word:

mai̅l̅ bi̅te̅ pa̅r̅t soi̅l shi̅p

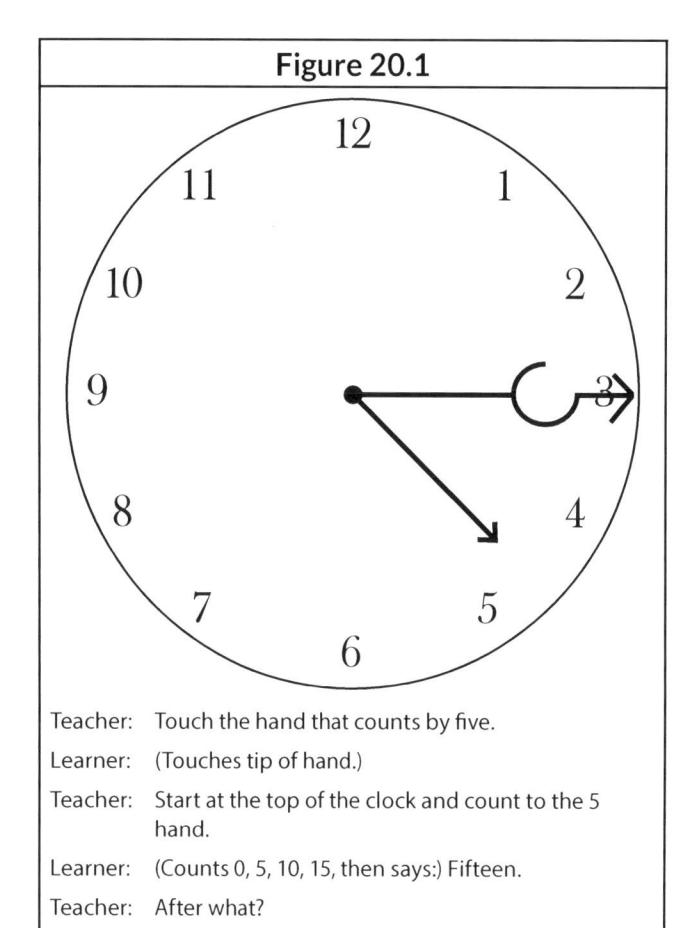

Figure 20.1

[Clock face diagram with numbers 1-12, minute hand pointing to a stylized 3, hour hand with arrow pointing toward 5]

Teacher:	Touch the hand that counts by five.
Learner:	(Touches tip of hand.)
Teacher:	Start at the top of the clock and count to the 5 hand.
Learner:	(Counts 0, 5, 10, 15, then says:) Fifteen.
Teacher:	After what?
Learner:	Five.

Because the same prompt is used for various subtypes, it cannot signal a specific response. It merely points out that the prompted element is "unusual" in some way. To determine how it is unusual, the learner must attend to the features of the prompted element and apply knowledge of the response that the prompted letter combination calls for.

The semi-specific prompt may be used as an initial prompt or as a transitional prompt for groups of previously prompted elements. For example, after **th**, **sh**, **ai**, and **i-e** have been taught with individual prompts, this type of transitional exercise might be introduced:

Examples	Teacher Wording
tha̅t̅	First tell me the sound of the part of each word that has a line over it. Then tell me the word.
wi̅sh̅	(Point to the overlined part of each word and ask:) What sound?
ma̅i̅l	(Point to the beginning of each word and ask:) What word?
bi̅te̅	

Figure 20.2

Original Prompt	Semi-Specific Prompt	Unprompted
Prompt I Prompt II Prompt III	Prompt N Replaces Prompts I-III	(no prompts in exercise)

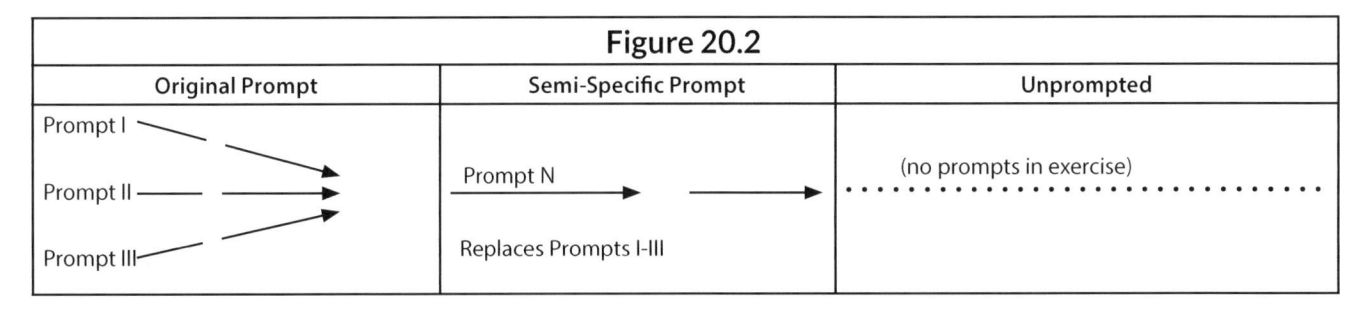

Figure 20.2 is a flow diagram indicating how the semi-specific prompts can be used in a transition.

The three original prompts are replaced by a single semi-specific prompt (**N**) after the learner has met acceptable criteria of performance with the original prompts. The semi-specific prompt requires the learner to attend to the non-prompted features of the examples. Finally, the unprompted examples are introduced. No prompt signals that the element requires special processing.

For most situations, the use of semi-specific prompts presents too much new teaching to be efficient as transitional devices. They may be used as initial prompts for sophisticated learners. If the set of examples for a system is only partially regularized, some symbols may have specific prompts. Others may have semi-specific prompts. For instance, the same specific prompt may be used for a group of sound combinations (**ar**, **al**, **oi**, **er**, **ou**). In addition to the semi-specific prompts, specific prompts may be used for "joined letters" such as **th**, **sh**, and **ch**. The specific prompts direct the learner to make a unique response for each pair of joined letters. The semi-specific prompt merely alerts the learner that the letters make a variant sound.

Prompting Through Juxtaposing or Grouping Examples

A final type of prompt is achieved by grouping examples together and indicating that all examples in the group are the same in some way. The grouping strategy is appropriate when the learner has been taught some examples of a particular subtype and we want the learner to: (1) learn new examples of that subtype, or (2) learn an unprompted form of the prompted examples.

Both situations involve some form of *standard transformation*. Therefore, a variation of the double-transformation program can be used to teach the desired behaviors.

If we have taught a prompted **th** and we want the learner to respond to unprompted **th**, we could present the sequence shown in Figure 20.3. To introduce the sequence, the teacher might say:

"You're going to read some words that have the sound '**thththt**.' Then you're going to read the same words when the letters for '**thththt**' look different."

Figure 20.3

Prompted	Unprompted	Integration
1. that	5. with	11. top
2. math	6. math	12. bat
3. than	7. then	13. math
4. with	8. that	14. hat
	9. the	15. than
	10. these	16. that
	11. bath	17. mat
	12. those	18. hen
		19. tan
		20. bath
		21. then

The sequence is different from the double-transformation sequence in two ways: (1) additional examples appear at the end of the unprompted set; and (2) the integration of types consists of the unprompted examples and examples that have **t** or **h**, but that do not have the sound combination **th**.

Figure 20.4

Prompted	Unprompted	Integration	
1. she	5. me	12. at	19. reed
2. seem	6. seem	13. peep	20. she
3. weed	7. she	14. ship	21. sand
4. me	8. weed	15. red	22. met
	9. see	16. sat	23. sit
	10. peep	17. me	24. seem
	11. seed	18. mad	

Figure 20.4 shows a possible sequence for dealing with long-**e** words. The sequence ends with an integration set consisting of the unprompted examples and other words that are not minimally different from the new type.

The juxtaposition prompting strategy is particularly appropriate for teaching families of irregulars. If the learner has been taught the words **other**, **come**, and **some**, we could use the sequence below to introduce new words.

come	brother
some	done
other	won
mother	

To introduce the sequence, the teacher could say: "The **o** in all these words makes the same sound."

For such skills as spelling, the juxtaposition strategy is probably the most important prompt we can use. The learner must learn that the **e** sound in some words is represented with the letters **ee**, in other words with **ea,** and in still other words with **e**. No before-the-fact rules are adequate for describing which spelling is appropriate for a new word that makes the sound. By grouping the words, we can establish the "generalization" of using a particular spelling, and *we can limit the generalization* to the examples we show.

Let's say that the learner can already spell **bean** and **seal**. The following is a possible juxtaposition sequence:

Teacher Wording

You know how to spell some words that are spelled with the letters **e-a**. You're going to spell some new words that have the letters **e-a**.
Seal. What word?
How is the sound **ee** in **seal** spelled?
Spell **seal**.
Bean. What word?
How is the sound **ee** in **bean** spelled?
Spell **bean**.
Eat. What word?
How is the sound **ee** in **eat** spelled?
Spell **eat**.
Seat. What word?
How is the sound **ee** in **seat** spelled?
Spell **seat**.
Meat. What word?
How is the sound **ee** in **meat** spelled?
Spell **meat**.
Leap. What word?
How is the sound **ee** in **leap** spelled?
Spell **leap**.

Note that this routine is quite powerful in prompting the desired behavior because it establishes a three-step attack with familiar examples. The same steps are then presented with unfamiliar examples, starting with **seat**. This sameness suggests to the learner that the new examples are the same.

Although grouping is a powerful strategy for showing how members of a family are the same, the grouping must be followed by practice with non-grouped examples. The grouping strategy involves creating "blocks" or groups of examples, all of which are the same with respect to a particular operation. We saw variations of the strategy in designing worksheet items (Chapter 16). After items appear in a block, the items are dispersed. By breaking up the groups, we create contexts of increasing difficulty. The transition from grouped to dispersed examples does not necessarily occur as a single all-or-none change. Rather, the larger blocks might first be broken into smaller blocks, each of which is dispersed. After the learner performs well on the smaller blocks, the final dispersion occurs.

As a further transition from the grouped examples, we can mix examples of the prompted type with other examples in a way that still prompts the desired responses. If we retain a high percentage of the previously prompted examples in a particular block, we prompt the desired response. For instance, if we mix 50 spelling examples, half of which involve the letters **ea**, the mixed group continues to prompt the **ea** spelling, simply because the examples of this spelling occur very frequently, although examples are not juxtaposed. This unprompting strategy shapes the *context in which the response occurs*, starting with the most highly-prompted context (the juxtaposed examples) and proceeding to the least-prompted context (the unpredictable mixture of the previously prompted examples with other familiar examples). We will encounter this context-shaping strategy again when we deal with non-cognitive operations (Section VII).

Complete Regularizing Versus Partial Regularizing

Regularized elements are inventions. We should not become enamored with inventing, without considering ultimate effectiveness. The ultimate effectiveness of a regularized set of elements depends greatly on the future curricula slated for the learner. If we could design the learner's future so that everything the learner read followed orthographic conventions that we specified, we could design a perfectly regularized code. We could redesign letters, spell phonetically, rename letters as sounds, and generally design the set of elements so that there are no highly similar members, and so that learning to read is a simple variation of learning to spell. For this code, spelling words would involve nothing more than saying them slowly.

Unfortunately, the learner is expected to read conventional orthography. Spelling English words is not perfectly congruent with reading them. Therefore, we must consider the number and type of misrules associated with different regularizing conventions. If we make everything in the reading code regular, we are inducing a possibly serious misrule, which is that written words have a perfect correspondence to spoken words. To teach the learner a basic tenet of our conventional orthographic code, we *must introduce some early words that are irregular.* These words teach the learner that there is a type of word that is not pronounced as the spelling would suggest. This code is only partly regularized.

Questions about the future skills that are scheduled for the learner determine the extent to which arithmetic may be regularized. Arithmetic notions are perhaps as irregular as those associated with conventional orthography used in reading. To convert a fraction notation into a notation of division, rotate the fraction ninety degrees in the clockwise direction:

$$\lfloor \tfrac{1}{4} \qquad 4\overline{)1}$$

To convert a fraction into a fraction that uses this "divide by" sign: ÷, the fraction is rotated in the *opposite* direction:

$$\lfloor \tfrac{1}{4} \qquad 1 \div 4$$

If the learner is expected to deal with this horrible inconsistency, we must design the teaching so that both notations are taught. However, the job would be much easier if the notation 1 ÷ 4 were completely discarded.

If we are assured of working with the learner for the first four or five years of arithmetic instruction, we can create notations far superior to those used in traditional arithmetic, and we will have ample time to transition the learner from these to the traditional notations. Furthermore, we will be able to teach skills in an order that is far more efficient than that of traditional sequences. One thing we might do is regularize the notation system so that any problem can be read (and worked) by approaching them from the left or from the right. The traditional notation does not permit the learner to approach this problem from the right:

$$2J + 5 = 7 - 15$$

If we read the problem from the right, the problem says: "Fifteen minus seven." The minus sign, however, belongs to the fifteen. We could change the notation system so that the act of "combining" is separated from the sign of the number. Here is such a notation:

$$\begin{array}{cccc} + & + & + & - \\ 2J + 5 & = & 7 - 15 \end{array}$$

Multiplication problems would have similar notations, but use a different sign between the numbers to indicate that the values are combined through multiplication.

$$\begin{array}{ccccc} + & + & - & + & - \\ 2 \times R & = & 5 \times 4 \times \tfrac{3}{7} \end{array}$$

All numbers have signs. The sign between numbers tells how the groups are to be combined. The learner can work the problems from the right or from the left.

Perhaps the biggest advantage of this notation is the conceptual one. It shows that there is a difference between the sign of the number and the sign used to combine the numbers. One sign stands for an absolute value, while the other signals an operation–information that is poorly conveyed by conventional notations.

No matter how attractive a system may be, our decision to use it must be based on the learner's future. If the learner will soon be required to engage in conventional arithmetic, it may be more efficient to work with the conventional notation setup.

The beginning Distar Arithmetic program (*Distar Arithmetic I*) uses little zeros as place-value indicators. These are faded or dropped after the learner has been taught to respond to the digits. A great advantage of the little zeros is that it makes the operation of carrying very easy and regular. What is carried to the tens column is never a one, but a ten. Figure 20.5 shows a routine that introduces carrying.

Figure 20.5

Teacher:	Read the problem.
Learner:	37 plus 28.
Teacher:	Where do we add first?
Learner:	In the ones column.
Teacher:	Listen: If you ever see a ten in the ones column, say: "Ten go over to the other side." This dotted line shows the sides. What are you going to say if you see a ten in the ones column?
Learner:	Ten go over to the other side.
Teacher:	How many ones are we adding?
Learner:	Seven plus eight.
Teacher:	What does seven plus eight equal?
Learner:	Fifteen.
Teacher:	(Write 1⁰5 and says): Oh-oh.
Learner:	Ten go over to the other side.
Teacher:	(Erases 1⁰ and writes it above the 3⁰.) Now what do we do?
Learner:	Add the tens.
Teacher:	How many tens are we adding?
Learner:	One plus three plus two.
Teacher:	How many is one plus three?
Learner:	Four.
Teacher:	How many is four plus two?
Learner:	Six.
Teacher:	What numeral do I write for six tens?
Learner:	Sixty.
Teacher:	(Writes 6⁰.)

The operation of carrying is much easier, because the learner can see that the carried digit *belongs* in the tens column. It has sameness features that are shared by the other digits in this column (the little 0's). Reversals in carrying (carrying the wrong digit) are minimized. Also, the concept of what is happening when carrying occurs is made obvious.

Regularizing the operation of carrying and similar operations can be achieved within a relatively short period of time (one or two school years). The regularization, therefore, is reasonable. If the regularization requires a greater amount of time, however, its appeal of efficiency is seriously tempered by practical problems.

Transitions to Unprompted Examples

Two important transition issues are:

1. How quickly should the prompt be faded?
2. How are new examples introduced after the prompts have been removed?

Two strategies are used in transitioning to unprompted examples: *removing prompts* and *modifying prompts*.

Here is an illustration of *prompt removal*. The learner has been taught to decode words that have joined letters. After the learner has become proficient at decoding joined-letter words, such as that, the joined letters are removed. The learner now reads the word **that**. Removal of prompts is an all-or-none procedure.

When prompts are *modified*, they are changed in the direction of the unprompted example. If the learner has been taught to read with small, silent letters, the size of the silent letters are increased (from havₑ to have). The prompt is still present; however, since the "small letter" is now less discriminable from regular-sized letters, the learner is provided with less of a prompt. *If the prompt is still present, but the prompted element is less discriminable from its unprompted counterpart, the prompt has been modified in the direction of an unprompted element.*

Here is a test to determine whether prompt modification is advisable: *If a particular detail that appears in prompted examples also appears in the unprompted example, it can be faded through prompt modification.* The word **shave** is an unprompted example that contains the detail **e**. Since the **e** appears in the unprompted example, we may use a series of fades to modify a small **e** in the prompted example. *If our prompt is a box around the* **e**, *however, we should* **not** *modify the box through a series of fades*. Instead we should simply remove the box. The unit **sh** is a discriminable element that is present in unprompted examples of the word **shave**, which means that we can fade a prompted **sh** through modification. If our initial prompt involves italicized letters, *sh*, we can reduce the degree of italics. If our initial prompt is a joined **sh**, we can unjoin the letters through a series of fades.

If the prompted variation of the word is:

shāve →

details have been added to the **a** that have no counterparts in the unprompted word **shave**. Also, the arrow does not appear in the unprompted word. Therefore, prompt modification is not appropriate for the **a** or the arrow. The reason is that if we modified the prompts, the final fade before the removal of the prompts might be:

shāve

This example provides the learner with as much information as the original prompted example. There is a marker to distinguish the **a** from short-vowel counterparts. Another marker shows the beginning of the word. The learner may rely as completely on these marks as on longer marks. *So long as any detail of a prompt that is not in the unprompted example is present, the learner may rely on the part.* (Note that it would be possible to introduce a prompt for the long-**a** that could be modified rather than be removed, perhaps an italicized **a**.)

Illustration 1. The following are prompts that have been introduced in a reading program. For some prompts, modification is possible. For others, removal is implied.

1. **moon**   2. **sister**
3. **fARm**   4. **sing**

1. A series of prompt modifications is possible for **moon**. The reason is that the elements **oo** appear in the unprompted words **moon**, **soon**, **loot**, etc.

2. Prompt-removal is the most appropriate for **sister** because the unprompted counterpart, **sister**, does not have an element that corresponds to the wiggly line.

3. Prompt removal is required for **farm** because the unprompted word **farm** has no shapes like those in the capital letters **AR**. Therefore, it is probably not practical to deal with prompt modification. Although it would be possible to superimpose the lower-case letters over the originals and fade out the originals, the learner could respond to the presence of the capital letters until the removal of the upper-case letters had been achieved.

4. Prompt modification for **sing** is possible, because the prompted detail (the tail) appears in the unprompted word **sing**.

Illustration 2. Figure 20.6 shows prompts that are used on clock faces.

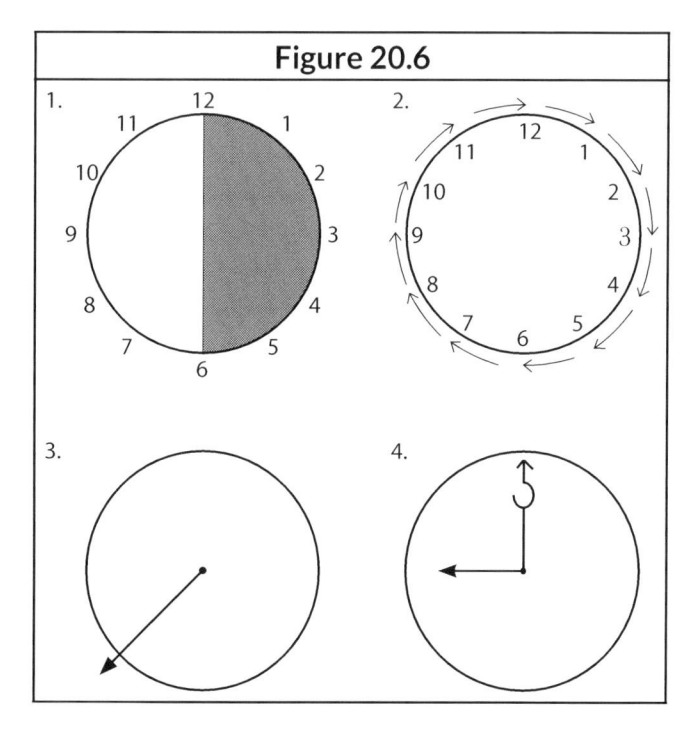

Figure 20.6

1. Prompt removal is called for on clockface 1. There is no line down the middle of an unprompted clockface and no shading on one side.

2. Prompt removal is called for with clockface 2. The unprompted clock has no arrows outside the face.

3. A prompt modification series could be used with face 3. The minute hand is present on the unprompted clock, and the minute hand is "longer" than the other hand. Therefore, it would be possible to create a series of fades from the prompted hand to the unprompted counterpart.

4. Although the 5 is not present on the unprompted clockface, prompt modification could be used for face 4. If we treat the 5 as an arrowhead, we can achieve the following type of modification:

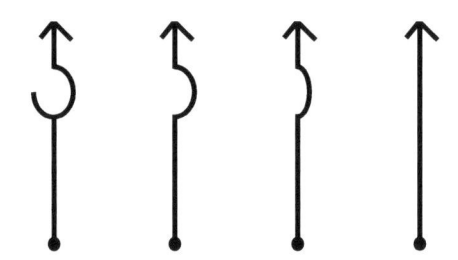

It may be argued that so long as there is difference between the points of the long hand and the short hand, it is possible for the learner to discriminate between the hands by attending to this difference, not to length. This shape difference is therefore "spurious" because it does not appear on the unprompted clockface. According to this argument, prompt modification is not advised. Since modification is questionable, we should probably not use it.

Remember, if it is possible for the learner to discriminate successfully by attending to *some feature other than the one that will be present when the prompts have been removed*, a misrule is possible. The misrule is possible as long as the feature exists. The feature, therefore, should be eliminated through prompt-removal.

Illustration 3. We indicated earlier that the double-transformation strategy provides the simplest procedure for prompt removal. First the learner goes through a series of prompted examples, then the learner goes through the same examples with the prompts removed. The learner is also introduced to new unprompted examples. The double transformation juxtapositions show the differences between prompted examples and their unprompted counterparts.

Figure 20.7 shows a possible series of examples involving a prompted clockface. The first two examples are prompted. The third example is the same as the preceding example except that the prompts have been removed. Example 4 is the same as example 1. It is followed by a new example.

The same basic double-transformation strategy is effective for nearly all types of prompt removal. Note that the prompted and unprompted sets are followed by the integration set.

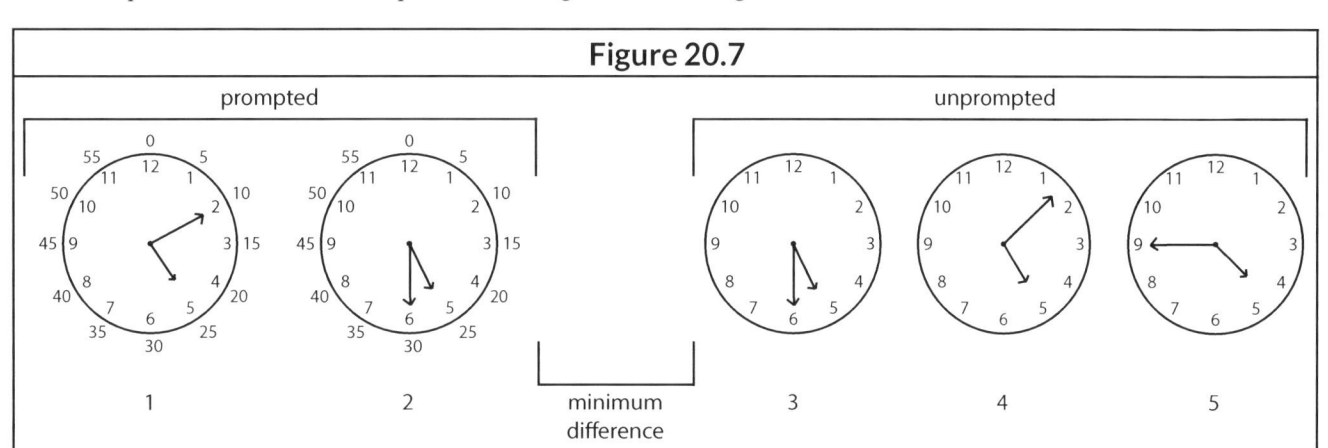

Figure 20.7

prompted | unprompted

1   2   minimum difference   3   4   5

The overtized routine for the prompted example 1:

1. Teacher: Touch the hour hand.
   (Learner touches short hand.)
2. Teacher: Figure out the hour.
   (Learner touches 5 and says, "Five.")
3. Teacher: Figure out the minutes.
   (Learner touches 0, 5, 10, and says, "Ten minutes.")
4. Teacher: Tell me what time it is.
   (Learner says: "Five ten.")

Before the first unprompted example is presented, the teacher explains: "You're going to figure out the same times you just worked, but the clock doesn't show the numbers that you count by. Pretend that they are there. Start at the top of the clock with zero and touch where each numeral should be.

Prompt modification versus prompt removal. It is possible to modify the prompt if the detail or feature that is prompted occurs in the unprompted example. *Merely because prompt modification is possible does not mean that it is either desirable or efficient in a particular situation.* The guiding rule should be to fade prompts as quickly as possible and with the least elaborate procedure. In some situations, prompt modification is a reasonable technique. For instance, if we are trying to maintain rate behavior (such as reading rate), prompt modification through a series of small changes in the program would be desirable because it would not disrupt the learner's rate performance. For most situations, however, we should try to remove the prompt. If the removal program leads to an obvious regression in the learner's performance, a series of prompt modifications might be tried.

Correcting mistakes on unprompted examples. If the learner can respond appropriately to fully-prompted examples, but is making mistakes on unprompted examples, the correction should present a juxtaposition prompt or a semi-specific prompt.

Let's say that the learner makes a mistake on the unprompted word **tooth** by calling the word "Toot." The word occurs in the sentence, "She had a sore tooth." The correction using a semi-specific prompt is as follows:

Teacher:	(Point to the last two letters.) These two letters go together. What sound do they make?
Learner:	Thththth.
Teacher:	So what word?
Learner:	Tooth.
Teacher:	Let's go back to the beginning of the sentence and read it again.

The semi-specific prompt *merely pointed out that the two letters go together.* It did not tell what sound they made. Note that the last step in the correction involves rereading the sentence—the context in which the mistake occurred.

The following shows the same correction with the addition of a juxtaposition prompt:

Teacher:	(Point to the last two letters.) These two letters go together. What sound do they make?
Learner:	Thththth.
Teacher:	So what word?
Learner:	Tooth.
Teacher:	(Writes on board: booth math them.) See if you can read each of these words.
Learner:	(Reads words.)
Teacher:	Now let's go back to the sentence that begins, "She had…"

The addition of the grouping step would be called for only if the learner tended to make the mistake frequently or failed to read the sentence correctly as the last step of the semi-specific-prompt correction.

The following shows the correction with no semi-specific-prompt, merely a juxtaposition prompt:

Teacher:	The word is tooth. What word?
	(Writes on board: booth math them mother this.) Read these words
Learner:	(Reads.)
Teacher:	Now let's go back to the sentence that begins, "She had…"

A pre-correction that provides a juxtaposition prompt consists of a number of examples that share the same features. For instance, the teacher presents the words **math**, **tooth**, **thing**, and **other**. The instructions: "Read these words." This prompt reduces the probability of a mistake on the examples that follow.

Summary

Prompts are devices that increase differences in examples. Prompts simplify the use of cognitive routines and increase the range of a routine's application.

Prompts permit the guidance of behavior that is more overtized, more precise.

Prompts permit the set of examples to be regularized, which means that fewer cognitive routines are needed to process all the examples in the set.

If a prompt is designed to show the *difference* between two elements that are minimally different, the prompt must involve the features that are different between these two elements. The prompt consists of a modification of the unprompted elements. If the prompt is designed to show an *operational sameness*, the prompt may involve the creation of some new element or detail that is not found in the prompted example.

If the set of examples is completely regularized, every element or symbol used has a fixed value (signals only one response). Since there are no irregular examples (variant values) for the elements in a fully-regularized set, the learner does not need rules, routines, or reminders for processing irregular examples. Elements are always processed in the same manner.

Regularization establishes the behavior across a range of types that will later become "irregular." A problem occurs because the same behavior will not be used for all examples when the prompts are removed.

The prompted, regularized set will have more symbols or types than the unprompted set, because it will contain all elements of the original set and as many additional elements as are needed to accommodate all examples that are created.

The transition from prompted to unprompted examples may be achieved through *prompt modification* or *prompt removal*.

Prompt modification may be used if the detail that is being modified is retained in the unprompted example. If the detail is not present in the unprompted example, however, prompt removal is most appropriate.

Two types of prompts have extensive application in the transition process—the *semi-specific prompt* and the *juxtaposition or grouping prompt*.

The semi-specific prompt provides the learner with the location of the prompted element and an indication that the part of the example contains an irregular element.

This prompt, however, does not suggest a *fixed value* for the prompted elements. The same semi-specific prompt may be used to process examples of various subtypes.

The juxtaposition prompt is based on the assumption that if new examples in the group have the same set of features as a familiar unprompted example, the juxtaposition makes common features more obvious. The grouping prompt may be used as part of the prompt-removal procedure. This prompt also serves to introduce new, unprompted examples of a particular type.

The juxtaposition prompting procedure is modeled after the double-transformation program. By grouping the prompted examples together and by following the set with the same examples in their unprompted form, we show the learner the standard transformation that converts prompted members into their unprompted counterpart.

The best prompts to use for corrections are the juxtaposition prompt and the semi-specific prompt. Both prompts require the learner to attend to the features of the unprompted example. At the same time, they provide the learner with information that part of the example is to be treated in a special or irregular way. For chronic errors, the semi-specific prompt or the juxtaposition prompt can be used to pre-correct possible errors.

Chapter 21
Covertization

Instruction that involves prompts shifts progressively from highly-prompted examples to unprompted examples. Stated differently, the instruction *shapes the context* in which the responses occur. First, the responses are established in the simplest context. Then, the context is changed (as the prompts are either modified or removed) as the responses are maintained.

Cognitive routines run a course parallel to that of prompts. The routines that are created for initial instruction are like prompted examples in that they make the context for solving the problem as easy as possible. The initial routines are designed so that the learner produces overt responses to specific teacher directions; however, the ultimate goal is for the learner to internalize a problem-solving operation. The program must therefore provide a transition from a highly-structured routine to one that contains very few directions. *This process shapes the context in which the responses occur.* It assures that some form of the original behavior is maintained as the steps in the routine are removed or modified. In the end, the responses are to be produced *covertly* by the learner, with no direction from the teacher.

Covertized Routines

The highly overtized routine is an initial-teaching communication. It is followed by a series of routines that provide for fewer overt responses or fewer responses that are signaled by specific directions from the teacher. Each routine in this series is similar enough to the preceding one to prompt the appropriate behavior.

The process of replacing the highly overtized routine with less structured routines is *covertization*. The routines are referred to as *covertized routines.*

As a rule:

1. Each covertization calls for one-half to three-fourths the overt responses as the preceding routine.

2. The learner should usually work on a covertized routine for at least two days before the next covertization is presented.

3. The covertization process should be no more elaborate than is necessary to assure that the transition from highly overtized routines to independent work is relatively errorless.

An illustration of an initial routine and four covertizations (**A, B, C, D**) follows. Note that these covertizations show the different covertization strategies. The illustration is not necessarily good at demonstrating how many or what kind of covertizations should be used. It simply shows the types of covertization strategies.

Original routine: □ = / / / /

1. Teacher: Touch the equal.
   Learner: (Touches.)
2. Teacher: What's the rule about the equal sign?
   Learner: We must end up with the same number on this side and on the other side.
3. Teacher: Touch the side you can start counting on.
   Learner: (Touches side with the lines.)
4. Teacher: Count how many are on that side.
   Learner: (Touches each line as he counts: "One, two, three, four.")
5. Teacher: How many did you end up with on this side?
   Learner: Four.
6. Teacher: So how many must you end up with on the other side?
   Learner: Four.
7. Teacher: Write 4 in the box.
   Learner: (Writes.)

The initial routine contains overt steps to assure that the learner can: (1) say the rule about the equal sign; (2) identify the side on which he is to count; and (3) apply the equality rule by "ending up with the same number on the other side."

Four covertization sequences follow after the learner has responded successfully to about eight applications of the original routine.

Covertization A

1. Teacher: What's the rule about the equal sign?
   Learner: We must end up with the same number on this side and on the other side.
2. Teacher: Touch the side you can start counting on.
   Learner: (Touches the side with vertical lines.)
3. Teacher: Count how many are on that side.
   Learner: (Touches each line as he counts: "One, two, three, four.")
4. Teacher: Make the other side equal.
   Learner: (Writes 4 in the box.)

Covertization B

1. Teacher: What's the rule about the equal sign?
   Learner: We must end up with the same number this side and on the other side.
2. Teacher: Touch the side you start counting on.
   Learner: (Touches side with lines.)
3. Teacher: Count the lines and make the other side equal.
   Learner: (Counts lines and writes 4 in the box on the other side.)

Covertization C

Teacher: You're going to make the sides equal in this problem. First you're going to touch the side you start counting on. Then you're going to count everything on that side. Then you're going to make the other side equal. Do it.
Learner: (Counts lines and writes 4 in the box.)

Covertization D

Teacher: Make the sides equal in this problem.
Learner: (Completes problem.)

The following strategies were used in the **A, B, C,** and **D** covertizations:

1. **Dropping a step or steps.** In covertization **A**, step 1 was dropped from the original routine ("Touch the equal sign").

2. **Regrouping a chain of instructions and responses, so the interaction between teacher and learner changes from T^1-L^1, T^2-L^2 to T^1-T^2, L^1-L^2. (T** stands for a teacher instruction; **L** stands for a learner response.) Covertization **B** contains the teacher instruction: "Count the lines and make the other side equal." This instruction involves two instructions that had been presented separately in Covertization **A** ("Count how many are on that side" and "Make the other side equal.") This interaction pattern is T^1-L^1, T^2-L^2. The interaction in Covertization **B** followed the pattern: Teacher instruction (T^1-T^2) followed by learner responses (L^1-L^2).

3. **Replacing a series of specific instructions with one inclusive instruction.** In covertization **A**, steps 5, 6 and 7 of the original routines were replaced by a single step (step 4). The wording of this replacement step, "Make the other side equal," was *not identical* to the original wording in steps 5, 6, or 7. The replacement step simply functioned as 5, 6, or 7 had functioned in the original routine.

4. **Creating pairs of equivalent instructions.** In Covertization **C**, the teacher begins by saying: "You're going to make the sides equal in this problem." The teacher then provides instructions *that are equivalent* to the first statement. "First you're going to touch the side you start counting on; then you're going to count everything on that side; then you're going to make the other side equal." These directions are simply another way of saying, "You're going to make the sides equal in this problem." In Covertization **D**, only part of the equivalent instructions appear. ("You're going to make the sides equal in this problem.")

Uses of the Covertization Techniques

Dropping Steps

Steps that are not critical once the learner has developed some facility with the routine may be dropped from the subsequent covertization. Also, *parts of steps* may be dropped when they make the routine awkward.

Here's the first-step of a routine: Teacher says, "Read the problem." Possibly, this step could be dropped for the next covertization. The decision to drop depends on the learner's reading performance. If the learner only rarely makes mistakes in identifying numerals or signs, the reading could be dropped.

Parts of steps may also be dropped if they are part of a chain that is always produced in the same order.

Teacher: You're going to multiply across the top and write the answer.
Then you're going to multiply across the bottom and write the answer.
Do it.

After the learner has worked many problems in the same way, this chain needs less verbal prompting. Therefore, in a covertization we can drop reference to writing the answers.

The best guideline for whether steps or parts of steps can be dropped (without some form of replacement) is the learner's behavior. In the absence of information about learner behavior, we can follow this rule of thumb: *About one-fourth of all steps in a routine can be dropped after the routine has been presented on three consecutive sessions with a total of eight or more examples.*

Dropping steps, however, is not always the most appropriate covertization. The semi-overtized routine that follows illustrates this point. The routine is designed to prompt the learner to attend first to the bottom number and then to the top number of the fraction.

Example: $\frac{12}{4}$

1. Teacher: What's the bottom number of this fraction?
   Learner: Four.
2. Teacher: How many times bigger than four is the top number?
   Learner: Three.
3. Teacher: So what does the fraction equal?
   Learner: Three wholes.
4. Teacher: How do you know that it equals three wholes?
   Learner: Because the top is three times bigger than the bottom.

If step 1 were dropped, the first step of the routine (step 2) would tell the learner the bottom number (4), *but would not require the learner to attend to it in the fraction.*

If we drop step 2 instead of step 1, the resulting routine is difficult.

1. Teacher: What's the bottom number of the fraction?
   Learner: Four.
2. Teacher: What does this fraction equal?
   Learner: Three wholes.

The juxtaposition of questions is particularly misleading in this covertization. Both questions ask "what." The answer to the first question is based on inspection. The answer to the second involves a "figuring out." The juxtaposition may prompt a hasty and possibly wrong answer to the second question.

A slightly better routine would be:

1. Teacher: What's the bottom number of the fraction?
   Learner: Four.
2. Teacher: Figure out what the fraction equals.
   Learner: Three wholes.

Step 3 is necessary to make sure that the learner is discriminating between "numbers" that are parts of fractions (such as the denominator 4) and the "whole" number that the fraction equals.

Step 4 should not be dropped because it is the only step in which the learner responds with the statement about the relationship between top and bottom numbers. (In step 2, the teacher asked about the relationship, but the learner did not express the relationship.)

This illustration demonstrates the test for dropping steps. If we can identify possible problems created by dropping steps, we should consider alternative covertization techniques.

Regrouping a Chain of Instructions and Responses

When steps are regrouped, a single step provides the instructions that had been conveyed through two or more separate steps of the earlier routine. For this covertization strategy, the teacher tells the learner to do two or more things. The learner then does them.

The general rule for using the regrouping technique is: *Regroup separate steps that lead to the same goal or that are part of the same fixed series of steps.* When the learner figures out minutes on the clock the learner goes through a fixed series of steps that lead to this goal. Possibly, some of these steps can be grouped together. When carrying a number of a multiplication problem, the learner carries out a series of steps (writing one of the digits, carrying the other, multiplying and then adding the amount carried.) These steps *always occur in a fixed order*; therefore, it may be possible to regroup some of them.

Let's say that the learner has successfully responded to an overtized routine for multiplying factions and to a covertized variation. Here's the latter routine:

Example: $\frac{3}{4} \times \frac{2}{3} = \square$

1. Teacher: Read the problem.
   Learner: Three-fourths times two-thirds.

2. Teacher: Multiply across the top and write the answer to the top.
   Learner: (Multiplies three times two and writes six.)
3. Teacher: Now multiply across the bottom and write the answer on the bottom.
   Learner: (Multiplies four times three and writes twelve.)

The pattern of responses in the format is: T^1-L^1, T^2-L^2, T^3-L^3.

We could create the next covertization by regrouping the parts of the series.

1. Teacher: Read the problem.
   Learner: Three-fourths times two-thirds.
2. Teacher: You're going to multiply across the top and write the answer. Then you're going to multiply across the bottom and write the answer. Do it.
   Learner: (Multiplies across the top and writes six. Multiplies across the bottom and writes twelve.)

The instructions in step 2 tell the learner two things to do.

Earlier we observed that dropping steps might not be the most effective approach for covertizing the fraction-reducing operation. The regrouping strategy could be used more effectively. Here is a possible covertization of the fraction reduction routine:

1. Teacher: First look at the bottom number. When I signal, tell me how many times bigger the top number is.
   Learner: Three.
2. Teacher: So what does this fraction equal?
   Learner: Three wholes.
3. Teacher: How do you know it equals three wholes?
   Learner: Because the top is three times bigger than the bottom.

Note that two ideas conveyed by the original instructions are chained together in step 1; however, the wording is not identical to that of the original steps. The learner is told to *attend* to the bottom number, not to respond to it. The learner is also told to tell how many times bigger the top number is; however, the learner is not told to tell how many times bigger than *four* the top number is. These variations are permissible if it becomes either awkward or too highly prompted to regroup steps in a way that retains the precise wording of the original steps.

The regrouping strategy should be used judiciously, with awareness of the responses the learner is to make. We should avoid creating illogical responses or those that are difficult to correct. If we regrouped the first two steps of the more highly structured routine by retaining the first question of the original routine, the step would be: "Tell me the bottom number and then how many times bigger the top number is." The learner's response "four . . . three," is not very logical. It treats the numbers as if they are coordinate with no qualification about how they are related. If we regrouped the last two steps of the original routine, the resulting step would ask the learner about the number of wholes and about the evidence of this conclusion: "Tell me what the fraction equals and how you know how many wholes it equals." The response the learner is to produce is elaborate: "Three wholes because the top is three times bigger than the bottom." With this change, we would have to spend time teaching the learner the conventions for responding.

The following is an overtized routine for telling time. Steps 3 and 4 could be regrouped when the routine is covertized.

Example:

1. Teacher: Touch the minute hand.
   Learner: (Touches.)
2. Teacher: How do you figure out minutes?
   Learner: Start at the top of the clock and count by fives to the hand.
3. Teacher: Touch the top of the clock and say zero.
   Learner: (Touches 12 and says: "Zero.")
4. Teacher: Now count by fives to the hand.
   Learner: Five…ten…fifteen.
5. Teacher: Tell me what the hand shows.
   Learner: Fifteen minutes.

We could regroup steps 3 and 4 in this way: "Touch the top of the clock, say zero, and count by fives to the hand." This is not a particularly difficult step because it deals with a chain of behaviors that the learner has performed.

Not all juxtaposed steps can be regrouped. For instance, we would not provide combined instructions for steps 2 and 3. ("Tell me how you figure out minutes" and "Touch the top of the clock and say zero.")

Steps 4 and 5 could possibly be combined, and there might be some justification in such chaining. However, if we had desired this behavior, we should have taught it initially, not as a part of a covertization. The teacher could have structured the step in the overtized routine as follows: "When you count minutes, you stop at the hand then say the minutes. My turn: Zero, five, ten, fifteen. *Fifteen minutes.* Your turn . . ."

Inclusive Instruction

Inclusive instructions involve new wording. The wording presents *less detail* than the original instructions but results in the same set of behaviors. Inclusive instructions cover behaviors that had been treated as two or more steps in the original routine.

The original routine for the multiplying fractions can be covertized many different ways through the use of inclusive steps. Here is one possibility:

Example: $\frac{3}{4} \times \frac{2}{3} = \square$

1. Teacher: Read this problem.
   Learner: Three-fourths times two-thirds.
2. Teacher: Figure out the answer.
   Learner: (Multiplies across the top and writes the answer. Multiplies across the bottom and writes the answer.)

The instructions in step 2 do not provide the information about multiplying, or multiplying across the top and then across the bottom, but they lead to the same behavioral outcome as instructions in the original routine. Note the difference between inclusive steps and regrouped steps. When steps are regrouped, the resulting instructions tend to contain the same words as the original steps. For inclusive steps, *more general wording is introduced* (such as "figure out").

Although the inclusive step does not involve the exact wording of earlier routines, it should use vocabulary already familiar to the learner. For long routines, there are usually many possible uses of inclusive instructions. The following is an overtized routine for an addition problem.

Example: $7 + 3 = \square$

1. Teacher: Read the problem.
   Learner: Seven plus three equals how many.
2. Teacher: (Points to 7 + 3 side.) Can we start counting on this side?
   Learner: Yes.
3. Teacher: (Points to box side.) Can we start counting on this side?
   Learner: No.
4. Teacher: Why not?
   Learner: Because the box doesn't tell how many.
5. Teacher: Circle everything on the side you're going to count on.
   Learner: (Circles 7 + 3 side.)
6. Teacher: (Points to 7.) How many in this group?
   Learner: Seven.
7. Teacher: And what does the problem tell you to do next?
   Learner: Plus three.
8. Teacher: Do it.
   Learner: (Makes three lines under the three.)
9. Teacher: Now count everything on the 7 + 3 side.
   Learner: (Touches under seven and says, "Seven." Then touches each line under 3 and counts, "Eight, nine, ten.")
10. Teacher: So how many go on the side with the box?
    Learner: Ten.

We could provide an inclusive step for figuring out the side the learner starts counting on. This step would replace steps 2 and 3 with one that required a strong response: "Show me the side you start counting on," or "Read everything on the side you start counting on."

Steps 7 and 8 of the original routine involve making lines for 3. These steps could be replaced with the step: "Make the lines." Although this instruction may seem more specific than any in the original routine, the learner must figure out where the lines are to be made and how many are needed. (The learner makes lines only under the 3.)

This covertized routine utilizes inclusive steps for steps 2-3 and for steps 6, 7, and 8.

1. Teacher: Read the problem.
   Learner: Seven plus three equals how many.
2. Teacher: Read everything on the side you start counting on.
   Learner: Seven plus three.

3.	Teacher:	(Points to box side.) Why can't you start counting on this side?
	Learner:	Because the box doesn't tell how many.
4.	Teacher:	Circle everything on the side you're going to count on.
	Learner:	(Circles 7 + 3 side.)
5.	Teacher:	Make the lines.
	Learner:	(Makes three lines under the 3.)
6.	Teacher:	Now count everything on the 7 + 3 side.
	Learner:	(Touches under seven and says: "Seven." Then touches each line and counts to 10.)
7.	Teacher:	So how many go on the side with the box?
	Learner:	Ten.

The resulting routine is shortened to 7 steps.

Equivalent Pairs of Instructions

The use of equivalent pairs is more complicated than the use of the other covertization techniques because the equivalent pairs strategy generally requires three covertizations. *Equivalent pairing is necessary when the instructions that are to appear in a later covertization do not appear in the original routine.* For instance, the later covertization introduces the instructions, "Find the numerator." If this instruction does not appear in the original routine, equivalent pairing is needed. Equivalent pairs consist of two instructions—one that the learner has mastered (**A**) and another that calls for the same behavior, but does so with unfamiliar instructions (**B**). The equivalent pairing technique assures that the learner will respond to **B**.

The general procedure for introducing equivalent instructions is first to present them in the **A-B** order, then in the **B-A** order, and finally to present only **B**.

A-B pairing. The first pairing (in the first of the three covertized routines) is one in which **A** *appears first and* **B** *immediately follows.* The learner responds to the familiar instructions, after which the teacher introduces new wording. ("You're going to tell me the opposite of *big*. That is, an *antonym* for *big*.") The learner does not have to attend to the meaning of the word *antonym*. It comes *after the fact*—after the learner has already listened to the instructions that convey the necessary information.

A variation of the **A-B** pairing is one in which the new term (**B**) is presented *after* the learner has responded to the **A** instructions: "Tell me the opposite of big . . . Good, you told me the opposite of big. You told me an *antonym* for big."

The basic task may be embellished by adding tests of the new word. "What kind of word did you give me for big?" In either case, this basic pairing (**A** followed by **B**) has the least potential to teach the learner because the learner receives all the necessary information from the **A** instructions and therefore is not required to attend to **B**. (The learner *could* respond appropriately by attending only to the familiar instruction.)

B-A Pairing. The pairing for the next covertization is a **B-A** pairing in which the new instruction (**B**) comes *first*. "You're going to tell me the antonym for a word. To do that, you tell me the opposite." This pairing has a greater potential to teach the meaning of antonym because the learner is required to attend to it to a greater degree.

B Alone. Following two or three sessions of the **B-A** pairing would be the final covertization, in which the **A** is dropped completely and the learner is required to operate only from **B**. The step in the new operation would be, "Tell me the antonym for big." If the learner failed to respond or responded with the synonym, the basic correction would be to use the **B-A** pairing, "You're going to tell me the *antonym* for big. To do that, tell me the opposite."

Illustration: Multiplying fractions. Let's say that the learner performed well on the fraction-multiplication operation and we wanted the learner to operate from the instructions: "Find the product." The instructions provided in the original operation are treated as the familiar instruction **A** (multiply across the top and the bottom). We could introduce the following progression of covertization.

The A-B Pairing

1.	Teacher:	Read the problem.
	Learner:	Three-fourths times two thirds.
2.	Teacher:	Multiply across the top and across the bottom.
	Learner:	(Performs operation.)
3.	Teacher:	You multiplied across the top and across the bottom. So you found the product. What did you find by multiplying?
	Learner:	The product.

The A-B pairing occurs in step 3 above.

The B-A Pairing

1.	Teacher:	Read the problem.
	Learner:	Three-fourths time two-thirds.

2. Teacher: You're going to find the product. You do that by multiplying across the top and across the bottom. How do you find the product?

   Learner: Multiply across the top and across the bottom.

3. Teacher: Do it. Find the product.

   Learner: (Multiplies and writes: $\frac{6}{12}$)

The pairing is introduced in step 2. Note that the step is designed so the learner responds to the question, "How do you find the product?" The learner, however, has been told what to do (multiply across the top and the bottom). Although step 3 tells the learner to find the product, the learner is not actually required to operate from a knowledge of the meaning of *product* because of the pairing of instructions that occurs in step 2.

B Alone

1. Teacher: Read the problem.

   Learner: (Reads.)

2. Teacher: Find the product.

   Learner: (Multiplies and writes: $\frac{6}{12}$)

The **A** instructions are dropped and the learner must operate from the **B** instructions only.

Illustration: Expanded notation. The learner has been taught this operation for expressing two-digit numerals as addition facts:

Example: 37

Teacher: Tell how many tens and how many ones are in this numeral.

Learner: Three tens plus seven ones.

We want the learner to indicate the addition fact in response to the direction: "Expand this numeral."

A-B Pairing

Teacher: Tell me how many tens and how many ones are in this numeral.

Learner: Three tens plus seven ones.

Teacher: You told me how many tens and how many ones are in the numerals so you expanded this numeral.

B-A Pairing

Teacher: You're going to expand this numeral. To do that, you tell how many tens and how many ones are in this numeral.

Learner: Tell how many tens and how many ones are in this numeral.

Teacher: Do it. Expand the numeral.

Learner: Three tens plus seven ones.

B Alone

Teacher: Expand the numeral.

Learner: Three tens plus seven ones.

Illustration: Beginning word reading. The learner can respond to this routine:

Example: ●───mat──→

1. Teacher: You're going to sound out this word and say it fast. What are you going to do?

   Learner: Sound out this word and say it fast.

2. Teacher: (Touches ball of arrow.) Sound it out. (Teacher moves to each sound as learner says: "mmmmaaaat.")

3. Teacher: Say it fast.

   Learner: Mat.

A-B Pairing

1. Teacher: You're going to sound out this word and say it fast. What are you going to do?

   Learner: Sound out this word and say it fast.

2. Teacher: (Touches ball of arrow.) Sound it out. (Teacher moves to each sound as learner says: "mmmaaat.")

3. Teacher: Say it fast.

   Learner: Mat.

4. Teacher: You sounded out this word and said it fast. You showed you could read this word.

B-A Pairing

1. Teacher: You're going to read this word. To do that you sound it out and say it fast. How do you read a word?

   Learner: Sound it out and say it fast.

2. Teacher: (Touches ball of arrow.) Sound it out. (Teacher moves to each letter as the learner says: "mmmaaat.")

3. Teacher: Say it fast.

   Learner: Mat.

B Alone

1. Teacher: You're going to read this word. How do you do that?

   Learner: Sound it out and say it fast.

2. Teacher: (Touches ball of arrow.) Sound it out. (Teacher moves to each letter as learner says: "mmmaaat.")
3. Teacher: Say it fast.
   Learner: Mat.

Choice of Covertization Techniques

Here are general rules about using various techniques:

1. If the terminal operation involves instructions that are in the initial overtized routine, no equivalent pairing is required. The strategies will be limited to dropping steps, regrouping, and creating inclusive steps.
2. If different wording is called for by the terminal operation, equivalent pairing is needed in the covertizations.
3. If the original routine involves steps that relate to mechanical details that are assumed to be firmed through the practice with the original routine, drop the steps or parts of steps that refer to the mechanical detail.
4. If the original routine involves a large number of steps, first try to group these steps to form "units," or a series of logically related behaviors. Use regrouping and inclusive instructions.

Let us say that the learner has mastered the following overtized operation:

Example: $\frac{5}{8}(—) = (—) = 1$

1. Teacher: To change any fraction into one by multiplying, you turn the fraction upside down and multiply. How do you change any fraction into one by multiplying.
   Learner: Turn the fraction upside down and multiply.
2. Teacher: What fraction are we starting with?
   Learner: Five-eighths.
3. Teacher: What is five-eighths turned upside down?
   Learner: Eight-fifths.
4. Teacher: Multiply eight-fifths times five-eighths.
   Learner: (Writes five-eighths times eight-fifths and multiplies and writes forty-fortieths.)
5. Teacher: What's the answer for the top?
   Learner: Forty.
6. Teacher: What's the answer for the bottom?
   Learner: One.
7. Teacher: What does forty over forty equal?
   Learner: Forty.
8. Teacher: We changed five-eighths into one by multiplying.

Here's the terminal covertization that will be presented:

Example: $\frac{5}{8}(—) = (—) = 1$

Teacher: Change the fraction into one by multiplying.

By comparing the terminal covertization with the fully overtized routine, we see that the wording used in the terminal task appears in the highly overtized routine. Therefore, we will not use equivalent-pair strategies in the covertizations.

Our first covertization lumps component steps together and makes the learner responsible for producing the rule about multiplying.

1. Teacher: How do you change any fraction into one by multiplying?
   Learner: Turn the fraction upside down and multiply.
2. Teacher: What fraction are you starting with?
   Learner: Five-eighths.
3. Teacher: Change five-eighths into one by multiplying.
   Learner: (Writes eight-fifths and forty-fortieths.)
4. Teacher: What does forty over forty equal?
   Learner: One.
5. Teacher: We changed five-eighths into one by multiplying.

The most critical aspects of the covertization have to do with dropping the instructions from step 1, and the inclusive instructions for the behaviors of the multiplication process.

Step 1 tests the learner on the rule. Step 2 (which could possibly be dropped with no great loss) remains overt. Step 3 is an inclusive instruction including behaviors presented in steps 3 to 6 of the original operation. This lumping is permissible because the learner has already practiced the individual behaviors as a chain that occurs in a fixed order.

Following the covertizations above would be the terminal task: "Change this number into one by multiplying." It would be possible to interpolate other covertizations before presenting the terminal task; however, the reduction of steps would be somewhat trivial. We assume that the learner can read the fraction and can perform the step of turning the number upside down and multiplying. The learner can therefore perform all the steps covertly.

Timetable

We cannot provide a precise specification of how many covertizations should be introduced or how long the learner should be exposed to each. However, we can provide rule-of-thumb guidelines based on logical considerations.

1. To be safe, retain each routine for two days or lessons. The two-day exposure guarantees that the learner works the sequence of steps frequently enough to make the subsequent covertization safe.

2. Process at least two examples through the routine each time it appears. For some routines, four or five examples should be processed each lesson.

3. For routines of 8 steps or more, do not change the preceding routine more than 25-30% for relatively naive learners and no more than 50% for experienced learners. To be safe, the 30% rule can be followed for all learners. For routines shorter than 8 steps, as much as 50% of the routine can be changed.

As the rules-of-thumb indicate, the longer routines require a larger number of covertizations than shorter routines. An 8-step routine can be reduced first to 5 steps, then possibly to 3, and finally to 1—the goal operation. A 20-step routine, on the other hand, would be reduced first to around 15 steps, then to 10, then to 7, then to 5, then to 1. If each variation of the routine is retained for 2 lessons (and if there is no overlapping of the routines presented on each lesson), the covertization process would require 12 lessons.

Overlapping Schedule

The problem associated with longer routines is stipulation. Since teacher directs the activities in an atomic manner, the learner may understandably have trouble working independently if the process of covertization takes too long. To hasten it, *routines at different stages of covertization may be introduced in the same lesson.* (This procedure is analogous to the response-shaping procedure that is described in Section VII.)

The basic overlapping procedure is to introduce two routines during the same lesson, *the first of which is more highly structured than the second.* The first-presented routine functions as the "familiar" routine. It prompts the series of behaviors that is to be followed in the subsequent routine. By juxtaposing the routines so that the less-highly structured one immediately follows the more highly-structured one, we prompt the learner to perform on the less-highly structured routine. (The learner does "the same thing" on juxtaposed examples.) This procedure helps to avoid stipulation because it shows the learner the "direction" in which instruction is progressing.

Table 21.1 gives a timetable for overlapping covertization of a long routine.

Figure 21.1									
Components	Lessons								
	1	2	3	4	5	6	7	8	9
Routine A	4	2	1						
Routine B		2	4	4					
Routine C				2	4	2			
Routine D					2	5	8	8	8

The numbers in each cell indicate how many examples are processed through the routine. Each routine is presented on three successive lessons; however, in nine lessons, the learner is taken through four routines. By the seventh lesson, the learner is performing on independent work exclusively. On nearly every lesson before 7, the learner works on two routines. On lesson 6, for example, the learner is presented with two examples of the **C** covertization, followed by five examples of the **D** covertization (which is independent work). The work on the **C** covertization prompts the skills that are called for by the independent work.

Correcting Mistakes in Covertized Routines

The correction for mistakes in covertized routines always involves overtizing the part of routine on which the mistake occurred using overt steps presented previously in the covertization series.

The correction involves:

1. Presenting those steps from an earlier covertization that relate to the learner's mistake.

2. Repeating the entire covertized *problem* on which the learner made an error.

Step 1 of this correction procedure is designed to "prompt" the behaviors called for. Step 2 is designed to test the learner in the context in which the mistake originally occurred.

Note that the correction takes the form similar to that of an **A-B** pairing. The **A** is the familiar routine; the **B** is the covertized routine. When the learner makes a mistake on **B**, **A** is introduced to prompt the appropriate behavior. **B** is then presented to assure that the learner can perform on the covertized routine.

Let us say that the learner is performing on this covertization:

Example: $\frac{5}{8}\left(\frac{}{}\right) = \left(\frac{}{}\right) = 1$

1. Teacher: How do you change any fraction into one by multiplying?
   Learner: Turn the fraction upside down and multiply.
2. Teacher: What fraction are you starting with?
   Learner: Five-eighths.
3. Teacher: Change five-eights into one by multiplying.
   Learner: (Writes $\frac{5}{8}\left(\frac{5}{8}\right) = \left(\frac{}{}\right) = 1$)

The teacher stops the learner at this point and provides a correction:

1. Teacher: What fraction are we starting with?
   Learner: Five-eighths.
2. Teacher: What's five-eights turned upside down?
   Learner: Eight-fifths.
3. Teacher: Multiply five-eighths times *eight-fifths*.
   Learner: (Writes: $\frac{8}{5}$ and multiplies.)
4. Teacher: (Praises, erases work.)
5. Teacher: What fraction are you starting with?
   Learner: Five-eighths.
6. Teacher: Change five-eighths into one by multiplying.
   Learner: Writes: $\frac{5}{8}\left(\frac{8}{5}\right) = \frac{40}{40} = 1$)
7. Teacher: What does forty over forty equal?
   Learner: One.
8. Teacher: We changed five-eights into one by multiplying.

Summary

To transport the learner from the highly overtized routine to one that requires independent work, a series of covertizations or routines of decreasing structure are introduced. Each routine in a covertized series is similar enough to a preceding one to prompt the appropriate series of steps, but different enough to represent a significant movement toward making the routine more independent.

The four covertization techniques are: *dropping steps, regrouping interactions, providing inclusive instructions,* and *providing equivalent instructions.*

Step-dropping, regrouping, and inclusive instructions are appropriate for virtually any routine. The equivalent-pair strategy is more elaborate than the others and is appropriate when the original overtized routine does not contain the words that will appear in the final routine.

Typically, more than one technique is used in designing a covertization for a routine.

The steps may be regrouped so the learner performs a logically related set of behaviors in response to the instructions for the set.

Steps or parts of steps that are needed for any but the introductory routine are dropped.

Inclusive instructions may be presented to alert the learner to a group of related steps that are to be performed.

When appropriate, the equivalent pairing prepares the learner for new vocabulary that will signal responses in later routines.

Both the inclusive instructions and the equivalent pairing introduce new words into the covertizations. The instructions processed through the inclusive-instruction technique are "familiar" to the learner in other contexts. The instructions introduced as equivalent pairs present new vocabulary.

As a general rule, covertizations of longer routines should involve an initial shortening of 30%. When inclusive instructions or equivalent pairs of instructions are introduced, the part of the routine in which they occur is lengthened. Other parts, however, are dropped, regrouped, or changed. Routines of 8 steps or fewer may be shortened initially by 50%.

If the learner works on highly structured, teacher-directed routines for a long period of time, the learner may understandably expect to be led through the operation, without initiating the various steps. To buttress against this type of stipulation, the covertizations of initially long routines are overlapped, so that on many lessons, the learner works problems of *more than one covertization*. The more-highly-structured routine is presented first. It serves as a prompt. After the learner has successfully worked one or more problems using this routine, the less-structured routine is introduced. This juxtaposition of a more highly-structured routine and a less-structured one implies to the learner that the same operation is used by the less-structured routine.

As a rule of thumb, each routine should be presented for at least two days, and each routine should process a total of at least ten examples.

The basic correction procedure involves making the steps involved in the operation overt. If the learner misses a step in a later covertization that had earlier been processed through four steps, the teacher takes the learner through the four steps, then presents the routine that requires only one step. By making the steps overt, the teacher can provide a precise diagnosis of the learner's problem. By returning to the less-structured routine, the learner is tested on applying the steps to the context in which the mistake occurred.

SECTION VII
RESPONSE-LOCUS ANALYSIS

So far, we have dealt with sequences and presentations that are based primarily on the analysis of stimuli. Although the pure stimulus-locus assumption has been modulated somewhat, it remains paramount in these communication forms. The design of communication forms has been dominated by the notion that the learner is a perfect receiver and that if we present a communication that is consistent with a single interpretation, the learner will learn. Evidence of the learning will be the pattern of responses the learner produces and generalization to examples for which generalization is logically implied.

As noted earlier, the response-locus analysis is an analysis of the learner, not of the stimulus. The analysis is based on the lawful tendencies of the learner's behavior to change in response to practice. It is used when the learner does not respond to a logically faultless communication. For example, we present a faultless communication that *shows* the learner exactly how to perform a back somersault in the air. When we test the learner on the understanding of what is to be done, we observe that the learner is able to *describe* the motor response, discriminate it, and label it. However, when asked to perform, the learner fails to produce the response. Repeatedly and in response to various reinforcers or punishers, the learner fails.

The response-locus analysis now comes into play because we must teach the learner *how to produce the response.* This process is slow, requiring many, many trials. The focus of this teaching is on the production of the motor response (doing a backward somersault in the air), not on verbal discriminations.

Parallels Between Stimulus-Locus and Response-Locus Communications

Although the emphasis of the response-locus communication is different from the ones we have dealt with in the preceding sections, there are parallels.

1. The procedures for inducing generalization of a new response are basically the same as those used to induce generalization for discriminations. To show how a particular motor response applies to a range of variation, we juxtapose applications that are greatly different. If the learner responds "in the same way" to these applications, the learner should be able to respond to any new application that falls within the range of variation that had been practiced.

2. The problem of stipulation has a counterpart in new-response teaching. Just as extended practice on a range of examples that presents a very limited range of variation induces stipulation, practice on a range of new-response applications that presents a very limited range of variation tends to produce responses that are *distorted*. These responses do not readily generalize to new applications.

3. Juxtaposed practice examples present the simplest context for new responses. Just as juxtaposed examples of the same discrimination present the least demanding context for showing what is the same and what is different about the various examples of a discrimination, juxtaposed practice with a new response prompts what is the same about the various examples of the new response.

4. The various applications that the learner is to respond to admit to a subtype analysis. This analysis suggests subtypes that are relatively simple (involving applications that require fewer responses, less coordination of responses, or shorter chains of responses), and subtypes that are relatively difficult (requiring a greater number of responses, more coordination of responses, or longer chains of responses). This analysis suggests details of a program for teaching the new response.

Differences Between Stimulus-Locus and Response-Locus Communications

There are three major differences between stimulus-locus communication and response-locus communications:

Section VII | Response-Locus Analysis

1. The goal of response-locus teaching is to teach specific responses. The stimulus-locus analysis is concerned with teaching a "pattern" that would be manifested with a variety of responses (pointing, verbal, manipulative). Through any of these responses, the learner could demonstrate knowledge of what is the same about the various examples. The analysis, therefore, is one of the *stimulus quality* that is the same across all examples, and the teaching is designed to induce knowledge of this sameness. The new-response teaching, on the other hand, has a completely different objective: to teach specific responses the learner cannot produce. The analysis therefore begins with the specific task that the learner cannot produce. The response that is called for may not be substituted for other responses. The teaching focuses on inducing the response. Much of the information that is relevant to the efficient induction of the new response comes from an analysis of the learner, what type of fatigue patterns are typically associated with different types of practice, what rate of learning can be expected, what type of reinforcers are relatively efficient, and so forth. Certainly, not all of the information that is relevant to new-response teaching comes from an analysis of the learner. The learner who is trying to learn a back somersault in the air is the same learner who learns qualitative samenesses and who generalizes on the basis of these samenesses. The learner can therefore be expected to apply this same generalization strategy to responses and to learn "misrules" if they are implied by instruction. However, the instructional procedures are basically different because the task is mandated as something the learner must do. The focus of instruction is on modifying the learner and inducing the response to the task.

2. The end product of response-teaching is a specific set of overt behaviors. When we teach the learner to write, the learner continues to produce the overt writing response after the program has terminated. These responses are not faded, covertized, or changed. This situation is quite different from instruction associated with concepts. For concept learning, no particular behavior is implied, and the goal of the program is usually to covertize the skill as much as possible. The responses that the learner produces are not the same responses the learner will produce after the program is completed. The routine that had been constructed to guide the learner and to permit feedback is replaced by some kind of internalized counterpart that may bear little resemblance to the overtized series of steps in the routine.

3. The juxtaposition pattern of examples cannot be controlled for response teaching the way it can be controlled for concept teaching. This difference is the most serious and carries the most extensive implications for the specific techniques used to teach responses.

Because the learner does not produce a new response appropriately during initial teaching, we are faced with a double problem: the first is to induce appropriate response *to some examples*. The second is to induce generalization to a range of examples. When we deal with concepts, we do not face a problem of first inducing the response with some examples. The learner is usually able to produce the responses on the first trial. *When the learner produces the responses for different examples on the first trial, there is a close correspondence between the juxtaposition pattern of the examples and the learner's pattern of correct responses.*

When we deal with response-teaching, we find *a great discrepancy between the juxtaposition of the examples and the pattern of correct trials the learner produces.* The reason is that the learner requires many trials on each example before producing an appropriate response to that example. Since we do not know how many trials will be required for the learner to master the early trials, we have very little control over the precise juxtaposition of *correct-trials*.

Figure VII.1
Comparison of Juxtaposed Examples and Pattern of Trials

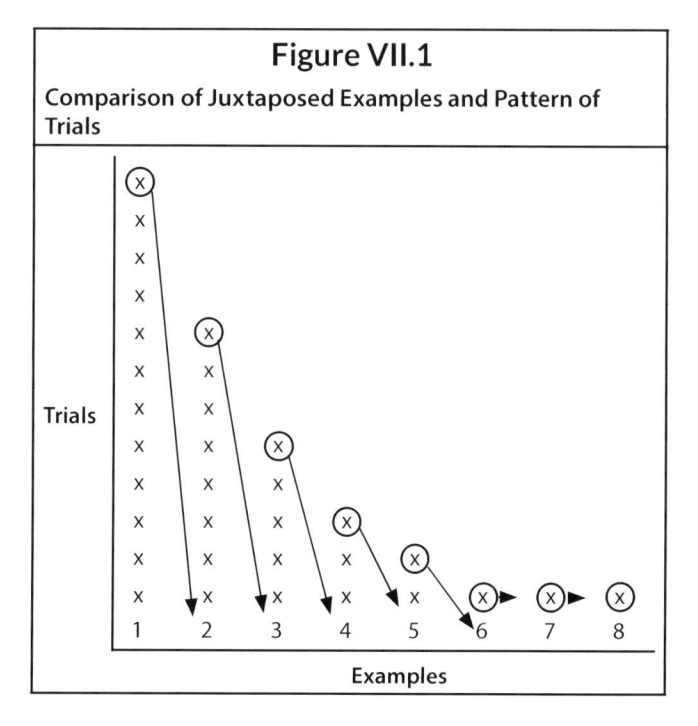

Figure VII.1 illustrates the discrepancy between the

juxtaposition of the learner's correct trials with the juxtaposition of examples. The circled X's are successful trials. The learner is presented with trials on test example 1 until an acceptable response is produced. Then the learner practices on example 2, and so forth. The examples (1-8) are sequenced to show sameness and difference.

The pattern of juxtaposition *for the successful trials* is completely different from the juxtaposition of the examples. The successful performance of examples 1, 2 and 3 are not juxtaposed. Following the twelfth trial with example 1, the first trial for example 2 is presented. This trial is not followed by example 3, but by seven more trials on example 2. Near the end of the sequence, a parallel evolves between the juxtaposed examples and juxtaposed trials. We would therefore predict that whatever sameness between examples exists at the end of the sequence (examples 5 through 8) would be conveyed to the learner. During the first part of the sequence, however, the discrepancy between the juxtaposition of examples and juxtaposition of successful trials creates a presentation that is not well designed to demonstrate sameness or difference. The practice trials with the first examples in the sequence are designed to induce *stipulation* in some form. (The learner repeatedly practices the same example.)

Avoiding Traps

Problems of teaching new responses are well designed to lead us into four traps.

1. The first trap is that of displacing the problem from a new response to some sort of discrimination. Instead of teaching the learner how to operate a handsaw, we require the learner to work on *labeling parts of the handsaw* or on other trials that have nothing to do with the central behavior of operating the machine. The goal of response teaching is to establish words about the behavior.

2. The next trap is that of *identifying the entire event* in which the new response is embedded as the objective of instruction. Instead of teaching the child how to tie a shoelace, the program begins with a long chain of behaviors—finding the shoes, putting them on, then tying them. Although we ultimately want the learner to perform the shoe-tying behavior in the context of a chain, we do not begin with this chain to teach shoelace-tying. We first teach the behavior of tying a shoe, and after it is taught we incorporate it into a longer chain. The distinction is not whether the chain of behaviors will be taught, but rather how we begin instruction. The shoe-tying should be removed from the chain because massed practice on shoe-tying is not provided easily within the longer chain.

3. The third trap is that of *sequencing examples from easy to hard*. It seems reasonable to assume that if we were teaching the learner to operate with screwdrivers, we would bring the learner to a high criterion of performance on the screwdrivers that involve the simplest behavior (those like hexagonal wrenches that fit tightly onto the nut that is being turned). The strict easy-to-hard progression is usually spurious. It fails to show the learner what is the same about the range of applications. The learner will learn inappropriate behaviors that work with simple examples. Later, the learner will have to relearn the behaviors. By following the principle of demonstrating sameness, we avoid the teaching of inappropriate responses. To the extent that it is possible, we sequence examples so that the learner works on juxtaposed examples that are greatly different. This work requires the learner to perform the same operation with "easier" examples and with juxtaposed harder examples. Knowledge of sameness is therefore induced.

Obviously, the demonstration of sameness must be modulated by practical considerations. If the learner cannot produce even an approximation of the response called for by the more difficult applications, work on these applications will not demonstrate sameness. We must therefore limit the sameness description to the range of applications to which the learner can respond with approximations of the desired response.

4. The final trap is that of *practice*. Most programs for teaching responses like cursive writing do not provide for the amount or type of practice needed to induce the desired behaviors. Without practice, the behaviors will not develop. With practice they will, even if the practice is not provided as elegantly as possible. Just as there is a tendency to provide inadequate practice, there is the opposite tendency to recognize practice as the only variable. On-task time and trials are not the only variables affecting performance. Good programs make substantial differences in the learner's performance; however, these programs may show no particular advantage at first.

A related practice issue concerns the criterion that we use for judging that the learner is "successful" on a particular task that involves new-response learning. A single successful performance does not imply that the learner has achieved an acceptable criterion of performance. The learner must demonstrate consistency in the appropriate response. The fact that the learner is able to produce the desired response in a highly prompted context (following the teacher's demonstration and help in producing the response) does not imply that the learner can produce the response consistently or in various contexts. A much more convincing performance is needed before we judge the learner to be successful.

Perspective

Chapters 22, 23, and 24 deal with different facets of teaching new responses. Chapter 22 presents the basic response-induction technique. Chapters 23 and 24 deal with complex physical operations like throwing a ball, tying a shoe, or performing the chain of behaviors required to get on a bus.

The range of new-response-teaching applications is very broad, but all applications are the same in an important way. The immediate goal of instruction is to change the learner so that the learner can perform appropriately on the task. A clearly understood assumption is that we will proceed as rapidly as possible. We will not attempt to see how many "steps" we can introduce in instruction, how many discriminations we can teach, or how much practice we can present. Our goal is scrupulous efficiency, which means that we will be very careful about the *starting point* for each program, the order and type of examples, and the various techniques that we may be able to use to achieve the desired behavior as quickly as possible.

Chapter 22
New Response Teaching Procedures

Identifying New-Response Problems

To identify a new-response problem, we first determine what the learner is to do. We then provide reasonable evidence that the learner cannot do it. As part of this process, we "reduce" or simplify the task so that we strip the unessential details from it.

Selecting a Single Objective

Initial teaching for responses is like that for discriminations in that it teaches only one thing at a time. The teaching may involve a complex response such as shoe-tying, or it may deal with a simple response, such as holding something between the thumb and forefinger.

We can appreciate the problem of specifying objectives by observing a naive learner eating. We do not like the way the learner is sitting, the inappropriate use of the fork, the slobbering, the spilling from the cup, the eating with fingers, etc. We may change all this behavior, but we do not *start* with "eating properly" as our objective. We must be far more precise. What aspect of eating properly do we wish to select for instruction? We are provided with many options, and our ultimate selection will be arbitrary, but we must identify one specific objective from the array of possibilities.

The good way to identify objectives is to group behavior *by goals*. What is the learner trying to do with the fork? (Transport green beans from plate to mouth.) What is the learner trying to do with the glass? (Transport milk to the mouth.) Each behavioral goal implies activities that are associated with particular goals.

By viewing objectives according to what the learner is trying to do, we automatically identify the *functional behaviors*. Furthermore, we avoid the peripheral behaviors.

Demonstrating Behavioral Deficiency

After we identify units of behavior related to a specific goal, we test to make sure that the learner cannot produce the behavior. For instance, if we identify the behavior of drinking from the glass without spilling, we must now demonstrate that the learner cannot do it. The demonstration serves as a placement test or pretest for the program.

Our strategy is to rule out all possible variables that could account for the observed behavior. Perhaps the learner is not trying. Perhaps we observed a non-representative sample of behavior. Perhaps the learner can perform on the particular behavior when it is removed from the context of the activity in which we observed it. Perhaps the learner does not understand what to do. To provide evidence that the observed performance is not controlled by these possibilities, we should:

1. Remove the behavior from the chain in which it occurred. Remove the drinking from eating a meal.

2. Remove all unnecessary discriminations from the task, and model the exact behavior that is expected of the learner. Do not use questionable verbal explanations. Simply show the learner what is expected, possibly with verbal explanations after the fact—as statements that describe what you did.

3. Arrange the testing setup so that trials of the task can be juxtaposed and presented quickly. If consecutive trials require more than 10 seconds, something is probably wrong with the skill that had been identified or with the setup. If you can identify the part of the response that prevents the learner from completing the trial, discard the original test and test the learner on the troublesome part.

4. Control reinforcement or attention variables if there is a question about whether the learner is trying. A number of techniques are available, including presenting a series of familiar tasks, which is immediately followed by the target task. If the learner performs appropriately on consecutive trials of the familiar task, and if the learner fails the new task, the probability is great that the learner cannot produce the response. For the tasks

that precede the target tasks, the teacher directs and the learner complies. Therefore, the learner will probably try to "do the same thing" (comply) with the target task.

The learner's performance on the four-step task above not only provides strong evidence about the behavior the learner cannot perform; it also helps us modify the task so that:

1. Juxtaposed trials can be presented quickly to the learner.
2. Trials do not require great understanding of verbal instructions or discriminations that are irrelevant to the new response.
3. There are reinforcing contingencies for trials that are judged reinforceable.

These requirements are essential for response teaching.

Reducing Tasks to a Simpler Form

When we design tasks, we try to find a simpler form. Obviously, we cannot simplify tasks indefinitely. We reach a point at which the simplified task no longer requires the intended response. A simpler form is one that requires the intended response and that has these features:

1. It shares all the essential response features with all other examples of the response.
2. It contains as few component behaviors as any example of the response we can identify.

The response that we design shares all essential response features if it possesses those features observed in *all* positive instances of the response, but in *no* negative instances. Judgment about whether the instance contains no more components than any other instance of the response depends on our ability to produce "creative" examples.

The point of applying the tests is to avoid infinite reduction of the operation or response. At some point, the operation of shoe-tying ceases to be shoe-tying. We want to identify a simple example of shoe-tying, but it must be an example of shoe-tying, not of making an Indian knot, of holding the teacher's hands as she ties, or of dealing with a component of shoe-tying, such as making a loop or pulling on the ends of the laces.

If the objective of the response is to transport food on a fork to the learner's mouth, the simplest form of the response is one in which the learner is not required to spear the food, to pick up the fork, or to do any behaviors except transport the forkful of food from the plate to the mouth. All other behaviors are removed. If we carry the removal of behaviors to an extreme, we could eliminate some of those associated with *holding* the fork. Perhaps the fork is attached to a glove the learner wears. The learner is still responsible for transferring the material, but the response requires coordination of fewer behaviors.

If the goal of an operation is to throw a ball, the learner should be responsible for the *throwing*, not for *picking up* or any other ancillary behaviors.

Continuous Parts and Non-Continuous Parts

Some responses involve *non-continuous behaviors* that are strung together. Others consist of *continuous behaviors* that cannot be stopped. Tying a shoe involves various non-continuous parts. We can cross the laces and then stop. We can next loop them and then stop, etc. Throwing a ball, saying the word *me*, spinning a top, and doing a somersault, require continuous behavior. We cannot stop (or start) in the middle. The idea is not to reduce all responses to a continuous behavior, merely to reduce them to a simple form. The ultimate form may have non-continuous responses chained together; or may consist of continuous behaviors. In either case, the simple form will have no unnecessary components.

Response-Teaching Strategies

There are three response-teaching problems. Each suggests a different strategy.

1. The learner is capable of producing the response that is called for, but *cannot produce the response in the context of the task* that we present. Although the response has been observed in other contexts, the learner apparently does not understand the new context, cannot remember the response that is called for, or is not attending to the appropriate details of the example. In any case, the learner does not produce the response in the new context.

2. The learner apparently understands the directions of the task but *is incapable of producing the response* and has never produced it in any context.

3. The learner apparently *does not understand the directions* and *has never produced the response called for by the task* in any context.

The implied remedy for type 1 is to first establish the behavior in a simpler context, then to modify the context so that it progressively approximates the desired context. This program works on teaching the learner *when* to produce a particular response. It shapes the *context*.

Type 2 suggests shaping the *response*. The learner gives indications of knowing what to do; however, the learner cannot produce the response under any reinforcing condition or in any context. Therefore, the instruction must help the learner form the response. The learner does not need information about *when* to produce the response, but needs information about *how* to respond and needs practice designed to change the learner's ability to respond. The program shapes the *response* through successive approximations.

Type 3 presents a double problem. The learner does not give any indication of knowing what kind of response is called for and the learner has never demonstrated the response in question. The strategy must make the learner aware of the type of response called for and must shape the response.

Type-1 Strategies:

Teaching When to Produce Responses

Type-1 strategies show the learner when to produce the response. The learner has a problem in "associating" a particular response with the signal or cue. For whatever reason, the learner does not decode this signal as a prompt or does not recall it, and therefore does not produce the response that is called for.

Teaching highly unfamiliar discriminations calls for type-1 strategies. Let us say that we were interested in teaching the learner to identify notes that we play on the piano. The correct responses are "A," or "C," or "G." The learner has no trouble producing these responses (saying "A" or "G"). However, after repeated trials, the learner may not produce the appropriate response when presented with an "A" note or a "G" note. The same problem is observed with mentally retarded and autistic children, who often require many trials before successfully responding to a task such as, "Come here." Yet the behaviors of *coming here* are not difficult for the learners to produce.

The strategy for remedying type-1 deficiencies is to provide *systematic interruptions of trials of the task being taught*. The strategy is based on a fact of juxtaposition, which is that if the learner is required to do the same thing on juxtaposed examples, the series requires less attention and less memory. Conversely, if the learner is required to do different things on juxtaposed examples, the series is more difficult—requiring more attention and more memory. Accordingly, *we can make an item or task relatively easy or relatively difficult according to how the task to be taught is juxtaposed with other events.*

Let's say that we wish to teach task **A**. Here's the type of juxtaposition that would make performance on task **A** relatively easy:

A ⟶ A ⟶ A ⟶ A ⟶ A ⟶ Ⓐ

The tasks are presented in rapid sequence. The circled **A** is the target task. As the sequence shows, the circled **A** is preceded by repetitions of the same task. The probability of appropriate performance of the circled **A** is great if the learner has performed successfully on the preceding **A**'s.

A more difficult pattern of juxtaposition is one that increases the amount and type of interference between the presentation of **A**'s. Here is a pattern of juxtaposition that requires the learner to attend to another task before returning to **A**.

A ⟶ B ⟶ Ⓐ

Assume that the learner performed successfully on the first **A** and assume that **B** is a familiar task (one the learner can perform consistently) that is greatly different from **A**. The probability that the learner will perform correctly on the circled **A** is reduced *because the circled **A** is more difficult* by virtue of the juxtapositions. The reason is that the learner's attention is pulled from **A** by the presentation of **B**. The learner must now remember more details of how to discriminate **A** or about how to produce the response that is called for.

We can make the task even more difficult by creating greater separations of the **A**'s. The more interference we introduce between the presentations of **A**, the more difficult the circled **A**. To create additional interference, we can pause a longer period of time, introduce a greater number of interpolated tasks, or make the interpolated tasks more similar to **A** or more difficult with respect to attention and response demands.

Here is a sequence that is more difficult than those illustrated above.

A ⟶ B ⟶ C ⟶ D ⟶ Ⓐ

The separations of **A** are created by presenting familiar tasks **B**, **C**, and **D**.

The most difficult sequence, with respect to the juxtaposition of examples, would be one in which the initial **A** is removed by perhaps hours from the presentation of the circled **A**. All the interpolated activities that occur between occurrences of **A** serve as potential interference for **A**.

The relative difficulty based on the patterns of juxtaposition provides the basis for designing teaching that proceeds from relatively easy tasks to those that are more difficult. Below are three levels of difficulty:

1. A ⟶ Ⓐ
2. A ⟶ B ⟶ Ⓐ
3. A ⟶ B ⟶ C ⟶ D ⟶ Ⓐ

The three levels of difficulty imply a three-level strategy. Since level 1 is the easiest level, it is the starting level. The pattern shown for level 1 is repeated until the learner performs successfully on three or four consecutive trials. Note that they *must be consecutive*. The fact that the learner performs once in a while is not an indication that the learner has worked out whatever operation is required to respond consistently to that task.

The number of trials presented for a given learner varies according to the learner's performance, which means that one learner may require 18 trials and another may require 5.

Here is the presentation of level 1 to a learner:

Teacher	Learner
Your name is Henry. What's your name?	No response.
Henry, what is your name?	Henry.
Good. What is your name?	No response.
Henry. Your name is Henry. What is your name?	Henry.
Good. What's your name?	Henry.
That's right. What's your name?	Henry.
I like the way you say that. What's your name?	Henry.

The learner performed correctly on four consecutive trials. *Immediately following this performance*, the teacher presents level 2 juxtapositions. This level is characterized by the interpolation of **B** tasks. These are familiar tasks that are greatly different from the **A** tasks.

Immediately following Henry's level-1 performance, the teacher presents these tasks. (Note that the sequence begins with Henry's last successful performance on level 1.)

Teacher	Learner
I like the way you say that. What's your name?	Henry.
Touch your head. Good.	(Learner performs.)
What's your name?	Henry.
Put your hand down. Good.	(Learner performs.)
What's your name?	Henry.
Stand up…Good.	(Leaner performs.)
What's your name?	Henry.
Sit down…Good.	(Learner performs.)
What's your name?	Henry.

The learner performed correctly on four consecutive trials, so the teacher may immediately proceed to the next level of difficulty–level 3 juxtapositions. (Note that the sequence begins with Henry's last successful performance on level 2.)

Teacher	Learner
Sit down…Good. What's your name?	Henry.
Touch your nose…hand down…stand up…Good. What's your name?	Henry.
Sit down…Clap…Stop. What's your name? Good job.	Henry.
Touch your nose…hands down…close your eyes…What's your name?	Henry.
Good working. Point to your teacher…Good. Stand up…Sit down…What's your name?	Henry.

Tasks introduced as **B**, **C**, and **D** in the level-3 pattern are tasks that have been pretaught.

The learner performed successfully, so the basic program has been completed. The teacher now introduces integration activities.

Features of the Strategy

The three-level context-shaping strategy has the following advantages:

1. It does not make assumptions about how much practice will be required for the learner to perform on the task when it is presented in the juxtaposition pattern of level 3. The learner's performance is the sole guide to whether the teacher stays on a particular level or moves to the next level.

2. Its design assures that if the teacher follows the rules, the learner will receive reinforcement on at least 70 percent of the trials once the learner masters level 1. Initially, the learner may not receive positive reinforcement at this rate; however, in most cases, the learner very quickly performs on level 1 with enough consistency to earn reinforcement on at least 70 percent of the trials.

3. A variation of the strategy can be used in any situation that involves teaching when to produce a response. Whether we are working with a traumatic stroke victim, an autistic child, or a person learning a new and difficult discrimination, we can design the practice according to the three-level strategy. We simply begin with level 1 and work on it until the learner performs on three or four consecutive trials, then immediately proceed to level 2 using the same criterion of performance, then to level 3. Also, the procedure can be individualized to any rate of learning. If the learner requires 2,000 trials to complete the program, the learner receives the necessary trials.

4. The three-level strategy permits the teacher to predict *when mistakes will occur and why they will occur*. When the learner proceeds from one level of difficulty to the next, the probability is increased that a mistake will occur. It will occur because the task is more difficult than the preceding task.

5. Given the relative difficulty of the levels, the appropriate corrections for mistakes is implied. Return to an easier level. More specifically, if the learner makes a mistake on level 3, return to level 1 until the learner performs on two consecutive trials, move to level 2 until the learner performs on two consecutive trials, then present level 3 tasks. Through this type of correction, the learner still receives reinforcement on most trials.

6. The procedure permits the massing of practice. One problem with discriminations that are highly unfamiliar to the learner is that the learner will require many practice trials before reaching an acceptable level of performance. If we mass trials the practice is *less efficient* than it is if we distribute the trials. However, if we mass the trials, *we can reach our objective in far less clock time than we could by distributing practice*. Let us say it requires 500 practice trials if we distribute practice and 800 if we mass the practice. Let us say that when we distribute the practice, we present 20 trials a day. With the massed procedure we reach procedure criterion in four days. The distributed practice requires 25 days.

The three-level sequence is different from any that we have dealt with in that it does not specify *a number of examples*. Instead it specifies a procedure and a criterion of performance. This feature follows from the nature of new-response teaching. We do not have perfect control over the juxtaposition of *successful trials* the learner receives. Therefore, we design the juxtapositions that are relatively more difficult and less difficult. The pattern that is presented is governed by the learner, not by a specified order of different examples.

Integration

The integration steps that we will describe involve two separate types of activities. The first is a careful *context integration*. The newly-taught item is first integrated with instructions that are highly unlike those of the target task and that call for responses that are greatly different from those signaled by the target task. Later, responses that are increasingly similar or that are signaled by instructions highly similar to those for the new response are juxtaposed with the new response.

As this integration goes on, *event-centered applications* are introduced. These applications associate the newly taught response with a situation or event that calls for the response. They also associate the newly-taught response with other familiar responses typically involved in the situation.

Context Integration. Context integration consists of *test* sequences composed of the new item and other items familiar to the learner. The tests are ordered so that later tests are more difficult than earlier tests.

The progression of initial teaching events and context integration is outlined in Figure 22.1. Each letter represents a different task. Tasks **X** and **Y** are highly similar to **A**. The others are not highly similar. Each integration sequence is repeated until firm. The first integration sequence may be presented during three or four sessions before the learner performs on the sequence without a mistake. If the sequence must be repeated many times, however, *the order of items in the sequence should be changed to prevent the learner from memorizing the sequence of events*.

Figure 22.1

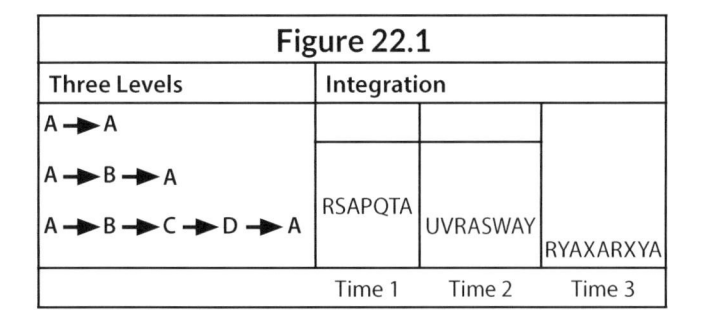

Three Levels	Integration		
A → A			
A → B → A	RSAPQTA	UVRASWAY	
A → B → C → D → A			RYAXARXYA
	Time 1	Time 2	Time 3

As soon as the learner finishes one integration sequence, the next is presented. The last sequence contains the two tasks that are most similar to **A** (**X** and **Y**). The non-similar task, **R**, is included to prevent the series from being entirely composed of highly similar discriminations or responses.

Before the final integration, the learner deals with **X** and **Y** in one context and with **A** in another. The learner is not alerted to the fact that all may occur in the same context or activity and that there are specific features of **A** that distinguish it from **X** and **Y**. Although we have used a variation of this strategy for introducing coordinate members into a set, a strict logical analysis suggests that it is not efficient. From a logical standpoint, **X** and **Y** should be introduced very early. The reason is that if the learner can discriminate between **A** and those discriminations that are most highly similar to **A** (**X** and **Y**), the learner will automatically be able to discriminate between **A** and any discrimination that is less similar to **A** than **X** and **Y**.

We do not follow a strict logical course when introducing coordinate members, and we do not follow it here because of the problems associated with firming the learner on an early set consisting of highly similar discriminations (**A**, **X**, **Y**). The set would be extremely difficult, particularly for the naive learner. (Facts about the learner support this contention.) We therefore shape the context that occurs in the integration, following the same procedures used for introducing coordinate members into a set. We first place **A** in the simplest context. We then modify the context by introducing discriminations that are more highly similar to **A**. Although this strategy may not always result in a savings in terms of the number of trials needed to achieve consistent performance on the set of **A**, **X**, **Y**, the ratio of successful trials to unsuccessful ones will be much higher, suggesting that the instruction will be more reinforcing. Although we remain aware of the problem created by this easy-to-hard progression, the learner's performance gives us little choice. We must demur logic to the facts about the learner.

Event-centered applications. The initial teaching provided by the three-level sequence prompts the new response through careful manipulation of the context in which the response occurs. The integration sequences remove many of these prompts. The purpose of the event-centered applications is to provide the learner with a different set of prompts for producing the response. A given prompt, such as "What's your name?" predictably occurs in situations that involve somebody for the first time. The question, "What's your name?" is not the only question that will probably occur in this situation. Other probable questions include, "Where do you live? . . What school do you go to? . ." and similar questions.

To present these event-centered applications, we create a mock situation that calls for the newly-taught response and other responses that are called for by that situation. For example, after teaching Henry his name, we include the question "What's your name?" in the context of questions such as, "How old are you?" and "Where do you go to school?" These questions would not always be presented in the same order; however, all would be presented. The teacher would frame the event as a "pretend" situation. "I'm going to walk into the room. Pretend that I don't know you . . . Hello. What's your name? . . Where do you go to school? . ."

These event-centered applications are effective for two reasons:

1. They prompt the various responses by virtue of their association with the same event.

2. They often help to solve problems of highly similar items because these items may not occur in the same event-centered application.

If the event does call for highly similar items (such as "What's your name?" and "What's your teacher's name?") we can make the discrimination easier by creating a response difference for one of them. For instance, we could get Henry to *initiate* the response, "Hello, my name is Henry." This initiation creates a difference between the response for "your name" and for "your teacher's name." The response to "What's your teacher's name?" is produced only as an answer to the question. Therefore, there are both differences between the tasks that call for the response, and differences between the responses.

The procedures for using event-centered applications are fairly simple. As soon as the learner completes the three-level sequence, these applications may be introduced (as the other integration activities are proceeding). We create a mock situation similar to those in which the response would frequently occur. We add to this situation responses to the other items that could occur in this situation. These responses would be familiar to the learner. We then present the situation frequently. A more detailed discussion of these "rehearsals" and their final application to real life situations is provided in Chapter 24.

Corrections

If the learner makes a mistake on the newly-taught task in any integration context, we use a shortened variation of the three-level strategy to firm the learner. We then return to the integration activity in which the mistake occurred. For example, if the learner failed to remember the sound for the letter l in the integration exercise, the teacher would first tell the learner the sound and would then present the level 1 juxtapositions. "Yes, what sound? . . . Good, what sound? . . ." followed by a level 2 and 3 juxtaposition ("What's your name? . . . What's my name? . . . What sound? . . . Good").

The steps in executing this correction are:

1. We tell the learner the correct response.
2. We present one level 1 task.
3. If the learner makes no mistakes, we follow with one level 2 task and one level 3 task. If the learner makes a mistake, we present a larger number of tasks for each level.
4. We repeat the activity in which the mistake occurred.

A shortened version of the three-level sequence is usually sufficient for the correction because the learner has already demonstrated successful performance on level 3. The correction therefore simply prompts the correct response through a few items and then returns to the context in which the mistake occurred.

Type-2 Strategies:

Teaching How to Produce Responses

Type-2 strategies cover a large range of responses, from simple grasping responses to executing a giant swing on the high bar. They apply to various situations in which:

1. *The learner can produce the response in some form but cannot produce it at the desired rate.*
2. *The learner cannot produce a simple response.*
3. *The learner cannot produce a complex response.*

Different strategies are appropriate for prompting the learner and for simplifying complex operations. However, the common feature of these teaching situations is that the learner cannot produce the response or cannot produce the response at a desired rate-accuracy criterion. The teaching strategies parallel those for teaching the learner *when* to produce the response. To teach the learner when to respond, we manipulate when (or in which juxtaposition context) we present the task. To teach the learner how to provide the response, we manipulate the criteria for reinforcing the learner's performance.

This procedure shapes *how* the response is produced and is appropriate only when we train the learner to perform at a higher rate, with greater accuracy, or with a different response configuration. It is not appropriate for teaching concepts or discriminations.

When we shape responses, we begin with a criterion of performance that the learner is capable of meeting on at least some of the trials. We reinforce trials that meet the criterion. As the learner practices the response, the responses tend to improve. We change the criterion of the performances that are closer approximations of the ultimate criterion of performance.

If we wanted a learner to sit on a chair and *if the learner is perfectly capable of producing the response*, we would not shape. (We would *not* reinforce the learner every time the learner got closer to the chair.) The reason is that *shaping induces misrules*. The learner is reinforced for some behavior. The reinforcement signals that the responses are appropriate and therefore should be retained and repeated. Every time we reinforce an approximation, we run the potential risk of suggesting to the learner that the behavior we reinforced is the behavior we desire. Therefore, we use shaping only when the learner is not able to produce the desired response under any reinforcing conditions, which means that we have no alternative other than working from approximations.

If the learner cannot say, "I am thirsty," at an acceptable rate, shaping is implied. Let's say that the learner can say "I," can say "am," and can say "thirsty," when these words are presented in isolation. Furthermore, the learner can say "I am" and "Am thirsty." The learner, however, cannot say "I am thirsty," without stumbling, pausing, or distorting one of the words. This situation meets the criteria for shaping. Although the learner can produce components, the learner cannot produce the response. This point is important. The fact that the learner can produce the components does not imply that the learner can produce the whole response.

Shaping the Response

Here are workable procedures for shaping simple responses.

1. Take baseline data on the learner's performance. Present the signal that you will use throughout the program. Possibly have another person model the response for the learner by producing the appropriate behavior in response to the signal. Present nine trials to the learner. Provide some sort of encouragement or reinforcement to insure that the learner is trying to produce the response. Carefully record the learner's performance, either by noting the details of the responses or by using some sort of recording that you can study later (such as video tape). The responses will vary, with some approximations "closer" to being appropriate and some not as good. (Some responses will be faster than others. Some will be less distorted.)

2. Use the baseline sample to assign three groups of responses.

   a. **Non-reinforceable responses.** These are the worst three responses produced. During the initial shaping, you will not reinforce responses of this type.

   b. **Single-reinforceable responses.** These are the middle three responses. Responses of this type will receive single-reinforcement during initial shaping.

   c. *Double-reinforcement responses.* These are the best three responses. Responses of this type receive double reinforcement.

3. Present trials and reinforce responses according to the criteria above. The resulting reinforcement schedule is designed *to show the learner the direction in which the shaping will move.* Some responses lead to no reinforcement. Each type of response has different features. By creating a correspondence between the features of the response and the amount of reinforcement, we communicate precise information about how reinforcement changes as the responses change.

Furthermore, the reinforcement procedure provides the learner with a sufficient amount of reinforcement to assure that the practice will not become unduly punishing. If the learner performs no better than the baseline performance, the learner will receive reinforcement on about 66% of the trials. With only 10% improvement (the elimination of some non-reinforceable responses), the learner will receive reinforcement on over 70% of the trials.

4. Change the criterion for awarding the reinforcement when the learner receives reinforcement on about 90% of the trials. The simplest procedure would be to look at the learner's last nine trials and assign the trials to three groups, the lowest group exemplifying the new standard for no reinforcement, and the highest group providing the criterion for double-reinforcement.

5. Repeat the cycle of reassigning criteria for reinforcement each time the learner consistently receives reinforcement on about 90% of the trials. Each cycle brings the learner closer to the desired response. After three or four cycles, the learner is typically responding in the acceptable range.

The procedure refers to double-reinforcers. A double-reinforcer is not necessarily two times a single, but may be quite different from the single. The double-reinforcer is something that is *more desirable to the learner than the single.* The test of which reinforcers are more desirable is to give the learner a choice of various reinforcers. The one that is consistently picked over the others is the strongest or most desirable reinforcer. In most situations, verbal statements and praise work perfectly well as reinforcers.

For singles, the teacher says something like, "Not Bad."

For doubles, "I can't believe that," or "Fantastic."

Points can also be used. For singles, the teacher might award one point or two points (somewhat randomly).

For doubles, the teacher might award 5 points. If points are used, the teacher should also use verbal praise: "Five points again. Terrific." If necessary, the points can be exchanged for tangibles.

Reinforcers should not satiate the learner. A wedge of cake is a very poor reinforcer. A sip of juice may be a good one. Verbal praise is probably the best and may be used in connection with other reinforcers.

Illustrations. If the learner cannot color within spaces, we take baseline on 9 simple examples (coloring inside 9 small boxes). We then identify the top three, middle three, and bottom three responses.

We then present trials of coloring inside outlines (perhaps starting with circles and then changing to something else). We model how to do it and help the learner with a box or two. The examples should be designed so the learner is able to complete one in 15 seconds or less. (For repetitive activities, such as making the back-and-forth strokes used in coloring, we can waive the 10-second limitation.) After each reinforceable trial, the learner gets points, praise, privileges, candy, or whatever the reinforcers are. After trials that do not earn reinforcers, we simply acknowledge it. "Okay, let's try another one." We do not punish the learner for non-reinforceable responses.

As the learner improves (achieving reinforcement on 90% of the coloring trials) we change the criterion of performance based on the learner's latest performance. The procedure is repeated until the learner's performance is judged acceptable.

We would use the same procedure to shape the learner's typing rate to 100 words per minute. We would first establish baseline performance by requiring the learner to type for nine 20-second samples. We would then examine each, identifying the rate-accuracy characteristics for the slowest three passages (the non-reinforcement samples), assigning the rate-accuracy range for the middle three as single-reinforcement status, and identifying the range for the top three as double-reinforcement.

We would now proceed with the program by giving the learner one-minute typing tests or longer tests that are rated on the word-per-minute basis. When the learner receives reinforcement on about 90% of the trials, the schedule changes based on the latest 9 trials. The procedure continues until the learner has achieved the goal.

Applying the Skill That is Taught

Just as applications follow the teaching of when to respond, applications should follow the shaping of the response. The purpose of shaping is to induce capabilities the learner did not previously possess. Once a particular skill has been shaped to the desired criterion of performance the skill should be used or applied. The situations in which it is applied should provide for reinforcing the learner. Often reinforcing applications for shaped responses are achieved with less effort than for the type-1 skills (learning *when* to respond). The reason is that the skill that is shaped often becomes a component of a physical operation. The physical operation provides feedback to the learner on all trials so long as the learner knows what the objective of the operation is. Therefore, the learner can practice the physical operation "independently" without direction or reinforcement from the teacher. When performing the operation, the learner uses the component skill. Therefore, the component skill is reinforced. For instance, if the learner is taught to press against the edge of a button with a thumb, the learner is taught a component skill that may later be used in the operation of buttoning. When pushing the button through the hole, the learner uses the component response. The learner receives reinforcement from the physical environment on each successful trial of buttoning. (Additional reinforcers may be added during the initial practice applications.)

Type-3 Strategies:

Teaching When and How to Produce Responses

In some situations, the learner is incapable of producing the response and is not firm on when to produce the response. For example, a deaf child who is learning responses to questions may not acceptably say "Henry," and may *not remember* how to produce even an approximation of the response to "What's your name?" Obviously, a great deal of teaching is involved in bringing the learner to an adequate criterion of performance.

The guiding principle for type-3 training situations is that the *learner must receive reinforcement on at least two-thirds of the trials.* Unless this principle is followed, the program will probably be ineffective. To assure this level of performance, we may consider three strategies:

1. Teach *when* to respond first and then shape the response.

2. *Shape* the response first (using cues or prompts so that the learner does not have to remember *when* to produce the response) and then teach when to respond.

3. Initially use separate teaching for *when* and for *shaping* the response, then put them together.

Choice 3 is preferable. It probably achieves the objective with the fewest misrules because it shows the learner very early in instruction both what type of response is called for and when the response is to be produced. In addition, the procedure is manageable. When the teacher works on when to produce the response, the criteria for reinforcing and correcting the learner are clear. A different set of reinforcement criteria is introduced when the teacher works on shaping the response. Although the teachings are separate, instruction in both how and when to respond can be presented during the same day. First the teacher works on one aspect of the task (*when*). At a later time, the teacher works on *how*. When the learner reaches an acceptable criterion of performance, the teacher presents applications. If the learner masters when to produce the response before learning to produce it correctly, the teacher introduces applications for *when* while continuing to work on the form of the response.

The type-3 training does not introduce anything new with respect to techniques for teaching *how* or teaching *when*. These skills are independent of each other and will probably be learned at different rates.

Firming Responses that Require Modest Practice

The basic strategies that we have presented for establishing responses are appropriate for responses that require hundreds of trials. While it is important to understand the procedures for establishing these responses, the response-teaching situations most frequently encountered by the teacher are not severe enough to warrant taking baseline data and carefully establishing the program. Most frequently, the learner has some trouble producing the response and remembering the response that is to be produced; however, the remedy requires fewer than 100 trials. For these situations, the teacher needs efficient techniques that teach the learner both when to produce the response and how to produce it.

There are two common situations that call for the abbreviated response-teaching procedures:

1. Statement and rule-saying.

2. Producing all the steps in a routine without prompting from the teacher.

Rules and statements. One of the most frequent new-response teaching applications involves rule-saying or statement saying. The learner may be required to say: "When things get hotter, they expand," before working on a series of correlated-feature examples. The learner may be required to point to the bottom number of the fraction ¾ and say: "Four parts in each group," then point to the top number, saying, "And we have three parts." The learner may be required to produce the statement, "The ball is under the table." The rule saying or statement saying may occur as part of a complex routine, or it may be a simple task. In any case, it often requires new-response teaching.

The steps for establishing verbal responses are:

- Model
- Lead
- Test

For the model step, the teacher says the rule or statement exactly as the learner is to produce it—at the same rate, and with the same inflection. Possibly the teacher presents a *multiple model* by presenting the model more than one time before the learner performs. The presentation of multiple models is a powerful technique because it impresses on the learner the pattern that is to be followed: "My turn. Four parts in each group . . . and we have three parts. My turn again: Four parts in each group . . . and we have three parts." The model should have: (1) unique inflection, and (2) unique pausing patterns.

The teacher might stress the words **group** and **have** in the sentences above. Also, the teacher might pause before and after **three**. The pauses and the unique inflections make various parts of the sentences *different from each other* and therefore easier to produce. If all parts of the sentence sound the same, the learner will have more trouble differentiating the parts. So we try to say the sentence in a way that conveys the information and that anticipates problems the learner will have in repeating it. (Expect the learner to reverse the words **groups** and **parts** and forget to say ". . . and we have . . ." Design the model to compensate for these problems.)

The lead step immediately follows the model. For the lead step, the teacher says the response with the learner at the same rate that the model had been presented. "Say it with me: Four parts in each group . . . and we have three parts. Again . . ." The lead step is repeated and alternated with the model step. If the learner simply tries to imitate the teacher's response, the teacher presents the model step several times before returning to the lead step. Usually, the model step helps the learner produce the response. Lead steps are weak if they are presented too frequently. As a rule, model and test steps should each be presented twice as frequently as lead steps.

The test step immediately follows presentations of the lead step. The test step is presented when the learner seems to be performing well on the lead step. There is no assumption that the learner will pass the "test" step the first time it is presented. "Your turn . . ." The teacher points to the bottom number and then to the top as the learner says, "Four parts in each group and we have three parts."

If the learner fails to perform on the test step, the teacher models the correct answer and repeats the test step. If the learner fails again, the teacher goes back to the model step followed by the lead step.

Chaining Parts of Statements

If the statement is too long for the learner to repeat, we present only part of the statement at a time. Some practitioners suggest the use of backward chaining—a procedure that first teaches the learner to respond to the last part of the sentence and then increases the length of the response by adding parts that precede the last parts.[*] We do not recommend the use of backward chaining for statement-saying because the procedure of ten prompts mislearning. For example, if we backward chain on the fraction-analysis sentence, *the learner would respond to the top number first.* The instruction is carefully designed to assure that the learner is strongly prompted to refer to the bottom number first. In this way, the learner finds out about the properties of the groups before referring to the top number and finding out how many parts have been used. Not only does the backward chain weaken the procedure of the bottom first then top; it also muddles what the learner will say. The first thing the learner is saying in the backward chain is: "And we have three

---

[*] Backward chaining was developed for non-verbal organisms to insure adequate reinforcement (the end of the chain). With verbal prompting of the chain elements, this procedure is not necessary and, as noted in the text, often creates additional problems.

parts." When the learner later tries to work the whole chain starting with the bottom, the learner may have serious reversal problems, saying something like, "We have four parts . . . and we have three groups," or "We have four parts and we have four groups."

The simplest and least complicated procedure for teaching long statements is forward chaining. To present a forward chain, simply have the learner say the first part of the sentence. Present the model, lead, and test for this part:

> "My turn: Four parts in each group . . . Again, four parts in each group . . . Say it with me: Four parts in each group . . . Pretty good. Your turn: Four parts in each group. Say it. Once more. Four parts in each group. Say it . . . Sounding good. Listen: Four parts in each group. Say it . . . Almost perfect. Listen: Four parts in each group. Your turn . . . That's it. Once more . . ."

The teacher does not stop as soon as the learner produces a perfect trial. If the learner requires quite a few repetitions to meet criterion on saying the part, the learner should not be considered firm until the learner is able to say the part on three or four consecutive trials. Use the same criterion that you would for level 1 of the three-level strategy for firming responses.

When the learner is firm on the first part, the teacher introduces the entire sentence, modeling, leading, and testing:

> "My turn. Four parts in each group . . . and we *have*, three parts.
>
> Listen again: Four parts in each group . . . and we *have*, three parts.
>
> Say it with me: Four parts in each group . . . and we *have*, three parts.
>
> Good. Now listen to the whole thing:
>
> Four parts in each group . . . and we *have* three parts.
>
> Say it with me: Four parts in each group . . . and we *have* three parts . . . You're getting it.
>
> Listen: Four parts in each group . . . and we have three parts. Say it . . .
>
> Yes, and we have three parts . . . Say the whole thing . . ."

Note that the pause (. . .) is quite long between parts. The purpose of this pause is to prevent the parts from being amalgamated or jumbled. The pause shows the learner that you first say the familiar part, then you say the new part.

If the learner has serious problems saying the second part of the statement, the teacher could introduce a variation of a backward chain. For this variation, the teacher *says the first part very quickly*, then pauses, and presents the second part at the regular rate and with the regular inflection. "My turn: (four parts in each group) and we have, three parts. Say the last part with me. (Four parts in each group) and we have, three parts."

To indicate that the learner is not to respond to the first part of the sentence, the teacher simply points to herself while saying the first part. To signal for the learner to respond, the teacher points to the learner just before presenting the second part of the sentence.

The same three steps—model, lead, test—are used with the last part of the sentence. As soon as the learner is firm on the last part of the sentence, the teacher models, leads, and tests on the entire sentence. If the learner seems to get into a mistake pattern, we model the correct sentence and do something else for a few minutes. When you return to the sentence, the learner may perform better. As a rule, present ten trials, then take a small break (perhaps no more than half a minute) before presenting another block of ten trials. Always try to end a block of trials with the appropriate response. If the learner's performance on the last trial is poor, model the correct response before terminating work on the sentence.

Applying the Three-Level Strategy

If the learner requires more than seven trials to say the sentence, we treat the sentence as a task in the three-level series.

A ⟶ A ⟶ A ⟶ A .... Ⓐ

We repeatedly juxtapose the same task until the learner performs on three or four consecutive trials. Because the learner had trouble achieving this criterion of performance, the learner will probably "forget" how to produce the response if we present the task ten minutes later. To provide the learner with the kind of practice needed to make the response firm at a later time, we design a transition that shapes the context. First create simple interruptions:

A ⟶ B ⟶ Ⓐ

Then create more elaborate ones.

A ⟶ B ⟶ C ⟶ D ⟶ Ⓐ

We work on each level until the learner performs on three or four consecutive trials. We can illustrate the procedure with the fraction-statement examples. After the learner has said the statement about the fraction, the teacher provides an interruption. "Add these numbers in your head. Thirty, fifty, and ten. What's the answer? ... Good job. Now say the whole statement about this fraction again. Get ready ..."

The teacher presents similar single-task interruptions until the learner performs on three or four consecutive trials. The teacher then introduces more lengthy interruptions: "Do all the addition problems on part three of your worksheet. Then we're going to come back and say the statement about the fraction again ..." Following the intervening activity, the teacher presents the fraction-statement task. The teacher continues to present level-three activities until the learner is firm.

Chaining Parts of a Routine

The most typical problem with rule-saying or statement saying is that the learner is capable of saying the individual words or individual phrases of the rule or statement, but is unable to produce the entire response. A similar situation occurs when the learner is working on cognitive routines. This problem is perhaps most noticeable when the routine is being covertized. Before covertization, the learner is not required to produce the entire chain or routine in response to a simple instruction. When covertization occurs, however, the directions for the different parts are removed and the learner may fail to perform, even though the learner is firm on the component steps.

The solution is to apply the three-level strategy. First, the teacher models exactly what the learner is to do. "Here's how I figure out if this fraction is more than one whole group. First, I touch the bottom number and say, 'seven parts in each group,' and then I touch the top number and say, 'and we have eight parts.' Then, I ask if we have more than there are in each group. Yes. So this fraction is more than one group. Watch how I do it." Teacher models the behavior, talking to herself and pointing to the parts of the fraction before writing "more than one group." "Your turn. Let's see you do it just like that. Start with the bottom number and talk to yourself ...

Good. Next problem..." This is level 1 of the three-level strategy.

After the learner has performed on three or four applications, the teacher provides an interruption to create a level-two difficulty of juxtaposition. "Time out, Henry. I notice that you've been doing a good job in your reading. How many points did you earn this morning?... Wow, that's really good. Are you going to do that well in your arithmetic?... Let's see if you remember to talk to yourself. Do problem three..." Note that the interruption is nearly as long as a task. Follow this procedure for longer tasks.

The teacher repeats level-two juxtapositions until the learner performs adequately. For the level-three presentation, the teacher presents a variety of problems with the fraction problems consisting of about one-fourth of the total problems. The fraction problems are distributed among the others.

Teaching the learner to perform independently should be considered as both an accuracy and rate problem. The strategy involves first making sure that the learner performs adequately, then shaping the learner's rate. In the illustration above, the learner may become quite accurate but may continue to say the steps aloud and process each problem relatively slowly. So long as the performance tends to be accurate, we can begin to shape the rate. Note, however, that we would not generally shape rate until we secure accuracy. The procedure for rate-shaping is the same as that outlined earlier. The teacher takes baseline data on the amount of time required to complete a worksheet. Criteria are established for no reinforcement (or points), singles and doubles. Note that the criteria may involve a combination of rate and accuracy performance. For doubles, the learner may be required to complete the worksheet in no more than five minutes, making no more than two mistakes. Possibly, the teacher could design a point schedule that involves different possible combinations of rate and accuracy outcomes. This schedule provides for more than single and double reinforcement. Perhaps four to six different point totals could be earned for a given worksheet.

Although the schedule might be a little more elaborate than other response shaping routines we have discussed, the shaping procedure follows the same general guideline outlined earlier. As the learner's rate-accuracy performance improves (manifested by higher average point totals), the schedule changes so that the learner must work faster to receive reinforcements.

Summary

When the learner does not behave like a perfect receiver, we use a response-locus analysis to identify the learner's deficiency. Three possible problems emerge:

1. The learner is capable of producing the response, but cannot produce the response in the context that is called for by the task the teacher specifies.

2. The learner is not capable of producing the response (under any reinforcing conditions), but does produce some approximation of the response in the context of the task.

3. The learner is not capable of producing the response (under any reinforcing conditions) and cannot perform in the context of the task.

Each deficiency suggests an instructional solution. We assume that the learner's behavior will be modified if we provide the learner with adequate practice. Many trials may be necessary before the learner meets an adequate criterion of performance.

Any techniques used to support the learner during these trials must be designed so the learner receives reinforcement on at least two thirds of the trials. If reinforcement drops below this level, the schedule may induce delayed responding, superstitious behavior, and a "dislike" of the training sessions.

The strategy for teaching *when* to respond (1 above) involves manipulation of the juxtapositions in which the task occurs. We identify three levels of juxtaposition difficulty:

1. A ⟶ Ⓐ
2. A ⟶ B ⟶ Ⓐ
3. A ⟶ B ⟶ C ⟶ D ⟶ Ⓐ

When the learner performs at a specified criterion of performance for level 1, the teacher immediately proceeds to level 2. The same procedure is repeated as the teacher moves from level 2 to level 3. When the learner has performed acceptably on level 3, the skill is integrated with other skills that have been taught. An integration series presents the new task (A) and other tasks. At first, integration series contain the new task and highly dissimilar tasks. Later, tasks that are similar to the new task are included in the integration.

In addition to the integration series, event-centered applications are presented. These provide a new set of cues that increase the difference between the new task and all other tasks. They also provide a format that permits the learner to use the skills in situations that are reinforcing.

Teaching the learner how to produce the response involves shaping the response by changing the criterion for reinforcing performance. We first take baseline and identify the poorest responses, middle responses, and best responses. The middle and best responses receive reinforcement during initial training, with the best responses receiving "double" reinforcement (reinforcement obviously more desirable to the learner). When reinforcement is provided on 90% of the trials, the teacher shifts the criterion of performance. The shift is based on the learner's most recent set of trials. Shifting the criterion is repeated until the learner's responses are consistently acceptable.

Teaching the learner both when to produce the response and how to produce the response involves double teaching. The most efficient and manageable way is to teach *when* at specified times of the day and *how* at other times. As the learner meets an acceptable criterion of performance on either *how* or *when*, the teacher presents applications.

If shaping the response does not require a great many trials, but more than seven, a workable procedure is to shape the response first so the learner performs appropriately on the task, then to process the task through the three-level strategy to assure that the learner is able to perform on the task when it occurs in an unprompted context. To establish the response, the teacher typically uses three steps: *model*, *lead*, and *test*. The model step shows how the response is produced. The lead step provides a prompt for the response. The test step gives the learner unassisted practice in producing the response.

Chapter 23
Strategies for Teaching New Complex Responses

Chapter 22 introduced the basic procedures for inducing new responses. These procedures play a role in the teaching of *complex responses*, such as buttoning, swimming, throwing a ball, turning a somersault, and similar complex responses. Complex responses are those for which we can identify parts of component responses. Because complex responses consist of component responses that are to be coordinated, we have a number of teaching options. Just as it is possible to treat skills taught through a cognitive routine as discriminations, it is possible to use basic response-teaching techniques to teach complex responses. Instead of using a program of events for teaching swimming, we could simply treat swimming as a response that is to be shaped. We could model the response, reinforce approximations, and in the end the learner would probably learn to swim.

The advantages of an analysis and accompanying techniques that go beyond simple shaping parallel the advantages of the cognitive routine over a discrimination sequence for teaching the same skills. By using a program for complex responses, we gain greater control over what the learner does. We make the learning easier and faster. Concepts that should be processed through a cognitive routine are not as obvious as simple discriminations. In a parallel way, complex responses should be processed through procedures more complicated than shaping because they are involved responses that are not easy to produce.

Misrules and Distortions

One of the great concerns in teaching new responses has to do with generalizations. We want the learner to generalize to a full range of applications, and we want these generalizations to come about as quickly and efficiently as possible.

The problems of establishing generalizations of new responses parallel those of establishing generalizations for discriminations or concepts. When teaching concepts we must avoid misrules. The two major types of misrules result from:

1. Presenting a set of examples that is consistent with more than one interpretation.

2. Stipulating that the discrimination is limited to a very narrow range.

The presentation that is consistent with more than one interpretation does not "guarantee" that a particular learner will pick up a misrule. It simply provides the learner with the option of attending to features of the presentation that are irrelevant to the desired generalization. The stipulation that can occur with initial training examples is that *all features of these examples are necessary*. The learner tends not to generalize to examples that do not have all the features of the training examples.

Both types of misrule have parallels in the teaching of response generalizations.

1. A presentation that is consistent with more than one set of responses leads to distortion. When teaching the new response, we present examples or applications. If the series of examples on which the learner initially practices are easy examples, they provide the learner with behavioral options (just as the easy examples in a discrimination context provide many options of features the learner may attend to). When presented with the easy-response example, the learner may produce the response in a way that will permit generalization to all other instances of the response; however, the learner may learn to perform on the easy examples in a way that will not generalize. In this case, the learner's responses are distorted. If the communication presents examples that permit many response options, the communication may induce distortion.

2. The communication that presents a very narrow range of differences in the initial-teaching applications for the response is guilty of stipulation. Following mastery on this set, the learner may not respond to applications that differ from those in the initial-teaching set. The initial instruction stipulates that a certain set of features must be present

before the response is to be produced. Absence of some features implies that the response is not to be produced. This situation parallels that of inducing stipulation in concept teaching.

Remedies

The problem of stipulation results because the learner has not been shown what is the same about *the range of applications* that call for the response. The remedy is to show the sameness. To show how applications of a response are the same, we juxtapose applications that are greatly different and we treat each application in the same way. When instruction violates this principle, stipulation occurs. We can use the sameness principle to diagnose programs that are guilty of stipulation. If the learner is capable of producing responses, but tends not to produce them for new applications, the program probably provided stipulated practice. Let us say that following programs designed to teach "creative responses" the learner produces unique, creative responses with hammers, but tends both to use *the hammering response* when producing "creative responses" with other objects and tends not to produce many creative responses with these objects. We can describe the program that induced this behavior. The use of the hammer was strongly stipulated, which means that the learner worked on hammering initially and for a relatively long period of time. The learner received a great deal of reinforcement for this work. The result was stipulation. A program that avoids stipulation would have required the learner to work with juxtaposed applications that are quite different from each other (hammers, lamps, pillows, books) and to treat them in the same way (by producing creative responses).

The problem of distortion is quite different. Unlike stipulation, the learner is not capable of producing the responses that are called for by some subtypes of examples, although the learner can produce the response for other subtypes. The problem is not one of "understanding," but of being able to produce the response.

All applications of the response are the same in some ways; applications for subtypes also differ in critical ways. And these critical differences preempt the learner from responding to some subtypes of examples.

Consider the generalization of buttoning buttons. Some buttoning tasks are easier than others. The smaller the button, the more difficult the response. Figure 23.1 presents a diagram of responses for three buttons–large, medium, and small. The height of each column represents the behavioral options that are available to the learner. The column for the large button is the highest, signaling that this application is the least demanding with regard to *specific behaviors*. The application permits many response options, all of which will lead to successful completion of the task. The height of the column for the small button is the shortest, indicating that this application provides the learner with the fewest behavioral options. Unless the learner produces certain, precise responses, successful buttoning is not possible.

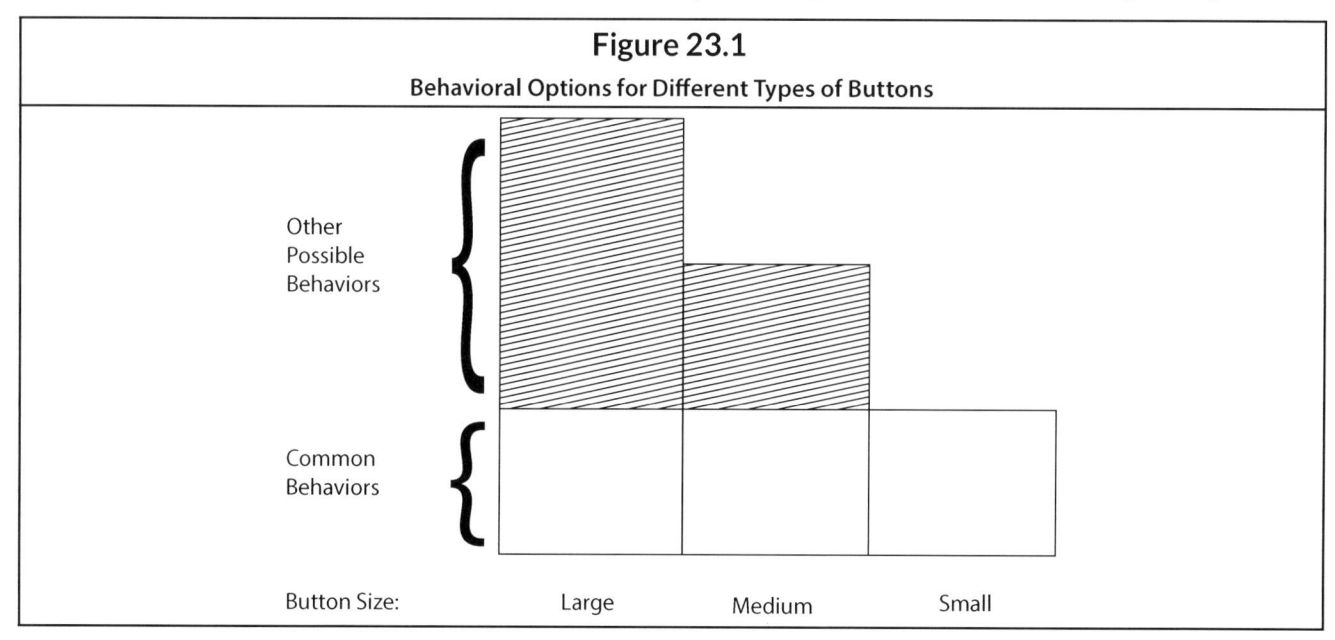

Figure 23.1
Behavioral Options for Different Types of Buttons

The unshaded area of each column shows that there are possible common responses for the three subtypes. Whether the button is large or small, it is possible for the learner to perform in a way that involves the same responses. By pressing against the edge of the button with the thumb and aligning the button with the button hole, the learner could button all three types.

The shaded area in the first two columns indicates the extent to which other possible behaviors may be employed to achieve the outcome. The height of the shaded area gives an indication of how "easy" the example is. The large button is easier than the medium and the small buttons because it provides the largest range of behavioral options that will lead to a successful outcome. Possibly, the learner grasps the flat sides of the large buttons between thumb and forefinger, an option that is not readily available with the small button. Possibly, the learner holds the large buttons by the edge (thumb and forefinger holding opposite edges of the button). Other options are also possible.

These options are unfortunate because they are not options for all subtypes of the response. They therefore imply non-generalizable learning. If the learner learns an option that permits successful outcomes only with the large buttons, the learner must later learn new options for the medium-sized buttons, and ultimately new options for the small buttons. The amount of learning would be greatly reduced if the instruction initially taught the learner to produce the response options that are common to all subtypes.

Analysis of Examples Versus Analysis of Learner

The button diagram suggests the universal dilemma for sequencing applications that involve subtypes of behavior. The smaller button is more difficult, simply because it provides the learner with no behavioral options. Unless the learner masters the set of behaviors that will lead to the desired outcome for all buttons, the learner will fail to perform with this button. Once the smallest button has been mastered, *the common behaviors for all applications have been learned, which means that it is relatively easy to achieve generalization to new examples.*

The analysis of the examples suggests, therefore, that the most efficient approach would be to present the application that has the least "margin of error," or that provides the fewest behavioral options. These applications, therefore, function a great deal like a discrimination sequence that is consistent with one and only one interpretation. The learner who masters the application will have learned the essential features that apply to all applications. Theoretically, no misrules are possible except that stipulation may occur if we work too long on the application.

The analysis *of the learner*, however, leads to quite different conclusions. The learner may have to work on the example for hundreds of trials before producing a successful response (that of achieving the desired buttoning outcome). Instruction is judged appropriate from the standpoint of the learner when that instruction permits successful trials on at least two-thirds of the total trials. Working on an application that does not admit to behavior options does not meet this standard. The use of shaping does not entirely solve this problem, because the idea behind working on the hard application is that successful completion of this application would assure generalization to "easier" examples (all of which can be processed with the same set of behaviors as those used for the more difficult application). When we shape the response on the more difficult application, the learner cannot benefit from more difficult examples because these benefits are possible *only if the learner successfully processes the examples.*

Another option is to start with easy examples. Possibly, the learner can perform the buttoning operation in 15 trials with an easy example. If so, the learner will be performing the operation *in some form* after only modest practice. Practicing some form of a successful application is usually far better than practicing an approximation of the application. The approximation is usually capable of generating more possible misrules and greater possible distortion.

Here is a summary of the issues in teaching complex physical operations:

1. If we work initially with difficult applications (those that permit no behavioral options):
   a. We provide a presentation that is consistent with a single interpretation, and therefore generalization to new and easier applications will be achieved very easily.

b. But we make the task very difficult for the learner because there is no latitude in the behaviors permitted by the application.

2. If we try to reinforce the learner on two-thirds of the trials:

   a. The learner does not produce the responses that would lead to the generalization.

   b. The work on approximations of a difficult example probably does not teach the learner as much as producing successful responses with a simpler example.

3. If we initially introduce an easier example instead of a difficult one:

   a. The learner will probably produce successful responses with fewer trials because the example permits a wider range of behavioral options.

   b. The probability is great that the learner will learn a response that is distorted and that will not generalize to new and more difficult applications.

   c. However, this application provides successful practice, which usually teaches more, and more rapidly than approximations.

Programs for Complex New Responses

The program for the complex new response (like buttoning, shoe-tying, and swimming) should be designed to bring the learner to applications with the fewest behavioral options as quickly as possible. Note that although the program may begin with easy examples, the program does not proceed from easy applications to hard ones in progressive steps. The easy-to-hard progression systematically teaches possible misrules of diminishing proportions. The hard applications are the ones that are capable of assuring the generalization to all other examples. The longer it takes to present these applications, the more work it requires to teach the generalization. Therefore, the goal is to reach the more difficult application quickly. The problem inherent in the easy-to-hard sequence can be illustrated by referring to a similar problem in teaching a simple discrimination.

If the positive examples are circles, and the negative examples are ovals that are very similar to circles, we would not shape the context by first having the learner discriminate between these examples: ◯ ⌇

then these examples: ◯ ⌇

and finally these examples: ◯ ()

The context shaping would probably induce serious misunderstanding. The reason is that *any difference* between the first pair of examples would permit the learner to discriminate reliably between the examples. The learner could attend to the waviness of the lines, the open form, the "branches," or any other difference. The second pair of examples rules out some of the possible misrules because this example is closed and has no "branches." However, there are many differences that the learner may attend to and reliably discriminate. Not until the learner is required to discriminate between the third set of examples is the learner provided with information about which features of the positive example are relevant to the discrimination.

The problem with the easy-to-hard sequence *for physical operations* provides a parallel. The easy example permits a wide range of "options." The intermediate example reduces some of the options. However, not until the learner encounters the most difficult example is the learner provided with information about the constraints of the operation. In the meantime, the learner is reinforced for learning behaviors that work for the easier examples, but will not generalize to more difficult examples.

Analyzing Complex Responses

The mechanics of engineering rapid progression to the difficult examples begins with an analysis of complex responses. Responses such as shoe-tying, using a screwdriver, soldering, riding a bicycle, and other operations are the same as cognitive routines in two ways:

1. All behaviors that account for the successful achievement of the outcome are overt.

2. The operation provides for feedback on every trial (given that the learner understands the goal of the operation).

Complex physical operations differ from cognitive routines in the following ways:

1. The overt behaviors *will never be covertized.*

2. The feedback is provided *by the physical environment.*

These unique features of physical operations suggest that the learner can benefit from practicing the routine independently. Furthermore, this approach should be designed so that the learner engages in independent practice as quickly as possible.

The job of designing instruction for complex responses is less complicated than designing instruction for cognitive routines. To design instructions for cognitive problems, we must first design the routine and make sure that it applies to the full range of examples; then we identify the various preskills implied by the routine. The behaviors for complex routines already exist. Therefore, we simply observe the full range of applications and then design the instruction that leads to the complex responses. Note that we do not have to design the routine—merely analyze it.

The analysis of complex responses involves identification of *temporal parts* and *simultaneous components.*

A *temporal part* is *everything that goes on during one identifiable segment of the response.* For instance, everything that goes on when you pull the shoe laces before starting to tie the shoe is a temporal part. Everything you do to loop one lace around the other is a temporal part. A temporal part should have a clearly-marked beginning and a clearly-marked end.

It is easy to identify temporal parts for responses that have discontinuous parts. A part is discontinuous if it can be executed outside the context of the operation as an isolated task without distortion of any sort. Although the parts may be run together, they may also be separated in time. (The learner can perform some parts of the shoe-tying operation and then stop before starting the next part. The learner can stop after printing part of the letter **b**.)

Some operations are composed primarily of *continuous parts.* Parts are continuous if they can be produced only within the context of the operation or within a similar operation. The follow through of a golf swing may be identified as a part if it has distinguishable behaviors not observed in the other parts of the swing. However, the follow through cannot be removed from the context of a swing. It cannot be practiced in isolation. It shares the movement of the preceding part, and differs only in some behavioral details that overlay this movement.

The implication of discontinuous parts is that they can be practiced as units or steps that may later be chained together. The implication of continuous parts is that they must be practiced within the context of the operation in which they occur (or in a simplified variation of the context, which has the same continuous part).

In addition to identifying temporal parts, we also identify simultaneous components. A *component* is a response detail that can be created in contexts other than the context of the operation. For example, a component of shoe-tying is grasping the ends of the shoe lace. This particular component occurs in various temporal parts of the response. This component, however, can be completely removed from the context of shoes, shoe laces, and any temporal part of shoe-tying. We could present the learner with a hanging string that is to be grasped between the thumb and index finger and that is to be held against a certain amount of resistance. The behavior is the same one that is called for in various temporal parts of the shoe-tying operation; however, when we remove the component from the operation, we try to present it in a context that is simplified.

The context of a component is relatively simplified if:

1. There are fewer simultaneous components that occur with the target component.
2. Trials of the component may be juxtaposed faster.

In the context of the shoe-tying operation, the learner grasps the ends of the two loops and pulls them in opposite directions. If we removed the component of grasping ends of looped strings, the learner could practice trials that involve only one hand. The requirements of coordinating this component with others is therefore simplified. Also, we could juxtapose trials of loop-grasping because the learner would not have to perform the preceding parts of the shoe-tying operation before practicing the grasping component. A trial of grasping could be followed by another trial of grasping.

Simultaneous components occur in temporal parts that are continuous or discontinuous. It is usually possible to identify ways of removing components from discontinuous parts. We simply identify the behavior that occurs within that part. We then design a simpler context for the target behavior. When we deal with parts that are continuous, simultaneous components present a far more challenging problem when they are not common to the preceding temporal part of the operation. Because they are not common to the preceding part and are produced within a continuous-part context, we must retain the continuous-part context. We can illustrate the problem with the response of saying the word **mess**. This response has parts–saying three sounds. Each part has simultaneous components. For the sound **m**, the simultaneous components are:

1. Making a *voiced* sound.
2. Keeping the lips closed.
3. Allowing air to escape from nose.

Each of these behaviors can be performed independently of the others. For instance, we can perform behaviors 2 and 3 without performing 1. (Simply breathe through the nose.) We can do 1 and 2 without doing 3. (With your nose held and lips pursed, make a voice sound.) We can do 1 and 3 without doing 2. (Make the sound for **n**.)

The three components are not produced within a continuous context; therefore, they can be practiced in isolation, removed from the word **mess**. For instance, if the learner was not closing the lips when saying the word **mess**, it would be quite easy to give the learner practice in imitating lip closing. The learner would simply imitate the teacher on trials that required separating the lips and closing them. This component can be removed from the context of **mess** because it is a component of **m** *that does not have anything to do with the fact that the* **m** *sound is a part that is joined continuously to the next sound.* Many components cannot be removed from the continuous context. For instance, the learner may be able to produce the **s** sound in isolation. When saying the word **mess**, however, the learner may voice the **s** sound–saying the sound for **z** instead of **s**. Stated differently, the learner has trouble stopping the voicing component for the **s** when it occurs within the continuous context of the word **mess**.

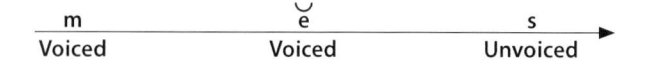

m	e̯	s
Voiced	Voiced	Unvoiced

We cannot work on this particular behavior apart from the continuous context of *a word*. We may be able to construct simpler examples or examples which have fewer temporal parts or fewer additional changes. For example, if the learner said, "es," there would be a shorter chain:

e̯	s
Voiced	Unvoiced

Possibly, we can find a context for the unvoicing of the **s** sound that is "easier" than the one above. For instance, we could require the learner to whisper the word **es**. This example requires the learner to produce the unvoiced component for the **s** sound; however, it does not require the learner to produce it in a context that goes from a voiced sound to an unvoiced sound, because the **e** sound is unvoiced also. The parts in this example vary only in other components, not in voicing.

The opposite approach is also possible, that of presenting continuous parts that vary *only* in the voice component. The word **zs** fulfills this requirement:

z	s
Voiced	Unvoiced

The only difference between the **z** sound and the **s** sound is the voicing. Work on this example would certainly show the learner how to control the voice component. It might not be a very easy example, however, because there is only one difference between the responses for the **z** part and the **s** part. The learner may have trouble manipulating this difference.

In summary, there are three options for finding a simpler example of components that must be joined to preceding continuous parts. They are:

1. Try to shorten the chain of events that precedes the part with the component in question.
2. Create an example in which the preceding part *shares* the component in question (all parts in the whispered word share the unvoiced feature).
3. Create an example in which the preceding part shares all details except the component in question (all components of the **s** sound except the unvoiced features are shared by **z**).

The type-2 strategy is the easiest for the learner, but is least capable of teaching the behavior, because it actually eliminates the problem. The type-3 strategy is the most capable of communicating the behavior; however, it may be difficult for the learner because it involves the most precise manipulation of the component. The introduction of type-3 continuous part should be experimental. If the learner performs on it with modest practice, a great deal is gained. If not, the example may be dropped and not a great deal is lost.

If we carefully analyze the complex response, we can often discover a way to apply the different strategies. For instance, if a learner is having trouble with a golf swing and if the problem has to do with the learner's left arm, the option of making the chain shorter is not a significant one. By requiring the learner to wear a brace on the left arm so that it could not bend, we would create an example in which the preceding part of the swing *shares* the component in question with the problem part of the swing (strategy 2). If we require the learner to swing a light object using only the left hand, we create an example in which the left arm must be totally responsible for any changes in the latter part of the swing. This example therefore functions as an example of strategy 3, with the parts the same except for a single response component. (Although we might have some trouble categorizing particular applications as either a type-2 strategy or a type-3 strategy, we can either eliminate the critical response through the choice of example or we can make the critical response the most prominent aspect of the application.)

Three Program Types

There are three basic programs for teaching new, complex responses. The three types are distinguished on the basis of how they start—the nature of the first step. Two programs begin with the learner being taught skills *within the context of the operation that is being taught*. One begins with the learner performing on components or parts *that have been removed from the context of the operation*.

The three programs are:

1. **Essential-response-features program.** At the beginning of this program, the learner works *within the context of the operation*, performing those features of the response *that are essential to the outcome*; the non-essential features that are involved in the operation are not performed by the learner.

2. **Enabling-response-features program.** The learner begins by working within the context of the operation; however, the learner does not produce the essential features. The learner produces *the non-essential features* while the essential features are supported.

3. **Removed-component-behavior program.** The first step in this program presents a context different from that of the operation. The learner first works on some part of the response or some component of the operation in this removed context.

Essential-response-features. To test whether the learner is producing the essential-response-features, we ask two questions:

1. What is the objective of the operation?
2. Who actually performs the behaviors that achieve that objective?

If the answer to 2 is "the learner," the learner produces the essential response features. Let's say that the objective of an operation is to hammer nails into a board. Who actually performs the act of hammering? If the learner performs the actual hammering—that behavior that accounts for the nail being driven into the board—the program is an essential-response-feature program. Possibly, the learner wears a glove and the handle of the hammer is affixed to this glove. Possibly, the learner's arm is raised by the teacher. These are not essential details or features. The essential features of the behavior are those that bring the hammer into contact with the nail head.

Let's say that the learner is screwing screws with a screwdriver. If the learner turns the screwdriver, the program is an essential-response-feature program. Again, the operation may be designed so that other behaviors are removed or supported. The blade of the screwdriver may be modified so that it fits easily into the slot. The handle of the screwdriver may be modified. But if the learner produces that part of the operation that turns the screw in the appropriate direction, the learner produces the essential response features.

Deciding on the essential features of a response is sometimes difficult and sometimes arbitrary. What are the essential features of riding a bicycle? The essential features are those aspects that distinguish the operation from all others. For bike-riding, we would judge that they have to do with maintaining the balance. The other behaviors—pedaling, steering, etc.—can be done with other vehicles that do not require the kind of balance called for by a bicycle.

The first part of the essential-response-feature program requires the learner to produce the essential response features in the context of the operation that is being taught. If the operation is riding a bike, the learner actually performs the balancing—perhaps on a coasting vehicle—while some of the non-essential behaviors (pedaling) are eliminated. The learner begins, in other words, *with a simplified version of riding*. The program then adds additional response features as the learner becomes proficient with the essential-response features in a context that is simplified.

If the operation involves hammering, the learner strikes the nail with the hammer. This essential-response feature is produced by the learner. Other behaviors, such as gripping the hammer, are removed or supported. Again, the strategy is to begin with a simplified example of hammering and then to add in details.

Enabling-response features. These behaviors are not essential to achieving the objective of the operation, *but occur in every instance of the operation.* They are enabling responses that permit the essential responses to be performed. For example, putting toothpaste on a brush is a feature that may be involved in every instance of tooth-brushing; however, it is not essential to the act of brushing teeth. Pedaling is not essential to "riding a bike." Holding a hammer is not essential to hammering. Placing a screw in position is not essential to driving the screw with a screwdriver.

The enabling-response-feature program is the opposite of the essential-response-feature program. Initially, the enabling-response-feature program requires the learner to perform some non-essential aspects of the operation. If the operation is tooth-brushing, the learner does not produce the behaviors of brushing teeth. Someone (or something) performs this part of the operation, while the learner performs enabling behaviors, such as putting toothpaste on the brush, holding the brush as it is manipulated, orienting the brush to different positions. The learner's role is passive *with respect to the essential behavior.* The learner does not actually brush the teeth.

In bike-riding, the learner who is engaged in an enabling-response-feature program would perform the ancillary behaviors, such as pedaling, steering, etc., while some other agent performed the essential part of the operation—balancing the bike. For swimming, the learner would swing arms or kick legs; however, something else would support the learner's body as it moved through the water. If the response involved making the letter **A**, the learner might passively hold the crayon as the teacher forms the letter. If the response involved walking, the learner would simply move one leg and then another, perhaps pushing backward, as the stroller or similar device achieves the essential-response features.

The enabling-response feature program slowly shifts responsibility for producing the essential part of the response. Note, however, that the entire process takes place within the context of the operation that is being taught. From the beginning of the program, the learner works on examples that involve shoe-tying, swimming, bike-riding, or hammering. At the beginning, the learner does not produce the behaviors essential to the outcome. Later, the learner assumes responsibility for these behaviors.

Removed component behaviors. The removed component program first presents a behavior that is removed from the context of the operation that is being taught. Those components or parts that are identified for such removal are those that prevent the learner from performing correctly on applications of the operation. For instance, we may identify that the learner fails to tie shoes because of a poor grasp on the ends of the strings when pressing the doubled-over strands between thumb and forefinger. This component can be removed from the context of shoe-tying. We can present relatively simple examples of the skill that involve wide strips of paper. (Hold a strip on edge. Touch the ends together. Instruct the learner to "fold" the paper by grasping it between thumb and index finger.) We can proceed from this example to those that involve smaller targets, more pliable material, and different orientations in space.

Similarly, if we note that the learner is not able to screw properly because the wrist turns inappropriately, creating torque that flips the blade from the slot in the screw head, we can remove the component of turning the hand appropriately. One variation would require the learner to hold a penlight and flash it on a target. The learner is then required to rotate her wrist without moving the beam from the target. The target may be placed in different positions so the learner must point ahead, down, and up.

Perhaps we notice that the learner fails to "crimp" smaller wires, but does an adequate job on larger ones. Further investigation discloses that the learner does not press the crimper tight against the base of the wires before squeezing the handle. We can remove part of the operation from the total operation. We might design a device that "beeps" if something presses against it with enough pressure. The learner takes the device, pushes it against each of the targets with enough force to make the "beep." When the learner has become proficient at "beeping" targets of different sizes in various positions, we introduce crimping. Although the setup for crimping may be quite similar to that for the preskill, the preskill does not involve crimping. It involves only a component behavior and that behavior is removed from the context of crimping.

The removed-component-behavior program introduces the actual operation after the learner has reached mastery on the removed component. Perhaps more than one component or part is removed from the operation and is pretaught. Following the completion of the removed-behavior work, the learner practices the operation. Possibly, it is simplified (essential-response-feature strategy).

The removed-component strategy may make it possible for us to accelerate the introduction of difficult subtypes of an operation. We noted earlier that we may induce distortion if we work too long on easy examples of operations like buttoning. If we identify a component-behavior problem—possibly that the learner does not have precise control over where to press on the smaller buttons—we may be able to design removed component exercises that strengthen this skill. An exercise for pressing might be to grasp a suspended disk between thumb and index finger. The disc hangs from a string and may be moved by pressing the thumb against the disc's edge. The index finger is on the other side of a "barrier." (See Figure 23.2.) The goal is to move the button to the index finger, then lift it over the top of the barrier.

Figure 23.2
Removed-Component Exercise for Buttoning Preskill

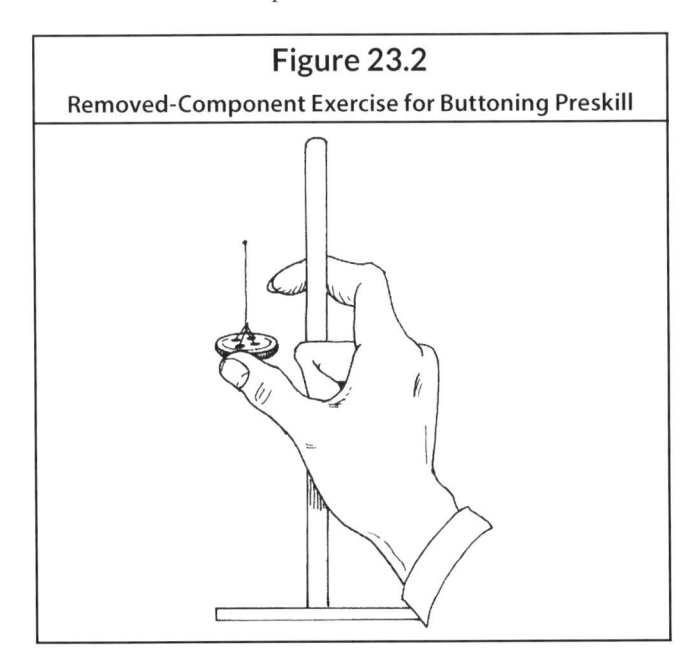

A variation of this activity is achieved by changing the barrier so that it is a fabric with a slit in it. The learner must now swing the disc through the slit in the fabric and press it against the index finger.

Typically, if we identify why the learner is failing particular subtypes of examples, we discover some precise behavioral problem. We can frequently design preskill activities that require only that behavior. Following completion of the preskill we can then present a full range of applications and solve the generalization problem. Instead of working only with relatively large buttons and then progressively working toward small ones, we may now introduce smaller buttons relatively early in the sequence (perhaps not as early as the first applications, but quite soon).

Illustrations. We can usually design all three types of programs for teaching operations such as shoe-tying, ball throwing, swimming, etc. To teach overhand-ball throwing, we could begin with a number of essential-response-feature programs. Possibly, the instruction begins with the learner standing on marks that position the feet properly. The "mark" for the front foot may be a sponge that is to be stepped on lightly (not flattened). A string hangs above and behind the learner. The learner moves the hand that holds the ball back until it touches the string.

At this time the feet are properly positioned; the weight is distributed properly. The elbow is positioned correctly. Now the learner swings the arm forward and "throws" the ball. Note that most of the non-essential features have been controlled, so they require minimum distraction from the central operation, throwing. Another possible essential-response-feature approach might begin by requiring the learner to sit at a table and throw by moving only the lower arm. The elbow would be held in place on the table. The arm would be bent, the hand extended back over the top of the shoulder. An object is placed on the fingertips, and the learner brings the arm forward, propelling the object. The elbow stays in place. Not only is this a simplified version of throwing; it is one that works on the most crucial feature of throwing—use of the wrist. If the learner is reinforced for throwing the object further, the learner will quickly learn that more velocity is achieved by "snapping" the wrist as the arm comes forward. The most difficult part of throwing is taught.

An enabling-response-feature approach might involve *passive throwing*. The learner is instructed to position his weight so that the foot opposite the throwing hand is off the floor (which means that all weight is on the back foot) and the throwing arm is brought back all the way. The teacher then brings the learner's arm forward to achieve the throwing. To achieve the appropriate position for the throwing, the teacher could use the same marks on the floor used for the essential-response-feature program. The learner stands on the marks, lifts the front foot off the ground, brings his arm back, and then the teacher effects the throwing.

A removed-component approach is one that deals with one of the more critical components of the response. One such component is the swing. To teach a transferable version of the swing, we could require the learner to stand in a certain position and then strike a target (such as a small punching bag) with a certain amount of force. The device could be rigged so that if it swings up, with a certain force, a bell rings. We could use markers on the floor to assure that the learner stands in the right position. These marks would place the learner far enough from the target to discourage all swings but a roundhouse. They would also assure that the learner starts with the weight on the appropriate foot and with the appropriate foot forward. (The marks would be arranged so that the foot opposite the throwing arm is forward.) The learner would be permitted to leave the mark for the back foot while swinging. This convention assures that the learner is "following through" on the swing. The program teaches the learner to swing a roundhouse blow, using the body for additional leverage—important components in achieving a hard throwing motion.

Teaching the learner to ride a bike could be taught as an essential-response-feature program, an enabling response feature program, or a removed component program. The enabling-response program would begin with training wheels. The learner performs the non-essential features of pedaling and steering, while the essential-response features of maintaining balance have been removed. The first step of the essential-response-features program would begin with the learner being propelled. The learner would steer and maintain balance—the essential features of the operation. The removed-component program would begin with some response components removed from the context of riding a bike. Possibly, the learner would balance on a pogo stick, or practice standing in different positions while only one foot is on the floor. These activities would teach the balancing component, removed from the context of bike riding.

With all programs, there would be a change in the examples after the learner mastered the first applications. After performing adequately on the first application in essential-response-features programs, the learner would work on examples that require increasing numbers and types of enabling-response features. The second stage of the enabling-response-features program would integrate more of the essential-response features. Following mastery of the removed-component, this program would proceed as either an essential-response-features program or an enabling-response-features program.

Distortion

Programs for complex physical operations involve stages of training. We must look at the early stages in a program very carefully with respect to the amount of distortion that is implied by work on the early applications. As noted earlier, we can determine the potential amount of distortion by analyzing the range of response options that lead to the goal and comparing this range of options with the range that will be permitted by the more difficult examples. The greater the discrepancy in response options, the greater the possibility that the learner will learn to produce a response that is successful for the easier examples, but that will not transfer to the more difficult ones.

This analysis of potential distortion must be referenced to the examples that are to be introduced, not to the learner. This point is extremely important. If we simply analyze the learner's performance while proceeding through a program, we may be completely deceived about the problems the program is creating. The learner may perform very well on the early examples. It is not until later examples are presented that we discover that the learner has a great deal of trouble. If the later examples are not mastered in fewer trials than the earlier examples, the earlier examples apparently did not facilitate generalization to the later ones. The reason that the generalization was not facilitated, however, is completely revealed only by analyzing the early examples and the distortion they imply. Without this information, we observe the learning progressing well through the program and then suddenly "regressing" when faced with more difficult examples.

The beginning steps for all three programs that we have described induce a certain amount of distortion that will be evident with more difficult examples. However, the most serious distortions result from the enabling-response features program. The reason is that at the beginning of this program, the learner produces the non-essential features in a context that supports the essential features. Therefore, these features may be produced in a way quite different from the way they must be produced when they are coordinated with or subsumed by the essential response features. When the essential responses are added, the learner is required to: (1) learn to produce the essential features, and (2) relearn the non-essential features that had been produced in the context of the earlier examples. This double learning may be as great as the learning that would be required if we merely started with the more difficult example. (The double learning would be particularly great if the learner practiced the earlier examples until achieving a high criterion of performance.) Consider the operation of walking with a "walker" or device that supports the learner's weight and relieves the learner of the central responsibility of maintaining balance. The learner can produce the response of moving one leg forward and pushing it back in a context that requires no balance. Therefore, the learner will probably learn to produce the enabling responses in a way that will have very little transference to walking without support.

The distortion problem is not as great for the essential-response-feature approach because:

1. The learner first masters a legitimate example of the complex operation.

2. The addition of enabling features requires the learner to modify the essential-response features only to the extent that is required to accommodate the non-essential features. (In other words, the learner learns a variation of the operation, not a totally new operation.)

3. The introduction of enabling features may be staged so that they provide a gradual introduction of new-learning demands.

Although the distortion is theoretically less for the essential-response-feature program, distortion may be induced if the learner works too long with the easy examples.

The amount of distortion implied by the removed-component program is not as great as that implied by the enabling-response-features program because the initial practice is not produced within the context of the operation. The variation of the component taught in isolation implies some distortion when it is placed in the context of the operation; however, the learner is required to learn a variation of this component, not to learn the entire component. Therefore, the preteaching with the isolated component should facilitate the learner's performance with the first examples that involve the operation. Again, however, if the component is practiced too long in isolation (or practiced to a very high criterion of performance), the transition to the operational context will probably be more difficult for the learner.

Combining Programs

The guiding principle for teaching complex responses or any physical skill is to achieve the terminal behavior as quickly as possible. It is a mistake to think of physical operations as if the total operation is a sum of the various parts. It is not. The sum is unique and not a simple addition of steps or parts. A learner may not be able to perform on a removed component or part, but will perform the complex operation. (A learner may not be able to say some component sounds for a word, *but may be able to say the word.*)

If our program proceeds atomically, it will not be totally effective. We may have to work on atomic details—parts, component behaviors—because the work on parts provides us with a more manageable instructional unit. The decision to work on a part, however, should come about only after we have determined that the learner cannot perform on the whole. In other words, we may develop a program for working on saying isolated sounds when teaching the speech-language delayed child. We may work on chaining sounds together, once they have been mastered in isolation; however, we must treat this approach as *one track* of a total program. The work on parts will teach the learner how the various sound parts retain their identity, how they are transformed when joined to other sounds, and how they affect the total word. These learnings are important. But other learnings that cannot be derived from work on the isolated components is equally important. The atomic approach does little to teach how to match inflection, match stress, and match tones. Initial work on the total word would not require the learner to produce the component sounds correctly. It would reinforce the learner for producing approximations, for attempting to match patterns of inflection and stress. When working on the production of isolated sounds and chaining them together, the program would reinforce the learner for saying the sounds properly and would not be concerned with stress and inflection.

A single-track program that teaches only the atomic chaining or only imitating the gross prosodic features of the word will have serious weaknesses. The atomic approach will produce slow, mechanical behavior because the learner will be so strongly prompted to chain the parts carefully. The gross-feature approach will be ineffective in teaching the learner to produce the parts or sounds that occur in different words.

Our first attempt should be to teach the total operation without teaching parts. We should try to design some essential-feature applications that would permit the learner to practice the operation quickly. However, if we see that the learner is having great difficulty with a particular part of the operation or with a particular behavioral component, we should introduce a removed-component program for that part. (At one time during the lesson, we would present practice trials on the removed behavior. At another time, we would practice the easy form of the total operation.)

If the operation is particularly complex, a different combination of approaches is possible. We may coordinate a non-essential features program and an essential-features program (the learner working on both tracks during each lesson). For some trials, the learner produces only the non-essential responses called for by the operation, and for other trials, the learner initiates the essential features. This approach is useful in operations such as bike-riding that require the learner to coordinate many details.

Just as the juxtaposition of greatly different examples that are treated in the same way demonstrates sameness, the juxtaposition of greatly different applications of operations that are treated in the same way suggests a response sameness.

Here is the simplest pattern for prompting this sameness:

1. Sequence practice so the learner spends about two-thirds of the time on easy applications and one-third on more difficult applications.

2. Use a different criterion of performance for easy and for difficult examples (higher criterion for the easy and lower for the more difficult).

3. Juxtapose practice blocks of examples—possibly six easy applications followed by three difficult ones—so the learner goes quickly from one block to the next.

4. Use the same instructions for all blocks to show that the blocks involve the same response.

Immediately after practicing on a block of trials involving the easy application, the learner would work on a smaller block that involves a more difficult application. The teacher would indicate that the responses are the same. "Here are some more buttons to button. These are small. I'll bet you can't even get them started." Note that the teacher uses a different criterion of performance. For the easier example, the learner buttons them. For the difficult application, the learner is reinforced for "getting them started," (or lining them up, or doing some of the behaviors associated with buttoning).

Note also that it is not important that the learner succeeds on the more difficult examples. It is important that the learner produces some behaviors that are involved in the buttoning responses. If the learner attempts to treat the examples from the two blocks in the same way, the juxtaposition of examples will have achieved its objective—that of prompting the learner to treat the different examples in the same way.

In summary, we present the learner with the terminal, difficult operations as early as we can. We do not teach parts or components unless we have to, because we recognize that we cannot readily generate a whole if we "stack" these parts (particularly when we deal with responses that have continuous parts). The whole has features that do not derive from the parts. And the simplest way to work on these features is to work on the whole. If the response is complicated, like swimming the crawl stroke, we may superimpose different programs on each other. We may use an essential-features program that presents operations of increasing complexity (based on the amount of coordination that is required). The simplest application may require the learner to float face-down, arms extended. A more complicated application may involve starting in the same position, pulling one arm down, and simultaneously turning the head away from the arm. All these variations build around the basic "balance" and orientation that is involved in the crawl stroke (legs basically straight, face-down floating position, arms extending full-length as part of the stroke).

In addition, components may be identified–such as kicking while holding a kick board. The program for each component represents a track.

Within each track, there is not a rigid step-by-step progression in difficulty. Rather, there is a systematic skipping around, with most of the initial practice provided with easy applications, but with more difficult examples interspersed. The criterion of performance is adjusted so that the learner receives reinforcement on most trials of the difficult applications.

Note that empirical evidence will provide us with information about which applications are better than others. We will certainly modify the program on the basis of this information. However, the twin problems of distortion and of the learner's inability to produce the response acceptably after only a few trials dictates the general direction that our program should follow. We may discover that requiring the learner to try to move arms when floating face down does not work as well as requiring the learner to move one arm–down, then straight out again. We may find that we can introduce an application that requires even more coordination of responses, such as kicking first, then stopping the kick and moving the arms–all while floating face down. The specifics are not given by the analysis, merely the direction that should lead to the most effective transmission of the skill.

Summary

The principles for teaching new and complex responses are complicated because we must somehow wed techniques for showing sameness of examples with techniques that will permit us to introduce approximations of operations. The guiding principle is to design the program so the learner performs on fully detailed applications as quickly as possible. The program should contain the fewest possible steps–the sequence that is least elaborate.

Some examples or applications are easier than others. These should be introduced early. Their advantage is that they provide the learner with practice in the operation that is targeted for instruction. Their disadvantage is that they permit a wider range of acceptable behavior than more difficult examples. Therefore, extended work on them will:

1. Create distortion in the response called for by more difficult examples.

2. Stipulate that the operation involves only applications of the type practiced.

To discover the options that are available for sequencing examples, we analyze examples of the operation. We identify those applications that are more difficult (those involving the more precise behaviors and coordination of a larger number of behaviors) and those applications that are easier. We analyze the responses according to their temporal parts and their simultaneous components. The analysis shows us whether parts are joined continuously or discontinuously. If they are joined discontinuously, they are easy to work on in isolation. If they are chained continuously, they must be worked on within the context similar to that of the operation being taught.

To work on a behavior that occurs within in a continuous context, we can:

- Shorten the chain of events that precedes the component being taught.
- Design the preceding event so that it also shares the behavior being taught.
- Design the preceding event so that it differs from the next part only in the behavior that is being taught.

For many physical operations, not all options are readily available.

The three basic programs for teaching complex responses or operations are:

1. Essential-response-features program.
2. Enabling-response-features program.
3. Removed-component-behavior program.

Each program has a different first step. The essential-response-feature program requires the learner to perform the behavior that accounts for the outcome of an operation while the non-essential features of the application are eliminated from the example or are performed by someone else. Think of the essential-response-feature program as one that begins with an easy (perhaps contrived) example of the operation being taught.

The enabling-response-features program also begins with an example of the operation; however, the learner does not produce those responses that lead to the outcome. These responses are supported or performed by somebody else while the learner performs the ancillary or component behaviors associated with the goal-achieving behaviors.

The first step of the removed-behavior program is not presented within the context of the operation that is being taught. A totally different setup is introduced to practice the particular component or part that is a potential stumbling block to making the learner proficient.

All programs proceed from the first step to the terminal or goal operation.

To reduce the problems of response distortion that results if we work too long on a limited range of examples, we use a combination of programs.

Each program becomes a track in a total program.

We juxtapose practice blocks within a lesson. This juxtaposition shows that the various activities involve the same operational steps.

A different criterion is used for the hard examples. About two-thirds of the practice is devoted to work on the easier examples, and about one-third to the harder applications.

If we provide a very logically-designed program that buttresses against distortion and stipulation, the program may require fewer trials and the learning will go more smoothly than it will if we simply require practice. However, the difference will be seen in the manageability of the sequence, the reinforcing quality of the practice blocks, and the relative smoothness of the progression from activity to activity. There should also be a savings in trials and an improvement in the generalizations.

Chapter 24
Expanded Chains

An expanded chain is a program designed to teach a central physical operation and the discriminations associated with this operation. The basic program for tooth-brushing deals with those behaviors that are most immediately associated with brushing teeth–the manipulations that account for the teeth being effectively brushed. Similarly, the basic program for operating the radial arm saw deals with the manipulations directly associated with sawing the wood. Associated with each basic operation are other discriminations and behaviors that are typically produced in the same context as the central operation. An expanded chain for tooth-brushing may involve everything from taking the brush from the rack to replacing the cap on the tube of toothpaste. The expanded chain for operating the radial arm saw may include putting on safety glasses, checking the equipment, selecting stock, turning on and turning off the machine.

An expanded chain has two features that set it apart from the other forms we have worked with:

1. The expanded chain consists of a chain of behaviors that does not become completely covertized. Often, the central behavior remains overt throughout all applications of the chain.

2. The chain consists of both discriminations and new motor responses.

The description of expanded chains suggests that expanded chains are not limited to motor operations like sawing or brushing teeth. The line between a cognitive operation and an expanded chain is fuzzy. The clear examples of expanded chains are those that deal with physical operations. Putting money in the soft-drink machine is the physical operation for an expanded chain that involves "counting out" money. Typing a business letter is an expanded chain, built around the physical operation of typing. Sweeping the floor is an expanded chain. In all cases of expanded chains, there is an integration of discriminations and motor responses. You do not sweep the floor where you have already swept. You do not type the heading on the letter three times.

And you do not stick pennies in the soft-drink machine. These discriminations feed the central operation. You discriminate whether the floor has been swept. Then you perform the appropriate response. You determine which coins are appropriate for the machine; then you place them in the machine. You determine which part of the letter you have typed; then you type the next part.

Expanded Chain Programs

Think of an expanded chain program as a *series of separate tracks, each dealing with a particular skill.* Ultimately, the tracks converge. The tracks that need the most work should begin earlier. These tracks typically involve the new motor responses. Motor skills will require more time to induce than the discriminations. Therefore, by starting them early, we enable the other components of the terminal expanded chain to be introduced sooner.

First, we teach each skill within a juxtaposition pattern that permits rapid repetition of the skill. If the skill is screwing the cap on the toothpaste tube, we work on repeated examples of this skill. We do not require the learner to complete the entire chain of brushing the teeth before practicing this behavior.

Following the initial juxtaposition, we introduce the skill into a *small chain* that is composed of the new skill and several skills that occur with the new skill. When the learner becomes increasingly proficient with this chain, we introduce a longer chain and so forth until the learner is performing the entire operation. The strategy is not new. In one respect it is a variation of the 3-level strategy. First, the easiest juxtaposition is presented; then, more interruptions are presented between examples of the newly-taught skill. For the expanded chain, the interruptions are other parts of the chain. They will always tend to occur in the same order and therefore the teaching is somewhat different from earlier forms. However, the procedure is one of going from repeated juxtapositions of a single task or part to a chain consisting of many parts.

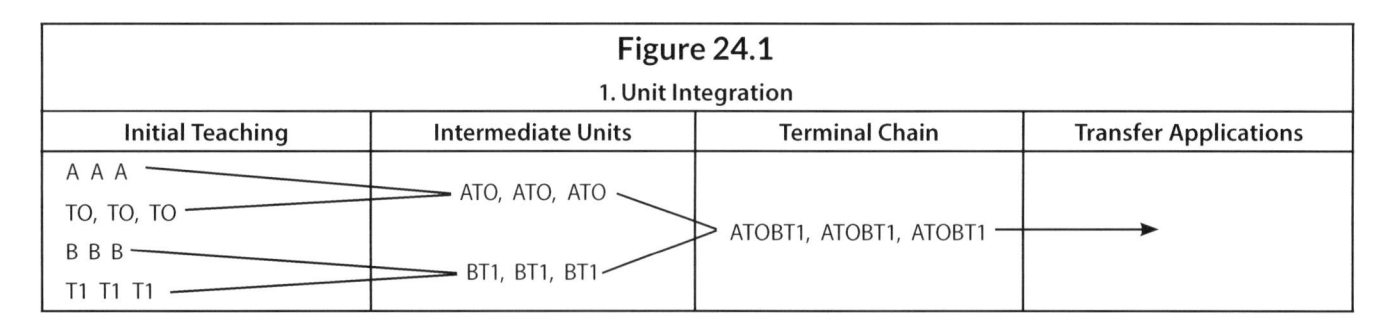

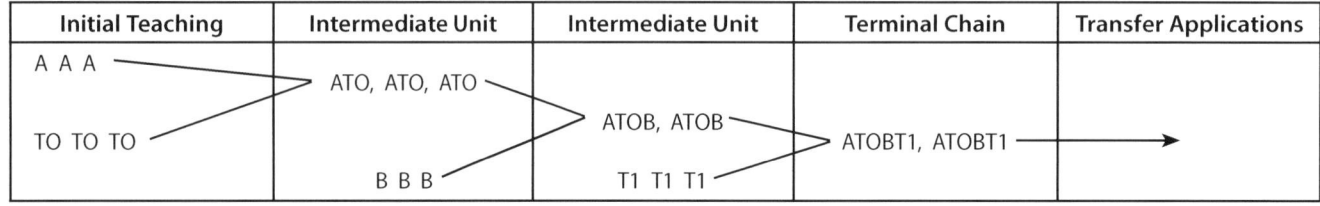

Figure 24.1

1. Unit Integration

Initial Teaching	Intermediate Units	Terminal Chain	Transfer Applications
A A A TO, TO, TO B B B T1 T1 T1	ATO, ATO, ATO BT1, BT1, BT1	ATOBT1, ATOBT1, ATOBT1	→

2. Trunk Integration

Initial Teaching	Intermediate Unit	Intermediate Unit	Terminal Chain	Transfer Applications
A A A TO TO TO	ATO, ATO, ATO B B B	ATOB, ATOB T1 T1 T1	ATOBT1, ATOBT1	→

Integration Strategies

Figure 24.1 shows two different patterns for initial teaching and integration of expanded chains. The first pattern is a *unit integration*. Individual skills (**A**, **TO**, **B**, **T1**) are taught and are then chained into intermediate units (**ATO** and **BT1**) and are finally combined to form the terminal chain (**ATOBT1**). The second pattern is a *trunk integration*. A trunk is established (**ATO**). New elements are added to the trunk until the terminal chain (**ATOBT1**) is formed.

At each stage in the trunk integration, the learner is working on the chain that contains **A** and another response (**TO**, **B**, and then **T1**). When the learner becomes firm on each skill in isolation, the skill is added to the trunk. In the trunk integration shown in Figure 24.1, the newly-taught skill is always added to the end of the chain being taught. The new skill, however, could be added to the beginning of the chain as well.

The schedule does not show all the teaching that is possible for each time period. A general rule is that the learner may practice the chain that has already been developed or any part of that chain. For instance, when the chain **ATO** has been established as a trunk, the learner may work on **A** in isolation, **TO** in isolation, and **ATO** as a chain. This convention follows from the general correction procedures. If the learner has serious trouble with **A** when it occurs in the context of **ATO**, the teacher removes **A** from the chain, practices it in isolation, and then reintroduces the chain **ATO**.

Scheduling Parts of the Expanded Chain

The principles for scheduling the skills that appear in an expanded chain are:

1. Do not attempt to introduce the skills in the order in which they will occur in the terminal chain.
2. Begin instruction on the central operation as early as possible.
3. Schedule the teaching of new responses (either as removed components or as part of the operation) as early as possible.
4. Make the program as simple as possible.

There are three reasons for teaching the central operation early, regardless of its position in the terminal chain. The first reason is that the central operation provides the motivation or justification for the other behaviors. The justification for checking traffic is much more easily communicated if it is linked to the actual behavior of riding the bike.

The second reason is that the central operation requires new responses. Because new responses imply a great deal of practice, the sooner we start on the central operation, the sooner we will achieve the amount of practice needed to establish independent behavior for the central operation.

The third reason is that the central operation can be practiced independently once it is mastered. (The physical environment provides feedback.) The scheduling of later skills is easier if the learner continues to work independently on that central skill.

Principle 4 suggests that the program should be as simple as possible. As we observed earlier, we should not see how elaborate the program can be, but how simple we can make it. The programs that we will illustrate may seem to violate this principle. These programs are designed for the learner who would be relatively hard to teach. Therefore, the programs provide for the careful teaching of each skill. More sophisticated learners will not need all the steps that the programs specify.

Illustration: Bike Riding

Bike riding is not a particularly difficult skill to teach; however, the skill serves to illustrate the process of integrating various components. Ultimately, we want the learner to exhibit the following behaviors:

- Check apparel.
- Check traffic to assure that riding is safe.
- Mount bicycle.
- Stay in marked lanes.
- Follow traffic rules, including giving signals.
- Turn and brake appropriately.
- Start and stop on level surfaces and hills.

We could add to the list. The more we add, however, the more we may obscure that central thrust of instruction. To find that central thrust, we answer two questions:

1. Which skill (or skills) do the other skills tend to assume?
2. What is it about this skill that the learner cannot do?

The answer to the first question is "ride the bike." All the information about following traffic rules, stopping and starting, etc., assume the basic skill of riding a bicycle.

The second question asks, "What is it about this skill that the learner cannot do?" Let's mentally put the learner on the bicycle, make the machine move, and think about what the learner would do if the learner does not have to worry about clothing, checking traffic, and other details of the chain that may complicate the operation. The learner would probably wobble from side to side, take one foot from the pedal to maintain balance, place it on the ground, thereby tipping the bike in the other direction, overcompensate with the handle bars, and fall over.

The purpose of mentally constructing the simplest possible example, removed from the events that precede the critical part of the operation, is to determine the setup for the central operation. If the learner probably cannot perform the operation described above, a simplified variation of this activity would be the central new response of the program. Although it would not be expedient to start all skills at the same time, *we can simultaneously introduce some skills that do not interfere with the actual riding operation or that depend on the operation.* Our choices include discriminations about safety, checking traffic, possibly even mounting the bicycle or pedaling, if these operations can be designed in a way that they do not assume the riding ability. Figure 24.2 shows a possible schedule that shows the strategy for the first five lessons.

Figure 24.2					
Tracks		Lessons			
		1	2	3	4
Riding	(R)	R	RP	MRP	TMRP
Pedalling	(P)	P			
Mounting	(M)	M	M		
Traffic checking	(T)	T	T	T	

As we observed earlier, the central skill is maintaining balance on a moving bicycle. We will refer to this skill as "riding."

The schedule does not show all the activities that occur on a given lesson, merely *the most complicated chain* that is presented on that lesson. The arrows show the progression of the different activities. First, each skill is taught in isolation and then added to the chain. The program involves a trunk integration of skills. Traffic checking is taught as a discrimination. The teaching may involve a correlated-features sequence.

Mounting is taught as an independent operation during the first two days. Practice in this operation could be made independent of riding by designing a device that would not fall over, but would move forward in the way a bike does when the pedal is pushed down. The learner could practice pushing the pedal down and swinging into a sitting position. This program would be a nonessential response program because the essential balance features of the response have been removed from the operation. Therefore, we should not retain the practice too long in this form. If we teach mounting through an essential-response program, we would have to present it in a context that required the learner to balance the bike. The learner might learn to scoot the bicycle (like a scooter) while keeping one foot on the pedal. When this operation is firm, the learner could learn to mount. Or the mount could be delayed until the riding had been firmed and then added as a part at the beginning of the riding operation. The schedule in Figure 24.2 assumes that we are presenting mounting through a non-essential program. The mounting is integrated with the central operation (on the third lesson); however, *not all trials* of riding would involve the three steps of mounting, pedaling, and riding.

The schedule introduces pedaling through a non-essential-response-features program. Part of the pedaling operation could involve standing and pedaling (with the pressure adjusted so that the learner would have to exert quite a bit of pressure on the pedals). The pedaling operation is taught as a non-essential-response features skill so that it may be introduced early. On the second lesson, it is integrated with some practice in riding. The quick integration of pedaling and riding assures that the pedaling response is not seriously distorted.

The schedule for riding in Figure 24.3 shows the various practice blocks and indicates how the activities from the other tracks may be juxtaposed with riding. This schedule specifies activities not presented on the general schedule for this program.

Within the riding track are skills that are taught within the context of riding (turning and stopping).

The juxtaposition of the early practice blocks is designed to permit rapid practice. On lessons in which skills are to be integrated, the skill that is to be added to the trunk is first practiced in isolation. Immediately following the successful practice of the skill in isolation, the skill is integrated into a chain. For instance, on lesson 2 the learner first practices pedaling in isolation, then practices pedaling within the chain of straight riding and pedaling. The work on the pedaling in isolation serves as a *precorrection*. The idea is to make sure that the learner is firm on the component to be integrated and is prompted on producing it. Note however, that the precorrection becomes counterproductive if the learner becomes fatigued while working on the component or begins to produce poor responses. In these cases, the introduction of the chain would be delayed. A break would be scheduled, followed by more work on pedaling in isolation.

Figure 24.3

	Trials
Lesson 1	
Mounting	5
Straight riding (no pedaling)	10
Pedalling	100 revolutions
Straight riding (no pedaling) stopping	10
Traffic check	Discrimination sequences
Straight riding (no pedaling)	5
Mounting	5
Straight riding (no pedaling) stopping	5
Lesson 2	
Straight riding (no pedaling)	5
Straight riding (no pedaling) stopping	100 revolutions
Turning (no pedaling)	10
Pedalling	5
Straight riding (pedaling)	5
Traffic check	Discrimination sequences
Mounting	5
Turning (no pedaling)	5
Straight riding (pedaling) stopping	5
Lesson 3	
Straight riding (no pedaling) stopping	5
Mounting	5
Mounting, riding, pedaling	5
Riding, turning	5
Traffic check	Test segment of discrimination sequence
Riding (pedaling), turning, stopping	5
Mounting, riding (pedaling), turning, stopping	10
Lesson 4	
Traffic check	1
Traffic check, mounting, riding, pedalling, stopping	5
Mounting, riding, pedaling, turning, stopping	5
Mounting, riding, pedaling, turning, stopping	5
Traffic check, mounting, riding, pedalling, turning, stopping	5

Illustration: Driving Screws with a Screwdriver

The expanded chain that we wish to teach involves the following behaviors:

1. Picking up screws and inserting them into predrilled holes on a surface that may be oriented so that the screw head is up, down, parallel to the floor, or in some intermediate orientation.

2. Turning the screw in with a screwdriver until the screw head is flush with the surface of the material in which the screw is embedded.

3. Meeting a rate-accuracy criterion for a minimum number of screws per minute.

Only two major behaviors are involved in the operation; however, each of these behaviors has many component behaviors. The act of screwing the screw with a screwdriver involves aligning the screwdriver, applying pressure, turning in the appropriate direction, and continuing to turn until the screw is set. The implication is that the learner knows the difference between a screw that has not been completely set and one that is completely set.

As the first step in designing the program, we answer the questions: "Which skills do the other skills tend to assume?" and "What is it about this skill that the learner cannot do?"

The essential part of the chain is operating a slot (or blade) screwdriver appropriately. The operation that the learner cannot do consists of aligning the instrument, pushing, and rotating the handle in a clockwise direction.

The *sameness* that we wish to teach is the basic operation of manipulating the screwdriver (aligning, pushing, and turning). The range of variation is accounted for by the orientation of the screw, the type of head, the type of screwdriver. Although these features vary, the basic operation (aligning, pushing, and turning) is not affected.

Figure 24.4 shows the relationship between the sameness (align, push, turn) and the range of variation for the operation of manipulating the screwdriver.

The diagram implies that we must design the operation so it is obviously the same operation across all possible variations of orientation, head type, and size.

Figure 24.4

Type of Variation	Range of Variation
Spatial orientation Type of head Size of screw	turn, turn, turn, turn, turn → push, push, push, push, push → Align, Align, Align, Align, Align →

Adding behaviors to make the operation unique. The orientation of screws presents a double problem. If we teach the learner to perform the operation with screws that are oriented head-up, and if the learner works on these examples for a fairly extended period of time, the learner will probably reverse the turn when we present screws that are head-down. An apparent solution to this problem is to introduce variations of head-up and head-down screws early. The problem with this solution is that it involves a very difficult discrimination, turning clockwise (in relationship to the ground) when the head is up, and counter-clockwise (in relationship to the ground) when the head is down.

We can solve this problem by adding stipulated behaviors to the operation. The purpose of these is to permit the learner to *do the same thing*, regardless of the screw's orientation. Possibly, the learner is taught to aim the screwdriver at the screw head (sighting down the shaft in the same way that you would aim a rifle). The learner holds the screwdriver so that the thumb is facing the screw head (not the learner's face). The learner inserts the screwdriver and turns it in a clockwise direction.

By following these steps, the learner will always turn the instrument in the appropriate direction, whether the screw is oriented head-up, head-down, or head-horizontal. No reversals are possible, because the screw head (not the ground) determines which direction is clockwise.

Note that this strategy involves adding behaviors to the operation. These stipulated behaviors permit us to introduce variations in spatial orientation very early. Instead of working only on head-up examples, we can work on examples in a variety of orientations.

The potential problem associated with the other variables (type of head and size of screw) is *response distortion*. We looked at this problem in Chapter 23. There are easy and hard examples of head types. The easy examples have the head of a bolt. (The screwdriver handle is attached to a socket that fits over the head.) This example is easy because the learner can succeed while performing a wide range of turning behaviors. The learner may create great lateral torque while turning the handle. If this behavior is performed with a blade screwdriver, the blade would disengage from the screw head and slip to the side. With the socket driver, however, the distorted lateral-pressure response does not affect the outcome, although the turning response is inappropriate for the blade screwdriver. If we introduce the socket variation at the beginning of the program, the program actually becomes a non-essential-response features program, because the learner is not responsible for alignment. (The learner initially aligns the screwdriver; however, continuous alignment is not necessary during the turning operation. Therefore, great distortion in the turning response is prompted by this example.)

The solution to the problem of a distorted-turning response is to juxtapose examples that are greatly different from each other, but that require the same basic operation. Here are examples that we will use. They are arranged in order of increasing difficulty.

1. socket driver
2. phillips
3. big blade
4. small blade

We begin by presenting examples of the easy type, *and* the most difficult type for which the learner can produce approximate responses. We present some examples of the socket driver and juxtapose these with examples of the big blade screwdriver. We set a different criterion of performance for both applications. (We might reinforce the learner for each complete rotation of the handle when working with the big blade and reinforce the learner only after setting the bolt with the socket driver.) As the learner improves, we change both criteria of performance, moving in the direction of increasingly difficult examples. This juxtaposition should prompt the learner to treat the diverse examples in the same way (particularly if the same unique operational steps are taken with each example).

Figure 24.5 is a possible schedule for high-criterion and low-criterion activities that would be juxtaposed during different time units (which could be weeks or days).

Note that the low criterion is used for more difficult examples and the high criterion for easy examples. At time 1, the high criterion problems involve a socket driver, and the low-criterion problems involve large-blade screwdrivers. As the learner improves, the context for both high and low criteria shift. At time 2, the most difficult examples the learner works on are small-blade examples. During the same lesson range, the learner also engages in high criterion practice with a phillips screwdriver (an example that is harder than a socket driver, but not as hard as a blade) and a large blade. At time 3, the high criterion track presents only large blades. At time 4, the low criterion track drops, because the learner is now performing at a high criterion on the most difficult examples (small blades).

The review track picks up the various skills that had been taught earlier to a high criterion. After high-criterion performance has been achieved with socket drivers, they move to the review track (time block 2) followed by phillips, large-blade, and small-blade applications. For all review items, the high criterion is retained.

The setup would be designed to accentuate the operational sameness. The various screws and bolts would already be started for the learner. All would be mounted on a board that rotates or changes position after each screw or bolt has been set. The learner first screws two or three bolts with the socket driver. Immediately following the last socket application, the learner screws one large screw with the large-blade screwdriver. As noted earlier, the criterion for reinforcing responses is different for

Figure 24.5						
Time Units:	1	2	3	4	5
High Criterion:	socket	phillips and large blade	large blade	small blade	
Low Criterion:	large blade	small blade	small blade		
Review with High Criterion:		socket	socket, phillips	socket, phillips, large blade	socket, phillips, small blade, large blade

the two examples. Perhaps a light goes on if the learner performs an acceptable trial (screwing the bolt all the way in a specified time period, or completing one rotation with the large-blade screwdriver).

The rules for the variation in the orientation of the board might follow a pattern of changing within the range of 45° during time phase 1. After each example has been completed, the board would change from 0° to 45°. During time phase 2, the range of variation might increase to 90°, during phase 3 to 135°, and for the remainder of the program to 180°. It may be expedient to introduce this range of variation only on some blocks of practice trials during the different time periods. (Just as the learner does not have to engage in every aspect of bike riding for every practice trial, the learner does not have to work on "difficult examples" on every trial.)

In addition to directing applications involving screwdrivers, the program should account for other aspects of the chain–placing the screws in by hand, selecting the appropriate screwdriver for the screw, aligning the screwdriver (a preskill to the operation of manipulating the screwdriver) and pushing against the screwdriver (another preskill).

The introduction of these skills follows the same pattern as the various secondary skills that were added to the chain for bike riding. For instance, to teach the behavior of turning, we could use the same board on which the screws are mounted, a flashlight, and a polarized lens.

After each trial, the board changes orientation. The learner must turn on the beam, and aim the flashlight at a polarized lens that is mounted on the board. Then the learner rotates the flashlight a half turn so that the light continues to strike the lens throughout the turning process. This movement is the same that is used in turning the screwdriver. The flashlight is therefore held in the same manner, with the thumb pointing to the target. A simple electric device could indicate whether each trial is successful. Rate criteria could be introduced. (The learner would have to perform "so many" trials during a specified time period.)

We might add component skills when we observe particular problems that the learner has. One such skill could be pressing the blade of the screwdriver into a slot and maintaining a certain amount of pressure. To teach this important component, we could design a screwdriver that must be aligned with the screw and pressed with a certain amount of pressure to sound a buzzer, which indicates a successful trial. The slots on the screw heads could be arranged so that the learner would have to first rotate the screwdriver and align the blade with the slot, then press with a certain amount of pressure, maintaining the screwdriver so that the shaft is parallel to the shaft of the screw.

The work on these operations would be superimposed on the work with the combined operations that occur in time periods 1 through 5. Figure 24.6 shows the various skills feeding into the main trunk of operating the screwdriver.

The preskills of placing, aligning, and turning are started in the first time unit. Placing continues through the third time unit. The combined operation of placing, aligning, and turning starts in the second time unit and continues to the end of the program. When performing this operation, the learner would place the screw with fingers, then set it using a screwdriver. This work would be performed in addition to the massed practice of working with screws that have already been placed.

	Figure 24.6			
Skills	Time Units			
	1	2	3	4
Placing	X	X	X	
Aligning	X			
Turning	X			
Align and turn	X			
Place, align, and turn		X	X	X
Screwdriving	socket and large blade	socket, phillips, large blade, small blade	socket, phillips, large blade, small blade	socket, phillips, large blade, small blade

This program calls for various automated devices—flashlights that give feedback, possibly pressure devices that "beep," boards with screws that change position from time to time. The program could be devised so that these devices are not needed. If the teacher is working with a group of learners, however, the devices become very important, because they permit the learners to work without continuous supervision from the teacher. The devices simply perform the feedback role for operations that involve discriminations the learner may not know. The learner may not know, for instance, how hard to press against the screw when turning. A device can be designed to provide feedback. Similarly, the learner may not know what the limits are for turning the handle while maintaining a true orientation. Again, a device that provides feedback can be designed. These devices have the potential of changing a program from one that requires constant teacher monitoring to one that provides more practice with far less monitoring.

Poorly Designed Expanded Chains

An expanded chain is an elaborate communication. If it inadequately conveys information to the learner, the learner will have trouble, which may not become obvious until later in the program.

The major communication flaws that are most typically observed in poorly designed programs are:

1. Inappropriate juxtaposition of examples for the initial teaching of a component or skill.

2. Introduction of events in a way that implies a false operation.

3. An order of introduction that arranges subtypes in a progressive, easy-to-hard series.

Juxtaposition Flaws

When a new skill is being taught, it should be possible to present repeated trials of that skill at least every 10 seconds. If much more time is required, something is wrong with the presentation. The problem is probably that the skill is embedded in too large a chain, or that the logistics and setup are not well-designed for initial teaching. The prediction based on poor juxtapositions is that some learners will experience chronic or persistent regressions.

Juxtaposition flaws typically occur when the only initial teaching of a skill occurs as the skill is added to the chain of behaviors already taught. Typically, this type of program introduces the skills either in the order in which they occur in the terminal chain or in the reverse order (backward chaining procedures). If the temporal parts are **A**, **B**, **C**, **D** (in that order), an inappropriate procedure would be the one diagrammed below.

(A) - - - ➤ (A + B) - - - ➤ (A + B + C) - - - ➤ (A + B + C + D)

Note that **B**, **C**, and **D** are not first taught in isolation and then integrated into the chain. The introduction and integration occur at the same time. The only time that **C** is taught is when it occurs in the context of **A** + **B** + **C**. The juxtapositions become very inappropriate for teaching skills that occur late in the chain. If the skill **E** is introduced only in the context of the chain **A** + **B** + **C** + **D** + **E**, the practice is poorly designed to teach **E**. We can illustrate the problem with a chain for teaching the learner to cut a series of boards the same length, using a radial arm saw.

A.	Teacher:	Tell me the rule for cutting boards on the radial arm saw.
	Learner:	The board must have a straight edge and must be long enough to hold against the fence.
B.	Teacher:	Cut one end of the board to square it.
	Learner:	(Cuts board.)
C.	Teacher:	Clamp the stop 12 inches along the fence.[1]
	Learner:	(Clamps stop.)
D.	Teacher:	Move the board to the stop and then cut it.
	Learner:	(Moves the board and cuts it.)
E.	Teacher:	(Repeats step **D** for each cut.)

Assume that the teaching for this operation occurs in the order of the events described in the routine above. First, the learner learns to recite the rule. The learner then learns to recite the rule and square the end of the board. The learner then learns to recite the rule, square the board, and operate the clamp. And so forth. Not only is the juxtaposition pattern inappropriate for performing the actual operation of making repeated cuts; it is inappropriate for the teaching of the other skills in the chain. To teach the learner to select stock appropriate for the sawing operation, a simple discrimination series is implied. The rule recitation should be

---

[1] The fence is a guide that orients the board. The stop is a device positioned at the end of the board so that there is a fixed distance from the saw blade.

dropped completely from the chain. The learner should be provided with massed practice in squaring the end of boards. The learner should receive massed practice in setting the stop at different distances along the fence. ("Set the stop at four inches" . . . "Set the stop at nine inches" . . . Etc.) Furthermore, the operation of making repeated cuts (moving the board to the stop and cutting, removing the piece that had been cut and again moving the board to the stop and cutting) should be introduced early. It is the central operation, and it should not be delayed until the learner learns the rule, stop-setting, selecting stock, and squaring.

The two major flaws in this program are very common. The program introduces skills in the same order they occur when the chain is completed. The program adds skills to the chain. These two flaws mean that the initial practice for many of the skills violate the ten-second rule. The simplest way to identify the flaws is to determine whether the learner would be capable of producing repeated responses to the entire chain used for initial teaching in no more than ten seconds. The remedy for the problem is to eliminate as much of the chain as necessary to create an appropriate pattern of juxtapositions for initial teaching. After the initial teaching has occurred, the newly-taught skill may be integrated into a larger chain.

If we follow the procedure of identifying the central operation and teaching it as quickly and simply as possible, the program for repeated cuts involves one sequence that deals with the stop and then an operation that meets the juxtaposition criterion. The following illustrates a possible program sequence:

Teacher Wording

To make repeated cuts that are 17 inches long, I set the stop 17 inches along the fence.

Where do you set the stop along the fence for repeated cuts that are 18 inches long?

Where do you set the stop along the fence for repeated cuts that are 28 inches long?

Where do you set the stop along the fence for repeated cuts that are 13 inches long?

Let's say you are going to make repeated cuts that are 9 inches long. So where do you set the stop along the fence? Do it.

Let's say you are going to make repeated cuts that are 20 inches long. Where do you set the stop? Do it.

Let's say you are going to make repeated cuts that are 30 inches long. Where do you set the stop? Do it.

This skill in integrated into a chain that involves only the new behavior and the sawing (**C** and **D**).

Teacher Wording

You're going to make repeated cuts that are 15 inches long. Where do you set the stop? Do it.

Now make 4 repeated cuts.

Implying False Operations

Another type of problem occurs if the program attempts to teach both a new-response skill and a discrimination in the same context or chain. This treatment may not effectively communicate to the learner whether the learner is expected to learn a discrimination or a motor response. Two types of false operations are possible. For the first, we are trying to teach a new motor skill; however, we emphasize discriminations or concepts to a degree that implies that we are actually trying to teach discriminations or concepts.

The second type of false operation involves the opposite situation. We are trying to teach a discrimination or concept; however, our emphasis on motor responses implies that the learner is supposed to learn a motor skill.

The radial-arm saw operation presented a false operation of the first type. The emphasis on verbal behavior (recitation of the rule) implied that the operation of making repeated cuts *requires* these verbal discriminations. The emphasis is displaced to talking about sawing.

We can illustrate the second type (teaching a discrimination, but implying that we are teaching a motor response) with a program designed to teach basic language skills to naive learners. The teacher presents objects. For each, the teacher says, "What is this?" The learner responds by naming the object within a statement form: "That is a ____." The learner may not know the name of some objects. The learner also may have trouble producing the complete statement (even for objects that are familiar to the learner). The typical correction is for the teacher to model the correct response: "That is a lamp," and require the learner to repeat the statement until firm. The reinforcement is provided with the words "Good talking."

The inappropriate strategy that the learner may develop from this presentation (particularly if there are many unfamiliar objects) is to talk (produce the motor responses) without paying attention to the features of the object. To remedy this flaw, we separate the motor skill from the discrimination. We first present the discriminations. When the learner is firm on these, we present the motor skills. Let us say the learner is to identify five objects—lamp, dog, cup, chair, and phone. The teacher first presents pictures of these, asking the question that requires a relatively simple response: "What is this?" Response: "Lamp." Reinforcement: "Good." The reinforcement now is clearly linked to identifying the object. The type of behavior the learner is performing is the same as that performed in other situations that call for looking at things and identifying them.

After the learner has performed on juxtaposed examples of identifying the objects with single-word responses, the teacher can work on the responses. The teacher points to an object. "What is this? . . . Yes, a lamp. Here's how to say the whole thing about the lamp: That is a lamp. Say the whole thing about the lamp . . . Again . . ." Reinforcement: "Good saying the whole thing."

Now the separation is clear. The reinforcement for "saying the whole thing" shows that the teacher is dealing with a new skill. If the teacher corrects a statement-saying response, the chances are greatly reduced that the learner will be confused about what sort of behavior the correction deals with. The correction does not imply that the learner should stop discriminating and simply produce "talking" responses.

Easy To Hard Examples

If the program sequences examples from easy to hard in a linear progression, we would predict serious response distortion. In fact, the learner would probably learn better if the sequence were random. In an easy-to-hard series of examples for screwdriving, the learner works first on bolt heads followed by phillips, large-slot heads, and finally small-slot heads. As we observed earlier, the prediction implied by the sequence is that the learner will have serious difficulty when the large-slot screws are introduced. The reason is that the preceding examples permit the learner to exert inappropriate lateral force while turning the handle. The large-slot screw does not permit this behavior. Therefore, the learner may learn an inappropriate turning behavior and may have trouble with the slotted screws because the blade pops out as the handle is rotated.

A similar prediction of distortion results if easy-to-hard examples are used for the spatial orientation of screws.

The easiest examples are those in which the screw head is up. Gravity tends to hold the screwdriver in place. If the screw head is horizontally oriented, gravity tends to force the slotted screwdriver to slip out. If the screw head is down, the learner must apply pressure to keep the screwdriver in place. By working on the easy examples of screwing until the learner is proficient, we not only teach a slight motor-response distortion (which results because of the gravity effect); we also set the stage for possible reversals. The learner may have trouble when confronted with upside-down screws and may turn the handle in the wrong direction.

Illustration: SCUBA-diving. A program for using SCUBA equipment may be introduced in a way that leads to possible problems if the sequence proceeds progressively from easy to hard examples. Underwater breathing with SCUBA gear is achieved by inhaling through a tube held in the mouth. Breathing can be accomplished when wearing a mask that covers the nose, or without a mask. If the instruction arranges examples in the order of easy-to-hard, the first examples the learner practices involve wearing the mask. Like other easy examples, this one permits the desired outcome with responses that are common to the entire range of examples or with responses that work only for the easy example. In other words, the easy examples may induce distorted responses. The possible distortion has to do with the involvement of the nose in breathing. While the mask is worn, the learner has the option of inhaling so that only the mouth is involved in inhaling, or breathing so that the nose is also involved. So long as the mask is fitted properly, the involvement of the nose makes no real difference in the outcome. The underwater breathing is successful. The slight pull on the mask caused by the involvement of the nose does not hinder the breathing. In fact, the learner may be quite unaware of using the nose.

Breathing underwater while using only the air tube—no mask—is more difficult because any involvement of the nose will lead to a nose full of water. Note that this example is more difficult because the outcome may be achieved only if the learner performs within a narrow range of behavioral limits. Underwater breathing while wearing a mask is easier because of the behavioral options it provides. However, it is possible to use exactly the same set of behaviors to breathe in both situations. The objective of instruction would be to induce this sameness in behavior as quickly and efficiently as possible. Teaching the behavior early is important because unintended examples may come into the sequence. Let us say the learner begins with "easy" examples that involve breathing with a mask and air tube. Suddenly, the learner's mask fills with water. In effect, the learner is presented with a difficult example—one that had not been scheduled in the sequence. Unless the learner knows how to breathe in this situation, the learner may inhale water through the nose, panic, and have an unpleasant experience.

The problem can be avoided if the sequence of examples teaches the behavior that is common to all underwater breathing situations. *The first examples in this program involve no mask.* The learner sits in shallow water with head under water, breathing *with only an air tube.* After demonstrating proficiency with this example, the learner performs the same operation in deep water, while swimming and carrying out a variety of maneuvers. Next, the learner is required to go underwater without a mask on, but with an air tube. The learner is not allowed to clear the mask. (The mask remains full of water.) Finally, the learner puts the mask on underwater and clears it (achieved by leaning back and exhaling through the nose). The skill of breathing without a mask is reviewed by a water entry routine that the learner uses for some time. The learner enters the water without a mask, goes underwater, puts on the mask, and clears it.

With this training the learner is not in jeopardy if the mask fills with water. The learner does not become excited, because the type of breathing that the program teaches is the same for all underwater situations.

When we violate the easy-to-hard order of introducing examples, we do not overlook the fact that some examples are harder than others. We do not place the learner in a situation that induces failure. Breathing without a mask may be more difficult than breathing with a mask; however, there are gradations of task difficulty for the no-mask situation. We could initially place the learner in deep water without a mask. Obviously, this situation would be dangerous. We therefore try to make it easy by manipulating the setup. When the learner sits in shallow water, the example has the properties of a good example. We can work on a breath at a time. The quick examples of inhaling and exhaling can be juxtaposed. There is very little interference that hinders this juxtaposition.

We made the harder examples in the screwdriver program easier by changing the *criterion* of performance.

We made the harder example of the underwater breathing situation easier by changing the *setup* so that the only behaviors required of the learner are those that are essential to breathing underwater. Swimming and other behaviors that are produced simultaneously in some examples of underwater breathing were removed, leaving only the behavior of breathing.

Both techniques are important for making harder examples easier. We follow this general guide:

- If possible, we eliminate the non-essential details of the harder example so that only the essential details remain.

- If it is not possible to design such examples, we change the criterion for the harder examples.

Rehearsal and Transfer

Teaching some expanded chains involves establishing the chain in an appropriate instructional setting, then transferring the behavior to a variety of other situations. The problem of transfer is particularly acute for these chains because we must often construct practice situations for initial teaching that are not highly similar to the transfer situations. This condition occurs when:

1. The transfer situation is not available for practicing the initial teaching.

2. The situation in which the learner is to respond occurs only infrequently.

3. The situation in which the learner is to respond does not permit juxtapositions that are appropriate for initial teaching.

An example of (1) above would be behavior that we expect the learner to perform in the doctor's office. The office is not available for rehearsing the behavior; therefore, we teach the behavior in some situation in a way that will prompt transfer to the doctor's office.

An example of (2) would be the sheet-and-clothing-tearing behavior of a learner that occurs only at night and only for a short period during the night. Rather than waiting for these infrequent situations, we must construct practice or rehearsal situations that permit a massing of trials on some behavioral chain that should transfer to the low-frequency situation. The rehearsal would involve following instructions to tear and not tear things on command. The "no-tearing" command would then be transferred to the bedtime situation.

An example of (3) would involve teaching a blind person to respond to directions that tell how far to go and in which direction. Because it is nearly impossible to carry out applications of this routine in 10 seconds or less, the pattern of juxtaposition is poorly designed for initial teaching. Therefore, we must create a "model" or rehearsal situation that permits manageable juxtapositions of examples. We expect the learner to transfer from this situation to the "real life" applications.

Some teaching assignments may involve all three problems—unavailability of transfer situation, low-frequency behavior, and poor juxtapositions.

Inducing Transfer

When we design instruction that will lead to transfer of an expanded chain to a situation different from the practice situation, we must create *sameness*. The learner must be shown that some feature in the transfer situation is also in the rehearsal situation and that this sameness triggers the same behavior in both situations. The simplest technique is to design the practice so that the *first steps* in both the practice situation and the transfer situation are identical. If the learner carries out the first steps, the learner will be strongly prompted to carry out the remaining steps in the chain. In designing the first steps so they serve as a prompt for transfer, we find things that are the same in the practice situation and in the application setting. We arrange the chain so that it starts with these shared features.

We can illustrate this procedure with rehearsal for a visit to the doctor's office. The purpose of the visit may be that the learner is getting a shot. The purpose of the rehearsal situation is to give the learner a number of things to do so that the shot will not be frightening. We can establish the chain in a way that will displace the learner's attention from the fear and provide the learner with behaviors that will lead to reinforcement.

For the chain to be efficient, it should begin with a detail that is common to both the doctor's office and the practice situation, possibly with the door to the doctor's office.

"We're pretending now. There's the door to the doctor's office. You open the door for me. You let me go in first and then you go in . . ." This part of the chain is practiced and the directions are replaced with questions. "What's on the other side of the door? . . . Who's going to open it? . . . Okay, let's go."

The beginning part of the chain is then linked with the other parts and practiced until the learner is proficient. The learner is reinforced during the practice sessions for carrying out the various behaviors. To practice the "shot," the teacher pinches the learner on the arm.

The chances are good that the learner will perform appropriately in the transfer situation. By beginning the chain the same way in the application setting, we imply that the behaviors practiced earlier apply to this setting. "Okay, there's the door to the doctor's office. What's on the other side of it? . . . Who's going to open it? . . . Let's go . . ." By constructing the two situations so they are the same with respect to trivial details, we imply that they must be the same with respect to the *relevant* details. If a reasonable parallel exists between the situations the learner will probably perform appropriately in the application setting. (The learner will not cry when getting the shot.)

The chain with common first steps is very powerful for prompting the behavior because it establishes compliance on details that are *not critical* to what happens in the application setting; however, since these first steps are chained to subsequent steps, compliance on the first steps implies compliance on the later steps.

If the learner needs a prompt to begin the behaviors called for by the chain, this prompt is provided in connection with details that are not critical to the operation. If the chain had been designed without a beginning that involves details not critical to the central operation, the prompt would have to be given during the critical part of the application, which is not an ideal time to try to establish compliance.

The following is a summary of the procedures for establishing the practice situations that promote transfer to application situations.

1. Begin the chain with behaviors that are common to both situations but that are not critical to the application situation (like opening the door).

2. Follow the first part with requirements for frequent responses. (Intermittent behaviors reduce the probability of continued compliance.)

3. Practice the entire chain in the practice situation until the learner can perform with a minimum of prompting.
4. Prompt the first part of the routine in the application setting (pointing out the details that trigger the chain of behavior) and reinforce the learner for performing appropriately.

Creating Rehearsals for Low-Frequency Behaviors

To deal with inappropriate behaviors that occur infrequently, we create a situation in which we can work on the behavior in a way that places it under instructional control (which means that the learner does it on command) and also work on the opposite behavior, which is also placed under instructional control. The logic of the program is that we can "tempt" the learner in this rehearsal situation. If the learner overcomes the tendency to be tempted in the controlled situation, and if the learner consistently responds to the instructions the teacher provides in this situation, the chances of the learner performing in the problem situation are greatly increased.

We can illustrate the procedure with the tearing behavior of an autistic child that occurs only at night. We design a situation in which we have many objects that can be torn or broken. (This training would occur in a classroom or a room of the house other than the bedroom.) We present objects to the learner and give the command, "Tear it," or "Break it." We insist that the learner must wait until we give the instruction to tear or break. We provide no reinforcement for tearing or breaking. Also, we issue the command, "No tearing" or "No breaking" when we hand the learner some objects. If the learner fails to comply (by tearing or breaking), we present the learner with a long series of commands, "Stand up . . . sit down . . . stand up . . . sit down . . ." After we present possibly 40 such commands (and the learner complies with at least the last 5), we return to the task the learner had non-complied with. We again present the same object and say, "No tearing."

Once the learner is firm on massed trials of "Tear it" and "No tearing," we introduce "temptation tasks." We present the learner with the kind of objects that he apparently delights in tearing and we issue new commands with these: "Hold it . . . no tearing," or "Take it to Ms. Brown. No tearing." We increase the degree of temptation by making the tasks longer and increasing the time interval between tasks (following the same progression that is used for shaping the context of a task). Any non-compliance is followed by a long series of stand-up, sit-down tasks and repetitions of the task that had been non-complied with. Note that during the "temptation" training the child is given no commands to tear, only to do different things with objects that are tempting candidates for tearing.

When the learner is firm on "temptation" tasks, we present a series of similar tasks in the bedroom setting before the child goes to bed at night. The child would receive a series of commands associated with the objects that he typically tears. "Touch your pajamas. No tearing . . . Good. Hand me your pillow . . . Good. Touch your blanket. Remember, no tearing . . . Good," etc.

In this final stage, we are treating the bedroom setting in the same way that we had treated the original training setting. The learner should therefore transfer to the bedroom situation. Of course, this transfer assumes that we had brought the learner to a hard criterion of performance in the classroom and had presented tasks that allowed the learner to be in the presence of tempting objects for long periods of time during which there was no direct supervision from the teacher.

If tearing occurs during the night, the learner is put through a series of "stand-ups" and is then rehearsed in the bedroom on "no tearing."

Creating Improved Pattern of Juxtaposition

We have already illustrated the problem of poor juxtapositions. The illustration that we will present next differs from those that we have dealt with because it involves creating a "model" for practicing a skill, but doing so in a way that transfer to the application settings is strongly implied.

To teach a blind learner to respond to instructions for going places in the school, we would design a chain that permits massed trials in the practice situation. We begin by presenting the learner with paper on which there are tactually perceptible marks. The paper is oriented so the direction the learner is facing is at the top of the paper. A dot in the middle of the paper marks the learner's position. The bottom of the paper represents the space behind the learner.

For the simplest exercises, we would inscribe lines from the center dot to different parts of the sheet. The learner would first feel the line, then point in the direction shown by the map. (The pointing does not involve the paper.)

The learner is next presented with applications that involve both distance and direction information. For instance, an example such as the one illustrated above is presented. The learner is told the number of steps (five) and is then presented with these tasks: "Show me the direction you're going to move . . . Good. And how many steps are you going to take in that direction? . . . Yes, five."

Note that the learner does not move, but merely describes what will happen. Note also that the wording of the tasks clearly implies that application situations will require the execution of these behaviors.

For the final set of rehearsal examples, we use a game format. "I'm going to put the ball some place in this room. Then I'm going to use the map to tell you where it is. See if you can find it . . ." The objects are in place before the game begins. We present the learner with various map examples and tell the distance for each. "Show me the direction you're going to go . . . Good. And how many steps are you going to take in that direction? . . . Yes, seven. Do it . . ."

The practice situations present the same format that would be used in the transfer situations. The only major difference is that the examples in the transfer situation cannot by presented rapidly. "Here's a map that shows where Mr. James' room is. Feel it and then point in the direction you'll go first . . . Point in that direction. You'll go about 50 steps. Then you'll come to a door. You'll turn at the door. Show me which way you'll go after you turn . . . You'll go about 20 steps. Then you'll come to another door on your right . . ." Although the example is more complicated than those used in the rehearsal situation, it is composed of simple components. (We assume that the learner has already been taught left and right.) If the learner performs in the transfer situation, the learner should have no trouble dealing with the transfer applications.

Rehearsal for Field Trips

Often the procedures used for field trips are backward. The teacher expects the learner to recognize the significance of things observed on a field trip and to retain this information. Actually, a more reasonable procedure would be to rehearse what will occur on the field trip, point out the significance of things that will be observed, and then use the field trip as both a transfer situation and a reinforcing experience. For instance, if the learner is to go to a museum, the teacher describes things the learner will see and do. These occur in a relatively fixed order. As part of the introduction, the teacher may use pictures.

"The first thing you're going to do is get your ticket stamped at the ticket window. Then you go straight inside and wait. Right in front of you, you'll see two dinosaurs. Here are their pictures . . . What's the name of this dinosaur? . . . What's the name of the other dinosaur? . . . And to your left, you'll see . . ."

The verbal routine is repeated until the learner can answer a series of questions about the topic. "What's the first thing you're going to do? . . . Where do you get it stamped? . . . Then where do you go? . . . There will be something right in front of you. What's that? . . . What's the name of the biggest dinosaur? . . . What's the name of the other dinosaur? . . . If you're standing just inside, point to where the dinosaurs would be . . . Now point to where the African elephant will be . . . Good."

Since the series of verbal questions can be presented in both the rehearsal situation and the transfer setting, the teacher can assure transfer by presenting the same questions in the transfer setting. "Okay, what's the building we're standing in front of? . . . And what's the first thing you're going to do? . . . And then what are you going to do? . . ."

If the learner is pretaught, the transfer situation is reinforcing. The learner has performed successfully on the various questions in the rehearsal situation; the learner has received reinforcement from the chain of questions. The same chain is presented in the transfer situation; therefore, the transfer situation is established as a reinforcing situation. Note that if a great deal of content is involved in the event that is to be presented, the teacher might use a visual-spatial display for communicating this information. The technique can be combined with the technique of acting out the first part of the chain. This variation would be appropriate for young or naive learners.

Chains with Divergent Responses

Let us say that we want children to play a dress-up game in which the teacher "auctions" different articles of clothing to a group of children. Each child selects those articles that would be worn by a particular character (a cowboy, a dancer, etc.). If the child chooses to dress up as a cowboy, the child selects cowboy clothes.

Initially, an aide plays auctioneer while the teacher sits with the children and directs the activity. The teacher models the behavior that the children are expected to produce, asks questions, and prompts them to respond.

First, the teacher models a role that she will play. "I'm going to be a cowboy. Boy, I like a cowboy. What are you going to be?" (A mailman.) "You're going to be a mailman? That's great." The teacher models great excitement. (If the teacher effectively models excitement, the learners will produce excited responses.)

The teacher continues to ask the various children what they are going to be and to brag about her role until all children have responded at least two times by telling what they will be.

Next, the game begins. The auctioneer holds up an article of clothing that the teacher will wear. The teacher says, "Oh boy, there's a cowboy hat and I'm going to be a cowboy. So I say, 'I want it! I want it...'" The auctioneer quickly gives it to the teacher. The procedure is repeated for the next object, chaps.

The teacher struts and shows off her outfit, making the point that she operated according to the rules of getting the cowboy clothes. "I'm a cowboy. I got the cowboy clothes... Wow, look at me." Quickly, the clothes are returned to the auctioneer and without hesitation the game starts over. This time, articles of clothing for the different roles are held up in an unpredictable order. For each article that is held up, the teacher says: "Who wears that?" Then she asks the child who selected that role, "So what do you say?" (I want it.) "You got it..." If the child does not respond immediately to both questions, the object is returned to the auctioneer. "You can do better than that," the teacher observes. The child is told to remember that object. It is returned to the auctioneer and is presented after one or two other objects are presented. (This pattern of juxtaposition is like level 2 of the three-level strategy. The learner has successfully responded to examples that are not interrupted by interference. Now another activity is interpolated between the presentations of the object.)

The procedure is repeated. If any children give spontaneous comments about their role ("I've got the fireman's hat and I'm going to be a fireman"), the teacher reinforces the response. "He sure does look like a fireman already... That's great."

After the children have their outfits, the teacher reinforces them and permits them to show off for a few minutes. "Wow, I see a cowboy and a pretty dancing girl, and who is that big fireman over there?..."

The game is repeated with the teacher providing fewer instructions. First, the teacher makes sure that the children have selected roles and remember their roles. "Remember what you're going to be. Who's going to be the farmer?... Right. Who's going to be the fireman?... Who's going to be the cowboy?... Who's going to be the queen?..." The teacher selects a role, sits with the children, and models the sort of responses the children are to produce. She talks to her neighbors. "I'm going to be the cowboy. So I get all the cowboy clothes."

The teacher praises the children. "Boy, they really know which clothes they're going to get. They are smart..."

As the children become proficient, the teacher no longer sits with the children. Children continue to receive praise for selecting new roles and for selecting the clothes for that role.

Variations of the procedures indicated for the dress-up game can be used to establish any chain that involves divergent responses. Although the procedure may seem quite different from those we have worked with earlier, the introduction of the modeling is the only new technique. To establish behavior on a divergent-response chain, we follow four steps:

1. We design the steps of the chain so that we can:
   a. *model the type of behavior* we expect the learner to produce;
   b. *present questions and tasks* to overtize what the learner does;

c. *provide reinforcement* for responding to the tasks and for spontaneous responses that are consistent with the role.

2. We introduce the steps in the easiest context and then we proceed to more difficult contexts. We follow the three-level strategy for controlling the context—first presenting repeated presentations of a step (level 1), followed by presentations of that step when it is chained to one or more of the other steps (levels 2 and 3).

3. When the learner can perform on the entire chain without requiring prompts or corrections, we modify the chain by removing the tasks and questions. We continue to model (play the role of a learner) and reinforce, but not to ask the structured questions.

4. After successful performance on this chain, we modify it again by removing the model. (The teacher no longer plays the role of a learner.) We maintain reinforcement. The chain is now operating as an independent activity or as one that does not require teacher involvement.

The most important ingredient in the procedures for establishing divergent responses is the modeling. The reason is that there is something that is the same about all examples. For the dress-up game, the sameness is that you are going to behave like a particular person. You are going to do what that person does. "I'm going to be a _____. So I'm going to pick the things a _____ wears." If the teacher makes this equation very strong for one role, each of the other roles is a kind of transformation of the role the teacher models. Many behaviors are the same for all roles—the excitement, the naming of what you are going to be, the selecting of things that the selected character would wear. The only difference is the particular role that is selected and consequently the specific articles that are selected.

Summary

Expanded chains consist of various discriminations and motor responses that are built around a central *physical operation*. The physical operation is the "reason" for the chain.

The basic strategy that we follow is to teach parts of the chain and then join the parts together, forming an increasingly longer chain. The two strategies for integrating the parts of the chain are the *unit integration* (which establishes smaller chains that become juxtaposed units in larger chains) and the *trunk integration* (which establishes a trunk that grows by the addition of single parts that are first taught in isolation and are then added to the chain).

The trunk integration is usually the most manageable if we follow basic scheduling rules:

1. Do not introduce skills in the order in which they appear in the chain.

2. Begin instruction on the central operation as early as possible.

3. Teach other new responses as early as possible.

4. Try to make the program simple.

For chains that involve the introduction of many new skills, a given lesson would include juxtaposed practice blocks for the various skills that have been taught. Skills being introduced are practiced in isolation. Skills that have already been integrated into a chain are presented in variations of the chain (some variations involving only some of the parts that have been taught and other variations involving all the parts that have been taught).

The most serious problems associated with designing expanded chains are: inappropriate juxtapositions for the initial teaching of a skill; a teaching emphasis that implies a false operation; and the ordering of examples from easy to hard.

If the examples that are introduced for initial teaching require more than ten seconds (or possibly more than six seconds for most skills), the juxtaposition of examples is not well designed for initial teaching. A smaller part of the chain should be identified or a new setup should be designed so that the examples may be presented more rapidly.

A false operation is implied if the skill being taught is a motor response and the introduction emphasizes discriminations that are associated with the response. Also, a false operation is implied if the new skill is a discrimination that is paired with a related motor response, suggesting that motor response is relevant to the discrimination. The remedy for the false operation is to separate the discriminations and related motor responses during initial teaching.

A progressive, easy-to-hard order of introduction for the applications of a physical operation creates both distortion and stipulation. The remedy is to introduce harder examples early and to juxtapose them with easier examples of the same operation. This juxtaposition conveys the sameness in the applications and therefore reduces the stipulation and distortion.

Many expanded chains are practiced in one situation with the expectation that they will transfer to other situations. The transfer may not be automatic because the rehearsal situation is different from the transfer situation. The solution is to add sameness to both situations. The chain that is rehearsed should begin with behaviors that are not critical to the central operation. The chain should permit a relatively high rate of learner response. When the chain is applied to the transfer situation, the teacher prompts the first part of the chain. Since this part is the same as the first part in the transfer situation, and since the rest of the chain always follows the first part in the practice setting, the entire chain is implied for the transfer setting.

To design a chain for divergent responses, we should model a particular example and present the kind of questions that permit the learner to produce a variety of responses.

Expanded chains are complicated. They present very little that is new, however, if we remember that the order of events that occurs in a chain does not imply the order for teaching the skills or necessarily the form for their initial teaching. We can usually identify sensible teaching for the skills. By following the basic rules for demonstrating sameness, we can engineer transfer to specified situations.

Chapter 25
Expanded Programs for Cognitive Skills

Expanded programs deal with broad subjects or topics that imply more than a single discrimination or cognitive routine. The subject may be expressive writing, solving elementary physics problems, basic fraction operations, geology, etc. Expanded programs are the cognitive counterpart of expanded chains. An expanded chain centers around a physical operation of some sort. (The central operation is never fully covertized.) The central operation in an expanded program is a cognitive skill—a discrimination or cognitive operation. Like the expanded chain, the expanded program consists of more than a single operation. New responses (motor skill teaching) may be involved. An elaborate chain may be created to support the central operation; however, in the end, the operation is a cognitive one and the chain of events is therefore an invention, created to make the discriminations overt and obvious. The procedure may be complicated by the requirements to teach particular vocabulary, facts, and behaviors. These requirements are subsumed by the central thrust of the cognitive program, which is to teach an idea. Because of this somewhat strange structure, we have a strange interplay of strategies. In one respect, we have great latitude about how we will teach the idea. We can adjust the examples, group or create the subtypes, use prompts, and possibly even create unique wording and other response conventions. In other respects, we are constrained by convention. In the end, the learner will be expected to perform in the framework already established for the idea that we teach. We must therefore temper our efforts to teach effectively with the facts about the conventions the learner must be taught.

Expanded programs involve all the formats that we have examined. Basic discriminations, joining forms, subprograms for teaching different skills, new motor responses, cognitive routines, visual-spatial displays, prompting-fading—all become tools in the expanded program. Although the total expanded program is largely a coordination of smaller, simple programs, the total program cannot be reduced to the various components. The expanded program deals with a unique organization that provides impetus for the components to come together.

The focus of this chapter is on the strategies for organizing the various component programs (or tracks) into an efficient whole. Although the rules for specifying what should be done are fairly simple, the execution of the program is not. Sometimes years of testing the strategy takes place before the simple solution inevitably emerges. The efficient solution is always a simple one. If the program is characterized by ambiguities, vagueness, and "profundity," the program is the product of poor analysis. There is order in what we wish to teach, just as there is order in the pattern observed in clouds, sea shells, or traffic moving down a freeway. Our task is to discover it and to communicate this order. If we do it properly, the development of the skills will seem so easy that it might strike the naive observer as "cheating." The program will not be difficult, will involve a minimum of brow-furrowing discriminations, and will not present severe road blocks that preempt all from learning but the intuitively gifted and the lucky.

Once we understand what the program ideally should be, we can judge whether the one that we have created is a close approximation or not. Sometimes we may recognize that our emerging program is not what it should be; however, we may not know how to change it. In these situations, we must judge whether it is better than those already available, and if it is, use it with the full understanding that it is not an excellent program, but a useful one. In time, and with observations of the problems that teachers and students have with the program, we may be able to reshape it into a strong, simple pattern. (Techniques for such reshaping are outlined in Chapter 28.)

Some aspects of an expanded program are similar to those of expanded chains; therefore, some basic facts and strategies apply to both expanded chains and expanded programs.

1. Examples range from easy to hard, and the problems of sequencing examples exist for the

expanded program and the expanded chain. We create stipulation if we adhere to a rigid, easy-to-hard sequence.

2. The strategies for integrating the newly-taught skills with the skills that have been taught derive from the problem of integrating the skills of an expanded chain. The problem of creating juxtapositions of appropriate examples for the newly-taught skill suggests that the skill should first be taught in isolation and then integrated with the skills that have already been taught.

3. The development of the various cognitive skills runs parallel to the skill development for the new-response programs. We can teach skills as removed components. We can present a non-essential-feature program or we can present an essential-features program. Often, we use removed components because we follow the procedure of teaching one thing at a time; however, we temper teaching one thing at a time with the goal of achieving the program objective with the least amount of teaching.

4. We design the activities to account for transfer, following the same basic rules that we use in designing expanded chains. We create sameness in responses to show how applications are the same. We modify the situations to reduce irrelevant details so that the apparent sameness is increased. We create rehearsal situations so that we can control the juxtapositions of the events. We then introduce the application or transfer situations in which the skill is to be used.

The Basic Strategy

The strategy that we will follow for designing expanded programs for cognitive skills is not complicated in its major steps. Only three steps are involved:

1. We first organize the content according to response dimensions, and we identify an operation for communicating the idea that we wish to teach.

2. We next identify the range of examples for which the operation applies.

3. Finally, we identify the related operations for sequencing subtypes of examples and for processing exceptions that are not handled by the "main" operation.

This three-step procedure becomes complicated because each step requires a very careful treatment, analytically. First, we will outline the general procedure; then, we will apply it to different content problems.

Organizing Content by Response Dimensions

For initial teaching of discriminations and motor responses, we use an approach that juxtaposes different examples involving the same response dimension. If we extend this approach to broad content areas, we radically reorganize the traditional content because the traditional content areas are organized around *topics—not common operations*. For instance, a topic in physics is optics. There are many facts about optics, each implying different arithmetic operations. Traditionally, the learner studies optics and learns a variety of facts and operations that are called for by this topic. Later, the learner may discover that some operations used in optics are also used in other topics.

The response-dimension approach is different. Instead of trying to exhaust a topic, it deals with individual *operations*, and it presents each operation so that it cuts across a variety of topics. Following the same basic procedure used with simpler forms, juxtaposed examples of the operation are applied to a variety of contents to show what is the same about all instances of the operation. In the end, topics emerge; however, the initial teaching focuses on response-dimensions, not on events.

An illustration of the response-centered orientation is the operation of "squaring." As the distance of an object from the light source increases, the amount of light striking the object decreases by the square of the object's distance from the light source. This relationship, however, is not confined to optics. Springs work in the same way. The amount of energy generated by a spring increases by the square of the "distance" that the spring is compressed. Also, centripetal force of an object increases by the square of the increase in the object's velocity. There are many other applications of the squaring relationship. To maintain a response-dimension orientation, we would introduce variations of a basic squaring routine and then apply it to problems from a variety of topics.

The rationale for organizing content around a response-dimension is the same as that for the design of simpler communications. By grouping examples of the same type, we can more effectively communicate samenesses and differences. Instead of encountering one example of the squaring operation now and another example perhaps weeks later, the learner encounters many examples immediately. The juxtaposition of the examples prompts the operation and therefore makes it initially easier for the learner to perform. We face the same responsibility for removing the prompts that we face with simpler communication forms. However, when the unprompted practice is introduced, we know that the learner has the capabilities of performing in prompted situations. The procedure for integrating the new skill is basically the same as that used for simpler forms. We place the operation in increasingly difficult contexts.

Finding the Range of Examples

To approach content as a response-dimension endeavor, we must group operations. To group operations, however, we must extend our analysis of examples.

The major difference between examples of simple discriminations and examples of operations (such as the operation of long division or the operation of writing a good first sentence for a paragraph) is that the features of operational examples are *facts* about the ways in which we can operate on the example.

To determine the "features" of an operation, we make up facts about examples of the operation. The procedure is the same as that used in the subtype analysis. The difference is that the analysis is now applied to examples of an operation. If we make up six facts for a given example of an operation, we are provided with an operational definition for identifying other examples that are in the same class as the original operation. If the six facts apply to another example of the operation, that operation has the same features as the original operation and is therefore in the same class. If only five of the facts hold, we are dealing with two subtypes of examples.

To identify examples that are in the same class:

1. We begin with an example that is a "mainline type," one that is unambiguously an example of the type we are concerned with.
2. We make up a set of facts about the operation.
3. Then we check the facts by seeing if they hold for other mainline examples.
4. If the facts do not hold, we adjust the set until we develop a set that holds for the mainline examples.
5. Now we test the range of examples by using the set of facts we have developed as a *criterion* for judging whether *non-mainline* examples are actually members of the set to which the operation applies.

This procedure involves two phases. During the first phase (steps 1 through 4), we develop the criterion for classifying examples. Step 5 is an application of the criterion to other examples. The assumption is that if another example possesses all the features that are expressed by the criterion, the example is *the same as* the mainline examples with respect to the operational details.

The procedure not only permits us to identify the range of variation of examples for a particular operation. It also: (1) helps us clarify the operation by forcing us to refer to specific features of the operation; and (2) provides a means by which we can discover unsuspected examples that are in the same class as mainline examples. With the information about the range of examples, we are in a much better position to offer the introduction of examples and types so that stipulation is reduced, relatively easy examples are presented early in the program, and examples of a given type are juxtaposed in a manner that will clearly imply the operational sameness that obtains across a range of example variation.

Identifying Subtypes

When we organize examples according to a common response dimension, we will identify some examples that are relatively easy and some that are analytically more complicated. The more difficult examples will involve more mechanical details and may require more knowledge.

In addition to the range of example variation, we will discover that some important types of examples do not lend themselves to the operation that we have designed. Since these example types should be taught, a variation of the operation must be designed to process them.

Both the range of examples to be processed by a single routine and the relationship between the main routine and related routines to process specific subtypes of examples may be expressed as transformations. The more difficult examples processed by the main routine are transformations of the simpler examples. The modification of the routine that is needed to accommodate examples that are not processed through the main routine involves a transformation. By viewing the problem of dealing with the full range of examples and the full range of routines as problems in designing transformations, we are provided with specific guidelines about how to achieve efficiency in design.

Illustration: Product Conservation

We can illustrate the procedure by referring to the physics concept of **conservation**. There is conservation of energy, conservation of mass, and other conservations. These conservations are either the same from an operational sense, or they are not.

To discover if an important sameness exists, we follow the procedures outlined above–starting with a mainline example (an example of conservation of momentum, for instance) and making up non-trivial facts about that example. A non-trivial fact is one that would not be true of *everything* or of a range of things far beyond the example under investigation.

Here are some non-trivial facts about conservation of momentum:

- Conservation is achieved through the product of values. (Simple momentum equals the *rate* times the *mass* of the object.)
- If the product remains the same and if one value is made larger, the other value is made smaller. (If the momentum of an object remains the same after the mass is increased, the object must have slowed down.)
- The product changes only if something is added or taken away from one of the values. (If the momentum is increased, the mass has increased or the rate has increased.)

We can use the set of facts that we have constructed as a *criterion* for identifying other examples. Each statement applies to conservation of energy, so this type of example falls into the same set as conservation of momentum.

By applying the set of common facts to a range of mainline examples, we can modify the set of facts—add facts, change some, delete some—until we get what appears to be a good set for the mainline members of the set—those examples that obviously seem to be the same in their operational structure.

We may also develop different ways of expressing the facts. For instance, we may express the product conservation (one dimension increases as the other decreases) by this type of equation:

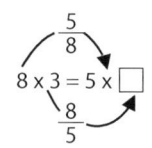

$$8 \times 3 = 5 \times \square$$

with $\frac{5}{8}$ and $\frac{8}{5}$ shown as the transformations.

The idea is to change the pair of values on the left side of the equation into the corresponding values on the right. The first number on the left changes into the first number on the right. The second number on the left changes into the second number on the right. To change 8 into 5, we multiply 8 by $\frac{5}{8}$. If we multiply the first number (8) by $\frac{5}{8}$, we have to multiply the second number (3) by $\frac{8}{5}$ (not by $\frac{5}{8}$) to find the missing value, which is $\frac{24}{5}$. We are multiplying the left side by $\frac{5}{8} \times \frac{8}{5}$, which equals one. Therefore, we are not changing the initial amount on this side. That the answer is correct can be seen by cancelling the 5's on the right side of the equation (5 × $\frac{24}{5}$), leaving 24, which is the value on the left side of the equation.

Although this equation holds for all simple product conservations, it is not the only way that we can express the facts about conservation. It is perhaps the most operationally salient, however, because it permits us to test the various examples with a precise procedure. Each example either shares the feature expressed by this operational "fact" or it does not. If it does, it is an example of **product conservation**.

When we apply the set of criteria for **conservation** to other examples, we find that a rectangular display of squares has all the basic conservation properties of the other examples. The rectangular display is the product of two values (the length times the width). If the product remains the same and one value is made larger, the other value is made smaller. For instance, if the total number of squares remains at 24, but the width is increased from 2 to 3, the length must change from 12 to 8.

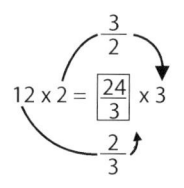

$$12 \times 2 = \boxed{\frac{24}{3}} \times 3$$

with $\frac{3}{2}$ and $\frac{2}{3}$ shown as the transformations.

The rectangular display does not possess irrelevant features of the other examples, only the operational features. It is therefore an "easy" example of product conservation.

Ordering Example Types

With the knowledge of the range of examples, we can now sequence the introduction of example types. We introduce each example *in the same way* (using the same routine) to signal the sameness in the examples. We begin the program with relatively easy examples that are manageable. The rectangular display meets these criteria. It also permits verification. The outcome or answer to each problem can be verified by arranging the component squares according to the pattern suggested in the problem (12 x 2, for instance). Juxtaposed examples involving this rectangular setup can be presented quite quickly. Therefore, the display could serve as a primary type of example for the initial teaching of the concept.

Once the initial teaching is achieved, we require the learner to transfer the skill to various other examples. Transfer is achieved if there are observable details of new problems that are the same as those of familiar problems. To make the sameness as obvious as possible, we design the routine with the initial example in the same way we design chains that are used in a rehearsal situation. We include unique details in the first part of the chain. If the learner is prompted to treat the first part of an unfamiliar example in the same way that the first part of a familiar example is treated, the learner will most probably transfer the operation to the new example. The transfer will occur for the same reason the transfer occurs when we deal with well-designed rehearsal chains. The operation is a chain of behaviors. The first part of the chain is prompted for both examples. Since the first part holds for the new example, transfer for the remainder of the chain is implied once the first part has been performed.

The remainder of the strategy parallels that used for expanded chains.

- We design a chain or a routine capable of processing all examples.
- We teach the preskills called for by that chain, scheduling the teaching of the motor skills early and designing the teaching so that we can introduce applications of the entire operation as quickly as possible.
- We provide applications of the chain that permit juxtapositions appropriate for initial teaching, examples that permit the learner to do the same thing with juxtaposed examples.
- We next shape the context in which the operation occurs by systematically introducing interruptions between presentations of the operation.
- We try to include early examples of all subtypes that present no great mechanical problems.
- We delay the presentation of highly irregular examples until the learner is firm on the other subtypes. Then, we introduce the irregulars either through a double-transformation program or through some other procedure that permits the massed practice with the new type and integration with the other types that have been taught.

Except for some details, the strategy is the same as that for expanded chains. The difference is that the determination of range of examples for the expanded chains is much easier than for expanded programs. For example, analyzing examples of using a screwdriver is relatively easy because:

1. We deal with only mainline examples as examples of using a screwdriver.
2. The variations in the operation that are possible can be discovered through observations of physical manipulations.

When we deal with cognitive skills, we must focus attention on non-physical details of the examples and *functional* samenesses. Once we have discovered a sameness (the operational features that are shared by various examples) we can arrange the examples in much the same way we would do with examples of physical operations.

Illustration: Averages

The operation of figuring out where a balance beam will balance illustrates how unsuspected examples of an operation may be discovered. Let's say that in our search for examples of the basic conservation relationship, we experiment with the formula for levers: **E x D = R x D**[1] (effort times its distance from the fulcrum equals the resistance times its distance). We discover that this relationship is an instance of **product conservation**. Consider this problem. If a force of 6 pounds moves 5 feet, 10 pounds of resistance would move how far?

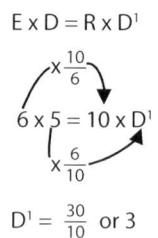

$$E \times D = R \times D^1$$

$$6 \times 5 = 10 \times D^1$$

with $\times \frac{10}{6}$ and $\times \frac{6}{10}$ compensation

$$D^1 = \frac{30}{10} \text{ or } 3$$

The problem is solved using the same compensation operation used for rectangular displays.

When we move to another type of balance problem, we see that the same conservation relationship holds. For these examples, the board does not move to create leverage. It simply balances. We put weights on one side of the balance. We then figure out how much weight would have to be put on the other side of the balance to effect a balance.

For instance, we start with this problem:

Three equal weights are placed 2 units from the fulcrum on the left. The X above the 3 indicates where we are to place weights on the right to achieve a balance. The question is, how much weight goes in this position? The same equation used for the preceding problem works for this problem: **E x D = R x D¹**.

These are the values: $3 \times 2 = \square \times 3$

The solution: $3 \times 2 = \boxed{\frac{6}{3}} \times 3$

The product of 6 is conserved on both sides of the balance; therefore, 2 units of weight must be placed at 3 on the right side of the balance.

We discover that a different operation is needed when we try to find the balance for a beam that has counters on it. For instance, where is the specific balancing point for this beam (given that the weights are of the same value)?

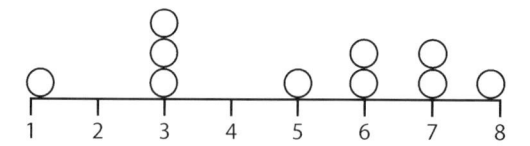

There are ten counters on the beam. Counting ten times at the unknown balance point is the same as counting one time at 1, three times at 3, one time at 5, two times at 6, two times at 7, and one time at 8. In other words:

$$10 \times BP = (1 \times 1) + (3 \times 3) + (1 \times 5) + (2 \times 6) + (2 \times 7) + (1 \times 8)$$
$$10 BP = 1 + 9 + 5 + 12 + 14 + 8$$
$$10 BP = 49$$
$$BP = \frac{49}{10} = 4.9$$

For problems of this sort, we add the various products. The number of counters tells the number of times we must count at the unknown balancing point, BP, which is 4.9.

When we search for other problems that have the same operational features as this problem, we find other types. Here is a problem with the same numbers as the problem above.

- Jane drank water on 10 occasions. On 1 occasion, she drank 1 glass. On 3 occasions, she drank 3 glasses. Once, she drank 5 glasses. On 2 occasions, she drank 6 glasses. On two occasions, she drank 7 glasses. And once she drank 8 glasses. What is the *average* number of glasses that she drank?

The solution:

$$10N = (1 \times 1) + (3 \times 3) + (1 \times 5) + (2 \times 6) + (2 \times 7) + (1 \times 8)$$
$$10N = 49$$
$$N = 4.9$$

Average problems and basic balance problems are the same because they have the same operational features. Instead of being taught as logically separate types, therefore, they should be juxtaposed, included in the same set of examples, and taught through the same operational steps (through a routine that prompts the sameness in the operation and that stresses the conservation of the products). Unless such instruction occurs, stipulation will take place and the learner probably will not have an intuitive understanding that balance-beam examples and averages are the same.

Here is a routine that could be used to prompt the operational sameness. The problem involves ten counters.

Teacher	Learner
We have to find the middle of the distribution. So what's the first thing we do?	Count the counters.
Do it.	(Counts.)
How many counters?	Ten.
So what do you write first?	Ten N equals.
Do it.	(Writes 10N =)
Now what do you do?	Add the products.
Do it.	(Adds 1 + 9 + 5 + 12 + 14 + 8)
What's the sum of the products?	49.
How do you find the middle of the distribution?	Divide by the number of counters.
Do it.	(Divides 10)‾49)
Where is the middle of the distribution?	4.9.

The wording, "We have to find the middle of the distribution," serves as a prompt for all problems of this type—including simple statistics problems. It permits the same operational steps to be applied to diverse problems. The prompting, as noted above, is the same type used for expanded chains. Through the double-transformation strategy, we could later introduce conventional wording. For example, the familiar set of problems might refer to the middle of the distribution, while the new set refers to the "average" or the "mean." Once we have introduced an operation across the range of examples we have performed the most important step, which is to establish the generalization.

Summary of Procedures

The conservation problems illustrate the basic approach to organizing content. First an operational sameness is discovered. Examples that share this sameness are members of a set. Those that don't share it are members of another operational set. When we test examples for product-compensation features, we discover that some unsuspected examples are in the set. Lever problems and some balance problems have the product compensation features, expressed as:

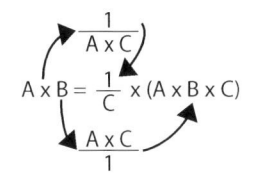

$$A \times B = \frac{1}{C} \times (A \times B \times C)$$

with transformations $\frac{1}{A \times C}$ and $\frac{A \times C}{1}$

Some problems that do not have this feature belong to a set of find-the-balance problems. The simplest way to assure that the learner is shown the operational samenesses for each of the two operations we have identified is to use a response-dimension approach and juxtapose various examples of a particular type, using a unique routine to prompt the operational samenesses across the range of variation in examples. We would first teach the basic product-conservation operation, then the discrimination for using the find-the-balance operation.

Illustration: Expressive Writing

Expressive writing is one of the most difficult skills to teach and certainly one of the most thoroughly mistaught. The problem seems to be that teachers expect the learner to simultaneously produce writing that exhibits sentence variety, uses stylistically and grammatically appropriate expressions, follows spelling and punctuation conventions, and adequately develops ideas. Obviously, any new learning situation that presented all these criteria (or even half of them) would overwhelm most learners and produce the type of writing behavior observed in many adults—a laborious attempt to try to create, compress, edit, and polish at the same time.

To organize expressive skills, we must recognize that we will not achieve the final development in writing skills at the beginning of the program. Just as the learner does not begin reading instruction by reading something like Plato's *Republic*, the learner should not start writing with applications that are too difficult.

We should *not* begin expressive writing by having the learner write about make-believe or imagined events because:

1. We have no way of knowing whether learners are precisely reporting about the things they imagine.

2. Therefore, we would not be in an ideal position to work on the better use of language.

If we begin with objective referents, we solve the problems associated with fantasy writing. We can observe what the learner is referring to; therefore, we can determine whether the learner's use of language is precise, and we can help the learner work on better wording. Another advantage of an objective referent is that it permits us greater control over the juxtaposition of examples.

We begin the expressive writing by using action pictures as the common referent. The simplest example of writing would involve a sentence that tells about something depicted by the picture. The simplest sentence is a subject-predicate one. This sentence has the following operational features:

1. It starts by naming or identifying something shown in the picture.
2. It then tells more about that entity.

The operational features imply how to make examples relatively easy or relatively difficult. Easy examples for the first part of the sentence would involve illustrated articles for which many labeling options are available or labeling which involves very familiar words. Easy examples for the second part involve pictures of entities that show a variety of possible actions or actions that are very familiar. More difficult examples are those that call for descriptive precision. We use minimum differences *in the wording* of sentences to create negative examples of the sentence. For example, a task requiring the learner to make up sentences using the word *only* could be very difficult if the learner had to describe *only the big boys* in the picture and *the only big boy* wearing a hat. A minimum difference in the wording of either examples creates a different meaning.

To teach the precise use of language with relatively easy examples, we begin by requiring the learner to write only parts of sentences, not entire sentences. For instance, we present a picture showing two entities (**A** and **B**) engaged in the same action (running). We require the learner to complete the sentence: "_____ was running" by telling about entity **A**. The learner must describe entity **A** in a way that will not permit confusion of **A** and **B**. This activity builds the skill of identifying the entity, using descriptive words, using appropriate class names, and referring to the details that make **A** different from **B**.

We use a variation of the activity to work on the predicate details. The picture shows identical entities (**A** and **B**) doing different things. The learner is required to complete the sentence: "The little girl _____," by describing **A**'s *action* (not **B**'s action). The description must be accurate enough to avoid possible confusion of **A** with **B**; therefore, the learner is required to use appropriate verbs and descriptions of position and objects that are receiving the action.

Part of the operation that the learner follows in writing simple sentences about the picture is to tell more about it. When we test to discover other possible examples that have this feature, we find that a variation of these features is shared by the regular-order paragraph, by outlines, and by a variety of sentence types.

The simple, regular-order paragraph begins with a sentence that first tells what somebody was doing and then tells more. For example, a paragraph for the picture in Figure 25.1 could begin with this sentence: The children ran from the monster. This sentence names a topic. To create a paragraph, we simply tell more about that topic—more about how the children ran from the monster. For initial teaching, we could refer to this activity as "reporting." For reporting, the writer is not permitted to interpret, merely to deal with the objective facts shown by the picture. The sentences could tell what they did, what their expressions were, what they did while running, and what happened as they ran.

The sentence that we begin with ("The girl ran down the pier") is a good sentence because it efficiently summarizes the action with a few words. We must recognize that this criterion for a good sentence is not necessarily consistent with the traditional criteria (many of which require the learner to embellish the sentence until becoming lost in its infractions). The use of two types of telling-more sentences make it clear which aspect of the original sentence is being amplified. If the sentence tells about *how* the girl *ran down the pier*, we underline the part that starts with the verb *ran* and we begin the part that tells more with another verb, and that amplifies running down the pier. If the sentence tells more about the last part of the sentence, we underline *the pier* and we begin the part that tells more with another word that describes the pier.

Here are the examples for the initial-teaching set that involve telling more.

Sentences	Paragraphs
Simple: She ran down the pier.	**Starts with the sentence:** She ran down the pier.

Figure 25.1

More about how she ran: She ran down the pier, trying to move as fast as she could.

More about the object: She ran down the pier, a structure made of posts and planks.

Tells more about how she ran: She kicked high into the air as she moved forward. She glanced back at the monster.

Tells more about the pier: The pier was wet and slippery. It wobbled under her feet.

The telling-more story strategy is also used in making an outline. A major heading provides the summary. Points that are included under the heading tell more.

With this range of examples, we are able to sequence relatively easy examples (sentences) and harder ones (paragraphs). We mix the task of writing sentences and writing simple paragraphs to induce the notion that there is a sameness in the skill of telling more.

An actual writing program would be concerned with much more information than the central thrust of telling more. Four basic skill tracks would be coordinated: *sentences, paragraphs, mechanical details,* and *editing.* All new skills would be integrated into the editing track and ultimately into the paragraph track. The editing track serves as a rehearsal track for the paragraph track. We expect learners to check the passages they write for punctuation, sentence types, tense, and possibly other details. By presenting passages that need editing, we provide easier examples that require the same basic behavior called for in writing. The editing is actually a removed-component of the total paragraph-writing task. When writing paragraphs, the learners must perform many other operations in addition to editing; however, if the learners are well practiced in reading over material and scanning for errors, the probability is greatly increased that learners will be able to edit their own writing.

One test of efficiency is the extent to which we can teach other writing skills as simple transformations of skills that we teach earlier. If a transformation is involved, the later skills are subtypes of the skills taught earlier. The extent to which we must engage in either teaching that contradicts what we taught earlier or teaching that is new is the extent to which the earlier teaching was not efficient.

When we apply the transformation test to the skill of telling-more-through-subject-predicate sentences, we can generate a large number of sentence forms through simple transformations of the subject-predicate type.

By moving parts of the regular-order sentence, we can create sentences that do not start out by naming the actor. Instead of writing, "They sat on the porch after they ate," the learner later writes, "After they ate, they sat on the porch." Instead of writing, "The monster came out of the water, grabbing a post," the learner later writes, "Grabbing a post, the monster came out of the water." A parallel transformation occurs for the paragraph writing. Regular-order paragraphs start with the "topic sentence" and then tell more. To create a simple transformation the learner deletes the first sentence, creating a description of a topic without first identifying it.

Also, groups of paragraphs are created by instructing the learner to frame the topic as a *problem* or a *solution* rather than a report of what somebody did. For example, the learner reads "Jane and Bill went on a vacation to a place that was far away from any town. They had planned to reach their campsite by three o'clock in the afternoon. But at 3 o'clock in the afternoon, they were not at their campsite because of a problem. The picture shows that problem." The illustration shows the car with a flat tire. Jane and Bill have emptied the trunk. Bill is holding a jack handle, but his expression suggests that there is no jack.

The learner follows the same procedure used with simple paragraphs, except that the first paragraph begins with a good sentence that tells about the problem *that Bill and Jane encountered.* (Their car had a flat and they did not have a jack.) The rest of the first paragraph tells more about the problem. The second paragraph tells how they solved the problem. (The picture contains details that suggest a solution—such as several long, thick branches next to the road and a stump next to the car.) Note that this context permits the learner to interpret (telling *why* the people did what they did to solve the problem). However, the context is safe. Inferences are based on specific details of the picture and the scenario that frames the picture.

A final transformation occurs with the instructions of fantasy-writing assignments. Once we have reason to believe that the learner has the ability to describe things that we can observe, we encourage the learner to apply this skill to describing other things that we cannot observe. Fantasy writing is an extension of interpreting pictured events. The difference is that the "pictures" are no longer available for our inspection.

The most difficult part of the program is not to teach the various skills, but to organize them so that: (1) the learner uses what has been taught; and (2) the subsequent skills clearly build on what is taught.

Main idea. In addition to teaching writing skills, the program we have been describing teaches critical skills for **outlining** and **main idea**. The teaching of **main idea** develops very naturally in the writing context. The learner makes up a simple sentence about the picture. If the sentence succinctly expresses the "main action" of the picture, the sentence expresses the main idea. The learner next tells more. The sentences that serve this function are supporting sentences for the main idea. It is possible to teach **main idea** in different ways—as a choice-response discrimination rather than a production-response skill. For such teaching, we present the learner with a passage and with choices of sentences that express the main idea. The presentation is fraught with potential communication problems and misrules. The major communication problem is that we have trouble juxtaposing examples appropriately. The reason is that the examples are long. The learner must read a passage before making the choices. The major misrule problem is that if we presented repeated paragraphs of the initial type developed in the writing program, the main idea would be expressed in the first sentence of every passage. The naive learner, therefore, might develop the spurious strategy of assuming that the first sentence of a paragraph *is* the main idea. Only later, and painfully, would the learner discover that the matter is more complicated. Teaching **main idea** in the writing context does not imply the misrule because *the learner designs the first sentence so that it meets certain specifications.*

The analysis of sameness of applications of **main idea** discloses the problem with the traditional system for teaching **main idea** as a reading-comprehension skill. Virtually all real applications of **main idea** require the learner to make up the main idea or the summary, not simply respond to choices. In other words, it is a language skill or a writing skill, not a reading skill. The simplest way to avoid distortion and stipulation is to teach **main idea** as a production skill.

Certainly we can devise programs that teach **main idea** as a reading-comprehension skill. A set of passages would be presented. All passages would: (1) deal with the same topic; (2) have many of the same sentences; and (3) begin with the same sentence. The learner could not learn the misrule that the first sentence expresses the main idea, because the first sentence never expresses the main idea. Some parts of the passages change, and the main idea changes. Therefore, the details that change must account for the change in the main idea.

Once the learner has mastered various sets of examples, we introduce passages in which the first sentence expresses the main idea. (These would be integrated with the type in which the main idea is not the first sentence.) This approach has a potential of working far better than that of barraging the student with passages and hoping that the learner develops the "concept" of **main idea**. Beyond raising performance on achievement tests, however, the approach has little justification. **Main idea** teaching may be used in reading; however, it is most naturally *taught* through writing. The use of **main idea** is not only functional in the writing context–it is essential.

Illustration: Analogies

Teaching analogies is far less complicated than teaching writing; however, the skill is elusive because analogical reasoning occurs in many forms, and even the direct expression of analogies shows great variation.

All analogies can be reduced to a form that involves sentences.

> A dog runs
> as a fish swims.

That analogy transforms into:

> A dog is to running
> as a fish is to swimming.

We can introduce variations that involve different types of things and different classifications. For instance, we can create analogies that name the class that the things are in:

> A dog is to mammals
> as a parrot is to birds.

Other analogies deal with location:

> A dog is to the ground
> as a fish is to the water.

Other analogies deal with analogous or homologous parts:

> A dog is to lungs
> as a fish is to gills.

Still other analogies deal with function:

> A dog is to guarding things
> as a horse is to carrying things.

All these analogies follow the same form. The names that appear at the beginning of the analogy are coordinate members of the same class. For example, **dog** and **fish** are coordinate members of the class of **animals**.

The relationship between the name that appears first in the analogy and that which follows are *correlated in the same way*. How are **dog** and **running** correlated? Running is an action that dogs perform when moving from place to place. How are **fish** and **swimming** correlated? Swimming is an action that fish perform when moving from place to place.

If we apply these facts, we see that many other types of analogy forms are simply *analogies with unstated parts*. For example, "His secretary was a little bit of sunshine on a cloudy day." The fully-stated analogy could be expressed as: "His secretary is to a dismal environment as a little bit of sunshine is to a cloudy day." Both parts of the analogy begin with pleasant things. The parallel correlation is that both pleasant things exist in a gloomy setting.

Here is a possible routine for teaching the basic analogies.

Example: A fish swims as a dog does something.

Teacher	Learner
This analogy is about a fish and a dog. What class are a fish and a dog in?	Animals.
This analogy tells how the animals move. What does it tell?	How the animals move.
Name the first animal.	A fish.
Tell how it moves.	Swims.
Say the statement about the fish.	A fish swims.
Now name the other animal.	A dog.
What is the analogy going to tell about that animal?	How it moves.
How does a dog move?	Runs. (Walks.)

Teacher	Learner
Once more: What does the analogy tell about the animals?	How they move.
Say the whole analogy. First tell about a fish, then tell about a dog. Get ready.	A fish swims, a dog runs.

The routine reflects the sameness revealed by analysis of the examples. The learner first indicates a class for the fish and dog. The learner then follows the rule of telling how the animals move. The same routine is used for other analogies:

Teacher	Learner
This is an analogy about a fish and a dog. What class are a fish and a dog in?	Animals.
This analogy tells what the animals breathe in. What does it tell?	What the animals breathe in.
Name the first animal.	A fish.
Tell what it breathes in.	Water.
Say the statement about a fish.	A fish breathes in water.
Now name the other animal.	A dog.
What is the analogy going to tell about that animal?	What it breathes in.
What does a dog breathe in?	Air.
Say a statement about a dog.	A dog breathes in air.
Once more: What does the analogy tell about the animals?	What they breathe in.
Say the whole analogy. First tell about a fish. Then tell about a dog. Get ready.	A fish breathes in water; a dog breathes in air.

A variation of the analogy would require the learner to make up analogies that tell how a bird, a fish, a kangaroo, and a lion move. The learner could make up analogies that tell the material used to make a coin, a bat, a belt, and a window. Also, the learner identifies *the rule* for various analogies.

Teacher	Learner
Listen to these analogies. They are going to tell different things about vehicles.	
Listen: A boat is to a boat dock as a train is to a train station. What does the analogy tell about the vehicles?	Where you get on them.
Listen: A boat is to water as a train is to tracks as a bus is to a street. What does that analogy tell about the vehicles?	What they move on.
Listen: A boat is to sails as a train is to a steam engine as a bus is to a diesel engine. What does that analogy tell about the vehicles? Etc.	What makes them move.

Note that these examples are designed according to the rules for a single-transformation sequence. Minimally-different examples show the learner how the rule changes as a function of the changes in the analogy. After basic routines have been introduced, we present variations in which more divergent responses are possible.

Teacher	Learner
Here's a strange analogy: "Moving fast is to something as moving slow is to something else."	
Name something that moves fast.	(Bullet. deer, etc.)
Say the first part of the analogy.	Moving fast is to a bullet.
Name something that moves slowly.	(Snail, turtle.)
Say the next part of the analogy.	Moving slow is to a turtle.
Say the whole analogy.	Moving fast is to a bullet as moving slow is to a turtle.

After introducing variations of this type, the learner operates on applications that require identification of how the things in an analogy are the same.

Teacher	Learner
Listen: The word *like* tells you that things are the same. The hero moved like a bullet. How could the hero and the bullet be the same?	They both move fast.
Her eyes were like the sky. How could her eyes and the sky be the same?	They're both blue.
The air inside the jungle was like a sponge. How could the air and the sponge be the same?	They're both damp.
The salesman was like a shark that smelled blood. How could that salesman and a shark be the same?	They're both mean.

Cursive Writing

The next expanded program that we will overview deals with the teaching of cursive writing. Obviously, writing in cursive is a motor skill, not a cognitive one. Therefore, the effective teaching of the skill must involve practice, shaping, and techniques appropriate for teaching motor skills. Far less obvious, perhaps, is that cursive writing may be presented largely as a transformation of skills that are known to the learner. To achieve efficient transfer, therefore, the program should prompt the transformation.

To discover that a transformation is involved, we analyze examples of cursive letters and their manuscript counterparts. This analysis reveals the following: The middle part of many cursive letters is the same as the middle part of corresponding manuscript letters. By adding a stroke from the baseline and adding a tail, we change the manuscript letters (see Figure 25.2).

Figure 25.2
a *a*
c *c*
e *e*
g *g*
j *j*
m *m*
n *n*
o *o*
p *p*
t *t*
x *x*
y *y*

Another transformation involves the slant. By starting with manuscript letters that are straight up and down and rotating them in the clockwise direction, we create manuscript letters that slant the same way that cursive letters slant.

Original Set   Transformed Set
    a   a
    j   j

We can achieve this transformation in slant most easily not by rotating the letters, but by rotating the paper on which the letters are to be written. If we rotate the paper slightly in the counterclockwise direction and require the learner to write the same up-and-down letters that are in the familiar manuscript set, the learner will make letters that slant in the appropriate way:

a j

Note that this transformation occurs whether the learner is right-handed or left-handed. We make this point because a number of traditional cursive-writing programs require right-handed students to rotate their paper in a counterclockwise direction (the correct way) and left-handed students to rotate it in a clockwise direction. This incredible requirement is based on a complete misanalysis of writing skills. Left-handed students who rotate the paper in a clockwise orientation must learn to write *sideways* to achieve the appropriate slant.

a j

The analysis on which this convention is based apparently does not take into account the idea that cursive letters are simple transformations of manuscript letters and that rotating the paper is supposed to facilitate the transformation. Instead, the analysis seems to be based on the idea that left is the opposite of right; right-handers rotate in a clockwise direction; therefore, lefties should rotate in the opposite direction.

Stroke descriptions. Many traditional approaches to cursive also make serious mistakes with respect to stroke descriptions. The purpose of stroke descriptions is merely to establish a basis for communicating with the learner, not to "teach" the stroke. When the learner makes a mistake, communication is made much easier if the teacher is able to say something like, "You didn't go all the way up to the top line." The stroke description should be simple, not elaborate. Figure 25.3 shows the stroke descriptions for the cursive letters in the *E-B Press Cursive Writing Program*. The letters appear in their order of introduction.

The basic cursive forms referred to in the descriptions above are the **i**-form, the **e**-form, the **c**-form, the **hump**-form, and the **j**-form. The letters finish in either a "tail" or a "shelf." By referring to forms and letters that have

Section VII | Response-Locus Analysis

Figure 25.3

Letter	Strokes	Lesson	Letter	Strokes	Lesson
⟨ (i form)	Up to the half line. Down to the baseline and tail.	1	h	Start like an l. Trace up with a hump form.	34
i	Make an i form with a dot.	1	g	Start like a c. Close and finish like a j.	37
u	Make an i form. Join it with another i form.	1	m	Start like an n. Trace up with another hump form.	40
t	Make an i form that touches the top line. Cross it.	2	s	Start like an i form. Close and tail.	42
c	Bend over at the half line. Make a printed c.	4	b	Make an l. Shelf.	48
w	Make a u, tail up to the half line. Shelf.	8	y	Start like a v. Finish like a j.	50
⟨ (Hump form)	Bend over at the half line and tail.	11	d	Start like a c. Close with an i form that touches the top line.	53
v	Make a hump form, tail up to the half line. Shelf.	12	k	Start like an h. Close like a printed r and tail.	56
e	Start like an i form, come back, and tail.	14	g	Start like an a. Go down to the subline. Finish like an f.	59
n	Start like a hump form and stop at the baseline. Trace up with a hump form.	16	z	Make an n that sinks below the baseline. Finish like a j.	62
o	Close a c at the half line. Shelf.	18	x	Make a hump form. Cross it going down.	65
j	Start like a i form. Go down to the subline. Come around like a printed j, and tail.	20	p	Start like a j. Close and tail.	68
l	Make an e that touches the top line.	22			
a	Start like a c. Close with an i form.	24			
f	Start like an l. Go down to the subline. Finish like an o at the baseline.	28			
r	Start like an i form. Shelf and tail.	32			

For letters that pose possible problems, such as the letter f, the stroke description makes reference to a known behavior—making an o. That behavior assures that the student will finish like an o, which means curve upward in a counterclockwise direction, not in a clockwise direction (like the letter *j*) as students often do when trying to make *fo* .

been taught, stroke descriptions for later letters are uncomplicated.

Sequencing cursive skills. Some forms are relatively easy for the learner to make—particularly **i** and **e**. Working on these gives the learner a sense of success; however, if we work too long on these, the presentation may induce distorted responses. The learner will make good **i**'s and **e**'s; however, the learner will have difficulty making forms that are based on **c**, the **hump**-form, or possibly **j**. The most serious problem will probably occur with **c** because **c** requires a response more complicated than the others. To avoid serious distortion, we try to introduce **c** early. We also try to introduce the **hump**-form fairly early. The strategy for introducing letters and integrating them involves the following steps:

1. Introduce the **i**-form with variations. Cursive **u** shows the repeated-stroke nature of cursive. Cursive **t** shows the height variation.

2. Introduce **c**-form early. Integrate this form with the **i**-form. Present exercises in which the learner writes joined letters, such as: *ci*

360   Theory of Instruction: Principles and Applications

3. Introduce the shelf variation early and integrate. Give practice with joins such as: *wi*

4. Introduce **hump**-form and integrate. When this form is combined with the shelf, cursive *n* is formed.

5. Introduce the two other forms (**e** and **j**) as quickly as possible and integrate.

6. Intersperse letters of each type so that the order of introduction presents juxtaposed letters that are not highly similar.

Once the learner has been introduced to at least one variation of a particular type, the probability of distortion has been reduced. When **c** and the **i**-form letters are juxtaposed in practice, distortion is counteracted because the learner must develop those responses that are common to writing both **c** and the **i**-form letters.

Joined letters. The final economy in the program comes from the introduction of joined letters. By practicing particular joined letters, the learner is actually practicing a simple transformation of another cursive letter. For instance, if the learner practices writing *ci*, the learner is actually practicing a transformation of another letter. By bringing the parts together and dropping the dot from the **i**, we make the letter *a*. The strategy is to work on the joined letters **ci** and **cu** before introducing the **a**. The work with the joined letters teaches the combination of behaviors called for by the letter. The introduction of **a** should go quite smoothly if the preteaching has been effective. Figure 25.4 shows other joins that set the stage for later letters.

In summary, the teaching of cursive involves four major transformations.

1. The form transformation from manuscript letters to cursive letters.

2. The slant transformation from manuscript to cursive.

3. Transformations achieved by introducing early forms that can be modified to form more complicated letters.

4. The joined letter to single-letter transformations.

The program is complicated only because it must proceed in two directions at the same time. If we initially introduced all members of a given type (such as all **i**-form letters), we could make the practice relatively

Figure 25.4	
Joins	Set the Stage For
ci	*a*
ii	*u*
ct	*d*
cj	*g*
br	*h*
ni	*r*
rj	*y*
nj	*z*

easy; however, we would probably introduce serious distortion that results from protracted practice with a small range of example variation. Therefore, we must trade-off the easy examples (the **i**-forms) with the harder examples, particularly those that present generically new writing behaviors (the **c**-forms). By introducing one **c**-form early, we buttress against distortion. At the same time, we continue to introduce the relatively easy examples. The strategy is similar to that of the **A-Z** integration approach.

The introduction of examples is modeled after that of the screwdriver program or the bike-riding program. Different practice blocks work on different skills, so that during a lesson the learner works on letters in isolation, joined combinations, sentences, reading cursive sentences and possibly some tracing or activities that require answering questions in cursive. Each activity is continuously integrated with the newly-taught skills. The program will not eliminate the need for practice, or even reduce practice by a half, over a program not ordered as carefully. However, the program will result in savings for both teacher and student.

Problem Solving

The theory of instruction that we have developed frames the psychology of learning within the domain of a logical analysis. We have applied the theory to a wide range of skills, from the teaching of simple discriminations to elaborate programs. The final illustration is the induction or "problem-solving" skills.

According to stimulus-locus principles, effective problem-solving programs derive from an analysis of the problems to be solved, not from an analysis of the learner. A particular problem-solving strategy will hold only for problems of a particular type. The problems that admit to the same strategy have a common quality, which is their problem-solving features. By analyzing problems and grouping them according to common features, we gain an understanding of these common features. This analysis is the same analysis of subtypes that we have used for analyzing other cognitive skills.

Let us say that we want to teach the learner how to handle problems that involve identifying which of the possible causes for failure in the system accounts for an observed failure. All problems that are in this group have this common feature: outcomes could be the result of more than one possible cause. For instance, the sink is plugged. The cause could be something in the drain, in the system of pipes that the drain feeds into, etc. Another example is: Your car will not start. This outcome could result from failure of the distributor, the gas line, or one of many other parts. Medical diagnoses thrive on examples of this problem-solving type. The patient exhibits some symptoms. The observed symptoms could be caused by many possible malfunctions.

To apply the failure-diagnosis strategy to an automobile problem, the learner should understand that three broad systems may account for the failure: The fuel system, the electrical system, and the mechanical system. The learner should also understand the parts of the broad systems, such as the basic components of the electrical system (battery, coil, distributor, wires, spark plugs, etc.). This information would be effectively taught to the learner through visual-spatial displays that show the higher-order nature of the larger systems and how the smaller systems make up the larger ones. (The electrical system would be a higher-order label, under which would be the various components of the system.)

To apply the problem-solving strategy to the diagnosis of diseases related to the circulatory system, the learner should understand that there are three types of major sources of failure—blocks in the pipes, leaks in the pipes, or malfunction of the pump (heart). The learner should also understand subtypes of each larger class—for instance, the types of pump malfunction. As the language implies, the same diagnostic procedures used for heart systems may be used for other hydraulic systems.

Understanding the major categories is important, because *the strategy involves ruling out large categories through binary tests or questions.* One test or question (possibly two) should permit us to rule out whether the problem with the car is an electrical failure. Ideally, one or two tests of the patient should rule out whether the symptoms are caused by a failure of the pump (heart). With a very few tests, therefore, the learner would know which major system was involved in either a heart problem or an automobile failure.

After determining the larger system that caused the failure, the learner rules out the various lower-order possibilities until the lower-order system that caused the failure is identified. The same steps that were conducted with the higher-order systems is now repeated with the lower-order systems. For example, if the electrical system of a car is involved with the failure, the learner must now determine whether the problem was caused by the battery, the coil, the distributor, etc. Ideally, we should be able to conduct one or two tests that rule out each possibility.

At each point, we present a test that is binary. If the system passes the test, we know that the problem is not caused by the component tested. For instance, our test of the battery determines either that the battery is the cause of the problems or the battery is not the cause of the problem.

With an understanding of this procedure, we can design a general cognitive routine. Here is the first part of a possible routine.

Teacher Wording	Student Response
Your car does not start. What are the main systems that might make your car not start?	Electrical, fuel, mechanical.
Which would you test first?	Fuel.
How?	First check the gas gauge. Then check the gas at the carburetor. Then check it at the cylinder by removing the spark plug.
What if the fuel seems okay?	Test the electrical.

Chapter 25 | Expanded Programs for Cognitive Skills

How?	Check the spark at the spark plug.
What if there is no spark?	Check the coil.
Etc.	

Note that the learner has been pretaught all system information needed for the diagnosis.

A variation of the same routine would be applied to different systems, such as the circulatory system. Here is the first part of a possible application.

Teacher Wording	Student Response
A person suddenly becomes pale. Pulse goes up. Person is dizzy. What are the main cardiovascular problems that could cause these symptoms.	Blocked vessels, leak in the system, heart malfunction.
Which you would you test first?	Leak in the system.
How?	Blood pressure test.
What if the blood pressure was near normal?	Test the heart.
Etc.	

This routine is the same one used for the car diagnosis. The only difference is the particular system that is dealt with. The range of applications, therefore, is limited only by the learner's understanding of different systems.

A variation of the routine may be used in a highly technical field. The variation is not generically different from the one above, simply more complicated because of the interaction of "systems" that can cause failure. If we are dealing with medical diagnosis, for example, *we might consider each disease a system that causes failure.* The symptoms are the outward manifestations of the diseases; however, symptoms are not uniquely affined to specific diseases. A dozen diseases share many of the same symptoms (high fever, fast heart rate, flushed appearance, dizzy, etc.). To deal with this interaction of symptoms and diseases, we present the various symptoms to the learner and begin with this question: "What are the main diseases that *could* cause these problems?" The learner must list *all* the diseases that have the symptoms. The learner then specifies tests for ruling out the different diseases. A good test may rule out many of the candidates. The learner continues until all but one of the diseases have been ruled out.

- The learner is presented with symptoms: 1, 2, 3, 4, 5.
- The learner would name the diseases that have this set of symptoms: diseases **A**, **B**, **C** and **D**.
- "How would you rule out disease **B**?"
- The learner indicates the test.
- The learner then receives information about the outcome.
- "Which disease would you rule out next?"
- The learner selects a disease, indicates the test, and then receives the results of the test.

The major differences between this routine and that for the simpler examples is that: (1) the same set of "causes" for failure are not involved in all examples; (2) more than one "symptom" is involved in the diagnosis.

With the simpler diagnosis, the first step involves the identification of the same three causes of failure–leak in pipes, block in pipes, pump. The more sophisticated applications do not always involve the same causes of failures and therefore require more knowledge. Symptom 1 may suggest that the "cause" is either disease **A** or **C**. Symptom 2 may suggest a completely different set of diseases–**A** or **B**, for instance. The learner who performs the diagnosis must know which diseases are suggested by which individual symptom or set of symptoms.

The routine used for sophisticated examples implies preteaching quite different from that which is traditionally provided. Instead of teaching various diseases with a list of symptoms for each, we would teach different *symptoms* and the diseases that each symptom occurs in. (The learner would not memorize the symptoms of chicken pox. The learner would learn the various diseases that have a specific symptom.) The reason for treating symptoms in this way is that the learner will never encounter the disease, merely the symptom. The categorization that lists symptoms for each disease, however, implies that all symptoms of the disease will be observed. Only some symptoms are typically observed. The learner who had been taught the implied relationship: *If symptoms 1, 2, 3, 4, and 5 are observed, the disease is* **X**, may be misled. A more reasonable approach is to identify the set of diseases associated with a particular symptom or set of symptoms. These suggest possible causes. By testing them, we can identify the single cause.

The point of this illustration is that even operations such as diagnosis can be approached following the general guides for organizing expanded programs for conveying cognitive skills. Mainline examples of diagnosis have a common set of features. If we express these features, we establish a criterion for classifying other possible examples. Once we have grouped the examples, we can identify the preskills that are needed for the learner to engage in the operation. We can express the operation as a routine. We can order the examples or applications so they induce samenesses or a generalized understanding of how the same problem-solving steps apply to a wide range of examples. Finally, we introduce variations (such as the medical diagnosis that involves symptoms of different possible diseases) as simple transformations of the basic type.

Subtypes and Transformations

The programs that we have outlined illustrate the relationship between the subtypes for a given skill and the organization of the expanded program. If we begin with the analysis of sameness, we find the features that are common to the mainline example. We next try to find the simplest examples that have the set of features. These are the most ideal for initial instruction. *We then view the other subtypes as simple transformations*, which means that they share many features with the original set of examples, but not all features. If we view these subtypes as transformations, we are provided with guidelines about how to introduce them. We teach a type of example. By changing the various members of the set in the same way, we can create a set of transformed members. The double-transformation program provides a model of how to communicate this transformation. Therefore, the introduction of the later subtypes may be modeled after the double-transformation strategy.

Summary

Expanded programs are the cognitive counterpart of expanded chains. At the center of the expanded program is a cognitive skill. This feature distinguishes the expanded program from the expanded chain.

Expanded cognitive programs are created to teach "ideas," or subjects such as the main idea of a passage, the idea of analogical reasoning, or the idea of diagnosing failures in a system by referring to symptoms. All skills, vocabulary, and specific behaviors required to teach idea or subject are part of the expanded program. The most difficult part of the program, however, is the means by which the central idea is developed. The idea must be analyzed, refined, and adjusted. The set of examples associated with the idea must also be identified, refined, and adjusted.

The procedure that we outlined for developing ideas and examples is to follow these steps:

1. Organize the content according to response dimensions (not according to traditional classifications of "topics" or content").
2. Identify the range of examples to which the operation applies.
3. Identify the important subtypes of examples that are not processed by the central operation.

Illustrations of this three-step procedure showed how content is organized in a new way if the content is ordered around a central operation. The central product-conservation problems included rectangular displays, level problems, and some balance-beam problems. The central operation could not accommodate problems involving averages; therefore, a related procedure was needed to solve these problems (and their balance-beam counterparts).

Expressive writing illustrated that both sentences and paragraphs are generated from the same idea of first naming something and then telling more. A number of related routines permitted the generation of related writing operations. The illustration pointed out that the related writing skills could be generated as simple transformations of earlier-taught skills. The expressive writing illustration also pointed out that teaching of main idea and outlining skills is very naturally presented as a subtype of naming and then telling more. Expressive writing, however, is not a graceful extension of reading (the "subject" in which main idea is traditionally taught).

Basic analogical reasoning was presented as a series of related operations that require the learner to express parallel relationships, identify the rule that indicates how the parallel parts of the analogy are the same, then use the knowledge of sameness to create similes.

Cursive writing was presented primarily as transformations from manuscript writing. The transformations included transformation by adding "tails," transformation in slant, transformation from earlier-taught forms, and transformations created by practicing joined-letter combinations.

Finally, a paradigm for both general and specific diagnostic skill showed that more complicated diagnostic procedures are simple transformations of easier ones. The major difference between the procedures is that the one uses more complicated situations and requires more elaborate steps to eliminate possibilities. The more complicated procedure was illustrated with medical diagnosis; however, the same procedure could be applied to any system in which given symptoms could be caused by different maladies.

Although the procedures for identifying operations and organizing examples of operations is complicated, it guarantees that the initial teaching will be efficient and will present the central operation so that it is applicable to a full range of examples. It also guarantees that related operations are clearly framed according to sameness and differences in operational steps. This type of organization ensures a smooth development of related skills.

SECTION VIII
DIAGNOSIS AND CORRECTIONS

This section presents topics that are related to the implementation of programs. When the teacher implements in the classroom, mistakes occur. The program that the teacher uses may have reasonable instructional provisions for buttressing against mistakes, but still mistakes occur. How the teacher corrects mistakes when the program provides for corrections is the subject of Chapter 27. Chapter 26 deals with the situation that occurs when the program does not have adequate provisions for buttressing against mistakes and for specifying corrections. In this case, mistakes must be classified and appropriate remedies must be developed. A diagnostic-remedial strategy is used.

Chapter 28 presents a paradigm for using field-tryout information to shape the instructional program.

Chapter 26
Diagnosis and Remedies

When we deal with problems of learning, we use two different diagnostic strategies. The first is a diagnosis of instruction the learner receives. The goal of this diagnosis is to predict future learning problems. The second diagnosis is a diagnosis of the learner. This diagnosis identifies current problems the learner is experiencing and corrects them.

Diagnosis of the Problem

This diagnosis assumes that if the instruction has flaws in it, some learners will respond to those flaws and will mislearn. Conversely, if the instruction is corrected, the kind of mislearning that was possible with the original instruction would no longer be possible. *This type of diagnosis is used to predict future problems, even when the learner is apparently performing well*, which is often what happens when the learner performs on the tasks presented in a poorly-designed sequence. In this case, the problem is not that the learner is failing, but that the learner probably *will* fail when presented with tasks that are not yet in the program. Program diagnosis is logical, based on the communications the learner receives. Predictions rest on the assumption that any misrules or stipulations conveyed by the communication will be learned, and will affect performance on subsequent activities. Predictions become increasingly valid when learners are more naive and when the flaw is more obvious. Suppose that we observe the teacher presenting a series of "following instructions" tasks to a language-delayed child. The child performs on all items; however, the items we observe occur in exactly the same order each time the sequence of tasks is presented ("go to the table . . . pick up the glass . . . take it to the counter . . ." etc.). The communication is flawed because the learner could perform correctly either by attending to the features of the instruction (the appropriate processing response) or by memorizing the sequence of events (an inappropriate strategy).

If we observe such a flaw, we can test it in one of two ways:

1. We can eliminate the relevant stimuli and show that the same response persists.
2. We can change the context or setting for the relevant stimuli and show that the response does not occur.

For the first type of test, we could present the learner with a series of nonsense commands, presented in the same context as the originals ("Go to the table...flam over the glosser . . . umble um orgona . . ."). The prediction would be that the learner will perform with the same responses produced for the original chain of instructions (responding to "flam over the glosser" with the response the learner produces for "pick up the glass," and so forth). For the second type of test, we could present parts of the chain in a different context. "Hold this dish . . . put it down here . . . good. Now go to the table . . . come on back . . . take this to the counter . . ."

The prediction for the second test is that the learner would fail to perform appropriately. The predictions are not based on knowledge of the learner; rather the diagnosis is based on the communication the learner has received. Note that this type of diagnosis is extremely difficult to achieve from a strict behavioral model. The learner is performing adequately on the series of tasks that is presented. From what the learner does, the problem is not obvious. It becomes obvious only if we consider the *logical* flaws in the presentation. These flaws suggest a way that the learner could perform as observed and yet not understand what the teacher supposes the learner understands.

The test of whether the learner has learned the misrule involves introducing tasks that are not part of the program. We can either change the relevant stimuli and predict the same response, or we can change the irrelevant stimuli (context details) and predict no response. We can derive the same sort of program-related information without introducing new tests. We simply note any problems the learner experiences later in the program and then attempt to confirm that each is caused by the earlier communications provided by the program. The disadvantage of this approach is that problems are not predicted; rather, they are discovered after they have become problems. If the learner later fails to generalize, we assume that the program provided inadequate instruction to assure the generalization. If the learner tends to behave as if a subset of examples had been stipulated, we can assume that the program in fact caused the stipulation. After making these assumptions, we check the program sequence to determine whether the program is actually responsible for the observed mislearning.

In summary, the procedures for figuring out what is wrong with the program involves two approaches:

1. The program-flaw-prediction looks for flaws in the program and tests to see whether these are transmitted to the learner.

2. The learner-performance approach looks for inadequate performance and then attempts to verify the causes by referring to the program.

A model for applying the learner-performance approach appears in Chapter 28.

Diagnosis of the Learner

The primary goal of diagnosing the learner is to identify the learning problem and correct it. *This diagnosis should imply an instructional remedy.* Therefore, it must be expressed in terms that translate into instruction. Regardless of how strange the learner may seem, we cannot refer to history, culture, neurology, chemistry, or other variables that are not directly associated with instruction. If the diagnosis is to imply a remedy, the diagnosis must express the learner's problems as a *skill deficiency*.

1. It expresses exactly what it is the learner is supposed to do; and

2. It expresses exactly how the learner actually performs.

The difference between the two statements is the problem—a specification of what the learner must be taught. This difference may imply an intervention that is modest or one that is relatively extensive. We can teach any skill by following the appropriate procedures. Therefore, we can specify a remedy for any difference that is identified.

Six Learner-Problem Types

When we examine the range of situations in which a learner diagnosis is called for, we identify six learner problem types. For each problem there is a remedy. The remedies for three problems involve application of the stimulus-locus analysis; remedies for two types derive from the response-locus analysis; the final remedy is appropriate for situations in which there is a question about whether the learner is actually trying to respond appropriately.

Nearly all the techniques used in these remedies are variations of techniques discussed earlier in different sections. The present classification provides a new focus for these techniques because it groups them according to the type of failure that the learner exhibits (the difference between what is expected of the learner and what the learner actually does). The following are the six types of learner problems.

Stimulus-locus problems

1. The learner does not transfer from one situation to another.

2. The learner does not differentiate between two situations or applications.

3. The learner can perform from some instructions, but not from the instructions provided by the task under consideration.

Response-locus problems

4. The learner can produce a particular response in some context, but cannot do it without prompting when it is presented in the context of the activity under consideration.

5. The learner cannot produce the response that is called for.

Possible compliance problems

6. Possibly, the learner is purposely not complying with the task requirements.

The following is a summary of the remedy implied by each stimulus-locus problem and an illustration of the development of the remedy.

Stimulus-Locus Problems

The learner does not transfer from one situation to another. This problem implies that the instruction has not been effective in showing the learner how the two situations are *the same*. The remedy is to increase the apparent sameness possessed by the two situations. The technique for showing that events are the same is to treat them in the same way.

Illustration. The learner has been taught spelling behavior, and the learner performs well in the spelling lesson. When writing reports for social studies, however, the learner does not use the spelling skills. The learner's behavior implies that the learner has not been effectively shown that the two situations *are the same* and that they call for the same behavior. To show how the situations are the same, the teacher must treat the situations in the same way. By treating the social studies content in the same way that spelling content is treated, the teacher shows that both call for the same behaviors.

For instance, as part of the spelling lesson, the teacher passes out copies of a social studies paper. Some of the words studied in spelling are misspelled in the paper. "See if you can find each misspelled word, cross it out, and write the correct word above the misspelled word."

Just as the teacher brings social studies into the spelling lesson, the teacher could also require spelling behavior in the social studies lesson. The teacher assigns a paper. "Use at least 10 words from your spelling list when you write about Holland. Make sure that you spell all words from your list correctly."

To prompt the spelling behavior further, the teacher could require the students to make a box at the top of their assignment sheet and check the paper for spelling. After checking the paper, the students are to make a check mark in the box. The addition of this prompt facilitates establishing the same behavior (checking spelling) in different content areas. The content areas become the same with respect to spelling because the learner is required to treat them the same way.

Perhaps more instructional confusion centers around transfer (or lack of it) than around any other topic. If the learner does not transfer spelling, the incorrect conclusion is that the spelling program failed because it didn't provide for the transfer. Actually, if the spelling behavior has been established in one context, the program has not failed to achieve its primary objective of communicating the skill. The failure is one of expansion. The remedy is to show the range of application for the skill. If a failure occurs in the social studies context, the failure is that the teacher has not required the same behaviors that are performed in spelling periods. The learner is behaving in a perfectly reasonable and predictable manner. Two situations are discriminably different, and the learner is responding to this difference. The failure is that of not showing that the two situations are the same in an important way.

The learner does not differentiate between two situations or applications. When we identify the specific situations that the learner "confuses," we identify a *discrimination* the learner has not been taught. The remedy is to teach the discrimination and then to give the learner further practice on this discrimination in the context of the original situation.

Illustration. The learner does not correctly work all division problems. The only problems the learner works correctly are those that have one-digit answers. The learner does not complete problems with two-digit answers. Instead, the learner writes the first digit in the answer, multiplies and subtracts, and then stops. Since the learner does not respond differentially to the two different problem types, the learner demonstrates a lack of knowledge about how these types are different. To teach difference, we juxtapose examples that are similar and treat them differently. To teach the discrimination– "Is the problem completed?"–we use examples where some problems are completed and some are not. A correlated-feature sequence could be used to convey the "rule" for determining whether an example is completed. Here is the first part of a sequence:

Example	Wording
	Listen. If a number is written over the last digit in the problem, the problem is completed.
79 37)2950 259 36	What is the last digit in this problem? Is there a number over it? My turn: Is this problem completed? No. How do I know? Because there is no number over the last digit in the problem. Your turn: Is this problem completed? How do you know?
79 37)2950 259 360 333 27	My turn: Is this problem completed? Yes. How do I know? Because there is a number over the last digit in the problem. Your turn: Is this problem completed? How do you know?
5)2950 25 45 45 0	Your turn: Is this problem completed? How do you know? Etc.

Note that the sequence is a correlated-feature sequence with some additional questions to assure that the learner is responding to the appropriate numerals. The complete remedy must go beyond teaching the learner to identify whether problems are done. It must teach the steps in working problems, which implies a cognitive routine. The discrimination is contingently linked to a cognitive routine. If the judgment is that the problem is not completed, the learner takes the conditional steps and completes the problem. The learner does not take the steps if the problem is completed.

When the routine is taught and covertized, we may discover that the learner still does not perform. The problem would not be a simple discrimination problem at this point, but one that implies a response-locus remedy. When we deal with the original instruction problem, however, we respond first to the most obvious problem, which is that the learner does not apparently know how to distinguish between problems that are complicated and those that are not. The immediate remedy is to teach this discrimination, then to attach a conditional routine to it. We first try to make the communication faultless before we deal with possible response-locus problems because we cannot be certain about classifying the problem as a response-locus problem until we have ruled out the possibility that the communication is faulty.

All differentiation problems take the same form and imply the same remedial strategy. We identify a detail that the learner is supposed to respond to. Teaching the discrimination involves applying one of the familiar forms. The choice of sequences depends on the nature of the discrimination.

The learner can perform from some instructions, but not from those provided by the task under consideration. The statement of the problem indicates that there is a single difference between the task that the learner can perform and the task that is required. We can, in other words, transform the task the learner can perform into the other task by changing only the instructions. Therefore, the remedy must show the learner the relationship between the familiar and the new instructions.

The statement of the problem suggests three possible forms that we have studied:

1. The equivalent-pairing covertization technique.
2. The correlated-feature sequence.
3. The double-transformation program.

If we are dealing with a single item or if that item is embedded in a chain, the equivalent-pairing technique is appropriate. The familiar and new instructions are paired first in the **A-B** order, then in the **B-A** order. Finally, the familiar instructions (**A**) are dropped.

If we are dealing with generalized applications, the correlated-features sequence or the double-transformation program may be adapted to the specific problem. Both provide means of showing the learner the "rule" for using the new instructions.

If the learner does not understand the instructions, "Express the numeral as an expanded notation," and similar references to expanded notation, but is reasonably proficient at addition, we could present the following correlated-features relationship:

> My turn: What's the expanded notation for 35? 30 plus 5. How do I know? Because 30 plus 5 equals 35.
>
> My turn again: What's the expanded notation for 71? 70 plus 1. How do I know? Because 70 plus 1 equals 71.
>
> Your turn: What's the expanded notation for 72? How do you know?
>
> Etc.

Various other correlated-features wording could be devised. Also, a short variation of the double transformation program could be introduced. We would alter the program so that the familiar set was quite small. Also, we would not integrate the sets. We would simply present a small familiar set, minimum difference to the new set, and possibly generalization examples for the new set.

Below is a possible sequence:

Example	Wording
35	Say the addition fact for this number. (30 plus 5)
182	Say the addition fact for this number.
56	Say the addition fact for this number.
56	My turn to say the expanded notation for this number: 50 plus 6. Your turn: Say the expanded notation.
182	Say the expanded notation.
35	Say the expanded notation.
279	Say the expanded notation.

In summary, all problems that require the teaching of

a new "label" or signal for a familiar discrimination are remedied by showing the relationship between the familiar and the new. Because the learner is not required to learn the discrimination from scratch–but merely to learn the new label–the appropriate techniques are those that establish the precise relationship between the familiar and the new.

Response-Locus Problems

All response-locus problems assume that there is a persistence in the learner's behavior despite attempts to change it. These problems may be linked with communication problems. For instance, the communication may have seriously stipulated a behavior and the learner may have practiced this behavior until it became habitual (highly resistant to extinction). The fact that a poor communication caused the problem is irrelevant. We must remedy the problem. Merely showing the learner what to do does not work. The learner repeatedly lapses into a behavior that had been stipulated, implying a response-locus remedy. Below is a summary of the two response-locus problems and illustrations of the remedies implied by each.

The learner can produce a particular response in some context, but cannot do it without prompting when it is presented in the context of the activity under consideration. This problem comes about in two different ways. In some cases, the instruction the learner had received stipulated a particular behavior for particular situations. When the learner is required to produce a new response in a situation that had been stipulated, the stipulated response persists. For example, if the learner speaks Spanish in particular situations, replacing the speech with English involves replacing highly-stipulated behaviors.

For the other type of context problem, the instruction the learner had received is not responsible for the problem. The learner simply cannot perform the response in the targeted context. The learner may "forget" the response that is called for or may produce the wrong responses, even though the learner can produce the response in other contexts.

The two types of context problems imply different responses *to the program used to teach the learner*. If we identify that the program induces serious stipulation, we would try to change the program for future students. For the type of context problem that is apparently a learner inability, no adjustment of the program for future students is implied. Regardless of the program the learner received, the learner's behavior shows whether serious stipulation has occurred and whether the learner has been reinforced for producing the stipulated responses. Merely showing the learner how to produce the new response in the different situations does not change the learner's behavior. The response is persistent. The instructional problem is one of replacing an established response pattern with one that is incompatible. The introduction must provide not merely for the establishment of the new response, but also for the extinction of the habitual response.

Note, however, the immediate remedy is the same for both types of context problems. The learner must be taught to perform within the context of the targeted activity. The paradigm that is followed is that of teaching the learner when to perform (by using the 3-level series.) Additional prompts may be useful for pointing out to the learner that the behavior called for is the same as that used in other situations.

Illustrations. The first illustration deals with the transfer problem that results when established behaviors must be replaced. The learner has been taught to speak English in school. Despite suggestions and demonstrations, the learner continues to speak Spanish on the playground and in the corridors and lunchroom. The teaching would be adequate to induce generalization if no behavior had already been established in these situations. The teaching problem, however, involves replacing a set of behaviors with an incompatible set. As soon as the learner becomes involved in an activity, the habitual behavior emerges.

To remedy this problem, we structure some playground activities in a way that permits us to present trials rapidly and to monitor the learner. Perhaps we make up a list of the various things that we want the learner to say. "Throw me the ball . . . Cover second base . . . Watch out . . . He's going to pop up . . ." and so forth. These are first practiced as symbolic exercises. The teacher describes the situations for which the various utterances are appropriate: "What are you going to say when you want the ball? . . . What are you going to say to make the batter miss the ball?" This context is something like a level 3 of the 3-level strategy. The learner produces various utterances. Each occurs intermittently, separated by other utterances. The context, however, is quite a bit simpler than the one required on the playground.

Immediately before the learner goes onto the playground, the teacher reviews the various utterances and reminds the learner to use these expressions during the game. The teacher then monitors the playground situation and surreptitiously reinforces the learner for using the appropriate expressions. The teacher continues to monitor the playground situation and to expand the range of expressions required on the playground. Before a particular expression is used on the playground, however, it is first rehearsed in the rehearsal context.

Note that the remedy involves increasing the number of ways that the playground situation and the classroom situation are the same. The statements that are used in each are the same. A variation of the events that evoke the responses are presented in both situations. The teacher describes those events during the rehearsal sessions ("What are you going to say when . . . ?"). The same events will occur in the playground; the teacher is in both situations.

In addition to the sameness, the instruction attempts to make the responses as fluent and easy as possible by rehearsing them in a 3-level strategy until they are quite firm. (If they are weak, characterized by great effort and latency, they will be very difficult for the learner to produce appropriately on the playground.)

In summary, the strategy involves four steps:

1. First firm the learner on the various responses in the 3-level strategy.
2. Frame the practice as rehearsal for the events that will happen in the application situation.
3. Monitor the learner in the application situation and provide reinforcement for using the targeted behaviors.
4. Expand the range of application and reduce the degree of monitoring as the learner becomes increasingly proficient.

This formula would apply to any situation in which the learner is to replace stipulated behaviors with new ones. For instance, the corrective reader would be "rehearsed" in a practice situation that permits controlled juxtaposition of words. This context is the list of unrelated words that does not prompt the learner to guess on the basis of the syntax or story context in which the word occurs. It functions like level 3 of the 3-level strategy. Following successful performance on this level, the learner engages in the reading of connected sentences. This situation is analogous to a game. The learner will probably revert to guessing as soon as the context becomes interesting, or as soon as the pattern of the sentences suggest what the next words will be. The learner's performance in this situation must be monitored carefully. The learner must be reinforced for accurate reading, but must not be expected to change immediately. Change will occur as a slow replacement of stipulated guessing behaviors with the new decoding behaviors.

The second type of situation in which the learner cannot perform in a particular context does not involve replacing stipulated behaviors with new behaviors. It involves making the learner facile in responses that are difficult for the learner. The learner can produce the response in a simplified context, but not within the context of the new activity.

For example, the learner gets on the bus, looks around, and apparently does not remember to put the coin in the coin box. The response can easily be prompted by showing the learner how to respond; however, the learner's behavior does not change after repeated trials. The learner apparently forgets what comes next in the expected chain of responses.

We cannot present repeated trials of this chain while the learner is on the bus. Also, the chain is too long. If we repeated the entire chain, the behavior of putting coins in the box could occur once in about 15 seconds. This interval is too long.

Since the behavior of putting the coin in the box always occurs within the context of a chain, we will use the technique described in Chapter 24 for promoting transfer with expanded chains. We will begin with a small chain and then we will lengthen the chain. The final chain that we design will start with a behavior that can be produced in the practice situation or in the transfer situation. This behavior serves as a device to demonstrate that the situations are the same.

For practice, we may construct a "mock bus," which consists of a platform, steps leading to the platform, something that resembles the coin box, and a person who is positioned next to the coin box and who plays the role of bus driver.

The initial chain requires the learner to climb the stairs with coin in hand and place the coin in the receptacle. Before each response, the teacher provides a *verbal signal*.

This part of the teaching is very important because it prompts the sameness of the practice situation and the real-life situation.

The basic signal could be, "Climb the stairs of the bus and put your money in the coin box." The learner does not have to understand precisely what these words mean because the practice will assure that the learner discriminates this instruction from others. The instructions simply work as a unique signal.

The teacher's assistant sits in the "driver's" seat, wearing a driver's cap and sitting behind a mock steering wheel. Note that every attempt should be made to provide the practice situation with parts or features that are shared with the real-life situation. The teacher directs the child. "Here's a bus. There's the driver. Look—next to the driver there is a coin box." The teacher then models the behavior. "My turn to climb up the stairs of the bus and put money in the coin box."

Immediately following the model, the child practices. Each trial is preceded by the instructions, "Climb up the stairs of the bus and put your money in the coin box." The money is placed in the child's hand. After a successful performance, the teacher and "driver" praise the child. The child is returned to the "starting position" and the next trial is presented. "Climb up the stairs of the bus and put your money in the coin box."

After three or four successful trials, an intervening activity that requires about as much time as the trial is introduced as a level-2 task (**A ▶ B ▶ A**). For instance, "That was really good. Let's hear you count to 10. Go . . . good job. Now let's see you climb up the stairs of the bus and put your money in the coin box."

After three or four level-2 tasks, the teacher can introduce a wider variety of intervening activities (creating a pattern of **A ▶ B ▶ C ▶ D ▶ A**). "Let's see if you remember how to do some of the things we've worked on. Touch your head . . . good. Touch your foot . . . good. What are you touching? Say the whole thing about what you are touching . . . Do you remember how old you are? . . . Good remembering. Now let's see you climb up the stairs of the bus and put your money in the coin box . . . Good remembering."

After the learner has performed successfully on three or four trials of level-3 difficulty, additional parts can be added to the chain. Each new part should be signaled by a new command. "I'm going to climb up the stairs of the bus and put money in the container. Then *I'm going to say hello to the driver...*" (The activity of saying hello can be practiced in isolation and then integrated with the other parts of the chain if the learner makes a mistake.) The teacher gives a command for the new behavior, creating an interaction pattern **T1-L1, T2-L2**. Later the interaction pattern becomes **T1-T2, L1-L2**. For example, at first the instructions are: "Climb the stairs of the bus and put your money in the coin box." After the learner drops the coin, "Good, now say hello to the driver." Later, the instructions are "Climb the stairs of the bus and put your money in the container. Then say hello to the driver . . . Good job."

This pattern is repeated with additional commands until the learner can perform an entire chain of behaviors from a single chain of instruction. "First take the money from your pocket and hold it in your hand. Then climb the stairs of the bus and put your money in the container. Then say hello to the driver and take a seat near the front of the bus."

After the learner is able to perform on level-3 context-difficulty for this activity when it is presented in the mock bus situation, the learner is ready to perform in a real-life situation.

Transfer will probably occur to the real-life situation because:

1. A form of some things that are named in the instructions appear in both situations—**coin, pocket, hand, stairs, coin box, seat**.

2. The behaviors are taught as a chain, which means that if the chain is started, it will tend to be continued.

3. The first behavior that occurs in the chain is exactly the same in both situations—taking the money from the pocket and holding it in the hand.

4. The presence of the teacher and of the instructions in both situations further prompts the sameness—particularly since these instructions are presented only in connection with a unique chain of behaviors.

All that remains is for the teacher to prompt the learner that the situations are the same. "Look, here comes the bus. You're going to take your money from your pocket and hold it in your hand. Then you're going to climb the stairs of the bus and put your money in the container.

Remember to say "hello" to the bus driver. Then you're going to take a seat near the front of the bus. Do it. Take your money from your pocket . . . good. Now climb the stairs . . ."

The learner cannot produce the response that is called for. If the learner gives evidence of not being able to produce the response that is called for, we must shape the response, starting with the behavior the learner exhibits and moving toward the goal behavior. Before we begin the response-induction process, however, we should be certain that the learner's problem is one of not being able to produce the response. Specifically, we must rule out the possibilities that the learner does not understand the instructions and that the learner cannot produce the response in some other context.

Illustration. The learner is required to copy the word **cat** and the learner fails. To make sure that the learner understands what the task requires, we could ask questions or model the behavior. Also, we would try to reinforce the learner for trying, in an attempt to get a sample of the learner's best effort. If the learner apparently tries and apparently understands the instructions but cannot produce an acceptable variation of **cat**, the problem is one of inducing a new motor response, a behavior that the learner has never produced before.

The specific program that we institute will depend on the level of response sophistication the learner demonstrates. The program for the learner who has trouble holding a pencil would be quite different from that for the learner who makes backward letters. Regardless of the program's starting point, it would be characterized by:

1. The use of shaping techniques—shifting the criterion for reinforcing the learners so that response requirements change as the task remains basically the same.
2. Provisions for a great deal of supervised practice.
3. Possibly the identification of behavioral components or parts of the copying tasks.
4. Possibly an essential-response-features program that presents a variation of copying that requires less behavior. (Perhaps the learner copies by using an index finger rather than a pencil.)

Everything the learner cannot do when trying to perform on the targeted task describes a specific skill that we can teach. Therefore, if we carefully observe what the learner cannot do when trying something like copying a word, we will be provided with the specific details for our program. For instance, the learner may have a habit of repeatedly looking at the model word and what is being written. This behavior suggests that the learner does not remember what is to be copied. The deficiency implies a program that shapes the memory. The teacher may make letters in the air. Immediately following the tracing of each letter, the learner traces it in the air. When the learner becomes proficient at this task, the teacher requires the learner to wait a few seconds before forming each letter. "Watch this . . . remember how that letter looked . . . your turn . . ."

As the learner becomes proficient at forming single letters that are delayed, the teacher introduces pairs of letters, the teacher first forming **oi** in the air, then telling the learner to make both letters. The program would continue until the learner was able to reliably form two letters following the teacher's model.

At the same time that the air-tracing tasks are presented, the learner would continue to practice tracing with a pencil. At first the learner would copy single letters. The teacher would permit the learner to look at each; then the teacher would cover the letter and the learner would copy it below. This procedure would assure that the learner does not continue to look back and forth between the model and what the learner is trying to write. As an additional prompt, the learner could be directed to trace each letter before the teacher covers it. Later the learner would be shown a series of letters, such as **cat**. The learner would be instructed to look at each letter the teacher points to and to say that letter. The teacher would then cover all the letters. The learner would be required to say the letters that are to be written, in order. When the learner is firm on saying the series, the learner would write the series of letters. (This technique combines the procedure used for visual spatial displays with the procedures for combining instructions T1, T2-L1, L2.) *The general rule is that everything the learner cannot do implies a specific intervention.*

Possible Compliance Problems

The learner may not be trying. A diagnosis of the learner's problem may be inaccurate if the learner is not actually trying. There are many techniques for getting the learner to try. When working with low performers or learners who exhibit a variety of inappropriate behavior, the best technique for assuring that the learner is trying is the task of *stand-up*. The activity is based on juxtaposition prompting. We present a series of stand-up and sit-down tasks to the learner in rapid succession. We continue until the learner performs without hesitation on four consecutive trials. *Immediately* following the last trial, we present the task about which we had questions. The learner's performance on this task following the stand-up sequence may be regarded as a sample of what the learner does when trying to perform. The rationale is as follows.

The series of tasks, "stand-up" and "sit-down" are presented in the same setting by the same person. All are examples of the same instruction-following behavior (the teacher tells you what to do and you do it). Presenting the tasks in rapid succession further assures the juxtaposition prompting of how the examples are the same. By the time the learner has produced four behaviors in a row, the learner has demonstrated compliance—willingness to perform on examples of the tasks in which the teacher says it and the learner does it. If another task immediately follows the fourth consecutive successful stand-up task, the probability is overwhelming that the learner will treat it as if it is the same as the other tasks—another example of complying with what the teacher says. The assurance of learner compliance may be further increased by providing the learner with reinforcement when complying on stand-up tasks.

For instance: "Stand up . . . that's good. Sit down . . . three more. Stand up . . . good. Sit down. Now you're doing it . . . Stand up . . . Sit down . . . Good job. Only one more. Stand up . . . Sit down. Good job. Read this sentence . . ." Any mistake the learner makes at this point is not the result of indifference. The learner is trying.

Diagnosis of a Complex Activity

The diagnosis of the learner may be difficult if the learner is engaged in a complex activity, particularly if the teacher is "mother henning" the learner through the various parts of the activity. The teacher may be prompting parts of the operation, helping the learner produce different responses, and generally obscuring what the learner does not know.

For example, the learner may be performing a task such as putting on a coat. The teacher first directs the learner to get his coat. The learner stares blankly. The teacher points to the coat rack and goes through some wriggling motions as if she is putting on the coat. "Put on your coat. Your coat," she says. The learner turns around and looks toward the coat rack where other children are busily dressing. The learner runs over and grabs the wrong coat. The teacher intercepts the learner and directs him to his coat. The learner then grabs the coat and proceeds to put his left arm through the wrong armhole. As he stands there, somewhat puzzled about why the coat is tending to go on backward, the teacher prompts some of the behavior—first orienting the coat, then pushing the second arm through the sleeve, then operating the zipper.

Just as we teach only one thing at a time, we should test one thing at a time to discover what the learner cannot do.

First test skills that are essential to the operation. Can the learner put on the coat unassisted if we start the first arm through the appropriate armhole? This activity virtually removes all discriminations from the task. What remains is part of the **putting-on** operation. If the learner cannot perform on this part of the operation when it is not confounded with the discrimination of orienting the coat, we have identified the central starting point.

To find out where the program should start, we may begin with an "easy" example—an over-sized coat with one sleeve marked. The coat is on a hanger. The learner wears a wristband that is marked with the same mark that appears on the sleeve. Without removing the coat from the hanger, the learner places the marked sleeve into the marked armhole. Because the coat is over-sized, the learner is relieved of some problems associated with putting on a coat. The learner simply rotates and puts his second arm through the other armhole.

It is important to test the central physical operation apart from the chain of events because (as we noted earlier) this operation will probably require quite a few trials to teach if the learner has not mastered it. As soon as the learner masters the central operation, independent (or semi-independent) practice can be started.

Each of the other discriminations should be tested separately, starting with additional motor operations (in this case, zippering). Can the learner perform an easy example of zippering (a large zipper that has already been started)? The discriminations should be tested in their simplest form.

If we show the learner his coat and then pause a few seconds, can he point to his coat? If the learner performs on this task (a level-1 task on the 3-level series), we can test on levels 2 and 3 to determine the learner's ability to recall which coat is his.

In summary, to diagnose the learner's performance on a complex activity that is responded to poorly we follow these procedures:

1. If we are in doubt about the learner's compliance, establish compliant behavior; then immediately follow successful trials with the test.

2. If the learner fails this test, we test on the component discriminations in the chain.

   a. Start with a simple variation of the central operation, stripped of discriminations (using models or very simple signals to indicate the operation that is to be performed).

   b. Test other motor responses in the chain and discriminations.

3. We design a program that starts with any central motor behaviors not mastered by the learner, teaches the various discriminations, and integrates components and parts into a chain.

Perspective

Both this chapter and the one that follows, "Mechanics of Correcting Mistakes," deal with identifying specific learning problems and solving them. The difference is in the latitude of the remedy. The product of the diagnosis developed in this chapter is a *remedial program*, something entirely new.

The perspective for mechanics of correcting mistakes assumes that a program already exists and that the learner is going through that program. Because neither the program nor the learner are perfect, mistakes will occur. How are they corrected in a way that assures that the learner will be able to take the next steps specified in the program? The idea is not to make up a program, but to intervene in a manner that is quick and effective and that permits the learner to continue in the program. Think of corrections as responses to unanticipated mistakes that the learner makes when being taught a program. The program is *given* and our job is to help the learner through it using corrections. The procedure or diagnosing and remedying learning problems does not assume that a program is given, and therefore creates new programs.

Summary

Diagnostic and remedial procedures may be directed at the instructional program. Diagnosis of instruction identifies problems with the programs. The remedy that follows eliminates the problem. The two approaches to diagnosis of the instruction are:

1. The program-flaw-prediction approach, which identifies flaws in the program and tests to document whether these flaws have been transmitted to the learner.

2. The learner-performance approach, which documents specific learner problems and then determines whether the instructional program was capable of creating the problem.

The program-flaw-prediction approach requires a test that is not part of the program. This test involves either changes in the relevant stimuli (with the prediction that the learner will respond in the same manner) or changes in the irrelevant stimuli (with the prediction that the learner will respond differently).

The learner-performance approach does not require the construction of additional tests; however, this approach identifies problems after the fact. The approach, therefore, is well-designed to shape an instructional program. (See Chapter 28.)

We may diagnose the learner as well as instruction. Diagnosis of the learner leads to an instructional program.

The program derives from a description that states what the learner is supposed to do and what the learner does.

The difference between the statements is the objective of the remedy.

The basic learner problems fall into six types, each implying a remedy.

1. The learner does not transfer from one situation to another. *Remedy*: Show how the situations are the same.

2. The learner does not differentiate between two situations. *Remedy*: Show how the situations are different.

3. The learner can perform from some instructions, but not from those provided by the task under consideration. *Remedy*: Teach the transformation.

4. The learner can produce a particular response in some context, but not without prompting in the task under consideration. *Remedy*: Use the 3-level strategy to shape the context of the task.

5. The learner cannot produce the response that is called for. *Remedy*: Use shaping procedures to shape the response.

6. Possibly the learner is not complying. *Remedy*: Use juxtaposition prompting with "stand-up" tasks.

The first three problems suggest stimulus-locus remedies—discriminations that are to be taught. Problems 4 and 5 are response-locus problems. Problem 6 is one of possible non-compliance. The form of each remedy is quite simple. If the learner is not performing because of an inability to produce the response, we use those procedures that will induce the response. If the learner's problem is one of performing the operation within a particular context, we shape the context starting with one that is relatively easy. If the learner is not complying, we use prompting techniques that induce compliance.

When the learner makes a variety of mistakes on a complex operation, an involved program may result. When attempting to formulate such programs, we test one thing at a time, starting with simple examples that involve the central operation. We test the learner on other discriminations. We construct a program that introduces the central motor response early.

The procedures for diagnosing the learner suggest that if the learner has a learning problem, the problem can be described. If it is described, the remedy is implied. (The problem will fall into one of the categories, and the direction of the remedy follows from the nature of the problem.)

Chapter 27
Mechanics of Correcting Mistakes

The learner may make a discrimination mistake, a response mistake, or a combination mistake (involving both a mistaken discrimination and a faulty response). A discrimination mistake occurs when the learner is capable of producing the response called for in the task, but produces another response. There is no question about the learner's ability to *discriminate*. A response mistake occurs when the learner cannot produce the response. If you were told to do a backward somersault in the air and land on your feet, you would probably have a perfect idea of what you are supposed to do; however, you would probably fail the task because you are unable to produce the response that is called for. You have never produced the response and you are not capable of producing it under any condition. To correct response mistakes, we *shape*. To correct discrimination mistakes, we give information by showing the learner what controls the response.

Despite the differences in correction procedures, the analysis of communications suggests common features of all logically designed corrections. These features are:

1. The correction should be designed to remedy one primary problem.
2. The correction should create juxtapositions that permit rapid repetition of the skill of discrimination that is to be corrected.
3. The correction should provide for adequate practice.
4. The confirmation of the correction should follow the correction and should demonstrate that the learner performs on the task in the context in which it had been originally presented.

The following is a brief rationale for the four common features of various corrections.

1. If the correction attempts to correct more than one thing, it may become so complicated that it never ends. Suppose the teacher tries to correct several behaviors in a chain of responses; and the learner then begins to make new mistakes, prompting the teacher to correct these. This elaboration may prompt new mistakes.

2. The creation of adequate juxtapositions reduces the memory requirements for the task because the learner does not have to attend to as much detail. The juxtaposition of examples that involve the same response dimension prompt the sameness in examples. In terms of clock time (not trials), the faster the examples can be presented, the faster the learner will produce the number of correct responses required to learn the skill.

3. If the correction does not provide a sufficient number of trials, it may not provide enough training for the learner or enough information for the teacher. The latter point is particularly important. The teacher who views an inadequate sample of the learner's performance may conclude that the learner is "firm" on the skill when the learner is not.

4. Finally, the justification for returning the learner to the precise context in which the mistake occurred is that this context may present unobserved problems. If we correct the learner in a simpler context without confirming that the performance transfers to the original context, we may have presented only a partial correction. The learner's failure on the original context and successful performance on a simpler context (during correction) suggests that the final objective of the correction must be to *shape the context* for the skill, changing it in the direction of the more difficult original context. By ending the correction with the original context, we convey a very important point to the learner: The correction prepares the learner for the situation in which the learner had failed earlier. If we end the correction in a context other than that of the original activity, the learner receives no compelling demonstration that the correction has such a purpose.

Correcting Discrimination Mistakes

A discrimination mistake occurs either within a sequence or within some other activity. The mistake is either chronic or not chronic. The context of the mistake and the relative frequency of the mistake determine the details of the specific correction procedures. We will illustrate both simple firming procedures and more elaborate remedies.

Non-Chronic Mistakes Within Context

The first step in correcting a mistake is to *firm it within the context in which it occurs*. The procedure involves these steps:

1. Model the correct *answer*.
2. Test on the missed *item*.
3. Back up several tasks or items and *test the tasks in the order in which they originally occurred*.

Illustration. The learner misses the first test example in a sequence for *getting hotter* (example 6). The learner indicated that "it got hotter" when it did not. Here is the correction:

Example		Teacher Wording
a. 110°		It didn't get hotter.
b. 112° }Repeat of example 6 110°		Let's do it again. Feel it now. Did it get hotter?... Good.
c. 55°		Feel it now.
105° }Repeat of example 4		Did it get hotter?
112° }Repeat of example 5		Did it get hotter?
110° }Repeat of example 6		Did it get hotter?

The teacher first modeled the answer to example 6 (step a). The teacher then repeated example 6 (step b). To present this example, the teacher had to present the temperature of 112° (example 5). Finally, the teacher presented example 6 within the context of examples 4, 5, and 6 (step c). Note that 4 and 5 were not tested when the sequence was originally presented. These were modeled examples. *They became test examples as part of the correction.*

If the learner performs adequately on example 6 when it is presented within the context of the other examples, the teacher continues with the remaining examples in the sequence. If the learner again makes a mistake, the teacher follows the same procedure—modeling the correct answer, testing on that item, then backing up several examples and testing on the examples in the context in which they were originally presented.

This firming procedure is used when the learner makes a mistake in an activity other than an *initial-teaching sequence*.

Let's say that the learner makes the mistake specified below:

Teacher Wording	Response
Which of these objects is taller?	The glass.
What do you think is in the cup?	Cocoa.
Which is hotter, the cup or the glass?	The glass.

Here's the correction:

1. The cup is hotter. The glass has ice in it, so it's not hot at all.
2. Which is hotter, the cup or the glass? ("The cup.")
3. Good. Which of these objects is taller?...What do you think is in the cup?

 Which is hotter, the cup or the glass?

 What is in the glass?

 Are ice cubes hot? Etc.

The firming procedure is the same as that used for a mistake in the sequence. First, the correct answer is modeled. Then, the learner is tested on the example missed. Then, the teacher backs up two or three tasks and tests on the tasks in the order in which they originally appeared.

Rationale for basic firming procedure. As noted above, the purpose of a correction is to assure that the learner can perform on the task when it appears *within the context* of a particular activity. The mistake occurred within a particular juxtaposition of events. Therefore, it is important to back up and present the missed item within the pattern of juxtaposition in which it originally occurred.

If the sequences are adequately designed, this correction procedure usually deals effectively with the specific problems the learner experiences when responding to the sequence. The sequences are designed so that the pattern of juxtapositions is carefully controlled. The learner is shown samenesses and differences. Then, the learner is tested on mixed examples. If the learner makes a mistake within the context of items that show samenesses, the learner is not attending to the basic sameness features. The remedy is to show how the items are the same. This is precisely what happens if the basic firming procedure is followed. By backing up several tasks and presenting the items in their original order, the missed item is now presented within a pattern of juxtaposition that shows sameness. Similarly, if the learner makes a mistake on a minimum-difference item, the most logical remedy is to show the difference, which is what the firming procedure will do by repeating the missed item within a context that shows a single difference between the missed item and the item that immediately precedes it. Finally, if the learner misses items in the test segment, the response implies that the learner is not using the information about the discrimination that had been demonstrated earlier in the sequence. The most logical remedy is to require the learner to apply the discrimination to items presented in the test context. (By returning to an easier pattern of juxtaposition, we are not providing the learner with the needed information. The learner has already shown the ability to perform on items in the easier context. What the learner cannot do is perform within the test segment, which is the context that should be firmed.)

Remedies for Chronic Errors

The procedures above apply to simple firming. Any learner can be expected to make mistakes from time to time, and these mistakes do not necessarily imply serious problems. Signs of serious problems are:

1. A high percentage of mistakes on a particular sequence or activity.
2. A high percentage of mistakes on a particular subtype or item within a sequence activity.

Corrections for chronic mistakes are more complicated than those for non-chronic mistakes. The Figure 27.1 shows the three basic procedures for chronic discrimination errors.

As the figure indicates, each remedy may call for the construction of additional sequences. If the mistake is a *general confusion* (Correction I), the remedy is to construct sequences that are parallel to the original. If the mistake is a *subtype mistake* (Correction II), a sequence containing only examples of the missed type is presented. If the mistake does not occur within a sequence, but within the *context of another activity* (Correction III), the missed item

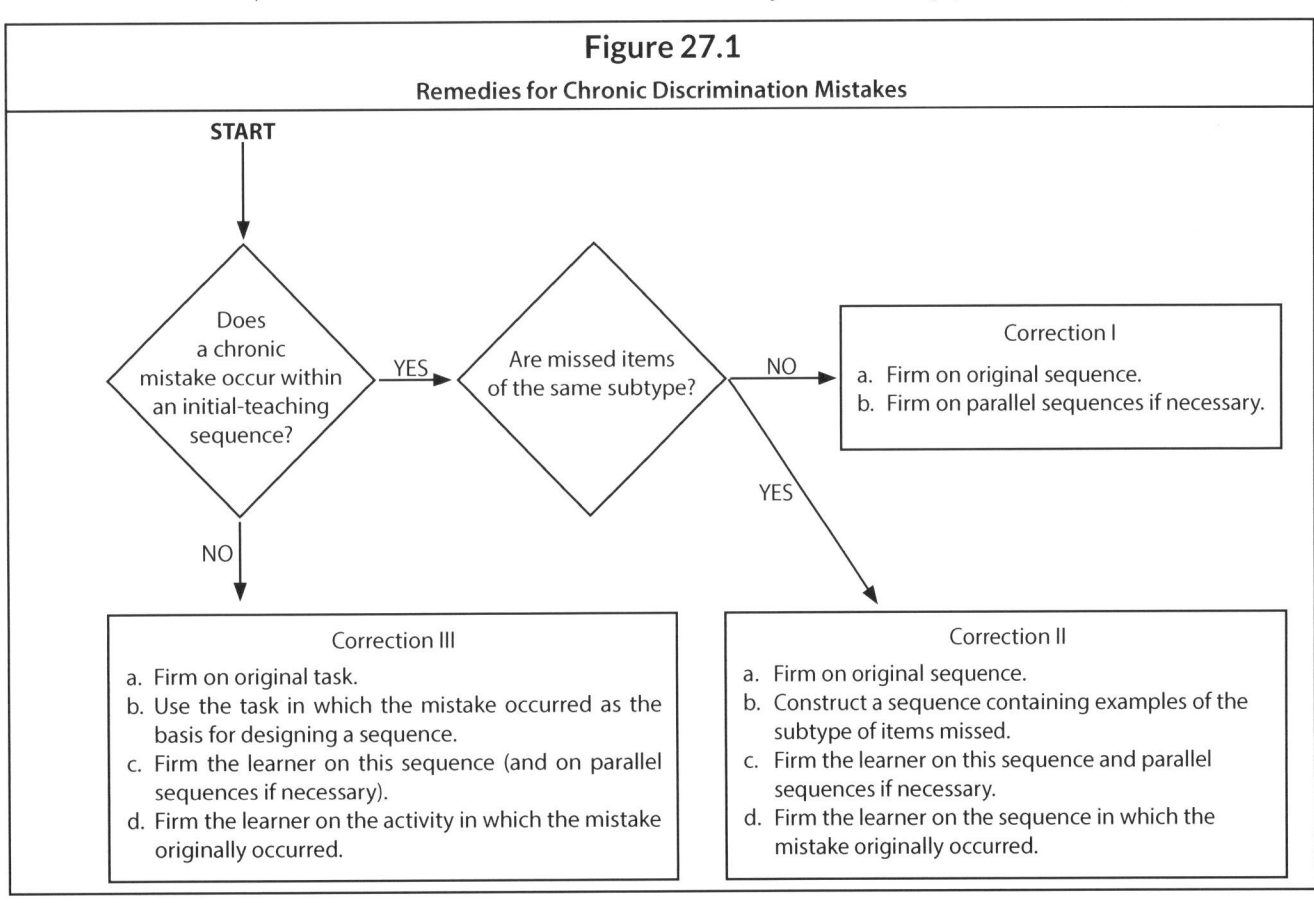

Figure 27.1
Remedies for Chronic Discrimination Mistakes

START

Does a chronic mistake occur within an initial-teaching sequence?
- YES → Are missed items of the same subtype?
  - NO → **Correction I**
    a. Firm on original sequence.
    b. Firm on parallel sequences if necessary.
  - YES → **Correction II**
    a. Firm on original sequence.
    b. Construct a sequence containing examples of the subtype of items missed.
    c. Firm the learner on this sequence and parallel sequences if necessary.
    d. Firm the learner on the sequence in which the mistake originally occurred.
- NO → **Correction III**
  a. Firm on original task.
  b. Use the task in which the mistake occurred as the basis for designing a sequence.
  c. Firm the learner on this sequence (and on parallel sequences if necessary).
  d. Firm the learner on the activity in which the mistake originally occurred.

Section VIII | Diagnosis and Corrections

is treated as a task that is used as a basis for designing an initial-teaching sequence.

Remedies for Chronic Mistakes that Occur Within a Sequence

Corrections I and II present the remedial procedures for mistakes that occur within a sequence.

Correction I. Consider the percentage of errors on a sequence unacceptably high (suggesting "general confusion") if the learner initially misses 25 percent or more of the test items.

1. Firm on original sequence. Each time a mistake occurs within the sequence, follow the basic firming procedures of modeling the correct response, testing on the missed item, and backing up several tasks and repeating the tasks in order. Although the learner has been "firmed" on the sequence at this time, we would still suspect the learner to make mistakes on new items if they were presented.

2. Firm the learner on a *parallel sequence*. A parallel sequence is one that presents a different set of examples and different specific juxtapositions, but that presents the same discrimination and the same wording for test items. The parallel sequence is capable of providing us with information about how firm the learner is and of providing the learner with the additional practice that will firm the response. When we present this sequence, we model fewer examples than the original and present fewer test items.

If the learner performs acceptably on the parallel sequence (making errors on less than 15 percent of the test items), consider the learner firm on the discriminations. If the learner makes mistakes on more than 15 percent of the items, present another parallel sequence. Repeat the procedure until the learner meets criterion of at least 85 percent correct on the test items.

Correction II. The correction for subtype errors involves four steps:

1. Firm on original sequence.
2. Construct a sequence containing examples of the subtype of items missed.
3. Firm the learner on this sequence and parallel sequences if necessary.
4. Firm the learner on the sequence in which the mistake originally occurred.

If the learner makes no more than 25 percent errors on the test items, and if the mistakes are of the *same* subtype, use the subtype correction. If the errors exceed 25 percent, *provide Correction I*, even if the mistakes are of the same subtype.

Like the remedy for a high percentage of mistakes, the subtype remedy begins by firming all mistakes in the original sequence. (We model the answer to each missed item, then test that item, then repeat the part of the sequence in which the mistake occurred.)

The subtype correction requires the introduction of a *new sequence* (step **b**), not a parallel sequence. The new sequence contains only examples of the missed subtypes (or a heavy predominance of these examples).

If the learner misses all no-change negatives in a sequence, the subtype sequence would consist predominantly of no-change negatives. Figure 27.2 shows a possible sequence.

Figure 27.2

Example	Teacher Wording
1	Watch the space. I'll tell you if it gets wider.
2	Did it get wider? Yes.
3	Did it get wider? Yes.
4	Did it get wider? No.
5	Your turn: Did it get wider?
6	Did it get wider?
7	Did it get wider?
8	Did it get wider?
9	Did it get wider?
10	Did it get wider?
11	Did it get wider?
12	Did it get wider?
13	Did it get wider?

If the learner consistently fails to identify one of the members presented in a noun sequence (**truck**, for instance), the subtype sequence would be a sequence in which that particular type predominated.

Chapter 27 | Mechanics of Correcting Mistakes

Example	Teacher Wording
red truck	My turn: What kind of vehicle? Truck.
black truck	Your turn: What kind of vehicle?
yellow truck	What kind of vehicle?
car	What kind of vehicle?
red truck	What kind of vehicle?
blue truck	What kind of vehicle?
car	What kind of vehicle?
black truck	What kind of vehicle?
car	What kind of vehicle?
red truck	What kind of vehicle?
yellow truck	What kind of vehicle?

If the subtype occurs in a single-transformation sequence, the subtype would be presented in a single-transformation sequence. It would be the only type in the sequence.

The following is a single-transformation sequence for teaching "numerical expansion." Mistakes are indicated with an asterisk.

Teacher Wording	Response
My turn: What does fifty-seven equal? Fifty plus seven.	
My turn again: What does seventy-one equal? Seventy plus one.	
Your turn: What does seventy-two equal?	Seventy plus two.
What does sixty-two equal?	Sixty plus two.
What does twenty-six equal?	Twenty plus six.
What does twenty equal?	Twenty plus twenty. *
What does ninety-four equal?	Ninety plus four.
What does thirty-three equal?	Thirty plus three.
What does eighty equal?	Eighty plus one. *
What does forty-five equal?	Forty plus five.

The subtype is two-digit numerals that end in zero. Unlike the others in the sequence, names of these numerals do not provide instructions for specifying the second digit. (The teacher does not say, "What does fifty-zero equal?")

The subtype sequence would consist totally of items of this type:

Teacher Wording	Response
My turn: What does thirty equal? Thirty plus zero.	
Your turn: What does twenty equal?	Twenty plus zero.
What does thirty equal?	Thirty plus zero.
What does ninety equal?	Ninety plus zero.
What does fifty equal?	Fifty plus zero.
What does seventy equal?	Seventy plus zero.

The following shows a different type of error pattern on the original sequence.

Teacher Wording	Response
My turn: What does twenty-six equal? Twenty plus six.	
My turn: What does twenty-seven equal? Twenty plus seven.	
Your turn: What does twenty-eight equal?	Twenty plus eight.
What does thirty-eight equal?	Thirty plus eight.
What does eighty-three equal?	Eighty plus three.
What does eighteen equal?	Eighty plus… *
What does forty-five equal?	Forty plus five.
What does fifteen equal?	Fifty plus… *

The subtype is the teen numerals. This type is potentially difficult because the convention for naming these numbers is the opposite of that for other two-digit numerals. Instead of naming the teen number first (teen-eight), the convention calls for saying, "**eighteen**." This sequence presents the teen subtype:

Teacher Wording

My turn: What does eighteen equal? Ten plus eight.
Your turn: What does nineteen equal?
What does fourteen equal?
What does twelve equal?
What does thirteen equal?
What does fifteen equal?
What does eighteen equal?

Note. For single-transformation or double-transformation concepts, the subset sequence contains *only* the subtype that is missed. All other subtype sequences contain a *predominance* of the subtype item.

Step **c** in the subtype remedy calls for firming the learner on the sequence and on parallel sequences. We use the same criterion of performance specified for Correction

I. We consider the learner firm only when the learner makes mistakes on no more than 15 percent of the test examples.

After the learner has performed adequately on the subtype sequence, we firm the learner on the sequence in which the mistake originally occurred (step **d**). Note that this step has no parallel in the remedy for a high percentage of errors. The reason is that we must return the learner to the context in which the original mistake occurred. This step is taken naturally for the Correction I mistakes because the parallel sequences that we construct present the same context as the original sequence. The situation is different with the subtype sequence, because this sequence is not like the original.

Optionally, a more involved process of integrating a subtype with the familiar type may be designed. This procedure is the integration procedure specified for integrating frequently missed worksheet items with low-mistake items (Chapter 16). The integration is modeled after the double-transformation sequence. First, the new set (subtype) is presented. Then examples of a familiar set are presented. Finally, the sets are mixed. The value of this procedure is that it permits the learner to deal with the members of the new set first in a relatively simple pattern of juxtapositions, then in a more difficult pattern. The procedure would be effective for subtypes that are fairly large or fairly difficult.

Chronic Errors Outside of a Sequence

Correction III. A chronic error may occur outside of a sequence. To provide a remedy, the teacher first firms on the missed task by modeling the correct answer, testing on the task, backing up several tasks, and repeating the tasks in the same order they had been presented initially. The teacher then presents a sequence designed from *the task* the learner missed.

To design a sequence from a task, we use the wording of the original task. We classify the task as either a choice-response task or a production-response task. We classify the task as one dealing with a non-comparative, a comparative, a noun, a transformation, or a correlated-feature relationship.

The cognitive routine below illustrates the procedure. Each step may be the cause of a chronic mistake. We can classify each step as a task that clearly implies a sequence.

Teacher writes on the board: 9 - 14 = ☐

1. Read this problem.
2. How many are you starting out with?
3. Will the answer be positive or negative?
4. How do you know?
5. Fourteen is five bigger than the number you're starting out with. So what is the number in the answer?
6. Read the problem and the answer.

Step 1 requires the learner to "Read this problem." The task is a production-response, single-transformation task. (If the same task were applied to different problems, the response would be different. Also, there are no negative examples for "Read this problem.")

If the learner is chronically weak on this step, we would firm the learner through a single-transformation sequence with the instructions, "Read this problem."

Here is the first part of a possible test sequence:

Example	Teacher Wording
9 - 9 = ☐	Read this problem.
9 - 10 = ☐	Read this problem.
10 - 9 = ☐	Read this problem.
10 - 4 = ☐	Read this problem.
10 - 14 = ☐	Read this problem.
9 - 21 = ☐	Read this problem.

Note that this sequence contains no models. The particular symbols that appear in the problems would depend on the learner's performance. If the learner had trouble with 9 and 10, the sequence above would be appropriate; however, it would not serve the learner who confused 4 and 5.

Step 2 in the problem presents the task, "how many are you starting out with?" This is a single-transformation task. If the learner identified the other numeral in the problem as "How many you start out with" (saying, "fourteen" instead of "nine"), we could use this sequence.

Example	Teacher Wording
9 - 7	This problem starts out with nine. How many does this problem start out with?
8 - 7	This problem starts out with eight. How many does this problem start out with?
8 - 6	How many does this problem start out with?
6 - 8	How many does this problem start out with?

12 - 5	How many does this problem start out with?
1 - 3	How many does this problem start out with?
5 - 4	How many does this problem start out with?
9 - 4	How many does this problem start out with?
14 - 1	How many does this problem start out with?
24 - 3	How many does this problem start out with?

Step 3 ("Will the answer be positive or negative?") is followed by **step 4** ("How do you know?"). The pair of items presents a correlated-feature relationship ("When the number you minus is greater than the number you start out with, the answer will be negative.").

Here is a sequence:

Example	Teacher Wording
9 - 8	My turn: Will the answer be positive or negative? Positive. How do I know? Because we're minusing less than nine.
9 - 10	My turn: Will the answer be positive or negative? Negative. How do I know? Because we're minusing more than nine.
9 - 11	Your turn: Will the answer be positive or negative? How do you know?
12 - 11	Will the answer be positive or negative? How do you know?
11 - 12	Will the answer be positive or negative? How do you know?
5 - 12	Will the answer be positive or negative? How do you know?
14 - 12	Will the answer be positive or negative? How do you know?
15 - 3	Will the answer be positive or negative? How do you know?
6 - 4	Will the answer be positive or negative? How do you know?
4 - 6	Will the answer be positive or negative? How do you know?

Step 5 is a variation of a correlated-feature relationship with part of the relationship not stated. ("Fourteen is five bigger than the number you're starting out with. So what is the number in the answer?")

Example	Teacher Wording
10 - 14	My turn: Fourteen is four bigger, so what's the number in the answer? Negative four.
13 - 14	Fourteen is one bigger. So what's the number in the answer?
14 - 14	Fourteen is zero bigger. So what's the number in the answer?
13 - 14	Fourteen is one bigger. So what's the number in the answer?
0 - 14	Fourteen is fourteen bigger. So what's the number in the answer?
8 - 14	Fourteen is six bigger. So what's the number in the answer?
11 - 14	Fourteen is three bigger. So what's the number in the answer?
-1 - 14	Fourteen is fifteen bigger. So what's the number in the answer?
-4 - 14	Fourteen is eighteen bigger. So what's the number in the answer?
7 - 14	Fourteen is seven bigger. So what's the number in the answer?

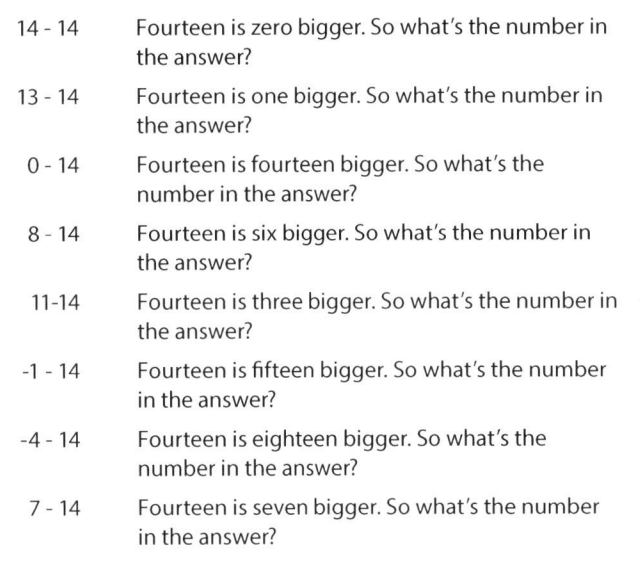

The same task analysis procedure is applied to the illustration in Figure 27.3. However, for this illustration the firming sequences do not derive as directly from the routine in which the chronic mistake occurred.

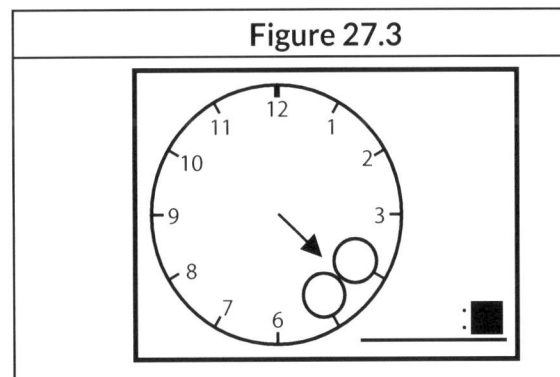

Figure 27.3

1. Look at this clock. Start at the top and say twelve. Count and write the number in the first circle and in the next circle.
2. Touch the little hand. Remember, if the little hand is between numbers, we write the first number. Is the little hand between numbers?
3. What number do we write for the little hand?
4. Write that number on the line.

There are two problems with the routine:

1. The tasks involve writing, which means that a sequence based on them would be slow and possibly would be failed if the learner is a poor writer.

Section VIII | Diagnosis and Corrections

2. A deduction is involved in steps 2 and 3; however, it is not set up in the standard correlated-feature form.

The solution to these problems involves modifying the tasks before creating the sequences. The final step, however, would be to return the learner to the wording in the routine.

Step 1. A possible juxtaposition problem occurs if the learner has trouble writing numerals. Since the writing is central to the operation, we would first test the learner on this skill as a component removed from the context of the routine. "Write the numeral 5 . . . write the numeral 6 . . ." The procedure of removing the discrimination and testing the motor response in a direct manner is basic to diagnosing the learner. (See Chapter 26.)

To test the learner's understanding of which numeral to write, we would change the sequence to permit quick juxtaposition of examples. Figure 27.4 shows a possible sequence.

The wording for the original task is modified. The word *say* has to be substituted for *write*. The sequence is a single-transformation.

The sequence above could be treated as the familiar set for a double-transformation sequence. The transformed set would consist of the same examples, but different instructions: "Count and *write* the number in the first circle and in the second circle." Upon completion of the transformed set, the learner would have performed on the instructions that appear in the original task and would have done so with a sufficiently large sample of examples to imply adequate understanding of the concept.

Step 2. "Is the little hand between numbers?" The task is a choice-response task, and it suggests a non-comparative sequence that presents the discrimination *between numbers* and *not-between numbers*. Figure 27.5 shows a possible sequence.

To make the response stronger, we might use two questions with examples that show the hands between. "Is the hand between numbers? . . . Which numbers?"

Steps 2 and 3 are linked through a rule: "Remember, if the little hand is between numbers, we write the first number . . . Is the little hand between numbers? . . . What number do we write for the little hand?"

Example	Teacher Wording
	Figure 27.4
	You're going to start at 12. Move to the circled numbers. Say the numbers that go in the first circle and the next circle.
clock (6,5 circled)	Say the numbers that go in the first circle and the next circle.
clock (7,6 circled)	Say the numbers that go in the first circle and the next circle.
clock (8,7 circled)	Say the numbers that go in the first circle and the next circle.
clock (2,3 circled)	Say the numbers that go in the first circle and the next circle.
clock (10,9 circled)	Say the numbers that go in the first circle and the next circle.
clock (12,1 circled)	Say the numbers that go in the first circle and the next circle.
clock (9,8 circled)	Say the numbers that go in the first circle and the next circle.

The rule creates a correlated-feature link between the little hand being between numbers and writing the first number. Although the questions are not presented in a standard form, we can use the wording of the question that occurs in step 3 ("What number do we write for the little hand?") and add the question, "How do you know?" (See Figure 27.6.)

The sequence contains only examples in which the hand is between numbers. A variation could be presented in which some hands were not between numbers. The second question could be dropped for these examples.

Note that the sequence contains a fair sample of examples involving numbers 7 through 12, usually the most

Chapter 27 | Mechanics of Correcting Mistakes

Figure 27.5

Example	Teacher Wording
(clock, hand on 3)	My turn: Is the hand between numbers? No.
(clock, hand between 2 and 3)	My turn: Is the hand between numbers? Yes.
(clock, hand between 1 and 2)	Your turn: Is the hand between numbers?
(clock, hand between 3 and 4)	Is the hand between numbers?
(clock, hand on 3)	Is the hand between numbers?
(clock, hand between 8 and 9)	Is the hand between numbers?
(clock, hand on 6)	Is the hand between numbers?
(clock, hand on 9)	Is the hand between numbers?
(clock, hand between 11 and 12)	Is the hand between numbers?

Figure 27.6

Example	Teacher Wording
(clock)	My turn: What do I write for the little hand? Four. How do I know? It's the first number.
(clock)	Your turn: What number do we write for the little hand? How do you know?
(clock)	What number do we write for the little hand? How do you know?
(clock)	What number do we write for the little hand? How do you know?
(clock)	What number do we write for the little hand? How do you know?
(clock)	What number do we write for the little hand? How do you know?
(clock)	What number do we write for the little hand? How do you know?
(clock)	What number do we write for the little hand? How do you know?

Example	Teacher Wording
50	Write that number on line **a**.
0-five	Write that number on line **b**.
0-one	Write that number on line **c**.
10	Write that number on line **d**.
25	Write that number on line **e**.
50	Write that number on line **f**.
15	Write that number on line **g**.
35	Write that number on line **h**.

troublesome. When the learner deals with numbers 1 through 6, the *first* number is the one on top. When dealing with 7 through 12, the *first* number is on the bottom.

For the last step in the routine, the learner writes the number for the little hand on a line. A variation of a single transformation sequence firms this skill.

We would adjust the sequence to the particular writing problems the learner was experiencing. (In the sequence

Section VIII | Diagnosis and Corrections

above, we stress two of the common confusions—0-one versus 10, and confusions on 50, 15, and 0-five.)

The final illustration of creating corrections sequences for chronic mistakes that occur outside a sequence comes from an intermediate math series.

a. Write: $2\frac{5}{7} =$
LET'S CHANGE THIS MIXED NUMBER INTO A FRACTION. HOW MANY PARTS WILL BE IN EACH WHOLE? "Seven."

b. Write: $2\frac{5}{7} = \frac{}{7}$
HOW MANY WHOLES DO WE HAVE? "Two."

c. A FRACTION EQUALS TWO WHOLES WHEN THE TOP IS HOW MANY TIMES BIGGER THAN THE BOTTOM? "Two."

d. WHAT IS THE BOTTOM OF THE FRACTION WE'RE WRITING? "Seven."

e. SO THE TOP MUST BE TWO TIMES BIGGER THAN SEVEN. TELL ME THAT NUMBER FOR THE TOP.

f. Write: $2\frac{5}{7} = \frac{14}{7}$
WE USED THE TWO WHOLES. HOW MANY PARTS ARE LEFT? "Five."

g. Write: $2\frac{5}{7} = \frac{14+5}{7}$
AND HOW MANY PARTS DO WE HAVE ALTOGETHER? "Nineteen."

h. Write: $2\frac{5}{7} = \frac{14+5}{7} = \frac{19}{}$
AND HOW MANY PARTS ARE IN EACH WHOLE? "Seven."

i. Write: $2\frac{5}{7} = \frac{14+5}{7} = \frac{19}{7}$

We could use a variation of the same sequence for firming each step—the single-transformation sequence. However, it is also possible to combine the steps that involve deductions and present them as correlated-feature sequences.

Below are the first parts of the various single-transformation sequences. In step **a**, the teacher asks: "How many parts will be in each whole?" Here are the first few examples in a possible sequence.

Example	Teacher Wording
$2\frac{5}{7}$	How many parts in each whole?
$2\frac{4}{7}$	How many parts in each whole?
$2\frac{7}{4}$	How many parts in each whole?
$2\frac{7}{5}$	How many parts in each whole?

In step **b**, the teacher asks, "How many wholes do we have?" Here are the first few examples.

Example	Teacher Wording
$2\frac{5}{7}$	How many wholes do we have?
$2\frac{7}{5}$	How many wholes do we have?
$1\frac{7}{5}$	How many wholes do we have?
$21\frac{7}{5}$	How many wholes do we have?

In step **c**, the teacher asks, "A fraction equals two wholes when the top is how many times bigger than the bottom?"

Here are the first examples in a possible firming sequence.

Teacher Wording

A fraction equals two wholes when the top is how many times bigger than the bottom?

A fraction equals three wholes when the top is how many times bigger than the bottom?

A fraction equals thirteen wholes when the top is how many times bigger than the bottom.

A fraction equals nine-R wholes when the top is how many times bigger than the bottom?

Step **d** asks, "What is the bottom of the fraction we're writing?" Here is the first part of a possible sequence.

Example	Teacher Wording
$2\frac{5}{7}$	What's the bottom number of the fraction we're writing?
$2\frac{7}{5}$	What's the bottom number of the fraction we're writing?

In step **e**, the teacher says: "So the top must be two times bigger than seven (the bottom number). Tell me that number for the top." To simplify this task, we could change the wording slightly.

Teacher Wording

If the top is two times bigger than seven, what's the top number?

If the top is two times bigger than six, what's the top number?

If the top is three times bigger than six, what's the top number?

If the top is five times bigger than four, what's the top number?

In step **f**, the teacher says: "We used the two wholes. How many parts are left?"

Example	Teacher Wording
$2\frac{5}{7}$	If we use the wholes, how many parts are left?
$2\frac{4}{7}$	If we use the wholes, how many parts are left?
$2\frac{7}{4}$	If we use the wholes, how many parts are left?
$5\frac{7}{14}$	If we use the wholes, how many parts are left?
$8\frac{3}{9}$	If we use the wholes, how many parts are left?
Etc.	

In step **g**, the teacher asks: "And how many parts do we have altogether?" If the learner has been taught an operation for adding, this step could be firmed through a sequence like the one below.

Example	Teacher Wording
$\frac{14+5}{7}$	How many parts do we have altogether?
$\frac{14-5}{17}$	How many parts do we have altogether?
$\frac{14-5}{1}$	How many parts do we have altogether?
$\frac{14-5}{1+2}$	How many parts do we have altogether?
$\frac{7}{J+3}$	How many parts do we have altogether?

The learner's problem may not be with the individual steps, but with the relationships between the steps. For most of these relationships, it would be possible to create correlated-feature sequences; however, each would do some violence to the wording or the order of the steps in the routine. A far more manageable alternative is to identify *clusters* of steps and schedule them according to the procedures specified in Chapter 19, *Scheduling Routines and Their Examples*. For instance, if the learner tended to make mistakes on both steps **b** and **c**, we would use the wording of steps **b** and **c** to create a cluster.

Example	Teacher Wording
$2\frac{5}{7} = \frac{}{7}$	How many wholes do we have?
	A fraction equals two wholes when the top is how many times bigger than the bottom?
$3\frac{5}{7} = \frac{}{7}$	How many wholes do we have?
	A fraction equals three wholes when the top is how many times bigger than the bottom?

It is possible to design other clusters and to incorporate the two steps above into a longer cluster. Also, the same step may be involved in more than one cluster. For instance, we might design a cluster that involves steps **c**, **d**, and **e** in addition to the one that involves **b** and **c**. The step **c** is common to both clusters. Here's the **c-d-e** cluster:

Example	Teacher Wording
$2 = \frac{}{7}$	A fraction equals two wholes when the top is how many times bigger than the bottom?
	What is the bottom number of the fraction we're writing?
	So the top number must be two times bigger than seven. Tell me that number.
$2 = \frac{}{8}$	A fraction equals two whole numbers when the top is how many times bigger than the bottom?
	What's the bottom number of the fraction we're writing?
	So the top number must be two times bigger than eight. Tell me that number.

Following the practice with the clusters, the entire routine would be reintroduced. Note that we would follow the cluster remedy whether or not the program had provided for the teaching of clusters before introducing the routine. However, if the program had provided for such teaching, our correction of the chronic mistake would simply involve returning to the part of the program in which the clusters had been taught and firming the learner on them.

Summary for firming chronic errors that occur outside a sequence. We have presented a large number of examples of correction problems that occur outside an initial teaching sequence to demonstrate that the procedures for analyzing tasks and classifying discriminations will permit a fairly rigorous treatment of any discrimination mistake. The mistake occurs in response to a specific task or series of tasks. The constraints are the *wording* of the task, *form* of the example, and the *"meaning"* of the particular discrimination that is intended.

Creating the sequence involves classifying the type of discrimination called for by the task and creating an initial-teaching sequence for that type. In some cases, we alter the wording somewhat or change the nature of the examples. However, we return to the original wording after the learner is firmed on the variant task form. (We can use a variation of the double-transformation program for achieving this transition.) The final step of the firming is to return the learner to the activity in which the chronic mistake originally occurred. The proof of the firming is that the learner can perform

Section VIII | Diagnosis and Corrections

within the juxtaposition pattern of tasks presented by the original activity.

Correcting Chronic Response Problems

The situations in which *response firming* is needed parallel those in which discrimination firming is implied. The chronic mistake may occur within a sequence or activity that is designed for initial teaching, or in some activity that is not designed for initial teaching. When a chronic problem occurs in an initial-teaching sequence: (1) the learner is not performing acceptably on at least 70 percent of the trials; and (2) the poor performance is persistent. When the response problem occurs outside the initial-teaching situation, the learner does not perform an activity acceptably because a particular response is: (1) omitted from the activity or (2) produced unacceptably. The problem is persistent.

The remedies indicated for the various cells in Figure 27.7 are not new. They have been outlined in earlier chapters. Their specific application to correction situations, however, is new. The particular remedy that is provided must be designed not only to correct the problem, but also to return the learner to the activity in which the problem occurred.

Remedies for Errors that Occur Within Response-Teaching Programs

As Correction I indicates, the problem may be that the learner cannot produce a response. There are two possible avenues for remedying this problem. We may change the response by simplifying it, or we may change the *criterion* for reinforcing the response. We should look first at the possibility of changing the response. We do this by:

1. Eliminating any complicated or unnecessary discriminations from the response chain.

2. Shortening the chain to the part that immediately precedes the part on which the error occurs.

3. Substituting the examples presented with those that are easier (in the sense that they can be processed through a wider variety of response options).

The elimination of the unnecessary discriminations improves the juxtaposition of practice examples and *focuses* the activity so the learner works with only that part that presents a problem. Shortening the chain improves the juxtaposition of practice trials. The use of

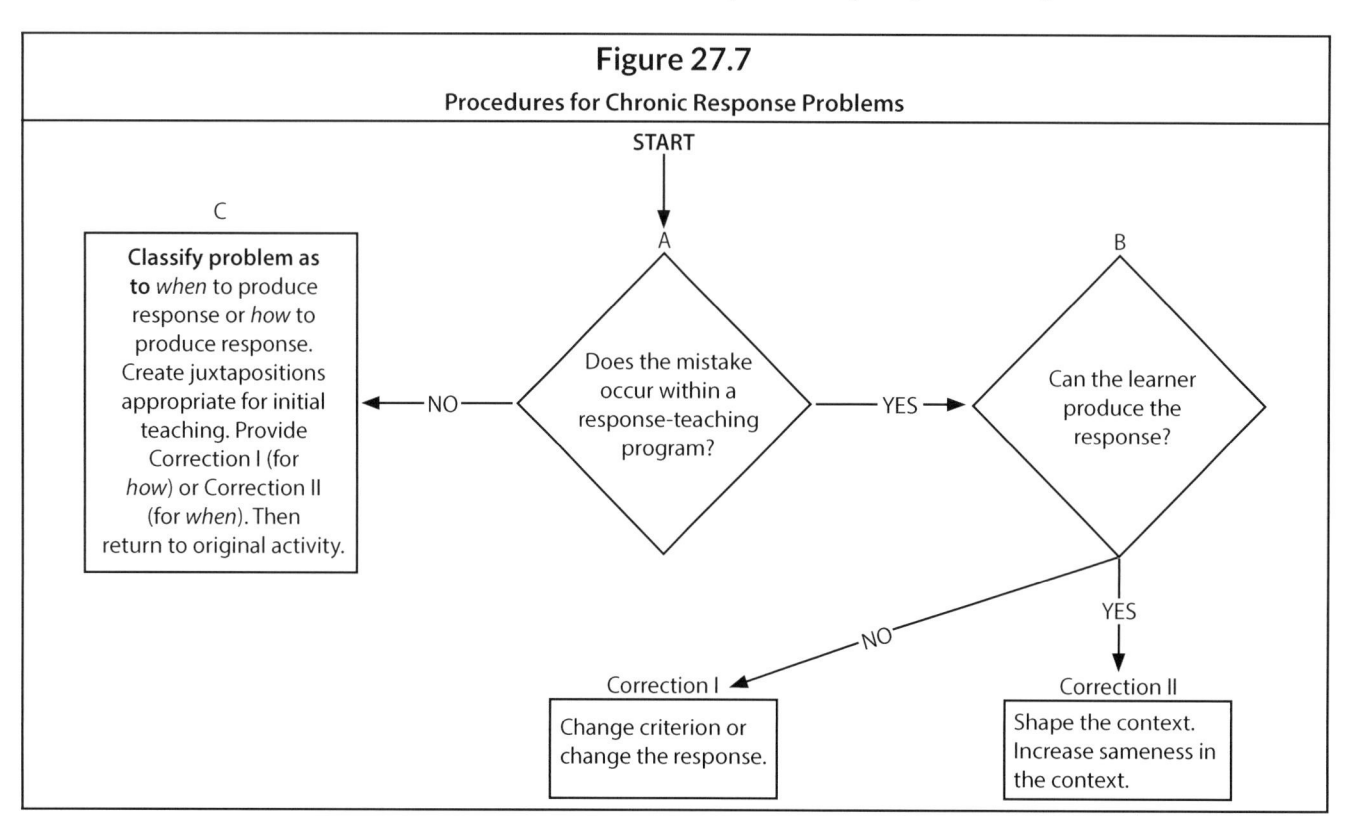

Figure 27.7
Procedures for Chronic Response Problems

START → A: Does the mistake occur within a response-teaching program?

- NO → C: Classify problem as to *when* to produce response or *how* to produce response. Create juxtapositions appropriate for initial teaching. Provide Correction I (for *how*) or Correction II (for *when*). Then return to original activity.

- YES → B: Can the learner produce the response?
  - NO → Correction I: Change criterion or change the response.
  - YES → Correction II: Shape the context. Increase sameness in the context.

easier examples assures that the learner will perform the operation more quickly on some examples.

The final step in the remedy for motor response problems is to shape the response from the simplified version described above to that which occurs in the response-teaching sequence.

The two avenues indicated by Correction I (change the criterion or change the response) are not exclusive remedies. We should consider the possibility of doing both. By changing the response, we redesign the activity so that it creates a greater possibility of success. In addition, however, we should adjust the criterion of performance so the learner succeeds (receives reinforcement) on at least 70 percent of the trials. The procedures for establishing such criteria are described in Chapter 22.

Correction II indicates the remedial steps implied if the learner can produce the response that is called for, but the response fails to occur in the program that is designed to teach the learner *when* to respond. The remedy involves two steps: shaping the context and increasing the sameness elements in the context. We use a variation of the 3-level strategy to shape the context. To increase the sameness across applications, we add unique behaviors to all examples. These behaviors may be perfectly irrelevant to any task. "Let's say that I walk up to you and say, 'Hi, what's your name?'" ... The introduction of this sameness ("Let's say that I walk up to you and . . .") has two functions. The first is to prompt sameness. (A unique and obvious behavior is attached to each presentation of the task; therefore, each presentation task must be the same and must call for the same type of response.) The second function of the added behavior is to create a non-failure set for the activity. Remember, the learner had failed this task repeatedly. The task is likely to be punishing. If our remedy is to be effective, we must create a reinforcing set. By using the added-behavior prompt with examples that are easy, we associate the prompt with reinforcement and success. If we present the same prompt with more difficult examples (those increasingly similar to the original activity with respect to context difficulty), we imply that these tasks are also relatively reinforcing. They have the same feature that predicts reinforcement with simpler tasks. After the learner has performed successfully with the sameness prompt, the prompt is dropped. Reinforcement continues and a positive set is created for the original activity.

Remedies For Problems That Do Not Occur Within Response-Teaching Programs

The problem that occurs outside the response-teaching program is either a problem of *when* to produce the response or *how* to produce the response. Therefore, the first step in effecting a remedy is to classify the problem. We then use the basic procedures specified for either Correction I (for how-to-respond problems) or Correction II (for when-to-respond problems). Finally, we return the learner to the original activity (which may happen automatically as part of the procedure for Correction I or Correction II).

Implying false operations. Perhaps the biggest potential problem that occurs if we do not create appropriate juxtapositions for firming responses is that we may *imply false operations.* False operations are implied if the juxtaposition of events suggests we are dealing with a motor response rather than a discrimination.

Consider this situation. The teacher points to an object and says, "What is this?"

The learner replies, "Du u car."

The teacher then works on the *response.* "Listen. *This is a car.* Say it with me . . . again . . . again . . . All by yourself, what is this? . . . Yes, what is this? . . . Yes, what is this . . ."

The correction implies a false operation. The question "What is this?" is repeatedly presented in a context of *saying,* not of discriminating between car and not-car. Therefore, the question "What is this?" implies saying words—not saying words that are based on the feature of the examples. The naive learner can therefore be expected to learn serious misrules about the nature of the response.

By creating appropriate juxtapositions, we solve the problem. We separate the discrimination from the elaborate response:

Teacher: What is this?

Learner: Car.

Teacher: Good. Say the whole thing.

Learner: Du u car.

Teacher: Not bad. Listen to me: This is a car. Listen again: This is a car. Say it with me. Get ready . . . This is a car. Again with me: This is a car . . . Pretty good. All by yourself. Say the whole thing . . ." etc.

The signal for the discrimination is "What is this?"

The signal for the motor response is "Say the whole thing."

The repeated trials of "Say the whole thing" can be presented without implying a false operation. (If the learner becomes confused, a series of "What is this?" tasks can be presented to demonstrate that the response for these is a single word or phrase.)

The inappropriate juxtapositions of responses and discriminations characterize many teaching activities. The learner may be reinforced for sitting properly, looking at the teacher, and other "proper" behaviors. When these responses are worked on repeatedly, a false operation is implied. The implied goal of instruction appears to be to sit with both feet on the floor, to look at the teacher, and to engage in other irrelevant activities. If the response of looking at the teacher is to be shaped in a way that does not imply a false operation, it should be framed in a way that *requires* the learner to look at the teacher. The formula is fairly simple:

1. Place a highly reinforcing contingency on *the discrimination* or skill that is to be taught.
2. Design the task so that the learner can perform only if the learner observes what the teacher does.

For instance, the learner may be inattentive while the teacher is pointing to different objects and asking "What is this?" Here is a possible solution:

"I'm going to go very fast. I'm going to point to different things and ask the question. If you get them all right, you get 10 minutes of extra recess. Here I go . . ." Now the learner has some functional reason for watching the teacher. Watching becomes a necessary step in getting extra recess. Given that the learner wants extra recess, the learner will watch. Of course, the teacher should adjust the task so that if the learner does watch and respond, the learner will succeed.

In summary, the problem of implying false operations is largely solved if we create juxtapositions that are appropriate. If the learner has problems in producing the response, work on the response production through tasks that do not imply discriminations (as in "Say the whole thing"). If the problem is one in which the learner can produce the response, but is not producing it, introduce a context that provides the learner with the appropriate reason for producing the response (as in the case of watching the teacher).

Creating a success set. Chronic response failures that occur in activities other than initial-teaching situations tend to make these activities punishing. For example, if the learner has had problems saying a series of addition statements such as, "Five plus one equals six; five plus two equals seven; five plus three equals eight," the learner may develop symptoms that are associated with chronic failure. These include: long response latency; frequent checks of the teacher's expression for confirmation of the response's correctness; and various superstitious or nervous behaviors.

Part of the correction should be to establish a positive set for the statement-saying. A solution for this aspect of the correction is an *add-on*. In addition to simplifying the operation and creating adequate juxtapositions, we create a new basis for treating all examples in a positive manner. For instance, we may press the learner's palm with one finger as a signal to say the first statement in the sequence; two fingers for the second statement; and three for the third. Or we may introduce some other behavior that is perfectly extraneous to the task, but that can be produced with all examples of saying a series of addition facts. For instance, "Hold your hands way over your head and get ready to say some statements." Or, "Close your eyes and get a picture of the statements you say."

The general rule is that if the easier examples and harder examples are the same in some observable ways, we can create add-on behaviors to imply that they are the same *in other ways that are not observed*. The diagram below shows how the implication is created:

Easy Examples	Hard Examples
Involve new behavior **A**.	Involve new behavior **A**.
Lead to reinforcement.	Therefore: they must lead to reinforcement.

Some traditional remedial procedures that involve using a new modality or combination of modalities tend to work, but not because of any direct influence of the new modality. When we introduce a new modality, we are actually requiring the learner to perform a new behavior (new behavior **A**). If the new behavior happens to be associated with success (which is what happens when the learner is taken back in the arithmetic program and is taught the new facts through multiple-modality inputs), the basic requirements for easy examples has been established. When more difficult examples are presented, particularly those that were formerly associated with chronic failure, the probability is increased that the learner will respond to the new prompt and approach these problems in a way that does in fact lead to success. The cause of the success is then falsely attributed to the introduction of new modalities, when the program simply introduced a new sameness that permitted the classification of all applications as "reinforcing applications."

Summary

The correction of a mistake occurs as an immediate response to the learner's inappropriate response to a task. The correction is designed to assure that the learner will perform correctly in subsequent presentations of the activity in which the mistake occurred. The correction may involve *non-chronic* or *chronic* mistakes. Different procedures are used for each type of mistake.

For correcting non-chronic *discrimination* mistakes, the teacher:

1. Models the correct answer.
2. Tests on the missed item.
3. Backs up several tasks or items and tests on the tasks in the order in which they were originally presented.

Step 1 provides the learner with information about the correct response; step 2 provides the most direct tests on whether the information had been effectively communicated to the learner; step 3 tests whether the learner is able to perform on the item when it is again placed in the context in which it originally occurred.

The 3-step firming procedure is used when a mistake occurs in any activity—an initial teaching sequence or some other activity.

For discrimination mistakes that are chronic, a more elaborate procedure is called for (because the simple firming procedure has apparently failed).

For correcting mistakes that occur within a sequence, we first determine whether the mistakes are predominantly of a particular subtype. If they are, we first firm on the original sequence, firm on one or more sequences composed entirely of the subtype (or predominantly of the subtype) and finally return to the original sequence.

If the mistakes are not of a particular subtype, the learner tends to miss items of different subtypes, which means that the learner has a general lack of understanding about the discrimination. To correct chronic mistakes of this type (high percentage of errors that do not involve the same subtype), we firm on the original sequence and firm on parallel sequences if necessary. Parallel sequences are those that require the same discrimination, and use the same wording, but present a different juxtaposition of items.

If the mistake occurs outside the sequence, we firm on the *task* in which the mistake occurred (using the 3-step firming procedure). We then construct a sequence that uses the task as the basis for the teacher wording and that presents the same meaning as the task. (If the task is a choice-response, the sequence is a choice-response. If the task is a production-response, the sequence presents production-response tasks.) The learner is firmed on the sequence and parallel sequences, after which the learner is returned to the original activity in which the mistake occurred.

If the mistake occurs within a cognitive routine, the firming may become elaborate and may resemble the preskill teaching that should precede the introduction of a cognitive routine. Juxtaposed steps of the routine may be presented as a *cluster*. More than one cluster may be designed. When the learner is firm on the clusters, the entire routine is presented and firmed.

In addition to discrimination mistakes, the learner may make response mistakes. The two basic types of response problems are those of not being able to produce the response acceptably, and those of not producing the response *when* it is called for. We have examined both types in earlier chapters. The new element that is introduced when we deal with corrections for these responses is that of potential punishment. If the learner is consistently failing at a high rate, the activity is likely punishing and the learner has probably developed avoidance behaviors and superstitious behaviors for dealing with the activity.

If the mistake occurs within a response-teaching activity, we should follow the usual procedure of shaping the response or the context. We should also try to change the activity so that it is reinforcing. The basic procedure for doing this is to *add some unique behavior to all examples.* If we start with easy examples, the unique behavior serves as a signal for a reinforcing activity. The implication is that when the behavior occurs with other activities, these activities are also reinforcing.

The same strategies apply to situations that are not designed to teach responses. We can create a success set by adding unique behavior to the tasks that involve the response and by assuring that the learner achieves a fairly high percentage of successful trials with these novel tasks.

The problem of appropriate juxtapositions is also important for response-teaching. The reason is that the context of a complex activity may imply a false operation. The repeated work on the response may convey the idea that the production of the response *is the operation* called for by a discrimination task. The remedy for this problem is to make sure that the part of the operation that involves a response is removed from the other parts and that there is a discriminable instruction for working on the response and a different instruction for "figuring out the answer."

Chapter 28
Program Revision and Implementation

Implementation involves a number of issues: (1) the field testing of material; (2) the training of teachers and aides; and (3) the use of data to monitor teacher and student performance. A full discussion of these issues is beyond the scope of this work. However, program implementation is relevant to the full development of programs. This chapter, therefore, describes a system of logically-based principles for achieving consistent implementation.

The Logical Ingredients

For implementation to occur, three ingredients are essential: (1) a *standard*; (2) *teacher behavior* that can be compared to the standard; and (3) expected *student outcomes*.

The standard is a very precise statement about what the teacher is supposed to do (according to the program) and the anticipated student outcomes. Note that the standard is not necessarily correct. The specified teacher behaviors may be inane and the predictions or assumptions about student outcomes preposterous. The standard serves as a standard only in the sense that it provides a basis for comparing the actual teacher behavior with that suggested by the standard and for comparing the actual student outcomes with those implied by the standard. The student outcomes may not be stated by the standard; however, they are implied by the activities the students are expected to do. If students work independently on a particular skill, the teaching provided for that skill by the program is assumed to be adequate.

Teacher behavior is the actual behavior we observe in the classroom. If the program is fully implemented, the assumption is that we would see teaching that corresponds precisely to the standard.

Student outcomes are the actual changes in student behavior. If the standard is accurate, the student outcome should be consistent with the predictions of the standard.

A model of an *ideal* implementation would look like this:

```
Standard        ⎤
   ↓            ⎥  No discrepancy
Teacher behavior⎦
   ↓            ⎤  No discrepancy
Student outcome ⎦
```

This ideal shows no discrepancy between the standard and the teacher's behavior and no discrepancy between the teacher behavior and the student outcome. In other words, the teacher behavior that we observe is perfectly consistent with the standard (predicted in every detail by the standard) and the student outcomes are those that are predicted. If this implementation were observed, the standard would be perfect in every respect and so would the teacher's performance.

If there are discrepancies between the standard, the teacher behavior, and the student outcomes, we can draw inferences about the nature of the problem. The following diagram shows a situation in which there is no discrepancy between the standard and the teacher behavior, but a discrepancy exists between the teacher behavior and the student outcomes:

```
Standard        ⎤
   ↓            ⎥  No discrepancy
Teacher behavior⎦
   ↓            ⎤  Discrepancy
Student outcome ⎦
```

This situation shows that *the standard does not work*. The teachers are performing in accordance with the standard; however, the predicted student outcomes do not occur.

Both diagrams above are greatly simplified, because they do not deal with the fact that both teachers and students exhibit a range of variation in performance. The following diagram shows a possible range of variation in teaching behavior.

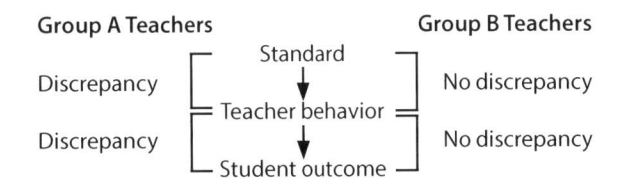

```
Group A Teachers                          Group B Teachers

                    ⎡    Standard     ⎤
Discrepancy         ⎢       ↓         ⎥      No discrepancy
                    = Teacher behavior =
Discrepancy         ⎢       ↓         ⎥      No discrepancy
                    ⎣  Student outcome⎦
```

Theory of Instruction: Principles and Applications

This model shows that the teachers who perform according to the standard (Group B) achieve the desired student outcomes; those teachers who do not perform according to the standard do not achieve the desired student outcome. The standard is valid. Those teachers who are not performing according to the standard need training.

The following pattern of teacher behavior leads to the conclusion that the standard is poor:

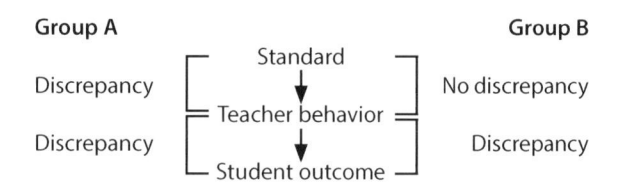

```
Group A                                          Group B
              ┌─ Standard       ─┐
Discrepancy   │         ↓        │   No discrepancy
              ├─ Teacher behavior ┤
Discrepancy   │         ↓        │   Discrepancy
              └─ Student outcome ─┘
```

Although there is a range of teacher behavior, the performance of students did not change in the predicted manner for teachers who follow the standard (Group B); therefore, the standard is poor.

Another model shows variability in student outcomes within teachers who implement:

```
    Standard         ┐
       ↓             │  No discrepancy
Teacher behavior     ┤
       ↓             │  Discrepancies with
Student outcome      ┘    some students
```

When teachers perform according to the standard, they achieve the desired student outcomes with some students, but not with others. The implication is that the standard is not fully valid. It must be modified if it is to work with all students. Note that the modification of the standard does not necessarily involve a prescription for all students. It may be that the revised standard specifies procedures for students who have trouble with particular tasks presented in the unrevised standard. The standard then specifies some new procedures for those students (specific "firming techniques," different forms of practice, etc.).

Another variation in the model shows that some activities within the program are invalid:

```
    Standard         ┐
       ↓             │  No discrepancy
Teacher behavior     ┤
       ↓             │  Discrepancy on
Student outcome      ┘    some activities
```

All students tend to succeed on some tasks and fail on others. The implication is that specific parts of the standard are faulty. These parts do not achieve the outcomes predicted from them, even though the teacher behavior is in strict accordance with the standard.

From all the situations we have described, we can draw specific implications about the validity of the standard. The reason is that in all variations, the teacher behavior corresponds closely to the standard. If the teacher behavior deviates from the standard, we are left with ambiguous information about the validity of the standard. Consider this situation:

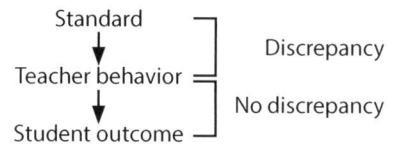

```
    Standard         ┐
       ↓             │  Discrepancy
Teacher behavior     ┤
       ↓             │  No discrepancy
Student outcome      ┘
```

Exactly what implication does the student outcome hold for the standard? The outcome does not show that the standard is *invalid*, merely that it is possible to achieve the desired student outcomes through a different standard (or the variety of standards that describe the observed teacher behavior). We do not know how effective the stated standard is because the standard is not tested in this implementation. The outcome, therefore, is not of great value for learning about the standard or about procedures for training teachers to achieve the specified behavior for that standard.

In the following model the teacher behavior does not correspond to the standard:

```
    Standard         ┐
       ↓             │  Discrepancy
Teacher behavior     ┤
       ↓             │  Discrepancy
Student outcome      ┘
```

The fact that the students do not achieve according to the standard provides us with no information about the potential of the standard to effect the desired student outcomes. The standard was not tested. The teachers used some other standard and the student outcomes show that the standard they used was ineffective in achieving the student outcomes predicted by the original standard. It would be appropriate, however, to judge the observed standard(s) (based on teacher behavior) on the basis of the observed student outcomes (just as it would be appropriate to judge the observed standards for the preceding example as being successful).

Is the Standard Manageable and Trainable?

Let us assume that we begin with the situation depicted in the last diagram. To test the standard in question, we train the teachers and provide whatever kind of monitoring of teachers we judge necessary to maintain their behavior in the classroom. We must use our best judgment about how to train. At this point, we are not immediately concerned with the student outcomes, merely with establishing teacher behavior that is specified by the standard.

By observing the variability in teacher behavior after training, *we can draw conclusions about the effectiveness of our training remedy.* Let us say that we exhaust different training and monitoring possibilities and none has a substantial effect on the teacher behavior. The teachers uniformly do not perform according to the standard.

Standard
↓   ] Discrepancy
Teacher behavior

Although a possibility exists that we are very poor at training, a more compelling conclusion is that our standard, regardless of its potential for teaching the student, is unmanageable and must be discarded or revised. There is little point in retaining a standard that we cannot reach through training.

After training on the standard, however, a different result may occur. Some teachers perform according to the standard and others do not.

Group A   Group B
Discrepancy [Standard ↓ Teacher behavior] No discrepancy

This situation raises questions about our standard and our teaching procedures. The fact that the training we used worked with some teachers permits us to take the next step of looking at student outcomes for the no-discrepancy teachers. If these students are not performing according to predictions, we would not retain the standard in its present form. If the teachers who teach according to the standard achieve predicted student outcomes, however, the implication is that the standard is valid, but that the training procedures do not work for all teachers. We would try to find better training procedures for the teachers who did not respond to the previous efforts.

A situation similar to the variability in teachers occurs if, after training, teachers generally perform on some activities or parts of the standard, but not on others.

Part A   Part B
Discrepancy [Standard ↓ Teacher behavior] No discrepancy

This outcome suggests that the teacher training for some components is weak. Possibly the weakness results from poor training techniques, possibly from an unmanageable or unreasonable standard. Before refining the standard or the teacher-training procedures, however, we should observe the student outcomes. If they are the outcomes predicted by the standard, refinement of weak parts of the standard or of teacher-training behavior for these parts is implied. However, if student outcomes for the non-discrepant students are not as predicted, the standard should be discarded.

The basic implementation strategy followed for all situations is to create a situation in which there is no discrepancy between the standard and the teacher behavior with at least some teachers or at least some tasks. Then we:

1. Compare the student performance on the no-discrepancy components with the predicted performance.

2. Respond to the information provided by these observations (producing teacher-training refinements, refinements in the standard, or both).

Without detailed knowledge of both the teacher performance and student outcomes, we cannot intelligently deal with specific possible weaknesses in either the training procedure or the standard.

Implementation Designed to "Shape" the Standard

Some implementations involve programs and training procedures that are not fully developed. These are field tryouts of programs. Simple procedures based on the discrepancy model can be used to "shape the standard" until it is workable. We save a great deal of time, however, if we begin with two assumptions about the standard. These assumptions are expressed as two constraints.

Constraint 1: The standard must specify or clearly imply teacher and student behaviors. It should specify the exact tasks the teacher is to present or the exact procedures that are to be executed. Unless the details of the standard are explicated in a manner that is apparent to a trainer and teacher, the standard will need further "shaping." If the standard merely indicates that the teacher will "carry on a discussion about a particular topic," there will be an unacceptable range of variation among teachers. The reason is logical. It is possible to "discuss" a topic in a way that will not induce the student outcomes called for by the activity. Therefore, the specification that the teacher should discuss is not sufficient.

Constraint 2: The standard must analytically account for the induction of the various student behaviors. In addition to being specific, the standard must be non-magical. We should be able to inspect it and determine that there are provisions for achieving the student outcomes. The program should provide teaching demonstrations, clear communications, tasks that deal with the topic, and provisions for practice. We should be able to see that preskills of complex tasks are identified and pretaught, and that the teaching at any given time does not seem burdened with new skills.

If the initial development of programs provides the degree of standardization and specificity suggested by the two constraints, many problems of implementation or field tryout are obviated, and the program will be close enough to being adequate to benefit from the field tryout.

Designing Field Tryouts

Field tryouts of instructional programs can be used to shape details of the program further and to provide information about what is needed for adequate teacher-training. To be successful, however, the tryout must not follow traditional procedures which use standardized tests, large samples, and modify the program according to *learning tendencies* of students. The traditional approach is inefficient and usually incapable of providing the designer with the type of information needed to modify the program intelligently.

Logical strategies for gathering tryout information are based on two assumptions about the nature of implementation:

1. The primary focus of all information gathering must be on failures, not on successes, and the information must permit us to investigate the cause of the failure. We must know the *qualitative* errors students and teachers make, because the only changes we make will be qualitative. All changes we will make will be designed to *improve* the program. We therefore need information about where the program fails. We will manipulate parts of the program that are associated with observed problems. We cannot manipulate the program intelligently if we know only that students tend to achieve a particular score on an achievement test, or even that they *tend* to miss a particular item. This information is merely a signal for us to secure more precise information about the mistake. Once we know the precise mistake in the context of the instructional situation, we can identify the causes of the mistake.

2. Our second assumption is that relatively lower performers make all the mistakes that higher performers make and additional mistakes that higher performers tend not to make. It follows that if the mistakes made by the lower-performing groups tend to include all mistakes made by higher performers, the lower groups provide the best information about program problems. Therefore, tryouts should concentrate on these groups. Low performing groups make the program problems and teacher-performance problems far more obvious than higher groups do. Higher groups may yield the error information at such a low rate that we cannot easily determine the pattern.

The two assumptions about implementation—the focus on faults and the idea that lower performers provide the best information about program weakness—determine the general orientation of the tryout. The design, perforce, will be different from that suggested by classical statistical evaluations. We are interested in *qualitative* problems. Statistics direct us to quantitative problems. We are concerned with the context in which a particular mistake occurs, because our assumption is that the events correlated with the mistake are possible causes of the mistake (or provide information about the causes). Statistical procedures (as they are traditionally used in tryouts) direct us away from such information. The manipulations that we will institute to correct mistakes have to do with specific wording changes and specific changes in responses, but aggregated data give us little information that helps us identify the specific types of changes that we should make.

The Too-Difficult Program

We can design a field tryout so that a relatively few teachers yield a great deal of information about the program. This goal is achieved if the program provides a high information yield and if the tryout employs efficient data-collection techniques.

To achieve a high information yield, *we violate our best guess about what would be perfectly appropriate for the learner.* We try to design the program so it errs in the direction of providing too little repetition and structure and of moving too fast for the "average" student who will use the program.

This strategy is important because *of the paradox of the perfect program.* If we design a perfect program and the field tryout information suggests that no students have trouble with the program, we do not really receive information that the program is perfect. We know only that it is easy for the students who use it. But why? Is the program far too easy for them? Would they have been able to progress at twice the rate? We have no basis for answering these questions. If we design the field-test program so that it does move too fast for some students, we have a basis for identifying the optimum rate of presentation for the final program.

By following a similar strategy, we can determine the extent to which preservice or inservice training is necessary for adequate teacher performance. Instead of providing all the information and training that we think should be necessary to perform in the program, we initially provide teachers with less information, so that we again err in the direction of providing what we feel is too little information. If all teachers perform perfectly following our training, we will not know whether our training was far too laborious or whether it was appropriate. If the training leaves some teachers in trouble, we receive precise information about areas in which training is needed.

Analyzing Failures

If teachers have trouble teaching a particular type of exercise, there are two solutions: (1) change the activity, or (2) provide training that permits the teachers to perform better.

A clue about whether training is needed is provided by teachers who follow the program closely. If these teachers succeed, the standard (program) is apparently manageable. Therefore, the problem probably has to do with training. If the only teachers who succeed *deviate* from the program, the standard is highly suspect. (There is still a possibility that training would remedy the situation; however, the successful teachers provide us with a solution that is probably more effective: change the standard.)

If most tasks in the program work as anticipated, teachers who succeed on some tasks and fail on others provide very articulate feedback about which tasks or activities are not well designed. Their performance on successful exercises in the program provides the teacher with baseline information about how well-designed activities should work. The teacher presents the exercises; the students respond as specified. Most students have no serious problems with the task, so no great amount of repetition and firming is needed. The poor task stands in stark contrast. The teacher cannot maintain good pacing on the activity, either because the task wording is awkward or because the students are not producing the desired responses. The task requires much repetition and firming. Because these tasks stand in contrast with successful trials, the teachers are generally quite accurate at identifying them as poor tasks.

The strategy of erring on the "too little" side does not mean that we leave the program or the teacher training this way. We want to find the *minimum set* of training activities and program activities that serves most teachers. We must revise as we learn about specific failures in the program.

Designing Lesson Blocks for Tryout

An efficient way to respond to weaknesses in the program is to develop the program in small chunks, perhaps 20 lessons at a time. If lessons are taught every day, 20 lessons should last teachers about one month. If problems with a particular strand or track within the program become evident early in the 20-lesson block, we can provide the teacher with replacement activities for those in the suspect tract. Providing substitute lesson parts for perhaps 15 lessons is far easier than providing replacements for an entire school-year program (140 to 160 lessons). If the problem emerges near the end of the 20-lesson block, we can design the lessons in the next block so they compensate for the problem. (Often, the type of compensation that we provide at this time is stop-gap. Our primary concern is that the teachers have lessons for every day they need them. Later, when we revise the program, we can integrate revised parts of lessons into a streamlined sequence.)

Some activities or procedures specified by the tryout program may have to be discarded or changed, even though the teachers who follow the specifications for these activities succeed. The program interacts with the training. We may discover that the amount of training needed to remedy the problem is impractical. Our choice is to modify the program or accept the fact that most teachers will not perform according to the standard. The most reasonable solution is to modify the program, because the activities are of no value if they are not communicated to the student.

Tryout Data

The goal of data in a tryout is to help identify flaws in a product, not to discover a population tendency. To identify flaws we use the type of tools that are implied by quality control. We inspect instruction through direct observations. We also augment this effort with data-collection tools. We respond to observed faults in instruction by providing quick responses, either in the form of replacements for parts of the program, or training.

Observations. During field tryouts, we observe the teacher working with groups of students. The observer should note:

1. Whether the teacher is following the specified procedures, and if not, what types of deviations occur.
2. Which activities are apparently unsuccessful because of task wordiness or some other problem with the standard.
3. Which activities are apparently unsuccessful because of poor student responses and other teacher-delivery problems.
4. Which activities are apparently unsuccessful because of sequencing or programming errors.

Note that errors in the program are inevitable. The program may schedule an introductory activity for too many days. The examples presented for some activity may not precisely fit the wording of the task. Necessary teacher directions may not have been included. *Careful observations of a few teachers should disclose nearly all these errors.* The simplest procedure is for the observer to sit with a copy of the program and follow along as the teacher presents. The observer marks each place at which the program is "lumpy." The observer does not try to solve the problems, but merely to report them. Observations of the problems predictably shape programs in the following ways:

1. We modify procedures that require the teacher to present a series of examples *using some material not provided by the program* (presenting a series of examples using a pencil to show **slanted, not-slanted**, for example). Although teachers can be trained to present these sequences, the training is difficult because tasks introduce variables not controlled by printed-page examples. Replacing the examples with a simplified presentation that appears on the printed page is a much more manageable alternative (even though the sequence may not be as precise for communicating with the students).

2. We reduce the number of variations in wording for a series of fades or covertizations of a particular activity. It is generally better to have fewer covertizations and to have each run longer than it is to have more frequent covertizations. From the students' standpoint, a greater number of covertizations is desirable; however, teachers have mechanical problems learning the subtle variations for activities that are highly similar.

3. We present a given procedure longer than is needed to teach the students. Two problems exist: (a) students are absent, and (b) teachers should be reinforced for following the program. If the program activities change too frequently lesson to lesson, teachers tend to be punished and often stop following the program precisely. If the program is as tightly sequenced as it should be for optimum instruction, students who are absent for a day or two tend to fall behind. In a traditional setting, absence does not present a problem because the program does not permit teaching to mastery. A tight program sequence, however, makes the returning student's deficiencies apparent and frustrating. The situation can be appeased somewhat if there is unnecessary repetition in the program.

Error data. The basic assumption about diagnosing errors is this: If the teacher follows the program and if the students have trouble with specific items, the program is faulty and must be changed. For error data to be of value, therefore, we must know that the teacher follows the specifications of the program. The teacher must not tell students answers when they are working independently. If the teacher helps students, their worksheet performance does not reveal performance problems; furthermore, it does not imply what students know about attending to the teacher presentation, retaining the information, and applying it to independent work.

The analysis of errors on the worksheet reveals items that tend to be missed more frequently than other items. The more frequently missed item may be poorly worded or may present "unusual" examples. The students may have answered correctly, but the scoring key may not consider their answers correct. This type of problem is common in field-test programs. For example, a story for a field-test teaching program told about Joe Williams, who is a red, number 4, wide, felt-tipped pen. The item: "What was Joe Williams?" The item is poor because the scoring options are enormous. To solve the problem, a series of items replaced the original: "What color was Joe Williams? What type of tip did he have? . . ." A range of acceptable responses still exists for the second question; however, the range is substantially reduced.

The best instrument for recording error data on worksheet exercises is a copy of the student worksheet. The use of a coding procedure helps the recorder to classify the different types of errors. Separate tallies should be kept for NR (no response) and for each substantive type of error. Those errors that cannot be classified as a type should be recorded. The worksheet page in Figure 28.1 shows error summary for ten students on a worksheet. All items that are missed by more than 20 percent of the students receive scrutiny (item 9).

A second check on item problems comes from the analysis of the high-performing students. The probability is high that any items they miss are weak items. If we use six high performers as our target group, we simply note any items that are missed by two or more students in this group. Usually these will be items missed by many other students. Responses of higher performers often give clues about the cause of the problem.

The percentage of all students missing an item provides a general warning signal that an item may be poor. However, the fact that a high percentage of students misses a particular item does not imply that the item is poor or that it should be changed. A 25 percent error-rate may not represent a serious problem, particularly if it occurs on the first day that a new skill has been transitioned to independent work. Often, students' error-rate on similar items drops to 10 percent on the following day. The 25 percent item might warrant no more than bonus points for students who make no mistakes on the newly-transitioned items (which are marked with stars on the worksheet).

Teachers' verbal reports about program problems. In addition to direct observations of teaching and error data, teacher verbal reports provide information about program problems. An interesting phenomenon associated with programs that are well-designed is that teachers who have never taught effectively before being involved in the tryout can, with a minimum of training, tell about tasks or activities that are relatively poor. They may be wrong about the *cause* of the problem; however, their identification of weak tasks is surprisingly accurate and reliable.

The reason is that the teacher is provided with a baseline against which to measure the effectiveness of various tasks. Given that most of the tasks in the program are reasonably well-designed and that the teacher follows them fairly closely, the teacher learns very quickly about how students respond to these tasks. For the poor tasks, the pacing is wrong, the students do not respond in the specified manner, and corrections are awkward. The teacher does not receive good information from traditional programs because these programs do not provide well-designed tasks that serve as a baseline for judging poor tasks.

Summary: Designing Field Tryouts

If we start with the assumption that the teachers and students will provide us with information about the weaknesses in our program, we can use field-tryout information to shape the program. We must design our information-gathering techniques so that they are sensitive to *problems*. The techniques must then identify them quickly and accurately. We must then respond by remedying the program.

Weaknesses in the standard or program specifications are indicated by unpredicted student outcomes. If the students do not learn the intended discriminations or skills, the program does not work. For this judgment to be valid, however, we must know that the teachers are following the program specification, or trying to. If they are trying but are unable, we must consider redesigning

Section VIII | Diagnosis and Corrections

Figure 28.1

The pilot took off and flew to Japan. She left her plane and took a vacation. She went to a place where there was a water wheel. Every second, one liter of water hit the blades of that wheel. How much weight is that? <u>(1 gram)''' (1 pound) (5 kilograms)</u> Around the water were insects that were born in the water and sucked blood.

What kind of insects were those? <u>(NR) (flea)</u>
The pilot stayed away from those insects. Why did she stay away from them? <u>Because she didn't like them.</u>
She had a nice vacation.

7. Look at the map.
   a. What part of the world is shown on the map? <u>South America</u>
   b. The map shows how far apart some cities are. Some cities are two thousand kilometers apart and some cities are four thousand kilometers apart.
   - Write **2** in the box if the line stands for two thousand kilometers.
   - Write **4** in the box if the line stands for four thousand kilometers.

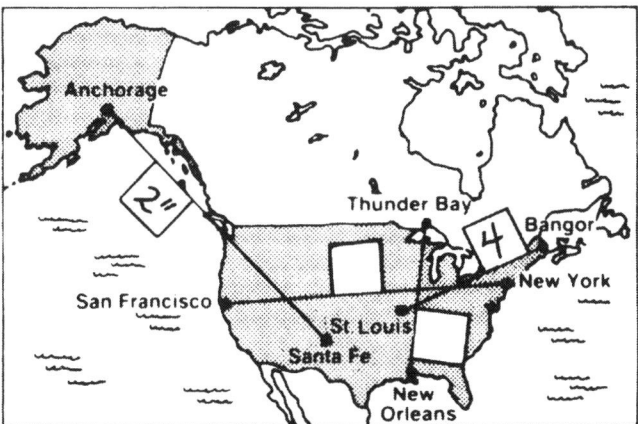

8. **Figure out what is being described.** It is made to carry passengers. It is a very large ship. It has a prow, a stern, decks, and bulkheads.

   What is it? _____

9. Name five insects. ① <u>spider</u> '''   ② _____
   ③ _____   ④ _____   ⑤ _____

From *Reading Mastery,* Workbook IIIB, by Siegfried Engelmann and Susan Hanner. Copyright ©Science Research Associates, Inc. 1982. Reprinted by permission of the publisher.

the standard so that it becomes more manageable. By designing the tryout so that both teachers and students will tend to make more errors (because the program moves too fast or provides insufficient information), we will discover precisely where additions are needed and what kind are needed. By analyzing error data, we identify weak parts of the program. We revise specific tasks and items. Through careful observations of teachers, we can shape the training for specific skills and skill clusters. If we continue to pursue the fairly simple procedure of attending to program failures, assuming that these failures are caused by inadequacies in the program, and changing the program, we will "shape" the details of the program until the program approximates a faultless one. Of course, it will never actually become faultless; however, the various details will have been improved and the program will certainly perform far better than the original.

The Role of Trainers

Training teachers is a microcosm of implementation. Like the larger implementation, training involves a *standard*, *behaviors*, and *outcomes*. The difference is that the standard is the specifications for preparing the teacher to teach; the behaviors are the behaviors of the *trainer* who works well with the teacher; and the outcomes are the changes in *teacher behavior* caused by training.

The same problems that characterize the larger implementation characterize the training program, and the same sorts of information shape the training program. Also, the same constraints are introduced to make the instructional program more manageable and to facilitate the training.

The training program is primarily concerned with inducing the desired *presentation behavior* in the teacher. The *standard* should provide clear specifications about how the teacher is to perform after training. The *training* should pass the test of logical inspection with respect to provisions for inducing the behaviors that are required. The training *should be standardized* with provisions for working with different types of teachers.

The most sobering constraint for training is *time*. Typically, a trainer must work with as many as 20 to 30 teachers. This situation is parallel to one in which one teacher must work with 20 to 30 students. The available time must be used efficiently if substantial teaching is to occur.

Effective training is possible only if the instructional programs used by the teachers are standardized across all teachers. We will arrive at this conclusion if we seriously pursue training in a situation that permits each teacher to use a different program to achieve instructional objectives. Here are facts about this situation:

1. If the tasks designed by the teacher are poor, they must be changed before the trainer works on specific presentation behaviors. We cannot work on presentation behaviors if the best possible presentation will lead to student failure. Working with poor tasks will provide the teacher with very poor information about presentation variables and about what the students are capable of learning. The tasks must have the potential to communicate unambiguously.

2. The probability is great that the trainer would have to repeat *the same basic program remedy* with different teachers. If one teacher has problems designing a program to teach a specific skill, other teachers will experience the same problem. The mistake patterns for teachers parallels that for students. If one tends to make a particular mistake, others will make the same mistake.

3. When different program sequences are used in different classrooms, the trainer is provided with no warning signals about which teachers are falling seriously behind in the rate at which they are teaching skills.

4. The possibility of the trainer responding to problems quickly is further reduced because of the time associated with remedying the teaching problems. First the trainer must specify program modifications; then train the teachers in the execution of appropriate procedures; then monitor the tasks. If this process is to work with teachers who use various programs, extensive monitoring is required in each classroom to determine precisely what each teacher is teaching and the effective rate of skill teaching.

5. The work that the trainer does on program modification does not relieve the trainer of working on specific presentation behaviors.

In this situation, the trainer will fail. The trainer will not receive adequate information about the nature of problems, will not be able to work on common training problems, and will certainly not be able to fix up the sequences the various teachers design.

If the program is standardized, the situation becomes far more efficient. Ideally, the program is divided into lessons, each of which can be handled by the average teacher in a specified period of time. Ideally, all tasks in the program are manageable, which means that the teacher should be able to achieve the responses that are specified without having to repeat them an inordinately great number of times. Ideally, all responses and teacher behaviors are specified in a way that presents no ambiguity.

The advantages of a standardized program are:

1. The trainer has pre-knowledge of tasks in the program that are typically failed by teachers. The trainer knows that teachers need training in the specific behaviors called for by these tasks. The trainer also knows that the teacher's presentation of potentially troublesome tasks should be monitored in the classroom.

2. Efficient classroom monitoring is possible because the trainer does not have to look at entire lessons, merely parts that provide the most information about the teacher's problems. The trainer can use the lessons as a guide for scheduling classroom observations.

3. With the removal of program-development responsibilities, the trainer's basic job is now reduced to working on presentation behaviors; a job that is made even easier if the program is well designed and does not have a great many rough spots.

4. The content of in-service training can be responsive to the more common problems the teachers are experiencing. If teachers tend to have trouble with specific procedures or tasks, the trainer can work on these relatively effectively *in a large group*, rather than individually. The group work represents a great time savings.

5. The fact that the rate of teaching can be reliably expressed in terms of *lessons taught* implies that projections can be made on the basis of lessons. By comparing the number of lessons taught by a teacher with the number of available school days, the trainer can quickly determine whether teachers are progressing at the projected rate.

6. Assessing the progress of teachers (and students) is easier because *lessons serve as mastery tests*. If we wanted to know, for example, whether a student has skills that were taught by lesson 60 in a program, we would simply sample skills that appear in a lesson (tasks similar to those presented on lesson 60). Formal mastery tests can be designed so they indicate the lesson range in which a student would be appropriately placed; however, a quick observation of the teacher reveals the mastery level of students.

Training is necessary for good implementation. If the district or school does not provide for relevant training, no vehicle exists to assure that teachers are taught to the standard of the program, or that they are required to meet criterion of student performance.

Implementations of "Final" Programs

The purpose of the field tryout is to shape the standard (the program). After the program has been revised and the training procedures have been refined, the program is implemented on a broad scale. This implementation is similar to the field tryout in some ways. The focus remains on failure and on efficient techniques for identifying failure. Usually, the remedies provided for failure will not involve great changes in the standard, but will be teacher-training remedies. For some students, the program may move too slowly, implying acceleration of part or all of the activities. Some groups may need firming or repetition in addition to that provided by the program. These and similar problems constitute the main focus of the implementation; however, modification of program sequences is also undertaken. (The program may have mistakes that somehow slipped through the field tryout—a situation that is more common than program designers like to see.)

The major difference between the typical on-site implementation and the tryout of an instructional sequence is the availability of knowledgeable trainers. If we are to use titles as a guide, we would conclude that the school districts have people who can serve as trainers (curriculum specialists, etc.). However, these people typically have no training expertise and no precise knowledge of program development. If training and monitoring are to succeed in typical school settings, most of the monitoring and training functions must be performed by personnel who have limited training skills—building supervisors, school psychologists, and people in similar roles. Here are general guides for effectively using available personnel and outside trainers.

1. If possible, use experienced trainers who have detailed understanding of teaching the program for formal training sessions (preservice training). Preservice should give the teachers practice in the actual behaviors or procedures that are called for by the first part of the instructional program they are to use. (Note that there is no pressing need to train teachers in skills or procedures that occur late in the instructional program. The teachers will probably forget the procedures before using them. Over practicing the early program procedures is more efficient. If these procedures are nearly automatic—at least in mock-presentation situations—the teachers will be in a far better position to present in a classroom situation.) Preservice training should not be handled by people who are unfamiliar with the program. Inexperienced people cannot identify potential problems of teaching pacing, corrections, praising, and various mechanical details.

2. Train *on-site personnel* for performing classroom monitoring and specifying routine remedies. Principals and others not familiar with the program can provide a very useful program-implementation function by monitoring classrooms and observing what the teachers do. The facts below suggest how an inexperienced person can serve a useful program-implementation role.

   a. *The skills that are observed tend to be those maintained by the teachers.* If the pacing of teachers is observed on a regular basis, teachers will tend to maintain better pacing. If the teachers' scheduling of time is observed, teachers will tend to maintain more exact time schedules.

   b. *Observations do not always support teachers' verbal reports.* Some teachers report that things are going quite well; however, observation discloses serious presentation problems. If we assume that things are going well in a particular classroom and therefore do not monitor it, we will make serious mistakes.

   c. *Many performance problems result from violations of very basic procedures.* Perhaps the most typical problem causing poor student performance is an inadequate daily schedule. The teacher is trying to teach the program in unreasonably short or infrequent periods. Often, the remedy is appallingly simple and involves starting earlier, specifying large-group instruction, or opening activities, etc.

As the facts suggest, people who are not familiar with details of teacher-training or program design can be effective in three broad areas:

1. They can demonstrate there is real interest in specific areas of teachers' performance. They can reinforce teachers who attend to these areas.

2. They can deal with simple problems—scheduling, basic classroom management procedures, and mechanical problems.

3. They can *identify* problems that are serious (without solving them). The monitor can report these problems to a trainer.

Unless the monitor observes frequently, the monitoring role is not very effective. When behavior problems have escalated or students have been mistaught a difficult skill, remedies are awkward. To assure that the monitoring goes quickly, each classroom should be set up so that basic program information is immediately accessible to the monitor.

Key information should be posted in the classroom. The posted information includes the *daily schedule* and *error data of students* (or points earned) for each major subject. This information tells the observer:

- What the teacher is supposed to be doing at the time of the observation (according to the schedule).

- Whether the teacher has been teaching a "lesson" each school day (inferred from the number of lessons on which there is error data for the students).

- Which individual students or which instructional groups tend to have trouble (or are progressing relatively slowly).

- Which activities tend to be missed by a relatively high percentage of students.

To augment the information that is provided by the posted data, the classroom monitor should identify possible serious flaws in the teacher's presentation. By watching the teacher teach, the observer can identify these types of gross problems:

- The teacher is not doing the activities called for by the schedule.

- The teacher does not follow lesson script.

Section VIII | Diagnosis and Corrections

- The teacher's pacing is poor.
- The teacher ignores student errors (instead of correcting immediately).
- The teacher does not reinforce students.
- The teacher has serious management problems.

Some problems call for a trainer. Others, however, can be solved by another teacher. If the monitor knows that teacher **B** works with the same sorts of children as teacher **A**, and that teacher **B** does not experience some of the problems that teacher **A** has, the monitor may be able to arrange for teacher **B** to take over **A**'s group. After **B** has taught them (and **A** has observed the teaching), **A** receives assignments about holding the students at the level of performance established by **B**.

If the problems observed are serious and cannot be handled by on-site teachers, outside trainers should be brought in as quickly as possible. (Sometimes they can specify remedies on the phone; however, they cannot usually provide a perfectly adequate remedy unless they observe the problem.)

Performance Testing

Traditional evaluation with standardized achievement tests has only an oblique place in systematic instruction. The tests are quite poor because they are designed from an aptitude model, which means that the items on a particular test bear no necessary relationship to what is taught in the classroom. Items are included on the test if they spread the distribution and exaggerate the individual differences (creating a normal distribution curve). This type of test may play a role in categorical funding (determining on a "norm" basis whether a particular student qualifies for a program for mentally retarded). The standardized nature of the tests may also serve to provide a district with some universal yardstick for comparing the performance of students in the district with others. (We cannot readily compare the students in different districts if we use different tests or if we used tests that used with one group do not correlate highly with the tests used with the comparison group.)

Norm-referenced evaluation (the type provided by the standardized tests) is not appropriate for designing quality-control measures. *Primary measures used to evaluate instruction must identify failures that may not be obvious to the monitors.* If a monitor makes efficient use of time, the monitor will certainly miss some problems, because the monitor will not observe all teaching activities. The teacher may be "helping" the students on their independent work. The error data are low, which suggests the students are learning well, and observations in the classroom may not disclose the problem.

To identify problems that may be missed by monitors, we use *criterion-referenced measures*. These measures should be designed so they test what is taught and should be correlated with the program the teachers use. For instance, if a skill is introduced on lesson 50, it would be possible to test the skill before the students reach lesson 60. The test items should be the same type of examples provided by the program. This type of test is a *continuous progress test*. It is the most useful test for program implementation because it identifies specific problems and clearly implies what must be done to remedy these problems.

1. It suggests whether the teacher is inadequately firming students. If the posted lesson in the classroom is always ahead of the performance on the continuous test, the teacher is not adequately firming students. For example, the posted information shows that the teacher has taught lesson 60. The test of student performance, however, reveals that the students generally cannot perform on skills introduced after lesson 40 in the program. The teacher is teaching 20 lessons beyond the performance level of the students. *The implied remedy is for the teacher to return to the lesson at which the students perform and to teach to a higher criterion of performance.*

2. Test results also imply whether individuals within a group are being firmed. If one or two children in a group consistently do not score at the lesson range the teacher is presenting, these children are not being taught in the group. The remedy is to provide additional teaching for these children—perhaps transferring them to a different group.

3. Also, the tests can be used to draw conclusions about specific tracks or groups of related exercises in the program. If students score many lessons behind the lesson being taught in one track, the teacher must be provided with techniques that permit more consistent firming within this track.

4. A parallel set of inferences derive for skipping groups of students ahead in the program, skipping individual students, and for skipping specific tasks in the program. If tests show that the group is ahead of the lesson on which the teacher is teaching, the group may be skipped.

(Note that this remedy does not always follow from the fact that the group performs on a higher lesson than the teacher is presenting. Some skills, such as reading, are not merely "teaching" new information, but are providing practice. If the practice is to facilitate reading fluency, the material that is read should be relatively easy, which means that the students would be able to perform on a higher lesson than the teacher is presenting. Typically, students should perform 20-40 lessons beyond the one that is being taught. Moving students to the point at which the learner can just manage the material is not a good strategy.)

5. Trends across different teachers show teacher problems and difficult tasks. If teachers tend to have problems with a particular task, a group remedy is implied. Teachers should be trained to teach the track. If only a small percentage of teachers have problems with a particular track, an individual remedy is implied. Some one-on-one training is needed and perhaps it can be provided by another teacher.

In summary, continuous tests do not provide norms, but document the extent to which the program delivers the skills it is supposed to deliver. The tests provide trainers and monitors with back-up information about problems or failures. If used properly, continuous tests can provide timely information about teachers who need additional training, groups that are weak, individual children who are not properly placed in the program, and parts of the program for which additional training is needed. They can also be used to provide long-range projections of student performance. By extrapolating on the basis of the teacher's effective rate of teaching (lessons mastered during so much time), we can determine how far the teacher will get by the end of the year. (If a group has mastered 60 lessons in 80 school days, we would project the group to master 130 lessons by 160 days, the end of the year.)

Other tools help the implementation and monitoring processes. Monitors should keep records of when they see teachers and what sorts of comments or assignments they provide the teacher. The monitor's summary of teacher observations should be kept in a log, so that the trainer or monitor can follow up on a regular basis and can provide those teachers who need more help with more frequent visits.

Copies of assignments or comments should be left with teachers, perhaps on a type of teacher-performance summary form. Figure 28.2 shows a possible form. Note that it has places for assignments and for checking the various behaviors that are being monitored.

Additional tools and more sophisticated ones may be used in implementation; however, their purpose must not be subverted. Continuous test information is

---

Figure 28.2

TECHNICAL ASSISTANCE FORM

Observation of: Date: Subject: Arithmetic   Language   Reading

Observer: Lesson: Level: I II III

IMPLEMENTED > Formats _____   Reinforcement _____   Individual turns _____
WELL!   Signals _____   Correct non-responding _____ End-of-lesson
               Pacing _____   Correcting errors _____   Individual test _____
                                                                  Firm-up _____

                                    Will check back (date)

Assignment:
_____
_____
_____
_____

Checked back on:
_____

valuable if it is received currently. Remedies based on problems that have existed for months are not intelligent remedies. Teacher performance forms and summaries of monitor's visits are useful only if they are used to identify problems and to solve them. All tools and procedures must reflect the basic theme of implementation, which is to identify failures and problems—and to respond to them quickly.

The Corrective Reading Program—A Case History

The development of SRA's *Corrective Reading Program* illustrates the use of tryout strategies to refine the program and to identify teacher-training needs.

Phase 1 of the program's development involved four groups of students, most of whom were in junior high schools. Four co-authors of the program taught groups of students and trained and monitored several other teachers.

The initial version of the program was designed to provide information about how much the student behavior would change if students received directed practice in reading stories. This version of the program contained only the simplest instructions about management, and no teacher-directed word-attack exercises (work with words not in the context of the stories). Stories were developed according to the error analysis of students. The early stories focused on regular words (those that have clear sound-symbol relationships for all letters). Later, stories attempted to provide practice on specific words the students confused, such as **big** and **dig**. (Several stories about "The Bug That Dug" focused specifically on **b** and **d**.) A series of stories involving "Chee" presented fairly heavy practice on those words and strategies that were most difficult for students. Chee was a dog who spoke in gibberish when she became flustered, uttering such things as, "Oh, to do so if go what then there who where." The words that appear in these sentences are those the students tended to miss the most.

The stories failed to change some aspects of the students' behavior. Additional stories were interpolated into the original sequence of stories and a second wave of students began the program. When the error patterns of the students showed which behaviors were *still* changing at an inadequate rate, word attack exercises were introduced. These exercises focused on the most frequently missed words that the students read in the context of the stories. The addition of the word attack exercises represented an educated guess about what would be needed to change some of the behaviors that persisted.

The next tryout wave focused on complete training for teachers—a management system with points, complete word-analysis exercises, and training presentations on management.

Later research by Linda Meyer (1979) suggests that some of the correction procedures specified in the edition of the *Corrective Reading Program* (the fourth major revision of the program) are not entirely satisfactory from the standpoint of teacher training or of student performance. Other improvements in the sequences, the stories, and the word-attack exercises have been suggested by specific program problems. In all, however, the strategies used to develop the program were quite efficient. The initial tryout disclosed the number of errors students made on words like **a** and **the**, **what** and **that**. It showed that, typically, more than a thousand practice trials were needed before the students performed at a highly accurate level when reading these words in sentences. The tryout showed the consistency of progress across students of different ages (showing that the older students require more practice to learn how to decode accurately). The tryout suggested words and word-families that should be practiced. It demonstrated the typical problems that the teachers had in presenting exercises to students, and it implied the kind of training or orientation that teachers needed to present the program. The field tryout, in other words, shaped the specific content presented to the students, shaped the kind of tasks the teacher was to present, and shaped the communication needed to train or orient a teacher.

The tryout for the *Corrective Reading Program* relied heavily on empirical data because there is no prima-facie or logical way to determine the difficulty students will encounter when trying to relearn accurate decoding. The initial development of a new-teaching program relies far less on empirical information and more on the analysis of the skills; however, a new-teaching program should go through the same sort of shaping received by the *Corrective Reading Program*. It should be put through the type of test that shows which parts of it work, which do not, and why some parts do not. The tools needed to document the performance of the teachers and students are those that show specific errors and when they are made. Tools needed for the trainer are those that permit the fastest, most effective observations of teachers.

Microcomputers

If a program is standardized, we can identify problems with the program (inadequacies of the standard) and deficiencies of the teacher behavior. Without standardization, we lose information. With the loss of information goes a loss of ability to respond intelligently to problems. When the program is standardized we know where it is weak, which parts present problems, and where both teacher and student failure will most likely occur. *Standardization begets simplified procedures for teaching and training.*

Microcomputer technology is capable of achieving greater standardization, of eliminating many teacher-presentation problems, and of providing a better medium than the printed page. The computer terminal can display continuous changes, pace presentations very precisely, and respond to a variety of contingencies that are not easily handled through the medium of the printed page.

The model below shows how the computer simplifies implementation:

Standard—teaching
↓
Student outcomes

No discrepancies can exist between the standard and the teaching because the standard and the teaching are inseparable. A variable has been eliminated from the implementation paradigm. The microcomputer has incredibly great potential for achieving standardized excellence, if the technology of instructional communication is intelligently combined with the computer technology.

At the present, computers are used primarily for drill and practice. This application may be reasonable, but certainly does not exploit the potential that computers have for eliminating teacher-presentation variables (including training variables) for exercises that are difficult to present. Higher math, physics, sophisticated comprehension skills, and similar activities are typically very difficult for teachers to present. However, a very realizable possibility is a computer presentation that could convey these difficult communications in a nearly faultless manner.

Summary

For field tryouts to be successful, they must identify problems and they must do so efficiently. By identifying the *standard*, the *teacher behavior*, and the *student outcomes*, we become aware of the logical problems associated with drawing conclusions about the program.

- If teachers do not perform according to the standard, the outcomes cannot tell us about the program that is being implemented.
- If extensive training does not bring the teachers' behavior into compliance with the standard, we can assume that the standard is unreasonable and should be changed.
- If teachers who perform according to the standard achieve the predicted student outcomes, the standard is reasonable.
- If parts of the standard are consistently failed by teachers who perform according to the standard on other parts, the standard must be revised or training must be provided for the weak parts.

By taking into account the pattern of teacher behavior and the pattern of outcomes, we can draw inferences that shape the standard and shape the training program. The field tryout will tell us which parts of the standard are weak, and it will suggest specifically how those parts are weak. Similarly, the tryout will imply what kind of training is needed.

Training procedures are shaped in the same manner that the program is shaped, because the implementation of training parallels that for student instruction. Like the instructional program, the training procedures become standardized as we receive information about the types of training problems that exist and the range of individual variation among the teachers to be trained. The outcomes suggest the parts of our standard that are weak and the parts of the trainers' behaviors that are deficient.

The data collection tools used in a sensible tryout are those that provide the most detailed information about what is going on. If we observe problems, we assume that they are the product of our standard or of our teacher training. Without observing the events that are correlated with specific problems, however, we will not have the type of information needed to draw qualitative conclusions about problems.

If we know only that the students missed an item, we may assume that the program caused the problem, but we do not know the cause because we do not know the specific mistake.

If we know the type of error the students made, however, we have much more specific information about how the program or training failed.

To secure the maximum amount of information, we try to work with teachers who will disclose problems at a reasonably high rate. These are relatively unsophisticated teachers who work with lower-than-average students.

We also design the program so that it is slightly less structured and faster-moving than we think it should be. To establish a reasonable rate for the revised program, we must have this information about the program limits.

For implementation of a program that has already been shaped through field tryouts, training and monitoring are needed. Both must be designed from the standpoint of quality control. They must focus on failure. They must be designed to identify problems quickly and in a way that implies a remedy.

A great deal of monitoring can be handled by a staff that does not have extensive teaching or training skills. Their classroom observations of a lesson disclose whether:

1. The teacher has been teaching at the prescribed rate (based on the number of the lesson being taught).

2. The teaching follows the standard (based on the teacher performance).

3. The students are responding as the program predicts.

The tools that are needed for such monitoring are fairly simple. They include performance forms that are given to the teachers and information that is posted in the classroom—the schedule and the error data for different subjects being taught.

To identify problems that an observer misses, criterion-referenced tests are needed. The tests should be administered frequently. Their results provide information about trends and problems. When used with classroom-observation data, they permit projections of how far students will progress during the school year, which groups of children need special work, and which teachers need additional training.

When effective quality control measures are used, a school district has a basis for serving teachers and students. The formula works, however, only if all quality-control ingredients are present. The instructional programs must be standardized and must work well. Training must be provided for the teachers. Some form of classroom monitoring and continuous-progress testing must be used to provide current and accurate information about specific problems. Finally, there must be immediate responses to the observed problems. As ingredients are removed from this formula, the probability of a quality implementation decreases, very quickly reaching an unacceptably low level.

SECTION IX
RESEARCH AND PHILOSOPHICAL ISSUES

This section answers two important questions that have not been dealt within preceding sections:

What database is there to suggest that the principles and procedures derived from the stimulus-locus analysis are valid?

To what extent are the philosophical underpinnings of the analysis consistent with the assumptions of science (inductive reasoning) and logical analysis?

Chapters 29 and 30 present summaries of studies that are based on the major details of the stimulus-locus analysis. Note that these chapters provide only brief summaries of the studies and do not include all the available studies.

Chapter 29 deals with the details of communications (juxtapositions, range of example variation, overtness of steps for complex operation, and related variables).

Chapter 30 presents:

- Studies that diagnose instruction and identify learner problems that are implied.
- Studies that achieve outcomes that would not be predicted from normative data of subjects.
- Studies concerned with the teaching of generically new skills and that therefore involve application of both principles for inducing new responses and stimulus-locus principles.

Chapter 31 discusses key theoretical issues that influence details of the stimulus-locus analysis—the departures from a strict behavioral analysis, methods of analyzing sets of stimuli, the relationship of the analysis to historically prominent theory, and the theory's relationship to current theories of cognition and learning.

Chapter 29
Instructional Research: Communication Variables

Basic-Form Communications

The studies in the first section of this chapter clarify the role of specific communication variables on basic learning outcomes. The studies are based on the logical assertions of the stimulus-locus analysis. The analysis provides assertions about the role of positive examples, the role of negative examples, the nature of differences between positives and negatives, the prediction of generalizations on the basis of samenesses, the effects of stipulated sets of examples, and the importance of consistent teacher wording.

Only Positive Examples

A stimulus-locus assertion is that it is impossible to convey a given sensory discrimination through the presentation of only one concrete example. A related fact is that it is very difficult to convey only one interpretation if *only* positive examples are used. To test this assumption, Williams and Carnine (1981) compared a positive-only treatment (consisting of 12 positive examples and no negatives) with a positive-negative treatment that involves the same number of examples (8 positives and 4 negatives). Twenty-eight subjects received training on the discrimination "Gerbie," positive examples of which are angles between 0 and 110 degrees. The transfer test included both positive and negative examples, none of which had been presented to either group during the training. The positive-only group scored 50 percent correct on transfer items; the positive-and-negative group scored 88 percent correct. The difference is statistically significant.

Sameness

According to the principle for showing sameness, if juxtaposed examples differ greatly and are treated in the same way, interpolation is implied. A study conducted by Carnine (1980a) tested this principle by varying the range of positive examples presented to different groups. The stimulus-locus prediction is that the group receiving the widest variation would perform best on a test involving new (generalization) examples.

Forty-seven students in grades 2-5 who had some knowledge of fractions, but not of decimals, were randomly assigned to two groups. Both groups received the same number of demonstrations about how to convert fractions with denominators of 100 into their decimal equivalents. The Full Range group received demonstrations with three types of fraction-to-decimal conversions of this form:

$$\frac{X}{100} \text{ to } .0X \qquad \frac{XX}{100} \text{ to } .XX \qquad \frac{XXX}{100} \text{ to } X.XX$$

The Restricted Range group received demonstrations of only this type of conversion $\frac{XX}{100}$ to .XX

The transfer items were fractions not presented during training with a denominator of 100 and 1, 2, and 3 digit numerators.

The Full Range group successfully performed on 80 percent of the transfer items, whereas, the Restricted Range group performed correctly on only 36 percent of the transfer items (a highly significant difference).

Correlation Between Same Behavior and Same Features

According to the stimulus-locus analysis, sameness is shown by treating examples that are the same in the same way. The same treatment prompts the learner to discover how the examples are the same. If this tenet of the analysis is correct, communications that are not precise in treating examples of the same concept in the same way will not communicate as articulately as presentations that clearly treat the examples in the same way.

Williams and Carnine (1981) investigated the hypothesis with 22 preschool students divided into two groups. All received the same positive and negative examples of diagonal (called "Blurp"). Twenty pairs of examples were presented, each on a separate page. For one treatment, students were presented the same wording for all test examples: "Is there a blurp on this page?"

The other treatment presented different questions with different examples of **blurp**. "Is there a blurp here?" or, "Do you see a blurp?" or "Are there any blurps on this page?" or "Can you draw a circle around the thing that is *not* a blurp?" The prediction was that this treatment would tend to obscure the basic sameness.

Students receiving the treatment in which the same response was produced for all examples reached criterion (ten consecutive correct responses) in half as many trials as students who received different instructions—a highly significant outcome.

Continuous Conversion

According to the analysis of communicating with the learner, continuous conversions increase the obviousness of the difference between positive and negative examples. Gersten, White, Falco, and Carnine (1982) compared continuous and non-continuous conversion sequences in four different studies. In the first study, 40 preschoolers were randomly assigned to a continuous or non-continuous presentation of the concept **diagonal**. In the second study, 40 different preschoolers were randomly assigned to continuous or non-continuous presentations of **convex**.

The third and fourth studies were replications of the first except the students were handicapped. The examples in all four studies were the same for both the continuous and non-continuous groups. In the continuous-conversion treatment for **diagonal**, a line segment was rotated to generate positive and negative examples. In the continuous-conversion treatment of **convex**, a wire was moved to create positive and negative examples of **convex** and **non-convex**.

The continuous conversion groups met the criteria of performance in significantly fewer trials. For example, the continuous-conversion non-handicapped group in the **diagonal** study achieved criterion performance in 20.6 mean trials, whereas the non-continuous conversion group required 56.4 mean trials. The continuous-conversion non-handicapped group for **convex** required 10.5 mean trials, whereas the non-continuous conversion group required 15.8 mean trials. Again, all differences were statistically significant.

Effect of an "Irrelevant" Difference

The stimulus-locus analysis asserts that if only one difference occurs between positives and negatives, that difference must account for the labeling of the examples as positives or negatives. Stated differently, the presence of the same features in both positives and negatives logically rules out possible interpretations. Carnine (1976a) investigated the extent to which college students respond to these logical implications. Thirty-eight students were assigned to three treatments. The same artificial concept was presented in all three treatments. Geometric figures with one, two, or three points were treated as positive examples; and examples with four or five points were treated as negative examples. In one treatment, a dot pattern appeared in both positive and negative examples. Since this feature appeared in both positive and negative examples, the dot pattern could not logically serve as a basis for determining whether an example was positive or negative. In a second treatment, the dots appeared *only* in positive examples (figures with one, two, or three points). In the third treatment, the dots appeared *only* in negative examples (figures with four or five points). Transfer test performance indicated that subjects learned the generalizations consistent with the different presentations. When dots appeared in both positive and negative examples, dots were ruled out as a basis for the concept on almost 100 percent of the trials. Subjects responded only to the number of points. When dots appeared only in positive examples, almost 100 percent of the subjects responded to the *presence of dots* and responded at a chance level to the presence of points. Similarly, almost all subjects in the third treatment group (dots present only in negative examples) responded to the *absence of dots* on a transfer test (treating items as negatives only if they had dots). The findings indicate that subjects responded to the logical possibilities. Related studies have been conducted by Gibson and Robinson, 1935; Harris, 1973; Overing and Travers, 1967; Rosenthal and Zimmerman, 1973; Samuels, 1973; Williams, 1969.

A Test of the Minimum-Difference Principle

A negative example logically rules out the maximum number of interpretations when the negative example is *least different* from some positive examples. To test the extent to which subjects responded to this logic, Carnine (1980a) developed five sets of examples for the concept **on**. (In the study a nonsense label was used for the concept.) All had the same positives, but different negatives (see Figure 29.1). Set **A** showed the minimum difference between positive and negative, while Set

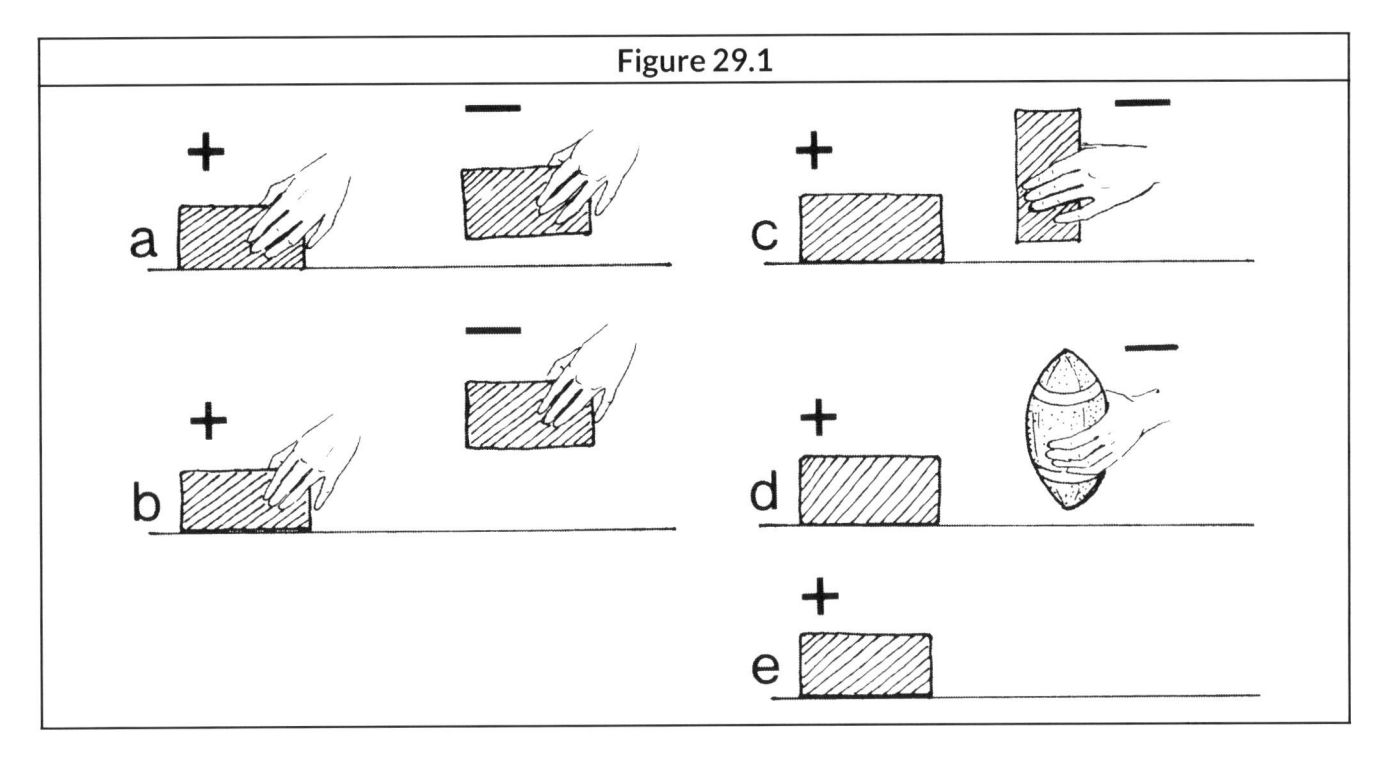

Figure 29.1

[Figure 29.1: Sets a–e showing positive (+) and negative (−) examples with hands manipulating blocks at various angles]

E contained *no* negative and therefore generated the largest number of possible interpretations.

Five groups of 13 preschoolers (65 children aged 4 to 6 years) received training, each group working on one of the sets of examples. After receiving a fixed number of demonstration examples, all children received a transfer test. Carnine found a significant linear trend between the similarity of positive and negative examples and correct response on a transfer set. Children presented with Set **A** examples responded correctly to 10.2 transfer items, while children presented with Set **E** responded correctly to only 5.0 transfer items. The trend clearly suggests that the greater the number of possible interpretations consistent with the set of training examples, the greater the probability that some students will learn an interpretation that leads to an "inappropriate" generalization (from the teacher's point of view).

The Setup Principle

Continuous conversion is logically superior to non-continuous conversion because if one example is converted into the next, only some details of an example are changed to create the next example. A number of features remain unchanged from example to example. If a change in example leads to a change in label (from negative to positive), whatever details remain the *same* are irrelevant to the change in label. If a change in example does not result in a change in label (the example staying either positive or negative), whatever details *change* are irrelevant to the label.

The setup principle is derived from this logic. This principle implies that a communication will be most precise if the maximum practical number of details remain the same in all positive and all negative examples within the initial communication.

Tennyson, Woolley, and Merrill (1972) and Tennyson (1973) have suggested a different procedure, one that changes the setup features after every second example (two examples with the same setup features are presented, followed by two examples with the next setup features). To determine the relative effectiveness of different setups, Carnine (1980b) taught the discrimination of 90° or more to 30 preschool children using three different variations in the setup features. For the continuous conversion group, all examples were created through continuous conversion to assure that a maximum number of details remained the same. For the non-continuous conversion group, the same set of examples and the same order of examples were used; however, the examples were shown on cards and were not created through continuous conversion, thus, the sameness from example to example would be less obvious. For the paired-setup group, as suggested by Tennyson, et al, the same setup features appeared in two juxtaposed examples and were replaced by different setup features in the next pair of examples.

Following initial training, all students were trained to a criterion on the same set of transfer examples. These examples were non-continuous and contained setup features that were found in *none* of the earlier training examples.

The most efficient procedure proved to be the continuous conversion presentation. Mean trials to criterion for students in this group was 10.6. The non-continuous procedure was the next-most efficient (with mean trials to criterion of 15.8). The least efficient procedure was the paired-setup presentation. Students required an average of 26.0 trials to meet the specified criterion of performance. The linear trend was statistically significant.

Juxtapositions for Showing Differences

The difference principle asserts that when minimum-difference examples are juxtaposed and treated differently, the intended interpretation is made most obvious. Granzin and Carnine (1977) conducted two studies that compared the effects of minimum-difference juxtapositions of positive and negative examples. In the first study, 44 first graders were randomly assigned to two treatment groups. Both groups received the same set of positive and negative training examples. The only difference was the juxtaposition of the examples. *Minimally* different positive and negative examples were juxtaposed for one treatment; *maximally* different examples were juxtaposed for the other treatment. A conjunctive concept (positive examples requiring the presence of more than one feature) was taught to all students.

The number of training trials needed for students to reach a specified criterion of performance was significantly lower for the minimum-difference juxtaposition group. This group required 17.4 mean trials to meet criterion. The students in the maximally different juxtaposition group required 29.9 mean trials to meet criterion.

In a second study conducted by Granzin and Carnine (1977), a disjunctive concept (the presence of at least one of a possible set of features) and a conjunctive concept were taught to second graders. The pattern of significant differences was the same as that for the first-grade study. Children who received the minimum-difference-juxtaposition treatment reached the training criterion for the conjunctive concept in significantly fewer trials than the children in maximum-difference juxtaposition treatment (means of 8.1 versus 19.1). Differences were also significant for the disjunctive concept. The minimum-difference children required 21.1 mean trials while the maximum-difference children required 37.1 mean trials.

Stipulation

Sprague and Homer (1981) investigated stipulation with six severely handicapped subjects of high school age. Subjects were first taught through procedures that stipulate behaviors that are relevant to operating a vending machine. Following stipulated practice, subjects worked on a second set of examples sequenced to demonstrate sameness across all vending machines. Three additional vending machines were practiced in this set. The machines differed greatly from each other with respect to those features that are relevant to operating the machine (the location of the coin slot, selection buttons, etc.). Throughout the training, subjects were tested on ten "probe" machines that were judged to sample a very wide range of variation in vending machines.

The results are consistent with the stimulus-locus prediction. No subject successfully operated more than two of the ten probe machines following their practice with the first machine or practice with machines highly similar to the first one. Furthermore, the specific errors subjects made in trying to operate the ten probe machines were fully accounted for by the feature differences between the probe machines and the machine(s) that had been practiced. On the final probe following the second set of examples (designed to show sameness across different machines), no subject successfully operated less than eight of the ten probe examples.

Homer and McDonald (1981) used a similar multiple-baseline design to test the effects of stipulation and sameness training for the skill of crimping biaxle capacitors. Subjects were first trained on a set of capacitors that were highly similar in size, shape, lead, color, etc. Following work on this *stipulated set*, subjects worked on a *sameness set*—a small number of capacitors that differed greatly from each other in size, shape, lead, color, etc.

The generalization of performance was tested through probes. Each probe presented 20 capacitors that had not been presented during training. During the training on the stipulated set, none of the four subjects correctly responded to more than five of the generalization items. During the sameness training, no subject responded correctly to fewer than 15 generalization items on any probe. The length of time that subjects worked on the stipulated set had no apparent effect on the number of generalization items responded to correctly during this phase of the training.

A specific prediction based on stipulation is that if all examples of decoding of connected sentences are immediately followed by comprehension activities, the association of comprehension with the decoding of connected sentences is strongly stipulated. The procedure, in other words, will stipulate that connected sentences are to be read for meaning. The most direct way of assessing such stipulation would be to ask the student questions and see if the decoding has resulted in "understanding." An indirect way is to analyze the type of errors the students make and determine the tendency to "self-correct" on the basis of syntax. Errors students make should tend to "make sense" if students read for meaning. The tendency should be quite independent of whether the children learn to read through "sounding out" or through "look-say."

To test this assumption, Linda Carnine (1980) applied Goodman's (1965) miscue analysis to 55 children in grades K through 3, who were taught DISTAR® reading, which teaches sounding-out and which stipulates strongly that sentence reading is reading for understanding. Goodman's analysis shows the extent to which the errors make sense grammatically and contextually. The percentage of errors that made sense grammatically and contextually for the kindergarten children was 21; in first grade it was 24; and in third grade it was 84. This trend suggests that although the children continue to work on the analysis of words in isolation, the stipulation provided by sentence reading leads to acquisition of a "set" for anticipating meaning, self-correcting words that apparently make no sense, and making the type of mistakes that are probable only if the meaning context is understood.

Joining-Form Communications

A common prediction for communications is that if the presentation is relatively faultless, it will lead to superior learning. The following studies deal with this prediction as it relates to the teaching of correlated-features and transformations.

Correlated Features

The suggested tasks presented with each example of a correlated features task ask first about the *correlated* feature and then ask, "How do you know?" The answer to this second question relates the correlated features to the features of the example. The answer shows which aspects of the example predict this correlated outcome.

It is possible to present the same set of examples as basic discrimination tasks (without making the correlation overt) by asking only the first question. The stimulus-locus analysis predicts that this procedure would probably be ambiguous, because it would not show which features of the examples predict the correlation. The more overt procedure would show the correlation unambiguously.

To study the effect of overtly expressing correlations, Ross and Carnine (1982) taught the *binary duality* relationship to children in grades 2 and 3 and in grade 5. The same set of examples was presented to all children. The only difference was the overt treatment of the correlation.

The 44 children were divided into three groups. For the Discovery Group, the teacher presented each demonstration example this way: "Five times six equals thirty. Is thirty a binary duality? No." No reason was given to suggest why not. The Rule-Plus-Discovery group received the same presentation of examples; however, before receiving this communication, the group said the rule: "A binary duality is the answer you get when you multiply two numbers. One of the numbers you multiply must be exactly two more than the other number."

The Rule-Plus-Overt Steps Group received this communication: "Six times five is thirty. Is thirty a binary duality? No. How do you know? Because six is not exactly two more than five."

The fifth-grade comparison showed that the Discovery Group was significantly poorer than either the Rule-Plus-Discovery Group or the Rule-Plus-Overt-Steps Group. Only 26.6 percent of the Discovery Group children met the training criterion; 92.8 percent of the Rule-Plus-Discovery Group children met the criterion; 100 percent of the Rule-Plus-Overt-Steps Group met the criterion. There was no significant difference between the Rule-Plus-Discovery and the Rule-Plus-Overt-Steps groups.

With children in grade 2, however, the difference between the Rule-Plus-Discovery and Rule-Plus-Overt-Steps groups was significant. Only 20 percent of the children in the Rule-Plus-Discovery group achieved the training criterion, whereas 83 percent of the Rule-Plus-Overt-Steps children achieved criterion. Neither the fifth-grade children nor the younger children tended to *discover* the relationship, even though: (1) the range of examples logically needed to induce the generalization was provided; and (2) the examples were massed, which should make discovery of the rule easier.

Rules and Applications

The stimulus-locus approach to the teaching of complex tasks is to teach the preskills that could affect learner performance and to apply the rule to a range of examples so that sameness is demonstrated. Two studies investigated the extent to which this approach improves learner performance.

In the first study, Kameenui, Carnine, and Maggs (1979) presented the following rule to first and second graders: "The lower you eat on the food ladder, the more protein you get." The students were divided into three groups, two containing 12 students each, and one containing 24 (12 average and 12 above-average students). The Rule-Only Group (12 students) received practice in saying the rule. The Rule-Plus-Concept Group (24 students) received practice in saying the rule and exercises designed to teach the component concepts expressed by the rule (lower on the food ladder, protein, etc.) The Rule-Plus-Concept-Plus-Application Group (12 students) received the training presented to the Rule-Plus-Concept Group and also received exercises in applying the rule to different factual situations.

The test following instruction consisted of ten application items, such as "Which has more protein, a worm or a fish?" No test item had been presented to any group during training.

The results show very little difference between the two groups that did not practice application (4.67 and 5.13 mean items correct). The group that practiced applications of the rule achieved 8.75 mean items correct. There was very little difference between the average and above-average students (as defined by test performance) on the transfer test. The means were: 5.08 for the average students and 5.17 for the above-average students. This lack of difference suggests that for these children, knowledge of the component concepts and the ability to state the rule were insufficient to induce understanding of how the rule *applies* to examples. A corollary is that although the presentation of applications items may require slightly more time, the items are more likely to assure that the communication will be effective.

In the second study, Ross & Carnine (1982) investigated the relationship between the clarity of a rule and learning. Stimulus-locus analysis predicts that a more clearly-stated rule would lead to better performance. Ross & Carnine presented two rules to different groups of children. One rule made the application steps fairly explicit. "A binary duality is the answer you get when you multiply two numbers. One of the numbers you multiply must be exactly two more than the other number." The other rule did not specify the steps as clearly: "A binary duality is the answer you get when you multiply one number that is exactly two more than the other." The prediction would be that the children would tend to learn better from the rule that makes the steps more obvious.

The study was conducted with 26 fifth-graders. Ninety percent of the children who received the more explicit rule met the training criterion; fifty percent of the children who received the less explicit rule met the criterion. This highly significant difference suggests the importance of a clear statement of steps to the learner. Related research has been conducted by Anderson and Kulhavy, 1973; Bourne, 1979; Bourne and O'Banion, 1971; Crist and Petrone, 1977; Feldman, 1972; Johnson and Stratton, 1966; Klausmeier and Feldman, 1975; Klausmeier and Voerwerk, 1975; Markle and Tiemann, 1974; Merrill and Tennyson, 1971; Swanson, 1972; and Voerwerk, 1979.

Transformations

Transformations are important to the credibility of the stimulus-locus analysis because they are among the more difficult "concepts" to describe verbally, which leads to the intuitively compelling conclusion that they are unteachable or difficult to teach. The stimulus-locus analysis contends, however, that if the presentation of examples show the basis for the transformation, the desired generalization will occur.

To test the importance of juxtapositions in inducing a single-transformation relationship, Carnine and Stein (1981) presented juxtapositions of arithmetic facts to two groups of six preschoolers (four to six-year-old children). The groups received instruction on eight sets of related facts. Each set contained three consecutive problems: 6 + 1, 6 + 2, 6 + 3, 7 + 7, 7 + 8, 7 + 9, etc. One set was introduced at a time, followed by a review of *all facts* that had been taught. The children were tested on the facts within a set by presenting the facts in random order. Criterion of performance for mastering a set was ten consecutive correct responses.

For the *Transformation Group*, the facts were presented in order. The rationale is that the systematic changes in the presentation show the learner more about: (1) what is the same about the various facts; and (2) the parallel between response changes and changes in the problems. For the *Non-Transformation Group*, the facts within each set were presented in random order.

Although the Non-Transformation Group completed the study in less total time (50 minutes compared to 74 minutes), the Transformation Group performed significantly better on a delayed test of the facts. The mean number of correct responses for the non-strategy group was 6.0 correct responses, compared to 13.8 correct responses for the strategy group. The ratio of number correct over time of instruction is one-and-a-half times greater for the Transformation Group. This ratio indicates the number of correct delayed-test items that are accounted for by each minute of instruction. The efficiency of the transformation instruction is therefore considerably greater than that of the non-transformation instruction. This outcome suggests that once learned, the transformation permits the learners to place individual facts in a framework rather than having to remember all details of all facts.

The procedure for communicating a double-transformation relationship is to first present a series of examples that show within-set sameness and then present examples that show across-set differences. An alternative approach would be to present examples in pairs. The learner responds first to an example from one set and then responds to a corresponding example from the transformed set. This approach was rejected because it does not juxtapose examples in a way that shows how examples within a set are the same. It also prompts a possible "elimination strategy."

To test the importance of juxtaposing examples, Carnine (1978) taught the transformation "Make a statement" and "Make a command" to preschool children. For each example, the child was presented with a picture and was told to "Make a statement" or "Make a command."

Three groups received the same amount of instruction. For the Across-Set Difference Group, the child was always required to perform on two tasks with each picture "Make a statement . . . Make a command . . ." The order of the tasks was randomized.

The juxtaposition of examples for the Within-Set-Sameness Group was designed to show sameness about examples within each set. Children first worked on a group of different examples in which they made a command, and then on a group of examples in which they made a statement.

The Transformation Group received the sequence that shows first within-set sameness and then across-set differences and then a mixture of examples from both sets.

The Transformation Group and the Within-Set Sameness Group performed equally well on a transfer test to new examples (60 percent correct for the Transformation Group and 61 percent correct for the Within-Set Sameness Group). The Across-Set Difference Group performed significantly more poorly (41 percent correct on transfer items).

The treatment received by the within-set sameness group is the same as the first part of the double-transformation sequence. The results suggest that when within-set sameness information is clearly provided, the transformation is mastered and generalizations occur. If this information is not presented clearly, the desired generalization tends not to take place.

Complex Form Communication

Visual-Spatial Displays of Fact Systems

According to the present analysis, the communication of facts that are related to a *topic* are most efficiently communicated through a visual-spatial display that shows the coordinate relationships of entries, higher-order relationships, and important "details."

Engelmann and Niebaurer (personal communication) compared two methods for transmitting study-skill information to students in grades 4 through 6. One method involved a program that presented various routines for showing students where to write their name on the paper, where to write the title, how to indent, etc. For each skill, a rule and applications were presented. The other method presented the same information, but consisted of a single visual-spatial display that showed the position of the name, date, title, procedure for indenting paragraphs, lines skipped, etc.

A test of application followed responses to questions about the display. The stimulus-locus analysis prediction is that if the students understood the information presented through the visual-spatial display, the display would be a more effective teaching procedure. The use of the *verbal rules* and operational steps provided by the routine are unnecessary. The results confirmed the prediction. Over 90 percent of the students in both groups reached criterion (appropriate application). The Visual-Spatial Group reached criterion in an average of 20 minutes. The Overt-Routine Group required an average of more than 180 minutes.

To investigate the relative effectiveness of the visual-spatial presentation over a presentation that was visual but not spatial, Sprick (1979) conducted an experiment with two groups of children, each composed of 24 children in grades 4, 5, and 6. Both groups received the same presentation of information and tasks. The only difference was the nature of the displays. For the Visual-Spatial Group, visual-spatial displays were presented. For the Visual-Only Group, each cell was presented in isolation, so that subjects did not receive information about the spatial relationships of one cell and other cells. To provide subjects in this group with information that paralleled spatial information, each cell was keyed with a symbol. If three cells were coordinate, each would have a coordinate symbol (possibly an orange strip in the corner). The symbols also suggested differences between cells. (No two coordinate cells were marked with the same shade of orange. Cells that were not coordinate were marked with another color or another symbol.)

Although the information provided by the two treatments was logically equivalent, the Visual Spatial Group showed a significant learning advantage on a test of information that immediately followed each presentation, but not on a retention test one week later.

Another study of visual displays was conducted by Darsh & Carnine (1981). The purpose of the study was to investigate the importance of three instructional variables when combined into various instructional packages designed to teach factual information in five content areas (i.e., weather, geographical information, etc.). The subjects were 86 sixth graders. Subjects were randomly assigned to one of four instructional groups by the school principal. The instructional package for Group 1 contained: (1) a teacher script (the teacher carefully followed the script; (2) a visual display (graphic display which presented the material in a logical form); and (3) an instructional game which required the students to separate into groups and review information in a highly motivating context. Group 2 was taught exactly the same as Group 1 except that the instructional game was replaced with self-study. Students were required to practice on their own, using their visual displays. Students taught in Group 3 read four written texts adapted from the scripts that were used with Groups 1 and 2. Included in the instructional presentation was the graphic display information. Finally, students were asked to self-study the visual display. The students taught in Group 4 were taught with the same text as presented to Group 3 and these students were required to self-study from the text material rather than the visual display. (Group 4 modeled traditional instruction. Several teachers evaluated these instructional units and considered them to be very powerful for teaching the material.) Instruction lasted 25 minutes a day for 15 days for each of the treatment groups.

The dependent variables for this study were: (1) a 15-item posttest which included a sampling of the factual material covered during instruction, and (2) a 4-item generalization test developed from content taken from a social studies text. This test was used to evaluate the students' ability to take textual information from traditional texts that included a visual display, and answer comprehension questions after study time. Planned comparisons were conducted with both tests on Group 1 versus each of the other three groups. For the posttest, all three comparisons were significant (percent correct for the groups were: 1 - 85%; 2 - 67%; 3 - 62 %; 4 - 70%). For the generalization test, only the comparison between Group 1 and Group 4 was significant (67% versus 48% correct).

These outcomes suggest that fact systems may be more readily conveyed if they are presented as displays that show the relationships in a fact system. However, more work is needed to carefully unravel the variables affecting teaching outcomes using visual displays.

Cognitive Routines

The stimulus-locus analysis of cognitive operations implies that communications are best if: (1) each step is made overt to provide evidence that the learner is attending to relevant dimensions of the problem; (2) feedback is provided; (3) the same operational steps are applied to a range of examples; (4) examples are presented in a manner that implies generalization; (5) the preskills involved in the operation are taught; and (6) the routine is systematically "covertized" (modified so that covert steps replace the overt ones).

Feedback for cognitive operations. Stimulus-locus analysis suggests that cognitive skills are generically different from physical operations with respect to the feedback provided by the environment. While the environment is capable of correcting or providing feedback with physical operations, no such feedback can logically occur with the naive learner who is trying to learn a cognitive skill. Therefore, independent practice with a cognitive skill may actually produce *decrements* in performance (because the learner may practice doing the wrong things and never receive feedback from the environment).

To test this position, Williams & Carnine (1981) presented a passage to two groups of 13 beginning readers. The children in both groups read the passage orally a total of three times. On the second and third readings, the Feedback Group received corrections as they read. The other group read with no feedback on these readings.

Errors on familiar words for the Feedback Group dropped from 4 percent to .7 percent between the first and third reading. Errors for the No-Feedback Group increased from 3 percent to 5.4 percent from the first to third readings. The differences are highly significant and tend to confirm analytical assumptions that independent practice on newly-learned cognitive skills seems to be ill-advised (as stimulus-locus analysis suggests).

In another study conducted by Carnine (1976b), a reversal design was employed during the teaching of arithmetic facts to 4 preschoolers. The treatments alternated from the Feedback Condition (during which mistakes were corrected) and No-Feedback Condition (during which no feedback was provided). Performance of all children varied predictably as a function of the condition used. During the Feedback Conditions, correct responses (both during the lesson and on posttest) averaged above 70 percent correct, while during the No-Feedback Conditions, the averages were below 20 percent correct. This difference is highly significant. As stimulus-locus analysis suggests, cognitive operations (in contrast to physical operations) are not learned through practice alone.

Research on the role of overt responding and feedback, not necessarily restricted to cognitive routines, has been conducted by Abramson and Kagan, 1975; Bourne, Ekstrand, and Dominowski, 1971; Durling and Schick, 1976; Frase and Schwartz, 1975; Tobias and Ingber, 1976.

Overtness of steps. The stimulus-locus analysis suggest that if the example has many features, it is possible for the unguided learner to perform correctly on a particular example by attending to inappropriate features of the example. If the learner is required to respond overtly to tasks that demand attention to relevant details, it is less possible for the learner to learn a "misrule." The study by Ross & Carnine (1982) discussed earlier suggested that the overt procedure tended to work best in teaching correlated features of examples (although the procedure was not significantly better than use of a rule followed by examples with fairly sophisticated learners. Does the same relationship maintain for cognitive operations that are more involved than correlated features? Studies were undertaken to answer the question: two studies involving arithmetic operations, one involving decoding, and several involving complex comprehension skills.

While these studies deal with instruction on overt cognitive routines, other studies have gathered descriptive data on the effects of different task variables, like vocabulary (Kameenui, Carnine, & Freschi, 1982). Data on these variables served as a basis for designing instructional interventions that are consistent with learner responses to the specific variables.

For each arithmetic study, two groups were identified. The group sizes were 12 to 13. One was taught a highly overtized operation; the other was taught the same skills and same set of examples through an "intuitive" procedure specified in an adopted mathematics textbook. Single-digit subtraction was taught to first-graders (Stein & Carnine, 1980). Long division was taught to fourth-graders (Kameenui & Carnine, 1980). The outcomes of both experiments were in accord with the stimulus-locus predictions.

The covertized subtraction group achieved a significantly higher percentage of correct answers on the training problems, transfer problems, and delayed test problems. The overtized long-division group achieved a significantly higher percentage of correct answers on the training problems, but not on posttest problems. (All students performed reasonably well on the posttest after several days of training. However, the overtized division group learned the skill more quickly, as indicated by the scores in daily tests.)

In another study comparing overt steps with covert procedures, Carnine (1977) taught two groups of preschoolers (15 in each group) to read a set of regularly-spelled words. They were later tested on generalization to both regularly-spelled and irregularly-spelled words (none of which appeared in training).

One group received instruction on component skills and instruction on performing a "sounding-out" operation for identifying words. The other group received only "look-say" practice on the words in the training set. The Sounding-Out Group reached the training criterion significantly faster (116.5 average minutes compared to 132.4 average minutes). On the transfer test, the Sounding-Out Group performed significantly better than the Look-Say Group—on both regular words and irregulars. The sounding-out subjects averaged over three times as many correct words as the look-say subjects.

The study clearly implies that if overt responses are made for the various elements that make one word different from another (the individual letters), the communication will more precisely communicate generalizable attack skills.

In a fourth experiment on the overtness of steps, Patching, Kameenui, Colvin and Carnine (1979) taught intermediate-grade students to identify three types of faulty arguments–faulty generalization ("Just because you know about a part doesn't mean that you know about the whole thing"); faulty causality ("Just because two things happen together doesn't mean that one thing causes the other"); and invalid testimony ("Just because a person is an expert in one field doesn't mean that the person's testimony is valid in another field"). Classifying and dealing with examples of these arguments assumes a number of steps; therefore, the prediction is that the highly-overtized routine would probably provide the best communication.

In the Overtized-Routine Group (consisting of three subjects), students went through a series of steps to identify the conclusion, the evidence, and to state any faults. This group performed significantly better than either the Feedback Group or the Comparison Group (26.8 mean correct for the Overtized-Routine Group compared to 17.5 for Feedback and 17.4 for Comparison). Note that the feedback and comparison groups perform almost identically, suggesting that the examples are consistent with many possible interpretations and therefore feedback was not sufficient to suggest the specific steps the learner would have to take to deal with the examples.

In the fifth experiment, conducted by Woolfson, Kameenui and Carnine (1979), 36 fifth-graders were presented with passages that were judged complex on the basis of variables that had been demonstrated to increase the "difficulty" of the passages. Information presented in these passages was separated so that the learner could not refer to a single place in the passage to answer particular questions; the material did not directly answer some questions, but provided only the evidence that could be used to draw the appropriate conclusions; the material also contained distractors, information that was not relevant to the questions asked, but appeared to be relevant; and the material did not begin with a statement about the point or the passage of the question that should be answered.

The Overt-Routine Group was taught a procedure for:

1. Finding out what the *problem* is.
2. Identifying the information or evidence that is relevant.
3. Transforming this information through deductions.
4. Answering the question (solving the problem).

The Feedback Group received feedback on the same set of passages presented to the Overt-Routine Group.

The Overt-Routine Group performed significantly better than the other groups (mean = 1.9 out of 3 correct compared to .7 for the Feedback Group, and .6 for the Comparison Group). It seems that the feedback condition did not work well because the examples were too complicated with too many possible features to suggest an appropriate strategy.

A study by Adams, Carnine and Gersten (1982) taught study-skill strategies to fifth-graders who had adequate reading (decoding) skills, but deficiencies in study skills. Forty-five (45) fifth-graders with reading scores on a standardized achievement test of less than one year below grade level, and scores of less than 50 percent on two individual tests of study skills, were randomly assigned to one of three samples. One group was taught to extract information using a cumulative-summary procedure. The performance of this group was compared to that of two comparison conditions. The Independent-Seatwork Group was presented with the same material and had the same opportunity time as the Cumulative-Summary Group to study the material. The Independent-Seatwork Group read the work passages independently, did worksheet items, and received feedback. The third group in the study received no instruction.

After four days of training, students were given a passage to study from a fifth-grade social studies text. They were then asked to retell important elements of the passage, and received a short-answer test on important facts in the passage. Two weeks later, the testing process was repeated. Results indicated students receiving systematic instruction in study skills performed significantly higher on a factual short-answer test on both occasions. No significant differences were found on the retell measures.

Dommes, Gersten and Carnine (1982) taught comprehension of pronoun-referent structures (identifying pronoun antecedents and answering factual questions based on this knowledge) to 45 fourth-grade students (identified as skill-deficient by a screening test) who were randomly assigned to one of the three treatment groups: Pronoun Specific Group, Retell Group, and a No-Intervention Group. Students in both the Pronoun Specific and Retell Groups received 20 minutes of individual instruction per day for three consecutive days. On the day following treatment, all three groups were given two tests, one assessing the ability to identify the word to which a targeted pronoun referred, and the second requiring the child to answer factual questions based on the comprehension of pronoun referent structures. Maintenance tests were given two weeks later. The Pronoun Specific Group performed better than the other groups on the Pronoun-Antecedent Identification Test.

In a final study on the overtness and organization of steps for complex operations (Fielding, 1980), a total of 42 high school students, 33 juniors and 9 seniors, were taught a two-week unit on the constitutional rights of youth. To assure equivalence of content across groups, all students received the same reading materials (summaries of legal cases) and viewed the same three filmstrips. Students were divided into the Direct Instruction Group and the Inquiry Treatments Group. The training for the two groups differed in teacher questions and review.

After six hours of instruction, all students completed two multiple-choice tests, an essay test of legal problem-solving, an "opinion" test, and an attitude questionnaire. The multiple-choice and essay tests were re-administered two weeks after the initial posttests as retention measures. All tests were reviewed by two third-year law students to establish content validity. These law students also rated the quality of subjects' essays.

Direct Instruction students significantly outperformed Inquiry subjects on the knowledge test and on the composite multiple-choice test. Direct Instruction students did significantly better on the initial essay, but not on the retention essay. No statistically significant differences were found between treatments on the opinion test, in which students wrote their views on legal policy issues relevant to the cases studied.

Related research on presentations for teaching complex operations has been conducted by Anastasiow, Sibley, Leonhardt and Borick, 1971; Baker and Brown, 1981; Brown, Campione, and Day, 1981; Egan and Greeno, 1973; Francis, 1975; Fredrick and Klausmeier, 1968; Gagne and Brown, 1961; Gordon, 1980; Hansen, 1981; Hansen and Pearson, 1982; Klausmeier and Meinke, 1968; Raphael, 1980; Rosenthal and Carroll, 1972; Rosenthal and Zimmerman, 1972; Tagatzh, Walsh, and Layman, 1969; Tennyson, Steve, and Boutwell, 1975; Tennyson and Tennyson, 1975; Wittrock, 1963.

Non-functional routines. Several experiments discussed have shown that if the learner is sophisticated, a presentation of the examples and a rule tend to work nearly as well as an overt strategy. For the less sophisticated learner, the overt steps make a significant difference in performance.

To investigate possible non-functional routines with reading comprehension skills, Coyle, Kameenui, and Carnine (1979) used three conditions to teach 36 intermediate-grade students a strategy for figuring out the meaning of words presented in the context of passages. The word to be analyzed was always underlined in the passage. One group received an explicit routine for dealing with this word. Students were told to look for other words in the sentence that could tell about the hard word. Students were also provided with a scanning strategy and with practice. A second group received the practice and feedback, but with no overt series of steps. A third group received no training. The analysis of the task suggests that:

1. The underlined word served as a stable signal for the learner to do something.
2. The other words in the sentence served as a high-probability source of information about the meaning of the underlined word.
3. The feedback on errors provided information about different strategies.
4. Therefore, the overt routine was probably not necessary.

The Overt Routine Group performed slightly better than the Feedback Group (6.25 to 5.33, a non-significant difference). Both groups were significantly better than the No Training Group, which scored 3.0. While the overt strategy had some effect, the information provided by the examples apparently served as primary influence in shaping the discriminations.

The three conditions used in the study above were also used to test the effectiveness of strategies for determining a character's motives (Clements, Stevens, Kameenui, & Carnine, 1979). The results were comparable, with the Feedback-Only Group performing slightly (but not significantly) better than the Overt-Routine Group. Both were significantly better than the No Training Group.

Preskills for clear communication. The stimulus-locus analysis implies that a communication is precise only if the learner "understands" the information that is being conveyed. The learner should therefore be pretaught those components of complex cognitive routines that possibly affect the communication. Other research related to preskills has been conducted by Gagne, Mayor, Carstens, and Paradise, 1962; Gollin, Moody, and Schadler, 1974; Jeffery and Samuels, 1967; Mayer, Stiehl, and Greeno, 1975; Royer and Cable, 1975.

To test this assumption, Carnine (1980d) taught 15 first-graders (divided into two groups) a complex cognitive routine for solving simple multiplication problems. The routine calls for the learner to "count by" the first number in the problem the number of times specified by the second number in the problem. To make the operation overt, the learner is taught to hold up the number of fingers indicated by the second number and then count by the first number. The answer is the number named as the last finger is counted.

An experienced Direct Instruction teacher taught both groups. The No-Preskills Group was taught everything as it came up in the operation. Each mistake the children made was corrected and firmed. The teacher modeled what the children were to do, led the children through the steps of the routine for each problem, and repeated the problem until the children performed adequately on it. The Preskills Group was taught in stages, with one new skill introduced at a time. The children were first taught to count by different numbers. Later, to count so many times (holding up the appropriate number of fingers), and taught how to translate written problems (such as 2 x 4) into the counting operation ("Count by 2, 4 times").

Both total teaching time to a specific training criterion and transfer tests were used to measure the relative effectiveness of the two approaches. The Preskills Group required significantly less total teaching time 105.5 mean minutes compared to 137.6 mean minutes for the No-Preskills Group). The difference on the transfer test was 6.5 items correct for the Preskill Group and 4.9 for the No-Preskills children. Similar results were obtained with older children who were taught a borrowing operation (Kameenui, Carnine & Chadwick, 1980).

Precise corrections. An assumption of the stimulus-locus analysis is that the more precise the feedback, the less ambiguous the correction and therefore the better the communication. Carnine (1980c) studied this assumption with three groups, each containing three preschool children who had learned to read by sounding-out regularly-spelled words and then identifying them. Before the experiment, all children had been taught to sound-out and identify five words. New words composed of sounds (letters) familiar to the children were introduced each day. The *initial correction* used for all groups was for the teacher to *say the correct word* and require the children to repeat it. A multiple baseline, single-subject design was used so that at different times, the groups were introduced to a new correction procedure. The *second correction* required the students to *sound out the missed word*, then identify it. The sounding-out correction is judged by the stimulus-locus analysis to provide a more precise communication because it shows which details of the word relate to the pronunciation of the word.

The results of the experiment corresponded closely to the analytical predictions. The performance of the groups showed great improvement only when the sounding-out correction was implemented. The longer the period of practice before the sounding-out correction was introduced, the more gradual the improvement. The group that remained in the whole-word correction the shortest period of time achieved 95 percent correct by the end of the experiment and the group retained in the whole-word correction for the longest period achieved only about 50 percent correct by the end of the experiment.

Covertization. An assumption of the stimulus-locus analysis is that the teaching of a highly overtized operation does not imply that the learner will perform problems of the operation covertly unless the learner receives the sort of communication that shows how a variation of the overtized operation can be performed covertly.

To investigate the necessity of specific covertization teaching, Paine, Carnine, White, and Walters (1982) used a multiple-baseline design in which three third-graders were given an opportunity to generalize an operation to a situation that was different from that in which the operation was taught. The children were taught a highly overtized procedure for solving column multiplication problems. During part of the lesson, the teacher directed the children in the problem-solving steps of various problems. During another part, the children worked worksheet items independently. This latter condition provided them with the *opportunity* to generalize the teacher-directed procedure even though this procedure was inadequate to imply such generalization.

Following the Opportunity Condition, children were directly taught how to handle the problems covertly. The worksheet performance of the students served as a dependent variable for the two phases of the experiment.

During the Opportunity Condition, the worksheet performance averaged 21 percent correct. By the third day of the covertization training for the group, worksheet accuracy improved to 76 percent correct. Following the formal covertization training, the performance went to 90 percent correct, suggesting that the children had generalized the overtized operation to independent applications.

Other Important Communication Variables

This book focuses on those instructional-design principles that relate to the content of communications, not to the behavioral details of communicating with a learner. Although we do not deal with specific teacher behaviors that affect the clarity of the communication, these variables may be considered as possible *pre-empting variables*. If we assume that the communication is faultless and has the potential to induce the desired generalizations, some things may happen during the transmission of information to the learner that effectively reduce the potential of the communication. Some of these variables are based on analytical consideration; some are based on empirically derived principles about the learner.

If the teacher does not juxtapose the examples in the manner called for by the communication, at least part of the communication's potential is pre-empted. If the teacher does not secure the learner's attention, the message may be further attenuated. If the teacher uses inappropriate wording, corrections, or reinforcement, further attenuation is likely for some learners. Even details about use of group turns and individual turns and the seating of the learners have the potential of overriding the message.

Becker, Engelmann, and Thomas (1975) have summarized experiments that show the relationship between the use of reinforcement, praise, behavioral rules, and other techniques and appropriate classroom behavior. Becker also observed (Madsen, Becker & Thomas, 1972) that the use of appropriate behavioral techniques is not enough to induce cognitive skills and that good management practices do not totally compensate for inadequate instructional sequences.

Teacher attention. One experiment demonstrated that the teacher can (through critical attention) actually *increase* the behavior he is trying to *eliminate*. This experiment involved the controlled use of disapproval statements in a reversal design (Thomas, Becker & Armstrong, 1968). When the rate of the teacher's disapproval statements to off-task behavior was high, the rate of on-task behavior was reduced to 65 percent. When the teacher reduced the rate of disapproval and gave approval to on-task behavior, relevant behavior went up to 85 percent. The disapproval statements apparently were reinforcing off-task behavior.

Teacher pacing. Carnine (1976b) showed that when teachers presented tasks at a higher rate to low first-graders, both on-task behavior and correct responses increased. When the teacher asked approximately 12 questions per minute in the fast-rate condition, the students answered correctly about 80 percent of the time and were off-task only about 10 percent of the time. When the teacher asked about 5 questions per minute (the slow-rate condition), the students answered correctly about 30 percent of the time and were off-task about 70 percent of the time.

Good-bad teaching behaviors. Carnine (1981) conducted a study using a reversal design in which the alternating conditions presented generically different teacher behaviors. One condition was judged analytically good because it controlled for pacing, signals, praise, and corrections. The other presentation was judged analytically "bad" because it presented contraindicated pacing, signals, praise, and corrections. Correct responding was 95.5 percent for the good condition versus 80.6 percent for the "bad." On-task behavior was 85.1 percent for the good condition and 50.6 percent for the "bad."

These and similar studies tend to confirm the general maxim that if a detail can be analytically demonstrated to affect the communication, that detail will be empirically demonstrated to be relevant to the effectiveness of the communication.

Summary

The stimulus-locus analysis is based on the idea that all details that are analytically capable of affecting the transmission of a communication will have an effect on learning rate, generalization of information, or retention. This chapter summarized studies that have investigated the effects of these details.

Studies on basic communication variables confirmed the analytically derived procedures for showing sameness and difference. They also demonstrated the effects of stipulated example sets across a wide range of applications.

Studies dealing with joining-form concepts (transformations and correlated-feature relationships) confirmed that the sequence of examples and the specific procedures for directing responses to the examples led to significant differences in learner performance.

The studies on cognitive routines demonstrated that practice without feedback does not improve performance, that the overtness of the steps greatly affects performance, and that preteaching critical information and systematically covertizing the operational steps improve learner performance.

As a group, the studies tend to show that a great deal of information about how learners will perform on an instructional sequence may be predicted before the fact by reference to the details of the presentation and by using as guidelines the principles of juxtaposition and the facts about the nature of cognitive learning.

Chapter 30
Instructional Research: Programs

Chapter 29 presented studies that suggest an empirical basis for the communications that derive from the stimulus-locus analysis. Those studies focused on specific communication issues. The studies that are presented in Chapter 30 deal with issues that are more complex. These studies are divided into three groups: those dealing with diagnosis of complex communications, those concerned with unpredicted normative outcomes, and those investigating the teaching of new skills and behaviors.

The diagnostic studies are based on the idea that it is possible to predict specific learning problems the student will encounter through an analysis of the communications the learner receives. (If the stimulus-locus analysis is useful, it should permit us to make such predictions.)

The studies dealing with normatively unpredicted outcomes suggest that some causes of student failure may not reside with students, but with the instruction they receive. If students receive instruction capable of teaching specific skills, students who would normatively not be expected to learn specific concepts should learn them.

The final group of studies, those involving new skills and behaviors, clarify the interactions between behavioral principles (based on the characteristics of the learner) and stimulus-locus principles (based on analysis of communications and skills). According to the stimulus-locus analysis, it should be possible to identify the influence of communication variables even if the new learning involves responses that are generically new to the learner and that require a great deal of shaping.

Diagnosis of Complex Communications

The stimulus-locus diagnostic assumptions are that:

1. Flaws in teaching communications can be identified through analysis of the communications.
2. Any flaws that are identified will be learned by some learners.

Studies have been conducted in which inappropriate learning is induced through presentations that have obvious logical flaws. In one study, Kyzanowski and Carnine (1980) designed a flawed drill sequence. The drill involved letters, which were identified by sounds. Two groups of preschoolers were identified. Each child was presented with 60 items (letters). Two target sounds were in the set—the letters **i** and **e** (responded to by the short letter sound). Each group received a different sequence of items. Both sequences presented **e** 15 times and **i** 15 times. However, the distribution of the letters differed for the two groups. In the **e**-Discriminated Group, the letter **e** was distributed (never followed by another letter **e**) and the letter **i** was always blocked (a group of **i**'s occurring as juxtaposed examples). The set of letters presented to the **i**-Discriminated Group reversed the roles of **e** and **i**. The **i**'s were never juxtaposed to other **i**'s, while the **e**'s were always juxtaposed.

A diagnosis of this communication for possible misrules suggests that the communication for the non-distributed letter in each block should *not* be learned as well as the distributed letter within each block. The reason is that the type of response called for within the non-distributed letter is that of repeating the letter sound again and again. Stated differently, the only letter that must be discriminated when the letters appear in blocks is the first letter in each block. Since the non-distributed letters were presented in only four blocks, the learner receives 15 discriminated trials for one letter and possibly only four effective trials for the other.

The results conform to the prediction. Although the distributed items were missed more frequently during training (56 percent correct versus 73 percent correct for the blocked items), they were identified correctly more frequently on a posttest (72 percent versus 30 percent). This pattern was consistent for both letters. Saying things over and over in a non-discriminated context is not an efficient procedure for teaching discriminations.

Theory of Instruction: Principles and Applications

Time-on-Task and Program Variables

Rosenshine and Berliner (1978) and others have suggested that time-on-task (engaged time in teaching) is the primary variable that accounts for differences in effectiveness of teaching sequence. The stimulus-locus analysis predicts that time-on-task becomes a highly relevant variable *only if the programmed sequences are designed so they effectively communicate the skills being taught*. A related prediction is that bringing the learner to a high level of performance on training examples will not induce desired generalizations if the communication is flawed. The additional practice may simply result in stipulation.

To test the relationship of engaged-teaching time and program variables, Darch, Carnine, and Gersten (1981) taught four groups of low-performing fourth graders (N = 74) procedures for solving multiplication and division story problems. Two program sequences were used. The one adopted from *Distar* and *Corrective Mathematics* was judged to be capable of communicating the skills needed to solve the problems. The other program sequence was adapted from commercial programs listed on the Oregon State-adopted list of approved programs. This sequence was judged to be ineffective. Two treatments were provided for each sequence. One received a fixed number of practice problems (60). For the other, additional practice was provided to all students who did not achieve 90 percent accuracy on a 10-item test following the program sequence.

Highly significant differences were observed on the 24-item posttest that followed instruction. Both the fixed-trials and mastery groups in the Direct Instruction sequence scored over 90 percent correct on the posttest (93.1 percent correct for fixed trials and 94.2 percent correct for mastery). The students receiving the traditional program achieved 69.2 percent correct for the fixed trials and 69.2 percent for the mastery. Note that the additional work with the mastery students (up to three extra lessons) did not produce improvement in the group's performance. Clearly, engaged time was not the primary variable associated with mastery in this experiment.

Another diagnosis study investigated the fact that the experimental approach used by Guess (1969) for teaching plurals to low-performers was consistent with possible misgeneralizations. The learners were always presented with two groups of objects. One group always contained only a single object, while the other group contained more than one object. All objects in the pair of groups had the same label and were from the same class (one dog and three dogs, for instance, never one dog and two cats and a dog). The implied misgeneralizations:

1. The repeated presentation of examples stipulates that the smaller group is singular.
2. The comparison always involves the same label for the pair of groups.

To study which of these misgeneralizations are learned, Flanders (1978) replicated the procedure used by Guess to teach a language-delayed child. Following the instruction, the child was presented with transfer tests.

Flanders found that when the child was presented with two groups of like objects, both of which were plural:

1	2
dog	dog
dog	dog
	dog

the child tended to respond to the smaller group as a *singular*. This outcome is consistent with the stipulation that the smaller group is always singular.

When tested with "spurious" plural groups:

1	2
dog	dog
	cat

the child tended to identify the second group as a plural (calling it either "dogs," or "cats").

Flanders corrected the presentation misrules by modifying the examples and overtizing the procedure for naming the individual objects before identifying the labels for the groups. If a traditional diagnostic procedure had been used rather than an analysis of the communication, the learner would have been labeled as one who fails to generalize, when in fact the presentation was guilty of teaching the inappropriate generalizations.

An elaborate diagnosis of instruction was conducted by Steely and Engelmann (1979). The analysis dealt with the specified instruction for teaching reading comprehension skills in grades 4 to 6 provided by the four widely-used basal reading programs–Holt, Scotts-Foresman,

Ginn, and Houghton Mifflin. The diagnostic strategy used in this study involved:

1. Analyzing the material presented to teach different skills and determining the extent to which the material had flaws.
2. Analyzing the actual teaching provided by the teacher and diagnosing it for possible flaws.
3. Comparing the program specifications, the actual teaching, and the performance of the students who received the communication.

The analysis of the instructional programs and of the teaching focused on features that are logically important and that have been shown through empirical studies to affect the clarity of the communication. For instance, consistency in wording is logically relevant to the communication and has been empirically demonstrated to be a factor affecting the communication. Other variables relevant to the clarity of the communication were analyzed, including: the set and range of examples presented, the number and types of examples, the possible misinterpretations implied by a set of examples, possible spurious prompts, the covertizations procedures that relate the structured presentations to the independent work.

Table 30.1 summarizes the analysis of the programs for teaching **main idea**. The summary is based on the analysis of all the exercises involving **main idea** that were presented over three years (grades 4 through 6).

The analysis discloses an almost total lack of concern with the logic of communications. The set of examples presented to the students for any given lesson supported four possible generalizations. (For instance, all the two-paragraph, main-idea examples presented in a reading series might have the "topic sentence" at the end. The examples are consistent with the generalization that if two paragraphs are involved in the example, the topic sentence appears as the last sentence.)

Spurious prompts were lavishly provided, particularly in the student material (which means that the students could answer items correctly by attending to the prompts and not to relevant features of the examples). Over three years, a total of only nine examples of main idea appeared in student materials on the same day that the teacher taught about main idea. The assumption seems to be that if the students are told once, they should understand. Perhaps the most telling feature of

Table 30.1
Program Analysis Results Across Programs

	Means Across Program	Ideal
Percentage of questions misleading or specified answers wrong	12	0
Percentage of questions relevant to concept, teacher presentation	62	100
Percentage of questions relevant to concept, student workbook	75	100
Number of possible interpretations based on examples presented for each skill	4	1
Percentage of visual distraction, student workbook	25	0
Percentage of academic distraction, teacher presentation, student workbook	31	0
Percentage of responses spuriously prompted, teacher presentation	24	0
Percentage of responses spuriously prompted, student workbook	49	0
Days since two examples of a topic were presented	62	?
Total number of examples over 3-year period	66	?
Total number of student examples presented on same day as teacher-presentation examples	9	?
Percent of student examples on same day as teacher-presentation example	14	?
Total number of lessons	22	50-80
Percentage of examples for which correction is specified	0	20-40

the programs is the extent to which corrections are specified. No program provided specific corrections.

The analysis of the programs leads to the conclusion that if the teacher follows them, they will not teach, which means that a large percentage of the students receiving the communication will not learn (although there is nothing to prevent any given student from "figuring out" the intended discriminations related to main idea).

To determine how the teachers taught, 17 teachers who had used one of the programs at least one year were videotaped for two half-hour periods. Different topics were taped to determine the consistency of teacher behaviors across topics. A comparison of what the teachers actually presented and what the program specified for a given lesson disclosed that the teachers tended to follow the programs very faithfully. Every teacher presented every example the program specified and presented every question and discussion topic. Their greatest deviation from the program was in the type and number of questions they asked. They asked 151 percent more questions than the programs specified; however, nearly all of the questions they added were judged irrelevant to the topic. Therefore, the teachers consistently taught slightly worse than the instructional programs specified. The instructional program, in other words, served as a model or limiter. The fact that teachers followed the programs much more closely than they reported following it strongly suggests that they did not know how to teach the various skills and relied heavily on the material.

Table 30.2 gives a summary of the teachers' behavior:

Table 30.2
Teacher Behavior Data Across Programs

	Grand Mean	Ideal
Total percentage of questions for which errors were made	27	0–12
Total percentage of questions that were group tests	16	25–60
Total percentage of questions that were individual	84	40–75
Total percentage of errors that were corrected	37	100
Total percentage of errors that were corrected and retested	10	100
Total percentage of tasks that were models or leads	34	0–25
Total percentage of responses that were given general praise	44	0–10
Total percentage of responses that were given specific praise	2	15–30
Total percentage of responses that were given negative feedback	1	0–2
Rate of tasks per minute	4.4	8–15

The analysis of the teacher material and the analysis of the communication provided by the teachers lead to the same diagnosis, which is that they would not teach the skills they purport to teach. They have far too little regard for the examples, the sequence, the tasks, and the manner in which the information is conveyed to the students.

To determine the extent to which the communications did actually teach, the students (middle-class children) were tested on the videotaped lessons immediately following the teaching. Eight topics were tested. The tests did not introduce anything new. The wording was as simple as possible; the generalizations were limited to those explicitly taught or assumed by the presentation; and the responses required by the students were straightforward. The results of the tests are summarized in Table 30.3.

Table 30.3
Student Performance

Topic	No. of Presentations	Mean Percentage of Students At or Above Criterion of:		
		90% correct	75% correct	50% correct
Main Idea	8	10%	33%	58%
Key Words	3	8%	32%	65%
Map Skills	3	30%	33%	56%
Inferences	2	15%	30%	62%
Context Clues	6	0%	0%	15%
Relevant Details	2	24%	82%	99%
Cause Effect	1	10%	30%	60%
Fact/Opinion	1	0%	25%	70%
Means Across All Topics		12%	30%	55%

Although there is great variation in the success of the various communications, the pattern of performance suggests that the teaching is well-designed to maximize individual differences. About half the children tended to fail half the items. An analysis of the mistakes that the students made revealed that the mistakes were largely consistent with the communication the students received.

Normatively Unpredicted Outcomes

These studies are based on the idea that if the communication is controlled to teach skills, it should be possible to teach skills to children who would not be expected to learn them, as indicated by normative trends. Inferences that derive from these studies are particularly strong because the predicted outcomes are highly unlikely. For instance, it is highly unlikely that preschoolers can be taught formal operations or arithmetic concepts that are typically not learned before the third grade. Because the outcome is highly unlikely, the probability is great that the intervention correlated with these outcomes was the cause and the only cause of the outcome.

Studies based on this rationale have demonstrated that disadvantaged preschoolers and middle-class preschoolers were able to learn concepts that are normatively unpredicted, that disadvantaged school-age children learn skills at a rate that is not normatively typical of these children, and that low-performing (low IQ) children learn skills at an unpredictably high rate.

Teaching Formal Operations to Preschoolers

According to Piaget's developmental hierarchy (1952), formal operations (the most sophisticated mental structures that develop) typically occur during puberty, although Piaget does not assert that everybody passes through this stage. According to Piaget, formal operations require the learner to make up propositions about propositions.

The stimulus-locus interpretation is that although the same skills do not normatively appear until a certain age, they could be induced at a much younger age if the communication with younger children is made precise. If the stimulus-locus proposition is accurate, it should be possible to induce formal operational "thought" or reasoning in children much younger than teenagers—possibly in preschoolers.

Through such an experiment, Engelmann (1967b) taught two groups of preschool children (a middle-class group and a disadvantaged group) a program designed to induce formal-operational generalizations. Daily instruction presented different examples of problems that required the same chain of reasoning. The test involved solving a new problem that had obvious differences from any problem practiced during training. The prediction was that the children would treat this problem in the same way they treated the training problems and successfully solve it. The training involved the following activities:

1a. You start with two lines that are the same size but when you come back to look at them, they look like this:

What are the two things the guy who changed them could have done? (Made the top line shorter or the bottom line longer.)

1b. If the guy did not touch the top line, what did the guy do? (Made the bottom line longer.)

2a. You start out with the bar sticking out just as far on either side of the wall. When you come back, the bar looks like this:

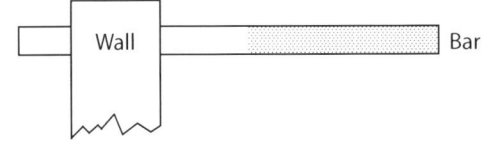

What are the two things the guy who moved the bar could have done? (Pushed in on the left or pulled out on the right.)

2b. *Half* the bar is painted (the darker part). If the guy who moved the bar did not get paint on his hands, what did the guy do? (Pushed in on the left side.)

The children worked a variety of these problems, following the same two steps with each problem. The test problem was also the same in some feature. The outcome that was shown could be achieved in two different ways:

You start with the teeter-totter level. When you come back, the teeter-totter looks like this:

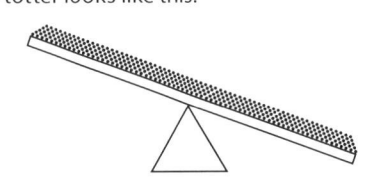

What could the guy have done? (Pushed up on the left or pushed down on the right.)

The top of the teeter-totter is painted. If the guy who moved the teeter-totter got paint on his hands, how did he move the teeter-totter? (Pushed down on the right side.)

Note that the children could not merely memorize a rote response pattern because the problems differed with respect to how the display had been changed (which side was down) and with respect to the information about what the person who changed the display had done (operated on either the top or the bottom).

Four of the five middle-class children passed the test of generalization; two of the five disadvantaged children clearly passed it; one possibly passed it; and two failed it. The middle-class child who did not pass the problem was three years old. The children were tested later on conservation of substance. Only one child passed.

A few weeks of daily instruction had induced a nontrivial generalization in children who were, by "developmental standards," preoperational. Their performance is accounted for only by the communication they received.

In addition to learning this generalization, the members of the middle-class group also learned to solve problems of relative direction and of reflection. The training on the reflection problems provided a good indication of how inductive reasoning is possible, if information about sameness is provided. The investigator first taught the children to predict the "path" of a ball that rolls against a wall. The investigator used this type of diagram:

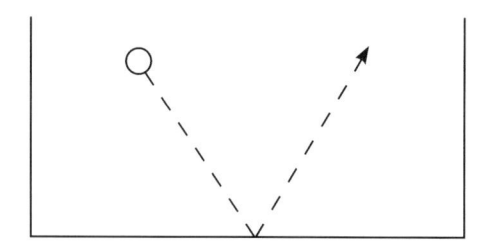

After the children had become proficient at predicting the angle of the ball's reflection, the investigator used a similar diagram for a new problem.

> The investigator . . . drew a map of the room and indicated a mirror against the wall. He asked the children if they could predict the path of their vision if they stood off to one side and looked into the mirror. He indicated the path of vision from the diagrammed child to the mirror. They were asked to indicate the reflected path. They could not. The investigator indicated the reflected path. He did not tie the problem in with the familiar rules about rolling balls. Instead, he wanted to see how long it would take for the members to see the analogy. He presented another problem (with the diagrammed person standing in a different position) and asked those who thought they knew the answer to raise their hand. All members raised their hand. The one called on to indicate the reflected path indicated it correctly. The investigator asked the other members to indicate where they would have to stand in relation to different mirrors if they wanted to see themselves. All but one answered correctly . . . (Engelmann, 1964, p.43).

In another experiment, Engelmann (1971) set out to teach a group of six-year-olds the skills needed to pass the Piagetian tasks of conservation of substance, speed, volume, weight, and the test of specific gravity. The test of specific gravity (an indicator of formal operational thought) was modified by the addition of a series of questions about mercury. After the children had worked with the two steel balls in water (predicting whether each ball would float or sink), the children were asked the same set of questions about whether the balls would float in mercury. (They first observed the smaller ball float and were asked what the larger ball would do. Next, they were asked to figure what was heavier, the mercury or the water. They were not permitted to touch either container.)

Engelmann attempted to teach the skills in a way that violated all those principles Piaget suggested were necessary for the induction of cognitive structures.

1. No real-life objects were presented because Piaget assumed manipulation of real-life objects to be necessary for cognitive growth.

2. No manipulation was presented during instruction.

3. No process of change was shown (either real or diagrammed) because Piaget suggests that knowledge of the process is necessary.

4. No long-time period for assimilation and accommodation was permitted (with the entire training involving less than five hours).

The children were taught logical rules about the relationship of things. The rules were rote. Their application was not, however, because the test required the children to apply these rules to situations quite different from any encountered during training.

The prediction that the children would handle the mercury problem as readily as the water problem was based on the fact that the instruction provided the rule for handling objects in *any* medium—water, air, gasoline, or whatever. The basic rule was: "It will sink if it is heavier than a piece of medium the same size. It will float if it is lighter than a piece of medium the same size." This rule implies applications such as, "A pin floats in air. So what do you know about the pin? . . . It's lighter than a piece of air the same size." Conversely, "A balloon is lighter than a piece of water the same size. So what's the balloon going to do in water? . . . That balloon is heavier than a piece of air the same size. So what's the balloon going to do in air? . . ."

A variation of the rule about sinking permits conclusions about the weight of the medium. "If the cork moves up in gasoline, which is heavier, the cork or a piece of gasoline the same size? So what do you know about the gasoline? . . . It's heavier than a piece of cork the same size."

Since the rule is framed to show what all examples of floating have in common, the prediction is that the children would be able to solve the problems correctly if they correctly perceived that the demonstration was providing information about the object and the medium.

Three of the five children in the experiment answered all primary questions about specific gravity correctly. They did not know, of course, that the small steel ball would float in mercury. Once they saw it float, however, they predicted that it would float again, and that the large ball would float. They also concluded that the mercury is heavier than the water.

One girl was absent on the day that the rules for compensatory change were introduced. These rules were designed to help children pass the test of conservation. The girl failed the test; however, during the Piagetian test of specific gravity, she showed that she was quite capable of applying what she had been taught in a perfectly new and creative manner. The experimenter asked whether a large candle would float or sink in water. The girl indicated that it would sink. The experimenter proceeded to saw it into two pieces of unequal length. The experimenter stopped sawing and asked the child whether the longer piece would float or sink. "Float," the child indicated. The experimenter asked about the shorter piece and received the same response. The examiner then asked about the entire candle. The child indicated that the whole candle would float. When asked why she had changed her mind, the girl explained that while the examiner was sawing the candle, a piece of the candle had landed in the pan of water. It floated, which means that the whole candle would float and that any part of it would float.

Another interesting relationship between the communication and the performance of the children was demonstrated on the test of the conservation of speed. It was impossible to teach anything about speed without showing movement. Therefore, the children were not taught about speed. They uniformly failed the test of conservation of speed. These aberrations in performance are explicable if we view learning as a reasonable response to communications. From a developmental standpoint, however, the children's performance was enigmatic.

In another experiment, Engelmann (1967a) demonstrated that the skill of conservation could be induced in non-conserving children by teaching them the "compensation argument" or the logic of how a change in one dimension is accompanied by a compensating change in another direction. After 54 minutes of instruction that did not involve real life objects, 10 of the 15 experimental subjects successfully passed the generalization test for conservation of substance.

Teaching Academic Skills to Preschoolers

Therese and Siegfried Engelmann (1966) taught preschool children academic skills, including reading and arithmetic skills. Four-year olds were taught to solve simple algebra addition problems (4 + □ = 7), multiplication, subtraction, fractions, and applications of multiplication, such as solving the area-of-rectangle problems. Although these children had not been taught addition or subtraction *facts*, they could solve problems by decoding each problem as a set of instructions for carrying out a counting operation and then carrying out the operation.

Bereiter, Washington, Engelmann, and Osborn (1969) presented four-year-old and five-year-old disadvantaged children with an intensive half-day academic curriculum which taught language skills, arithmetic, reading, and singing. The demonstration performed with the first group (entering as four-year olds in 1964) was that:

1. They could learn to read through the application of logical rules.

2. They could learn basic arithmetic operations that are typically not mastered by children in the third grade.

The second group of children (entering in 1965) received a more intensive language program, and the emphasis was switched from showing the extent to which they could learn sophisticated operations to implementing curricula that were effective in teaching the foundation skills in arithmetic and reading.

The results with the first group showed that two of the three instructional groups could learn the same kinds of arithmetic operations that had been taught to middle-class preschoolers.

The results with the second group (1965 to 1967) showed large IQ gains on the Stanford-Binet achieved during the children's first year (15 points), and additional gains of 9 points during the second year. The children's achievement test performance in arithmetic was grade level 2.5, and their reading grade level was 2.6. Upon graduating from the preschool, the children had an average IQ of 121. Middle-class children taught in the preschool achieved higher IQ scores and larger academic gains.

Stein (personal communication) taught 10 four- and five-year-old preschoolers in a half-day program. These children ranged from "behavior problems" to very gifted children. Their performance at the end of one year was grade level 4.3 in reading and 3.0 in arithmetic on the Wide Range Achievement Test.

Teaching Academic Skills to School-Age Children

In 1978, Engelmann taught a class of 4th, 5th, and 6th-grade average children for 16 sessions (12 hours total teaching time). At the end of these sessions the students averaged over 90 percent correct on independent problems of these types:

- $\frac{3}{4} a = \frac{2}{7}$
- $\frac{5}{3} a = \frac{}{}$
- If two tanks fill in 1.45 hours, how long will it take to fill 3½ tanks that are the same size?
- The elm tree is 15 meters tall and its shadow is 11 meters long. How long is the shadow of an oak tree if the oak tree is 6 meters tall?
- If it takes 4 men 3 days to build 5 houses, how long will it take 7 men to build 6 houses?

The results of the USOE Follow Through study provide crude measures of how the Direct Instruction approach (used by Engelmann, Becker, and Carnine) compares with other approaches to teaching disadvantaged children. Different sponsors worked with participating school districts, with a given district implementing a particular sponsor's program under the auspices of USOE Project Follow Through. The Direct Instruction Program was implemented in a variety of settings—large city (New York, Washington, D.C.), rural (Williamsburg County, S.C., Smithville, Tenn.), Indian (Cherokee, N.C., Todd County, S.D.), Spanish (Las Vegas, N.M.), Mexican (Uvalde, Tex.). The implementation of the program in most sites was far below the standards that could have been achieved if school districts were oriented toward performance and were responsive to classroom problems. This situation, however, was not one unique to the Direct Instruction Program. Sponsors of programs far different from Direct Instruction reported similar frustrations with attempts to implement (Nero, 1975).

Despite the problems of implementation, the USOE comparison of the Follow Through sponsors showed that the third-grade Direct Instruction students scored higher than all other approaches in reading, arithmetic, spelling, and language. The performance of D.I. students on measures of self-image suggested stronger self-images. They excelled both in academic skills designated as "basic" and those designated as "cognitive conceptual."

Figure 30.1 summarizes the third-grade performance of kindergarten-starting disadvantaged children for the major sponsors.

The line at the 20th percentile indicates the expected performance for disadvantaged children (and corresponds closely to the pretest performance level of the Direct Instruction students). The figure is divided in quarter-standard-deviation units. The difference between the 31 percentile and the 40 percentile, for instance, is one-fourth standard deviation. The University of Kansas Behavior Analysis is clearly the closest competitor. However, the Direct Instruction students are nearly one-fourth standard deviation above the Behavior Analysis Model in reading, one-half standard deviation in math, and three-fourths standard deviation in language. The other models, which tend to be based on more the current idiom of instruction, reach the 32nd percentile in only one skill—the rote skill of spelling.

Another analysis of the Follow Through comparison shows how the various sponsors performed on basic skills (those subtests identified by Abt Associates as being relatively heavy in their rote-learning component) and on cognitive-conceptual skills (those that involve drawing inferences and using chains of reasoning that

Figure 30.1
Comparison of Third-Grade Follow Through Children on the Metropolitan Achievement Test

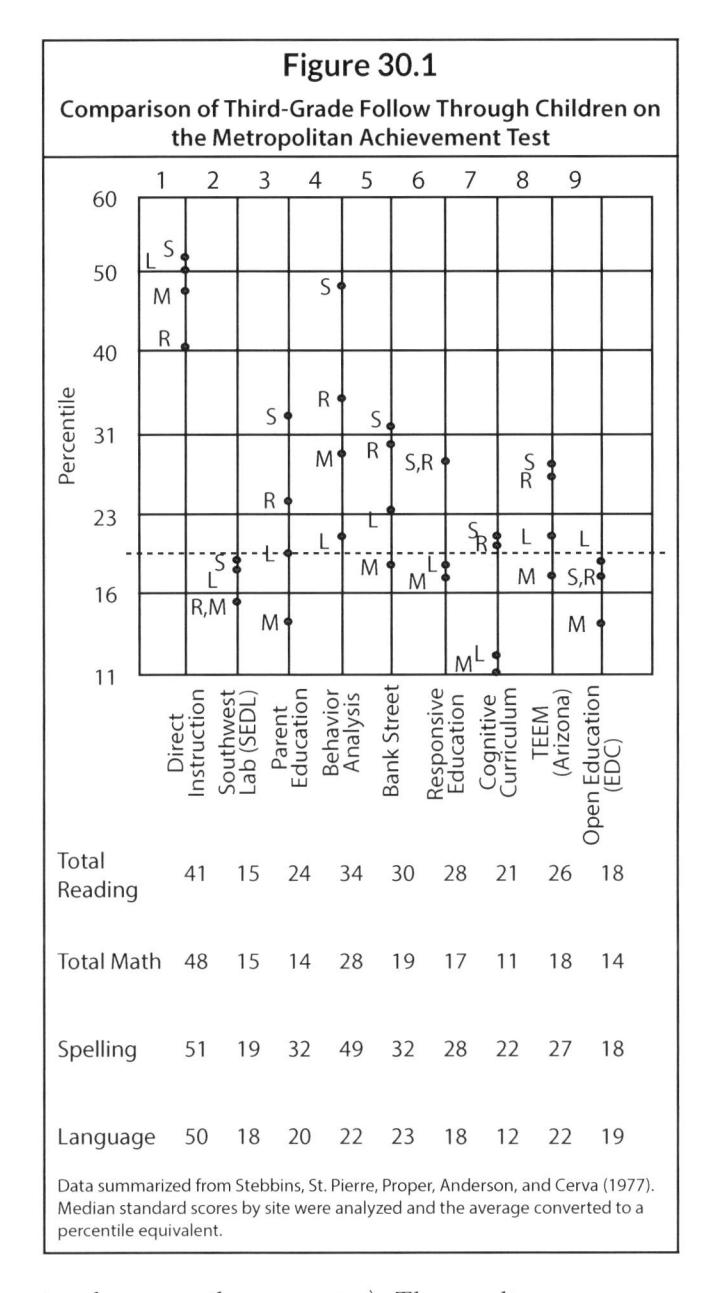

	Direct Instruction	Southwest Lab (SEDL)	Parent Education	Behavior Analysis	Bank Street	Responsive Education	Cognitive Curriculum	TEEM (Arizona)	Open Education (EDC)
Total Reading	41	15	24	34	30	28	21	26	18
Total Math	48	15	14	28	19	17	11	18	14
Spelling	51	19	32	49	32	28	22	27	18
Language	50	18	20	22	23	18	12	22	19

Data summarized from Stebbins, St. Pierre, Proper, Anderson, and Cerva (1977). Median standard scores by site were analyzed and the average converted to a percentile equivalent.

Figure 30.2
ISOs for Basic Skills (B), Cognitive Skills (C), and Affective Measures (A)

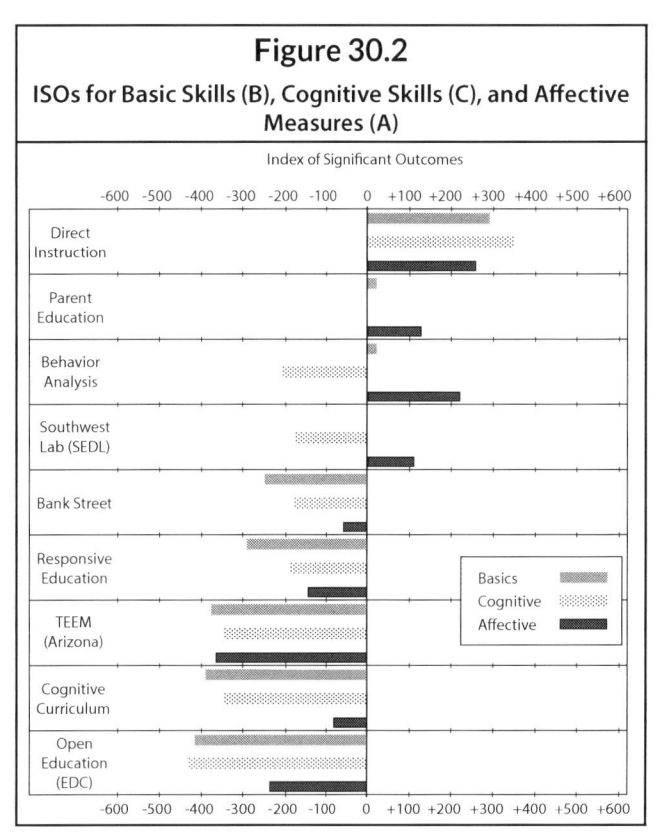

involve more than one step). The results are summarized in Figure 30.2 (after Stebbins, et. al., 1977).

The centerline of the figure is the null outcome, e.g., no difference between a Follow Through model and the comparison subjects. The further right the bar goes from the centerline, the higher the proportion of sites in which a model showed both educationally and statistically significant effects. Some models had positive impacts (bars on the right side of the baseline). Many had negative results. The Direct Instruction approach created the highest degree of positive impact in both cognitive-conceptual skills and in basic skills. Note that the values for the cognitive-conceptual skills are greater than those for basic skills. These findings strongly militate against the interpretation that Direct Instruction is "rote learning."

Significant gains in IQ are also found for DI students, and are largely maintained through third grade. Students entering the program with IQ's over 111 do not lose during the Follow Through years, although one might expect some regression phenomena. The low IQ children, on the other hand, display appreciable gains, even after the entry IQ has been "corrected"—students with IQ's below 71 gain 17 points in the entering-kindergarten sample and 9.4 points in the entering-first sample; gains for the children with entering IQ's in the 71-90 range are 15.6 and 9.2, respectively (Gersten, Becker, Heiry & White, 1981).

Studies of how low IQ students (under 80) perform under Direct Instruction show the program is clearly effective with students who have a higher probability of failure. As indicated in Figures 30.3, , and 30.5, these students *gain* nearly as much each year in reading (decoding) and math, as students with higher IQ's—a gain of more than a year per year on the WRAT, and a year for a year on MAT Total Math.

Section IX | Research and Philosophical Issues

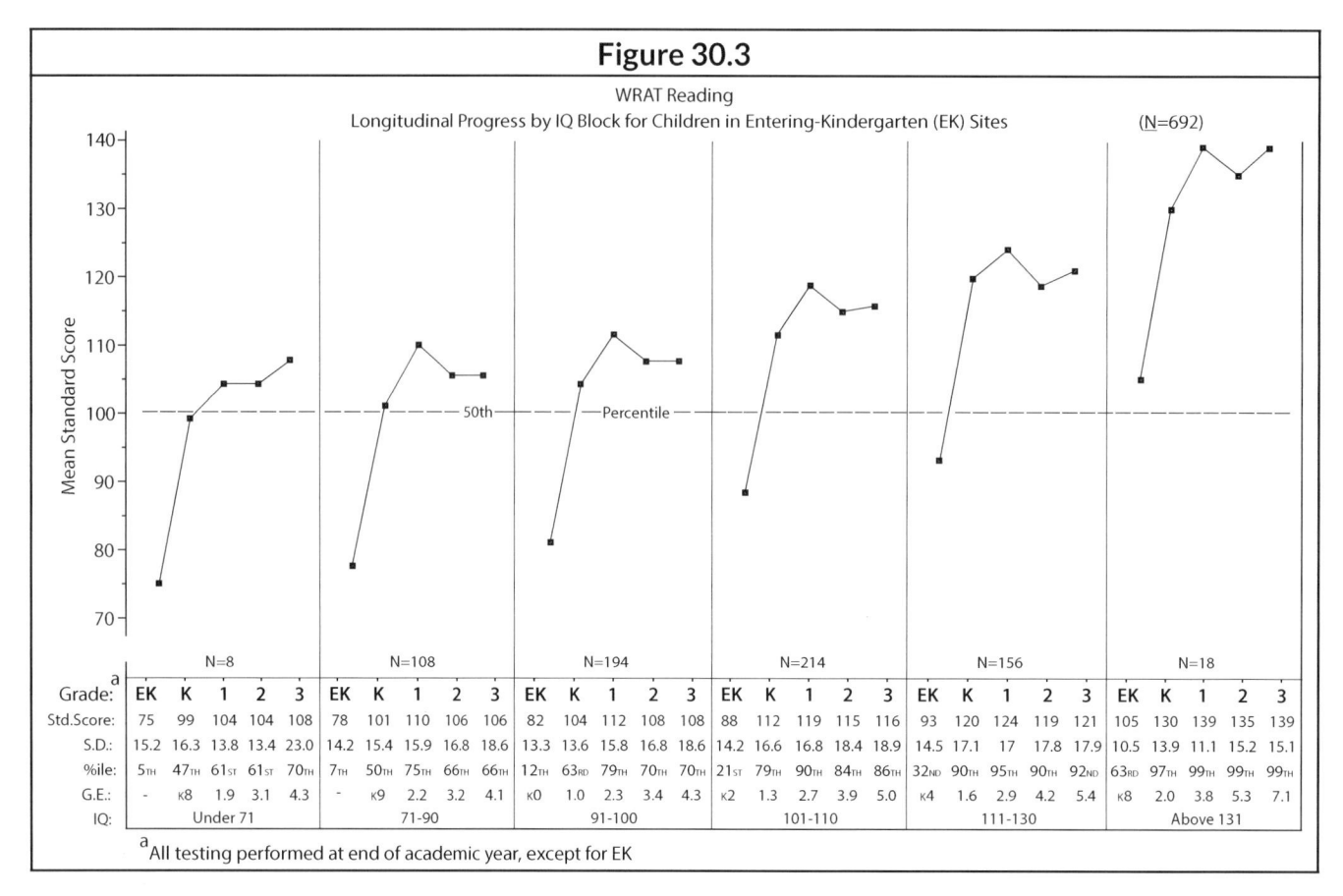

Figure 30.3
WRAT Reading
Longitudinal Progress by IQ Block for Children in Entering-Kindergarten (EK) Sites (N=692)

Grade:[a]	EK	K	1	2	3	EK	K	1	2	3	EK	K	1	2	3	EK	K	1	2	3	EK	K	1	2	3	EK	K	1	2	3
Std.Score:	75	99	104	104	108	78	101	110	106	106	82	104	112	108	108	88	112	119	115	116	93	120	124	119	121	105	130	139	135	139
S.D.:	15.2	16.3	13.8	13.4	23.0	14.2	15.4	15.9	16.8	18.6	13.3	13.6	15.8	16.8	18.6	14.2	16.6	16.8	18.4	18.9	14.5	17.1	17	17.8	17.9	10.5	13.9	11.1	15.2	15.1
%ile:	5TH	47TH	61ST	61ST	70TH	7TH	50TH	75TH	66TH	66TH	12TH	63RD	79TH	70TH	70TH	21ST	79TH	90TH	84TH	86TH	32ND	90TH	95TH	90TH	92ND	63RD	97TH	99TH	99TH	99TH
G.E.:	-	K8	1.9	3.1	4.3	-	K9	2.2	3.2	4.1	K0	1.0	2.3	3.4	4.3	K2	1.3	2.7	3.9	5.0	K4	1.6	2.9	4.2	5.4	K8	2.0	3.8	5.3	7.1
IQ:	Under 71					71-90					91-100					101-110					111-130					Above 131				
N	N=8					N=108					N=194					N=214					N=156					N=18				

[a] All testing performed at end of academic year, except for EK

On reading comprehension (MAT Total Reading), students with IQ's of 80 or less show as much gain from the end of first grade to the end of second grade as other IQ groups, but not as much from the end of second grade to the end of third grade. This latter effect may reflect the change in the Elementary Level MAT reading test to an uncontrolled (adult level) vocabulary (while the earlier tests used a controlled vocabulary). IQ is strongly influenced by one's vocabulary, which relates closely to parents' education.

Probably the most remarkable feature of Figures 30.3, 30.4, and 30.5 is that they show nearly parallel gain functions for the various IQ groups, with the one exception noted above. These parallel functions imply that how much a child can learn under Direct Instruction is largely unrelated to IQ (in the ranges shown). Children with lower IQ's start at lower levels and end at lower levels, but *gain as much* as the others in nearly every case. It should be noted that data from another 750 entering-first grade students (with more than 50 in the lowest IQ grouping) show remarkably similar results.

These results serve as a low-probability demonstration, particularly when they are compared with other large-scale attempts to implement effective programs for disadvantaged children. McLaughlin's (1975) book *Evaluation and Reform* summarizes the abortive results achieved by Title I implementations. Virtually all Title I programs that were evaluated showed no positive results. This theme recurs consistently in the evaluation of bilingual programs and other special programs for the disadvantaged. Against this background of failure, the Follow Through evaluation stands as perhaps the only one that suggests what might be possible with a complete implementation of resources. The results are low-probability in these respects:

1. The total time available would not predict superiority *in every subject* unless there was some generically different approach used to teach the various skills.

2. The relative uniformity of the outcomes across different school settings and administration types suggests that the approach is capable of making a

Figure 30.4

MAT Total Reading
Longitudinal Progress by IQ Block during 2nd and 3rd Grade for Children in Entering-Kindergarten (EK) Sites [b] (N=1,082)

Grade:[a]	1	2	3	1	2	3	1	2	3	1	2	3	1	2	3	1	2	3
Std.Score:	33.9	46.6	47.4	40.1	50.6	54.3	43.1	52.7	56.0	46.0	54.5	59.6	49.0	57.1	63.2	55.4	65.1	72.6
S.D.:	7.7	7.0	13.1	8.2	6.5	8.4	8.6	7.5	8.6	8.4	8.1	8.5	9.3	8.7	9.6	8.1	9.2	7.7
%ile:	30TH	22ND	11TH	50TH	41ST	29TH	66TH	51ST	34TH	78TH	59TH	44TH	88TH	70TH	58TH	94TH	88TH	81ST
G.E.:	1.6	2.2	2.3	1.9	2.5	2.8	2.0	2.7	3.0	2.2	2.9	3.4	2.4	3.1	3.7	2.9	3.9	4.9
IQ:	Under 71			71-90			91-100			101-110			111-130			Above 131		
N	N=19			N=181			N=271			N=310			N=265			N=36		

[a] All testing performed at end of academic year
[b] During Grade 3, the highest IQ block gained significantly more than the lowest block (which reflects the verbal content of the SIT and the Total Reading subtest of the Elementary Level MAT)

◀ Grade 1 National Median
◀◀ Grade 2 National Median
◀◀◀ Grade 3 National Median

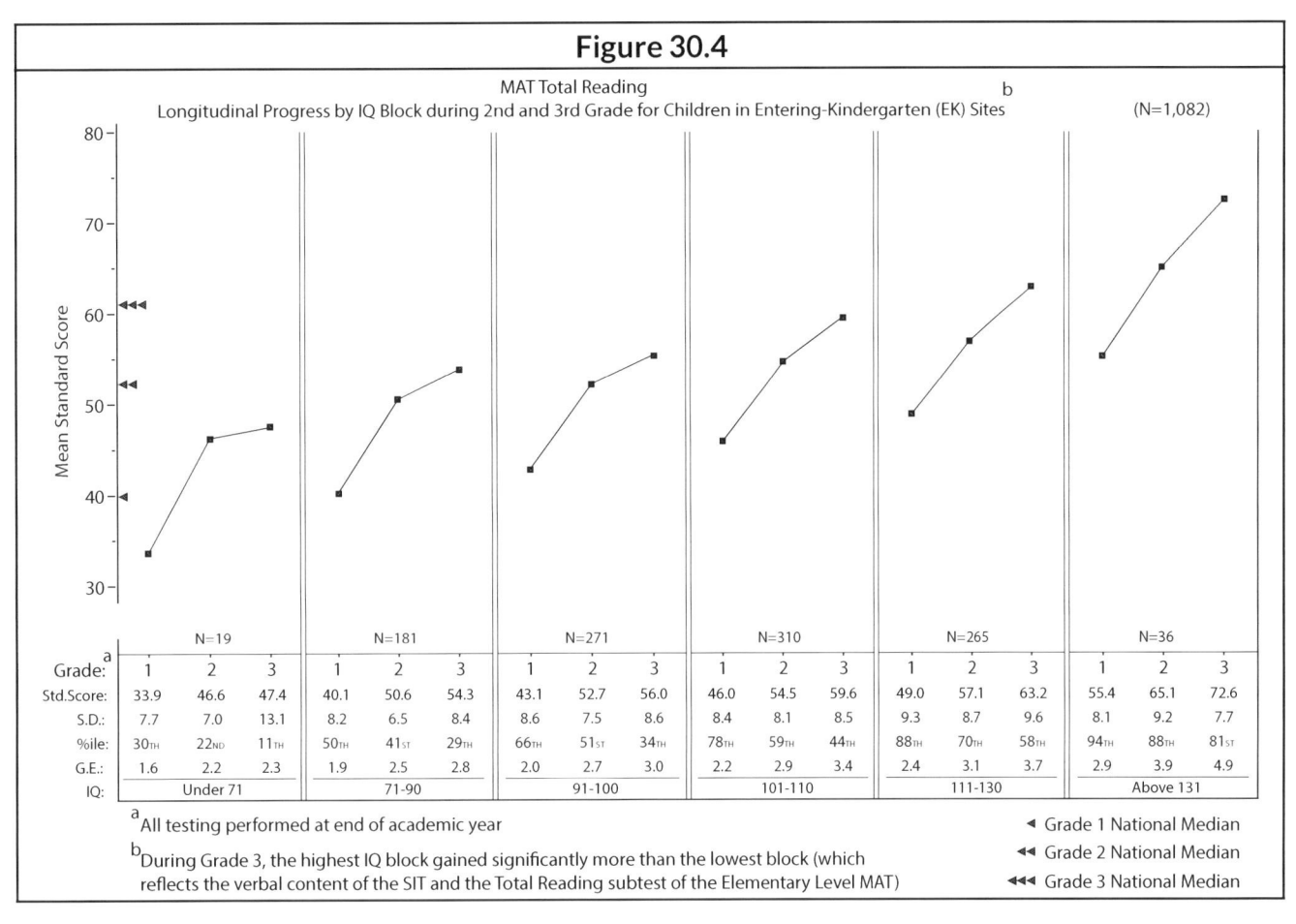

range of teachers and administrators more effective in delivering instruction to children.

3. The relative uniformity across children suggests that the program is effective with lower performers as well as middle-class children.

The summaries above are based on poor children only. Within each Follow Through site is a percentage of middle-class children. These typically enter somewhat higher and progress at a somewhat faster rate. Table 30.4 gives a summary of the test percentile means for non-poor kindergarten-starting children in the Direct Instruction model at the end of the third grade. (Data from Becker & Engelmann, 1978.)

To test the applicability of Direct Instruction to other hard-to-teach populations, Alex Maggs and his associates conducted a series of over 30 studies in metropolitan and rural areas of Australia, using Direct Instruction programs and teaching methods (*Distar, Corrective Reading, Morphographic Spelling*). Subjects included retarded, migrant, aboriginal, learning-disabled, and economically disadvantaged.

Table 30.4

Mean Standard Scores Converted to Percentiles on the Metropolitan Achievement Test

	N	Total Reading	Total Math	Language	Spelling
Poor Children	1800	40	52	50	47
Middle-Class Children	250	62	69	75	60

Alex Maggs and Robyn Maggs (1979) conclude their review of this work:

> There is no other major output of acceptable educational research in Australia that has shown the results obtained by this body of Direct Instruction research. There is concern being expressed at all levels of the Australian community that the schools are not making children sufficiently competent in their critical basic skills. The dramatic results of the Direct Instruction findings raise important questions of effective teaching and educational accountability. There is now a

Figure 30.5

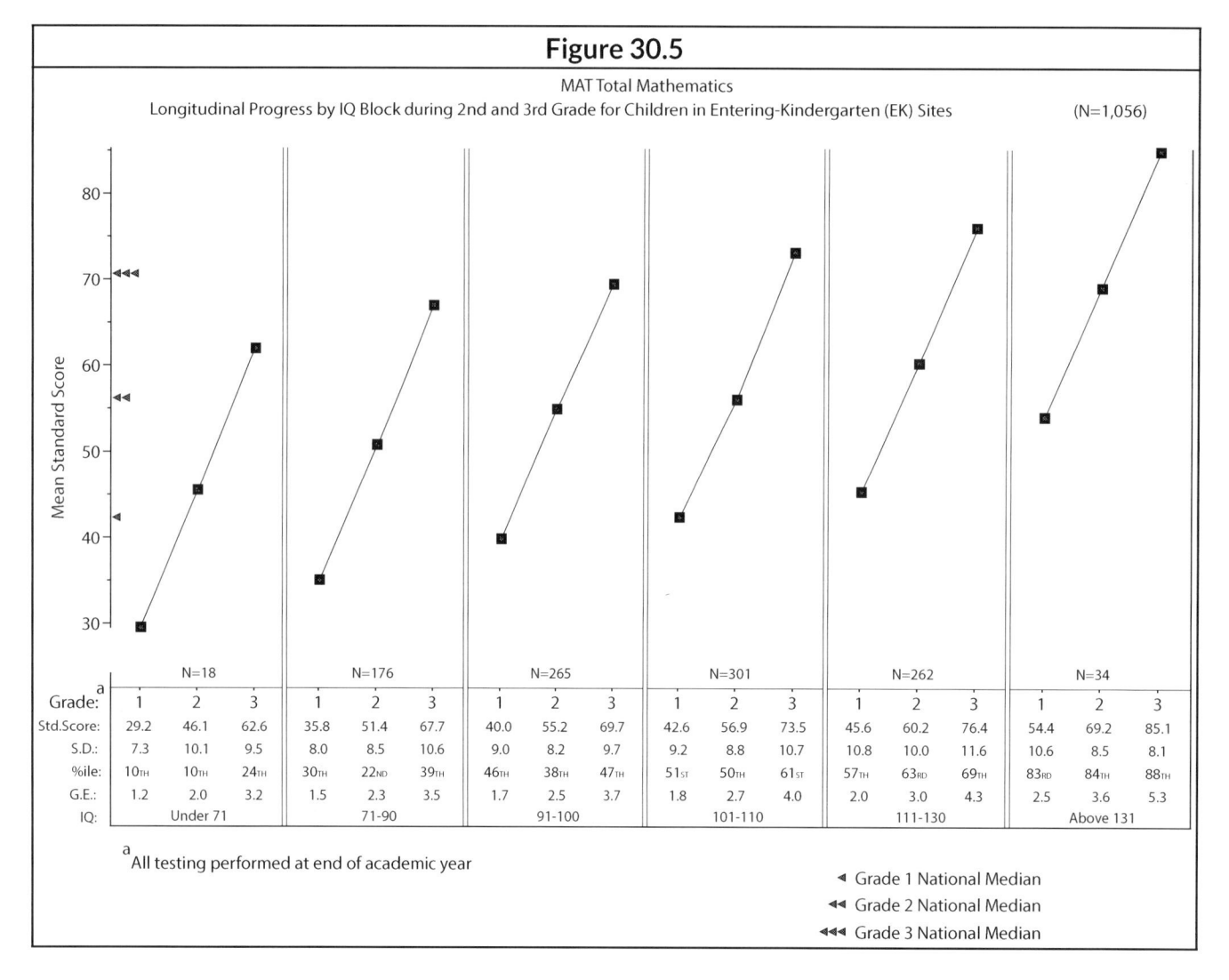

MAT Total Mathematics
Longitudinal Progress by IQ Block during 2nd and 3rd Grade for Children in Entering-Kindergarten (EK) Sites (N=1,056)

	N=18			N=176			N=265			N=301			N=262			N=34		
Grade:[a]	1	2	3	1	2	3	1	2	3	1	2	3	1	2	3	1	2	3
Std.Score:	29.2	46.1	62.6	35.8	51.4	67.7	40.0	55.2	69.7	42.6	56.9	73.5	45.6	60.2	76.4	54.4	69.2	85.1
S.D.:	7.3	10.1	9.5	8.0	8.5	10.6	9.0	8.2	9.7	9.2	8.8	10.7	10.8	10.0	11.6	10.6	8.5	8.1
%ile:	10TH	10TH	24TH	30TH	22ND	39TH	46TH	38TH	47TH	51ST	50TH	61ST	57TH	63RD	69TH	83RD	84TH	88TH
G.E.:	1.2	2.0	3.2	1.5	2.3	3.5	1.7	2.5	3.7	1.8	2.7	4.0	2.0	3.0	4.3	2.5	3.6	5.3
IQ:	Under 71			71-90			91-100			101-110			111-130			Above 131		

[a] All testing performed at end of academic year

◀ Grade 1 National Median
◀◀ Grade 2 National Median
◀◀◀ Grade 3 National Median

body of empirical data upon which decisions can be based. This evidence provides administrators, principals, and teachers with a basis for a choice of teaching strategies that have proven to be effective (p. 32).

New Skills and Behaviors

The stimulus-locus analysis assumes that the learner is a perfect receiver of information. In situations that require the learning of generically new skills, including new motor responses, however, the learner is not a perfect receiver. Primary questions associated with generically new learning have to do with the effectiveness of specific techniques and with the influence of the program on the learner's performance.

Tactual Hearing Experiments

The tactual vocoder is a device that transforms sound into patterns of tactual vibration, in much the same way sound is transformed when it travels on a long-distance phone connection. The tactual vocoder creates an analog of sound through frequency-to-locus patterns. The display used in experiments conducted by Engelmann and his colleagues consists of 24 vibrators arranged in order from high to low frequency. When a word is said verbally into a microphone, the device produces a series of vibratory patterns that theoretically should be a tactual counterpart of the word as it is experienced auditorially. Increases in loudness are expressed as more vigorous vibration; changes in pitch are expressed by a change in position; changes in phonemes result in changes of the vibratory pattern; changes in rate are reflected in rate of change of vibratory patterns.

In the first experiment four adult hearing subjects were taught a 60-word vocabulary (Engelmann & Rosov, 1975). Subjects also worked on identifying words that rhyme with known words, matching pitch and inflection of verbal patterns, identifying individual "sounds," and identifying novel sentences composed of words from their vocabulary. Three subjects had banks of vibrators placed on their forearms; one had the vibrators on her fingers.

The format for instruction was for the instructor to stand behind the subject and say words. The subject, who wore headphones that transmitted a high level of white noise, responded by trying to repeat what the instructor had said.

Subjects who practiced on the device for at least 20 hours learned to identify words, individual sounds, and sentences. They also learned to match pitch and inflection. Although the vocabulary presented to the subjects contained a number of minimally different words, as well as those that are not highly similar, the subjects generally achieved 90 percent accuracy on words when they were presented in a random order.

On about 40 percent of the trials that involved new sentences (sentences that had not been presented before), the subjects identified all words correctly on the first repetition. These sentences were spoken at a normal speaking rate. On about 40 percent of the trials, the subjects would request the sentence to be repeated (or part of it) and would then identify it correctly. On about 20 percent of the trials, they would make a mistake (usually on words at the beginning of the sentence).

The subjects could match unique musical inflections of vocabulary words, such as the name "Lori Skill-man" presented as a novel melody. The subjects consistently matched such unique patterns without deviating by more than a half-note on any part.

The learning of sounds, words, and sentences was not linear in difficulty. Words were not generally more difficult than sounds; sentences were somewhat more difficult than words, but not much more difficult.

The nature of what had been learned was further verified by location transfer tests. Subjects were tested on vocabulary words when the vibrators were placed on *their legs*, which placement had never occurred during training. For the subject who had worked with the vibrators on her fingers, performance on the transfer test was very poor (less than 20 percent accurate). The pattern of vibrators on her legs was not a perfect analogue to the pattern on the fingers. For subjects who had performed with the vibrators on their forearms, the transfer performance was about 85 percent of what their average performance had been with the vibrators on the arms, suggesting that *a pattern-identification skill* had been learned that was easily transferred to the legs.

A series of training studies was conducted with profoundly deaf subjects. These subjects predictably learned more slowly than the hearing subjects, because a much greater amount of new learning was implied. Instead of learning the transformation from a familiar spoken code, these subjects had to learn the spoken code (how to say the words); learn how to classify similar sounding words; learn to discriminate between them; and learn how to remember the association between a given tactual pattern and the spoken counterpart.

The data for one deaf subject appears in Figure 30.6.

The fact that the learner learned faster as the set of words became larger implies that the learner learned the *system of sameness and differences that characterizes the material.*

The plateau between 35 and 60 words (weeks 18 to 31) is typical of other deaf subjects. When the vocabulary reaches a certain size, the learner must apparently work out new "rules" for identifying words. Until this process is completed, learning is erratic. Once the consolidation has been achieved, however, learning proceeds very rapidly.

The general learning trend shown in Figure 30.6 is consistently observed in new-learning situations. Even work with autistic children is characterized by a "multiplier effect" with later members of a given set being mastered faster than earlier members of the set.

Sherman and Lorimer (personal communication) presented object-naming tasks to five- and six-year old autistic children. The children were taught to identify different objects. A large number of trials (of ten over 3000) was required to achieve the discrimination of the first-taught objects; however, the number of repetitions required to achieve discriminations dropped to an average of 60 after the sixth object had been discriminated.

An interesting fact about the performance of these children is that their progress was quite irregular and was

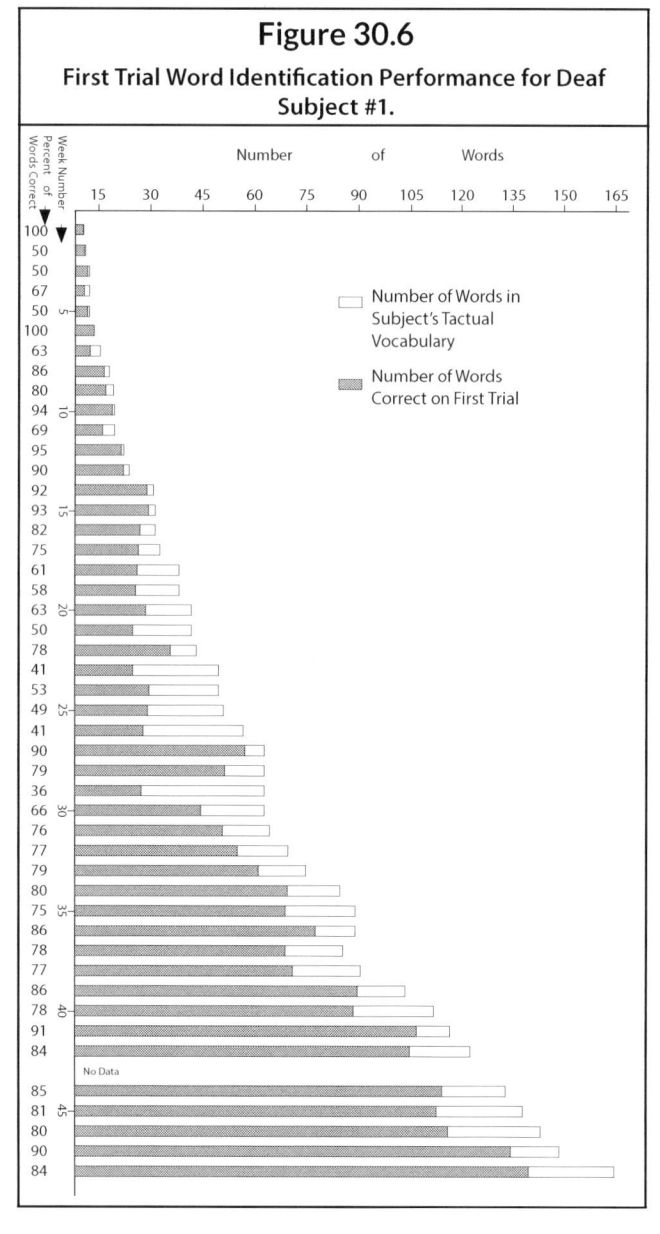

Figure 30.6
First Trial Word Identification Performance for Deaf Subject #1.

characterized by large regressions (objects whose name learning required unusually high numbers of repetitions). In every case, these "difficult" items were associated in a *container relationship* observed in everyday situations. All regressions involved discriminations like a glove (which bears a container relationship to hand), a cup (which bears a container relationship to juice or milk), a shoe (which is related to foot), etc. This outcome may illustrate a basic information-processing problem confronting the autistic child.

To provide a more precise understanding of the interaction between learner variables and communication variables in learning new skills, Williams, Engelmann, Becker, and Granzin (1979) designed a vocoder study that compared "communication predictions" with "learner predictions."

A set of 12 words was taught to four groups of hearing adults. The set contained minimally different words as well as some that were more greatly different. The criterion of performance the subjects were required to achieve and the sequence of the words were varied across the groups. The criterion was **high** or **low**. A **high** criterion required the learner to perform correctly on a larger consecutive number of items before a new word was added to the learner's set. A **low** criterion of performance required fewer consecutive correct responses. The sequence was designed either **hard** or **easy**. The **hard** sequence presented minimally different words early in the sequence, while the **easy** sequence distributed the difficult words, introducing one member of a minimally-different pair early and the other quite late.

Here are the words and the two sequences:

Hard sequence: eating, meeting, mile, smile, lag, log, toe, patrol, implement, geese, rung, up

Easy sequence: toe, eating, patrol, mile, implement, lag, geese, smile, rung, log, up, meeting

A pure stimulus-locus analysis would predict that the best sequence is the one that presents the high criterion of performance and the hard sequence. The rationale is that the high criterion assures that the learner is not responding to irrelevant features of the words. The hard sequence shows the learner quite early the minimum ways the words differ from each other. Therefore, it should more readily induce learning in a way that *does not imply misrules for later words*. (If the learner can discriminate between **mile** and **smile**, the learner will not confuse **mile** with **patrol**.) Note that the stimulus-locus analysis would be modified somewhat if the fact is given that the learner will proceed very slowly through the sequence. This situation will induce possible stipulation problems (working too long on the same small set of members).

A pure analysis of the learner leads to a different conclusion about which treatment should be best. This analysis would hold that the criterion should be relatively low because the learner is apparently incapable of attending to the degree demanded by a high criterion. For the hearing subjects in the initial vocoder study, mastery was inversely related to the criterion, with the subject working on a 60 percent correct criterion performing best; those on a 70 percent criterion performing next best; and the subject working on an 80 percent criterion performing most poorly. Not only do facts about the learner suggest that the low-criterion condition should work best, but also that the easy sequence should work best.

The group receiving the low criterion and the hard sequence performed the best by a considerable margin. Table 30.5 summarizes the means for the four groups. As the table shows, the sequence variables interact with the criterion variables. The same sequence (hard) is the best sequence when the criterion is low and the *worst* when the criterion is high. The treatments that involve the easy sequence are not so obviously affected by the change in the criterion, which means that these sequences are relatively "safe," if not capable of producing spectacular results.

Table 30.5
Mean Total Trials to Criterion by Condition

Criterion	Sequence	
	Easy	Hard
Low	1593 (N = 4)	984 (N = 4)
High	2361 (N = 5)	2602 (N = 5)
P Levels		
Sequence (S)		.49
Criterion (C)		.001
Interaction (SXC)		.05

All groups were given a transfer test in which the vibrators were placed on the subjects' legs and a sequence of 36 words was presented (12 words each three times in random order). The average performance was 72 percent correct (which was 85 percent of the performance achieved when the vibrators were placed on their arms) with no significant differences among the four groups, suggesting that modalities are not as important as the information. Transfer is predicted from the fact that the learners had generally mastered the words and could therefore perform on a tactual presentation that was analogous to the original.

The study shows that learner variables interact with communication variables. Even in situations that involve highly unfamiliar discriminations (those that are achieved only after an average of over 2,000 trials), the logical aspects of the presentation have some predictive value.

Easy-to-Hard Sequences

According to the logical analysis of *skills*, the easy-to-hard sequence will lead to distorted responses and stipulated responses. (The easy-word sequence in the vocoder study presented a sequence that proceeded from easy *discriminations* to hard ones.) To investigate the effect of the easy-to-hard sequence on learning new motor skills, Colvin (1981) predicted the generalizations that would occur if profoundly retarded students went through a program that taught using screwdrivers. This program required students to meet certain criteria on easy applications before moving to more difficult ones. Subjects worked first with socket drivers (for square-headed bolts) and last with slotted screwdrivers. Also they worked first on screws that were oriented vertically, with the head pointing up (0°), and they then worked on screws at different angles.

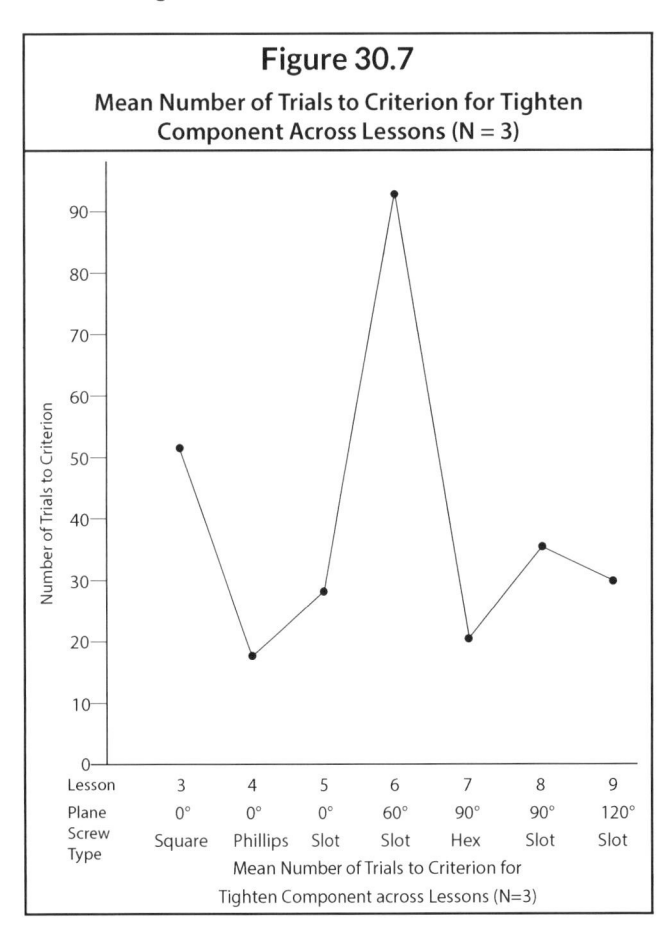

Figure 30.7
Mean Number of Trials to Criterion for Tighten Component Across Lessons (N = 3)

Lesson	3	4	5	6	7	8	9
Plane	0°	0°	0°	60°	90°	90°	120°
Screw Type	Square	Phillips	Slot	Slot	Hex	Slot	Slot

Mean Number of Trials to Criterion for Tighten Component across Lessons (N=3)

As Figure 30.7 shows, the work at 0° did not facilitate the

work at 60° with the slotted screwdriver (lesson 6). The variation in angle had not been implied by the earlier work. As a result, stipulation occurred and the learners produced responses that did not readily transfer to screw driving on an angle.

Figure 30.8 shows a different aspect of an easy-to-hard sequence. In lesson 1, the learners were taught to hand-turn screws that were already set in a board. In lesson 2, learners were required to place screws without turning them until they were hand-tight. Learners required many trials to meet criterion on placing in lesson 2 simply because they placed the screw and then hand-tightened it. If placing had been introduced in lesson 1, followed by *placing and turning* in lesson 2, this problem would probably have been avoided. Although it may seem to be analytically easier to place without turning, this skill is actually harder for low performers if they have already been taught to hand-turn the screws.

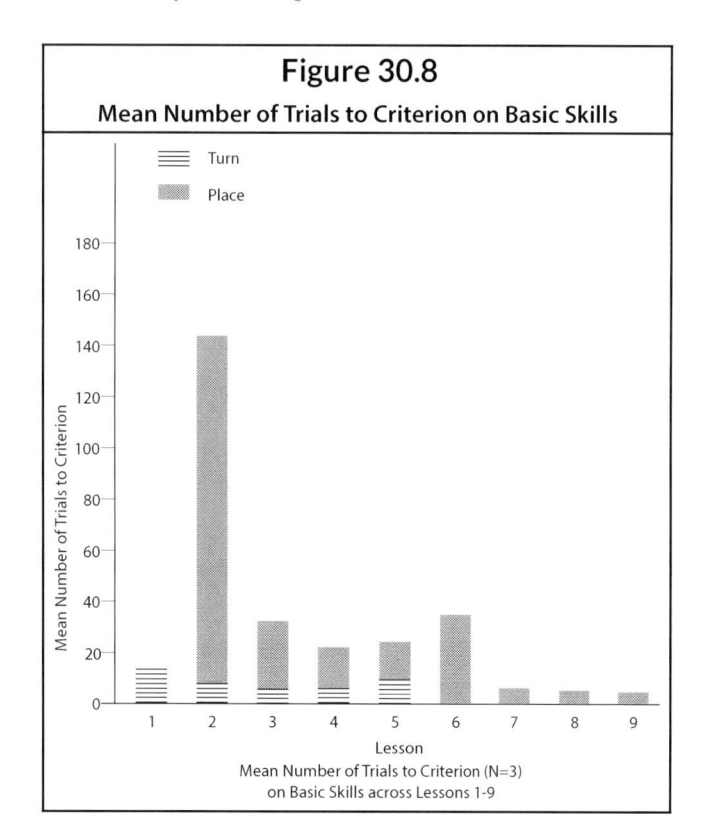

Figure 30.8
Mean Number of Trials to Criterion on Basic Skills

Mean Number of Trials to Criterion (N=3) on Basic Skills across Lessons 1-9

Teaching Generalized Compliance

According to the stimulus-locus analysis, generalizations are induced by demonstrating sameness across a range of applications. Generalizations are predicted for any example that clearly falls within the range. Engelmann and Colvin (1981) developed procedures based on this analysis for inducing compliance in highly non-compliant subjects. The training was designed not to induce specific compliant behaviors, but to teach a "compliance set"—a generalization about how a range of adult-learner situations are the same.

To induce the generalization, the program first established compliance to the commands "stand up" and "sit down." The purpose of this training was to demonstrate that compliance is required whether or not the learner wishes to comply. Subjects received no reinforcement for following the commands and were physically made to comply if they did not respond. Each presentation of this set of commands continued until learners met a criterion of performance (such as following four consecutive commands without requiring physical assistance or acting-out in any way).

In addition to this set of tasks, the program provided for a range of other tasks for which reinforcement could be received (such as "come here," "touch your nose," "walk to the chalkboard," and so forth). Appropriate performance on these tasks was reinforced. Also included in this set were tasks that related to behaviors expected of the learner in different situations (such as the lunch room). If the learner failed to perform on any task presented in this reinforcement set, the learner was taken through a series of "stand-up" tasks, followed by repetition of the task that had not been complied with.

Successful performance on the range of tasks for which reinforcement is provided implies that the learner will comply to receive the reinforcement. Successful performance on the stand-up tasks implies that the learner has learned that compliance is required. When the number of stand-up series diminishes to nearly zero and the learner performs consistently on the reinforcement activities, the learner's performance suggests that the learner will generalize compliant behavior to any situation that would fall within the range of tasks presented in training.

Figure 30.9 shows the summary of tearing and breaking behavior performed by an autistic child. At the beginning of training, the child broke things at the rate of about three items a day at home and two items per day at school. At night, he would tear up his pajamas, sheets, even the bed. The "stand-up" procedures were modified for this subject so that breaking was performed on command. (For instance, the trainer would hand the child a stick and say, "Break it," or "Don't break it.")

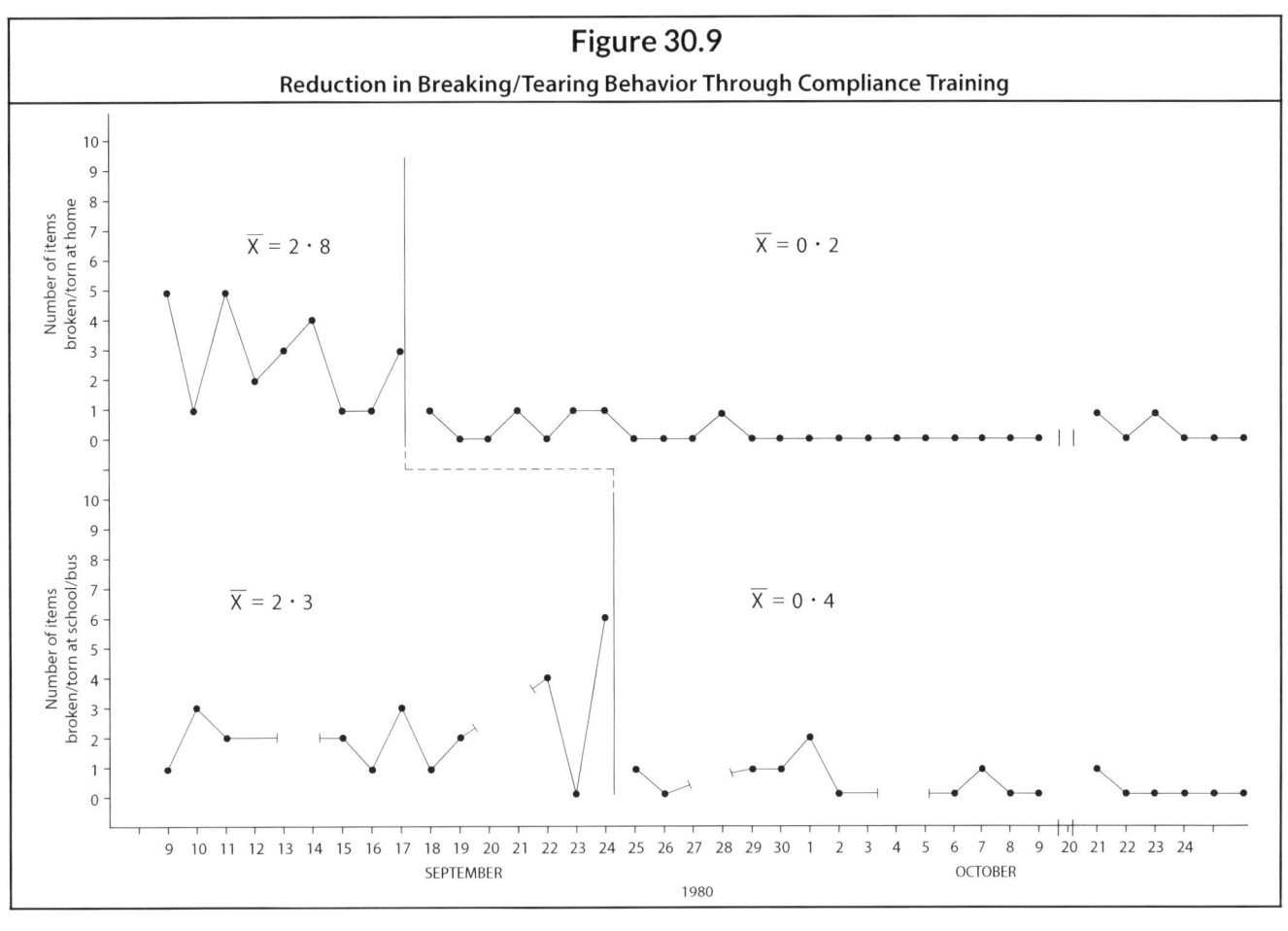

Figure 30.9
Reduction in Breaking/Tearing Behavior Through Compliance Training

[Chart showing number of items broken/torn at home (top) and at school/bus (bottom) from September 9 to October 24, 1980. Top panel: $\overline{X} = 2 \cdot 8$ before intervention, $\overline{X} = 0 \cdot 2$ after. Bottom panel: $\overline{X} = 2 \cdot 3$ before intervention, $\overline{X} = 0 \cdot 4$ after.]

The transfer on "No breaking" was generalized from the training situation to situations in which the learner was not supervised. As Figure 30.9 shows, the program was first implemented in the home, resulting in an immediate change in the rate of breaking and tearing. However, no transfer occurred to the school setting. (If anything, the rate of tearing in school increased.) When the program was implemented in the school, the rate quickly dropped in school. On only one day after the implementation of the compliance training was the rate at home or at school more than one break per day.

Similar results have been consistently achieved with a variety of non-compliant children. The program taught what was the same about compliance and showed that compliance was required for a range of situations. Knowledge of compliance transferred to situations beyond the specific tasks involved in training.

Introducing Similar Members to a Set

The vocoder experiment reported earlier by Williams, et al. (1979) showed that both criterion of performance and sequence of introduction are important. The experiment dealt with *highly* unfamiliar discriminations (evidence of which is the high number of repetitions needed to achieve the learning). In situations that do not involve highly unfamiliar discriminations, which are far more typical of the kind of learning that occurs in academic situations, minimally different members are not juxtaposed in their order of introduction. Rather, they are separated, so that the learner first receives practice on one name that has a highly similar counterpart before the second name is introduced. For instance, in *Distar Reading I* (Engelmann & Bruner, 1975), **d** is introduced early (on lesson 27) but **b** is not introduced until lesson 121. The idea is that the relationship of **b** and **d** is made most obvious if **d** is quite familiar when **b** is introduced. If the learner is not firm on **d**, the learner may become confused about which shape goes with which sound. The similarity between the members may lead to chronic errors (reversals).

To investigate the importance of separating highly similar members in their order of introduction, Carnine performed two studies. In the first (Carnine, 1976c) similar members were introduced successively to one group of first-graders and preschoolers and non-successively to another group (with the two similar members separated by a series of non-similar members). The children were taught the short sounds for **e** and **i**. When these two letters were separated, first graders made fewer errors during training (33 percent error rate for the Separated Group versus 52 percent for the Successive Group). Preschoolers reached criterion in fewer total trials when the letters were separated. (178 versus 293).

In the second study, the context was shaped (Carnine, 1980e). Children were required to match letters, all of which were highly similar (**p, q, b, d**). The children matched the letter shown by the teacher with letters on a "choice sheet." For the separated-members treatment, the children first worked from choices that presented only one highly similar member (one was correct; one was highly similar; two were not similar). Later the number of highly similar choices increased until all four were highly similar to the one presented by the teacher. The choices presented to the Successive Group were all highly similar. The Separated Group required 31 trials to reach training criterion while the Successive Group required 69 trials.

This experiment suggests that if it is possible to "shape" the context in a way that creates no serious misrules, the shaping may prove to be the most effective procedure. Note that even for the Successive Group, the number of trials is relatively small compared to that required by highly unfamiliar sets of discriminations (such as those in the tactual vocoder experiments). Related research has been conducted by Cheyne, 1966; Gruenenfelder and Borkowski, 1975; Houser and Trublood, 1975; O'Malley, 1973.

Teaching the second member of highly similar pairs. When highly similar members are introduced to the learner, the introduction of the second member is very important, even if the members are separated in time. The introduction of the second similar member can either involve both the similar members (new and familiar) or one of them (new). If the members are similar in features and similar in name, the problem of the *spurious transformation* may occur. If the learner has mastered **b** and the letter **d** is introduced, the *names* are similar and the *shapes* are similar.

To compare the effectiveness of the separated-set approach and the integrated-set approach with highly similar members, Carnine (1981a) introduced concepts labeled **bif** and **dif** to four groups of preschoolers. **Dif** referred to a left-leaning parallelogram, and **bif** referred to a right-leaning parallelogram. First **bif** was taught to four groups of preschool children. All groups were then taught **dif**. One group was immediately required to discriminate between examples of **bif** and **dif**. The second group was introduced to **dif** in the context of a circle and triangle. This introduction did not initially require discrimination of **bif** and **dif** in the same sequence.

For the third group, **dif** was not initially identified as **dif**, but as **not-bif**. Students were immediately required to discriminate between **bif** and **not-bif**. Later, students were taught the other name for **not-bif** (**dif**).

For the juxtaposition of the fourth group, **bif** and **dif** were included in the same sequence (following the introduction of **dif**). However, triangle and circle also appeared in this sequence. **Bif** and **dif** were seldom juxtaposed in this sequence.

The results showed that one treatment was significantly poorer than the others. That was the sequence that presented only **bif** and **dif**. The children performed about the same on the others. This study shows that if there is a strong basis for a spurious transformation, such as the one prompted by the relationship between the parallelograms and the names **bif** and **dif**, the similar names must be separated.

Semi-specific prompts. Darwin and Baddeley (1974) and others have conducted experiments showing that similarity in names causes the identification problem more than similarity in examples. The problem seems to be that the learner is aware of specific features of the example, but is unable to "associate" those features with the appropriate name. The appropriate name becomes "mixed-up" with the inappropriate one.

To investigate this phenomenon, Engelmann and Granzin (1980) conducted a reversal experiment with a deaf girl who was learning speech through tactual-vocoder practice. The words taught to the girl were not "highly" similar on an absolute scale; however, they were functionally highly similar, which means that the girl had a great deal of trouble discriminating between them. On the words most recently taught to her, she averaged 50 percent correct when she was required to "listen" to words (presented through tactual vibration) and identify them. Her performance with words that had been introduced earlier (those words not in the most recent 10) were identified correctly on over 80 percent of the items.

To determine the extent to which the learner's problem was one of recognizing the words, but not being able to produce the response that signals recognition, the investigators presented a *semi-specific prompt*. The last 10 words introduced were written on the chalkboard. The learner (who could read) was permitted to observe these words during the test. She was tested on *all* words that had been taught (as many as 85 words), 10 of which were the most recently introduced. The test words were presented in an unpredictable order. If the learner recognized a particular word as one of the last 10, but did not know how to pronounce it, she could look at the list, find the appropriate word, and use the spelling as a guide for pronouncing it.

During the semi-specific prompt condition, she performed at 65 percent correct on the most recently introduced words. Removal of the prompt resulted in the accuracy of these words dropping to 20 percent. The experiment showed that her problem was not one of recognizing the words presented tactually, but one of associating a word with a specific response and producing that response. Since she was not practiced in either phase of this operation, she tended to perform poorly on words that had not been practiced many, many times.

Related research on prompting has been conducted by Archer, 1962; Drotar, 1974; Imai and Garner, 1965; Lyczak, 1976; Restle, 1959; Silver and Rollins, 1973; Trabasso, 1963; Trabasso and Bower, 1968; Warren, 1954.

Summary

This chapter dealt with demonstrations of low-probability learning outcomes, studies that show the correlation between the diagnosis of flaws in programs and learning outcomes, and studies concerned with the interaction of stimulus-locus variables and learner variables.

The demonstrations of low-probability learning outcomes show that when communications are carefully controlled, different types of learners are consistently capable of learning much more than they would under "normal" circumstances. Demonstrations with preschoolers showed that they could learn both cognitive-conceptual skills (such as understanding of specific gravity) that were not normally learned by young children, and academic skills (reading, arithmetic, logic) far beyond normative expectations. Disadvantaged preschoolers performed on the second-grade level in academic subjects while their peers performed below the age norm for five-year olds. Low-probability demonstrations were also provided with school-age children. The most extensive was the Direct Instruction Follow Through Model. Children in this model outperformed all comparison children in *all* academic areas and in self-esteem measures. The children were taught from kindergarten through third grade. Those taught by other methods performed around the 20th percentile (on the average), while the Direct Instruction children performed near the 50th percentile. These outcomes were achieved in different geographical areas with children from different types of backgrounds. Low-IQ students (under 80) exhibited unpredictably large achievement gains, as did middle-class children.

Studies that deal with diagnosis confirm that when a teaching communication has analytically observable flaws, some learners will learn inappropriately (responding to the flaws). If programs are analytically incapable of providing a clear communication, they tend to be ineffective with learners. Furthermore, the type of learner failure that is exhibited tends to be predictable from an analysis of the communication.

Studies that deal with learner variables confirm that learning is characteristically slow. Even within the framework of a learning experience that requires hundreds of trials, however, the learner tends to be logical. Stated differently, although the overriding necessary condition for generically new learning is a large number of practice trials, different outcomes are predictable from the "logic" of the communication. The studies in this group tended to show that by applying the basic analysis of flawless communications to the learning of generically new skills, we can predict generalizations for diverse behaviors such as compliance and new motor responses. We can identify where problems will occur in a program that proceeds rapidly from easy to hard examples.

Singly, the studies cited in these research chapters are inconclusive. As a group, however, they lend strong support to the basic stimulus-locus premise, which is that the learner responds to the information conveyed by the communication. Therefore, it follows that unless the communication is controlled by making it as nearly flawless as possible, we will seriously misdiagnose learning problems and may falsely conclude that the learner is responsible for failing when in fact the learner responded imperfectly reasonable ways to the communication.

Chapter 31
Theoretical Issues

This chapter outlines the primary philosophical views that influenced the analytical system we have developed. The chapter also addresses more specific theoretical issues–the relationship of our analysis to traditional learning theories, the logical basis for some reinforcement and punishment phenomena, the logic of learning to learn, the theoretical problems associated with strict behavioral objectives, and the role of humanism in instruction.

Philosophical Underpinnings

Scientific theories rest on basic philosophical assumptions about knowledge, meaning, and rigor. The present work is obviously influenced by philosophical orientations quite different from those assumed by either strict behaviorism or cognitive developmental theories such as the one formulated by Piaget.

Behaviorism is perhaps best described as an extension of pragmatism. It seems to be heavily influenced by the rule presented by "the father" of pragmatism, C.S. Peirce (1935). The criterion that Peirce used to determine whether an idea was useful is: Does the difference make a difference? For example, two people express different positions on a point and may argue. There is an apparent difference. But does this apparent difference make a real difference in their lives or in some significant outcome? If not, Peirce would contend that the difference is not really a difference, because it does not result in any difference that is substantive.

By applying this principle of "differences that make a difference" to learned behavior, we might come up with a scheme quite similar to that developed by strict behaviorists. What are the important differences? Behaviors. Does it matter what goes on inside the head to produce given behaviors? No. Therefore, these internal differences do not make a significant difference, and we can deal with problems of human behavior in a direct, uncomplicated way by considering only the relationship between those differences in stimuli that cause differences in behavior. By following this line of reasoning, we are left with a system in which stimuli are the agents that make a difference, and the differences that are made are the responses.

The position adopted in the present work is that there is nothing wrong with behaviorism as far as it goes. It simply does not go far enough in permitting us to deal theoretically with stimuli. The guidelines that we use for analyzing stimuli are logical. When we say that they are logical, we use the term in a very broad sense. If something is not possible either through "induction" or "deduction," we will consider it impossible and will further assume that a learner could not learn it.

Our first problem in dealing with stimuli involves *sets of stimuli*. We know that we can present different shades of red to a naive learner and that the learner will appropriately classify new stimuli as **red** after exposure to the different shades we had presented. Since the new stimuli are not identical to any stimulus presented during the training, it is impossible for the learner to "memorize" a color. No such color was presented during the training. If it is impossible for the learner to simply "associate" one particular stimulus value with the word **red**, we must postulate a mechanism that makes the learner's performance possible. The simplest such mechanism is the capacity to learn *what is the same about all the stimuli in the set of demonstration examples* that were identified as red. For the learner to perform this feat, the learner must abstract this sameness from the various stimuli and must be able to use this abstracted sameness to identify new examples of red.

Interestingly enough, this particular problem of color generalization played an important role in the history of philosophy. David Hume (1975) had developed a highly mechanical system that explained how thinking took place. He suggested that the mind simply *recombined sensory impressions*, enabling the thinker to imagine such things as a golden tree, although the person had never experienced a golden tree. The person simply "combined" the idea of gold (which was familiar) with the idea of tree (which was also familiar).

Hume did demur about the perfectly mechanical nature of ideas and impressions, however. He indicated that he had little doubt that a person would be able to identify a new shade of blue, one that had never been experienced before. Hume added that this example was singular and unimportant. However, it proved to be important enough for Immanuel Kant (1899) to destroy Hume's theory. Kant pointed out that ideas and impressions are not totally determined by experience. Some preconditions must exist for the experience to be possible. The question of ideas, therefore, had to be considered within the framework of these prerequisites.

Although the details of Kant's system of prerequisites are not highly relevant to our discussion, Kant clearly pointed out the fallacy of trying to explain "ideas" by referring only to experiences (simple responses to stimuli). Some intermediary is necessary to explain how it would be possible for a person to identify something that had never been experienced.

A very good analysis of stimuli was developed by an English philosopher who came after Kant. This analysis dealt with *sets of stimuli* and provided specific guidelines for developing sets of examples so *they would rule out all but one possible interpretation*. The philosopher was John Stuart Mill (1950). The analysis that he developed was not designed as an educational theory. Instead, it addressed the problem of scientific inquiry. Perhaps the most interesting aspect of Mill's analysis is the failure of later investigators to recognize that it indeed provided a basic structure for a theory of instruction. Although educational investigators seem quick to adapt theories from various fields outside education (from information theories to developmental theories), the single theory that carried the most significant implications for instruction has had virtually no impact on instruction. Apparently, investigators generally failed to recognize the close correspondence between the instructional settings and one in which the investigator is trying to determine the precise cause of various outcomes. In both situations, we must deal with concrete examples and draw inferences from these "particulars." In both cases, the analysis must therefore focus on the features of the examples. In both cases, sets of examples are needed if we are to communicate the precise relationship between the features of the examples and the "outcome" (which is the behavior that accompanies the examples in the instructional setting). In both cases, the problem is one that involves *inductive reasoning*–proceeding from specific, concrete instances to a "concept" that applies to instances not observed as part of the communication that induces the concept.

Mill developed *methods* for showing sameness, for showing difference, for showing the relationship between sameness and difference, for dealing with concepts that are related to familiar concepts, and for presenting correlated-feature concepts. Below is a brief summary of these principles.

By substituting the word *feature* for *circumstance*, we can see the similarity between Mill's principles and the principles of juxtaposition that we postulated.

Mill's first principle is the principle of agreement (or sameness).

> If two or more instances of the phenomenon under investigation have only one circumstance in common, the circumstances in which alone all the instances agree is the cause (or effect) of the given phenomenon (Mill, 1950, p. 214).

Stated differently, if the examples are different except for a common feature and if the outcome is the same for all instances, the only possible cause of the common outcome is the common feature. This principle is logically irrefutable (if the cause or effect is associated with only a single feature). The fact that the various examples share only this feature rules out the possibility that another feature is a cause (or effect).

The juxtaposition principle of sameness is based on the same logic. The cause in question is the basis for labeling examples in the same way. If the examples vary greatly and have only one common feature, the set of examples communicates unambiguously what this cause is. If the examples are highly similar, however, the communication is ambiguous because it presents many possible causes.

Mill's second principle is the principle of difference.

> If an instance in which the phenomenon under investigation occurs and an instance in which it does not occur have every circumstance in common save one, that one occurring only in the former, the circumstances in which alone the two instances differ is the effect, or the cause, or an indispensable part of the cause of the phenomenon (Mill, 1950, p. 215).

Stated differently, if the positive and negative examples of a given outcome are the same in all features but one, the single feature must be essential to the outcome. Again, this principle parallels the juxtaposition principle of difference. If there is only one difference between two examples and if the outcome is different in any way, the difference in the examples must cause the difference in the outcome. (The cause here is the objective basis for treating the two examples differently.) If we violate the difference principle, we create communications that are guilty of implying false causes. If two examples are greatly different and are treated differently, the different treatment may be attributed to any single difference in the examples or any combination of differences. This principle, like the sameness principle, is logically unassailable (given a single cause is associated with the observed differences).

In some experimental situations, the cause may be complex enough to warrant the use of both the principle of agreement and the principle of difference. Mill refers to this principle as the joint method of agreement and difference.

> If two or more instances in which the phenomenon occurs have only one circumstance in common, while two or more instances in which it does not occur have nothing in common save the absence of that circumstance, the circumstances in which alone the two sets of instances differ is the effect or the cause, or an indispensable part of the cause, of the phenomenon (Mill, 1950, p. 221).

This principle describes the logic followed by the stimulus-locus analysis for demonstrating concepts in basic sequences. Minimum difference examples show the single difference between positive and negative examples while juxtaposed positive examples that differ greatly show the basis of sameness or agreement of the positive examples.

Mill's principle that suggests transformations is called the method of residues:

> Subduct from any phenomenon such part as is known by previous inductions to be the effect of certain antecedents, and the residue of the phenomenon is the effect of the remaining antecedents (Mill, 1950, p. 223).

Although this principle does not contain the detail necessary to derive the procedures for communicating either single-transformation or double-transformation concepts, the basic logic of demonstrating "residue" is used by both these sequences. The progressive minimum differences at the beginning of the single transformation sequence are designed so the part that is known from previous inductions is large, and the residue (or difference from example to example) is small and specific. In this way, the nature of the "residue" is made clear. Also, the double transformation is based on the idea that the transformation for one set is known. The procedures for juxtaposing instances of this set with instances of the new set shows the nature of the across-set transformation (or residue).

Mill refers to the principle for correlated features as the method of concomitant variations.

> Whatever phenomenon varies in any manner whenever another phenomenon varies in some particular manner is either a cause or an effect of the phenomenon, or is connected with it through some fact of causation (Mill, 1950, p. 227).

The goal is to show the correlation between two sets of events—one set of antecedent events and a set of outcome events—by determining "whether we can produce the one set of variations by means of the other" (Mill, 1950, p. 227). Note that this principle describes the correlated-feature logic. Two sets of events are related by a factual or causal link. By presenting examples of one set and requiring the learner to apply the causal link to each example in this set, the learner creates the instances of the correlated set.

When designing the principles of juxtaposition, we did not refer to Mill's logical principles. In fact, although we had studied Mill's scientific method years before, we were not consciously aware of the parallel until after the fact. The similarity of Mill's principles and our principles of juxtaposition occurs because *instruction is inductive in nature*. We therefore face the same induction problems that occur in the experimental situation—the problems of showing the single basis of sameness across the positive examples, showing the difference between positives and negatives, and providing special arrangements of examples for complicated concepts. The principles of juxtaposition (or some approximation of them) logically follow once we recognize that concepts are not the property of the mind, but are the inductions described by possible sets of examples.

Mill's analysis has apparently stood the test of time. Although the examples that Mill gave of correlated events were weak and although the principle of residue could have been amplified to deal with sets of examples, the system is basically sound, which implies that the principles of juxtaposition are logically sound.

The method that we used for *analyzing concepts* for their sameness was suggested by a philosophical school that developed a unique method for providing alternative explanations. The two most important proponents of this school were G.E. Moore (1903) and A.C. Ewing (1947). These philosophers were not interested in scientific investigation, but in the relationship between definitions or descriptions and reality. They focused their analysis on ethics or "the definition of good." Moore suggested that **good** was like the property **yellow**. This inference is based on the fact that both good and yellow are the same in some observable ways; therefore, a reasonable hypothesis is that they are the same in other ways. Specifically:

Yellow
1. Yellow is learned through experience.
2. We know that something is yellow through intuition.
3. Yellow is an irreducible property of events.

Good
1. Good is learned through experience.
2. We know that something is good through intuition.
3. Good is an irreducible property of events.

If the first two sentences are accepted, the third becomes compelling. Note that the reference that "yellow is known through intuition" is not a mystical statement. It means simply that there is no logical means by which one can explain the person's basis for identifying something as **yellow**. If a person says, "I know it's yellow because that's what I learned," the person is making a statement of history, not of one that explains *how* the person knows that it is yellow. If the person says, "I know it's yellow because it's a particular wave-length," the person has simply sidestepped the question. How does the person know that the object is of a certain wave-length if the person simply looks at the object? In the end, the person will say something to the effect of, "I know it's yellow because I know it's yellow."

Our purpose in presenting the argument about good is not to argue for it, but to point out the strength of the analysis. Any two things, no matter how different, are the same in some ways. (If two things were completely different in every possible dimension, they would both be in the class of things that were completely different from at least one other thing. Therefore, they would be the same in one way.) By constructing a set of statements that express the various samenesses, we are provided both with a profile of how the things are the same, and with the possible basis for drawing inferences about how these things may be the same in some unobserved ways. For example, if object **A** and object **B** are the same in eight ways and if object **A** has a ninth feature that is unobserved, but not contradicted in **B**, there is a possibility that **B** may also share this ninth feature. The only way to determine whether this inference is valid is to perform some sort of test or investigation. The analysis, however, suggests the test and suggests both the kind of evidence that would support the inference and the kind of evidence that would provide for possible falsification of the inference. Because the method permits us to develop possible classification systems for events that are superficially quite different, we used this analysis as the basis for formulating the classification of knowledge. For example, the concept of **book** and the concept of **moving faster** are apparently quite different from each other. Yet, by applying a variation of the sameness analysis suggested by Ewing and Moore, we can determine the extent to which they are the same.

Books
1. There are concrete examples of **books**.
2. There is a label for **books**.
3. There are negative examples of **books**.
4. The naive learner would not know the basis for the label **book** unless we present concrete examples of **book**.
5. The naive learner would not know the basis for **not-book** unless we present examples of **not-book**.
6. The naive learner would not know which examples were actually **books** and which were **not-books** unless we treated the examples differently.
7. The learner would not know what is the same about various books and what is different about **books** and **not-books** unless we design examples to show sameness and difference.

Moving faster
1. There are concrete examples of **moving faster**.
2. There is a label for **moving faster**.
3. There are negative examples of **moving faster**.
4. The naive learner would not know the label for **moving faster** unless we present concrete examples of **moving faster**.

5. The naive learner would not know the basis for **not-moving faster** unless we present examples of **not-moving faster**.

6. The naive learner would not know which examples are **moving faster** and which are **not-moving faster** unless we labeled the examples differentially.

7. The learner would not know what is the same about various instances of moving faster and what is different about **moving faster** and **not-moving faster** unless we design the examples to show sameness and difference.

We could certainly add to this list. In the end, however, we are provided with a set of common features that suggest both a common classification (basic forms) and common procedures (the labeling conventions, the setup convention, the principles for sameness and difference, the test of generalization).

By extending this analysis, we are provided with a precise basis for determining how the examples are *different*. A statement that can be made about one example but not about the other describes a specific difference. After determining a difference (such as the fact that examples of **moving faster** are not absolute), we can use this feature as a basis for finding other examples that share the relative feature observed in **moving faster**. With information about enough other examples, it is possible to determine a taxonomy that is reasonably precise for accommodating all knowledge and skills.

Both the analysis provided by Moore and Ewing, and that suggested by Mill, address the problem of dealing with sets of examples. But later philosophers have tended to shy away from the analysis of concrete examples in favor of an analysis of language.* For example, Wittgenstein referred to the use of examples in teaching. For Wittgenstein, the examples do not show the learner what is common about the examples, but show the learner how to use the words. Pitkin explains Wittgenstein's position about using examples:

> The place where explanation fails and training is called for is where the pupil lacks knowledge of how to use the word. And that kind of knowledge is completely contained in the examples . . . (Pitkin, 1972, p. 48).

But Wittgenstein seemed to miss the most important point about the examples, which is that we can show the common feature of the examples that are treated in the same way. Wittgenstein says,

> One gives examples and intends them to be taken in a particular way. I do not, however, mean by this that the learner is supposed to see in those examples that common thing which I—for some reason—was unable to express; but that he is now able to employ the examples in a particular way. Here giving examples is not an indirect means of explaining—in default of

---

* The movement from analysis of concrete examples is evident in the philosophy of science. Although the assumption of concrete examples is implicit in any discussion of hypotheses and the procedures by which they are corroborated or falsified, primary emphasis is on language. Popper (1959), for instance, argues that hypotheses must be designed so that they provide for their falsification. The reason is basically logical. It is never rigorously possible to show a cause or a concept by presenting only positive examples. On the other hand, it is possible to show with great rigor that something does not cause a particular outcome. Therefore, by designing the hypothesis so that it indicates the precise conditions (or set of conditions) that would lead to a negative outcome, the hypothesis provides a compelling basis for ruling out different possible causes and for lending greater support to the conclusion that the unique antecedents common to the examples in which the positive outcome occurred describe the sole cause of the positive outcomes. Although this idea is quite valuable, it can be directly derived from Mill's analysis. By using the joint method of agreement and difference, the investigator receives information about both positives and negatives, and the information should be quite precise about which antecedents were relevant to the different outcomes.

Mill's joint method of agreement and difference therefore suggests an operational model for constructing hypotheses that provide for possible falsification and that are very specific. If the investigator specified a possible set of examples to be tested, indicated a range of possible outcomes, and showed how the various examples insured that the specific cause would be evident regardless of the outcome, the "hypothesis" would be required to remain closely associated with the concrete realities of the experimental situation. It would not become a language problem that is at least partially divorced from the features of the experimental instances. This hypothesis would clearly demonstrate each possible basis for falsifying the hypothesis.

Our purpose here is not to get deeper into the philosophy of science, merely to point out that this field is preoccupied with the *propositions or statements*. Certainly, these are very important. However, the propositions are important only because they relate to possible concrete situations that may be misunderstood or interpreted in a way that will lead to possible problems (and paradoxes) unless particular language is used. So long as one understands the *concrete bases* for the language conventions, the conventions present no problem; however, the emphasis of modern theories of science tend to focus so strongly on the propositional level that the concrete examples are all but lost. And these theories often fail to suggest that there is probably always more than one linguistic solution to a specific concrete problem.

a better. For any general definition can be misunderstood too (1968, p. 208).

The final approach that influenced the stimulus-locus analysis was that of Sigmund Freud. Although our analysis is quite different from Freud's with respect to specific details, we used two aspects of Freud's (1938) approach to formulate theory:

1. Assuming an observation of an unexpected phenomenon is lawful.
2. Postulating an explanation for the phenomenon that is based on evidence, not on conscious impressions or introspection.

Freud would typically observe one instance of a strange behavior. Instead of treating this instance as an aberration, he would use evidence (in the form of the subject's reactions to different topics) to formulate a possible explanation. This explanation would typically run counter to the subject's conscious impressions of the situation.

Freud's approach involved first attending to the *qualitative* details of the subject's responses, because these details indicated what the subject was "hiding." The second step was to postulate a general mechanism that would describe the phenomenon (such as displacement, sublimation, etc.). Freud's tacit assumption was that if one subject used this mechanism, the mechanism was probably a universal one. This reasoning assumes that the subject's behavior is lawful.

A problem parallel to that confronting Freud is encountered in instruction. A tacit assumption of many investigators is that the specific nature of the mistakes a learner makes is relatively unimportant and that conscious impressions of how one thinks leads to valid assumptions about learning or teaching. Our analysis assumes that the mistakes the learner makes are perfectly lawful and are caused by the communication, not by aberrations of the learner. We are therefore quite concerned with these qualitative details of instruction, because these details are critical to understanding the learner's problem and must account for the specific error the learner made.

The stimulus-locus analysis further assumes that our conscious impressions play a very minor role in analyzing learning. Evidence plays the major role. And this evidence often flies in the face of conscious impressions. Stated differently, we cannot specify the basis that we use for identifying something as "yellow." We probably cannot verbally describe what we do when we walk. We are not clearly aware of the standard that we use to indicate when something is slowing down.

A weakness in Freud's theory was the suggestion that the unconscious was primarily associated with emotional problems. He failed to recognize that most of what we do when we perform the simplest acts of cognition are perfectly unconscious. Our impressions of what we learn are highly unreliable. Experiments with blind people who could avoid bumping into objects disclosed that these people gave a variety of explanations about the mechanism that they used to avoid these objects. The suggested mechanisms ranged from the use of the ears, to fingers, to sensitive spots on the forehead. Despite the conscious impressions provided by these subjects, an experiment revealed that all used only one mechanism—the ears. Just as their conscious impressions were basically unfounded in evidence, most of the other strong beliefs based on conscious impressions of learning are unfounded. If we learned long division a particular way, we may have the conscious impression that our way is the only natural way. However, we must recognize that *any* method that had been used may have induced the same impression.

The reason that we have indicated the major philosophical underpinnings of the analysis we have developed is that any theory rests on a foundation of philosophical assumptions, and the theory will be as weak as its foundation. A theory of learning or instruction cannot glibly ignore the issue of inductive reasoning, because, if the learner learns through examples, inductive reasoning is the only means by which the learner can learn a generalization. The theory cannot ignore the issue of the learner's capacity to organize particulars into integrated wholes by trying to reduce the question of learning to one of pragmatism and functional relationships. While the functional approach will permit some modest advancements in knowledge, it will ultimately try to reduce questions of logic (the logic implied by the examples and the communication the learner receives) to empirical facts about how learners respond and to apparent "laws" and "sublaws" that purport to be behavioral, but that have nothing to do with behaviors. Unless the theory provides an analysis that is philosophically sound, the theory will suffer in very predictable ways.

Relationship of the Stimulus-Locus Analysis to Theories of Learning

Traditionally, instructional theories have been stepchildren of psychological and medical theories. Nearly every development in psychology, neurology, or medicine has found its way into education. Theories of the brain have prompted instructional procedures. So have theories of intuition, theories of psycho-sexual development (such as the one formulated by Freud), learning theories, and theories of personality. Actually, however, an appropriate analysis of instruction is not subsumed by psychological theories of learning and development. The analysis of instruction provides the specific rules for changing behavior in virtually any situation—whether we are trying to induce new motor responses or provide some type of psychotherapy. In psychotherapy, the learner will be presented with specific stimuli. The design of these stimuli is assumed to exert a causal influence on the learner's behavior. The primary theory for designing such influences must provide guidelines about how to design communication capable of communicating the intended "concepts." The theory must provide a basis for providing adequate practice and describing an adequate test of generalization. Although different specific procedures will be applied to deal with specific new learning situations (such as learning a new motor response or learning new behaviors that relate to emotionally laden situations), and although the use of reinforcement and punishment plays an important role in these situations, any procedure will be relatively ineffective unless it is: (1) designed as a program that communicates what the learner is expected to do, and (2) follows the rules for unambiguously conveying this information. The theoretical foundation for this endeavor is not to be found through investigations of behavior, but through the analysis of concepts and communications.

Learning Theories

The stimulus-locus analysis is not continuous with the works of Skinner, Guthrie, Tolman, Hull, or other learning theorists (Hilgard & Bower, 1975); however, parts of it are compatible with aspects of these theories and with aspects of developmental explanations of learning. For example the response-locus analysis that we propose is largely compatible with Skinner's analysis of behavior (1953). Great departures from Skinner's orientation come about when we move to the sphere of discriminations or cognitive learning.

Of the prominent learning theories, Tolman's (1967) expectancy theory is probably the closest to the stimulus-locus analysis. Tolman suggested that when learning occurs in an operant learning situation, *the expectancy is conditioned*, not specific behaviors. Tolman produced some experimental data to support this notion. For instance, in a study conducted by Tinklepaugh (1928), a monkey who received a lettuce reward when he had been accustomed to receiving banana rewards reacted with a tantrum, although lettuce served as a reinforcer to the monkey in other settings. This outcome might suggest that indeed the monkey had an expectation that was not satisfied; however, the problem of operationalizing the notion of expectancy is not easily solved. If we try to express expectancy in terms of internal states, our definition relates to unobservable features and is therefore mere speculation. Another possibility is to describe expectancy in terms of observable signs. If we begin to interpret glances, expressions, or partial responses as expectations, we must provide some convincing validation that these "signs" are not mere accidents, that they are predictive, and that we can reliably identify them. In the end, we are required to develop a calculus of signs. This understanding would run into serious problems if we try to make the notion of expectancy operational, objective, and procedurally reliable.

If we explain expectancy in terms of units of behavior larger than signs, we merely play a word game in which the word **expectancy** is used in place of the word **behavior**. For instance, if the learner responds more rapidly, we say that the "expectancy" increased or strengthened. The notion of expectancy is now circular. How do we know that the expectancy changed? Because the behavior changed. What made the behavior change? An increase in the expectancy. Clearly, this sort of description is not rigorous.

To make the notion of expectancy rigorous, we must be able to describe it so that: (1) a particular expectancy is unambiguously manifested in behaviors of the learner; and (2) the expectancy must be described in non-behavioral operational terms. We must be able to predict the behavior that we will see by following specific operational steps. The description of an expectancy, therefore, would take the form: If we do operations **A**, **B**, and **C**, we will observe behaviors **X**, **Y**, and **Z**.

The stimulus-locus analysis provides the means for operationalizing expectancy. When this analysis is used, the investigator is not required to "hunt for signs" that are interpreted as expectancy. Rather, a large segment of behavior *is predicted*. This behavior is the generalization, or set of generalizations, implied by the sequence. The cause of the "expectancy" behavior (or generalization) is clearly specified and is described in non-circular terms. The method of analyzing the sequence to determine the specific expectancy (or the set of expectancies) that will be induced are reasonably reliable.

Furthermore, the probability is nearly zero that the learner could respond in the manner predicted by the stimulus-locus analysis unless an "expectancy" rather than specific stimulus-response associations had been conditioned by the presentation. Only an expectation or a concept could enable the learner to "anticipate" what is critical about the positive examples and generalize to new examples that possess this critical feature. For the series of generalization responses to occur by accident is hundreds of times less likely than the probability of the learner producing a "sign" or partial responses that may be spuriously interpreted as an expectancy. The predicted sample of generalization behavior is large; the causes of the generalization are singular; and the tests for determining the type of expectancy that will occur are reasonably rigorous. Therefore, the stimulus-locus approach tends to solve the most serious problems associated with Tolman's formulations.

Cognitive-Developmental Theories

Current emphases in cognitive theory that have developed from Piaget's developmental theory have the same sort of problems that Tolman's theory has. The emphasis of these approaches has been to describe the internal process by which the learner approaches specific cognitive problems. The explanations, in other words, suggest the expectancies that the learner possesses. The problem with this orientation is very basic. The internal scheme must be validated through observations of some types of behavior. The problem becomes one of designing these behaviors so they are: (1) consistent with the predicted scheme, and (2) consistent with *only* the scheme. The problem is basically the same one encountered with Tolman's theory. A monkey's response may indeed be consistent with the notion that the monkey had a particular expectation; however, merely being consistent with this possibility is not precise enough for scientific endeavors. The probability must be near zero that the response did not occur for any other reason. The only design that verifies expectation is one in which the behavior occurs *if and only if* a particular expectancy or schema or mental organization is present. The Piagetian model and those modeled after it are not constructed from the *if and only if* standpoint. Rather, only a *plausible* explanation is provided. If data that are *consistent* with the explanation are provided, those data are interpreted as supporting the explanation, even though it is possible to account for the observed outcomes with alternative explanations.

The stimulus-locus approach helps solve many problems associated with mapping the learner's knowledge, structures, and concepts by permitting us to induce these in a naive learner. If we deal with concepts for which the learner's only exposure is our experimental intervention, we can create a situation in which the probability is very low that the observed pattern of generalization was caused by anything but our intervention. The learner's pattern of behavior may now be used as a fairly reliable indicator of a cognitive structure. By plotting the learner's pattern of responses to a wide variety of tasks, we can create a fairly extensive map of the learner's cognition. By repeating this procedure with various learners, we can derive extended laws of cognitive learning and mental structures. Unless we start with a rigorous basis for inducing a given concept or expectation, however, our attempts to map knowledge will be characterized by false conclusions and abortive remedies for cognitive deficiencies in a learner.

Reinforcement and Behavioral Theory

The attraction that current behavioral theory has for dealing with problems of changing the learner's behavior is that it is simple, operational, and fairly rigorous. It suffers from none of the problems that characterize Tolman's and Piaget's explanations. The difficulty in determining what the learner is thinking is not a problem for the behaviorist because thinking is not an observable behavior and therefore is beyond the purview of behavioral theory. Skinner (1953) rejected definitions and substituted for them actual responses or behavior. This bold treatment assured that the behaviorists dealt with observables and that they did not interpret these speculatively. No interpretation was permitted beyond the observation of whether responses occurred, the rate at which they occurred, the consequent and antecedent conditions correlated with their occurrences, and possibly the changes in topography of the responses.

This system has a wide range of applications (sociopolitical behavior, instructional behavior, animal behavior, and therapy). It also reduces in a straightforward way to the use of numbers—a clear indication that it is in the same league as other number-oriented sciences. It permits us to express learning with numbers that tell us about rate, response latency, intensity, proximity, and the other legacies of Newton and the English empirical philosophers.

Although behavioral theory has much to recommend it and is applied well to situations that involve new-response learning, it is obviously not designed to deal with cognitive learning. The learner's behavior becomes the criterion that determines whether appropriate learning has occurred. Because the theory cannot predict *generalizations*, however, it provides no basis for designing the teaching in a way that assures the appropriate generalization. If we follow a strict behavioral orientation in teaching the concepts **on** and **under**, we may discover that when we use a cup and a table for examples of **on** and use a pencil and a chair for all examples of **under**, we can induce what we describe as appropriate behavior in fewer trials than we can achieve if we use the cup and the table for both **on** and **under**. We are using a spurious prompt, but to understand the problem, we must abandon a strict behavioral orientation and analyze the *possible* generalizations or stipulations that are implied by the communication (the common sameness of the examples that determines responses that have not yet occurred). Unless we employ this analysis of stimuli, it is not at all obvious that the teaching of **on** and **under** with different objects is inappropriate. Granted, the investigator may discover the problem by trying to apply **on** and **under** to new objects. Rules of "behavior" may result from such studies; however, the problem is that they are not actually rules of behavior, but rules of *communication*. By treating them as rules of behavior, we introduce circuity that both conceals their actual nature and displaces the problem from one of logic to one of brute empiricism.

If we further pursue the notion that the learner responds to the implied logic of the communication, we discover *alternative explanations* for some learning phenomena that are treated as behavioral laws. Certainly these phenomena are legitimately expressed as behavioral laws; however, they may be viewed more basically as predictable outcomes *implied by the communication*. We will present two examples of such alternative views—*schedules of reinforcement*, and *punishment procedures*.

Schedules of reinforcement. The communication for a *fixed-time schedule* of reinforcement shows the learner that every so often reinforcement for producing a response occurs (every 30 seconds, for instance). All examples of reinforcement have the *same quality*, which is that they come a half-minute after the preceding reinforcement had been presented. The generalization implied by the communication is that only these responses produced a half-minute after the preceding reinforcement will be reinforced. A law of behavior is that when fixed-time schedules are presented, the learner tends to respond at a higher rate immediately preceding the presentation of the next reinforcer. This behavior is predicted by the communication, implying that the law is not actually a behavioral law. It is a stimulus-locus corollary.

The common feature of reinforcers that are presented on a *variable schedule* is that the presentation of reinforcement is *unpredictable* with respect to the preceding reinforcer. The law of behavior is that this schedule induces a high, constant rate of response and the responses resist extinction. (The learner continues to produce the response after the reinforcers have been discontinued.) Both outcomes are perfectly predictable on the basis of the common quality of the reinforcers presented through the communication. If the communication demonstrates that the learner may produce as many as 20 responses (or some other "large" number) before receiving a reinforcer, a series of more than 20 trials without reinforcement provides the learner with *one* example that the schedule has changed and that the response is now on extinction. If the learner had been on a schedule in which reinforcement was presented continuously, after each response, each response that is produced during extinction has a quality of not leading to reinforcement. Therefore, the task of learning about this sameness of extinction trials logically requires fewer responses (20 responses for each variable-schedule extinction trial versus one response for each continuous-schedule extinction trial). Therefore, extinction is predictably slower following variable schedules.

Punishment phenomena. Just as the phenomena associated with extinction and schedules of reinforcement have a logical basis, punishment phenomena are grounded in the logic of the communication. Punishment tends to change the naive learner's behavior very quickly;

however, it may inhibit the learner from producing responses in various situations and may condition the learner to avoid entire situations in which punishment occurs. By diagramming a situation in which either reinforcement or punishment occurs, we see that there is a generic difference between punishment and reinforcement with respect to the information that is conveyed to the learner.

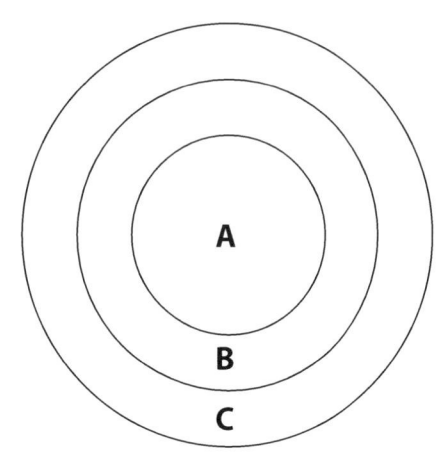

The letters refer to the behavioral context of a response. **A** is the most immediate behavioral context. Context **A** consists of the behaviors the learner produced immediately before the reinforcing or punishing consequence. Context **A** occurs within the behavioral context of **B** (which means that the learner *must be doing* **B** before the learner performs **A**). **B** occurs within the broader behavioral context or situation **C**. (The learner must engage in **C**, then **B**, before **A** is possible.)

When we *reinforce* **A**, our communication is always *relatively precise* in indicating the behavior that is reinforced. The behavior is one that occurs in the behavioral context of **B-C**; however, the **B-C** context itself is not sufficient to "cause" reinforcement. Some behavior within the **B-C** context must be produced. Although the learner may not immediately learn that behavior **A** causes the reinforcer, the learner discovers that the reinforceable response occurs within the **B-C** context and that *some* behavior within the context causes the reinforcer. Given this information, the learner experiments until discovering that **A** or **A** in combination with some other behaviors will lead to reinforcement. (The learning of **A** in connection with some other behaviors is the learning of a superstitious behavior.)

When reinforcement is used, the learner must respond with **A** *and only with* **A** *to receive reinforcement, which means that the communication shows the precise cause of the reinforcement. However, when punishment is involved, the communication is consistent with more than one possible interpretation.*

Consider the same context of **A-B-C**, but assume that **A** is a behavioral context for *punishment.* When the learner responds with **A**, punishment follows. The communication implies that **A** should be avoided. It also implies that **B** should be avoided and that **C** should be avoided. Note that all possibilities will lead to the successful avoidance of the punishing consequence. By avoiding context **B**, the learner successfully avoids the punishing consequence because **A** is avoided when **B** is avoided. By avoiding context **C**, the learner also avoids punishment.

According to an analysis of the communication, learning from punishment is logically easier than learning from reinforcement because the punishment communication permits the learner *many possible alternative concepts of strategies.* So long as **A** is avoided, punishment is avoided. But the learner may learn to avoid **A** by avoiding **B** or avoiding **C**. To learn that **A** is reinforcing, on the other hand, the learner must learn to produce **A** and only **A**.

The punishment situation is like a very easy example in a new-response teaching program. The example is relatively easy because it permits a variety of behaviors that lead to a successful outcome. Like other easy examples, the punishment example should produce faster learning because it presents a much wider range of behavioral options than the analogous reinforcement situation. The punishment situation, like other "easy" examples, may teach a successful response to the situation that later proves to be distorted and requires unlearning. Note that the punishment may lead to a non-distorted response just as an easy example of buttoning may lead to a non-distorted response. However, because the learner is provided with behavioral options, we may later encounter a problem if we want the learner to produce responses other than **A** in the behavioral context of **B-C**. If the learner avoids **B**, the learner cannot discover that some behaviors in the context **B-C** lead to reinforcement.

Learning to Learn

Harlow (1949), Kohler (1925), and others have demonstrated that the learner learns to learn. We have discussed this issue earlier; however, it deserves a final mention because it is the quintessence of generalization. As the learner learns different members of a set, the learning rate increases so that later members are learned far faster than earlier ones. (Obviously, this trend does not continue indefinitely.) The stimulus-locus explanation for the trend is: the savings in time for the learning of later members is possible *only because they are the same in some way as the earlier members*. The quality that is the same does not have to be relearned for the learning of each member; therefore, later members are learned in less time.

The proper analysis of the phenomenon focuses on the quality that is the same and on how to communicate this quality so that learning proceeds smoothly. Let's say that we wish to teach the learner to "generalize" a puzzle-solving skill to various puzzles that require fitting pieces together in either a two-dimensional or three-dimensional display. The faster program may be one that introduces greatly different puzzles, such as a simple jigsaw and a simple, three-dimensional "barrel" puzzle. The sequence could then possibly alternate between three- and two-dimensional displays, each track progressing slowly in difficulty and providing plenty of review (the learner working variations of the same puzzles many times as new ones are introduced).

The juxtaposition of greatly different examples would demonstrate the common quality shared by the puzzles. Once this quality is learned, the learner would be able to solve various puzzles that share the quality. The learner would not have to "relearn" the common quality of the various examples. This savings in the amount that must be relearned from puzzle to puzzle would be reflected in a decrease in the amount of time needed to solve new puzzles, until ultimately the learner would develop a "generalized" puzzle-solving skill and would be extremely proficient at solving any new puzzle that has the quality of the puzzles presented in the set of training examples. This prediction is possible by reference to the set of examples and the features common to all examples.

Behavioral Objectives

The stimulus-locus analysis implies that the use of "behavioral objectives" is appropriate only after a series of steps have been taken by the instructional designer. A behavioral objective describes *a task that is to be taught.* According to convention, the task must specify the behavior or response the learner is to produce.

In Chapter 12, we introduced procedures for analyzing tasks. We indicated the problems associated with treating tasks as immediate criteria for devising instruction. We suggested creating transformed tasks that deal with a broader range of application than a single task. The transformed task describes a variety of specific, concrete tasks of the same form. The transformed task therefore avoids miscommunication problems that may result if we simply accept the task as presented and teach it to the learner. In the chapters dealing with cognitive routines, complex responses, and diagnosis, we have used the general transformed-task strategy to create instruction that teaches generalized responses and that therefore avoids stipulation.

Our purpose here is to provide a more rigorous basis for demonstrating the problems associated with the use of non-transformed tasks, particularly for cognitive skills. The demonstration shows that although it is possible to use non-transformed tasks as a possible checklist or test of whether instruction is effective, they should not function as *directives* for specific teaching.

The two problems that may occur if we simply teach a task without considering how that task interacts with other tasks are:

1. We may stipulate that the response is limited to a particular context when in fact it should occur in a variety of other contexts.

2. We may stipulate that a particular context calls for only a certain response when in fact the context should support a variety of responses.

We can use diagrams to show the extent to which there are problems with the *context* and the *response* specified (or implied) by a stated task or behavioral objective. Each diagram consists of two circles that overlap—one circle representing the stated context and one for the stated response. The overlapping part of each diagram is shaded. The larger that part is, the less there is a problem with the context or the response. Conversely, the unshaded part shows the extent to which a problem occurs if the behavioral objective is taught as stated (without transforming it).

Figure 31.1 shows three diagrams. The context circle is largely unshaded in the first diagram, implying that if we teach the objective as stated (without transforming it), we will have problems with the context that the response occurs in. The second diagram shows the response circle largely unshaded, implying that if we teach the objective as stated we will later encounter problems with the

Section IX | Research and Philosophical Issues

Figure 31.1

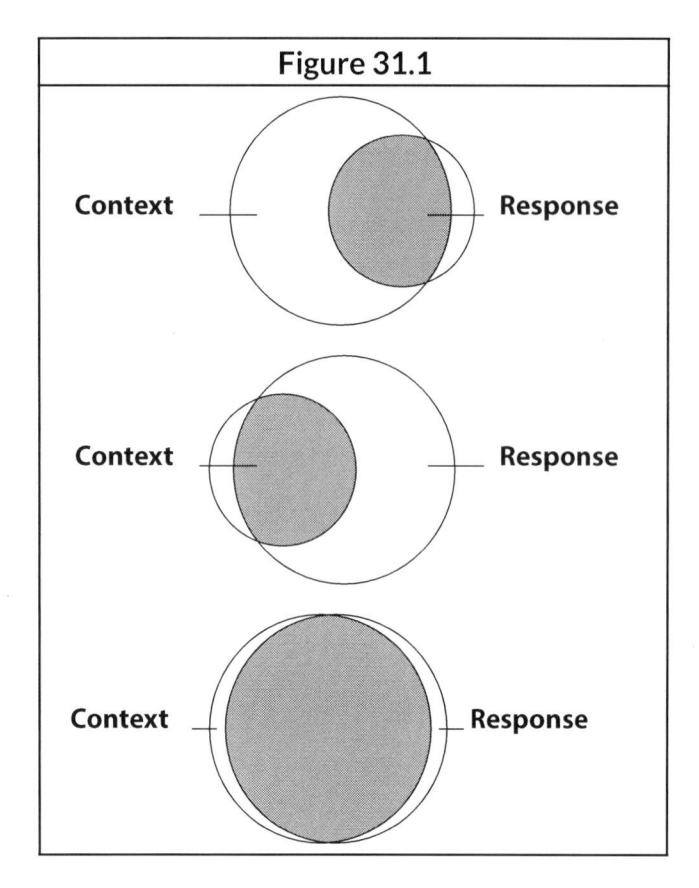

[Three diagrams showing Context and Response circles with varying amounts of shaded overlap]

response. The third diagram show very small, unshaded areas for the response and the context circles, implying that if we pursue the task as stated, we will not create problems with the response or with the context.

To determine problems with the context, we ask: *Could the context that is specified in the behavioral objective reasonably be expected to support responses other than those specified by the objective?* If the answer is "Yes," *part of the context circle is unshaded* (indicating potential context problems). If the answer is "No," all (or nearly all) of the context circle is shaded.

To determine problems with the response that is stated, we ask: *Would the response specified in the behavioral objective reasonably be expected to occur in contexts other than the context indicated by the objective?* If the answer is "Yes," part of the response circle is unshaded (indicating a potential response problem).

Illustration. Here is a behavioral objective: The learner will put her material away at 3:30.

The context is 3:30. The response is putting things away.

Context question: *Could the same context that is specified in the behavioral objective reasonably be expected to support responses other than those specified by the objective?* Yes, in other situations the context of 3:30 might function as a signal for the learner to catch a bus, to start dinner, to go to the movies, etc. Therefore, the context circle has an unshaded area (indicating that a context problem would occur if we teach only a single response in the context of 3:30).

Response question: *Would the response specified in the behavioral objective reasonably be expected to occur in contexts other than the context indicated by the objective?* Yes, we would expect the learner to understand how all situations of "At time **X** put your things away," are the same. We would expect the learner to produce the response of putting things away within the context of 9:00, 12:30, 4:10, etc. The response circle of the diagram therefore would have an unshaded area.

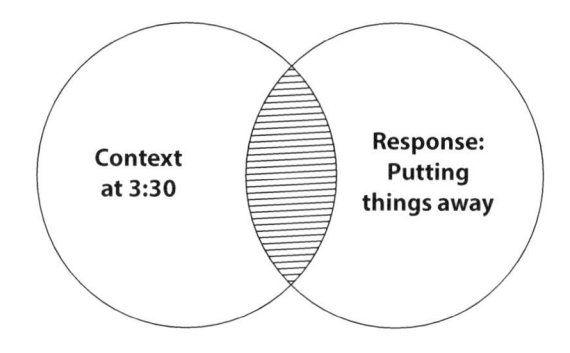

[Venn diagram: Context at 3:30 / Response: Putting things away, with overlap shaded]

The large amount of unshaded area shows that the objective does not take into account the fact that: (1) the context should support other responses, and (2) the response would occur in other contexts. The implication is that if we actually provide a communication that is capable of achieving *the stated objective*, the communication may create serious stipulation problems with respect to both the context and the response.

To communicate the objective "At 3:30 the learner will put away her things," without regard to other objectives that involve the context or the response, *we would condition the learner to respond at 3:30*. Possibly, strong adverse stimuli would be presented if the learner did not respond at 3:30 and a strong reinforcing consequence would be provided if the learner responded within a particular time span. The time span would be narrowed until the learner had been conditioned to produce the response of putting things away across a wide variety of situations. When 3:30 occurred, the learner would put things away, regardless of what the learner was doing at the time, what day of the week was involved, and where the learner was.

Obviously, this sort of instruction is absurd. The learner should be taught the skill as a "cognitive" skill, not through a mindless conditioning program. Note, however, that *the conditioning program is implied if we accept the behavioral objective and apply behavioral technology to achieving it.* To correct the instruction, we recognize that the learner should use the response in context other than 3:30 and should not be preempted from producing responses other than putting things away in the context of 3:30.

Just as the diagram of the non-transformed objective depicts the nature of the problem, it suggests what must be done to transfer the objective so that it is reasonable, which means adjusting it so there are no unshaded areas in the diagram.

There is an unshaded area in the context circle of the diagram, indicating that the context *should* support other responses. By listing other possible responses that we might expect to observe in the context of 3:30, we are provided with a list of things that should occur within the context.

Similarly, by listing other *contexts* in which the response of putting things away might be expected to occur, we fill in the unshaded area of the response circle. The various contexts that we list for the response suggest that the learner will perform at *some specified time* (not merely at 3:30). The various responses that are reasonably expected within the context of some specified time are best described as, "*Some specified behavior.*" Here is the transformed objective:

> *At some specified time, the learner will perform some specified behavior.* The statement of objective generates a number of specific applications, such as:
>
> At 9:00 the learner will sharpen her pencil.
>
> At 9:00 the learner will turn on the TV.
>
> At 1:00 the learner will turn on the stove.
>
> At 3:30 the learner will call Mrs. Anderson.
>
> At 3:30 the learner will turn off the stove.
>
> Etc.

The new objective implies appropriate teaching for *all examples*. Furthermore, the program that is used assures that the learner is taught the *cognitive skills* needed to perform the behavior. The learner is taught to tell time, to estimate time, and to do the various behaviors that are called for (turning off the stove, calling Mrs. Anderson, etc.).

The type of faulty diagram shown above (with two unshaded areas) results whenever a cognitive skill is expressed as a specific behavior. If we teach the behavioral objective without transforming it, there will be later problems with both the response and the context. Behavioral objectives, in other words, are perfectly inappropriate as mandates for communicating cognitive skills. A cognitive skill is best described not as a response, but as a pattern of *potential responses* that occurs regardless of the specific responses that are called for. When we view cognitive skills in this manner, we see that the basic description that must be used as an objective for teaching is a *general statement*, such as the transformed objective of doing things at some specified time. The general statement is an inclusive one that implies various concrete applications. It is, therefore, consistent with the nature of the cognitive skill. It leads to the teaching of specific behaviors; however, the type of teaching provided is consistent with the need to communicate *the pattern or quality that is common to all applications*. In the case of doing some specified behavior at a specified time, juxtaposed examples would be processed through a variation of the same cognitive routine to imply how the various situations are the same and how the same strategy applies to all—estimating time, anticipating what must be done, and carrying out the specified behaviors.

Analyses that are based merely on behavioral objectives *may well achieve the desired objectives*. The cost, however, becomes evident when we attempt to teach objectives that involve the response or the context of the objective presented earlier.

Humanism

Perhaps the greatest impediment to intelligent instruction comes from investigators who purport to be humanistic. Sociolinguists (e.g., Labov, 1972), and those espousing a natural-learning or general-stimulation approach to learning (e.g., Weikart, in Maccoby & Zellner, 1970), see the use of instructional technology as contrary to humanistic beliefs. A long-standing trend that dominates the post-sputnik era tends to reduce the problems of instruction to understanding the culture and language of the learner, to feelings of empathy, and to telling the truth. If there is a guaranteed formula for failure, that is it. Furthermore, it is probably no accident that this belief is prominent. It serves an inept educational establishment by reassuring teachers and administrators that there is no need to deal with the concrete realities of the *teaching failures* that occur in nearly every school. The humanistic position conveniently views these failures as non-failures. The philosophy further assumes that those who deal with instruction on a technical level—not an amorphous one—are ignorant of "theory," unenlightened about the facts of humans, and reactionaries concerned with the suppression and manipulation of children rather than with growth and creativity.

This attitude is not humanistic because it overlooks the basic fact that *instruction is manipulation* and instruction occurs through communications. However, communications are presented and communications teach whether they are designed by intent or whether they are the product of accident. The humanist in the classroom does not have the luxury of "not teaching." No matter what the teacher does, a model will be presented; the behavior of the teacher will suggest rules about the relative importance of particular material. The *teacher* is responsible for achieving student outcomes. If the teacher permits the children to progress "at their own rate," and "in their own style," some children may demonstrate slow rates and poor styles. In that end, a self-fulfilling prophecy is realized. Some children will indeed "prove" that they are slow, and the teacher will believe—out of ignorance, not humanity—that these children would have been slow no matter what type of instruction had been provided. From our perspective, many classroom demonstrations provided by people who express great concern for humanity are no more humane than the practice of using leeches to bleed diseased patients.

If we are humanists, we begin with the obvious fact that the children we work with are perfectly capable of learning anything that we have to teach. We further recognize that we should be able to engineer the learning so that it is reinforcing—perhaps not "fun," but challenging and engaging. We then proceed to *do it*—not to continue talking about it. We try to control these variables that are potentially within our control so that they facilitate learning. We train the teacher, design the program, work out a reasonable daily schedule, and leave NOTHING TO CHANCE. We monitor and we respond quickly to problems. We respond quickly and effectively because we consider the problems moral and we conceive of ourselves as providing a uniquely important function—particularly for those children who would most certainly fail without our concerted help. We function as advocates for the children, with the understanding that if we fail the children will be seriously preempted from doing things with their lives, such as having important career options and achieving some potential values for society. We should respond to inadequate teaching as we would to problems of physical abuse. Just as our sense of humanity would not permit us to allow child-abuse in the physical sense, we should not tolerate it in the cognitive setting. We should be intolerant because we *know* what can be achieved if children are taught appropriately. We know that the intellectual crippling of children is caused overwhelmingly by faulty instruction—not by faulty children.

Because of these convictions, we have little tolerance for traditional educational establishments. We feel that they must be changed so they achieve the goals of actually *helping all children.*

This call for humanity can be expressed on two levels. On that of society: Let's stop wasting incredible human potential through unenlightened practices and theories.

On the level of children: Let's recognize the incredible potential for being intelligent and creative possessed by even the least impressive children, and with unyielding passion, let's pursue the goal of assuring that this potential becomes reality.

References

Abramson, T., & Kagan, E. Familiarization of content and differential response modes in programmed instruction. Journal of Educational Psychology, 1975, 67, 83-88.

Adams, A., Carnine, D., & Gersten, R. Instructional strategies for studying content area texts in the intermediate grades. Reading Research Quarterly, 1982, 18(1), 27-55.

Anderson, R.C., & Kulhavy, R.W. Learning concepts from definitions. American Educational Research Journal, 1973, 9, 385-90.

Anastasiow, N.J., Sibley, S.A., Leonhardt, T.M., & Borich, G.D. A comparison of guided discovery, discovery, and didactic teaching of math to kindergarten poverty children. American Educational Research Journal, 1971, 7, 493-510.

Archer, A.E. Concept identification as a function of obviousness of relevant and irrelevant information. Journal of Experimental Psychology, 1962, 63, 616-620.

Baker, L., & Brown, A.L. Comprehension monitoring and critical reading. In J. Flood (Ed.), Instructional Reading Association Handbook on Reading, 1981.

Becker, W.C., & Engelmann, S.E. Analysis of achievement data on six cohorts of low-income children from 20 school districts in the University of Oregon Direct Instruction Follow Through model. Technical Report 78-1. Eugene, OR: University of Oregon Follow Through Project, 1978.

Becker, W.C., Engelmann, S.E., & Thomas, D.R. Teaching 1: Classroom Management. Palo Alto: Science Research Associates, 1975.

Bereiter, C., Washington, E., Engelmann, S., & Osborn, J. Research and development program on preschool disadvantaged children: Curriculum development and evaluation (Vol. 2). Final Report to U.S.D.H.E.W., Project #5-1181, Contract #0E6-10-235, 1969.

Bloom, B. (Ed.) Engelhardt, M., Furst, E., Hill, W., & Drathwaohl, D. Taxonomy of educational objectives. Handbook I: Cognitive domain. New York: McKay, 1956.

Bourne, L.E. Stimulus-rule interaction in concept learning. American Journal of Psychology, 1979, 92(1), 3-17.

Bourne, L.E., Ekstrand, B.R., & Dominowski, R.L. The Psychology of Thinking. New Jersey: Prentice-Hall, Inc., 1971.

Bourne, L.E., and O'Banion, K. Conceptual rule learning and chronological age. Developmental Psychology, 1971, 5, 525-34.

Brown, A.L., Campione, J.C., & Day, J. Learning to learn: On training students to learn from texts. Educational Researcher, 1981, 10, 14-24.

Carnine, D.W. Establishing a discriminative stimulus by distributing attributes of compound stimuli between positive and negative instances. Eugene, OR: University of Oregon Follow Through Project, 1976a.

Carnine, D.W. Correction effects on academic performance during small group instruction. Unpublished manuscript. Eugene, OR: University of Oregon Follow Through Project, 1976b.

Carnine, D.W. Similar sound separation and cumulative introduction in learning letter-sound correspondences. Journal of Educational Research. 1976, 69, 368-372.c

Carnine, D.W. Phonics versus look-say: Transfer to new words. Reading Teacher, 1977, 30(6), 636-640.

Carnine, D.W. Relating new learning to previous learning. In Becker, W.C., & Engelmann, S., Technical Report 78-1, Appendix A. Eugene, OR: University of Oregon Follow Through Project, 1978.

Carnine, D.W. Relationships between stimulus variation and the formation of misconceptions. Journal of Educational Research, 1980, 74, 106-110.a

Carnine, D.W. Three procedures for presenting minimally different positive and negative instances. Journal of Educational Psychology, 1980, 72, 452-56.b

Carnine, D.W. Correcting word identification errors of beginning readers. Education and Treatment of Children, 1980, 3, 323-330.c

Carnine, D.W. Preteaching versus concurrent teaching of the component skills of a multiplication algorithm. Journal of Research in Mathematics Education, 1980, 11, 375-378.d

Carnine, D.W. Two letter discrimination sequences: High-confusion-alternatives first versus low-confusion-alternatives first. Journal of Reading Behavior, 1980, 8, 41-47.e

Carnine, D.W. High and low implementation of direct instruction teaching techniques. Education and Treatment of Children, 1981, 4(1), 43-51.

Carnine, D.W., & Stein, M. Organizational strategies and practice procedures for teaching basic facts. Journal of Research in Mathematics Education, 1981, 12, 65-69.

Carnine, L.M. Analyses of oral reading errors made by kindergarten, first and third grade low SES students taught with a code-emphasis program. Paper presented at American Educational Research Association, Boston, Mass., April, 1980.

Cheyne, W.M. Vanishing cues in paired-associate learning. British Journal of Psychology, 1966, 57, 351-359.

Clements, J., Stevens, C., Kameenui, E., & Carnine, D.W. Instructional procedures for identifying and interpreting character's motives during narrative reading. Unpublished manuscript. Eugene, OR: Umversity of Oregon Follow Through Project, 1979.

Colvin, G.T. Experimental analysis of generalization: An evaluation of a general case vocational program to teach screwdriver use to severely handicapped high school students. Doctoral dissertation. Eugene, OR: University of Oregon, 1981.

References

Coyle, G.A., Kameenui, E., Carnine, D.W. A direct instruction approach to teaching the utilization of contextual information in determining the meaning of an unknown word embedded in a passage. Unpublished manuscript. Eugene, OR: University of Oregon Follow Through Project, 1979.

Crist, R., and Petrone, J. Learning concepts from contexts and definitions. Journal of Reading Behavior, 1977, 9(3), 301-303.

Darsh, C., & Carnine, D.W. Effects of explicit instruction, visual displays, and team games on acquisition of information from expository material. Unpublished manuscript. Eugene, OR: University of Oregon, 1981.

Darsh, C., & Carnine, D.W. & Gersten, R. Variation in type and amount of instruction on mathematics word problems. Unpublished manuscript. Eugene, OR: University of Oregon, 1981.

Darwin, C.J.; Baddeley, A.D., Acoustic memory and the perception of speech. Cognitive Psychology, 1974, 6, 41-60.

Dommes, P., Gersten, R., & Carnine, D.W. Instructional procedures for increasing skill deficient fourth graders' comprehension of syntactic structures. Educational Psychology, 1984, 4(2), 155-165.

Drotar, D. Discrimination learning in normal and retarded children as a function of instruction, cue locus and cue relevance. Child Development, 1974, 45, 1146-1150.

Durling, R., & Schick, C. Concept attainment by pairs and individuals as a function of vocalization. Journal of Educational Psychology, 1976, 68, 83-91.

Egan, D.E., & Greeno, J.G. Acquiring cognitive structure by discovery and rule learning. Journal of Educational Psychology, 1973, 64, 85-97.

Engelmann, S. Log for formal operational teaching. Unpublished manuscript. Urbana, IL: Umvers1ty of Illinois, 1964.

Engelmann, S. Cognitive structures related to the principles of conservation. In D.W. Brison and E.V. Sullivan, Recent Research on the Acquisition of Conservation of Substance. Toronto: Ontario Institute for Studies in Education, 1967, 25-51.a

Engelmann, S. Teaching formal operations to preschool children. Ontario Journal of Educational Research, 1967, 9(3), 193-207.b

Engelmann, S. Does the Piagetian approach imply instruction? In Green, D.R., Ford, M.P., & Flamer, G.B. Measurement and Piaget. Carmel, CA: California Test Bureau, 1971, 118-126.

Engelmann, S., & Bruner, E. DISTAR Reading Level I. Chicago: Science Research Associates, 1975.

Engelmann, S., & Colvin, G.T. Generalized compliance Training. Unpublished manuscript. Eugene, OR: University of Oregon, 1981.

Engelmann, S., & Engelmann, T. Give your child a superior mind. New York: Simon & Schuster, 1966.

Engelmann, S., & Granzin, A. Assessing labor cost of objectives. Directions, 1980, 1(4), 54-63.

Engelmann, S., & Rosov, R. Tactual hearing experiment with deaf and hearing subjects. Exceptional Children, 1975, 42, 243-253.

Ewing, A.C. The definition of good. N.Y.: Macmillin, 1947.

Feldman, K.V. The effects of number of positive and negative instances, concept definition, and emphasis of relevant attributes on the attainment of mathematical concepts. Technical Report No. 243, Madison, WI: Wisconsin Research and Development Center for Cognitive Learning, 1972.

Fielding, G. A comparison of an inquiry-oriented and a direct instruction approach to teaching legal problem solving to secondary school students. Doctoral Dissertation. Eugene, OR: University of Oregon, 1980.

Frase, L.T., & Schwartz, B.J. Effect of question production and answering on prose recall. Journal of Educational psychology, 1975, 67, 628-635.

Francis, E.W. Grade level and task difficulty in learning by discovery and verbal reception methods. Journal of Educational Psychology, 1975, 67, 146-150.

Frederick, W.C., & Klausmeier, H.J. Instructions and labels in a concept attainment task. Psychological Reports, 1968, 23, 1339-1342.

Freud, S. The basic writings of Sigmund Freud. Translated by Dr. A.A. Brill. New York: The Modem Library, 1938.

Gagne, R.M. The conditions of learning (Rev. ed.). New York: Holt, Rinehart, Winston, 1970.

Gagne, R., & Brown, T. Some factors in the programming of conceptual learning. Journal of Experimental Psychology, 1961, 62, 55-63.

Gagne, R.M., Mayor, J.R., Garstens, H.L., & Paradise, N.E. Factors in acquiring knowledge of a mathematical task. Psychological Monographs: General and Applied, 1962, 76(7).

Gersten, R.M., Becker, W.C., Heiry, T.J., & White, W.A.T. The relationship of entry IQ level and yearly academic growth rates of children in a Direct Instruction Model. A longitudinal study of over 1500 children. Paper presented at the American Educational Research Association Annual Conference, Los Angeles, CA, April, 1981.

Gersten, R., White, W.A.T., Falco, R., & Carnine, D. W. Enhancing attention of handicapped and non-handicapped students through a dynamic presentation of instructional stimuli. Analysis and Intervention in Developmental Disabilities, 1982, 2, 305-317.

Gibson, J.J., & Robinson, D. Orientation in visual perception; the recognition of familiar plane forms in differing orientations. Psychological Monographs, 1935, 46, 39-47.

Gollin, E., Moody, M., & Schadler, M. Relational learning of a size concept. Developmental Psychology, 1974, 10, 101-107.

Goodman, K S. A linguistic study of cues and miscues in reading. Elementary English, 1965, 42, 439-643.

Gordon, C.J. The effects of instruction in metacomprehension and inferencing on children's comprehension abilities. Unpublished doctoral dissertation. Minneapolis, MN: University of Minnesota, 1980.

Granzin, A.C., & Carnine, D. W. Child performance on discrimination tasks: Effects of amount of stimulus variation. Journal of Experimental Child Psychology, 1977, 24, 332-342.

Gruenenfelder, T.M., & Borkowski, J.G. Transfer of cumulative-rehearsal strategies in children's shortterm memory. Child Development, 1975, 46, 1019-1024.

Guess, D. A functional analysis of receptive language and productive speech: Acquisition of the plural morpheme. Journal of Applied Behavior Analysis, 1969, 2, 55-64.

Hansen, J. The effects of inference training and practice on young children's comprehension. Reading Research Quarterly, 1981, 16, 391-417.

Hansen, J., & Pearson, P.D. An instructional study: Improving the inferential comprehension of fourth grade good and poor readers. Technical Report 235, Urbana: University of Illinois, Center for the Study of Reading, 1982.

Harlow, H.E. The formation of learning sets. Psychological Review, 1949, 56, 51-65.

Hilgard, E.R., & Bower, G.H. Theories of learning, (4th Ed). Englewood Cliffs, N.J.: Prentice-Hall, 1975.

Harris, C.R. Concept learning as a function of type, identifiability, and variety of instructional instances. The Journal of Educational Research, 1973, 67, 182-189.

Horner, R., & McDonald, R. A comparison of the effectiveness of single instance training versus general case training on the acquisition of a generalizable vocational skill by four severely handicapped high school students. Unpublished manuscript. Eugene, OR: Specialized Training Program, University of Oregon, 1981.

Houser, L.L., & Trublood, C.R. Transfer of learning on similar metric conversion tasks. Journal of Educational Research, 1975, 68, 235-237.

Hume, D. Enquiries concerning human understanding and concerning the principles of morals. Oxford: Clarendon Press, 1975. (First published in 1758.)

Imai, S., & Garner, W.R. Discriminability and preference for attributes in free and constrained classification. Journal of Experimental Psychology, 1965, 69, 596-608.

Jeffery, W.E., & Samuels, S.J. Effect of method of reading training on initial learning and transfer. Journal of Verbal Learning and Verbal Behavior, 1967, 6, 354-358.

Johnson, D.M., & Stratton, R.P. Evaluation of five methods of teaching concepts. Journal of Educational Psychology, 1966, 57, 48-53.

Kameenui, E.J., & Carnine D.W. Deductive and inductive teaching of division. Unpublished manuscript. Eugene, OR: University of Oregon Follow Through Project, 1980.

Kameenui, J., & Carnine, D.W. An investigation of the ecological validity of fourth graders' comprehension of pronoun constructions. Reading Research Quarterly, 1982, 17(4), 556-580.

Kameenui, E.J., Carnine, D.W. & Chadwick, J. Simultaneous versus successive presentation of component skills for teaching borrowing. Unpublished manuscript. Eugene, OR: University of Oregon, 1980.

Kameenui, E.J., Carnine, D.W. & Fresihi, R. Effects of text construction and instructional procedures for teaching word meanings on comprehension and recall. Reading Research Quarterly, 1982, 17(3), 367-388.

Kameenui, E.J., Carnine, D.W., & Maggs, A. Concept and application training in relation to making inferences. Unpublished manuscript. Eugene, OR: University of Oregon Follow Through Project, 1979.

Kant, I. Critique of pure reason. Translated from the German by J.M.D. Mieklejohn. New York: The Colonial Press, 1899. (First published in 1781.)

Klausmeier, H.J., & Feldman, K.V. Effects of a definition and varying numbers of examples and nonexamples on concept attainment. Journal of Educational Psychology, 1975, 67(2), 174-178.

Klausmeier, H.J., & Meinke, D.L. Concept attainment as a function of instructions concerning the stimulus material, a strategy, and a principle for securing information. Journal of Educational Psychology, 1968, 59, 215-222.

Kohler, W. The mentality of apes. N. Y.: Harcourt, Brace & World, 1925.

Kryzanowski, J.A., & Carnine, D.W. Effects of massed versus distributed practice schedules in teaching sound-symbol correspondences to young children. Journal of Reading Behavior, 1980, 8(3), 225-29.

Labov, W. The logic of nonstandard English. In Language in the inner city. Philadelphia: University of Pennsylvania Press, 1972.

Lyczak, R.A. Learning to read: The redundant cues approach. The Journal of Educational Psychology, 1976, 68, 157-166.

Maccoby, E.E., & Zellner, M. Experiments in primary education: Aspects of Project Follow Through. New York: Harcourt Brace Jovanovich, Inc., 1970.

Madsen, C.H., Becker, W.C., & Thomas, D.R. Rules, praise, and ignoring: Elements of elementary classroom control. In K. Daniel O'Leary and Susan G. O'Leary (Eds.), Classroom Management. Elmsford, N.Y.: Pergamon Press Inc., 1972, 115-133.

Maggs, A., & Maggs, R. Direct instruction research in Australia. Journal of Special Education Technology, 1979, 2(3), 26-34.

Markle, S., & Tiemann, P. Some principles of instructional design at higher cognitive levels. In R. Ulrich, R. Stachnick, & J. Mabry (Eds.), Control of Human Behavior, Vol. 3. Glenview, Ill.: Scott, Foresman, 1974.

Mayer, R.E., Stiehl, C.C., & Greeno, J.G. Acquisition of understanding and skill in relation to subjects' preparation and meaningfulness of instruction. Journal of Educational Psychology, 1975, 67, 331-350.

McLaughlin, M.W. Evaluation and reform. Cambridge, Mass.: Ballinger, 1975.

Merrill, M.D., and Tennyson, R.D. Attribute prompting errors as a function of relationship between positive and negative instances (Working Paper No. 28). Provo, Utah: Brigham Young University, 1971.

Meyer, L.A. An experimental study of the treatment effects of word-analysis and word-supply correction procedures during word-attack. Doctoral dissertation, Eugene, OR: College of Education, University of Oregon, 1979.

Mill, J.S. John Stuart Mill's philosophy of scientific method. E. Nagel (ed.) New York: Hafner Publishing Company, 1950. (First published as A system of logic, in 1844.)

Moore, G.E. Principia ethica. Cambridge: The University Press, 1903.

Nero & Associates. A description of Follow Through sponsor implementation processes. Portland, OR: Nero & Associates, 1975.

References

O'Malley, J.M, Stimulus dimension pretraining and set size in learning multiple discriminations with letters of the alphabet. Journal of Educational Research, 1973, 67, 41-45.

Overing, R.L., & Travers, R.M. Variation in the amount of irrelevant cues in training and test conditions and the effect upon transfer. Journal of Educational Psychology, 1967, 58, 62-68.

Paine, S.C., Carnine, D.W., White, W.A.T., & Walters, G.C. Effects of fading teacher presentation structure (covertization) on acquisition and maintenance of arithmetic problem-solving skills. Education and Treatment of Children, 1982, 5(2), 93-107.

Patching, W., Kameenui, E., Colvin, G., & Carnine, D.W. An investigation of the effect of using direct instruction procedures to teach three critical reading skills to skill-deficient grade-5 children. Unpublished manuscript, Eugene, OR: University of Oregon Follow Through Project, 1979.

Peirce, C.S. Collected papers of Charles Saunders Pierce. C. Harshorne & P. Weiss (Eds.) Vol V. Pragmatism and pragmaticism. Cambridge: Harvard University Press, 1935.

Piaget, J. The origins of intelligence in children. N.Y.: International University Press, 1952.

Pitkin, H.F. Wittgenstein and justice. Berkeley: University of California Press, 1972.

Popper, K.R. The logic of scientific discovery. New York: Basic Books, 1959.

Raphael, T.E. The effects of metacognitive strategy awareness training on students' question answering behavior. Unpublished doctoral dissertation. Urbana, IL: University of Illinois, 1980.

Restle, F. Additivity of cues and transfer in discrimination of consonant clusters. Journal of Experimental Psychology, 1959, 57, 9-14.

Rosenshine, B.V., & Berliner, D.C. Academic engaged time. British Journal of Teacher Education, 1978, 4, 3-16.

Rosenthal, T.L., & Carroll, W.R. Factors in vicarious modification of complex grammatical parameters. Journal of Educational Psychology, 1972, 63, 174-178.

Rosenthal, T.L., & Zimmerman, B.J. Instructional specificity and outcome expectation in observationally-induced question formation. Journal of Educational Psychology, 1972, 63, 500-504.

Ross, D., & Carnine, D. Analytic assistance: Effects of example selection, subjects' age, and syntactic complexity. Journal of Educational Research, 1982, 75(5), 294-298

Royer, J.M., & Cable, G.W. Facilitated learning in connected discourse. Journal of Educational Psychology, 1975, 67, 116-123.

Samuels, S.J. Effect of distinctive feature training on paired-associate learning. Journal of Educational Psychology, 1973, 64, 164-168.

Silver, J.R., & Rollins, H.A. The effects of visual and verbal feature emphasis on form discrimination in preschool children. Journal of Exceptional Child Psychology, 1973, 16, 205-216.

Skinner, B.F. Science and human behavior. New York: Macmillan Co., 1953.

Sprague, J., & Homer, R. Vending Machine use: An analysis of stimulus features and the application of a general case programming strategy to induce generalization to a full range of examples by severely handicapped students. Unpublished manuscript. Eugene, OR: Specialized Training Program, University of Oregon, 1981.

Sprick, R.S. A comparison of recall scores for visual-spatial, visual-serial, and auditory presentation of intermediate grade content. Unpublished doctoral dissertation. Eugene, OR: University of Oregon, 1979.

Stebbins, L., St. Pierre, R.G., Proper, E.C., Anderson, R.B., & Cerva, T.R. Education as experimentation: a planned variation model (Vol.IV A-D). Cambridge, MA: Abt Associates, 1977.

Steely, D., & Engelmann, S.E. Implementation of basal reading in grades 4-6. (Final Report). Eugene, OR Engelmann-Becker Corporation, 1979.

Stein, M., & Carnine, D. W. Deductive and inductive teaching of subtraction. Unpublished manuscript, Eugene, OR: University of Oregon Follow Through Project, 1980.

Swanson, J.E. The effects of number of positive and negative instances, concept definition, and emphasis or relevant attributes on the attainment of environmental concepts by 6th grade children. Tech. Report No. 244, Madison, WI: Wisconsin Research & Development Center for Cognitive Learning, 1972.

Tagatz, G.E., Walsh, M.R., & Layman, J.A. Learning set and strategy interaction in concept learning. Journal of Educational Psychology, 1969, 67(6), 821-827.

Tennyson, R.D., Steve, M.W., & Boutwell, R.C. Instance sequence and analysis of instance attribute representation in concept attainment. Journal of Educational Psychology, 1975, 67, 821-827.

Tennyson, R.D., & Tennyson, C.L. Rule acquisition design strategy variables: Degree of instance. Journal of Educational Psychology, 1975, 67, 852-859.

Tennyson, R.D. Effect of negative instances in concept acquisition using a verbal learning task. Journal of Educational Psychology, 1973, 64, 247-60.

Tennyson, R.D., Woolley, R.R., & Merrill, M.D. Exemplar and nonexemplar variables which produce correct classification behavior and specified classification errors. Journal of Educational Psychology, 1972, 63, 144-62.

Thomas, D.R., Becker, W.C., & Armstrong, M. Production and elimination of disruptive classroom behavior by systematically varying teacher's behavior. Journal of Applied Behavioral Analysis, 1968, 1, 35-45.

Tinklepaugh, O.L. An experimental study of representative factors in monkeys. Journal of Comparative Psychology, 1928, 8, 197-236.

Tobias, S., & Ingber, T. Achievement-treatment interactions in programmed instructions. Journal of Educational Psychology, 1976, 68, 43-47.

Tolman, E.C. Purposive behavior in animals and men. New York: Apple-Century-Crofts, 1967.

Trabasso, T. Stimulus emphasis and all or none learning of concept identification. Journal of Experimental Psychology, 1963, 65, 398-406.

Trabasso, T., & Bower, G.H. Attention in learning: Theory and research. New York: John Wiley and Sons, Inc., 1968.

Voerwerk, K. Instructional design strategies for rule attainment in fifth grade students. Contemporary Educational Psychology, 1979, 4, 20-25.

Warren, J.M. Additivity of cues in visual pattern discriminations by monkeys. Journal of Comparative Physiological Psychology, 1954, 47, 290-292.

Williams, J.P. Training kindergarten children to discriminate letter-like forms. American Education Research Journal, 1969, 6, 501-514.

Williams, P., & Carnine, D. W. Relationship between range of examples and of instructions and attention in concept attainment. Journal of Education Research, 1981, 74(3), 144-48.

Williams, P., Engelmann, S., Granzin, A., & Becker, W.C. Teaching language to truly naive learners—an analog study using tactual vocoder. Journal of Special Educational Technology, 1979, 2, 5-15.

Wittgenstein, L. Philosophical investigators. Translated by G.E.M. Anscombe, (3rd Ed.) New York: Macmillan, 1968.

Wittrock, M.C. Verbal stimuli in concept formation: Learning by discovery. Journal of Experimental Psychology, 1963, 54, 183-190.

Woolfson, N., Kameenui, E., & Carnine, D.W. Direct instruction procedure for making inferences with variation in the explicitness, complexity, and dispersal of information: An experimental study. Unpublished manuscript. Eugene, OR: University of Oregon Follow Through Project, 1979.

Subject Index

academic skills, teaching to preschoolers, 435-436
academic skills, teaching to school-age children, 436-440
across-set differences, 175, 179-180
across-set juxtapositions, 176
add-on; add-ons, 196-197, 201, 398
analogies, 357-358, 364
analysis of behavior, 1
analysis of cognitive learning, 1-2
analysis of communications, 1
analysis of examples, 317
analysis of knowledge systems, 1
analysis of preskills (preteaching), 198-199
analysis of programs, 431
analysis of teacher behavior, 431-432
analysis of the learner, 317
analyzing failures, 401
averages, 351
A-Z integration procedure, 140-142
basic communication, structural requirements of, 5-8, 10
basic communications, analysis of, 11-22
    basic concepts, 12
    behavioral signal, 11
    complex concepts, 17
    concrete examples, 12, 13
    continuous conversion, 18, 21
    differences, 14, 21
    extrapolation, 16, 21
    faultless communications, 17, 18-19
    generalization, 11-12, 17
    interpolation, 15, 21
    juxtaposition, 15, 21
    learning failure, 20, 22
    learning sets, 12
    minimum difference, 15
    modeling, 18
    pattern of responses, 13
    positive examples, 11
    sameness; samenesses, 11, 12, 14, 21
    set of examples, 13
    stimulus-locus analysis, 11, 20
    stipulation, 16-17, 21
    generalization, test of, 12, 21
    test examples, 12, 21
basic concepts, 12
    basic forms, 23, 24-25, 38, 41-89
    comparatives; single-dimension comparatives, 42
    discrimination, 42
    generalization, 42
    non-comparatives; single-dimension non-comparatives, 42
    nouns, 42
    sensory-based concepts, 42-43
    set of examples, 42
basic-form communications, 415-419
behavior analysis, 3
behavioral objectives, 459-461
behaviorism, 449
behavioral signal, 11
binary-duality relationship, 419
blocks (sets of items), 222, 223, 224, 225
boundaries of variation, 6-7
cells (display), 188, 191-192
chaining a series of steps, 232, 237, 240-241
chaining parts of a routine, 312-313
chaining parts of statements, 311-312
choice responses, 237-238
choice-of-example items, 215, 217, 224
choice-of-label items, 215, 217-218, 224
choice-response items, 215, 220
chronic discrimination mistakes, 383-384, 395
chronic mistakes outside of a sequence, 386-392, 395
chronic mistakes outside of response-teaching programs, 393-395
chronic mistakes within a sequence, 384-386, 395
chronic mistakes within response-teaching programs, 392-393, 395
chronic response problems, 392-395
classifying components, 163-165
clusters of components, 258
clusters, scheduling, 258-260
codes, 188, 200
cognitive knowledge classifications; stimulus-locus classifications, 23-33, 38-39
cognitive operations, 228-229
cognitive problem-solving routines, 23, 27-30, 38-39

Subject Index

cognitive routines, 227-229, 231-243, 423-427, 428
    cognitive operations, 228-229
    cognitive routines, design requirements, 229
    discovery learning, 227-228
    physical operations, properties of, 228
    chaining a series of steps, 232, 237, 240-241
    choice responses, 237-238
    cognitive routines, constructing, 232-234, 242
    cognitive routines, properties of, 232
    cognitive routines, testing, 242
    component discrimination tasks, chaining, 240-241, 243
    component discrimination tasks, constructing, 239-240
    descriptive rule, 233
    descriptive rule components, designing tasks for, 237-240
    descriptive rule, identifying, 234-236
    descriptive rule, using familiar names in, 238
    operational sameness, 234-235
    production responses, 238
    range of examples, 232-233
    range of examples, identifying, 234-236
    responses that describe behavior, 238-239
    sameness; samenesses, 234-235
    set of examples, constructing a routine for, 236-237
cognitive routines and their examples, scheduling, 257-268
    clusters of components, 258
    clusters, scheduling, 258-260
    components, scheduling, 257-260, 268
    conditional parts, 265
    conditional parts, structure of, 265
    conditional-parts routines, scheduling, 265-268
    differences, 261
    examples with difficult responses, 261-262
    limited generalizations, design problems, 263
    limited generalizations, scheduling, 263-264, 268
    limited generalizations, testing, 264
    minimum-time schedules, 257-258
    range of variation, 262-263, 268
    sameness; samenesses, 261
    set of examples, designing and ordering, 261
    set of examples, scheduling, 260-264
cognitive routines, constructing, 232-234, 242
cognitive routines, design requirements, 229
cognitive routines, feedback for, 423
cognitive routines, illustrations of, 245-255
    confirmation, 245, 246, 253
    descriptive responses, 251-253
cognitive routines, properties of, 232

cognitive routines, testing, 242
cognitive-developmental theories, 458
combining programs, 325-327
communication variables, 442, 447
    communications about events, 23, 30, 39
comparatives, advanced applications, 84-86
comparatives, identifying and analyzing, 86-89
comparatives, when to convert from non-comparatives, 87-89
comparatives; single-dimension comparatives, 23, 25, 42, 79-89
    comparatives, advanced applications, 84-86
    comparatives, identifying and analyzing, 86-89
    comparatives, when to convert from non-comparatives, 87-89
    continuous-conversion comparative sequences, constructing, 89
    difference, 80, 84
    fewer examples, 84
    indirect sequences, 82, 85
    minimum-difference negative change, 79
    minimum-difference negatives, 79
    naïve learner, 85
    negative-first comparative sequences, 79-83
    negative-first comparative sequences, constructing, 81
    negative-first comparative sequences, variations in, 83
    no-change negative, 79
    non-comparatives, identifying, 87-89
    nouns, identifying, 87-89
    perceptible differences, 82
    positive-first comparative sequences, 83-84
    sameness; samenesses, 80, 84
    sensory qualities, 82
    setup features, 84
    two-choice wording, 84
    two-response comparative sequences, 85
    verbal explanation, 84
complete regularizing versus partial regularizing, 278-279
complete teaching, 159, 203-225
    different discriminations, 203
    expanded teaching, 204
    expansion activities; expanded activities, 204
    initial teaching sequences, 203
    juxtaposition prompting, problem of, 203
    stipulation, problem of, 203
    stipulation, types of, 203
complex (new) responses, teaching strategies for, 315-328
    analysis of examples, 317
    analysis of the learner, 317
    combining programs, 325-327
    complex responses, analyzing, 318-321

complex-response programs, 318
complex-response programs, types of, 321-324, 327-328
continuous parts, 319-320, 327
distortion, 324-325
enabling-response-features programs, 322, 324, 328
essential-response-features programs, 321-322, 323, 327
juxtaposition, 326, 328
misrules and distortions, 315-316, 327
misrules and distortions, remedies for, 316-317
removed-component-behavior programs, 322-323, 324, 328
simultaneous components, 319
temporal parts, 319

complex activity; complex operation, 377-378, 379
complex concepts, 17
complex forms, 23, 26-33, 38
complex physical problem-solving operations; complex physical operations; complex operations, 34, 36-38, 39
complex responses, analyzing, 318-321
complex-form communications, 421-427
complex-response programs, 318, 321-324, 327-328
compliance set, 444
component behaviors, 36
component discrimination tasks, chaining, 240-241, 243
component discrimination tasks, constructing, 239-240
component discriminations, 163, 165-168
components, scheduling, 257-260, 268
computer technology and implementation, 413
concrete examples, 12, 13, 147
conditional parts, 265
conditional parts, structure of, 265
conditional-parts routines, scheduling, 265-268
confirmation, 245, 246, 253
container relationship, 442
context integration, 305-306
context of another activity, 383
context problems, 459-460
context shaping; response-context shaping, 34-35, 39
continuous behaviors, 302
continuous conversion, 18, 21, 50-51, 95, 416
continuous conversion and pictorial illustrations, 60
continuous parts, 319-320, 327
continuous progress test, 408
continuous-conversion comparative sequences, constructing, 89
coordinate cells, designing, 192-198
coordinate cells, showing variation in, 197
coordinate higher-order classes, 157-158
coordinate members of a set, introducing, 131-146

A-Z integration procedure, 140-142
coordinate members, applications, 139-140
coordinate members, charting a schedule, 138-139, 146
coordinate members, ordering, 133-134, 135, 145-146
coordinate members, teaching procedures, 135-140
cumulative reviews, 131, 136, 137-138
cumulative reviews, designing, 136
discriminating between members, 132
expansion; expansion activities; expanded activities, 133, 135-136, 137, 146
initial teaching, 135, 136-137, 146
minimum differences, identifying, 134
minimum-difference introductions, 138
related subtypes, introducing, 140-145, 146
review sets, 136
subtype that counteracts stipulation, identifying, 142-144, 146
subtype-difference procedure, 140, 144-145
uncontrolled feature misrule, 132-133

coordinate members, applications, 139-140
coordinate members, charting a schedule, 138-139, 146
coordinate members, ordering, 133-134, 135, 145-146
coordinate members, teaching procedures, 135-140
corrections; correcting mistakes, 381-396, 426
add-on; add-ons, 394
chronic discrimination mistakes, 383-384, 395
chronic mistakes outside of a sequence, 386-392, 395
chronic mistakes outside of response-teaching programs, 393-395
chronic mistakes within a sequence, 384-386, 395
chronic mistakes within response-teaching programs, 392-393, 395
chronic response problems, 392-395
context of another activity, 383
discrimination mistakes, 381-392
false operations, 393, 395
general confusion, 383
juxtapositions, appropriate, 392, 393, 394, 396
non-chronic discrimination mistakes, 382-383, 395
subtype mistake, 383
success set, creating a, 394-395, 396

Corrective Reading Program, 410-411
correlated features, 419-420
correlated-feature sentences, 162-169
correlated-feature sentences, analysis of, 163
correlated-features and statements of fact, 111-112
correlated-features relationships, 23, 25-26, 91, 451-452
correlated-features sequences, 111-125
correlated-features and statements of fact, 111-112

Subject Index

    correlated-features sequences, corrections, 115-116
    correlated-features sequences, non-comparative, 116
    correlated-features transformation sequences, 119-124
    correlated-features transformation sequences, applications, 121-123
    correlated-features transformation sequences, constructing, 120-121, 124
    correlations involving and-or, 116-117
    discriminations, first-mentioned, 111
    discriminations, second-named, 112
    divergent responses, 123-124
    equivalent meanings, 117-118
    juxtapositions, 113
    negative wording, 116
    non-comparative correlated-features sequences, 116
    progressive minimum differences, 120
    representations rather than sensory presentations, 113-114
    sequence length, 113
    sequences, choice of, 121-122
    single-dimension correlated-features sequences, constructing, 112-119, 124
    unambiguous responses, 114
    verifying conclusions, 118-119
correlated-features sequences, corrections, 115-116
correlated-features sequences, non-comparative, 116
correlated-features transformation sequences, 119-124
correlated-features transformation sequences, applications, 121-123
correlated-features transformation sequences, constructing, 120-121, 124
correlations involving and-or, 116-117
covertization; covertizing, 30, 285-295, 427
    covertization techniques, 286-292, 294
    covertization techniques, choice of, 292-293
    covertized routines, 285-286
    covertized routines, corrections, 293-294, 295
    covertized routines, properties of, 285
    covertized routines, scheduling, 293, 294-295
    dropping steps, 286-287, 294
    equivalent pairs of instructions, 286, 290-293, 294
    inclusive instructions, 286, 289-290, 294
    regrouping a chain of instructions and responses, 286, 287-289, 294
covertization techniques, 286-292, 294
covertization techniques, choice of, 292-293
covertized routines, 285-286
covertized routines, corrections, 293-294, 295
covertized routines, properties of, 285
covertized routines, scheduling, 293, 294-295

created-part, created-whole system, 188
criterion-referenced measures, 408
cumulative review sequences, 153-154
cumulative reviews, 131, 136, 137-138
cumulative reviews, designing, 136
cursive skills, sequencing, 360-361
cursive writing, 358-361, 364
cursive writing transformations, 361, 364-365
cursive writing, stroke descriptions, 359-360
demonstrating behavioral deficiency, 301-302
descriptive responses, 251-253
descriptive rule, 233
descriptive rule components, designing tasks for, 237-240
descriptive rule, identifying, 234-236
descriptive rule, using familiar names in, 238
diagnosis and remedies, 369-379
    complex activity; complex operation, 377-378, 379
    diagnosis of instruction, 369, 378
    diagnosis of the learner, 369, 377-378
    learner problems, types of, 370-377, 378-379
    learner-performance approach, 370, 378
    possible compliance problems, 370, 376-377, 379
    program-flaw prediction, 370, 378
    response-locus problems, 370, 373-376, 379
    skill deficiency, 370
    stimulus-locus problems, 370-373, 379
diagnosis of complex communications, 429-432
diagnosis of instruction, 369, 378, 430-431
diagnosis of the learner, 369, 377-378
difference, 80, 84
difference principle, 48, 52, 450-451
difference prompts, 269-271, 284
differences, 14, 21, 261
different discriminations, 203
Direct Instruction, 425, 426, 430, 436-449, 437
discovery learning, 227-228
discriminating between members, 132
discrimination mistakes, 381-392
discriminations, 42, 70-71
discriminations, first-mentioned, 111
discriminations, preteaching, 169
discriminations, second-named, 112
displays, choice of, 195
displays, scheduling, 199-200
DISTAR Arithmetic program, 281
DISTAR Reading program, 419, 445
distortion, 37-37, 324-325

divergent responses, 123-124
divergent responses, reinforcing, 209
divergent tasks, 208-209, 213
divergent tasks, designing, 209
divergent-response chains, 343-344, 345
double transformation sets, identifying, 185
double transformation sets, types of, 174
double transformations, criteria for, 174
double-reinforcement responses, 308
double-transformation programs, 173-185
    across-set differences, 175, 179-180
    across-set juxtapositions, 176
    double transformation sets, identifying, 185
    double transformation sets, types of, 174
    double transformations, criteria for, 174
    double-transformation programs, designing, 181-184
    double-transformation programs, parts or cycles of, 175-176, 185
    double-transformation programs, strategy for teaching, 173
    double-transformation programs, structure of, 173-174
    double-transformation sequences, 176, 179, 185
    familiar set, 175, 181-182, 185
    full cycle, 176
    integration of familiar set and transformed set, 176-177
    juxtapositions, 175
    parallel set, 173
    partial cycle, 176
    separate sets, 182-183, 185
    sequence-derived program, 183, 185
    transformed set, 175, 182
    within-set juxtapositions, 175
double-transformation programs, designing, 181-184
double-transformation programs, parts or cycles of, 175-176, 185
double-transformation programs, strategy for teaching, 173
double-transformation programs, structure of, 173-174
double-transformation sequences, 176, 179, 185
dropping steps, 286-287, 294
easy-to-hard examples; easy-to-hard sequence, 338-339, 344, 443-444
E-B Press Cursive Writing Program, 359
enablers; non-essential components, 36
enabling-response-features programs, 322, 324, 328
environment, 3
equivalent meanings, 117-118
equivalent pairs of instructions, 286, 290-292, 294
error data, 402-403
essential behaviors, 36
essential-response-feature approach, 36

essential-response-features programs, 321-322, 323, 327
event-centered applications, 306-307
event-centered applications, effectiveness of, 306-307
event-centered task series, 210-211, 213
event-centered task series, designing, 210-211
Ewing, A. C., 452
examples with difficult responses, 261-262
examples, communicating through, 45-52
    continuous conversion, 50-51
    difference principle, 48, 52
    examples, facts about, 45-47, 51
    juxtaposition principles, 47-51, 52
    sameness principle, 48-49, 52
    setup principle , 47-48, 51-52
    testing principle, 49, 52
    wording principle, 47, 51
examples, facts about, 45-47, 51
expanded activities, using in programs, 211-212
expanded chains, features of, 329
expanded chains, integration of, 330, 344
expanded programs for cognitive skills, 347-365
    analogies, 357-358, 364
    averages, 351
    cursive skills, sequencing, 360-361
    cursive writing, 358-361, 364
    cursive writing transformations, 361, 364-365
    cursive writing, stroke descriptions, 359-360
    E-B Press Cursive Writing Program, 359
    expanded programs, designing, 348-351, 364
    expanded programs, similarity to expanded chains, 347-348, 364
    expressive writing, 353-358, 364
    functional sameness, 351
    joined letters, 361
    operational sameness, 349, 353
    organizing content by response dimensions, 348-349
    problem-solving skills, 361-364
    product conservation, 350-351, 352, 353, 364
    range of examples, identifying, 349
    set of examples, designing and ordering, 351
    subtypes and transformations, 364
    subtypes, identifying, 349-350
expanded programs for physical operations, 329-345
    divergent-response chains, 343-344, 345
    easy-to-hard examples; easy-to-hard sequence, 338-339, 344
    expanded chains, features of, 329
    expanded chains, integration of, 330, 344

Subject Index

expanded-chain parts, scheduling, 330, 344
expanded-chain programs, design problems, 336-339
    false operations, 337-338, 344
    juxtaposition, 341-343, 344
    juxtaposition flaws, 336-337, 344
    operational sameness, 334
    physical operations, 329, 344
    rehearsal and transfer, 339-341, 342, 345
    sameness; samenesses, 340
expanded programs, designing, 348-351, 364
expanded programs, similarity to expanded chains, 347-348, 364
expanded teaching, 204, 205-214
    divergent responses, reinforcing, 209
    divergent tasks, 208-209, 213
    divergent tasks, designing, 209
    event-centered task series, 210-211, 213
    event-centered task series, designing, 210-211
    expanded activities, using in programs, 211-212
    expansion activities, applications, 212-213
    expansion activities, types of, 205, 213
    expansion activities; expanded activities, 205-214
    fooler games, constructing, 210
    fooler games, responses for, 209-210
    fooler games; foolers, 209-210, 213
    implied-conclusion tasks, 207-208, 213
    implied-conclusion tasks, designing, 207-208
    manipulative tasks, 205-206, 213
    manipulative tasks, constructing, 205
    production responses, 205
expanded-chain parts, scheduling, 330, 344
expanded-chain programs, design problems, 336-339
expansion activities, applications, 212-213
expansion activities, scheduling, 222
expansion activities, types of, 205, 213
expansion; expansion activities; expanded activities, 133, 135-136, 137, 146, 204, 205-214
expansion functions, 221-222
expressive writing, 353-358, 364
extinction, 457
extrapolation, 16, 21, 195
fact system teaching, 188
fact systems, types of, 187-188
fact-system programs, 187-201
    add-on; add-ons, 196-197, 201
    analysis of preskills (preteaching), 198-199
    cells (display), 188, 191-192
    codes, 188, 200
    coordinate cells, designing, 192-198
    coordinate cells, showing variation in, 197
    created-part, created-whole system, 188
    displays, choice of, 195
    displays, scheduling, 199-200
    extrapolation, 195
    fact system teaching, 188
    fact systems, types of, 187-188
    game (expansion activities)188
    interpolation, 195
    juxtaposed displays, 199, 201
    natural-part, created-whole system, 187-188
    natural-part, natural-whole system, 187
    prompted chart and script, 188
    script, criteria for constructing, 198
    script, designing, 198
    selecting information for displays, 197-198
    spurious prompts, rules for avoiding, 193
    super display, 197
    unprompted chart and test, 188
    visual-spatial display, presentation format, 188-189
    visual-spatial displays, designing, 191-192
    visual-spatial displays; displays, 187
fading, 30
false operations, 337-338, 344, 393, 395
familiar set, 175, 181-182, 185
faultless communications, 3, 7, 8, 10, 17, 18-19, 297
fewer examples, 84
field tryouts, designing, 400-405
firming responses 310-311
firming sequence, high-order, 157-158, 159
Follow Through; Project Follow Through, 436-439, 447
fooler games, constructing, 210
fooler games, responses for, 209-210
fooler games; foolers, 209-210, 213
form shaping; response-form shaping, 34-36, 39
formal operations, teaching to preschoolers, 433-435
Freud, Sigmund, 454
full cycle, 176
functional sameness, 351
game (expansion activities), 188
general confusion, 383
generalization, 4, 5, 6, 8, 11-12, 17, 42, 444-445, 453, 455, 456, 457, 458
generalization, test of, 7, 10, 12, 21
generalized compliance, 444-445
hierarchical class programs, 147-159

Subject Index

complete teaching, 159
concrete examples, 147
coordinate higher-order classes, 157-158
cumulative review sequences, 153-154
firming sequence, high-order, 157-158, 159
hierarchical class programs, advanced applications, 154-155
higher-order class programs, 147-159
higher-order class programs, advanced applications, 154-155
higher-order class programs, constructing, 159
higher-order firming sequence, 157-158, 159
higher-order programs, teaching schedule, 150-151
higher-order progressions, 148-149
higher-order relationships, structure of, 147-148
higher-order sequences, 149-150, 151
lower-order sequences, constructing, 152-153
minimum-difference examples, identifying, 152
hierarchical class programs, advanced applications, 154-155
higher-order class programs, 147-159
higher-order class programs, advanced applications, 154-155
higher-order class programs, constructing, 159
higher-order firming sequence, 157-158, 159
higher-order noun sequences, constructing, 76-77
higher-order nouns, 65, 73-76
higher-order programs, teaching schedule, 150-151
higher-order progressions, 148-149
higher-order relationships, structure of, 147-148
higher-order sequences, 149-150, 151
highly unfamiliar discriminations, 305
humanism, 461-462
Hume, David, 451
identifying components, 163
implementation, principles of, 397-400
implied-conclusion tasks, 207-208, 213
implied-conclusion tasks, designing, 207-208
inclusive instructions, 286, 289-290, 294
indirect sequences, 82, 85
initial teaching, 135, 136-137, 146
initial teaching sequences, 203
instructional research: communication variables, 415-428
basic-form communications, 415-419
binary-duality relationship, 419
cognitive routines, 423-427, 428
cognitive routines, feedback for, 423
complex-form communications, 421-427
continuous conversion, 416
corrections; correcting mistakes, 426
correlated features, 419-420

covertization, 427
Direct Instruction, 425, 426
DISTAR Reading program, 419
irrelevant difference, 416
joining-form communications, 419-421, 428
juxtapositions, 418, 420-421
maximum-difference examples, 418
minimum difference principle, 416-417
minimum-difference examples, 418
non-functional routines, 425-426
overtness; overtized routines, 423-425
positive-only examples versus positive-negative examples, 415
preteaching components, 426
same behavior and same features, correlation between, 415-416
sameness set, 418
sameness; samenesses, 415-416
setup principle 417-418
stimulus-locus analysis, applications, 420
stipulated set, 418-419
stipulation, 418-419
teacher attention, 427-428
teacher behaviors, 428
teacher pacing, 428
transformations, 420-421
visual-spatial displays; displays, 421-422
instructional research: programs, 429-448
academic skills, teaching to preschoolers, 435-436
academic skills, teaching to school-age children, 436-440
analysis of programs, 431
analysis of teacher behavior, 431-432
communication variables, 442, 447
compliance set, 444
container relationship, 442
diagnosis of complex communications, 429-432
diagnosis of instruction, 430-431
Direct Instruction, 430, 436-439, 437
DISTAR Reading program, 445
easy-to-hard examples; easy-to-hard sequence, 443-444
Follow Through; Project Follow Through, 436-439, 447
formal operations, teaching to preschoolers, 433-435
generalization, 444-445
generalized compliance, 444-445
introducing similar members to a set, 445-447
learner variables, 442-443, 447
low-probability demonstrations, 447
new skills and behaviors, 440-447
pattern-identification skill, 441

Subject Index

    phonemes, 440
    Piaget's developmental theory, 433, 434
    semi-specific prompts, 446-447
    spurious transformation, 446
    stimulus-locus analysis and formal operations, 433
    teaching the second member of highly similar pairs, 446
    time-on-task variables, 430-432
    Title I programs, 438
    unpredicted normative outcomes; normatively unpredicted outcomes, 432-440
    vocoder study; tactual hearing experiments, 440-443, 443, 445, 446
    vocoder; tactual vocoder, 440

integration functions, 222
integration functions, purposes of, 224
integration of familiar set and transformed set, 176-177
integration, corrections, 307
integration, types of, 305-307
interpolation, 15, 21, 195
introducing similar members to a set, 445-447
irregular responses, 97
irrelevant difference, 416
joined letters, 361
joining forms, 23, 25-26, 38, 91-125
    correlated-features relationships, 91
    transformations, 91, 109
    transformations, types of, 91-92
joining-form communications, 419-421, 428
juxtaposed display, 199, 201
juxtaposition flaws, 336-337, 344
juxtaposition or grouping prompts, 276-278, 283
juxtaposition principles, 47-51, 52
juxtaposition prompting, problem of, 203
juxtapositions, 15, 21, 53, 95, 113, 175, 326, 328, 341-343, 344, 418, 420-421
juxtapositions, appropriate, 392, 393, 394, 396
Kant, Immanuel, 450
knowledge systems 23-39
    basic forms, 23, 24-25, 38
    cognitive knowledge classifications; stimulus-locus classifications, 23-33, 38-39
    cognitive problem-solving routines, 23, 27-30, 38-39
    communications about events, 23, 30, 39
    comparatives, 23, 25
    complex forms, 23, 26-33, 38
    complex physical problem-solving operations; complex physical operations; complex operations, 34, 36-38, 39
    component behaviors, 36
    context shaping; response-context shaping, 34-35, 39
    correlated-features relationships, 23, 25-26
    covertizing, 30
    distortion, 36-37
    enablers; non-essential components, 36
    essential behaviors, 36
    essential-response-feature approach, 36
    fading, 30
    form shaping; response-form shaping, 34-36, 39
    joining forms, 23, 25-26, 38
    non-comparatives, 23, 25
    non-essential-response feature approach, 36
    nouns; noun concept, 23, 25
    physical and cognitive operations, differences between, 28-29
    removed-component approach, 36
    response-locus classifications; physical operations classifications, 33-38, 39
    simple responses, 34-35
    symbolic event, 31
    system of facts, 31
    transformations, 23, 25

lead step, 310-311
learner problems, types of, 370-377, 378-379
learner variables, 442-443, 447
learner-performance approach, 370, 378
learning failure, 20, 22
learning mechanism, attributes of, 4
    learning sets, 12
learning to learn, 458-459
left-over pictures, 218
lesson blocks, designing, 401-402
limited generalizations, design problems, 263
limited generalizations, scheduling, 263-264, 268
limited generalizations, testing, 264
logical analysis, 3
lower-order sequences, constructing, 152-153
low-probability demonstrations, 447
manipulative tasks, 205-206, 213
manipulative tasks, constructing 205
match-of-labels-and-examples items, 215, 218, 224
maximum-difference examples, 418
meaning of words, 162-163
Mill, John Stuart, 450-451, 453
minimum difference principle, 416-417
minimum differences, 15, 67, 69, 70
minimum differences within a subtype, 102
minimum differences, identifying, 134

minimum-difference examples, 67, 418

minimum-difference examples, identifying, 152

minimum-difference introductions, 138

minimum-difference negative change, 79

minimum-difference negatives, 79

minimum-time schedules, 257-258

misrules and distortions, 315-316, 327

misrules and distortions, remedies for, 316-317

model step, 310

modeling, 18

Moore, G. E., 452

multiple-dimension concepts, 65

naïve learner, 67-68, 85

narrow-range concepts, 58

narrow-range sequences, 68

natural-part, created-whole system, 187-188

natural-part, natural-whole system, 187

negative examples, 6-7, 10

negative wording, 116

negative-first comparative sequences, 79-83

negative-first comparative sequences, constructing, 81

negative-first comparative sequences, variations in, 83

negative-first sequences, 53

    negative-first sequences, constructing, 54-55

new responses, applications, 300

new responses, teaching traps, 299-300

new skills and behaviors, 440-447

new-response problems, 301-302, 313

new-response teaching procedures, 301-314

    chaining parts of a routine, 312-313

    chaining parts of statements, 311-312

    context integration, 305-306

    continuous behaviors, 302

    demonstrating behavioral deficiency, 301-302

    double-reinforcement responses, 308

    event-centered applications, 306-307

    event-centered applications, effectiveness of, 306-307

    firming responses, 310-311

    highly unfamiliar discriminations, 303

    integration, corrections, 307

    integration, types of, 305-307

    lead step, 310-311

    model step, 310

    new-response problems, 301-302, 313

    non-continuous behaviors, 302

    non-reinforceable responses, 308

    reducing tasks to a simpler form, 302

    response-teaching strategies, 302-313

    rules and statements, 310

    selecting a single objective, 301

    shaping the response; shaping responses, 307, 308-309, 313

    single-reinforceable responses, 308

    teaching how to produce responses, 307-309

    teaching when and how to produce responses, 309-310

    teaching when to produce responses, 303-307

    test step, 311

    three-level strategy, 304-305, 312

no-change negative, 79

non-chronic discrimination mistakes, 382-383, 395

non-comparative correlated-features sequences, 116

non-comparative sequences, 53-63

    continuous conversion and pictorial illustrations, 60

    juxtapositions, 53

    narrow-range concepts, 58

    negative-first sequences, 53

    negative-first sequences, constructing, 54-55

    non-comparative sequences as component of complex communications, 61-63

    non-comparative sequences, constructing, 54-58, 63

    non-continuous conversion sequences, 59

    positive-first sequences, 53, 57

    positive-first sequences, constructing, 57

    stipulation, 56-67

    two-choice tasks, 60-61

    undergeneralization, 56

    variation within the setup, 55

non-comparative sequences as component of complex communications, 61-63

non-comparative sequences, constructing, 54-58, 63

non-comparatives, 23, 25

non-comparatives, identifying, 87-89

non-comparatives; single-dimension non-comparatives, 42

non-continuous behaviors, 302

non-continuous conversion sequences, 59

non-essential-response feature approach, 36

non-functional routines, 425-426

non-reinforceable responses, 308

norm-referenced evaluation, 408

noun sequences, 66-67, 70

noun sequences (not high-order), constructing, 77

nouns, 42, 65-77

    discriminations, 70-71

    higher-order noun sequences, constructing, 76-77

    higher-order nouns, 65, 73-76

    minimum differences, 67, 69, 70

Subject Index

    minimum-difference examples, 67
    multiple-dimension concepts, 65
    naïve learner, 67-68
    narrow-range sequences, 68
    noun sequences, 66-67, 70
    noun sequences (not high-order), constructing, 77
    selecting negatives for higher-order noun sequences, 74-75
    single-dimension concepts, 65
    test examples, 67
    wide-range nouns, 71
nouns, identifying, 87-89
nouns; noun concept, 23, 25
observations, 402
operational sameness, 234-235, 273, 283, 334, 349, 353
organizing content by response dimensions, 348-349
overtness; overtized routines, 423-425
parallel set, 173
partial cycle, 176
pattern of responses, 13
pattern-identification skill, 441
Peirce, C. S., 449
perceptible differences, 82
performance testing, 408-410
phonemes, 440
physical and cognitive operations, differences between, 28-29
physical operations 329, 344
physical operations, properties of, 228
Piaget's developmental theory, 433, 434, 456
positive examples, 5-7, 10, 11
positive-first comparative sequences, 83-84
positive-first sequences, 53, 57
positive-first sequences, constructing, 57
positive-only examples versus positive-negative examples, 415
possible compliance problems, 370, 376-377, 379
pragmatism, 449
prescriptive applications of programs, 169-170
preteaching components, 426
probing, 169-170
problem-solving skills, 361-364
product conservation, 350-351, 352, 353, 364
production responses, 205, 238
production-of-example items, 215, 219-220, 224-225
production-of-label items, 215, 219, 224
production-response items, 215, 220
program implementation, 397-412
    analyzing failures, 401
    computer technology and implementation, 411

    continuous progress test, 408
    Corrective Reading Program, 410-411
    criterion-referenced measures, 408
    error data, 402-403
    field tryouts, designing, 400-405
    implementation, principles of, 397-400
    lesson blocks, designing, 401-402
    norm-referenced evaluation, 408
    observations, 402
    performance testing, 408-410
    quality-control measures, 408, 412
    standard, 397, 399-400, 413
    student outcomes, 397, 411
    teacher behaviors, 397, 402, 411
    teachers' verbal reports, 403
    trainers; training, 405-408, 411
    tryout data, 402-403, 411
program-flaw prediction, 370, 378
programs, 127-171
    programs, types of, 127
    programs for coordinate members, 127
    programs for higher-order and lower-order members, 127-128
    programs that derive from a complex task, 128
    programs for showing the relationship between two single-transformations, 128
    programs for teaching systems of related facts, 128-129
    programs that reduce prompting and stipulation of initial teaching sequences, 129
programs derived from tasks, 161-171
    classifying components, 163-165
    component discriminations, 163, 165-168
    correlated-feature sentences, 162-169
    correlated-feature sentences, analysis of, 163
    discriminations, preteaching, 169
    identifying components, 163
    meaning of words, 162-163
    prescriptive applications of programs, 169-170
    probing, 169-170
    set of related tasks, 162
    strict task analysis, 161-162
    task, 161
    task analysis, 161, 170-171
    transformed task, 162
    transformed-task analysis, 162
    wording, 162-163
programs for coordinate members, 127
programs for higher-order and lower-order members, 127-128
programs for showing the relationship between two single-transfor-

mations, 128

programs for teaching systems of related facts, 128-129

programs that derive from a complex task, 128

programs that reduce prompting and stipulation of initial teaching sequences, 129

programs, types of, 127

progressive minimum differences, 96, 120

progressive minimum differences, 120

prompt modification, 279, 283

prompt modification versus prompt removal, 282

prompt removal, 279, 283

prompted chart and script, 188

prompts and cognitive routines, 273-282

prompts used with symbol systems, 274

prompts; prompting; prompted examples, 269-283

    complete regularizing versus partial regularizing, 278-279

    difference prompts, 269-271, 282

    DISTAR Arithmetic program, 279

    juxtaposition or grouping prompts, 276-278, 283

    operational sameness, 273, 283

    prompt modification, 279, 283

    prompt modification versus prompt removal, 282

    prompt removal, 279, 283

    prompts and cognitive routines, 273-282

    prompts used with symbol systems, 274

    regularized symbols for decoding, 274-275

    regularizing a set of examples, 273, 274-275, 283

    regularizing a set of examples, rules, 274

    sameness prompts, 272-273

    semi-specific prompts, 275-276, 283

    spurious prompts 270

    unprompted examples, corrections, 282

    unprompted examples, transition to, 271, 272, 279-280

punishment, 457-458

quality, 4, 5, 7

quality-control measures, 408, 412

range of examples, 232-233

range of examples, identifying, 234-236, 349

range of variation, 6-7, 10, 262-263, 268

recombined sensory impressions, 449

reducing tasks to a simpler form, 302

regrouping a chain of instructions and responses, 286, 287-289, 294

regularized symbols for decoding, 274-275

regularizing a set of examples, 273, 274-275, 283

regularizing a set of examples, rules, 274

rehearsal and transfer, 339-341, 342, 345

reinforcement, 457

reinforcement and behavioral theory, 456-457

related subtypes, introducing, 140-145, 146

removed-component approach, 36

removed-component-behavior programs, 322-323, 324, 328

representations rather than sensory presentations, 113-114

response problems, 459-460

response-locus analysis, 9, 297-300

    faultless communications, 297

    new responses, applications, 300

    new responses, teaching traps, 299-300

    response-locus analysis, 297

    stimulus-locus and response-locus communications, differences between, 297-299

    stimulus-locus and response-locus communications, parallels between, 297

response-locus classifications; physical operations classifications, 33-38, 39

response-locus problems, 370, 373-376, 379

responses that describe behavior, 238-239

response-teaching strategies, 302-313

review functions, 220-221

review sets, 136

rules and statements, 310

same behavior and same features, correlation between, 415-416

sameness principle, 48-49, 52, 450

sameness prompts, 272-273

sameness set, 418

sameness; samenesses, 4, 5, 7, 11, 12, 14, 21, 80, 84, 98, 99, 234-235, 261, 340, 415-416, 449

same-response minimum difference, 105-107

script, criteria for constructing, 198

script, designing, 198

selecting a single objective, 301

selecting information for displays, 197-198

selecting negatives for higher-order noun sequences, 74-75

semi-specific prompts, 275-276, 283, 446-447

sensory qualities, 82

sensory-based concepts, 42-43

separate sets, 182-183, 185

sequence length, 113

sequence-derived program 183, 185

sequences, choice of, 121-122

set of examples, 5-7, 10, 13, 42, 449, 450, 453, 459

set of examples, constructing a routine for, 236-237

set of examples, designing and ordering, 261

set of examples, designing and ordering, 351

set of examples, scheduling, 260-264

set of related tasks, 162

Subject Index

sets of stimuli, 449, 450
setup features, 84
setup principle, 47-48, 51-52, 417-418
shaping the response; shaping responses, 307, 308-309, 313
signals, 6-7, 10
similarity, 8
simple responses, 34-35
simultaneous components, 319
single-dimension concepts, 65
single-dimension correlated-feature sequences, variations, 114-115
single-dimension correlated-features sequences, constructing, 112-119, 124
single-reinforceable responses, 308
single-transformation sequences, 93-109
    continuous conversion, 95
    irregular responses, 97
    juxtapositions, 95
    minimum differences within a subtype, 102
    progressive minimum differences, 96
    sameness; samenesses, 98, 99
    same-response minimum difference, 105-107
    single-transformation sequences, constructing, 96-97
    subtype analysis, 100-102, 107-108, 109
    subtype errors, identifying, 103
    subtype variations, setup for, 99
    subtypes, 97-100
    subtypes, difficult, 98-99, 102-104
    subtypes, difficult, remedies for, 103-104
    subtypes, identifying, 99
    subtypes, irregular, 98-99
    subtypes, three types of, 101
    subtype-variation sequences, constructing, 107
    system of responses, 93
    transformation sequences, differences from non-comparative sequences, 93
    transformation sequences, structure of, 94-95, 108-109
    transformations, advanced applications, 104
    transformations, identifying, 94
    unique responses, 93
single-transformation sequences, constructing, 96-97
skill deficiency, 370
spurious prompts, 270
spurious prompts, rules for avoiding, 193
spurious transformation, 446
standard, 397, 399-400, 411
stimulus-locus analysis, 5, 9, 10, 11, 20
stimulus-locus analysis and formal operations, 433
stimulus-locus analysis and learning theories, 455-456

stimulus-locus analysis, applications, 420
stimulus-locus and response-locus communications, differences between, 297-299
stimulus-locus and response-locus communications, parallels between, 297
stimulus-locus problems, 370-373, 379
stipulated set, 418-419
stipulation, 16-17, 21, 56-67, 418-419
stipulation, problem of, 203
stipulation, types of, 203
strict task analysis, 161-162
student outcomes, 397, 411
subtype analysis, 100-102, 107-108, 109
subtype errors, identifying, 103
subtype mistake, 383
subtype that counteracts stipulation, identifying, 142-144, 146
subtype variations, setup for, 99
subtype-difference procedure, 140, 144-145
subtypes, 97-100
subtypes and transformations, 364
subtypes, difficult, 98-99, 102-104
subtypes, difficult, remedies for, 103-104
subtypes, identifying, 99, 349-350
subtypes, irregular, 98-99
subtypes, types of, 101
subtype-variation sequences, constructing, 107
success set, creating a, 394-395, 396
super display, 197
symbolic event, 31
system of facts, 31
system of responses, 93
tactual hearing experiments; vocoder study, 440-443, 445, 446
tactual vocoder, 440
task, 161
task analysis, 161, 170-171
teacher attention, 427-428
teacher behaviors, 397, 402, 411, 428
teacher pacing, 428
teachers' verbal reports, 403
teaching failure, 462
teaching how to produce responses, 307-309
teaching the second member of highly similar pairs, 446
teaching when and how to produce responses, 309-310
teaching when to produce responses, 303-307
temporal parts, 319
test examples, 7, 10, 12, 21, 67
test step, 311
testing principle, 49, 52

Subject Index

theory of instruction, overview of strategies, 1-10
    analysis of behavior, 1
    analysis of cognitive learning, 1-2
    analysis of communications, 1
    analysis of knowledge systems, 1
    basic communication, structural requirements of, 5-8, 10
    behavior analysis, 3
    boundaries of variation, 6-7
    environment, 3
    faultless communications, 3, 7, 8, 10
    generalization, 4, 5, 6, 8
    generalization, test of, 7, 10
    learning mechanism, attributes of, 4
    logical analysis, 3
    negative examples, 6-7, 10
    positive examples, 5-7, 10
    quality, 4, 5, 7
    range of variation, 6-7, 10
    response-locus analysis, 9
    sameness; samenesses, 4, 5, 7
    set of examples, 5-7, 10
    signals, 6-7, 10
    similarity, 8
    stimulus-locus analysis, 5, 9, 10
    test examples, 7, 10
theory of instruction, philosophical origins, 449-462
    behavioral objectives, 459-461
    behaviorism, 449
    cognitive-developmental theories, 456
    context problems, 459-460
    correlated-features relationships, 451-452
    difference principle, 450-451
    Ewing, A. C., 452
    extinction, 457
    Freud, Sigmund, 454
    generalization, 453, 455, 456, 457, 458
    humanism, 461-462
    Hume, David, 449
    Kant, Immanuel, 450
    learning to learn, 458-459
    Mill, John Stuart, 450-451, 453
    Moore, G. E., 452
    Peirce, C. S., 449
    Piaget's developmental theory, 456
    pragmatism, 449
    punishment, 457-458
    recombined sensory impressions, 449
    reinforcement, 457
    reinforcement and behavioral theory, 456-457
    response problems, 459-460
    sameness principle, 450
    sameness; samenesses, 449
    set of examples, 449, 450, 453, 459
    sets of stimuli, 449, 450
    stimulus-locus analysis and learning theories, 455-456
    teaching failure, 462
    Wittgenstein, 453
three-level strategy, 304-305, 312
time-on-task variables, 430-432
Title I programs, 438
trainers; training, 405-408, 411
transformation sequences, differences from non-comparative sequences, 93
transformation sequences, structure of, 94-95, 108-109
transformation worksheets, 223-224
transformations, 23, 25, 91, 109, 420-421
transformations, advanced applications, 104
transformations, identifying, 94
transformations, types of, 91-92
transformed set, 175, 182
transformed task, 162
transformed-task analysis, 162
tryout data, 402-403, 411
two-choice tasks, 60-61
two-choice wording, 84
two-response comparative sequences, 85
unambiguous responses, 114
uncontrolled feature misrule, 132-133
undergeneralization, 56
unique responses, 93
unpredicted normative outcomes; normatively unpredicted outcomes, 432-440
unprompted chart and test, 188
unprompted examples, corrections, 282
unprompted examples, transition to, 271, 272, 279-280
variation within the setup, 55
verbal explanation, 84
verifying conclusions, 118-119
visual-spatial display, presentation format, 188-189
visual-spatial displays, designing, 191-192
visual-spatial displays; displays, 187, 421-422
vocoder study; tactual hearing experiments, 440-443, 443, 445, 446
vocoder; tactual vocoder, 440
wide-range nouns, 71
within-set juxtapositions, 175

Subject Index

Wittgenstein, 453
wording, 162-163
wording principle, 47, 51
worksheet items, 215-225
    blocks (sets of items) 222, 223, 224, 225
    choice-of-example items, 215, 217, 224
    choice-of-label items, 215, 217-218, 224
    choice-response items, 215, 220
    expansion activities, scheduling, 222
    expansion functions, 221-222
    integration functions, 222
    integration functions, purposes of, 224
    left-over pictures, 218
    match-of-labels-and-examples items, 215, 218, 224
    production-of-example items, 215, 219-220, 224-225
    production-of-label items, 215, 219, 224
    production-response items, 215, 220
    review functions, 220-221
    transformation worksheets, 223-224
    worksheet items, advantages of, 215
    worksheet items, design strategy, 217
    worksheet items, designing, 217-220
    worksheet items, functions of, 220-224
    worksheet items, strategy, 215
    worksheet items, types of, 215-216
worksheet items, using in programs, 220-224

ABOUT NIFDI PRESS

The National Institute for Direct Instruction (NIFDI) is a non-profit organization focused on supporting Direct Instruction implementations with schools around the world. NIFDI also maintains a publication arm to the organization: NIFDI Press. Dedicated to publishing high quality works that support the development of effective implementations of Direct Instruction programs, the press publishes manuals and books designed to help a variety of audience purposes:

- teachers, coaches, and administrators implementing DI programs in their schools;
- parents preparing or supporting their children in academic success;
- researchers in search of theoretical and empirical studies regarding the development, efficacy and implementation of DI.

The Press also distributes other Direct Instruction and education-related titles, including:

- *Teach Your Child to Read in 100 Easy Lessons*
- *Teaching Needy Kids in Our Backward System: 42 Years of Trying*
- *The Science and Success of Engelmann's Direct Instruction*
- And more!

You can order through our website at http://nifdi.org/store or by calling toll-free 877.485.1973.

Made in the USA
Columbia, SC
06 February 2025

9463907e-c2b8-4080-baab-19b9195c7d0bR03